DISMANTLING DEMOCRACY IN VENEZUELA
The Chávez Authoritarian Experiment

Since the election of Hugo Chávez Frías as president of the Republic of Venezuela in December 1998, and during the past decade, the country formerly envied for its democratic accomplishments over the second half of the twentieth century has suffered a tragic setback regarding democratic standards, suffering a continuous, persistent, and deliberate process of demolishing institutions and destroying democracy, which had never before been experienced in the constitutional history of the country. The 1999 Constitution, although considered by some of its drafters as one of the best constitutional texts in contemporary Latin America, has been constantly violated by all branches of government, and more seriously by the Supreme Tribunal of Justice and its Constitutional Chamber. The chamber, completely controlled by the executive, has molded and accepted as legitimate all the constitutional violations that have occurred. Worse, the process has been conducted by defrauding the Constitution and the representative democratic regime in the name of a "participatory democracy" designed to be controlled by the central government. The result has been the complete lack of all essential elements of democracy, as defined by the 2001 Inter-American Democratic Charter: namely, access to power and its exercise subject to the rule of law; periodic, free, and fair elections based on the universal secret vote as an expression of the sovereignty of the people; a plural regime of political parties and organizations; separation and independence of branches of government; and respect for human rights and fundamental freedoms.

This book covers the Chávez authoritarian experiment on dismantling democracy, which has influenced other countries, like Ecuador, Bolivia, and Honduras. It is based on a series of essays written as the facts were occurring during Venezuela's decade of authoritarian government (1999–2009).

Allan R. Brewer-Carías has been Professor at the Central University of Venezuela since 1963. He also has been Simón Bolívar Professor at the Law Faculty of Cambridge University (1985–86), where he was Fellow of Trinity College; at the University of Paris II (1990); and at Columbia University, where he has been Visiting Scholar and Adjunct Professor of Law (2002–4, and 2006–7). He is Vice President of the International Academy of Comparative Law, and he is a member of the Venezuelan National Academy of Political and Social Sciences, where he served as President (1997–99); he was also Senator for the Federal District, Minister for Decentralization, and an elected member of the 1999 National Constituent Assembly.

DISMANTLING DEMOCRACY IN VENEZUELA

The Chávez Authoritarian Experiment

Allan R. Brewer-Carías

Professor of Law, Central University of Venezuela
Academy of Political and Social Sciences, Venezuela
Vice President, International Academy of Comparative Law

CAMBRIDGE UNIVERSITY PRESS
Cambridge, New York, Melbourne, Madrid, Cape Town, Singapore,
São Paulo, Delhi, Dubai, Tokyo, Mexico City

Cambridge University Press
32 Avenue of the Americas, New York, NY 10013-2473, USA

www.cambridge.org
Information on this title: www.cambridge.org/9780521145572

© Allan R. Brewer-Carías 2010

This publication is in copyright. Subject to statutory exception
and to the provisions of relevant collective licensing agreements,
no reproduction of any part may take place without the written
permission of Cambridge University Press.

First published 2010

Printed in the United States of America

A catalog record for this publication is available from the British Library.

Library of Congress Cataloging in Publication data

Brewer Carías, Allan-Randolph.
Dismantling democracy in Venezuela : the Chávez authoritarian experiment / Allan Brewer-Carías.
   p. cm.
Includes bibliographical references and index.
ISBN 978-0-521-19587-4 (hardback)
1. Democracy – Venezuela. 2. Venezuela – Politics and government. 3. Chávez Frías, Hugo – Influence. I. Title.
JL3831.B7318   2010
987.06′42–dc22   2010018536

ISBN 978-0-521-19587-4 Hardback
ISBN 978-0-521-14557-2 Paperback

Cambridge University Press has no responsibility for the persistence or accuracy of URLs for external or third-party Internet Web sites referred to in this publication and does not guarantee that any content on such Web sites is, or will remain, accurate or appropriate.

CONTENTS

AUTHOR'S NOTE — 1

INTRODUCTION
DEFRAUDING DEMOCRACY THROUGH NONCONSENSUAL CONSTITUENT ASSEMBLIES — 7

PART ONE
THE POLITICAL ASSAULT ON STATE POWERS AND THE FRAMEWORK FOR AUTHORITARIANISM — 33

Chapter 1
THE 1999 EXCLUSIONIST CONSTITUTION-MAKING PROCESS — 35

I. **THE 1999 NATIONAL CONSTITUENT ASSEMBLY** — 37
II. **THE 1998 CRISIS OF THE POLITICAL SYSTEM AND THE NEED FOR DEMOCRATIC RECONSTRUCTION** — 41
  1. *Party Domination and Demand for Participation* — 42
  2. *State Centralism and the Crisis of Decentralization* — 44
  3. *The Demand for Reform* — 46
III. **THE CONSTITUTION-MAKING PROCESS AND ITS DEFORMATION** — 48
  1. *The Choice of a National Constituent Assembly* — 48
  2. *The Constitutional Debate Regarding the Election of the Constituent Assembly* — 50
  3. *The Electoral Rule for the Election of the Assembly* — 55
  4. *The Seizure of the Constituted Powers* — 57
  5. *The Drafting Phase: Haste and Exclusion* — 60
IV. **THE PARALLEL TRANSITORY REGIME** — 64
V. **THE DEMOCRATIC FAILURE OF THE CONSTITUTION-MAKING PROCESS** — 65

Chapter 2

THE ENDLESS AND ILLEGITIMATE TRANSITORY
CONSTITUTIONAL REGIME   69

I.   **FAILED EFFORTS TO CREATE A CONSTITUTIONAL FRAMEWORK TO TRANSITION PUBLIC POWERS THROUGH AN APPROBATORY REFERENDUM**   69
II.   **THE ILLEGITIMATE REGIME FOR THE TRANSITION OF PUBLIC POWERS**   71
     1. *Elimination of Congress and Creation of the National Legislative Commission*   73
     2. *Dissolution of State Legislative Assemblies and Creation of State Legislative Commissions*   75
     3. *Control over Municipalities*   75
     4. *Intervention of the Judiciary*   76
     5. *Dismissal and Appointment of Officials of the Citizens' Power*   78
     6. *Dismissal and Appointment of Members of the National Electoral Council*   79
III.   **JUDICIAL ACCEPTANCE OF A DOUBLE CONSTITUTIONAL TRANSITORY REGIME**   79
IV.   **THE KIDNAPPING OF THE CONSTITUTION AND SUBJECTION OF THE JUDICIAL BRANCH TO THE GOVERNMENT**   85

Chapter 3

THE 1999 POLITICAL CONSTITUTION AND THE
REINFORCEMENT OF CENTRALIZATION   87

I.   **THE CONSTITUTION OF 1999: FRUSTRATION OF THE NECESSARY POLITICAL CHANGE**   88
II.   **THE NEW "BOLIVARIAN" REPUBLIC AND ITS PARTISAN CHARACTER**   91
III.   **THE PROBLEM OF A POLITICAL CONSTITUTION DRAFTED FOR CENTRALISM AND AUTHORITARIANISM**   95
IV.   **THE DEMOCRATIC REGIME AND POLITICAL PARTICIPATION**   100
     1. *Representative Democracy*   101
     2. *The Mixed Electoral System and Its Distortion*   103
     3. *Principles of Participative Democracy and Their Distortion*   105

	Democracy Institutions, Referenda, and the Distortion	
4.	Recall Referendum	110
	al Political Parties and the Move toward a Single-Party em	116
	titutions of Government Accountability and Liability	121
	YSTEM OF GOVERNMENT AND THE RATION OF POWERS	122
	'residential System and Its Reinforcement	122
	Unbalanced Powers Due to Concentrated Power in the National Assembly	123
	The State of Justice and Its Incongruence	126
	The Constitutional Base for Militarism	130

.pter 4

THE 1999 SOCIAL AND ECONOMIC CONSTITUTION AND ITS PROBLEMS ... 134

I. **CONSTITUTIONAL VALUES AND DECLARATIVE PRINCIPLES** ... 134
II. **THE GENERAL FRAMEWORK ON MATTERS OF HUMAN RIGHTS** ... 141
  1. *General Declarations* ... 141
  2. *Social Rights and the Social State* ... 147
  3. *Limits to the Exercise of Constitutional Rights That Can Only Be Established through Statutes* ... 151
  4. *Freedom of Expression and Its Limitations* ... 152
  5. *The New Indigenous People's Collective Rights* ... 155
III. **THE PROBLEM OF AN ECONOMIC CONSTITUTION CONCEIVED FOR STATE APPROPRIATION ("STATIZATION") OF THE ECONOMY** ... 156
  1. *The Mixed Economic System* ... 156
  2. *Reduced Property Rights and Economic Freedoms* ... 158
  3. *The Almost-Unlimited Possibility of State Intervention in the Economy* ... 160

PART TWO

INSTITUTIONAL DEVELOPMENT TOWARD CONSOLIDATING AUTHORITARIANISM

Chapter 5
CONSTITUTIONAL FRAUD AND DEFRAUDING DEMOCRACY

I. **POPULAR AUTHORITARIANISM AND CONCENTRATED STATE POWERS** 16

II. **THE PROCESS OF CONCENTRATING POWER SINCE 1999** 171
 1. *The Germ of Concentrated Power: The National Assembly's Authority to Remove State Officials* 173
 2. *The Political Supremacy of the Executive and the Absence of Checks and Balances* 175
 3. *Continuous Interference and Subjection of the Judicial Power* 177

III. **CENTRALIZING POWER AND THE ABSENCE OF EFFECTIVE POLITICAL PARTICIPATION** 183
 1. *The Meaning of Democracy and the Illusion of Participatory Democracy* 183
 2. *The Reaction against the Federation as a Decentralized State* 189
 3. *The Reaction against Local Governments and the Centralized Communal Councils* 191

IV. **THE FORESEEABLE OUTCOME: THE DICTATORSHIP OF DEMOCRACY** 193

Chapter 6
THE REINFORCED CENTRALIZATION OF THE FEDERATION 198

I. **HISTORY AND DEVELOPMENT OF THE VENEZUELAN FEDERATION** 200
II. **FEDERALIST CONSTITUTIONAL PROVISIONS IN THE 1999 CONSTITUTION** 202
III. **LIMITING THE CONTENTS OF SUBNATIONAL CONSTITUTIONS** 204
IV. **CONSTITUTIONAL DISTRIBUTION OF POWERS** 206
V. **THE FINANCING RULES OF THE FEDERATION** 208
VI. **THE RECENTRALIZATION OF THE FEDERATION** 209

Chapter 7

CONCENTRATION OF POWERS AND AUTHORITARIAN GOVERNMENT 212

I. THE SEPARATION OF POWERS IN MODERN CONSTITUTIONALISM AND THE VENEZUELAN CONSTITUTIONAL TRADITION 212
II. SEPARATION OF POWERS AND DEMOCRACY 215
III. DEFRAUDING POLITICAL PARTICIPATION IN APPOINTING OFFICIALS 217
IV. THE SUPREMACY OF THE EXECUTIVE AND THE ABSENCE OF CHECKS AND BALANCES 219
V. THE RUPTURE OF THE RULE OF LAW AND THE REJECTED 2007 CONSTITUTIONAL REFORM 220

Chapter 8

THE CATASTROPHIC DEPENDENCE AND POLITICAL SUBJECTION OF THE SUPREME TRIBUNAL OF JUSTICE 226

I. THE SUBJECTION OF THE SUPREME TRIBUNAL OF JUSTICE 226
   1. *The Confiscation of Civil Society's Right to Participate in the Appointment of the Magistrates of the Supreme Tribunal in 2000* 227
   2. *The Appointment of the Magistrates of the Supreme Tribunal of Justice* 230
   3. *The Consolidation of the Commission on the Functioning and Restructuring of the Judicial System and the Complete Political Control of the Judiciary* 231
   4. *The 2004 Reform of the Supreme Tribunal Organic Law and the Reinforcement of Executive Control over the Judiciary* 236
II. THE SUPREME TRIBUNAL AS A TOOL TO DISTORT THE CONSTITUTION AND RECOURSE FOR CONSTITUTIONAL INTERPRETATION 239

Chapter 9

STATE APPROPRIATION, NATIONALIZATION, EXPROPRIATION, AND CONFISCATION OF PRIVATE ASSETS 245

I. THE COMPULSORY ACQUISITION OF PRIVATE ASSETS 245
II. THE 2006–2007 STATE APPROPRIATION OF PRIVATE ENTERPRISES IN THE NATIONALIZED OIL INDUSTRY 250

III. THE 2008–2009 NATIONALIZATION AND STATE APPROPRIATION   254
1. The Nationalization of the Iron and Steel Industry   254
2. The Nationalization of the Cement Industry   256
3. The State Appropriation of Assets and Services Related to Primary Hydrocarbon Activities   258
4. The Reservation to the State of Petrochemical Activities   261

IV. THE STATE APPROPRIATIONS OF RURAL LAND AND ALIMENTARY INDUSTRIES   261

PART THREE
CONSTITUTIONAL REFORMS DESIGNED TO CONSOLIDATE AUTHORITARIANISM   263

Chapter 10
THE FAILED ATTEMPT TO CONSOLIDATE AN AUTHORITARIAN AND ANTIDEMOCRATIC POLITICAL SYSTEM IN THE CONSTITUTION   264

I. A NEW FRAUD ON THE CONSTITUTION   264
II. PROPOSED CHANGES TO THE FUNDAMENTAL PRINCIPLES OF THE POLITICAL SYSTEM   271
1. Bolivarian Doctrine   273
2. The Substitution of the Social-Democratic State for a Socialist State   274
3. The Elimination of Decentralization as a State Policy   276
4. Fragmentation of Public Administration   277
5. The Abandonment of Budgetary Discipline and the Unity of the Treasury   279

III. PROPOSED CHANGES IN THE POLITICAL SYSTEM: FROM REPRESENTATIVE DEMOCRACY TO PARTICIPATORY DEMOCRACY   280
1. The Elimination of Representative Democracy at the Local Level   280
2. Elimination of Republican Alternation in Office by Establishing the Possibility of Indefinite Reelection of the President   283
3. The Contradictory Restrictions on Citizens' Right to Political Participation   284
   A. The Elimination of the Civil Society's Participation in Nominating State Officials   284

        B. *Limits to Political Participation by Means of Referenda and Restrictions on Direct Democracy*   286
        C. *Limits on the Right to Political Participation in Constitutional Review Procedures*   287
    4. *Reducing the Right to Political Participation to Implementing Socialist Ideology*   288
    5. *Political Parties, Political Association, and Public Financing of Electoral Activities*   289

Chapter 11

THE FAILED ATTEMPT TO CONSOLIDATE A CENTRALIZED STATE IN THE CONSTITUTION   291

I. **PROPOSED CHANGES IN THE STATE FORM: FROM CENTRALIZED FEDERATION TO CENTRALIZED STATE**   291
    1. *The Destruction of the Federation*   292
        A. *Taking Away Territoriality from the Federation*   292
        B. *A Territorial Division of the Republic Tied to the Central Power*   293
        C. *The Capital City: No Political Autonomy or Democratic Government*   294
    2. *Abandoning Vertical Distribution of the Public Powers*   295
    3. *Nationalizing Federated States' Competencies*   296
    4. *Obligating States and Municipalities to Transfer Their Competencies to the Organs of the Popular Power*   298
    5. *Eliminating the Constitutional Guarantee of Municipal Autonomy*   299
II. **PROPOSED CHANGES IN THE ORGANIZATION OF THE NATIONAL LEVEL OF GOVERNMENT**   300
    1. *Proposed Reforms Regarding the International Activities of the Republic*   300
    2. *Proposed Reforms to the Executive Power and Reinforcing the Presidential System*   301
        A. *The Extension of the President's Term and Unlimited Reelection*   301
        B. *The New Executive Organs: Vice Presidents*   302
        C. *Extending the Powers of the President*   302
    3. *Proposed Reforms Regarding the Legislative Power and Political Permeability*   306

4. *Proposed Reforms Regarding the Appointing and Dismissing of the Head Officers of the Nonelected Branches of Government*   306

III. **PROPOSED CHANGES IN THE ARMED FORCES: FROM A CIVIL MANAGED STATE TO A MILITARIST STATE**   307

Chapter 12

THE FAILED ATTEMPT TO CONSOLIDATE A SOCIALIST CENTRALIZED ECONOMIC SYSTEM IN THE CONSTITUTION   311

I. **PROPOSED CHANGES ON MATTERS OF ECONOMIC FREEDOM AND PRIVATE PROPERTY**   313
1. *Eliminating Economic Freedom as a Constitutionally Protected Right*   313
2. *Eliminating Property as a Constitutionally Protected Right*   315
3. *The Elimination of the* Latifundio   317

II. **PROPOSED CHANGES ON MATTERS OF PUBLIC ECONOMY MANAGEMENT**   318
1. *The Regime Governing State Intervention in the Economy*   318
2. *Proposed Changes in the State's Fiscal and Economic Regime*   321
   A. *Eliminating the Autonomy of the Central Bank of Venezuela*   321
   B. *Macroeconomic Policy at the Mercy of the National Executive*   322

III. **PROPOSED CHANGES IN MATTERS OF HUMAN RIGHTS**   324
1. *The Extension of the Principle of Equality*   324
2. *Proposed Changes in the States of Exception*   325
   A. *The Expansion of States of Exception*   325
   B. *The Elimination of the Duration of a State of Emergency*   325
   C. *The Possibility of Suspending Constitutional Guarantees*   326
   D. *Changes Regarding the Constitutional Guarantees of Human Rights That Can Be Suspended or Restricted in Situations of Exception*   326
   E. *The Elimination of the Control Mechanisms of States of Exception*   327
3. *Proposed Changes in Education Rights: The Limits to University Autonomy*   328
4. *Proposed Changes in Labor Rights: A Useless Constitutional "Reform"*   328

Chapter 14. POPULAR FRAUDULENT IMPLEMENTATION OF THE 1999 CONSTITUTIONAL REFORM THROUGH THE ILLEGITIMATE MUTATION OF THE CONSTITUTION THROUGH JUDICIAL CONSTITUTIONAL INTERPRETATION 329

335

I. THE ACCEPTANCE OF A TRANSITORY CONSTITUTIONAL REGIME NOT APPROVED BY THE PEOPLE 337
II. FROM REVOCATION REFERENDA TO RATIFYING REFERENDA 339
III. THE ELIMINATION OF THE CONSTITUTIONAL PRINCIPLE OF ALTERNATE GOVERNMENT AND THE LIMITS TO CONTINUOUS REELECTION 341
IV. LIFTING THE PROHIBITION ON REPEATING REFERENDA FOR CONSTITUTIONAL REVIEW 344
V. ILLEGITIMATE TRANSFORMATION OF THE FEDERAL SYSTEM 346
VI. THE LIFTING OF THE PROHIBITION ON GOVERNMENT FINANCING OF ELECTORAL ACTIVITIES 349
VII. THE ILLEGITIMATE ELIMINATION OF THE SUPRACONSTITUTIONAL RANK OF INTERNATIONAL HUMAN RIGHTS TREATIES 351
VIII. THE ELIMINATION OF JUDGES' POWER TO IMMEDIATELY AND DIRECTLY APPLY INTERNATIONAL HUMAN RIGHTS TREATIES 354
IX. THE DENIAL OF THE PEOPLE'S RIGHT TO INTERNATIONAL HUMAN RIGHTS PROTECTION 355

Chapter 15

THE ALTERNATE PRINCIPLE OF GOVERNMENT AND THE 2009 CONSTITUTIONAL AMENDMENT ON CONTINUOUS REELECTION 359

I. THE REPUBLICAN PRINCIPLE OF ALTERNATE GOVERNMENT AND THE VENEZUELAN TRADITION OF NO REELECTION 360
II. THE LIMITS IMPOSED BY THE CONSTITUTION ON CONSTITUTIONAL REVIEW 362
III. THE BINDING CONSTITUTIONAL INTERPRETATION 364

FINAL REFLECTIONS

THE RIGHT TO DEMOCRACY AND ITS VIOLATION BY VENEZUELA'S AUTHORITARIAN GOVERNMENT: SOME RELEVANT FACTS FROM THE PAST DECADE

I.	REPRESENTATIVE DEMOCRACY AND THE VENEZUELAN AUTHORITARIAN GOVERNMENT	367
II.	REPRESENTATIVE DEMOCRACY AND ITS DEFORMATIONS	371
III.	PARTICIPATORY DEMOCRACY AND THE VIOLATION OF THE CITIZENS' RIGHT TO PARTICIPATION	380
IV.	DISRESPECTING HUMAN RIGHTS	386
V.	ACCESS TO POWER AND ITS EXERCISE CONTRARY TO THE RULE OF LAW	392
VI.	BROKEN REPRESENTATIVE DEMOCRACY	396
VII.	WEAKENED DEMOCRACY DUE TO THE ABSENCE OF PLURALISM	398
VIII.	VANISHING DEMOCRACY AND ABSENT SEPARATION OF POWERS	401
IX.	DEMOCRACY AND PROBLEMS OF TRANSPARENCY	406
X.	FEEBLE DEMOCRACY AND RESTRICTIONS ON FREEDOMS OF EXPRESSION AND THE PRESS	407
XI.	DEMOCRACY AND SUBMISSION OF THE MILITARY TO CIVIL POWER	410

INDEX 413

R'S NOTE

ᴐk deals with the dismantling of Venezuelan democracy from ،at the country's authoritarian government has accomplished the past decade using some democratic tools defrauding the ،ıtution.[1] This process began after the election of Hugo Chávez Frías ᴐresident of the Republic of Venezuela in December 1998, the result of hich was the tragic setback to democratic institutions and standards. Venezuela had been one of the most admired Latin American countries because of its stable democracy, which had consolidated during the second half of the twentieth century. During the past decade, the country has experienced a continuous, persistent, and deliberate demolishing of institutions and destruction of democracy, which has never before occurred in the constitutional history of the country.

The first step to subvert democratic principles and values materialized in 1999, with the forced convening of a constituent assembly – not established in the Constitution as a valid means for constitutional reform – through a consultative referendum to impose the "will of the people" over the Constitution itself (peoples' sovereignty over constitutional supremacy). The result was the interference and takeover of all recently elected branches of government by the newly elected Constituent Assembly, completely controlled by the president of the republic. For the election of the Assembly, an electoral system was adopted without any sort of agreements, the Constitution was sanctioned without any sort of consensus, and conditions were established for the imposition of an authoritarian and centralized government, which has since eliminated any checks and balances and, consequently, the rule of law.

The remote antecedent of the use of the constituent assembly procedure, not established in the constitution, to draft a new constitution without the

---

[1] See, in general, Allan R. Brewer-Carías, "La demolición del Estado de derecho y la destrucción de la democracia en Venezuela (1999-2009)," in *La democracia en su contexto. Estudios en homenaje a Dieter Nohlen en su septuagésimo aniversario,* coord. José Reynoso Núñez and Herminio Sánchez de la Barquera y Arroyo, Instituto de Investigaciones Jurídicas, Universidad Nacional Autónoma de México, Mexico City 2009, 477-517

interruption of the constitutional rule can be found in Colomb, the transition between the governments of President Virgilio Ba. President César Gaviria in 1990, after the Supreme Court of J. expressly accepted the constitutionality of the process. The Constitu Assembly was elected with a pluralistic composition, after the politic actors had agreed on the electoral system. The assembly drafted the 199 Constitution, also based on negotiations and consensus, thus contributin' to the further development of democratic institutions in the country.

However, it was after the 1999 experience in Venezuela that a new formula was developed in which the general bylaws for the election of a Constituent Assembly, also not established in the 1961 Constitution as a constitutional review method, resulted not from consensus and agreements among political actors but from those who took the initiative to convene the referendum. The result in this case was the establishment and development not of a democratic government but of a framework for developing an authoritarian government through democratic tools. In Venezuela, a popular consultation or consultative referendum was convened to subvert the Constitution itself, as President Chávez unilaterally defined the assembly in a way that impeded the configuration of a plural political body. In 2007, Ecuador's president Rafael Correa also implemented this "formula" to depart from the Constitution then in force, and in 2009, Honduran President Manuel Zelaya tried to implement it, but the Supreme Court of Justice of Honduras declared it unconstitutional.[2] Unfortunately, in Honduras, instead of waiting for the results of the judicial process initiated against the president, indicted for violating the Constitution, the military eventually expelled him unconstitutionally from the country. His expulsion led to an international uproar from the less democratic leaders of Latin America, including Hugo Chávez and Raúl Castro, supposedly to defend democracy and to impose the 2001 Inter-American Democratic Charter.[3]

In Venezuela, contrary to the Colombia in 1991 and Honduras in 2009 cases, the Supreme Court of Justice, though requested to issue a decision on the interpretation of the constitutionality of the convening of the assembly, refused to rule in a clear way and instead issued an ambiguous decision that ultimately allowed the president to impose his own rules for

---

[2]The formula has been referred to as the Chávez franchise or the Chávez brand because of his ostensible involvement in the political processes of the countries that have previously applied it, such as Ecuador. See, e.g., "The Wages of Chavismo" (Opinion), *Wall Street Journal*, July 1, 2009, A12.

[3]See, e.g., Moisés Naim, "Golpe en Honduras: Idiotas contra hipócritas," *El Pais*, Madrid July 5, 2009.

Chapter 13

THE IRREGULAR FRAUDULENT IMPLEMENTATION OF THE REJECTED CONSTITUTIONAL REFORM THROUGH LEGISLATION ... 329

Chapter 14

THE ILLEGITIMATE MUTATION OF THE CONSTITUTION THROUGH JUDICIAL CONSTITUTIONAL INTERPRETATION ... 335

I. THE ACCEPTANCE OF A TRANSITORY CONSTITUTIONAL REGIME NOT APPROVED BY THE PEOPLE ... 337
II. FROM REVOCATION REFERENDA TO RATIFYING REFERENDA ... 339
III. THE ELIMINATION OF THE CONSTITUTIONAL PRINCIPLE OF ALTERNATE GOVERNMENT AND THE LIMITS TO CONTINUOUS REELECTION ... 341
IV. LIFTING THE PROHIBITION ON REPEATING REFERENDA FOR CONSTITUTIONAL REVIEW ... 344
V. ILLEGITIMATE TRANSFORMATION OF THE FEDERAL SYSTEM ... 346
VI. THE LIFTING OF THE PROHIBITION ON GOVERNMENT FINANCING OF ELECTORAL ACTIVITIES ... 349
VII. THE ILLEGITIMATE ELIMINATION OF THE SUPRACONSTITUTIONAL RANK OF INTERNATIONAL HUMAN RIGHTS TREATIES ... 351
VIII. THE ELIMINATION OF JUDGES' POWER TO IMMEDIATELY AND DIRECTLY APPLY INTERNATIONAL HUMAN RIGHTS TREATIES ... 354
IX. THE DENIAL OF THE PEOPLE'S RIGHT TO INTERNATIONAL HUMAN RIGHTS PROTECTION ... 355

Chapter 15

THE ALTERNATE PRINCIPLE OF GOVERNMENT AND THE 2009 CONSTITUTIONAL AMENDMENT ON CONTINUOUS REELECTION ... 359

I. THE REPUBLICAN PRINCIPLE OF ALTERNATE GOVERNMENT AND THE VENEZUELAN TRADITION OF NO REELECTION ... 360
II. THE LIMITS IMPOSED BY THE CONSTITUTION ON CONSTITUTIONAL REVIEW ... 362
III. THE BINDING CONSTITUTIONAL INTERPRETATION ... 364

FINAL REFLECTIONS

THE RIGHT TO DEMOCRACY AND ITS VIOLATION BY VENEZUELA'S AUTHORITARIAN GOVERNMENT: SOME RELEVANT FACTS FROM THE PAST DECADE — 367

I. **REPRESENTATIVE DEMOCRACY AND THE VENEZUELAN AUTHORITARIAN GOVERNMENT** — 367
II. **REPRESENTATIVE DEMOCRACY AND ITS DEFORMATIONS** — 371
III. **PARTICIPATORY DEMOCRACY AND THE VIOLATION OF THE CITIZENS' RIGHT TO PARTICIPATION** — 380
IV. **DISRESPECTING HUMAN RIGHTS** — 386
V. **ACCESS TO POWER AND ITS EXERCISE CONTRARY TO THE RULE OF LAW** — 392
VI. **BROKEN REPRESENTATIVE DEMOCRACY** — 396
VII. **WEAKENED DEMOCRACY DUE TO THE ABSENCE OF PLURALISM** — 398
VIII. **VANISHING DEMOCRACY AND ABSENT SEPARATION OF POWERS** — 401
IX. **DEMOCRACY AND PROBLEMS OF TRANSPARENCY** — 406
X. **FEEBLE DEMOCRACY AND RESTRICTIONS ON FREEDOMS OF EXPRESSION AND THE PRESS** — 407
XI. **DEMOCRACY AND SUBMISSION OF THE MILITARY TO CIVIL POWER** — 410

INDEX — 413

AUTHOR'S NOTE

This book deals with the dismantling of Venezuelan democracy from within that the country's authoritarian government has accomplished during the past decade using some democratic tools defrauding the Constitution.[1] This process began after the election of Hugo Chávez Frías as president of the Republic of Venezuela in December 1998, the result of which was the tragic setback to democratic institutions and standards. Venezuela had been one of the most admired Latin American countries because of its stable democracy, which had consolidated during the second half of the twentieth century. During the past decade, the country has experienced a continuous, persistent, and deliberate demolishing of institutions and destruction of democracy, which has never before occurred in the constitutional history of the country.

The first step to subvert democratic principles and values materialized in 1999, with the forced convening of a constituent assembly – not established in the Constitution as a valid means for constitutional reform – through a consultative referendum to impose the "will of the people" over the Constitution itself (peoples' sovereignty over constitutional supremacy). The result was the interference and takeover of all recently elected branches of government by the newly elected Constituent Assembly, completely controlled by the president of the republic. For the election of the Assembly, an electoral system was adopted without any sort of agreements, the Constitution was sanctioned without any sort of consensus, and conditions were established for the imposition of an authoritarian and centralized government, which has since eliminated any checks and balances and, consequently, the rule of law.

The remote antecedent of the use of the constituent assembly procedure, not established in the constitution, to draft a new constitution without the

---

[1] See, in general, Allan R. Brewer-Carías, "La demolición del Estado de derecho y la destrucción de la democracia en Venezuela (1999-2009)," in *La democracia en su contexto. Estudios en homenaje a Dieter Nohlen en su septuagésimo aniversario,* coord. José Reynoso Núñez and Herminio Sánchez de la Barquera y Arroyo, Instituto de Investigaciones Jurídicas, Universidad Nacional Autónoma de México, Mexico City 2009, 477-517

interruption of the constitutional rule can be found in Colombia, during the transition between the governments of President Virgilio Barco and President César Gaviria in 1990, after the Supreme Court of Justice expressly accepted the constitutionality of the process. The Constituent Assembly was elected with a pluralistic composition, after the political actors had agreed on the electoral system. The assembly drafted the 1991 Constitution, also based on negotiations and consensus, thus contributing to the further development of democratic institutions in the country.

However, it was after the 1999 experience in Venezuela that a new formula was developed in which the general bylaws for the election of a Constituent Assembly, also not established in the 1961 Constitution as a constitutional review method, resulted not from consensus and agreements among political actors but from those who took the initiative to convene the referendum. The result in this case was the establishment and development not of a democratic government but of a framework for developing an authoritarian government through democratic tools. In Venezuela, a popular consultation or consultative referendum was convened to subvert the Constitution itself, as President Chávez unilaterally defined the assembly in a way that impeded the configuration of a plural political body. In 2007, Ecuador's president Rafael Correa also implemented this "formula" to depart from the Constitution then in force, and in 2009, Honduran President Manuel Zelaya tried to implement it, but the Supreme Court of Justice of Honduras declared it unconstitutional.[2] Unfortunately, in Honduras, instead of waiting for the results of the judicial process initiated against the president, indicted for violating the Constitution, the military eventually expelled him unconstitutionally from the country. His expulsion led to an international uproar from the less democratic leaders of Latin America, including Hugo Chávez and Raúl Castro, supposedly to defend democracy and to impose the 2001 Inter-American Democratic Charter.[3]

In Venezuela, contrary to the Colombia in 1991 and Honduras in 2009 cases, the Supreme Court of Justice, though requested to issue a decision on the interpretation of the constitutionality of the convening of the assembly, refused to rule in a clear way and instead issued an ambiguous decision that ultimately allowed the president to impose his own rules for

---

[2] The formula has been referred to as the Chávez franchise or the Chávez brand because of his ostensible involvement in the political processes of the countries that have previously applied it, such as Ecuador. See, e.g., "The Wages of Chavismo" (Opinion), *Wall Street Journal*, July 1, 2009, A12.

[3] See, e.g., Moisés Naim, "Golpe en Honduras: Idiotas contra hipócritas," *El Pais*, Madrid July 5, 2009.

the convening of the Constituent Assembly. In 1999, the executive unilaterally designed a constituent process that not only sanctioned a new Constitution in the name of the popular will but also proceeded with an aggressive takeover of the legislative and judicial branches.

Although many of its drafters consider it among the best constitutional texts in contemporary Latin America, to allow the intended institutional destruction, the 1999 Constitution has also been constantly violated under the watch of its own product, the Supreme Tribunal of Justice. The tribunal, particularly its Constitutional Chamber, is completely controlled by the government, and it has molded and accepted as legitimate all the subsequent constitutional violations.

Now in Venezuela there is a complete lack of the essential elements of democracy as defined by the 2001 Inter-American Democratic Charter: access to power and its exercise subject to the rule of law, the performing of periodic free and fair elections based on universal and secret vote as an expression of the sovereignty of the people, the plural regime of political parties and organizations, the separation and independence of all branches of government, and respect for human rights and fundamental freedoms.

I have been writing on the Venezuelan constitution-making process and its consequences over the past decade, since the process began in 1998, and have produced a series of essays that study the subversion of democracy from within and the violation of the Constitution.[4] This book is the result of those essays, mainly written from New York, where I have lived, able to continue my academic activities, since September 2005. My political opposition to Chávez's authoritarian government and the threats I received to my freedom unfortunately forced me to leave Venezuela in 2005.[5] I had begun such opposition in 1998, when Chávez became

---

[4]The text of all my academic works and papers and almost all my published books and articles can be downloaded from my website: http://allanbrewercarias.com/

[5]I was unjustly accused of "conspiring to change violently the Constitution" because I had given a legal opinion, as a lawyer, in the midst of the political crisis originated by Chávez's resignation on Apr. 11, 2002. I gave that opinion at the request of the head of the brief provisional government, established after such resignation was publicly announced. On those facts, see Allan R. Brewer-Carías, *La crisis de la democracia venezolana: La Carta Democrática Interamericana y los sucesos de abril de 2002*, Ediciones El Nacional, Caracas 2002 (full text available at http://allanbrewercarias.com/Content.aspx?id=449725d9-f1cb-474b-8ab2-41efb849fea5). Although my legal opinion defended the democratic principle and was contrary to what the provisional government eventually announced in its constitutive decree, the government immediately reacted against me and publicly condemned me, without trial, and accused me of having written the decree, which I did not. All this was in violation of my constitutional guarantees, particularly my right to defense and the presumption of innocence, and based on interested, malicious journalists' opinions. Thus, the government, using the public prosecutor as a tool for political persecution, as well as newspaper clippings as the sole evidence, accused me in a process that allowed the head of the Prosecutor

presidential candidate in the elections of that year after having led in 1992 a failed military coup against the democratic government. As president of the National Academy of Political and Social Sciences, I convened all the presidential candidates to explain their political projects for the state and the political system before the academy. When I introduced Chávez at an academy session on August 15, 1998, I stressed his "nondemocratic" way of entering the Venezuelan political arena and my opposition to his main electoral proposal of "convening the Constitutional Assembly without giving it constitutional basis by reforming the Constitution."[6] My opposition to that political project seeking the global take over of State power continued after his election as president, when in 1999 I personally went before the former Supreme Court of Justice to challenge his decree on the Constituent Assembly on the grounds of its unconstitutionality. After contributing to force the correction of the decree through judicial decisions, my opposition continued throughout the 1999 National Constituent Assembly, to which I was elected as an independent candidate. Myself and three other distinguished Venezuelan politicians and thinkers formed the very tiny but substantive minority opposition group of the assembly. I continued my opposition during the discussions on the draft 1999 Constitution because of the authoritarian trends it set forth to concentrate and centralize state powers. Since the approval of the Constitution, I have continued to denounce in books, essays, and speeches all the successive antidemocratic, centralistic, and militaristic decisions and measures taken by the government. This book and the essays that inspired it are part of that effort.

New York has been a formidable place to live, and being together with my wife, Beatriz, has helped us overcome the sadness of not having the

---

General's Office to violate my rights. See the letter I sent to the prosecutor general on the eve of my departure from Venezuela, on Sept. 28, 2005, in Allan R. Brewer-Carías, *En mi propia defensa*, Editorial Jurídica Venezolana, Caracas 2006, 573-90 (full text available at http://allanbrewercarias.com/Content.aspx?id=449725d9-f1cb-474b-8ab2-41efb849fea5). I could not have possibly expected a fair trial from the Venezuelan Judiciary. Consequently, in Jan. 2007, I filed a complaint against the Venezuelan State before the Inter-American Commission on Human Rights based on the violation of my due process, defense, presumption of innocence, and free expression rights, as established in the American Convention on Human Rights. The Commission admitted my petition in Sept. 2009 (Case: 12.724: *Inter-American Commission on Human Rights, Allan Brewer Carías/Venezuela*). Available at http://www.cidh.oas.org/annualrep/2009eng/Venezuela84.07eng.htm.

[6] It was my first and last personal encounter with Chávez. See my introduction to Allan R. Brewer-Carías, coord., *Los candidatos presidenciales ante la Academia: Ciclo de exposiciones 1998*, Academia de Ciencias Políticas y Sociales, Caracas 1998, 23, 38, 92, 95, 137, 138, 320. See my foreword to the same book: "A modo de presentación: Reflexiones sobre la crisis del sistema político, sus salidas democráticas y la convocatoria a una constituyente," in id., 9-66.

always very important direct contact with our family and friends. Beatriz, as always during the almost five decades we have been married, with all her generous love, has helped me in an unimaginable way in allowing me to continue with my writings. As always, I am very grateful to her for all her love, understanding, support, and loyalty.

Since our arrival in New York, good friends gave us companionship, helping us continues with our daily lives; and, most important, after having been in the academic life for fifty years, I immediately received the hospitality of Columbia University. As adjunct professor of law at the Columbia Law School, I have been able to continue teaching, giving over various semesters the course Judicial Protection of Human Rights in Latin America: A Comparative Constitutional Law Study of the Latin American Injunction for the Protection of Constitutional Rights (*Amparo* Proceeding). The text I wrote for the course was published in 2009.[7]

Of course, also from an academic point of view, New York has been an extraordinary launching pad that has allowed me to get in touch with many other universities in the United States and to continue, increasingly, my already well-established, long relations with universities and law professors in Europe and Latin America. This has allowed me to continue with my work and writings.

The truth is that if somebody in Venezuela at any moment considered that forcing me to leave the country would annihilate my academic work and life and press me to renounce my ideals and cease to diffuse them, they have noisily failed. It is enough to visit my Web site (http://www.allanbrewercarias.com) to appreciate the use I have made of my time in favor of freedom, of the rule of law and of democratic principles. In the end, they have allowed me to devote more time to continue analyzing the chaotic situation of Venezuela's constitutional and legal system that has resulted from the disorderly implementation of a supposedly "Bolivarian revolution," which, as Chávez confessed himself in January 2010, is no more than the phantasmagoric resurrection of the

---

[7]See Allan R. Brewer-Carías, *Constitutional Protection of Human Rights in Latin America: A Comparative Study of the Amparo Proceeding*, Cambridge University Press, New York 2009. The Appendix to the course, containing the text of all the *amparo* laws in force in Latin America, was also published in Mexico as *Leyes de amparo de America Latina*, 2 vols., Instituto de Administración Pública de Jalisco y sus Municipios, Instituto de Administración Pública del Estado de México, Poder Judicial del Estado de México, Academia de Derecho Constitucional de la Confederación de Colegios y Asociaciones de Abogados de México, Guadalajara 2009.

historically failed "Marxist revolution," but led by a president who has never even read Marx's writings.[8]

Nevertheless, on April 2010, the governmental United Socialist Party of Venezuela of which he presides, in its First Extraordinary Congress adopted a "Declaration of Principles" in which it officially declared itself as a "Marxist," "Anti-imperialist" and "Ant-capitalist" party. According to the same document, the party's actions are to be based on the "scientific socialism" and on the "inputs of Marxism as a philosophy of praxis," in order to substitute the "Capitalist Bourgeois State" by a "Socialist State" based on the Popular Power and the socialization of the means of production.[9]

With these declarations it can be said that, finally, the so called "Bolivarian Revolution" has been unveiled; a revolution for which nobody in Venezuela has voted except for its rejection in the December 2, 2007 referendum, in which the President's proposals for constitutional reforms in order to establish a Socialist, Centralized, Police and Militaristic state received a negative popular response.[10]

Allan R. Brewer-Carías
New York, August 4, 2010

---

[8] In his annual speech before the National Assembly on Jan. 15, 2010, in which Chávez declared to have "assumed Marxism," he also confessed that he had never read Marx's works. See María Lilibeth Da Corte, "Por primera vez asumo el marxismo," in *El Universal*, Caracas Jan. 16, 2010, http://www.eluniversal.com/2010/01/16/pol_art_por-primera-vez-asu_1726209.shtml.

[9] See "Declaración de Principios, I Congreso Extraordinario del Partido Socialista Unido de Venezuela," Apr. 23, 2010, at http://psuv.org.ve/files/tcdocumentos/Declaracion-de-principios-PSUV.pdf

[10] See on the constitutional reforms proposals, Allan R. Brewer-Carías, *Hacia la consolidación de un Estado socialista, centralizado, policial y militarista. Comentarios sobre el sentido y alcance de las propuestas de reforma constitucional 2007*, Editorial Jurídica Venezolana, Caracas 2007; *La reforma constitucional de 2007 (Comentarios al proyecto inconstitucionalmente sancionado por la Asamblea Nacional el 2 de noviembre de 2007)*, Editorial Jurídica Venezolana, Caracas 2007.

INTRODUCTION

DEFRAUDING DEMOCRACY THROUGH NONCONSENSUAL CONSTITUENT ASSEMBLIES

I

Democracy is much more than voting. It is a political regime in which, in addition to the holding of periodic, free, and fair elections based on secret balloting and universal suffrage as an expression of the sovereignty of the people, the following other essential elements are all ensured: respect for human rights and fundamental freedoms, access to and exercise of power in accordance with the rule of law, a pluralistic system of political parties and organizations, and separation of powers and independence of the branches of government.

This is what is set forth in Article 3 of the Inter-American Democratic Charter (*Carta Democrática Interamericana*), which members of the Organization of American States signed in Lima, Peru, on September 11, 2001 (the same day of the terrorist attacks in the United States). After so many antidemocratic and militarist regimes that have existed in Latin American history, and so many authoritarian regimes disguised as democratic that still have been developed there, adoption of a continental doctrine about democracy was an imperious necessity. That is why, in addition to the foregoing essential elements, Article 4 of the same charter included the following essential components of the exercise of democracy: transparency in government activities, probity, responsible public administration on the part of governments, respect for social rights, freedom of expression and of the press, constitutional subordination of all state institutions to the legally constituted civilian authority, and respect for the rule of law by all institutions and sectors of society.

For the purpose of adopting this charter, the General Assembly of the Organization of American States assumed that representative democracy is indispensable for the stability, peace, and development of the region, its purposes being to promote and consolidate representative democracy with due respect for the principle of nonintervention; and considering that solidarity among and cooperation between American states requires that the political organization of those states be based on the effective exercise of representative democracy; and that democracy as well as economic growth and social development based on justice and equity are interdependent and mutually reinforcing. The General Assembly furthermore recognized the contributions of the organization and other regional and subregional mechanisms to the promotion and consolidation of democracy in the Americas, as well as the facts that a safe environment is essential to the integral development of the human being, which contributes to democracy and political stability; that the right of workers to associate themselves freely for the defense and promotion of their interests is fundamental for the fulfillment of democratic ideas; and that all the rights and obligations of member states under the organization's charter represent the foundation on which democratic principles in the Western Hemisphere are built.

Without doubt, the Inter-American Democratic Charter is the most important international instrument adopted in the contemporary world regarding democracy and democratic principles.[1] Article 1 recognizes and declares that the peoples of the Americas have a "right to democracy" and that their governments have an obligation to promote and defend that democracy, which is essential for the social, political, and economic development of the peoples of the Americas.[2]

Article 2 of the same charter states that the effective exercise of representative democracy is the basis for the rule of law and for the constitutional regimes of countries, which must be strengthened and deepened by the permanent, ethical, and responsible participation of the citizenry within a legal framework that conforms to a respective constitutional order. For such purposes, Article 5 of the charter considers that the strengthening of political parties and other political organizations is a priority for democracy; Article 6 declares that it is the right and responsibility of all citizens to participate in decisions relating to their own

---

[1] The Member States of the African Union in its Eight Ordinary Assembly held in Addis Abeba, Ethiopia, on Jan. 30, 2007, have also signed the "African Charter on Democracy, Elections and Governance." Available at http://www.un.org/democracyfund/Docs/AfricanCharterDemocracy.pdf.

[2] See Asdrúbal Aguiar, *El derecho a la democracia: La democracia en el derecho y la jurisprudencia interamericanos: La libertad de expresión, piedra angular de la democracia*, Editorial Jurídica Venezolana, Caracas 2008. See also my foreword to that book "Sobre el derecho a la democracia y el control del poder" at 17-37.

development because doing so is a necessary condition for the full and effective exercise of democracy; and Article 7 of the charter proclaims that democracy is indispensable for the effective exercise of fundamental freedoms and human rights in their universality, indivisibility, and interdependence, which is embodied in the respective constitutions of states and in inter-American and international human rights instruments.

Consequently, democracy is not only a matter of voting and elections; it is a political system in which elections must be held with a pluralistic system of political parties, the principles of the rule of law are ensured, the separation of powers is guaranteed, and human rights and freedoms are protected. In this context, any violation of a country's constitution is undemocratic, and any constitution-making process that contravenes or defrauds[3] an existing constitution is contrary to democracy.

II

Undemocratic constitution making is precisely what occurred in Venezuela in 1999. That year began the dismantling of democracy that Venezuela has suffered, with the convening of an illegitimate, unconstitutional constituent assembly for constitutional review; the imposition of new election rules adopted in a nonconsensual way and without the participation of the country's political forces; and the takeover of all branches of government by an exclusionist group aiming to destroy its opponents and impose its own political project.[4] In 2009, attempts aimed to impose this method of assaulting power by using democratic tools but defrauding the Constitution, so successfully employed in Venezuela to destroy its democracy, were made in Honduras.

In effect, in the first half of 2009, inspired by the constitutional formula that President Hugo Chávez had used in Venezuela a decade earlier (in 1999), Honduras's President Manuel Zelaya decided to convene a consultative referendum to clear the way for the convening of the National Constituent Assembly, which the Honduran Constitution did not include as a

---

[3] I have used the word *defraud* (to cause injury or loss by deceit) in general, as it is used in civil law systems, referred not only to persons but also to institutions, in the sense that you can defraud the Constitution, you can defraud a provision of a statute, and you can defraud democracy itself.

[4] See, in general, Allan R. Brewer-Carías, "Constitution Making Process in Defraudation of the Constitution and Authoritarian Government in Defraudation of Democracy: The Recent Venezuelan Experience," in *Lateinamerika Analysen* 19, German Institute of Global and Area Studies, Hamburg 2008, 119-42; and "The 1999 Venezuelan Constitution-Making Process as an Instrument for Forming the Development of an Authoritarian Political Regime," in Laurel E. Miller, editor, *Framing the State in Times of Transition: Case Studies in Constitution Making*, United States Institute of Peace, Washington 2010, 505-32.

valid way to reform the Constitution. The purpose of such a proposal, which was conceived without any political consensus or agreements between political parties and political actors of the country, was to reshape Honduras's constitutional principles, including the change of traditionally solid provisions, like the one establishing the absolute prohibition on presidential reelection.

The attorney general of the republic challenged Zelaya's attempt before the courts, requesting judicial review of the administrative action. The courts did issue preliminary judicial measures to suspend the presidential acts that had been challenged on grounds of unconstitutionality. The president ignored the judicial decisions and publicly insisted on achieving his proposal through de facto means. After his prosecution before the Supreme Court of Justice for contempt of court and for violating express provisions of the Constitution,[5] Zelaya's detention was ordered. In Honduras, the president's actions provoked the functioning of the country's democratic checks-and-balances system (the Supreme Electoral Tribunal, the Supreme Court, the attorney general, the human rights commissioner, and the Congress declared the president's intentions unlawful); unfortunately, the Supreme Court's decision was not enforced as ordered. Instead, the same military in charge of detaining the president unconstitutionally expelled him from the country. With that action began the well-known international political crisis in which even the general assemblies of the United Nations and the Organization of American States intervened. Ironically, and suddenly, the crisis briefly converted the less democratic heads of state of Latin America, like Hugo Chávez and Raúl Castro, into political leaders defending democratic principles. That muddled many democratic leaders of the world in a discussion to qualify the events in Honduras as a coup d'état and resulted in the absurd dilemma of whether to impose international sanctions on a country in which the democratic institutions had worked – at least previous to the president's expulsion.[6]

---

[5] In Honduras, the Constitution expressly prohibits any public official, including the president of the republic, from proposing reforms to the Constitution to alter the principle of alternate government and to change the prohibition established for presidential reelection, which is considered an unchangeable, solid principle. The Constitution even establishes that any public officials who propose such reforms will immediately cease their public functions (art. 239). See, in general, Octavio Rubén Sánchez Barrientos, *Los extravagantes y el Caudillo que se sacó a sí mismo de la Presidencia. Un ensayo sobre la historia del Artículo 239 de la Constitución de la República de Honduras y del Principio de Alternabilidad en el Ejercicio de la Presidencia de la República* (forthcoming book), Tegucigalpa, June 2010.

[6] See Allan R. Brewer-Carías, "Reforma constitucional, asamblea nacional constituyente y control judicial contencioso administrativo: El caso de Honduras (2009) y el precedente venezolano (1999)," *Revista Mexicana Statum Rei Romanae de Derecho Administrativo: Homenaje de Nuevo León a*

The formula of forcing the convening of a constituent assembly not established in the Constitution by unilaterally imposing its bylaws without any consensual process or political agreement had been used a decade earlier, in 1999, in Venezuela. But in Venezuela, the Supreme Court, although requested to decide on the matter, abstained from adopting a clear interpretative decision on the constitutionality of such a proposal, thereby allowing the president to impose his rules for the election of the assembly. Something similar happened in Ecuador in 2007, where the president of the republic also convened a constituent assembly not established in the constitution by submitting to a popular referendum the rules for electing a constituent assembly, without any previous political agreement or consensual process. Nonetheless, in that case, no judicial decision on the matter was adopted by the Constitutional Tribunal and the constitution making continued without previous judicial review. All these cases and experiences are a contrast to the initial precedent developed in Colombia in 1991, where the convening of a constituent assembly not established by the Constitution was made only after political parties and political actors reached agreements to hold a consultative referendum on the matter, which only took place once the Supreme Court of Justice had ruled on the constitutionality of the procedure.

III

In any case, the convening of constituent assemblies for the purpose of reforming constitutions is not exceptional in Latin America. Latin American countries have a long history of constitution making by means of constituent assemblies, which have been convened and elected many times without indications for doing so in a constitution. Historically, such conventions have generally occurred after a de facto rupture of the legal constitutional order, produced by a coup d'état, a revolution, or a civil war. In such cases, those who have come to power have always convened the constituent assemblies, and according to the rules they unilaterally impose. Subsequently, a popular vote and the new leadership legitimized the newly sanctioned constitution. In such matters, Latin American countries have gained recognized expertise during their two hundred years of political turmoil.

Jorge Fernández Ruiz 3, Asociación Mexicana de Derecho Administrativo, Facultad de Derecho y Criminología de la Universidad Autónoma de Nuevo León, Monterrey, Mexico, 2009, 11-77; *Reforma constitucional, asamblea constituyente, y control judicial: Honduras (2009), Ecuador (2007) y Venezuela (1999)*, Universidad Externado de Colombia, Bogotá 2009.

Because of the rupture of the constitutional order, the elected constituent assemblies, according to the rules designed by the political winners, have usually exercised unlimited constitution-making power and have tried to represent the will of the people. However, they have not subjected themselves to provisions of the previous constitution, except regarding some solid or rocklike principles or traditionally preserved clauses imposed by the republican form of government.

It is in contrast with this traditional trend that, in the past decades, a new constitution-making process began to take shape in Latin America. This has occurred by means of electing unconstitutional constituent assemblies, particularly when there has been no previous rupture of the constitutional order. As a result, in many cases, the convening of a constituent assembly has occurred after issuing of a judicial interpretation of the constitution, which allows for the procedure to be applied without rupturing the constitutional order and through democratic elections, such that a plural entity can be figured to reshape the constitutional order. As already mentioned, this was the case in Colombia in 1991, where the rules and conditions for the election of the Constituent Assembly resulted from political agreements and consensus. In contrast, this was not the case in Venezuela in 1999, where the Supreme Court abstained from a clear and unambiguous decision on the constitutionality of the procedure, thereby allowing the president of the republic to impose his own rules and conditions for electing the Constituent Assembly. That process resulted in the election of a nonplural constituent assembly completely dominated by the president's followers. The assembly, far from just writing a new constitution, was the main tool of the newly elected president's assault on all branches of government to gain control, which violated the 1961 Constitution, whose supposed judicial interpretation helped to create the Assembly.[7] Consequently, the elected Constituent Assembly technically was a coup d'état,[8] unfortunately with the consent and complicity of the former Supreme Court of Justice. As always happens in cases of illegitimate institutional complicity, the Supreme Court was inexorably the first victim of the authoritarian government, which it helped to grab power. Just a few months

---

[7] See Allan R. Brewer-Carías, *Debate constituyente (Aportes a la Asamblea Nacional Constituyente)*, Fundación de Derecho Público–Editorial Juridica Venezolana, Caracas 1999, 1 (Aug. 8–Sept. 8):17-122.

[8] A coup d'état occurs, as affirmed by Diego Valadés, "when an elected constitutional organ ignores the Constitution." See Diego Valadés, *Constitución y democracia*, UNAM, México 2000, p. 35; and Allan R. Brewer-Carías, *Golpe de estado y proceso constituyente en Venezuela*, Universidad Nacional Autónoma de México, Mexico City 2002, 194-5.

later, that Supreme Court was eliminated from the institutional scene.[9] As a result, Venezuela has an authoritarian government created not by the classic Latin American military coup d'état but rather by a systematic process of destroying from within the state all the basic principles of democracy, its institutions, and the Constitution.

IV

The 1999 Constituent Assembly was, then, the instrument the president used to dissolve and interfere in all branches of government (particularly the judiciary) and to dismiss all public officials who had been elected just a few months earlier in November 1998: namely, the representatives to the national Congress, the state legislative assemblies, and the municipal councils, as well as the state governors and municipal mayors. The sole exception to this interference was the president of the republic itself, precisely the author of the constitutional fraud, whose tenure was not affected. In addition, the Constituent Assembly interfered in all other branches of government, particularly in the judiciary, whose autonomy and independence was progressively and systematically demolished.[10] The result was tight executive control over the judiciary, particularly regarding the newly appointed Supreme Tribunal of Justice, whose Constitutional Chamber has been the most ominous instrument for consolidating authoritarianism in the country.[11]

The new constitution-making process established in Venezuela in 1999 can be characterized as a defrauding of the Constitution, which was deliberately used and interpreted without any consensus of the interested political parties and actors to elect a body with the final purpose of violating that same Constitution whose ambiguous judicial interpretation birthed the

---

[9]On Dec. 1999, after the popular approval of the new Constitution, the Constituent Assembly dismissed the members of the Supreme Court of Justice, created the Supreme Tribunal of Justice and appointed its members. See the study about the effects of the Dec. 1999 Transitory Regime established by the Constituent Assembly after the approval, by popular referendum, of the Constitution of 1999, in Allan R. Brewer-Carías, *La Constitución de 1999*, Editorial Arte, Caracas 2000; and *La Constitución de 1999: Derecho constitucional venezolano*, Editorial Jurídica Venezolana, Caracas 2004, 2:1.150ff.

[10]See Allan R. Brewer-Carías, "La progresiva y sistemática demolición de la autonomía e independencia del poder judicial en Venezuela (1999–2004)," in *XXX Jornadas J.M Domínguez Escovar, Estado de derecho, Administración de justicia y derechos humanos*, Instituto de Estudios Jurídicos del Estado Lara, Barquisimeto 2005, 33-174.

[11]See Allan R. Brewer-Carías, "*Quis Custodiet ipsos Custodes*: De la interpretación constitucional a la inconstitucionalidad de la interpretación," in *VIII Congreso Nacional de Derecho Constitucional*, Fondo Editorial and Colegio de Abogados de Arequipa, Arequipa, Peru, 2005, 463-89; and *Crónica de la "In"Justicia constitucional: La Sala constitucional y el autoritarismo en Venezuela*, Editorial Jurídica Venezolana, Caracas 2007, 11-44, 47-79.

assembly. This assembly, which the president completely controlled, set forth the foundations for the enthroning of an authoritarian regime that has led the process of demolishing institutions in order to defraud democracy. That is, despite the relatively free but manipulated elections held for the purpose of allowing the president's supporters complete control of the assembly, the process began the destruction of democracy and the consolidation of an authoritarian government.

After defrauding the Constitution to gain power, once it controlled all the state branches of government, the government began another defrauding process, this time of democracy. It used processes of representative democracy to progressively eliminate the same and substitute it by a supposed "participative democracy" based on nonelected communal councils, which the president directly controls.

V

With different phrasing but the same sense and content of the 1999 Venezuelan convening of the constituent assembly to reshape the Constitution and the political system, in January 2007, the newly elected president of Ecuador, Rafael Correa Delgado, also convened a referendum to ask the people about the convening and election of a national constituent assembly not established by or regulated in the 1998 Constitution then in force, according to the rules and conditions Correa unilaterally established, again without previous political agreement or consensus. After three months of bitter political and institutional conflicts, particularly between Correa and the Congress, the referendum took place on April 15, 2007. Voters approved the president's proposal and the election of the assembly took place in September 2007, completely controlled by the president's supporters.

In modern constitutionalism, a constitution as a political pact sanctioned by the representatives of the people and their constitution-making process has always resulted from political conflicts, whether for their prevention or their solution, and consequently has tended to create democratic institutions to achieve political stability. This, of course, is the situation in democratic systems. In authoritarian systems, the Constitution, even with voter-approved veils of democracy, always remains the sole expression of a ruler's will. The question in democratic systems is the need to determine the extent to which constitutions can contribute to resolving conflict and creating stable democratic governments – in other words, how constitutions must be adopted to effectively prevent conflicts and build stable democratic institutions.

As constitutional history shows, those goals have not always been achieved. Constitutions are not the magical instrument that many think they are for guaranteeing the end of political conflicts or the founding of permanent stability. The real ability of a constitution to contribute to conflict resolution and prevention and to ensure stability depends on the way constitution-making processes are conceived of and developed and how constitutions are drafted and adopted.

During the past two hundred years, all kinds of constitutional review proceedings have occurred in the world, and the ideal path of constitution making so that a constitution contributes to conflict resolution and the creation of a stable democratic government has yet to be designed.[12] However, one thing is clear: No constitution-making process can endure in a given country when one political or social faction implements it to impose a way of life or a specific political and economic system to a given country. In such cases, conflicts are not resolved and constitution-making processes restart, sometimes over and over in an endless process.

In the events of Venezuela in 1999 and Ecuador in 2007, which have produced endless political conflicts, the commonality was that the constitution-making process began without any constitutional foundation and without agreement between political parties and actors but according to rules unilaterally imposed by the head of the executive branch. Moreover, they developed without any de facto rupture of the Constitution; that is, no coup d'état preceded the election of the Constituent Assembly, being the interpretation of the existing Constitution the fact that paved the way for it election. These same steps were found in the president of Honduras's failed attempt to establish a constituent assembly in 2009, which in that case was stopped by the judiciary.

In Venezuela, as mentioned earlier, it was the Constituent Assembly that resulted from the election in 1999, the one that gave the "constituent" coup d'état against the 1961 Constitution and against all existing elected constituted powers. In this case, the existing Constitution of 1961 and all democratic tools were fraudulently used to violate the Constitution, setting up the basis for the progressive undermining of the democratic form of government and allowing for authoritarian seizure of all state branches of government by the new political forces supporting the president – thereby crushing the traditional political parties.

The ultimate aims of the government regarding the Constituent Assembly were, of course, not previously announced, explained, or proposed to the people when the president convened it in February 1999. The publicly

---

[12]See, in general, Laurel E. Miller, editor, *Framing the State in Times of Transition: Case Studies in Constitution Making*, United States Institute of Peace, Washington 2010.

proposed aims of convening the assembly were to reform state institutions and to improve democracy, aims that hardly anybody could challenge and that nearly everybody was willing to support, particularly given the political crisis of the state institutions and the party system.

The Venezuelan people in January 1999, like the people of Ecuador in 2007, should have known before they voted what kind of institutions the president was proposing to conduct the constitution-making process. For example, in Honduran President Manuel Zelaya's failed attempt, the people knew some of the proposed constitutional reforms that the president was offering and could determine that they were contrary to the country's Constitution, which provoked challenges to his process.

In the case of Ecuador, the presidential decree of January 2007 proposed the election of the Constituent Assembly to draft not only the "new" Constitution but also one with full power to transform the institutional framework of the state. According to the assembly's bylaws, unilaterally drafted by the president, all decisions could take effect only after the new Constitution was approved through referendum. That provision, approved in the April 2007 referendum without clarification from the Constitutional Tribunal before the September elections, resulted (as in Venezuela in 1999) in the election of a nonplural constituent assembly with two different goals: first to transform the institutional framework of the state; second to write the draft of a new constitution. These were the goals assumed by a constituent assembly completely controlled by the president's followers, having full and unlimited powers to transform the institutional framework of the state and to interfere in all branches of government. With these powers, the assembly could, for example, remove or limit the government; dissolve the Congress and assume the legislative function itself; intervene in provincial and municipal powers; remove the magistrates of the Supreme Court, the Supreme Electoral Tribunal, and the Constitutional Tribunal, as well as the comptroller general of the state; and intervene in the judiciary and the Public Prosecutors' Office.

Thus, the main constitutional discussion that took place in Ecuador during the first month of 2007 was focused on limiting the full powers to be attributed to the Constituent Assembly to ensure that the recently elected (December 2006) branches would be respected. To realize the intensity of the bitter political conflicts that resulted from those discussions, it is enough to bear in mind the institutional decisions of the subsequent three months, from January to April 2007.[13] Once the Supreme Electoral Council received the presidential decree on January 16 convening the constituent assembly, the tribunal submitted the decree to Congress for its approval. Congress then issued a decision considering urgent the assembly's convening but modifying the original decree. The Supreme Electoral Tribunal ignored Congress's decision and, on March 1, it convened the referendum according to the original decree with some modifications proposed by the president himself. Congress, by a vote of fifty-seven members, dismissed the president of the Supreme Electoral Tribunal because he ignored Congress's decision, and Congress then challenged as unconstitutional the Supreme Electoral Tribunal's decision before the Constitutional Tribunal. In response to these actions, the Supreme Electoral Tribunal dismissed the congressional representatives who had adopted the decision for interfering with voting processes, even though the Constitution established only the possibility of a recall referendum for such purposes. Before the referendum took place on April 15, a few *amparo* actions were filed before the Constitutional Tribunal and before various lower courts, arguing that the representatives had been unconstitutionally dismissed. Some of the *amparo* judges granted constitutional protection to the dismissed representatives, ordering their reincorporation to Congress, a decision that the president of Congress accepted, even though he had sworn in their substitutes the previous week. Then, the Supreme Electoral Tribunal decided to dismiss the lower-court judges who had granted the *amparo* protection, ignoring the adjudication that protected the dismissed representatives, considering them invalid. The president also considered the *amparo* decisions invalid, even though the Constitutional Tribunal considered them as obligatory as any constitutional judicial decision. Members of the Supreme Electoral Tribunal threatened to dismiss the members of the Constitutional Tribunal because they admittedly considered some of the *amparo* actions filed against the convening of the referendum. Once the referendum took place on April 15, the Constitutional Tribunal, after reviewing one of the lower court's *amparo* decisions, ruled to constitutionally protect fifty of the dismissed representatives by ordering their reincorporation. Congress, this time with a different majority because of the recently sworn–in representatives, on April 23 considered exhausted the term of the magistrates of the Constitutional Tribunal from January 2007.

---

[13]See Allan R. Brewer-Carías, "El inicio del proceso constituyente en Ecuador en 2007 y las lecciones de la experiencia venezolana de 1999," in *Estudios sobre el Estado constitucional (2005-2006)*, Editorial Jurídica Venezolana, Caracas 2007, 767-806. See also Allan R. Brewer-Carías, *Reforma constitucional, asamblea constituyente y control judicial: Honduras (2009), Ecuador (2007) y Venezuela (1999)*, Universidad Externado de Colombia, Bogotá 2009, 13ff.

That decision gave rise to endless discussions on the validity of all the constitutional decisions the tribunal had adopted since January 2007.

Thus, as can be deduced from this intense, three-month institutional quarrel, the constitutional discussion on the powers of the Constituent Assembly did not end. On the contrary, because the matter was not resolved before the election of the assembly in September 2007, the bitter political conflict was aggravated after the assembly's installment, which eventually assumed all political powers, prevailing over all the other branches of government.

VI

The case of the 1999 Constituent Assembly, although it was not the first convened in Venezuelan constitutional history,[14] in contrast with all the other previous assemblies, it did not result from a factual rupture of the constitutional order because of a revolution, a war, or a coup d'état, but rather from a process developed under a democratic rule (as was the case of the 1991 Colombian process and the 2007 Ecuadorian one), though in the middle of the most severe political crisis of the country's democratic system.[15] In 1999, it was the same Constituent Assembly that carried out a coup d'état after its election in July 1999 and brushed aside the 1961 Constitution, whose ambiguous interpretation had served to allow its convening.

The Venezuelan process is important not only because it marks a new trend in Latin American constitution making (i.e., defrauding the Constitution) but also because of the lessons it offers to help avoid repeating it or to help understand it if something similar occurs again (i.e., fraudulent use of the Constitution and democratic tools to establish a system founded on violation of the former and demolition of the latter). In the Venezuelan case, the constitution–making process exploited the people's legitimate hopes and expectations regarding the state's political recomposition as a consequence of the decline of the party system.

---

[14]For the text of previous Venezuelan constitutions (1811–1961), see Allan R. Brewer-Carías, *Las constituciones de Venezuela*, Biblioteca de la Academia de Ciencias Políticas y Sociales, Caracas 1997. On the constitutional history of those texts, see my "Estudio Preliminar" in id., 11-256.

[15]See Allan R. Brewer-Carías, "La crisis de las instituciones: Responsables y salidas,"in *Revista del Centro de Estudios Superiores de las Fuerzas Armadas de Cooperación*, 11, Caracas 1985, 57-83. See also Allan R. Brewer-Carías, *Instituciones políticas y constitucionales*, Universidad Católica del Táchira–Editorial Jurídica Venezolana, San Cristóbal–Caracas 1996, 1 (Evolución histórica del estado):523-41.

The Venezuelan crisis of the politically centralized, democratic multiparty system that had functioned since 1958 imposed the need to redesign the system to ensure the democratic governance of the country. The situation required a search for new political instruments to ensure democratic conciliation between political forces by means of political pacts or consensus among all political actors and factions of society, which is why the convening of a constituent assembly could have been justified for those reasons.[16] Accordingly, in Chávez's presidential decree of February 1999, the issue submitted to popular vote was the election of a constituent assembly "with the purpose to transform the state and to create a new juridical order allowing the effective functioning of a social and participative democracy."[17] Such was the raison d'être of the 1999 process, a purpose that was difficult for anybody to contradict.

But, at that moment, the country expected a constitution-making process based on political conciliation with the participation of all sectors of society. That did not happen, and the convening actors never intended it to. Given the aggressive antiparty and anti-representative-democracy presidential campaign, the lack of effective popular participation, and the absence of any sort of political consensus, what resulted were accentuated differences among political sectors and reinforced factioning of the country. Far from being a mechanism for dialogue and peace, Venezuela's 1999 constitution-making process served to aggravate an existing political crisis.

VII

Eleven years after the 1999 constitution making, despite the political rhetoric and exuberant spending, which wasted the immense fiscal income of a rich state in a poor country, no effective reform of the state has been achieved. Instead of social and participatory democracy, the process resulted in the configuration of a centralized, militaristic, and concentrated authoritarian regime that seeks to impose a socialist model of society with a democratic veil – centralized populist programs and institutions that pretend to be participatory have almost completed the destruction of the direct representative democracy.

In this sense, from a democratic point of view, the 1999 constitution-making process was a failure. Any changes the country has experienced

---

[16] See Allan R. Brewer-Carías, "Reflexiones sobre la crisis del sistema político, sus salidas democráticas y la convocatoria a una Constituyente," in *Los candidatos presidenciales ante la academia*, Biblioteca de la Academia de Ciencias Políticas y Sociales, Caracas 1998, 9-66.

[17] Article 3, Decree N° 3 of Feb. 2, 1999, in *Gaceta Oficial* N° 36.634 of Feb. 2, 1999.

have accentuated the crisis of the democratic system by concentrating all power in the president's hands and centralizing all territorial and local governments, which have limited representation. There have been great changes among Venezuela's political actors, as new groups filled with extreme hate and resentment (fed by the president's well-orchestrated speeches and diffused by state media) have crushed traditional parties and accentuated differences among Venezuelans in a context of extreme political polarization, which makes conciliation even more difficult.[18]

From an authoritarian, antidemocratic point of view, the 1999 constitution-making process can be considered a success – it allowed one faction, person and party, to completely seize and take over political power, and subsequently use it to crush all others parties and opponents. That opened wounds and created social and political rivalries that had been unknown for decades in the country, thus reinforcing social and political conflicts and destroying the democratic institutions, including the Armed Forces that were created with so much effort during the second half of the twentieth century.

The 1999 crisis of the democratic and representative party system should have led Venezuela's leadership to seek transformation, not destruction. The democratic system needed to improve to give way to a more participative democracy, which, of course, can take place only at the level of autonomous local government. Such was the people's main objective in responding to the constitution-making process called for in 1999: to draft an effective decentralization framework of the federal state and to transform the country's decades' old centralized federation into a participatory, decentralized democracy.

In the modern world, consolidated democracies have always both resulted from and caused political decentralization; that is, decentralization has been a consequence of the democratization process and a condition for democracy's survival and improvement. Thus, decentralization is the political instrument designed into a democracy to articulate all intermediate political powers, thereby allowing for government accomplishments close to the regions, communities, and people. Decentralization is a matter of democracies; decentralized autocracies have never existed.

The convening of the Constituent Assembly in Venezuela in 1999, after more than forty years of democracy, was supposed to have accentuated the democratic principle by decentralizing power, not destroying it. However, in

---

[18]See Allan R. Brewer-Carías, "El proceso constituyente y la fallida reforma del Estado en Venezuela," in *Estrategias y propuestas para la reforma del estado,* Universidad Nacional Autónoma de México, Mexico City 2001, 25-48.

the past decade, the federal form of government has transformed into a simple constitutional rubber stamp to disguise a completely centralized state ruled by one person who is simultaneously head of the state, the executive, the public administration, the military, and the ruling United Socialist Party. He calls himself "the leader," to be "reelected" indefinitely.[19]

In 1999, other much-needed reforms included checks and balances among the branches of government. Achieving this, particularly reforming relations between the executive and legislative power, was why people accepted the constitution-making process of 1999. Paradoxically, the crisis of democratic governance in the 1990s was a result not of excess presidentialism but rather of excess party parliamentarianism, particularly given the tight political control that the traditional parties exercised over Congress. In particular, with respect to the exclusively partisan nomination and appointment of the nonelected public officials, like the magistrates of the Supreme Court, the head of the Comptroller General Office, the head of the Public Prosecutor's Office, and members of the Supreme Electoral Council, there were nasty criticisms given the excessive partisan character of those appointments, which were made without any possibility of civil–society participation. The reform of such matters aimed to ensure a better balance among independent powers and more effective checks among them, thus limiting their exclusive partisan conformation. Particularly, reform aimed to build a complete independent and autonomous judiciary. But none of these reforms was applied because of the absolute concentration of state powers that has developed during the past decade (1999-2010).

The fact is that the 1999 Venezuelan Constituent Assembly was not elected to govern the country or to substitute for all elected branches of government. According to the Supreme Court decision on the challenged bylaws, the assembly had neither full powers nor original constituent powers. In principle, it had the particular mission of drafting a new Constitution and was to function in parallel with the constituted branches of government that had been elected in November 1998: the national Congress, the states' legislatures and governors, and the municipal councils and mayors. Nonetheless, at its first session, through the vote of the overwhelming majority of its members and without any constitutional support, the assembly proclaimed itself as having original constituent power and, in particular, all the needed powers to "limit or to decide to cease the

---

[19] In the "Declaration of Principles" of the United Socialist Party (Apr. 23, 2010), the proposal is to assure the leadership of Chávez during the "Bicentennial Era: 2010-2030." Available at http://psuv.org.ve/files/tcdocumentos/Declaracion-de-principios-PSUV.pdf

activities of the authorities conforming the branches of government." It set forth in its internal bylaws that "all the State entities are subordinated to the National Constituent Assembly and are obliged to execute and to provide for the execution of the public acts issued by the Assembly."[20]

VIII

Despite all those powers, the result of the constitution-making process, the 1999 Constitution, from a democratic point of view did not turn out to be the document promised to the people in the April 25 consultative referendum to transform the state and the democratic system. It did not conform to the new vision of consolidating democratic principles and politically reorganizing the country, substituting the centralized party and state system for a decentralized one.

On the contrary, the result was an authoritarian framework of centralized government based on state intervention in the economy – helped by uncontrolled public oil income – which reinforced a presidentialism that has concentrated and controlled all state powers with a sharp antiparty tendency and a military force never before incorporated in the Constitution. Today, a single-party system is embodied in the state.

It has been within this constitutional framework that, during the past decade, an authoritarian government has arisen in Venezuela, with a president who, after ten years in office, has succeeded in amending the Constitution to ensure his continued and indefinite reelection, which was eventually approved by referendum in 2009. Also, in defrauding the Constitution, the president has progressively erased the federation; has suffocated local governments through the creation, in 2006, of communal councils directly dependent on the president[21]; and has been building a socialist state contrary to the will of the people – who discarded it in rejecting the 2007 constitutional reform proposals – imposed upon them above the debris of the demolished democratic institutions.

---

[20]See *Gaceta Constituyente (Diario de Debates), Agosto–Septiembre 1999*, Aug. 3, 1999, N° 1, 4. See my dissenting vote in *Gaceta Constituyente (Diario de Debates), Agosto–Septiembre 1999*, Aug. 7, 1999, N° 4, 6-13; Allan R. Brewer-Carías, *Debate constituyente (Aportes a la Asamblea Nacional Constituyente)*, Fundación de Derecho Público–Editorial Juridica Venezolana, Caracas 1999, 1 (Aug. 8–Sept. 8):15-39.

[21]See Allan R. Brewer-Carías, "El inicio de la desmunicipalización en Venezuela: La organización del poder popular para eliminar la descentralización, la democracia representativa y la participación a nivel local," in *AIDA, Opera Prima de Derecho Administrativo. Revista de la Asociación Internacional de Derecho Administrativo*, Universidad Nacional Autónoma de México, Mexico City 2007, 49-67.

All these trends found their origin in the exclusionist 1999 constitution-making process, which far from politically reconciling the country accentuated fundamental differences across social classes, multiplied and increased political division in the country, and provoked extreme polarization. The process also was the main instrument for ensuring that one and only one political group, in support of the president, could seize all state powers and take absolute control of all institutions – this was all fueled by the extraordinary increase in public funds that were dispensed without control. That is, the 1999 constitution-making process has been an instrument for excluding all political parties, especially those that dissent against the president's will, and for establishing hegemonic control.

IX

The assault, seizure, and takeover of power by the political group that controlled the Constituent Assembly did not finish with the drafting of the Constitution. It continued after the December 15 referendum. This time, the same assembly carried out a constitutional coup, this time against the new Constitution, to impose different constitutional provisions the people had never approved, which allowed for the complete seizure of all branches of government and the final assault on power.

On December 22, 1999, one week after the popular approval of the Constitution, paralleling the provisions of the Constitution but not submitted to popular approval, the assembly adopted the Decree for a Transitory Regime. Through the decree, as expected, only the president was ratified in his office; all other elected and nonelected state officials were definitively dismissed.[22]

To fill that institutional gap, the Assembly, again without following provisions of the new Constitution, appointed members of the Supreme Tribunal of Justice and of the National Electoral Council, the public prosecutor, the comptroller general, and the people's defender. In addition, also without any constitutional support, the Assembly created and appointed the members of the National Legislative Commission, not established in the Constitution, to act as a nonelected legislative body that would substitute for the dismissed Congress until a new National Assembly could be elected. The Constituent Assembly, again without constitutional authorization, directly

---

[22]See the Decree of Dec. 22, 1999, "Transitory Constitutional Regime," in *Gaceta Oficial* N° 36.859 of Dec. 29, 1999. See also Allan R. Brewer-Carías, *Golpe de estado y proceso constituyente en Venezuela*, Universidad Nacional Autónoma de México, Mexico City 2002, 354ff.; and *La Constitución de 1999: Derecho constitucional venezolano*, Editorial Jurídica Venezolana, Caracas 2004, II:1.003-117.

assumed legislative functions and sanctioned some statutes – among them, the Electoral Law – to govern the first general elections that took place in August 2000.

All these unconstitutional decisions, unfortunately, were covered up and endorsed by the new Supreme Tribunal of Justice, particularly its Constitutional Chamber, whose members had been appointed by the same Constituent Assembly in the same unconstitutional transitory regime with the mandate of giving that Assembly judicial support in judicial proceedings. Consequently, the new tribunal appointed by the assembly recognized the supposedly "original character" of the Constituent Assembly and its "supraconstitutional" power, thereby justifying all transitory political decisions adopted, many of which have subsisted to the present and serve to justify and cover up the endless unconstitutional interventions of the judiciary.[23]

X

The result of the 1999 Venezuelan constitution–making process, despite any political changes that have since taken place, has been the complete takeover of all levels of power and branches of government by supporters of President Hugo Chávez. This has imposed on the Venezuelan people a centralized form of government and a political socialist project whose aim is found in the phrase "motherland, socialism, or death," repeatedly pronounced since Chávez took his second oath in January 2007. That phrase is now the official military salute – though nobody voted on or approved it.[24]

___

[23] See, e.g., the Jan. 26, 2000, Decision N° 4 (*Caso: Eduardo García*), and the Mar. 28, 2000, Decision N° 180 (Case: *Allan R. Brewer-Carías et al.*) in *Revista de Derecho Público* 81, Editorial Jurídica Venezolana, Caracas 2000, 93ff. and 86ff. See also Allan R. Brewer-Carías, *Golpe de estado y proceso constituyente en Venezuela*, Universidad Nacional Autónoma de México, Mexico City, 2002, 354ff.

[24] See Alberto Muller Rojas (Military Presidential Chief of Staff), in Reuters, "Venezuelan military adopts Chavez socialism slogan" ("Venezuela's military has adopted President Hugo Chavez's 'Homeland, Socialism or Death' slogan as an official salute, a further sign of politicization of core institutions in the OPEC nation"), *El Universal*, Caracas May 13, 2007 ("Militares venezolanos adoptan lema socialista de Chávez), at http://www.reuters.com/article/idUSN1142580120070511; Vivian Castillo, "Chávez instó a la FAN a asumir el socialismo 'sin ambigüedades,'" in *El Universal* (Caracas), Apr. 13, 2007, at http://www.eluniversal.com/2007/04/13/pol_art_chavez-insto-a-la-fa_246899.shtml; Patricia Rivas, "Chávez: 'El 13 de Abril [2002] la revolución bolivariana se hizo antiimperialista y socialista,'" in Prensa Web YVKE Mundial, Caracas Apr. 13, 2009, at http://www.radiomundial.com.ve/ yvke/noticia.php?22791. See in the "Declaration of Principles" of the United Socialist Party (Apr. 23, 2010), the proposal regarding the "Bolivarian Socialism" and the "Socialist State," all based on the slogan "Socialist Homeland or death." Available at http://psuv.org.ve/files/tcdocumentos/Declaracion-de-principios-PSUV.pdf

In summary, the 1961 Constitution was fraudulently used to provoke the 1999 constitution making by means of the election of a constituent assembly not established in the Constitution. After the assembly was democratically elected according to bylaws that the president unilaterally imposed to gain complete control of the assembly, the assembly staged a coup d'état. Since 2000, under the authoritarian framework of the new Constitution, it has been the turn of representative democracy to be used to demolish democracy itself. That is, Venezuela's government moved from defrauding the Constitution to defrauding democracy. In the past decade, it has used representative democracy to eliminate democracy progressively and substitute for it a participatory democracy of popular power based on communal councils – a democracy that is participatory only in name.

In this way, a "state of the popular power" is progressively replacing the democratic rule of law, again through fraud. That substitute pretends to establish a supposedly "democratic" system based on a direct relationship between a leader and the people, basically through popular mobilization, populism, and organization of the aforementioned communal councils, whose members are not elected by the people but directly appointed by open citizens' assemblies, which are, of course, controlled by the government's single party, thus maintaining the populist system that has been developed from the uncontrolled distribution of oil wealth.[25]

The main identifier of such a system is that all power is concentrated in the head of state, who is surrounded by ministerial offices "of the popular power,"[26] not being discarded that, in the near future, he will pretend to be "president of the popular power." The system is not democratic, representative, or participatory, being completely controlled by the head of state through the United Socialist Party it has created.

All these proposals and reforms, officially announced in January 2007, tend toward what the then–vice president of the republic called the "the dictatorship of democracy."[27] Nonetheless, in democracy, no dictatorship is

---

[25] See Allan R. Brewer-Carías, "El autoritarismo en Venezuela construido en fraude a la Constitución (De cómo en un país democrático se ha utilizado el sistema eleccionario para eliminar la democracia y establecer un régimen autoritario de supuesta "dictadura de la democracia")," Report to *VIII Jornadas de Derecho Constitucional y Administrativo* and to the *VI Foro Iberoamericano de Derecho Administrativo*, Universidad Externado de Colombia, Bogotá, July 25–27, 2007, available at http://www.allanbrewercarias.com.

[26] See, e.g., the provisions of Decree N° 6670 of Apr. 22, 2009, on the Organization and Functioning of Public Administration, *Gaceta Oficial* N° 39163, Apr. 2, 2009.

[27] Vice President Jorge Rodríguez, in Jan. 2007: "Of course we want to install a dictatorship, the dictatorship of the true democracy and the democracy is the dictatorship of everyone, you and us together, building a different country. Of course we want this dictatorship of democracy to be installed forever." *El Nacional*, Caracas Jan. 1, 2007, A-2.

acceptable, not even a dictatorship of democracy. That harks back to a different context and time: the failed dictatorship of the proletariat that emerged from the Russian Revolution in 1918, based on the Soviets (Councils) of soldiers, workers, and peasants. With a ninety-year delay, something similar has been deigned and in process of being implemented in Venezuela, since the creation in 2006 of the aforementioned communal councils, directly dependent on the national executive,[28] to channel the popular power, with the alleged participation of organized people, to install the "dictatorship of democracy."[29]

History has shown that popular dictatorships have always been fraudulent instruments that circumstantial leaders have used to gain power and then, in the name of popular power, to demolish any trace of democracy and impose a socialist regime on a country without a popular vote. Some countries have learned nothing from Boris Yeltsin. Yeltsin, the first elected president of the Russian Federation, on the occasion of the burial of the Romanov family's remains, in reaching closure on the Russian Revolution, voiced one of the most bitter lessons of humanity: "The attempts to change life by means of violence are doomed to fail."[30]

Lesson learned or not, what is true is that any dictatorship, whatever its origin or kind, being inevitably the result of the exercise of violence, physical or institutional, is condemned to fail and collapse sooner or later.

XI

What has occurred in Venezuela since 1999 is a political lesson that must be known about and learned, particularly because Chávez has sold the formula as a magic one for resolving political crises in democratic regimes in Latin America. The recent applications of the formula by Ecuador's President Rafael Correa and the Honduras's former President Manuel Zelaya show the need for deep analysis, particularly of how leaders have defrauded

---

[28]See Allan R. Brewer-Carías, "El inicio de la desmunicipalización en Venezuela: La organización del poder popular para eliminar la descentralización, la democracia representativa y la participación a nivel local," in *AIDA, Opera Prima de Derecho Administrativo. Revista de la Asociación Internacional de Derecho Administrativo*, Universidad Nacional Autónoma de México, Mexico City, 2007, 49-67.

[29]That is why the political project of the Chávez's government has been identified as "communist." See Jesús Antonio Petit Da Costa, "La lucha en Venezuela es contra el comunismo," *La Razón*, Caracas Jan. 10, 2010. On Jan. 15, 2010, in his annual speech before the National Assembly on the government's accomplishments, President Chávez said: "For the first time, I assume Marxism." *El Universal*, Caracas Jan. 16, 2010, http://www.eluniversal.com/2010/01/16/pol_art_por-primera-vez-asu_1726209.shtml Dece16.

[30]See *Daily Telegraph*, London Aug., 8, 1998, 1.

the Constitution to demolish the rule of law and to destroy democratic values and standards.

This book is devoted to analyzing in detail the Venezuelan experience that began in 1999, with all its subsequent political consequences, to show how the Constitution in force at the time was used to violate that same Constitution and how the use of the existing democratic tools destroyed democracy in that country. It is based on a series of essays I have written during the past decade, as the facts were occurring, in which I studied the unfortunate process of subverting democracy from within and of violating the Constitution to consolidate authoritarianism – all accompanied by a systematic process of demolishing institutions and destroying democracy.

I have reworked all those essays for this book, which is divided into three parts and fifteen chapters. Part I is devoted to in-depth analysis of the tools used to develop the exclusionist 1999 constitution–making process as a means to assault state powers and completely reshape the Constitution. Chapter 1 is based on the paper "The 1999 Venezuelan Constitution–Making Process as an Instrument for Framing the Development of an Authoritarian Political Regime," which I presented on October 11, 2002, at the U.S. Institute of Peace Conference Project on Constitution-Making, Peace Building and National Reconciliation, in Washington, DC.[31] Chapter 2 covers the endless transitory constitutional regime that the Constituent Assembly illegitimately sanctioned in 1999, after the Constitution had been approved by popular vote. The regime has prevented the complete enforcement of the 1999 Constitution. Chapter 2 is based on an essay I wrote between 2001 and 2002 that was first published as "Illegitimate Constitutional Transitory Regime Adopted by the National Constituent Assembly after the Popular Approval of the New Constitution" in a book by the Universidad Nacional Autónoma de México.[32] The transitory constitutional regime resulted in state entities adopting various arbitrary decisions in violation of the Constitution, but the Supreme Tribunal of Justice, consisting of magistrates appointed by that regime, obediently endorsed those decisions.[33] Chapters 3 and 4 are a critical reflection on the

---

[31] The paper was later published as "The 1999 Venezuelan Constitution-Making Process as an Instrument for Forming the Development of an Authoritarian Political Regime," in Laurel E. Miller, editor, *Framing the State in Times of Transition: Case Studies in Constitution Making*, United States Institute of Peace, Washington 2010, 505-32.

[32] See Allan R. Brewer-Carías, *Golpe de estado y proceso constituyente en Venezuela*, Universidad Nacional Autónoma de México, Mexico City 2002, 343ff.

[33] The initial version of these reflections was published in my book *Golpe de estado y proceso constituyente*, Universidad Nacional Autónoma de México, Mexico City, 2002, 341-405, and in my book *La Constitución de 1999. Derecho constitucional venezolano*, Caracas 2004, 2:1.017-115.

political and socioeconomic provisions of the 1999 Constitution, from its exclusionary process to later distortions in its implementation. The chapters are based on a few essays I wrote during the month following its approval, beginning with one for the Conference on Challenges to Fragile Democracies in the Americas: Legitimacy and Accountability, organized by the Faculty of Law of the University of Texas, in Austin on February 25, 2000,[34] and another, on "Global Values in the Venezuelan Constitution: Some Prioritizations and Several Incongruencies," in which I contrasted the formal constitutional provisions and the political reality written for a presentation at a National Constitutional Jurisprudence conference in Bellagio, Italy, on September 22–26, 2008.

Part II is devoted to analyzing the most important institutional developments deriving from the 1999 Constitution. It is divided into five chapters. Chapter 5 summarizes the previously described process of consolidating authoritarianism and is based on a paper on "Authoritarianism in Venezuela Built Defrauding the Constitution" that I initially wrote for the Ninth Ibero-American Congress on Constitutional Law and the Seventh National Symposium on Constitutional Law, organized by the Associação Brasileira dos Constitucionalistas Demócratas, Seção Brasileira do Instituto Ibero-Americano de Direito Constitucional, and Academia Brasileira de Direito Constitucional, held on November 11–15, 2006, in Curitiba, Brazil.[35]

---

[34]An abstract of my presentation was published in *Texas International Law Journal* 36, 2001, 333-38. See in addition my critical comments on the new Constitution immediately after its approval, in "Reflexiones críticas y visión general de la Constitución de 1999," Inaugural Lecture, Curso de Actualización en Derecho Constitucional, Universidad Católica Andrés Bello, Caracas Feb. 2, 2000; "La Constitución de 1999 y la reforma política, Colegio de Abogados del Distrito Federal, Caracas Feb. 9, 2000; "The Constitutional Reform in Venezuela and the 1999 Constitution," Seminar, Challenges to Fragile Democracies in the Americas: Legitimacy and Accountability, organized by Faculty of Law, University of Texas, Austin, Feb. 25, 2000; "Reflexiones críticas sobre la Constitución de 1999," Seminar, *El constitucionalismo latinoamericano del siglo XXI en el marco del LXXXIII aniversario de la promulgación de la Constitución política de los Estados Unidos Mexicanos*, Cámara de Diputados e Instituto de Investigaciones Jurídicas UNAM, Mexico City, Jan. 31, 2000; "La nueva Constitución de Venezuela del 2000," Centro Internationale per lo Studio del Diritto Comparato, Facoltà di Giurisprudenza, Facoltà di Scienze Politiche, Universita'degli Studi di Urbino, Urbino, Italia, Mar. 3, 2000; "Apreciación general sobre la Constitución de 1999," *Ciclo de conferencias sobre la Constitución de 1999, Academia de Ciencias Políticas y Sociales*, Caracas May 11, 2000. These papers were published in Diego Valadés and Miguel Carbonell, coords., *Constitucionalismo iberoamericano del siglo XXI*, Cámara de Diputados, LVII Legislatura, Universidad Nacional Autónoma de México, Mexico City 2000, 171-93; in *Revista de Derecho Público* 81, Editorial Jurídica Venezolana, Caracas 2000, 7-21; in *Revista Facultad de Derecho, Derechos y Valores* 3, N° 5, Universidad Militar Nueva Granada, Santafé de Bogotá, D.C., Colombia, July 2000, 9-26; *La Constitución de 1999*, Biblioteca de la Academia de Ciencias Políticas y Sociales, Caracas 2000, 63-88.

[35]The essay was rewritten in 2007 and published in *Temas constitucionales: Planteamientos ante una reforma*, Fundación de Estudios de Derecho Administrativo, Caracas 2007, 13-74.

Chapter 6 covers the reinforcement of the centralization to which the state has been submitted. It is based on my paper, "Centralized Federation in Venezuela," presented at the seminar Federalism in the Americas and Beyond, at Duquesne School of Law in Pittsburgh, on November 13, 2004.[36] Chapter 7 discusses the concentration of power in the branches of government. It is based on an essay I wrote on the principle of separation of powers and authoritarian government in Venezuela, discussed in seminars at Fordham Law School in New York City (February 11, 2008), Duquesne University School of Law (November 7–8, 2008), and University of Pennsylvania Law School in Philadelphia (April 16, 2009).[37] Chapter 8 covers the catastrophic political subjection of the Supreme Tribunal and the illegitimate use of its jurisdictional powers to mutate the Constitution. The chapter is based on the essay I wrote for the Duquesne seminar Judicial Review in the Americas and Beyond in November 2006.[38] Chapter 9 deals with the state compulsory appropriation of economic activities, enterprises, and assets through expropriations and confiscations, with special reference to the oil industry. It is based on an essay on the state appropriation of Primary Hydrocarbons Joint Venture Exploitations established before 2001, their unilateral termination, and the confiscation of assets of their private parties, published in 2008.[39]

Part III deals with recent draft constitutional reforms that have been rejected (2007) or approved (2009) to consolidate the authoritarian, centralist, and militarist government that has been implemented during the past decade for the purpose of stringently controlling the state and all aspects

---

[36]The essay was published in *Duquesne Law Review* 43, Duquesne University, Pittsburgh, PA, 2005, 629-43. I wrote some of the reflections for the paper "The Centralized Federation in Venezuela and Subnational Constitutions" for the conference Federalism and Subnational Constitutions, Design and Reform, organized by the Center for State Constitutional Studies, Rutgers University, New Jersey, held in Bellagio, Italy, May 23–26, 2004.

[37]Published in *Duquesne Law Review* 47, Duquesne University, Pittsburgh, PA, 2009, 813-38. I wrote a first version of the reflections, "Separation of Powers and Authoritarianism in Venezuela," for a lecture in Prof. Ruti G. Teitel's course Constitutional Comparative Law, at Fordham Law School, New York City, Feb. 11, 2008. I further developed the essay for the lecture "Venezuela under Chávez: Blurring between Democracy and Dictatorship?" at the University of Pennsylvania Law School, Philadelphia Apr. 16, 2009.

[38]Published in *Duquesne Law Review* 45, Duquesne University, Pittsburgh, PA. 2007, 439-65.

[39]Published as "The 'Statization' of the Pre-2001 Primary Hydrocarbons Joint Venture Exploitations: Their Unilateral Termination and the Assets' Confiscation of Some of the Former Private Parties," in *Oil, Gas & Energy Law Intelligence* 6 (http://www.gasandoil.com/ogel/); and as "La estatización de los convenios de asociación que permitían la participación del capital privado en las actividades primarias de hidrocarburos sucritos antes de 2002, mediante su terminación anticipada y unilateral y la confiscación de los bienes afectos a los mismos," in coord. Víctor Hernández Mendible, *Nacionalización, libertad de empresa y asociaciones mixtas*, Editorial Jurídica Venezolana, Caracas 2008, 123-88.

of society. It also deals with the mutations (distortions) of the Constitution made by the Constitutional Chamber of the Supreme Tribunal. In Chapters 10, 11, and 12, I analyze the president's 2007 draft constitutional reforms, which fortunately the people rejected in the December referendum. The chapters are based on a 2007 essay published in Caracas by *Fundación Editorial Jurídica Venezolana*.[40] Chapter 13 deals with the irregular fraudulent implementation of the rejected constitutional reform through legislation, and mainly through decrees laws enacted in execution of the 2007 enabling law. Chapter 14 deals with the process of illegitimate mutation or distortion of the Constitution made by the Constitutional Chamber of the Supreme Tribunal of Justice, as Constitutional Jurisdiction, which via constitutional interpretation has modified the Constitution, even in order to implement the rejected constitutional reforms of 2007. The chapter is based on the essay "Judicial Review in Venezuela," which I wrote for the lecture "The Constitutional Judge and the Destruction of the Rule of Law" at the Administrative Law Seminar of Professor Eduardo García de Enterría, at the *Universidad Complutense de Madrid*, on April 1, 2009.[41] Finally, Chapter 15 discusses the 2009 Constitutional Amendment, approved by referendum on February 2009, which eliminates the alternating character of the government by establishing the possibility of the continuous, indefinite reelection of the president, which has been always prohibited. I initially wrote the essay, "Venezuela 2009 Referendum on Continuous Reelection: Constitutional Implications," for the panel discussion Venezuela Referendum: Public Opinion, Economic Impact, and Constitutional Implications for the Americas Society and Council of the Americas, held in New York on February 9, 2009.[42]

---

[40]See Allan R. Brewer-Carías, *Hacia la consolidación de un estado socialista, centralizado, policial y militarista: Comentarios sobre el sentido y alcance de las propuestas de reforma constitucional 2007*, Editorial Jurídica Venezolana, Caracas 2007, and *La reforma constitucional de 2007 (Comentarios al proyecto inconstitucionalmente sancionado por la asamblea nacional el 2 de noviembre de 2007)*, Editorial Jurídica Venezolana, Caracas 2007, 224. See also my essays "La reforma constitucional en Venezuela de 2007 y su rechazo por el poder constituyente originario," *Revista Peruana de Derecho Público* 8, *N°* 15, Lima, 2007, 13-53; and as "La proyectada reforma constitucional de 2007, rechazada por el poder constituyente originario," in *Anuario de Derecho Público 2007* 1, Instituto de Estudios de Derecho Público de la Universidad Monteávila, Caracas 2008, 17-65.

[41]Published as "El juez constitucional al servicio del autoritarismo y la ilegítima mutación de la Constitución: El caso de la Sala Constitucional del Tribunal Supremo de Justicia de Venezuela (1999-2009)," in *Revista de Administración Pública*, 180, Centro de Estudios Políticos y Constitucionales, Madrid 2009, 383-418.

[42]Published as "El juez constitucional vs. la alternabilidad republicana (la reelección continua e indefinida)," *Revista de Derecho Público* 117, Editorial Jurídica Venezolana, Caracas 2009, 205-14.

The entire process in Venezuela of institution demolishing and democracy destroying has gravely affected the country's democratic standards and accomplishments – democracy has been dismantled with democratic tools, and the Constitution defrauded in the process. Therefore, "Final Reflections," I provide a general overview of the right to democracy and the violation of that right by Venezuela's authoritarian government from 1999 to 2010. The text of that final chapter generally follows the lines of the essay on "The Inter-American Democratic Charter and the Situation of the Venezuelan Democratic Regime," written between December 2001 and January 2002 to denounce all violations of democratic principles committed by the Venezuelan government, a process that has continued to this date.[43]

A fact is definitive in these matters: All constitution–making processes developed in countries with durable democratic institutions, though generally resulting from conflicts, have been the product of political agreements and consensus among conflicting parties, with extended public participation and consultation. On the contrary, when those processes result from a political leader's, faction's, or party's own particular concept of the state and society, without dialogue or political participation, eventually those processes implode.

When they result from agreement and consensus, in which parties effectively talk to one another and where peace opens all doors to all, constitutions can be, at the eve of a political conflict or of a civil war, the main tool to avoid them, providing that they are the final product of a political pact of different forces of a society that are in conflict. When irrational conduct prevents the possibility to achieve those agreements and consensus before a conflict explodes, inevitably, at the end of a war, constitutions can then be the result of a political armistice also between parties in conflict. In both cases, when constitutions result from conflict, as political pacts, they tend to create conditions for stability and democratic government. But constitutions also can be imposed by one political force on the rest of society, by controlling power through institutional manipulations or through a revolution. In such cases, they do not result from agreement of forces in conflict; they express the sole will of the predominant faction of society, to be imposed on others. With such constitutions, no stability can be achieved in the post–conflict transition – and, of course, never the silence of the prisons or the graves could mean stability.

---

[43]The text of the original essay, which was initially diffused through the Internet, was published as a chapter of my book, *La crisis de la democracia en Venezuela: La Carta Democrática Interamericana y los sucesos de abril de 2002*, Libros El Nacional, Caracas 2002, 137-218.

The fact is this: Forced imposition of a specific political system, a specific economic or social system, a territorial artificial organization, or the predominance of one ethnic group or religion over others has never attained long life. Eventually, the state and political institutions are demolished or implode. In other words, in any constitution-making processes, any attempt to impose a political system or a territorial division or integration on society, through violence, – including institutional violence – that is, the one exercise by means of using state power and institutions – will fail.

PART ONE

THE POLITICAL ASSAULT ON STATE POWERS AND THE FRAMEWORK FOR AUTHORITARIANISM

The main trend of the Venezuelan experience of dismantling democracy from within is that the process, aimed to replace representative democracy with "participatory democracy," used democratic tools but defrauded democracy itself, and using constitutional mechanisms it also defrauded the Constitution.[1] The result has been a political assault on state powers by a new resentful political group that was formed; nonetheless, profiting from the democratic rules during Venezuela's four decades of stable democracy. That group has destroyed the traditional parties, all democratic institutions, and any sort of pluralism seeking to implement a socialist model for which the people did not vote.

The process began in 1999 with the convening of the Constituent Assembly not authorized in the 1961 Constitution. That assembly allowed a resentful political class to take over all branches of government and completely reshape the Constitution (Chapter 1). In addition, to facilitate the dismantling of democracy, after popular approval of the Constitution and before its publication, without any authority to do so, the Constituent Assembly sanctioned the Transitory Constitutional Regime, which allowed many provisions of the Constitution not to be applied and split provisions into two categories: those approved by the people and others

---

[1] In Dec. 2009, in a speech at an International Congress commemorating the tenth anniversary of the 1999 Constitution, the vice president of the Constitutional Chamber of the Supreme Tribunal of Justice (Francisco Carrasquero), considering that "it is impossible to construct socialism with the legal superstructure of representative democracy," proposed for the Parliament and the other branches of government together with the Executive to "start dismantling all that legal superstructure created by representative democracy elite," adding the role the Constitutional Chamber has "in order to dismantle all that megastructure of representative democracy statutes." Available at http://www.eluniversal.com/2009/12/09/pol_art_en-el-nuevo-constit_1687934.shtml.

not submitted to popular approval (Chapter 2). The result of this constitution-making process was a new Constitution that formally reaffirmed all the democratic values constructed during the previous decades but sowed the seeds for the reinforcement of centralization (Chapter 3) and state intervention in the social and economic life (Chapter 4), allowing the dismantling and destruction of democracy by the elected governments.

Chapter 1

THE 1999 EXCLUSIONIST CONSTITUTION-MAKING PROCESS

In December 1999, as a result of the constitution–making process developed during that year, a new Constitution was approved in Venezuela. A national constituent assembly elected that same year sanctioned the new Constitution, which was submitted to popular approval by referendum on December 15, 1999.

As a member of the National Constituent Assembly, participating in all its sessions and in all the constitutional discussions held, I opposed the Constitution and led the political campaign for a no vote in the referendum. This position was based on my multiple negative votes in the Constituent Assembly and on my publicly expressed fear that the new Constitution,[1] despite its advanced civil and political rights regulations,[2] was an instrument framed for the development of an authoritarian regime. This fear was due to the Constitution's provisions allowing for the possibility of the concentration of state power, state centralization, extreme presidentialism, extensive state participation in the economy, the general marginalization of civil society in public activities, exaggerated state social obligations reflecting state oil-income populism, and extreme militarism.[3]

---

[1] See my dissenting votes in Allan R. Brewer-Carías, *Debate constituyente (Aportes a la Asamblea Nacional Constituyente)*, Fundación de Derecho Público–Editorial Jurídica Venezolana, Caracas 1999, 3 (Oct. 18–Nov. 30):107-308.

[2] See my proposal on this matter in Brewer-Carías, *Debate constituyente, (Aportes a la Asamblea Nacional Constituyente)*, Fundación de Derecho Público–Editorial Jurídica Venezolana, Caracas 1999, 2 (Sept. 9–Oct. 17):76-155ff.

[3] See "Razones para 'no' firmar el proyecto" and "Razones para el voto 'no' en el referéndum sobre la Constitución," in Brewer-Carías, *Debate constituyente, (Aportes a la Asamblea Nacional Constituyente)*, Fundación de Derecho Público–Editorial Jurídica Venezolana, Caracas 1999, 3 (Oct. 18–Nov. 30):311ff.

Unfortunately, the warning signs of 1999–2000 have become reality, and the political system that resulted from the 1999 constitution making has turned out to be the current authoritarian regime, led by former Lieutenant-Colonel Hugo Chávez Frías, a leader of the failed 1992 military coup.[4] Chávez was elected president of the Republic of Venezuela in the general elections of December 1998,[5] elected in 2000 after the approval of the new 1999 Constitution, and reelected in December 2006.[6] After nine years of consolidating the existing authoritarian regime, in August 2007, he proposed before the National Assembly a radical reform to the Constitution to formally consolidate a socialist, centralized, militaristic and police state.[7] The Assembly sanctioned the reform on November 2, 2007, but the people rejected it in a referendum on December 2, 2007.[8] In any event, such fundamental transformations of the state could be sanctioned only by a National Constituent Assembly as expressly set forth in the 1999 Constitution (Article 347) and cannot be approved by a constitutional reform procedure (Article 342), as the president proposed in contravention of the Constitution.[9] Notwithstanding, even if the people did reject unconstitutional proposals, during 2008 and 2009, many of the rejected reforms were implemented by defrauding the

---

[4]On the Feb. 4, 1992, coup d'état attempt, see H. Sonntag and T. Maingón, *Venezuela: 4F1992. Un análisis socio-político,* Caracas 1992; Gustavo Tarre Briceño, *4 de febrero. El espejo roto,* Caracas 1994.

[5]In the 1998 presidential election, Hugo Chávez Frías obtained 56.20% of votes cast, followed by Henrique Salas Römer, with 39.99% of votes. Approximately 35% of eligible voters did not vote. See the references in *El Universal,* Caracas Dec. 11, 1998, 1-1.

[6]In the 2006 presidential election, Hugo Chávez Frías obtained 62.84% of votes, and the opposition candidate, Manuel Rosales, obtained 36.9% of votes. Approximately 25.3% of eligible voters did not.

[7]See *Proyecto de Reforma Constitucional. Elaborado por el ciudadano Presidente de la República Bolivariana de Venezuela, Hugo Chávez Frías,* Editorial Atenea, Caracas Aug. 2007, 58. See the comments on the draft in Allan R. Brewer-Carías, *Hacia la consolidación de un estado socialista, centralizado, policial y militarista. Comentarios sobre el alcance y sentido de la Reforma Constitucional 2007,* Editorial Jurídica Venezolana, Caracas 2007; *La Reforma Constitucional de 2007 (sancionada inconstitucionalmente por la Asamblea Nacional el 2 de Noviembre de 2007),* Editorial Jurídica Venezolana, Caracas 2007.

[8]The reform was submitted to referendum on Dec. 2, 2007. A majority of the people rejected it. The no votes comprised 51% (4.5 million) of votes cast (9.2 million); approximately 44.11% of eligible voters did not vote.

[9]See Allan R. Brewer-Carías, "El autoritarismo establecido en fraude a la Constitución y a la democracia y su formalización en Venezuela mediante la reforma constitucional. (De cómo en un país democrático se ha utilizado el sistema eleccionario para minar la democracia y establecer un régimen autoritario de supuesta 'dictadura de la democracia' que se pretende regularizar mediante la reforma constitucional)," in *Temas constitucionales. Planteamientos ante una Reforma,* Fundación de Estudios de Derecho Administrativo, Caracas 2007, 13-74; Allan R. Brewer-Carías, *Estudios sobre el estado constitucional 2005-2006,* Editorial Jurídica Venezolana, Caracas 2007, 79ff.

Constitution, by means of legislation, decrees, laws, and even convenient judicial interpretations of the Constitution issued by the Constitutional Chamber of the Supreme Tribunal.

The 1999 Constitution replaced the previous 1961 Constitution,[10] becoming the twenty-sixth in the history of the country.[11] As mentioned, it was discussed and drafted by a national constituent assembly called and elected for that purpose, and it was approved by referendum on December 15, 1999.[12]

I. THE 1999 NATIONAL CONSTITUENT ASSEMBLY

The 1999 National Constituent Assembly was not the first of its kind in Venezuelan history. Originally, the independent and autonomous state of Venezuela was created through two constituent assemblies. The first took place in 1811, after the Declaration of Independence (July 5, 1811) by the former Spanish colonies, which had been integrated in 1777 in the General Captaincy of Venezuela, creating the Confederation of States of Venezuela (1811 Constitution). The second took place in 1830, after the separation of the Provinces of Venezuela from the Republic of Colombia, which Simón Bolívar had created nine years earlier, in 1821, when he managed to integrate the former Spanish colonies of what is today Ecuador, Colombia, and Venezuela (1830 Constitution).

After those two original constituent assemblies, seven other constitution-making processes through similar elected institutions were carried out in 1858, 1863, 1893, 1901, 1914, 1946, and 1953. In each case, the constitution-making process through constituent assemblies resulted from a de facto rejection of the existing constitution, a coup d'état, a revolution, or a civil war.[13] In all these cases, the assemblies were never

---

[10]See Allan R. Brewer-Carías, *La Constitución y sus enmiendas*, Editorial Jurídica Venezolana, Caracas 1991; and *Instituciones políticas y constitucionales,* Universidad Católica del Táchira–Editorial Jurídica Venezolana, San Cristóbal–Caracas 1996, 1 (Evolución histórica del estado):455ff.

[11]See the text of all Constitutions (1811–1999) in Allan R. Brewer-Carías, *Las Constituciones de Venezuela*, Biblioteca de la Academia de Ciencias Políticas y Sociales, Caracas 2008. For the constitutional history behind those texts, see my "Estudio Preliminar" in the same book, 1:23-526.

[12]See Allan R. Brewer-Carías, *La Constitución de 1999*, Editorial Jurídica Venezolana, Caracas 2000; *La Constitución de 1999. Derecho Constitucional Venezolano,* Editorial Jurídica Venezolana, 2 vols., Caracas 2004. See also Hildegard Rondón de Sansó, *Análisis de la Constitución venezolana de 1999,* Editorial Ex Libris, Caracas 2001; Ricardo Combellas, *Derecho constitucional: Una introducción al estudio de la Constitución de la República Bolivariana de Venezuela,* McGraw-Hill, Caracas 2001; Alfonso Rivas Quintero, *Derecho constitucional,* Paredes Editores, Valencia, 2002.

[13]See Elena Plaza and Ricardo Combellas, coords., *Procesos constituyentes y reformas constitucionales en la historia de Venezuela: 1811-1999*, Universidad central de Venezuela, Caracas

elected peacefully under democracy, always serving as a political tool to reshape the political process of the country, in which they played a decisive role.

Thus, it is possible to define the basic political periods of Venezuelan constitutional history by those constituent assemblies: As mentioned, the first period began in 1811 with the Constituent Congress that declared independence from Spain. After the independence wars and the disappearance of Venezuela as an independent Republic because of being united with the former provinces of New Granada in the Republic of Colombia, a new constitutional assembly was elected in 1830 to restore the republic. This period of formation of the new state ended abruptly with the Federal Wars, which were preceded by the 1858 Constituent Assembly. At the end of the wars, a constituent assembly was again elected in 1863 to establish the constitutional basis of the federal state system.

This initiated the second political period, which once again ended abruptly after the *Revolución Liberal Restauradora* in 1899, which provoked the election of the Constituent Assembly of 1901. That assembly designed a radical change in the political system, giving birth to a centralized and autocratic state, which was consolidated by the Constituent Congress of 1914 and through other constitutional reforms approved during the first half of the twentieth century.

This third political period of Venezuelan constitutional history ended abruptly with the Revolution of October 1945. A new constituent assembly in 1946 assumed the task of designating the democratic political system of a centralized state, which prevailed for the second half of the twentieth century and was consolidated after a military interregnum (1948–58) in which a constituent assembly was also convened (1953). It was the system of state centralism and democracy of parties that at the end of the 1990s demanded a radical change. That was the change that should have been designed by the Constituent Assembly of 1999, which was to be convened, as never before, within a democracy and without a previous de facto constitutional break. That is why the Constituent Assembly and the constitution-making process of 1999 were different from all the previous ones in Venezuelan history and even from many similar processes in other countries in the past decades. It did not result from a de facto rejection of the 1961 Constitution or from a revolution, a war, or a coup. Rather, with

2005; Allan R. Brewer-Carías, "Las asambleas constituyentes en la historia de Venezuela," *El Universal*, Caracas Sept. 8, 1998, 1-5.

some similarities to the 1991 Colombian and 2007 Ecuadorian Constituent Assemblies,[14] the Venezuelan Constituent Assembly of 1999 resulted from a formal democratic process that did not involve a rupture of the previous political regime.[15] Nonetheless, in Colombia, the Constituent Assembly resulted from political agreements and consensus between the political forces of the country. In Venezuela and Ecuador, the Constituent Assembly was unilaterally conceived and submitted to popular vote by the president, without any previous political agreements or participation by political parties.

In all cases, but particularly Venezuela, the constitution making of 1999 took place in the context of a severe political crisis,[16] which was affecting the democratic regime that had been established in 1958.[17] The crisis had arisen as a result of a lack of evolution from a system of overly centralized political parties,[18] which existed then and still exists today. In fact, the call for the referendum on establishing the Constituent National Assembly, made by the newly elected president, Hugo Chávez, on February 2, 1999, intended to ask the people their opinion on a constituent national assembly "aimed at transforming the State and creating a new legal order that allows the effective functioning of a social and participative democracy."[19] That was the formal raison d'être of the constitution making and is why, with few exceptions, it would have been difficult to find anyone in the country to disagree with those stated purposes: transforming the state and putting

---

[14]See Allan R. Brewer-Carías, "El inicio del proceso constituyente en Ecuador en 2007 y las lecciones de la experiencia venezolana de 1999," in *Estudios sobre el estado constitucional 2005-2006*, Editorial Jurídica Venezolana, Caracas 2007, 766ff.

[15]See Allan R. Brewer-Carías, "Reflexiones sobre la crisis del sistema político, sus salidas democráticas y la convocatoria a una constituyente," in *Los candidatos presidenciales ante la academia*, Aug. 10–18, 1998, Biblioteca de la Academia de Ciencias Políticas y Sociales, Caracas 1998, 9-66.

[16]See Allan R. Brewer-Carías, *La crisis de las instituciones: Responsables y salidas,* Cátedra Pío Tamayo, mimeo, Centro de Estudios de Historia Actual, Facultad de Economía y Ciencias Sociales, Universidad Central de Venezuela, Caracas 1985. Also see Allan R. Brewer-Carías, *Instituciones políticas y constitucionales*, Universidad Católica del Táchira–Editorial Jurídica Venezolana, San Cristóbal–Caracas 1996, 1 (Evolución histórica del estado):523-41.

[17]On the democratic political process after 1958, see Allan R. Brewer-Carías. *Cambio político y reforma del estado en Venezuela. Contribución al estudio sobre el estado democrático y social de derecho*, Ed. Tecnos, Madrid 1975.

[18]See Allan R. Brewer-Carías, *El estado: Crisis y reforma*, Academia de Ciencias Políticas y Sociales, Caracas 1982; and *Problemas del estado de partidos*, Editorial Jurídica Venezolana, Caracas 1988.

[19]See the text of the decree at *Gaceta Oficial* N° 36.634, Feb. 2, 1999, and its modification in *Gaceta Oficial* N° 36.658, Mar. 10, 1999. See the criticisms of the decree as constitutional fraud, in Allan R. Brewer-Carías, *Asamblea constituyente y ordenamiento constitucional*, Biblioteca de la Academia de Ciencias Políticas y Sociales, Caracas 1999, 229ff.

into practice a form of democracy that would be social, participatory, and effective. For that purpose, undoubtedly, a political conciliation and participative process was necessary.

Unfortunately, Chávez did not formally conceive of the constitutional process as an instrument for conciliation, aimed to reconstruct the democratic system and to ensure good governance. That would have required agreements and consensus to reach a political commitment from all components of society, as well as the participation of all sectors in the design of a new, functioning democracy – that did not occur.[20]

The Constituent Assembly of 1999, in fact, served to facilitate the total takeover of state powers by a new political group supporting the president, which crushed all the others, including existing political parties. As a result, almost all opportunities for inclusion and public participation were squandered. Moreover, the constitution-making process became an endless and continuous constituent coup d'état when the Constituent Assembly elected in July 1999, before changing the existing 1961 Constitution, began violating it by assuming powers it lacked under that text and under the terms of the April referendum that created it.[21] As an independent candidate, I was elected to the 1999 Constituent Assembly and thus able to participate in all its discussions. I dissented orally and in writing to all unconstitutional and undemocratic decisions.[22] I witnessed the seizure of power, beginning with the convening of the referendum on the Constituent Assembly in February 1999, then the April 1999 referendum to approve the convening of the Constituent Assembly, the election of the Constituent Assembly in July 1999, the exercise of "supraconstitutional" power by the Constituent Assembly from August 1999 to January 2000, the drafting and discussion of the draft constitution between October and November 1999, and the approval of the new constitution through referendum in December 1999.

The result of this brief but intensive process was that 1999 saw the failure of the constitution-making process as an instrument for political reconciliation and democratization, in that the stated democratic purposes

---

[20]See the 1998 political discussion regarding the necessary inclusive character of the proposed constitution-making process in Allan R. Brewer-Carías, *Asamblea constituyente y ordenamiento constitucional*, Biblioteca de la Academia de Ciencias Políticas y Sociales, Caracas 1999, 38ff.

[21]See Allan R. Brewer-Carías, *Golpe de estado y proceso constituyente en Venezuela*, Universidad Nacional Autónoma de México, Mexico City 2002, 181ff.

[22]See my dissenting votes in Allan R. Brewer-Carías, *Debate constituyente, (Aportes a la Asamblea Nacional Constituyente)*, Fundación de Derecho Público–Editorial Jurídica Venezolana, Caracas 1999, 1 (Aug. 8–Sept. 8):17ff. and 3 (Oct. 18–Nov. 30):109ff.

of the process were not accomplished.[23] No effective democratic reform of the state occurred, just an authoritarian government; and no social and participatory democracy resulted, unless one can consider democratic the election of a populist government that concentrated all branches of government and crushed political pluralism. Thus, if it is true that there have been important political changes, then some of them have aggravated the factors that provoked the crisis in the first place.[24] New political actors have assumed power, but far from implementing a democratic conciliation policy, they have accentuated the differences among Venezuelans, thereby worsening political polarization and making conciliation increasingly difficult. The seizure of power has opened new wounds, making social and political rivalries difficult to reconcile. Despite Venezuela's extraordinary oil wealth gained during the first decade of the twenty-first century, the country's social problems have increased.

II. THE 1998 CRISIS OF THE POLITICAL SYSTEM AND THE NEED FOR DEMOCRATIC RECONSTRUCTION

To understand the failure of this constitution-making process as an instrument to reinforce democracy, it is essential to analyze its political background. As previously mentioned, the process began in the midst of a crisis facing Venezuela's political system, which had been established at the end of the 1950s. That system was established as a consequence of the democratic (civil-military) revolution of 1958, during which then–president General Marcos Pérez Jiménez, who had led a military government for almost a decade, fled the country.

Three main democratic political parties, whose consolidation began in the 1940s, mainly led the democratic revolution: the Social Democratic Party (Acción Democrática, AD), the Christian Democratic Party (COPEI), and the Liberal Party (Unión Republicana Democrática, URD) parties. The parties agreed to establish and consolidate democracy in Venezuela through a series of written agreements, the most important of which was the *Pacto de Punto Fijo* (1958).[25] That document is an

---

[23]See Allan R. Brewer-Carías, "El proceso constituyente y la fallida reforma del estado en Venezuela," in *Estrategias y propuestas para la reforma del estado*, Universidad Nacional Autónoma de México, Mexico City 2001, 25-48.

[24]See, in general, A.C. Clark, *The Revolutionary Has No Clothes: Hugo Chávez's Bolivarian Farce*, Encounter Books, New York 2009.

[25]These parties compromised on the maintenance of a democratic regime obtained with more than 92% of votes in the 1958 general elections. The Communist Party, which obtained no more than 5% of votes, was left out of the pact because of its nondemocratic program and doctrine. It cannot be

exceptional example in Latin American political history of an agreement among political elites to ensure the democratic governance of a country,[26] and it went on to produce one of the most stable democracies of Latin America during the second half of the twentieth century.[27]

The democratic political system strengthened during the 1960s and 1970s, precisely under that extraordinary political agreement, and evolved into a democracy of parties that functioned in a centralized state and a system of presidential government subject to parliamentary control.

1. *Party Domination and Demand for Participation*

Political parties increasingly monopolized the political regime established in the 1960s as a representative and pluralist democracy. They had established the democratic regime, but they did not understand, after establishing it, that the effects of democratization would require the system of governance to become more representative and more participatory.[28]

Democratic representation ended up being an issue exclusively for parties themselves. The d'Hondt method of electing party representatives according to the system of proportional representation resulted in the

---

considered "a considerable force in Venezuela politics." See Daniel Hellinger, "Political Overview: The Breakdown of *Puntofijismo* and the Rise of Chavismo," in *Venezuelan Politics in the Chávez Era: Class, Polarization, and Conflicts*, eds. Steve Ellner and Daniel Hellinger, Lynne Rienner, London 2003, 29. See the Venezuelan election data up to 1975 in Allan R. Brewer-Carías, *Cambio político y reforma del estado en Venezuela*, Editorial Tecnos, Madrid 1975. Forty years after the first election of 1958, in the general elections of 1998, the Communist Party obtained only 1.25% of votes. See Richard Gott, *Hugo Chávez and the Bolivarian Revolution*, Verso, London 2005, 139.

[26] On the Punto Fijo Pact, the origins of the 1961 Constitution, and the political-party system, see Juan Carlos Rey, "El sistema de partidos venezolano," in *Problemas socio políticos de América Latina*, Caracas 1980, 255-338; and Allan R. Brewer-Carías, *Instituciones políticas y constitucionales*, Universidad Católica del Táchira–Editorial Jurídica Venezolana, San Cristóbal–Caracas 1996, 1 (Evolución histórica del estado):394ff.; *Las constituciones de Venezuela*, Caracas 1997, 201ff.; and *La Constitución y sus enmiendas*, 13ff. The text of the pact was published in *El Nacional*, Caracas Jan. 27, 1998, D-2; Haydee Miranda Bastidas et al., *Documentos fundamentales de la historia de Venezuela 1777-1993*, Los Libros de El Nacional, Caracas 1999, 174ff.; *Documentos que hicieron historia*, Presidencia de la República, Caracas 1962, 2:443ff.

[27] See, e.g., Robert J. Alexander, *The Venezuelan Democratic Revolution: A Profile of the Régime of Rómulo Betancourt*, Rutgers University Press, New Brunswick, NJ, 1964; Daniel H. Levine, *Conflict and Political Change in Venezuela*, Princeton University Press, Princeton, NJ, 1973. For criticism of Venezuelan exceptionalism, see Steve Ellner and Miguel Tinker Salas, eds., *Venezuela, Hugo Chávez and the Decline of a "Venezuelan Democracy,"* Rowman & Littlefield, New York 2007, 3ff.

[28] See Allan R. Brewer-Carías, *El estado: Crisis y reforma*, Academia de Ciencias Políticas y Sociales, Caracas 1982, 7-89; and *El estado incomprendido. Reflexiones sobre el sistema político y su reforma*, Editorial Jurídica Venezolana, Caracas 1985.

elections of party representatives who felt they were more accountable to their own parties than to their constituents or community. In addition, political parties monopolized the possibility for people's participation and penetrated all of civil society, from trade unions to professional associations and neighborhood organizations.

It must be noted that the proportional representation system was established in the 1961 Constitution and applied to all representative elections at the national, state, and municipal levels, allowing for the statutory establishment of a different electoral method at the local level, which occurred in some places in the 1980s and 1990s.[29] The absolute dominance of Congress by representatives of two or three political parties who had no direct relationships to their constituencies provoked their rejection by the people and the rejection of Congress, which was viewed as an exclusive, partisan body, not as the House of Representatives of the people. As a consequence, electoral support for the two main parties (AD and COPEI) varied from 92.83% in 1988 to 45.9% in 1993, to 36.1% in November 1998, and to 11.3% in December 1998, when Chávez was elected president.[30]

Thus, at the beginning of the 1980s, the public began to make new and diverse demands for means of representation and political participation, but those demands were not met. Among other things, the public called for a reform of the electoral system. In general, they wanted to make democracy more participatory. There was thus an urgent need for local government reform, because it is the only effective way to ensure effective democratic participation. However, in general, this was not understood, particularly by the political parties and their leaders.

Municipalities in Venezuela were and still are so disconnected from the citizens that they are of sporadic benefit to them. They never managed to become the primary political unit, the center of political participation, or an effective instrument for managing local interests. They were accountable to no one; no one was interested in them, except the political

---

[29]See Allan R. Brewer-Carías, "La reforma del sistema electoral," *Revista Venezolana de Ciencias Políticas* 1, CEPSAL-Postgrado en Ciencias Políticas, Universidad de Los Andes, Mérida, Dec. 1987, 55-75; and *Ley Orgánica del Sufragio,* Caracas 1993. See also J. G. Molina and C. Pérez Baralt, "Venezuela ¿un nuevo sistema de partidos? Las elecciones de 1993," *Cuestiones Políticas* 13, 1994, 63-99.

[30]See *El Universal,* Caracas Dec. 11, 1998, 1–1.

parties, and they became a mechanism of political partisan's use and unpunished corruption.[31]

Thus, without eliminating political representation, the proposed reforms tended to create mechanisms that would have allowed people to participate on a daily basis in local affairs. That should have been one purpose of the constitution–making process of 1999, or at least many people thought it would be.[32] In any case, the aim was to reform the democratic system, on the basis of the Pacto de Punto Fijo, not to destroy democracy through policies based on the demonization of the pact, the parties that subscribed to it, and representative democracy itself.[33]

2. *State Centralism and the Crisis of Decentralization*

Democratic reforms were needed in relation to the organization of the state. Venezuela has been a federal state since the Constitution of the Confederation of the States of Venezuela, dated December 21, 1811. Just as federalism was the only constitutional force uniting the previously independent thirteen colonies of the United States in the eighteenth century, in 1811 in Venezuela, it was the only constitutional means of bringing together the dispersed and isolated seven provinces that constituted the General Captaincy of Venezuela. Subsequently, Venezuelan political history has been marked by the swing of the pendulum between centralization and decentralization.[34] In the early stages of the republic, despite the centralist orientations of Simón Bolívar

---

[31] See Allan R. Brewer-Carías, "Municipio, democracia y participación. Aspectos de la crisis," *Revista Venezolana de Estudios Municipales* 11, Caracas 1988, 13-30; and "Democracia municipal, descentralización y desarrollo local, *Revista Iberoamericana de Administración Pública* 11, Ministerio de Administraciones Públicas, Madrid 2004, 11-34.

[32] On this, see my proposal to the 1999 Constituent Assembly in Allan R. Brewer-Carías, *Debate constituyente, (Aportes a la Asamblea Nacional Constituyente)*, Fundación de Derecho Público–Editorial Jurídica Venezolana, Caracas 1999, 1 (Aug. 8–Sept. 8):156ff.

[33] This policy has characterized Chávez's actions to justify the takeover of all branches of government, including the attempted coup he led in 1992. On the justification of Chávez's demonization of the Punto Fijo Pact, see Nikolas Kozloff, *Hugo Chávez: Oil, Politics, and the Challenge to the United States*, Palgrave Macmillan, New York 2006, 47, 61; Richard Gott, *In the Shadow of the Liberator: Hugo Chávez and the Transformation of Venezuela*, Verso, London 2000, 17; Julia Buxton, *The Failure of Political Reform in Venezuela*, Ashgate, Aldershot, UK 2001, 19.

[34] On the evolution of the Venezuelan federation, see Allan R. Brewer-Carías, *Instituciones políticas y constitucionales*, Universidad Católica del Táchira–Editorial Jurídica Venezolana, San Cristóbal–Caracas 1996, 1 (Evolución histórica del estado):351ff.; 2 (El Régimen del Poder Público y su Distribución Vertical):394ff.

(contained in the 1819 and 1821 Constitutions),[35] in 1830, regionalist pressure led to the formation of a mixed central-federal state, which definitively consolidated as a federal system in 1864, when the United States of Venezuela was established.

However, the federation as it existed in the nineteenth century was abandoned in 1901, and throughout the twentieth century, the country experienced political centralization.[36] Centralized governance was autocratic in its first phase but, beginning in 1935, it started to evolve to the more democratic form of the second half of the twentieth century.

At the end of the twentieth century, Venezuela remained a centralized federation, with power concentrated at the national level and illusory delegations of power to the federal states. At the same time, the centralized state led to a centralized political system, as party leaders and party organizations that were governed from Caracas (the center) came to dominate the political parties.

Long after the regional and local leadership of caudillos in the nineteenth century and after the consolidation of the national state in the first decades of the twentieth century, the call for increased democratization and decentralization in the modern era faced formidable challenges. Not only was it difficult to enhance the autonomy of local authorities; there also was resistance to admit the need to devolve power even to intermediate levels of government.

This state of affairs impeded the complete democratization of the country. Decentralization is a consequence of democracy and, at the same time, a condition necessary to its survival and improvement. It is an instrument for the intermediate-level exercise of power in a territory, which should, in turn, link the activities of the center to communities and regions. There are no decentralized autocracies; decentralized power is possible only in a democracy.[37] Consequently, the public outcry of 1989

---

[35]See Allan R. Brewer-Carías, "Ideas centrales sobre la organización del estado en la obra del libertador y sus proyecciones contemporáneas," in *Boletín de la Academia de Ciencias Políticas y Sociales* 95–96, Caracas 1984, 137-51.

[36]See Allan R. Brewer-Carías, "El desarrollo institucional del estado centralizado en Venezuela (1899-1935) y sus proyecciones contemporáneas," in *Revista de Estudios de la Vida Local y Autonómica* 227–228, Madrid 1985, 487-514, 695-726; and *Instituciones políticas y constitucionales,* Universidad Católica del Táchira–Editorial Jurídica Venezolana, San Cristóbal–Caracas 1996, 1 (Evolución histórica del estado):351ff.; "La reforma política del estado: La descentralización política," in *Estudios de derecho público (Labor en el Senado),* Ediciones del Congreso Nacional, Caracas 1983, 1 (1982):15-39.

[37]See Allan R. Brewer-Carías, *Reflexiones sobre la organización territorial del estado en Venezuela y en la América colonial,* Editorial Jurídica Venezolana, Caracas 1997, 108ff.

called for parties to accelerate state reforms to political decentralization that were based on provisions in the 1961 Constitution. As a result, in 1989, state governors were directly elected for the first time in one hundred years; at the local level, the introduction of direct election of mayors superseded exclusive government by council.[38]

Such democratic "remedies" without a doubt breathed life into the system and allowed democracy to survive in the 1990s. Nevertheless, the decentralizing advances as of 1993 were abandoned,[39] and the political system entered a terminal crisis in the last years of that decade.[40] The crisis, as mentioned earlier, provoked the calling of a constituent assembly, whose main objectives should have been the realization of decentralized power and consolidated democracy, not the destruction of democracy.

3. *The Demand for Reform*

Latin American constitutionalism in recent decades has experienced an expansion of the traditional horizontal concept of separation of powers beyond the classic legislative, executive, and judicial powers. Many Latin American states have introduced a series of constitutional and autonomous institutions outside of the three classical branches of government, such as general controllerships, defenders of the people or of human rights, judiciary councils, and public ministries (public prosecutors). In addition,

---

[38] See Allan R. Brewer-Carías, "Los problemas de la federación centralizada en Venezuela," in *Revista Ius et Praxis* 12, Universidad de Lima, Lima 1988, 49-96; "Bases legislativas para la descentralización política de la federación centralizada (1990: El inicio de una reforma)," in Allan R. Brewer-Carías et al., *Leyes y reglamentos para la descentralización política de la federación*, Caracas 1994, 7-53. Also see Brewer-Carías, *Instituciones políticas y constitucionales*, Universidad Católica del Táchira–Editorial Jurídica Venezolana, San Cristóbal–Caracas 1996, 2 (El régimen del poder Público y su Distribución Vertical):394ff.

[39] See discussion of the 1993 efforts to reinforce the decentralization process in Venezuela in *Informe sobre la descentralización en Venezuela 1994. Memoria del Dr. Allan R. Brewer-Carías, Ministro de Estado para la Descentralización*, Presidencia de la República, Caracas 1994.

[40] See Pedro Guevara, *Estado vs. democracia*, Universidad Central de Venezuela, Caracas 1997; Miriam Kornblith, *Venezuela en los 90. Crisis de la democracia*, Ediciones IESA, Caracas 1998. See also, Allan R. Brewer-Carías, *Cinco siglos de historia y un país en crisis*, Academia de Ciencias Políticas y Sociales y Comisión Presidencial del V Centenario de Venezuela, Caracas 1998, 95-117; "La crisis terminal del sistema político," in *Una evaluación a estos cuarenta años de democracia, El Globo*, Caracas Nov. 24, 1997, 12-13; "La crisis terminal del sistema político venezolano y el reto democrático de la descentralización," in *Instituciones políticas y constitucionales*, Universidad Católica del Táchira–Editorial Jurídica Venezolana, San Cristóbal–Caracas 1996, 3 (La Distribución Horizontal del Poder Público):655-78; "Presentación," in *Los candidatos presidenciales ante la academia*, Academia de Ciencias Políticas y Sociales, Caracas 1998, 9-66; and *Asamblea constituyente y ordenamiento constitucional*, Academia de Ciencias Políticas y Sociales, Caracas 1999, 15-85.

to increase participation of citizens in the democratic order, they have introduced new remedies for the protection of rights. Such measures have included judicial review of the constitutionality of legislation and judicial guarantees of constitutional rights, together with improvement in citizens' ability to use the *amparo* action (a specific judicial remedy for the protection of constitutional rights),[41] all of which have required that the judiciary be more independent and autonomous. The reforms have brought about a significant transformation of the system of checks and balances that regulates the traditional powers in those states. There were demands to institute similar reforms in Venezuela in the late 1990s, which would have required a transformation of the balances among the traditional powers of the state. Without doubt, those reforms should have been accomplished through the constitution-making process of 1999.

There was a particular need for reform in Venezuela. Although the Venezuelan system, like other Latin American systems, has been characterized by presidentialism, it had been a moderate presidentialism because of a series of parliamentary controls on the executive. Paradoxically, the crisis of the Venezuelan system stemmed not from an excess of presidentialism but from an excess of parliamentarianism, which took the form of the political parties' monopoly on power.[42]

In the late 1990s, criticisms of that monopoly focused, in particular, on the appointment by Congress of the heads of the nonelected organs of public power (Supreme Court, Judicial Council, general controller of the republic, prosecutor general of the republic, Electoral Supreme Council). Serious criticism arose because of the excessive partisanship shown in those appointments and because of the lack of transparency and participation of civil society in them.[43]

Therefore, on the one hand, the demands for reform called for increased checks and balances to break the monopoly of the political parties and reduce partisanship and, on the other hand, for an increase in the judicial guarantees of constitutional rights to guarantee greater citizen participation in the democratic order.

---

[41] See Allan R. Brewer-Carías, *Constittuional Protection of Human Rights in Latin America: A Comparative Study of* the Amparo *Proceeding*, Cambridge University Press, New York, 2009; *El amparo a los derechos y garantías constitucionales (Una aproximación comparativa)*, Editorial Jurídica Venezolana, Caracas 1993; and *Instituciones Políticas y Constitucionales*, Universidad Católica del Táchira–Editorial Jurídica Venezolana, San Cristóbal–Caracas 1998, 5 (Derecho y acción de amparo):111ff.

[42] See Allan R. Brewer-Carías, *Problemas del estado de partidos*, Editorial Jurídica Venezolana, Caracas 1988, 92ff.

[43] *Id.*

Consequently, the 1999 Constituent Assembly should have been used as a vehicle for including and reconciling all political stakeholders beyond traditional political parties in the redesign of the democratic system.[44] The Constituent Assembly should have focused on establishing a system that would guarantee not only elections but also all the other essential elements of democracy, as were later set forth in the Inter-American Democratic Charter enacted by the General Assembly of the Organization of American States on September 11, 2001. Such elements include "the respect for human rights and fundamental freedoms, the access to power and its exercise subject to the rule of law, the making of periodic, free and fair elections based on universal and secret vote as an expression of the sovereignty of the people, the plural regime of parties and political organizations and the separation and independence of the public powers" (Article 3).

III. THE CONSTITUTION-MAKING PROCESS AND ITS DEFORMATION

1. *The Choice of a National Constituent Assembly*

Although the call for a constituent assembly materialized in 1999, the demand for such a body as a vehicle of conciliation or political reconstruction had actually arisen earlier. It had been proposed before and in the aftermath of the two attempted military coups of 1992,[45] which had been carried out, among others, by then lieutenant–colonel Hugo Chávez Frías, later elected president of Venezuela in 1998.

The subject, in fact, was publicly discussed from 1992,[46] but the leaders of the main political parties failed to appreciate the magnitude of the

---

[44]See my proposal regarding the convening of the 1999 Constituent Assembly in Allan R. Brewer-Carías, *Asamblea constituyente y ordenamiento constitucional*, Academia de Ciencias Políticas y Sociales, Caracas 1999, 56-60.

[45]See, e.g., Frente Patriótico, *Por una asamblea constituyente para una nueva Venezuela*, Caracas 1991.

[46]On the initial 1992 proposals, see Elías García Navas, "La Constituyente es la única salida a la crisis política" (Interview, Allan R. Brewer-Carías), in *El Nacional*, Caracas Mar. 1, 1992, D-2; Consejo Consultivo de la Presidencia de la República, *Recomendaciones del Consejo Consultivo al Presidente de la República*, Caracas 1992, 15; Oswaldo Álvarez Paz, *El camino constituyente,* Gobernación del Estado Zulia, Maracaibo, June 1992; Ricardo Combellas, "Asamblea constituyente. Estudio jurídico-político," and Ángel Álvarez, "Análisis de la naturaleza de la crisis actual y la viabilidad política de la Asamblea Constituyente," in COPRE, *Asamblea constituyente: Salida democrática a la crisis,* Folletos para la Discusión 18, Caracas 1992; R. Escovar Salom, "Necesidad de una asamblea nacional constituyente," *Cuadernos Nuevo Sur* 2–3, Caracas 1992, 156-60; Frente Amplio Proconstituyente *¿Qué es la Constituyente?, El Nacional*, Caracas June 30, 1994; Hermánn Escarrá Malavé, *Democracia, reforma constitucional y asamblea constituyente,* Caracas 1995.

political crisis. Instead of attempting to democratize institutions, they tried to maintain the status quo. This response served to discredit the leaders and their political parties, leading to a leadership vacuum in a regime that had been previously characterized by the hegemony of the political parties and their leaders.[47]

In the middle of this political crisis, in 1998, Chávez, as presidential candidate, raised the issue of calling a constituent assembly, only a few years after the removal of criminal charges against him stemming from his 1992 attempted military coup. Notwithstanding all the benefits of the proposal, some of the traditional political parties disputed the proposal and others rejected it; all political elements rejected the idea that the Congress elected in December 1998 could take the lead in the constitution-making process. That is, the political parties, although holding sufficient seats in Congress to shape the constituent process and assume the task of implementing the needed democratic political reforms declined to take on that role.[48] Their ignorance of the magnitude of the political crisis was pathetic; in the end, the Constituent Assembly turned out to be the exclusive political project of candidate Chávez,[49] and it remained such after he was elected president in December 1998 with an overwhelming majority of 60% of votes cast. Nonetheless, his proposal was not intended to reform the democratic system – he conceived of it as "revolutionary process which seeks to destroy this [democratic] system; unlike other project, ours does not seek to fix this system."[50] However, the call for a constituent assembly posed a seemingly insurmountable constitutional problem: The text of the 1961 Constitution did not provide for the institution of a constituent assembly as a mechanism of constitutional reform. That text set out only two procedures for the revision of the constitution, one that would apply in the case of a simple amendment and

---

[47]The progressive implosion of the Venezuelan democratic regime, which Enrique Krauze considered "one of the great mysteries of contemporary Venezuela. A mystery and a tragedy," was provoked by the "blindness of the political parties' leadership that did not understand the people's cry out for reform." This blindness was also a main cause of what Krauze called democracy suicide. See Enrique Krauze, *El poder y el delirio*, Tusquests Editores, Mexico City 2009, 47, 52.

[48]See my comments from Nov. 1998, in Brewer-Carías, *Asamblea constituyente y ordenamiento constitucional*, 78-85. See also Daniel Hellinger, "Political Overview: The Breakdown of *Puntofijismo* and the Rise of Chavismo," in Ellner and Hellinger, *Venezuelan Politics in the Chávez Era*, 29.

[49]See his "Propuestas para transformar Venezuela," in Hugo Chávez Frías, *Una revolución democrática*, Caracas 1998, 7.

[50]See Agustín Blanco Muñoz (Entrevistas a Hugo Chávez Frías), *Habla el Comandante*, Universidad Central de Venezuela, Caracas 1998, 287. See also A. C. Clark, *The Revolutionary Has No Clothes: Hugo Chávez's Bolivarian Farce*, Encounter Books, New York 2009, 61.

another that would apply in the case of a larger "general reform."[51] Both procedures required the vote of both houses of Congress, with additional approval by popular referendum or by the majority of the state assemblies, without any provision for the creation of a separate constituent assembly.

Consequently, the first fraudulent action committed against the then-in-force 1961 Constitution occurred in February 1999, when the then–newly elected President Hugo Chávez Frías, on the same day of his inauguration and after the Supreme Court of Justice had issued an ambiguous decision on the matter a few days before, convened a referendum without constitutional authorization and without any previous political agreement or consensual process, to ask for the opinion of the people on the convening and election of a Constituent Assembly not established in the Constitution to reshape the constitutional order of the country.[52]

2. *The Constitutional Debate Regarding the Election of the Constituent Assembly*

These constitutional impediments, the general claims of the people for political change, and the commitment of the elected Presdent with the constituent assembly proposal, provoked that after the presidential elections, political discussion ceased to be about the need to convene a constituent assembly and turned to be about how to do it and, particularly, whether it was necessary to amend or reform the existing Constitution to create the institution.[53] Particularly regarding the question of whether the election of the Constituent Assembly required a previous constitutional amendment to establish such an institution, and if the concept of popular sovereignty could allow the election of a constituent assembly in the absence of preexisting constitutional authority. In short, it was a conflict

---

[51]See Allan R. Brewer-Carías, "Los procedimientos de revisión constitucional en Venezuela" in *I Procedimenti di revisione costituzionale nel Diritto Comparato,* Atti del Convegno Internazionale organizzato dalla Facoltà di Giurisprudenza di Urbino, Apr. 23–24, 1997, Università Degli Studi di Urbino, pubblicazioni della Facoltà di Giurisprudenza e della Facoltà di Scienze Politiche, Urbino, Italy, 1999, 137-81; and in *Boletín de la Academia de Ciencias Políticas y Sociales* 134, Caracas 1997, 169-222. See also Allan R. Brewer-Carías, *Asamblea constituyente y ordenamiento constitucional,* Academia de Ciencias Políticas y Sociales, Caracas 1999. 84-149.

[52]On the political discussion regarding the proposed constitution-making process, see Allan R. Brewer-Carías, *Asamblea constituyente y ordenamiento constitucional,* Biblioteca de la Academia de Ciencias Políticas y Sociales, Caracas 1999, 38ff.

[53]See my 1998 proposal in Brewer-Carías, *Asamblea nacional constituyente y ordenamiento constitucional,* 56–69; see the contrary position of Carlos M. Escarrá Malavé, *Proceso político y constituyente. Papeles constituyentes,* Maracaibo 1999, 33ff.

between constitutional supremacy and popular sovereignty,[54] which has been a basic dilemma of all political crises, that is, constitutional review through either constitutional supremacy or popular sovereignty, and the weight that one or the other principle must have in modern constitutional states.

In hindsight, considerations of the rule of law should have resolved the debate. Viewed from that perspective, there is no doubt that a constitutional amendment was required. This was the only way the issue could have been resolved without violating the text of the existing Constitution.[55] On the contrary, the violation of the Constitution to establish a new constitution–making process that would allegedly give preference to the will of the people (popular sovereignty) over the rule of law (constitutional supremacy) always leaves the indelible imprint of doubts of political legitimacy, which eventually can serve to revert the situation.[56]

Because the matter of constitutional reform was more political than legal, before the Supreme Court could issue any ruling on the matter, as civil society had requested, the elected president announced his intention to convene the Constituent Assembly as his first act of government, to be issued on Inauguration Day (February 2, 1999). Buoyed by his popularity at the moment, Chávez publicly pressured the Supreme Court to decide the question submitted to it in an interpretative recourse on consultative referendums filed by a nongovernmental organization, according to the statute governing the Supreme Court.

---

[54]See Allan R. Brewer-Carías, "El desequilibrio entre soberanía popular y supremacía constitucional y la salida constituyente en Venezuela en 1999," *Revista Anuario Iberoamericano de Justicia Constitucional* 3, 1999, Centro de Estudios Políticos y Constitucionales, Madrid 2000, 31-56; and *Asamblea constituyente y ordenamiento constitucional,* 152ff.

[55]See Allan R. Brewer-Carías, "Comentarios sobre la inconstitucional de la convocatoria a referéndum sobre una Asamblea Nacional Constituyente, efectuada por el Consejo Nacional Electoral en febrero de 1999," *Revista Política y Gobierno* 1, Fundación de Estudios de Derecho Administrativo, Caracas 1999, 29-92. See also Brewer-Carías, *Asamblea constituyente y ordenamiento constitucional,* 229ff.

[56]Among the authors who thought the convening of the Constituent Assembly needed a prior constitutional provision establishing it was Ricardo Combellas, who in 1998 was head of the Presidential Commission on State Reforms. See Ricardo Combellas, *¿Qué es la Constituyente?. Voz para el futuro de Venezuela,* COPRE, Caracas 1998, 38. The next year, after having been appointed by Chávez as member of the Presidential Commission for the Constitutional Reform, he changed his opinion, admitting the possibility of electing the assembly even without constitutional support. See Ricardo Combellas, *Poder constituyente,* Presentación, Hugo Chávez Frías, Caracas 1999, 189ff. In 1999, Combellas was elected a member of the Constituent Assembly from the lists supported by Chávez, but a few years later, he withdrew his support for the president and became a critic of his antidemocratic government.

On January 19, 1999, almost two weeks before the president took office, the Court issued two ambiguous decisions that failed to expressly resolve the issue,[57] if there was a need to first reform the Constitution before the assembly could be convened; thus decreeing "the death of a Constitution."[58] The Court, in its decision, referred broadly to the traditional constitutional doctrine on constituent power, including quotations from the 1789 writings of Abate Sièyes, which those defending the possibility of convening the Assembly subsequently used to support their argument.[59] In this regard, the Court's ambiguous decision contrasted with the very clear and direct decision of the Supreme Court of Justice of Colombia in 1991, which allowed the Constituent Assembly to be convened, and with the clear decisions of the contentious administrative jurisdiction courts in Honduras in 2009. This is the main difference between the cases of Colombia in 1991 and Venezuela in 1999 – in the former, the Constituent Assembly was elected after the Supreme Court expressly allowed it. In the case of Venezuela, the Supreme Court's decisions acknowledged the possibility of a consultative referendum to seek popular opinion on the election of a constituent assembly and presented a theoretical summary of the constitutional doctrine of constituent power. However, the Court said nothing about the main issue of whether a previous constitutional amendment was required to elect a constituent assembly to give constitutional rank to its status.[60]

[57] See the texts in *Revista de Derecho Público* 77–80, Editorial Jurídica Venezolana, Caracas 1999, 56-73; and Allan R. Brewer-Carías, *Poder constituyente originario y asamblea nacional constituyente,* Editorial Jurídica Venezolana, Caracas 1999, 25ff.

[58] See Alessandro Pace, "Morte di una Costituzione," *Giurisprudenza Costituzionale* XLIV, Fasc. 2-Giuffrè Editore, Milan 1999, 1544-452; "Muerte de una constitución," in *Revista Española de Derecho Constitucional* 57, Centro de Estudios Políticos y Constitucionales, Madrid 1999, 271-83.

[59] On the decisions, see Allan R. Brewer-Carías, "La configuración judicial del proceso constituyente o de cómo el guardián de la Constitución abrió el camino para su violación y para su propia extinción," *Revista de Derecho Público* 77–80, Editorial Jurídica Venezolana, Caracas 1999, 453-514; Allan R. Brewer-Carías, *Asamblea constituyente y ordenamiento constitucional,* Academia de Ciencias Políticas y Sociales, Caracas 1999, 152-228; Allan R. Brewer-Carías, *Golpe de estado y proceso constituyente en Venezuela*, Universidad Nacional Autónoma de México, Mexico City 2002, 65ff.; Lolymar Hernández Camargo, *La teoría del poder constituyente: Un caso de estudio: El proceso constituyente venezolano de 1999,* Universidad Católica del Táchira, San Cristóbal 2000, 53ff.; Claudia Nikken, *La cour suprême de justice et la constitution vénézuélienne du 23 Janvier 1961,* Ph.D. diss., l'Université Panthéon Assas, Paris 2001, 366ff.

[60] See comments on the decisions in Allan R. Brewer-Carías, "La configuración judicial del proceso constituyente o de cómo el guardián de la Constitución abrió el camino para su violación y para su propia extinción," in *Revista de Derecho Público,* 77–80, Editorial Jurídica Venezolana, Caracas 1999, 453-514; Allan R. Brewer-Carías, *Asamblea constituyente y ordenamiento constitucional,* 152-228; Allan R. Brewer-Carías, *Golpe de estado y proceso constituyente en Venezuela,* Universidad Nacional Autónoma de México, Mexico City 2002, 65ff.; Lolymar Hernández Camargo, *La teoría del poder constituyente. Un caso de estudio: el proceso constituyente*

The ambiguous Supreme Court decision emboldened the president who, without constitutional authorization, issued his first official act on February 2, 1999: a decree ordering a referendum to propose that the people authorize Chávez, and him alone, to call the Constituent Assembly and to define its composition, procedure, mission, and duration.[61] Thus, he purported to hold a referendum on a constituent assembly in which people would vote blindly, without knowing the number of representatives to be elected; the electoral system to be applied and the procedure for the assembly's election, composition, or the nature or duration of its mission. That means that the president began the process to convene a constituent assembly to transform the state and the legal order, without any previous political consultation or consensus with the political parties and forces of the country, thus disregarding any constitutional or legal consideration.[62] In that way, he marked the process as one imposed by the president on the basis of his own popularity, without the participation of the political spectrum of the country. This was another main difference from Colombia's 1991 Constituent Assembly.

Because he tried to impose his exclusive and exclusionist proposal through the February decree, it is hardly surprising that the constitutionality of the decree was challenged before the Supreme Court,[63] which in a series of judicial review decisions ruled that the manner in which the president had acted in calling for the consultative referendum on the Constituent Assembly was unconstitutional. In one of the rulings, issued on March 18, 1999, the Supreme Court declared that the president

venezolano de 1999, Universidad Católica del Táchira, San Cristóbal 2000, 53ff.; Claudia Nikken, *La Cour Suprême de Justice et la Constitution vénézuélienne du 23 Janvier 1961,* Ph.D. diss., l'Université Panthéon Assas (Paris II), Paris 2001, 366ff.

[61]See *Gaceta Oficial* N° 36.634, Feb. 2, 1999, and its modification in *Gaceta Oficial* N° 36.658, Mar. 10, 1999. See comments regarding the decree in Allan R. Brewer-Carías, *Golpe de estado y proceso constituyente en Venezuela,* Universidad Nacional Autónoma de México, Mexico City 2002, 113ff.; Allan R. Brewer-Carías, *Asamblea constituyente y ordenamiento constitucional,* Academia de Ciencias Políticas y Sociales, Caracas 1998, 229ff.

[62]The same day, Feb. 2, 1999, in which he convened the Constituent Assembly, he said in a public rally: "[Many think] that the Decree on the Constituent [Assembly] does not fulfill provisions, I don't know of which law, or of which thing, or of which Constitution! Who cares that the Decree of the Constituent [Assembly] does not fulfill with, I don't know what thing of a law, or of the Constitution, if it is the people who is the one crying out for transformation; [the problem] is not legal, is political, and for those in the Congress [beware]: there is no walk back; for those in the political parties [beware]: there is no walk back." See Ana Teresa Torres, *La herencia de la tribu. Del mito de la independencia a la Revolución bolivariana,* Editorial Alfa, Caracas 2009, 224.

[63]See the text of the challenge I brought before the Supreme Court in Brewer-Carías, *Asamblea constituyente y ordenación constitucional,* 255-321. On the other challenges brought before the Supreme Court, see Carlos M. Escarrá Malavé, *Proceso político y constituyente,* Caracas 1999, Exhibit 4.

could not exclusively formulate the composition, procedure, mission, and duration of the Constituent Assembly, and that those details would at least have to be submitted to popular vote.[64] Consequently, the National Electoral Council was required to submit to popular vote whether to convene the Constituent Assembly and the complete text of its bylaws, from the president, which were not the product of any sort of political agreement, compromise, or consensus among political forces of the country. In contrast, in Colombia, the Constituent Assembly was convened after political parties had reached agreements and consensus. But Ecuador followed the example of Venezuela in 2007. In both cases, even with some judicial corrections, the president unilaterally imposed the bylaws of the Constituent Assembly. On April 13, 1999, Venezuela's Supreme Court ruled that the Assembly had to be elected within the framework of the Court's interpretation of the 1961 Constitution and could not have "original constituent powers," as the president had proposed. The Court expressly ordered the National Electoral Council to eliminate those full and unlimited powers from the bylaws to be submitted to the April 25 referendum.[65]

The members of the Supreme Court had been elected years before by the party-controlled Congress, and it was that same Court that, under tremendous political pressure from President-Elect Chávez, issued the aforementioned decision of January 1999, by which it gave way, without express ruling, to the possibility of the election of a constituent assembly without previously reforming the Constitution. After having freed the political constituent forces of society as a means for participation, when the Supreme Court tried to control them by ruling that the Constituent

---

[64] See the text of Supreme Court decisions from Mar. 18, 1999; Mar. 23, 1999; Apr. 13, 1999; June 3, 1999; June 17, 1999; and July 21, 1999, in *Revista de Derecho Público* 77–80, Editorial Jurídica Venezolana, Caracas 1999, 73-110. See the comments in Allan R. Brewer-Carías, *Poder constituyente originario y asamblea nacional constituyente,* Editorial Jurídica Venezolana, Caracas 1999, 169-98, 223-51; "Comentarios sobre la inconstitucional convocatoria a referendo sobre una Asamblea Nacional Constituyente efectuada por el Consejo Nacional Electoral en febrero de 1999," *Revista Política y Gobierno* 1, Fundación de Estudios de Derecho Administrativo, Caracas 1999, 29-92; and *Golpe de estado y proceso constituyente en Venezuela,* Universidad Nacional Autónoma de México, Mexico City 2002, 160ff.

[65] In particular, see Supreme Court decisions of Apr. 13, 1999; June 17, 1999; and July 21, 1999, in *Revista de Derecho Público* 77–80, Editorial Jurídica Venezolana, Caracas 1999, 85ff.; Brewer-Carías, *Poder constituyente originario y asamblea nacional constituyente,* 169-98, 223-5. Venezuelan constitutional law distinguishes between "derivative" constituent authority and "original" constituent authority, the latter being the kind of nonlimited authority such an institution would have at the very moment of conception of a new state. The 1811 General Congress of the Confederation of the States of Venezuela as a constitutional convention would be an example of the kind of institution that would be considered original in this sense.

Assembly to be elected had to observe and act according to the 1961 Constitution, it was too late.[66] After the election in July 1999, the Constituent Assembly crushed all the constituted powers, including the Supreme Court itself, violating the in–force 1961 Constitution.[67]

3. *The Electoral Rule for the Election of the Assembly*

Despite the Supreme Court's rulings and in the absence of any political negotiations, agreements, or consensus among various sectors of society, the president proceeded unilaterally with the consultative referendum to call a constituent assembly on April 25, 1999. In a voting process in which only 38.7% of eligible voters cast their ballots (62.2% of eligible voters did not turn out to vote), the yes votes obtained 81.9% and the no votes 18.1%.[68] The approved proposal provided for the election of a 131-member constituent assembly: 104 members to be elected in 24 regional constituencies corresponding to the political subdivisions of the territory (states and the federal district); 24 members to be elected in a national constituency, and 3 members representing the indigenous peoples, who constitute a small portion of Venezuela's population.

The referendum approved the electoral system that the president had proposed in which candidates were to run individually, allowing Chávez's supporters to easily dominate the Constituent Assembly.[69] The 104 regional constituency seats were allotted according to the population of each state and the federal district. A list of all the candidates in each regional constituency was placed on the ballot in each constituency, and the voters could vote for the number of candidates on their constituency's list that corresponded to the number of seats allotted to their constituency. The elected candidates were those who received the greatest number of votes. Voting proceeded in the same way on the national level for the twenty-four seats, except in that case, voters were allowed to choose only ten candidates from the list.

---

[66]In particular, see the Supreme Court decisions of Apr. 13, 1999; June 17, 1999; and July 21, 1999, in *Revista de Derecho Público* 77–80, Editorial Jurídica Venezolana, Caracas 1999, 85ff.

[67]See references to all those decisions in Brewer-Carías, *Debate constituyente, (Aportes a la Asamblea Nacional Constituyente)*, Fundación de Derecho Público–Editorial Jurídica Venezolana, Caracas 1999, 1 (Aug. 8–Sept. 8):11-124.

[68]See José E. Molina and Carmen Pérez Baralt, "Procesos Electorales. Venezuela, abril, julio y diciembre de 1999," in *Boletín Electoral Latinoamericano* 22, CAPEL-IIDH, San José 2000, 61ff.

[69] See Gregory Wilpert, *Changing Venezuela by Taking Power: The History and Policies of the Chávez Government*, Verso, London 2007, 21.

This electoral system was without any precedent in Venezuela. It amounted to a ruse by the president and his followers to ensure absolute control of the Constituent Assembly. In a campaign financed by Venezuelan insurance companies and foreign banks,[70] among others, the president appeared personally in every state of the country proposing his list of candidates for election in each constituency. On the national level, he proposed only twenty candidates for the twenty-four seats; dividing the country in two, he proposed a list of ten candidates to voters in the east and a separate list of ten candidates to voters of the west. This was rather unusual in Venezuelan political tradition. After more than a hundred years of the constitutional rule of no reelection, Venezuelans were not used to having presidents directly involved in electoral campaigns, and any governmental involvement in elections had been considered illegitimate.

The election was carried out on July 25, 1999, without the participation of the traditional political parties; only 46.3% of eligible voters cast ballots (53.7% of eligible voters did not turn out to vote).[71] The candidates supported by the president obtained 65.8% of the votes cast, but the election resulted in his followers controlling 94% of the seats in the Constituent Assembly. All of the president's supported candidates except one were elected, for a total of 123 – of the 104 candidates elected at the state level, only one belonged to a traditional party (Acción Democrática); of the 24 candidates elected at the national level, only 4 independent candidates who opposed the president were elected without his support, mainly because the president had proposed only 20 candidates of 24 to be elected. Because the voters could vote for only ten candidates nationally, all those proposed by the president (ten each in the east and west) were elected. It can be deduced that if the president would have proposed three sets of eight candidates – instead of two sets of ten – all twenty-four candidates would have been elected. In addition, three indigenous representatives elected to the assembly were followers of the president and his party.

The result of this electoral scheme was that instead of contributing to democratic pluralism, the Constituent Assembly was totally controlled by the newly established government party and the president's followers, to the exclusion of all traditional political parties. As mentioned, only one

---

[70] For which a few high former officials of the Banco Bilbao Vizcaya of Spain were criminally indicted on Feb. 8, 2006, by the Juzgado Central de Instrucción N° 5, Audiencia Nacional, Madrid (Procedure N° 251/02-N).

[71] See José E. Molina and Carmen Pérez Baralt, "Procesos Electorales. Venezuela, abril, julio y diciembre de 1999," in *Boletín Electoral Latinoamericano* 22, CAPEL-IIDH, San José 2000, 61ff.

member out of 131 belonged to the traditional parties (one regional member), and 4 others were elected independently, in opposition to the president.[72] Together, they became the opposition group in the assembly.

A constituent assembly formed by a majority of that nature was not a valid instrument for dialogue or for political conciliation and negotiation. It was a political instrument to impose the ideas of a dominant group on the rest of society and to totally exclude other groups.

4. *The Seizure of the Constituted Powers*

Meanwhile, and before the convening of the Constituent Assembly, President Chávez and all the representatives to the National Congress had been elected in November and December 1998, per the provisions of the 1961 Constitution. The governors of the 23 states, the representatives of the state legislative assemblies, and the mayors and members of the municipal councils of the 338 municipalities had also been elected in November 1998. That is, all the heads of the representative public entities set forth in the Constitution had been popularly elected before the constitution-making process of 1999 had begun. In addition, the nonelected heads of the organs of state, such as the judges of the Supreme Court of Justice, the prosecutor general of the republic, the general controller of the republic, and the members of the Supreme Electoral Council, had been appointed by the National Congress, again in accordance with the 1961 Constitution.

Therefore, by the time the Constituent Assembly was elected on July 25, 1999, the constituted public entities were functioning in parallel, with different missions. The Constituent Assembly was elected to design the reform of the state and to establish a new legal framework institutionalizing a social and participatory democracy, which was to be submitted for popular approval in a final referendum. It was not elected to govern, substitute, or interfere with the constituted powers. Moreover, as the Supreme Court of Justice declared in one of its decisions, it had no "original" constituent authority.[73]

However, in its first decision, which was the adoption of its own statute governing its functioning, the Constituent Assembly, in a contrary sense to what had ruled the Supreme Court a few months earlier, declared itself "an

---

[72] Allan R. Brewer-Carías, Claudio Fermín, Alberto Franchesqui, and Jorge Olavarría.

[73] See the decision of Apr. 13, 1999, in *Revista de Derecho Público* 77–80, Editorial Jurídica Venezolana, Caracas 1999, 85ff.; Brewer-Carías, *Poder constituyente originario y asamblea nacional constituyente,* Editorial Jurídica Venezolana, Caracas 1999, 169-98, 223-51.

As a result, the initial period of the Constituent Assembly was a period of confrontation and political conflict between all branches of government and the various political sectors of the country. The constituent process, in that initial phase, was not a vehicle for dialogue and peace or an instrument for avoiding conflict. On the contrary, it was an elected political instrument for exclusion and confrontation, crushing all opposition or dissidence. The Constituent Assembly was thus subject to exclusive domination by one new political party (Movimiento V República [MVR]), that of the government, which answered to the president. It was in that way that the constitution-making process was used to abolish the political class and parties that had dominated the scene in former decades.

5. The Drafting Phase: Haste and Exclusion

After the constituted powers had been either encroached on or entirely usurped, the Constituent Assembly entered its second phase (September–October 1999), which involved elaborating the text of a draft constitution. The extreme brevity of the second phase did not allow for any real public discussion or popular participation. The Constituent Assembly rejected the traditional method adopted by other constitutional processes throughout the world whereby a broadly representative and plural constitutional commission elaborates a draft, through negotiations and consent, which is later presented in plenary session.[85]

It is true that the president of the republic, just before he took office, had informally created the Constitutional Commission, which though composed of independent political figures who all were at that time his supporters, actually devoted its time to the issues surrounding the drafting of the method of electing the Constituent Assembly. It never worked to develop a coherent constitutional draft, and its proceedings were not public or participatory. It held no public meetings and met with the president only during the weeks prior and subsequent to the installation of his government. Soon after, all of its members were already in the opposition.

Thus, the Constituent Assembly began to work collectively without an initial draft. The president did publish and submit to the Constituent Assembly a document prepared with the assistance of his appointed

---

[85]Such a method was used, for instance, to develop the 1947 Constitution. See *Anteproyecto de Constitución de 1947. Elección directa de gobernadores y eliminación de asambleas legislativas*, Papeles de Archivo N° 8, Ediciones Centauro, Caracas 1987.

Constitutional Council. Its intention was to propose ideas for the new Constitution, but its contents were not completely coherent.[86] Even though the Constituent Assembly did not adopt the document as the draft constitution, the drafting commissions used parts of it, particularly because their members in general had no constitutional–studies expertise. Also, two draft constitutions were submitted to the Constituent Assembly, one by a small-membership left-wing party and another by the nongovernmental organization Primero Justicia, which in 2002 became a center-right political party. Neither of these was adopted as drafts for discussions and, because of their origins, the parties had no particular influence in the drafting commissions.

After two months of dealing with the interference of all the constituted powers, the Constituent Assembly began to elaborate a draft by appointing twenty commissions to deal with the essential subjects of any constitution. Each commission was charged with coming up with a proposed draft for its subject area. This all occurred during only a few days, between September 2 and September 28, 1999. During that period, each commission acted alone and in isolation, consulting only briefly with groups the commission considered appropriate.[87]

The president, once the Constituent Assembly had usurped all public power, urged it to quickly complete drafting the constitution to end the political instability provoked by the constituent process and to use the new constitutional framework to relegitimate the branches of government through new elections. The timetable to finish the drafting of the constitution was established not by the referendum of April 1999 or the Constituent Assembly but by its board of directors in response to presidential pressure.

As of September 1999, the twenty commissions sent their drafts to an additional Constitutional Commission of the Constituent Assembly, in charge of integrating the texts received. Collectively, the commissions' submissions included more than eight hundred articles. The Constitutional Commission was charged with integrating the submissions to form a single draft. Unfortunately, the board of directors of the Constituent Assembly gave the Constitutional Commission just two weeks to integrate

---

[86]See Hugo Chávez Frías, *Ideas fundamentales para la Constitución bolivariana de la V República,* Caracas Aug. 1999.

[87]I was president of the Commission on Nationality and Citizenship. See the Report of the Commission in Allan R. Brewer-Carías, *Debate constituyente (Aportes a la Asamblea Nacional Constituyente),* Fundación de Derecho Público–Editorial Jurídica Venezolana, Caracas 1999, 2 (Sept. 9–Oct. 17): 2:45-74.

all those drafts. The hasty process of elaborating the draft left no room for public discussion or the participation of civil society, whose input could have been incorporated into the discussions in plenary session.[88]

The draft that the Constitutional Commission submitted to the Constituent Assembly on October 18, composed of 350 articles, was a very unsatisfactory text, sometimes contradictory, and full of good intentions.[89] The draft followed many of the provisions of the 1961 Constitution, with the addition of some portions of the president's proposed document. Some foreign constitutional provisions, particularly copied from the Colombian and Spanish constitutions,[90] were included in the draft text, and part of the text of the American Convention on Human Rights enriched the draft as well. Nevertheless, it can be said that foreign experts or international or regional organizations played no specific publicly known role in the Constituent Assembly.[91] There was no time left for that possibility.

The government imposed an urgency to finish the constitutional draft, requiring the Constituent Assembly to discuss and approve the draft in just one month, from October 19 to November 17, 2000, to submit the constitution to referendum in December 1999. This schedule explains why only nineteen days were devoted to the first round of discussion sessions (October 20–November 9) and three days to the second round (November 12–14), for a total of twenty-two days. During that time, I proposed drafts and expressed my dissenting votes.[92] Together with the other opposition

---

[88] I was also a member of the Constitutional Commission of the Assembly. On the difficulties of participating in the drafting process, see Brewer-Carías, *Debate constituyente (Aportes a la Asamblea Nacional Constituyente)*, 2 (Sept 9–Oct. 17):255-86.

[89] See *Gaceta Constituyente (Diario de Debates)*, Oct.–Nov. 1999, N° 23, Oct. 19, 2009.

[90] See, e.g., Allan R. Brewer-Carías, "La Constitución española de 1978 y la Constitución de la República Bolivariana de Venezuela de 1999: Algunas influencias y otras coincidencias," in *La Constitución de 1978 y el constitucionalismo iberoamericano*, coord. Francisco Fernández Segado, Ministerio de la Presidencia, Secretaría General Técnica, Centro de Estudios Políticos y Constitucionales, Madrid 2003, 765-86.

[91] All suggestions I made to the board of directors of the Constituent Assembly to invite the most distinguished constitutional lawyers of Latin America and Spain to advise in the constitution-making process were systematically denied. Nonetheless, after the Constitution was approved, it became known that some faculty of the University of Valencia, Spain, helped the vice president of the Assembly in the Technical Committee. See Roberto Viciano Pastor and Rubén Martínez Dalmau, *Cambio político y proceso constituyente en Venezuela (1998-2000)*, Valencia, 2001.

[92] See the text of my 127 dissenting votes in Brewer-Carías, *Debate constituyente (Aportes a la Asamblea Nacional Constituyente)*, Fundación de Derecho Público–Editorial Jurídica Venezolana, Caracas 1999, 3 (Oct. 18–Nov. 30):107-308.

members, I participated in the political campaign for a no vote in the referendum on the Constitution because of its authoritarian content.[93]

After one month of campaigning, the Constitution was approved in the December 15, 1999, referendum. Turnout was low: only 44.3% of eligible voters cast votes (57.7% of eligible voters did not turn out), with 71.8% voting yes and 28.2% voting no.[94] This means that just 30% of Venezuelans with the right to vote approved the Constitution.

However, the approved text did not conform to the operational language of the consultative referendum of April 1999. It failed to provide the new democratic and pluralistic vision that society required, to define the fundamental principles required for reorganizing the country politically, and to create a decentralized state based on participatory democracy.

Despite some good intentions and brief attempts at public education, the hastiness of the process rendered any effective public and political participation impossible. It must be noted that one of the twenty commissions of the Constituent Assembly was the Participatory Commission, totally controlled by the president's followers, which did divulge some information, including to television programs, related to the drafting process and the content of the other commissions' drafts. The sessions of the Constituent Assembly were also directly broadcast on television, thus allowing the public to follow daily discussions. But the great debate that should have taken place in the Constituent Assembly, on such issues as the monopoly of the political parties, decentralization and the power of local government, expansion of institutional protections of human rights, and the basic mission of the constitution, never took place. There was no public education to encourage the submission of proposals from civil–society groups and nongovernmental organizations. The only minority group that was offered an opportunity to participate was that of the indigenous peoples, who were allowed three seats in the assembly.

Those who controlled the work of the Constituent Assembly were conscious that participation required time; instead, they chose the fast track, working without participatory procedures. The result was that political participation was reduced just to the vote cast by the public, in which most eligible voters did not vote: first in the April 1999 consultative referendum on the convening of the Constituent Assembly, in which only

---

[93]See arguments in Brewer-Carías, *Debate constituyente (Aportes a la Asamblea Nacional Constituyente)*, 3 (Oct. 18–Nov. 30):309-40.

[94]See José E. Molina and Carmen Pérez Baralt, "Procesos Electorales. Venezuela, abril, julio y diciembre de 1999," in *Boletín Electoral Latinoamericano* 22, CAPEL-IIDH, San José 2000, 67-68.

37% of potential voters participated; second, in the July 1999 election of members of the assembly, in which only 46% of voters participated; and third, in the December 1999 approval referendum of the new Constitution, in which only 44% of voters participated.

IV. THE PARALLEL TRANSITORY REGIME

The ramifications of the departure from the rule of law entailed in the deformation of the constitutional process can be perceived not only in the events that immediately followed but also in the crisis that continues to plague the political system.

In the week following the adoption of the new Constitution, the Constituent Assembly, without questioning the duration of its authority, on December 20, 1999, adopted a new decree establishing the Transitory Constitutional Regime,[95] which had not been approved by popular referendum and violated the newly adopted Constitution, including its transitional provisions.[96] According to it, the Constituent Assembly ratified the president in his post and, acting in violation of the new Constitution and in the absence of any participation by civil society, directly appointed the members of the new Supreme Tribunal of Justice, the new National Electoral Council, the prosecutor general, the people's defender, and the comptroller general, ending the tenure of those previously appointed. The Constituent Assembly, moreover, eliminated definitively Congress and created and appointed the new Legislative National Commission, which had not been provided for in the 1999 Constitution; the new commission assumed legislative power until the new National Assembly (supplanting the dissolved Congress) was elected. The unconstitutional transitional regime was challenged before the new Supreme Judicial Tribunal, created as part of the same regime. Deciding in its own cause, the tribunal upheld the transitional regime's constitutionality, justifying it on the basis of the Constituent Assembly's supraconstitutional powers.[97]

---

[95] See *Gaceta Oficial* N° 36.859, Dec. 29, 1999.

[96] See comments on this decree in Allan R. Brewer-Carías, *Golpe de estado y proceso constituyente en Venezuela*, 354ff.; *La Constitución de 1999. Derecho constitucional venezolano*, Editorial Jurídica Venezolana, Caracas 2004, 2:1.017.

[97] See the Jan. 26, 2000, Decision N° 4 (Case: *Eduardo García*), and the Mar. 28, 2000, Decision N° 180 (Case: *Allan R. Brewer-Carías et al.*), in *Revista de Derecho Público* 81, Editorial Jurídica Venezolana, Caracas 2000, 93ff. and 86ff. See comments in Brewer-Carías, *Golpe de estado y proceso constituyente en Venezuela*, 354ff.

The Transitional Constitutional Regime fixed the general framework for the subsequent concentration of powers and development of the current authoritarian political regime. This regime, which unfortunately has enjoyed the support of the Constitutional Chamber of the Supreme Judicial Tribunal, has taken shape in Venezuela as envisaged when President Chávez came to power in 1998 and is characterized by the president's complete control of all branches of government. In particular, the control of the Supreme Tribunal has lead to a judiciary composed of more than 90% provisional or temporary judges,[98] with no autonomy or independence whatsoever.[99]

V. THE DEMOCRATIC FAILURE OF THE CONSTITUTION-MAKING PROCESS

From all that has been stated herein, it is clear that the Venezuelan constitution-making process of 1999 failed to achieve its stated mission of political conciliation and improved democracy. Against a democratic principle, instead of offering the participation that so many sought, the process imposed the will of one political group on others and on the rest of the population.

Thus, as an instrument for the development of a constitutional authoritarian government, the Constitution can be considered a success. Undoubtedly, the democratically elected Constituent Assembly conducted a coup d'état against the 1961 constitutional regime, facilitated the complete takeover of all branches of government by one political group and crushed other political parties, and drafted and approved a constitution

---

[98] Almost two years after the Constituent Assembly's intervention in the judiciary, some magistrates of the Supreme Tribunal acknowledged that more than the 90% of judges in Venezuela were provisional. See *El Universal*, Caracas Aug. 15, 2001. In May 2001, other magistrates recognized that the so-called judicial emergency was a failure. See *El Universal*, Caracas May 30, 2001, 1-4. See also *Informe sobre la situación de los derechos humanos en Venezuela*; OAS/Ser.L/V/II.118. d.C. 4rev. 2, Dec. 29, 2003, para. 11. It reads: "The Commission has been informed that only 250 judges have been appointed by opposition concurrence according to the constitutional text. From a total of 1.772 positions of judges in Venezuela, the Supreme Court of Justice reports that only 183 are holders, 1.331 are provisional and 258 are temporary." The same Commission also said that "an aspect linked to the autonomy and independence of the Judicial Power is that of the provisional character of the judges in the judicial system of Venezuela. Today, the information provided by the different sources indicates that more than 80% of Venezuelan judges are provisional"; in id., para. 161.

[99] See Allan R. Brewer-Carías, "La progresiva y sistemática demolición institucional de la autonomía e independencia del poder judicial en Venezuela 1999-2004," 33-174; Rogelio Pérez Perdomo, "Judicialization in Venezuela," in *The Judicialization of Politics in Latin America*, eds. Rachel Sieder, Line Schjolden, and Alan Angell, Palgrave Macmillan, 2005, 145ff.

with an authoritarian framework that has allowed the installment of a government that has concentrated and centralized all state powers.

The durability of the new Constitution can be predicted to be the same as the durability of the power of those who imposed it and remain in control. That is why reforms of the political system, founded in the democratization and political decentralization of the country, remain pending tasks that the Constituent Assembly of 1999 was unable to accomplish.

In the meantime, on August 15, 2007, the president submitted to the National Assembly a constitutional reform proposal intending to consolidate a socialist, centralized, and militaristic police state, minimizing democracy and limiting freedoms and liberties.[100] The main purpose of the proposals can be understood from the president's speech at the presentation of the draft constitutional reforms,[101] in which he said that the reforms' main objective is "the construction of a Bolivarian and Socialist Venezuela."[102] This is intended, as he explained, to sow "socialism in the political and economic realms."[103] This is something that the Constitution of 1999 did not do. When the Constitution of 1999 was sanctioned, said the president, "We were not projecting the road of socialism. Just as candidate Hugo Chávez repeated a million times in 1998, 'Let us go to a Constituent [Assembly],' so candidate President Hugo Chávez said [in 2006]: 'Let us go to Socialism' and, thus, everyone who voted for candidate Chávez then, voted to go to socialism."[104]

Although this assumption was false, because in the 2006 election nobody voted for a socialist program, the draft constitutional reforms presented by the president, according to what he said in his speech, proposed the construction of "Bolivarian Socialism, Venezuelan Socialism, our Socialism, and our socialist model."[105] It is a socialism

---

[100]See *Proyecto de Reforma Constitucional. Elaborado por el ciudadano Presidente de la República Bolivariana de Venezuela, Hugo Chávez Frías,* 58. See comments on the draft in Brewer-Carías, *Hacia la consolidación de un estado socialista, centralizado, policial y militarista.*

[101]"Discurso de Orden pronunciado por el ciudadano Comandante Hugo Chávez Frías, Presidente Constitucional de la República Bolivariana de Venezuela en la conmemoración del Ducentésimo Segundo Aniversario del Juramento del Libertador Simón Bolívar en el Monte Sacro y el Tercer Aniversario del Referendo Aprobatorio de su Mandato Constitucional," special session of Aug. 15, 2007, Asamblea Nacional, División de Servicio y Atención legislativa, Sección de Edición, Caracas 2007.

[102]Id., 4.

[103]Id., 33.

[104]Id., 4.

[105]See "Discurso de Orden pronunciado por el ciudadano Comandante Hugo Chávez Frías...," 34.

whose "basic and indivisible nucleus" is "the community" (*la comunidad*), one "where common citizens shall have the power to construct their own geography and their own history."[106] This is all based on the premise that "real democracy is only possible in socialism."[107] However, the supposed democracy referred to is one that, as the president suggests in his proposed reform to Article 136, "is not born of suffrage or from any election, but rather is born from the condition of organized human groups as the base of the population." Of course, that is not democracy, as there can be no democracy without the election of representatives.

The president in his speech summarized all of the proposed reforms in this manner: "on the political ground, deepen popular Bolivarian democracy; on the economic ground, create better conditions to sow and construct a socialist productive economic model, our model; the same in the political field: socialist democracy; on the economic, the productive socialist model; in the field of Public Administration: incorporate new forms in order to lighten the load, to leave behind bureaucracy, corruption, and administrative inefficiency, which are heavy burdens of the past still upon us like weights, in the political, economic and social areas."[108]

All the 2007 constitutional reform proposals, although sanctioned by the National Assembly on November 2, 2007, were rejected by the people in the December 2, 2007, popular referendum, increasing the extreme polarization in the country that began in 1999.[109] In any case, and unfortunately for the constitutional process, the rejected reforms have been illegitimately implemented through legislation, through decree laws,[110] and by means of ex post facto judicial interpretations issued by the Constitutional Chamber of the Supreme Tribunal. In addition, in February 2009, after the Constitutional Chamber mutated the meaning of the Constitution, a constitutional amendment was submitted to popular vote to change the alternating form of government and allow the successive and continuous reelection of the president and all the elected

---

[106]Id., 32.
[107]Id., 35.
[108]Id., 74.
[109]See the collective works on the 2007 draft constitutional reforms in *Revista de Derecho Público* 112 *(Estudios sobre la reforma constitucional)*, Editorial Jurídica Venezolana, Caracas 2007.
[110]See the collective works on the 2008 delegate legislation implementing the rejected draft constitutional reforms in *Revista de Derecho Público* 115, *(Estudios sobre los Decretos Leyes)*, Editorial Jurídica Venezolana, Caracas 2008.

representatives and officials, also one of the rejected constitutional reforms.[111]

During 2008 and in 2009 and 2010, all the reforms adopted by the National Assembly regarding statutes related to the functioning of the state have incorporated the figure of the communal council and of popular power, as an important piece, precisely implementing the 2007 rejected constitutional reform, aimed to transform the state into a popular state.[112]

---

[111] See comments in Allan R. Brewer-Carías, "El juez constitucional vs. la alternabilidad republicana (La reelección contínua e indefinida)," in *Revista de Derecho Público* 117, Caracas 2009, 205-11.

[112] See, for instance, on the communal councils and the "Popular Power," in Allan R. Brewer-Carías, *Ley de los Consejos Comunales,* Editorial Jurídica Venezolana, Caracas 2010. In June 2010, the National Assembly began the discusión of the *Ley de Comunas* and the *Ley Orgánica de Contraloría Social* in order to complete the dismantling of the federation and the consolidation of the Popular Power.

Chapter 2

THE ENDLESS AND ILLEGITIMATE TRANSITORY CONSTITUTIONAL REGIME

The same Constituent Assembly that sanctioned the 1999 Constitution modified it one week after its popular approval through referendum, and more than one week before it began to be enforced through its publication in the *Official Gazette*.[1] The Constituent Assembly, evading any popular approval, issued a decree creating the Transitory Constitutional Regime preventing the effective enforcement of the Constitution, through which the country began to have two constitutions: one approved by the people and another without such approval.

I. FAILED EFFORTS TO CREATE A CONSTITUTIONAL FRAMEWORK TO TRANSITION PUBLIC POWERS THROUGH AN APPROBATORY REFERENDUM

The National Constituent Assembly, when sanctioning the new Constitution on November 15, 1999, included in its text just a few transitory provisions that were those approved by the people in the December 15, 1999, referendum. The Constitution does not contain any provision regarding the then-existing constituent powers or the situation of the head officials of branches of government elected in 1998, so the applicable principle was the continuation of the elected officials up to the election of new ones according to the provisions of the new Constitution.

---

[1] The Constituent Assembly sanctioned the 1999 Constitution on Nov. 15, 1999, and it was approved in the referendum on Dec. 15, 1999; formally proclaimed by the assembly on Dec. 20, 1999; and published in *Gaceta Oficial* N° 36.860 of Dec. 30, 1999. Nonetheless, in the interim, after popular approval and before publication, the Assembly on Dec. 22, 1999 modified the Constitution as to a transitional regime through a decree that was published in *Gaceta Oficia*N° 36.859 of Dec. 29, 1999.

Due to the fact that the draft constitution of November 15, 1999, did not contain any such provision regarding the tenure of those elected high officials, on November 19, 1999, the same day that the draft was signed for submission to approbatory referendum, the Constituent Assembly approved a decree seeking the convening of a parallel consultative referendum, which was to take place also on December 15, 1999 – that is, the same day fixed for the approbatory referendum of the new Constitution. The purpose of the proposed consultative referendum was for "the Venezuelan people to decide on the permanence (or not) of the President of the Republic, and of the governments of each of the 23 states, subject to popular election, in exercise of their functions."[2]

The underlying intention of the proposal was to convert the approbatory referendum of the Constitution into a plebiscite on the permanence of President Hugo Chávez Frías in power, thus distorting the significance of the popular approval of the Constitution. Nonetheless, in a very confusing way, a few days later, in its session of December 12, 1999, three days before the fixed approbatory referendum of the Constitution was to be held, the assembly revoked without any explanation the proposed consultative plebiscite, basing the decision only on a supposed prior one of revocation adopted in "plenary session," which actually never took place.[3] As a result, a first effort to change the transitory provisions of the 1999 draft constitution, which contained no clause that addressed the termination of terms of office of elected heads of branches of government, was frustrated. But this would be the case only for a short time.[4]

After the 1999 Constitution was approved by the people in the December 15 referendum, in the following ordinary session of the assembly, on December 20, 1999, the Constitution was formally proclaimed. That means that the assembly had accomplished its functions according to the basic rules (*bases comiciales*) adopted in the consultative referendum of April 25, 1999, that allowed the assembly to function for six months (from July to December 1999). But instead of ending its mission, the Constituent Assembly decided to self–extend its tenure and

---

[2] *Gaceta Constituyente (Diario de Debates), Noviembre 1999–Enero 2000*, Sesión 19-11-99, N° 46, 3.

[3] *Gaceta Constituyente (Diario de Debates), Noviembre 1999–Enero 2000*, Sesión 09-12-99, N° 48, 5.

[4] It should be emphasized that the representative Hermán Escarrá Malavé, in the Assembly's session of Nov. 15, 1999, distinguished the transitory provisions (*disposiciones transitorias*) from a transitory regime (*régimen transitorio*), which ought to have been approved by referendum and about which he asked not to be questioned. See *Gaceta Constituyente (Diario de Debates), Noviembre 1999–Enero 2000*, Sesión de 15-11-99, N° 45, 9.

convened for its session of closure to be held on January 30, 2000.[5] With the decree, and despite the prior popular referendum approving the Constitution, the constituent assembly provided clear signs of its intention to continue exercising the "original" constituent power that it had bestowed on itself, well beyond the terms established for its existence in the consultative referendum of April 2009.[6] To set its session of closure on January 2000, the assembly considered that the powers given to it "had been recognized by the Supreme Court of Justice, in a formal decision, as original and supraconstitutional"[7] – that is, even above the new Constitution. It eventually concluded, ignoring the new Constitution, by announcing that it was "necessary to decree constitutional acts required for the transition to the new State foreseen in the Constitution approved by the people of Venezuela." The fact was that the latter was the only text that could establish a regime for a transition to the new state, but the transitional provisions that the same Constituent Assembly had drafted addressed nothing on this matter.

The assembly has, in a certain way, tricked the people: it sanctioned a constitution and submitted it to popular approval without any provision for the termination of the term of the 1998 elected officials, and after the Constitution was approved by the people and proclaimed, it decreed its violation, announcing that it would remain, thus exercising supraconstitutional powers to dictate constitutional acts that were not authorized by the transitional provisions of the new Constitution.

II. THE ILLEGITIMATE REGIME FOR THE TRANSITION OF PUBLIC POWERS

The first violation of the Constitution took place by the National Constituent Assembly itself in the days after the December 15, 1999, referendum, precisely during the nationwide commotion caused by massive flooding in the country's central coast, in the state of Vargas. The

---

[5]*Gaceta Constituyente (Diario de Debates), Noviembre 1999–Enero 2000*, Sesión 20-12-99, N° 49, 6.

[6]See Lolymar Hernández Camargo, *La teoría del poder constituyente. Un caso de estudio: El proceso constituyente venezolano de 1999,* Universidad Católica del Táchira, San Cristóbal 2000, 76.

[7]Decision of Oct. 6, 1999, published Oct. 14, 1999 (Case: *Henrique Capriles, Decreto de regulación de funcionamiento del poder legislativo*), in which the Supreme Court of Justice ruled in an action filed by the president of the Representative Chamber of Congress, seeking to nullify the National Constituent Assembly Decree Regulating the Legislative Power, by attributing supraconstitutional rank to the provisions in the text approved in referendum on Apr. 25, 1999, for the election of the National Constituent Assembly but not to its acts.

Assembly sanctioned on December 22, 1999, a decree containing the Regime for the Transition of Public Powers.[8] This occurred just two days after the proclamation of the new Constitution but before the Constitution's entry into effect with its publication, which was deliberately delayed until December 30, 1999.[9]

In the context of political eagerness to name new officials without waiting for the election of the new National Assembly, on December 22, 1999, the Constituent Assembly, without any constitutional authority, sanctioned the aforementioned decree. In it, and to "make the process of transition to the regime established in the Constitution of 1999 effective" through the termination of the titular officers of the state, the Constituent Assembly once again relied on its supposed self-attributed powers as "original constituent," which it assumed in Article 1 of the Statute of Functioning, considering them as having supraconstitutional character.

The decree had the objective of establishing a "regime of transition" supposedly to "allow the immediate going into effect of the Constitution" (Article 1), which had not yet been published. In fact, nothing impeded the immediate effectiveness of the Constitution. Nonetheless, the Constituent Assembly decided to "develop and complement the Transitory Provisions of the new Constitution" (Article 2), but it had no authority to do so. This was not authorized in the new Constitution that it had drafted and sanctioned, that was approved in a referendum, and that was even formally proclaimed two days before, on December 20, 1999, by the same assembly.

Nonetheless, the new transitory regime decree, according to its text, was devoted to filling the vacuum that the Constituent Assembly had created in failing to incorporate into the transitory provisions of the draft constitution, such transitory regime for the transfer of power from the existing elected organs (1998) provided in the 1961 Constitution to the newly created organs in the new Constitution. In the absence of such provisions in it, the principle that then needed to be applied was one to ensure the continuity of government mentioned in Article 16 of the decree. Instead, the Constituent Assembly usurped the authority of the original constituent power (the people) and acted against what had been approved in referendum, violating, in addition, the basic text for its election

---

[8]See *Gaceta Oficial* N° 36.859, Dec. 29, 1999.

[9]See *Gaceta Constituyente (Diario de Debates), Noviembre 1999–Enero 2000*, Sesión de 22-12-9, N° 51, 2ff., Session of Dec. 22, 1999, N° 51, 2 et seq.; *Gaceta Oficial* N° 36.859, Dec. 29, 1999; *Gaceta Oficial* N° 36.860, Dec. 30, 1999.

approved by referendum on April 25, 1999 – this was another coup d'état, this time against the new 1999 Constitution.

1. *Elimination of Congress and Creation of the National Legislative Commission*

The Constituent Assembly, in its transitory regime decree, first decided to definitively dissolve the former Congress (Article 4) and dismiss its elected (in 1989) senators and representatives. This decision, adopted after the popular approval of the new Constitution, violated the democratic principle and created a constitutional vacuum, in which, until the election of a new National Assembly, the republic would have been without a national legislative organ. For that reason, to fill the self-created vacuum, the Constituent Assembly made another decision, also without constitutional basis or authority, to create the "National Legislative Commission" (called *Congresillo*) not provided for in the new Constitution as approved by the people. By doing so, it illegitimately granted to the commission the exercise of the legislative power, "until the representatives to the new National Assembly are elected and in office" (Article 5). The members of the commission were appointed by the Constituent Assembly (Article 5) from partisans of the new power and members of the political parties that supported the government.[10] The National Legislative Commission functioned "in a permanent form" from the date of its installation on February 1, 2000 (Article 7) until the date of the effective installment of the new elected National Assembly (August 2000) (Article 8), and it assumed all "the rights and obligations" of the former Congress (Article 9).

These decisions of the National Constituent Assembly violated the basic text adopted in the April 25 referendum for its election. The decision to terminate the popular mandates of elected representatives in democratic elections, to constitute a new legislative organ, even temporarily, and moreover to assign legislative functions to unelected persons, violated the principles of representative democracy and progressiveness of the political right to democratically participate and to have elections; it further violated international treaties requiring Venezuela to ensure the effective exercise

---

[10]The assembly, on Jan. 28, 2000, again "in exercise of the original constituent power" that it had conferred on itself, named additional members of the National Legislative Commission. See *Gaceta Oficial* N° 36.903, Mar. 1, 2000.

of representative democracy.[11] The result of all these decisions was the installment of the National Legislative Commission, composed of unelected members and in open violation of the new Constitution.

A month later, on January 30, 2000, the Constituent Assembly issued another decree to amplify the powers of the National Legislative Commission,[12] assigning it a series of special powers to legislate on various matters. The assembly issued the decree, again "in the exercise of the sovereign original constituent power," which later the new Constitutional Chamber of the Supreme Tribunal of Justice considered as having "constitutional hierarchy."[13]

All these unconstitutional acts of the Constituent Assembly violated the new Constitution and were, successively and unfortunately, laundered by the new Supreme Tribunal, whose magistrates had also been appointed by the same Constituent Assembly precisely in the same transitory regime. On the occasion of deciding the judicial review actions challenging an act of the commission (Resolution Recommending the Reincorporation to Their Jobs of Labor Leaders and Workers Unjustly and Unconstitutionally Dismissed in Different Regions of the Country) of May 19, 2000,[14] in exercise of the powers conferred on it by the Constituent Assembly through the amplifying decree, the Constitutional Chamber of the Supreme Tribunal of Justice considered that such Resolution had constitutional rank.[15]

---

[11]Charter of the Organization of American States, and the American Convention on Human Rights, Art. 23. See Allan R. Brewer-Carías, *Debate Constituyente (Aportes a la Asamblea Nacional Constituyente)*, Fundación de Derecho Público–Editorial Jurídica Venezolana, Caracas 1999, 1 (Aug. 8–Sept. 8):76-81.

[12]*Gaceta Oficial* N° 36.884, Feb. 3, 2000.

[13]See Decision N° 1454 (Feb. 18, 2001) (Case: *C.A. Good Year de Venezuela*).

[14]*Gaceta Oficial* N° 36.965, June 5, 2000.

[15]The Constitutional Chamber ruled the following: "Because the then Supreme Court of Justice, in plenary session, on the 14th of Oct. of 1999, ruled that the basic text [*bases comiciales*] submitted to the Consultative Referendum on Apr. 25, of that year, were of *supraconstitutional rank* with respect to the Constitution of 1961, it has been concluded that the normative and organizational acts of the National Constituent Assembly in execution of the *bases comiciales* have *constitutional rank*. Due to the fact that the National Constituent Assembly implicitly referred the *bases comiciales* in the 'Decree Amplifying the Powers of the National Legislative Commission' founding its authority on the '*referendum democratically approved on the twenty-fifth of April of nineteen hundred and ninety-nine*,' the Decree amplifying the powers of the Commission would also effectively have *constitutional rank*." See Decision N° 1454 (Feb. 18, 2001) (Case: *C.A. Good Year de Venezuela), in Revista de Derecho Público* 85–88, Editorial Jurídica Venezolana, Caracas 2001.

2. *Dissolution of State Legislative Assemblies and Creation of State Legislative Commissions*

The national Constituent Assembly, in its decree of December 22, 1999, also violated the new Constitution when it ordered the "dissolution of the Legislative Assemblies of the States" and the dismissal of the elected representatives (elected in 1998) who composed them (Article 11). The assembly had no constitutional authority to do so, as this was not provided for in the transitory provisions of the Constitution approved by the people.

At the state level, the Constituent Assembly created in each state the State Legislative Commission, empowering the Coordinating Commission of the National Constituent Assembly and not the assembly itself with the appointment of commission members (Article 12). This decision, not authorized in any constitutional or legal norm, also violated the previously mentioned democratic guarantee, one of the limits established on the Constituent Assembly.

On January 4, 2000, the Coordinating Commission of the Constituent Assembly, supposedly "in accordance with powers conferred to it by the Assembly in its session of December 22, 1999" (powers that were not identified), resolved to institute the Regime for the Creation of Legislative Commissions of the States,[16] for which purpose it created the National Nominating Commission to select candidates for the legislative commissions and conferred powers to those commissions. This was not even authorized by the Regime of Transition of the Public Powers, so the Coordinating Commission of the Constituent Assembly usurped the powers of constitutional regulation that the assembly had attributed to itself.

3. *Control over Municipalities*

With respect to municipalities, Article 15 of the decree on transition set forth that existing municipal councils were to exercise their functions "under the supervision and control of the National Constituent Assembly or the National Legislative Commission" until new popularly elected representatives were in office.[17] The decree further authorized the Coordinating Commission of the National Assembly or National Legislative Commission the power to partially or completely substitute

---

[16] *Gaceta Oficial* N° 36.865, Jan. 7, 2000.

[17] See *Gaceta Constituyente (Diario de Debates), Noviembre 1999–Enero 2000*, Sesión de 22-12-99, N° 51, 5.

members of the municipal councils and mayors in cases of serious administrative irregularities.

The provisions were contrary to the new Constitution, which in a contrary sense guarantees municipal autonomy, and to the democratic principle with respect to municipal authorities, who needed to be popularly elected.

4. *Intervention of the Judiciary*

Article 17 of the transitory regime decree also provided for the termination of the Supreme Court of Justice to give way to the Supreme Tribunal of Justice, even if the Constitution that created it was not still in force (it was published on December 30, 1999). For such purpose, the three chambers of the former Supreme Court of Justice (political-administrative, criminal, and civil cassation) were extinguished and its magistrates dismissed. In substitution, the Constituent Assembly, without any constitutional authority, created the new chambers of the Supreme Tribunal of Justice (constitutional, political-administrative, electoral, and social, civil, and criminal cassation), although the Constitution of 1999 was not yet in effect.

The Assembly also designated the new magistrates of the Supreme Tribunal of Justice (Article 19), but for such purpose did not hold itself to the conditions for those appointments established in the new Constitution (Article 263) or to the citizens' participation provisions established in Article 270 of the Constitution. Among the magistrates selected was the former president of the Supreme Court of Justice, who had occupied that position for the previous two months. His services to the new regime implementing, from the Supreme Curt, the unconstitutional framework used by the Constituent Assembly to usurp all branches of government, undoubtedly were acknowledged by the new political group that took over the control of the state.

In the text of the new Constitution, there was a glaring absence of transitory provisions regarding the functioning of the judicial power, with only one reference to the Commission on the Functioning and Restructuring of the Judicial System (fourth transitory provision) regarding the transitional system for public defense until relevant legislation had passed. Nothing more. Moreover, the referenced commission did not yet exist when the Constitution was drafted and submitted to referendum. It came into existence only later, through the aforementioned decree of transition (Article 27). In the new Constitution, however, this organ had competence only to develop a system for the public defense as stated in the fourth transitory provision.

The transitory regime decree, in any case, was completely incongruous. As mentioned, before the new Constitution came into effect (December 30, 1999), on December 22, 1999, the decree "created" the chambers of the Supreme Tribunal of Justice and appointed its judges (Articles 17 and 19), although provisionally (Article 20). In fact, those chambers had no constitutional existence, because the new Constitution did not provide for the number of its members and was not in effect. Thus, the assembly produced a constitutional act creating state organs (Article 17), something over which it had no constitutional authority.

The Assembly adopted a variety of transitory norms not provided for in the new 1999 Constitution to ensure the new Constitution's immediate effect, although as stated, the new Constitution was not yet operative. These included a provision that transformed the former Council for the Judiciary into the Executive Office of the Magistrature of the Supreme Tribunal of Justice, established in Article 267 of the new Constitution, not yet effective, and dismissed the members of the Council for the Judicature (Article 26).

Immediately following this, the Assembly provided for another transitional regime without any authority to do so, providing that until the Supreme Tribunal had organized the aforementioned executive office, the government, administration, inspection, and vigilance over the Courts, as well as all the powers that until that time had been legislatively lodged in the Council for Judicature, be exercised by the Commission on the Functioning and the Restructuring of the Judicial System (Article 21). The National Constituent Assembly thus confiscated from the Supreme Tribunal of Justice (whose members it had selected) one of the tribunal's new functions and attributed it to a commission whose members were appointed by the Constituent Assembly, not even by the Supreme Tribunal of Justice. The Supreme Tribunal accepted this situation even after the new Constitution went into effect, an irregular situation that the new Supreme Tribunal resignedly has accepted for the past decade (1999–2010).

Another unconstitutional provision adopted by the National Constituent Assembly in the decree was to attribute to the Commission on the Functioning and the Restructuring of the Judicial System the judicial disciplinary jurisdiction that Article 267 of the Constitution reserves to judicial courts or tribunals. This transitory provision was to be in effect "until the National Assembly approves legislation that determines the disciplinary procedures and tribunals," which through 2010 had never occurred.[18] In this way, during the past decade, no stability of judges had existed. In general, they are appointed temporarily and dismissed in a discretionary way by the aforementioned commission without any due process of law.[19]

According to the new Constitution, only judges can exercise judicial functions (Article 253), and it is totally illegitimate and contrary to the guarantee of due process (Article 49) to confer judicial functions to a commission, not a court. If the intention was to establish, even arbitrarily, a transitory regime of judicial discipline, the judicial diciplinary jurisdiction should have been vested in preexisting courts or judges, not in an ad hoc commission. The latter violated both the guarantee of due process and the right to a natural judge expressly regulated in the new Constitution (Article 49).

On January 18, 2000, also "in exercise of the sovereign original constituent power," the National Constituent Assembly issued two other decrees relating to the judicial power. These concerned the designation of the inspector of courts,[20] as well as the members of the Commission on the Functioning and the Restructuring of the Judicial System.[21]

5. *Dismissal and Appointment of Officials of the Citizens' Power*

The National Constituent Assembly, through the Decree on the Regime for the Transition of Public Powers,[22] also dismissed the comptroller general and the prosecutor general and appointed substitutes (Articles 35 and 36). It also appointed the people's defender (Article 34), which in fact was the only office that it was constitutionally authorized to designate under the transitory provisions of the 1999 Constitution. They were appointed until after the new National Assembly was elected and could

---

[18]In this regard, the Inter-American Commission on Human Rights in its *Annual Report 2009*, said that "even though the 1999 Constitution states that legislation governing the judicial system is to be enacted within the first year following the installation of the National Assembly, a decade later the Transitional Government Regime, created to allow the Constitution to come into immediate effect, remains in force. Under that transitional regime, the Commission for the Functioning and Restructuring of the Judicial System was created, and this body has ever since had the disciplinary authority to remove members of the judiciary." See Par. 481. Available at http://www.cidh.org/annualrep/2009eng/Chap.IV.f.eng.htm.

[19]The reorganization of the judiciary since 2000 has been a permanent situation. See the Resolution of the Supreme Tribunal of Justice N° 1009-0008 (Mar. 18, 2009), in which "all the Venezuelan Judicial Power" was declared in a process of "integral restructuring."

[20]*Gaceta Oficial* N° 36.878, Jan. 26, 2000.

[21]Id.

[22]See *Gaceta Oficial* N° 36.859, Dec. 29, 1999.

name officials to those posts. Nonetheless, appointments were made without any sort of citizen participation as established in Article 279 of the Constitution.

In addition, the decree assigned powers to the comptroller general that were not authorized by any constitutional or legal provision, as was the power to intervene in the functions of the state and municipal comptrollers and to provisionally name officials of those entities (Article 37). This was in violation of state and municipal autonomy as guaranteed in the new Constitution.

6. *Dismissal and Appointment of Members of the National Electoral Council*

Finally, with respect to the electoral power, the National Constituent Assembly, being wholly without competence or authority, and in an illegitimate way, by means of the Decree on Transition Regime of December 22, 1999, conferred unto itself the power to appoint members of the new National Electoral Council (Article 40). Consequently, a few days later, it dismissed the members of the Supreme Electoral Council and provisionally appointed to the council persons all tied to the new power and to the political parties that supported the government, without any citizen participation. This act failed to guarantee electoral impartiality, thus violating Articles 295 and 296 of the new Constitution.

The Constituent Assembly also conferred on itself the power to set the dates for the first elections to fill representative offices established in the new Constitution (Article 39). It assigned to itself the power to issue the electoral statute (*estatuto electoral*) intended to govern the first elections for all representative legislative bodies and executive organs within the public powers.

III. JUDICIAL ACCEPTANCE OF A DOUBLE CONSTITUTIONAL TRANSITORY REGIME

The Decree on the Regime for the Transition of the Public Powers was challenged on the grounds of its unconstitutionality before the then-existing Supreme Court of Justice on December 29, 1999, with respect to its provisions for the appointments of the prosecutor general, the comptroller general, magistrates in the Supreme Tribunal of Justice, the people's defender, members of the National Electoral Council, and members of the National Legislative Commission.

> After January 1, 2000, the files of the action for judicial review were transferred to the new Constitutional Chamber of the Supreme Tribunal of

Justice appointed in the same transitory regime decree, which decided the case in Decision No. 4 (January 26, 2000) (Case: Eduardo García), on the basis of the opinion by the same magistrate who was former president of the Supreme Court. The decision precisely recognized that the transition decree through which all the magistrates were appointed was "of constitutional rank and nature" and "of an organizational nature, producing the appointment of high officials in the National Public Powers, based upon the intent to re-organize the State, which purpose had been assigned to the National Constituent Assembly."[23]

On the basis of the latter, the Constitutional Chamber concluded its decision by determining "that given the original character of the power conferred by the people of Venezuela upon the National Constituent Assembly by means of Question No. 1 and the Eighth *Base Comicial* approved in the April 25, 1999, national consultative referendum, this power is not subject to the constitution then in effect [1961 Constitution], and the judicial challenge now proposed based on presumptive transgressions of the referenced constitution but not of the standards determined in the [April 25, 1999] referendum, is considered without merit to proceed."[24]

The Constitutional Chamber ruled similarly regarding the challenge on January 17, 2000, of the same decree. In Decision No. 6 (January 27, 2000), the action for judicial review unconstitutionally filed against the decree was also rejected on the basis of the following arguments:

> [T]his Chamber understands that until the date of publication of the new Constitution [December 31, 1999], the Constitution that preceded it (of 1961) was in force. This derives from the Single Derogatory Clause [of the 1999 Constitution]; and as the acts of the National Constituent Assembly were not subject to the derogated Constitution (1961), those acts were subject to supra-constitutional norms only, as was ruled by the Plenary Supreme Court of Justice as quoted above. Thus, by obverse argument, only those acts issued by the National Constituent Assembly after the publication of the new Constitution were subject to it.
>
> It arises from all the aforementioned that the act of the National Constituent Assembly that is challenged here, published in the Official Gazette on the 29th of December of 1999 [No. 36.859], before the

---

[23] See *Revista de Derecho Público* 81, Editorial Jurídica Venezolana, Caracas 2000, 91ff.
[24] Id.

Constitution of the Bolivarian Republic of Venezuela of 1999 entered into force, it is not subject to it, nor to the Constitution of 1961.[25]

The Supreme Tribunal of Justice, created by the challenged decree and the magistrates appointed for it, thus recognized the constitutional rank of the transitional regime invented by the National Constituent Assembly and contained in the decree, declaring that such decree was subject to neither the Constitution of 1961 nor to the Constitution of 1999 but rather to supraconstitutional norms. Being an act on which all the magistrates had personal and direct interest, the least the magistrates could have done would have been to recuse themselves, but they did not. This and other decisions in which they judged the transition regime violated the most elemental principles of the rule of law: No one can be a judge in his own case.

The Supreme Tribunal of Justice ratified the criteria of the paraconstitutional character of the decree in Decision No. 186 (March 28, 2000) (Case: *Allan R. Brewer-Carías et al.*), issued to resolve the challenge for judicial review of the Electoral Statute of the Public Powers,[26] approved by the National Constituent Assembly in its last session on January 30, 2000. The Supreme Tribunal rejected the action of unconstitutionality filed by former members of the Constituent Assembly, basing its decision on the argument that the Constituent Assembly, according to the basic rules approved in the referendum of April 25, 1999 – to fulfill its mission of transforming the state, to create a new legal order, and to draft a new Constitution to replace that of 1961 – had several alternatives with respect to regulating a constitutional transition regime. First was to draft transitory provisions within the text of the Constitution approved by the people in the December 15, 1999, referendum; second was to pass separate constituent acts, giving origin to a parallel transitory regime of constitutional nature and rank, approved by the people. The Supreme Tribunal, in effect, ruled as follows:

> The National Constituent Assembly, with the purpose of fulfilling the mandate conferred to it by the people, had several alternatives: one to draft a constitution with a set of transitory provisions in order to regulate as possible the juridical implementation of the transition regime between the institutions provided for in the Constitution of the Republic of Venezuela

---

[25] See *Revista de Derecho Público* 81, Editorial Jurídica Venezolana, Caracas 2000, 81ff.
[26] *Gaceta Oficial* N° 36.884, Feb. 3, 2000.

of 1961, and those provided for in the Constitution of the Bolivarian Republic of Venezuela of 1999.

Another alternative was not to include such implementation in the transitory provisions of the Constitution, and instead to effectuate it through a separate body of legislation [sic], complemented by acts aimed at filling the institutional vacuum that would be created when the new Constitution went into effect. This was the route chosen by the National Constituent Assembly, when it enacted the Decree on the Regime for the Transition of the Public Powers."[27]

This assertion had no constitutional or logical basis, and it violated the constitutional principle of the need for popular approval regarding the Constitution, set forth in the referendum of April 25, 1999, and particularly in its ninth basic rule (*base comicial*), which the former Supreme Court considered as having supraconstitutional rank. According to this provision, which the tribunal did not consider, any constitutional provision resulting from the constitution-making process of 1999 required popular approval through referendum. This was the will of the people as expressed on April 25, 1999: The National Constituent Assembly was not to place constitutional acts into force; only the people, by means of referendum, could place a new constitution into force. It was for that purpose that the Venezuelan people convened to vote in referendum on December 15, 1999 – to approve the new Constitution. In conformity with the people's will established on April 25, 1999, only the people themselves were authorized to approve the Constitution through an approbatory referendum. Thus, no other norm of constitutional rank could legitimately exist that the people had not approved.

Therefore, the Supreme Tribunal of Justice, by deciding that the electoral statute sanctioned by the National Constituent Assembly was of constitutional rank, enacted for the purpose of filling supposed gaps or vacuums in the transitory provisions of the 1999 Constitution – vacuums that had been both created and caused by the National Constituent Assembly itself, before publishing the 1999 Constitution – violated the people's sovereign will as expressed in referendum. The truth is that there was no point for Venezuelans to approve a constitution in the December 15 referendum if the National Constituent Assembly could pass other parallel constitutional texts not approved by the people.[28]

---

[27] See *Revista de Derecho Público* 81, Editorial Jurídica Venezolana, Caracas 2000, 86ff.
[28] See Allan R. Brewer-Carías, *La Constitución de 1999*, 3rd ed., Caracas 2001, 270ff.

The most important feature of the Supreme Tribunal's decision is that it established the principle that the National Constituent Assembly could enact norms of constitutional hierarchy not approved through popular referendum. This, beyond a doubt, violated the ninth basic rule (*base comicial*) approved by referendum on April 25, 1999, which the former Supreme Court of Justice considered supraconstitutional in the decision of October 14, 1999 (Case: *Henrique Capriles Radonski vs. Decreto de Regulación de Funciones del Poder Legislativo*).

This *base comicial* approved by referendum, which, it must be emphasized, was considered as having supraconstitutional rank, established that the new Constitution would enter into force only if approved in another referendum. From this, it can be deduced that the popular will in Venezuela as expressed on April 25, 1999, was that the National Constituent Assembly could not give effect to the new constitution or to any constitutional provision of act not approved by the people through referendum.

However, that was not the criterion the Supreme Tribunal employed in its decision, opening the door to arbitrariness and to an endless transitory constitutional situation that, in some cases, has endured for a decade, as with intervention in the judicial power.

The Supreme Tribunal, in effect, deduced the constitutional absurdity that a constitutional transitional regime could exist even if not foreseen in the 1999 Constitution approved by the people but dictated by the National Constituent Assembly. It did so without mentioning the ninth *base comicial* (its decision referred only to the first and eighth basic rules) of the April 25 referendum that imposed with supraconstitutional status the requirement that every provision of constitutional rank produced by the National Constituent Assembly must be approved by the people in referendum to take effect. This was what took place regarding the transitory provisions of the 1999 Constitution approved in the December 15 referendum but that never occurred with the Regime for the Transition of the Public Powers issued a week later (December 22, 1999). Nonetheless, the Supreme Tribunal, ignoring the will of the people, assigned to such a regime a "rank analogous to the Constitution" and a juridical status "parallel to the current [1999] Constitution."

From the aforementioned Decision No. 186 of the Supreme Tribunal (Case: *Allan R. Brewer-Carías et al.*),[29] the following irregular situation resulted:

1. On November 17, 1999, the National Constituent Assembly approved a Constitution with a transition regime established in its transitory provisions that implied the permanence of the organs of the public powers until new officials were elected. In the expression of public will (in the referendum of December 15, 1999) and the will of the National Constituent Assembly that approved and proclaimed the Constitution, therefore, there was no legal vacuum whatsoever with respect to the constitutional transition.

2. The Constitution of 1999, with the stated transitory provisions, was submitted to an approbatory referendum on December 15, 1999; was approved by the people; and was formally proclaimed by the National Constituent Assembly on December 20, 1999.

3. Two days later, the National Constituent Assembly changed its opinion and resolved to alter the transitory provisions foreseen in the 1999 Constitution already approved by the people. Before publishing it in the *Official Gazette*, on December 22, 1999, the National Constituent Assembly enacted the Regime for the Transition of the Public Powers, which substituted all officials of government branches (except the president) and modified the structure of the state. This transition regime created, therefore, a "vacuum" that the Constituent Assembly sought to fill with provisions of constitutional rank not approved by the people.

4. The Supreme Tribunal of Justice, in its decision of March 28, 2000, attributed constitutional rank and value to that transition regime enacted by the National Constituent Assembly without the approval of the people, in contravention of the ninth *base comicial* of the April 25 referendum, which allowed the election of the Constituent Assembly and had supraconstitutional rank, thus limiting the activity of the assembly.

5. In Venezuela, then, and as a consequence of the Supreme Tribunal's decision, two parallel constitutional regimes existed at once: one contained in the transitory provisions of the 1999 Constitution, approved by the people; the other, passed after that approval, by the National Constituent Assembly, without constitutional support. The latter was not approved by the people and of imprecise duration – it was deemed

---

[29]See *Revista de Derecho Público* 81, Editorial Jurídica Venezolana, Caracas 2000, 86ff.

to have legal effect until the passage of all implementing legislation foreseen by the Constitution of 1999, which could be a period of decades.

The Supreme Tribunal of Justice, unfortunately, instead of fulfilling its duty as guardian of the Constitution, wishing to resolve the supposed vacuum created by the same National Constituent Assembly after the popular approval of the 1999 Constitution, accepted the dual constitutional transitory regime in many aspects until 2009. For instance, it still prevails on judicial matters with the continuous interference of the Commission on the Functioning and the Restructuring of the Judicial Power.

IV. THE KIDNAPPING OF THE CONSTITUTION AND SUBJECTION OF THE JUDICIAL BRANCH TO THE GOVERNMENT

Transitory constitutional regimes defined by the Supreme Tribunal had different durations. The transitory provisions of the 1999 Constitution mainly devoted to define a legislative program that the new National Assembly was to develop had a "sunset clause" to take effect within a precise number of years. But the Decree of the Transition Regime was imprecise and, on that matter, the Constitutional Chamber issued contradictory rulings. For instance, in Decision No. 179 (March 28, 2000) (Case: *Gonzalo Pérez Hernández*), the tribunal decided that the constitutional transition regime created by the National Constituent Assembly was to last "until the constituted powers were designated or elected" (in 2000)[30]; however, in the aforementioned Decision No. 180 (Case: *Allan R. Brewer-Carías et al.*), also issued on March 28, 2000, the chamber stated: "The regime for the transition of the Public Powers projects into the future, not just until the National Assembly [Legislature] is formed, but even beyond that," until new legislation was approved. Consequently, "the norms and acts of the National Constituent Assembly remain in full effect, and will remain so until the legal regime that derogates the provisional regime is established in conformity with the Constitution, leaving without effects the norms and acts sanctioned by the Constituent Assembly."[31]

This situation implies that the 1999 Constitution has never been completely in force – in some respects, after a decade of application, the National Assembly has sanctioned no legislation; thus, an imprecise

---

[30] See *Revista de Derecho Público* 81, Editorial Jurídica Venezolana, Caracas 2000, 83.

[31] See *Revista de Derecho Público* 81, Editorial Jurídica Venezolana, Caracas 2000, 87-88.

transition regime remains in effect, applied according to the variable interpretations of the government and the Supreme Tribunal. This has been particularly shocking regarding the judicial branch of government, particularly the constitutional provisions on the conditions and procedures for the appointment of magistrates of the Supreme Tribunal, and on the stability of judges, by means of implementing the judicial carrier and the disciplinary judicial Jurisdiction, which up to 2010 are still inapplicable. As the Inter-American Commission on Human Rights has said in its *Annual Report 2009*:

> Furthermore, even though the 1999 Constitution states that legislation governing the judicial system is to be enacted within the first year following the installation of the National Assembly, a decade later the Transitional Government Regime, created to allow the Constitution to come into immediate effect, remains in force.[32]

---

[32] See IACHR, *Annual Report 2009*, Chapter IV, "Human Rights Developments in the Region: Venezuela," Par. 481, available at http://www.cidh.org/annualrep/2009eng/Chap.IV.f.eng.htm.

Chapter 3

THE 1999 POLITICAL CONSTITUTION AND THE REINFORCEMENT OF CENTRALIZATION

The 1999 Constitution kept many provisions of the 1961 Constitution and mixed them with new principles and intents, in some cases confused with constitutional rights, including some important contradictions like the declaration of the State as a "decentralized federation," paralleling provisions that have further centralized the centralized federation the country had for more than one hundred years. Regarding the democratic character of the government, it emphasized participatory means but eroded the representative nature of democracy in an antiparty framework. Furthermore, the Constitution formally declares the rule of law but within a militaristic framework never before established by any previous constitution. The separation of powers was formally expressed, adding to the traditional ones (legislative, executive, and judicial) two new additional branches of government, the electoral and citizens' branches, but with a clear prevalence of the legislative power (National Assembly) over the others.

I began to analyze the 1999 Constitution and to make critical comments on its contents as a member of the National Constituent Assembly that drafted the Constitution. I strongly opposed its approval in the December 15, 1999 referendum, and began to write on the matter just a few weeks after the approval of the Constitution.[1] The comments on the Constitution have been developed in further works, in which I have studied the

---

[1] See Allan R. Brewer-Carías, "Constitutional Reform in Venezuela and the 1999 Constitution," Symposium on Challenges to Fragile Democracies in the Americas: Legitimacy and Accountability, Faculty of Law, University of Texas, Austin, Feb. 25, 2000, in *Texas International Law Journal* 36, 2001, 333-38.

constitutional text in depth.[2] For the purpose of this book, I summarize in this and the following chapter the main aspects of the 1999 Constitution that can be considered as important reforms.

I. THE CONSTITUTION OF 1999: FRUSTRATION OF THE NECESSARY POLITICAL CHANGE

According to the referendum of April 25, 1999, which created the National Constituent Assembly, the institution had as its mission the elaboration of a new constitution to transform the state and create a new legal order, which would permit the effective functioning of a social and participatory democracy. For that purpose, the members of the assembly were elected on July 25, 1999.

The creation of the assembly and the election of its members responded to the requirements of political change in the country, provoked by the crisis of the political system of centralized government and parties, which was based first on the state centralism and second on the democracy of parties, which exercised a monopoly over participation and representation.

The democratic transformation to a decentralized and participatory state needed to be based on the political decentralization of the state's powers in the territory and local governments, and on people's participation. For this purpose, the assembly needed to introduce the following: to transform the state to make it more democratic, demolishing centralism and constructing a decentralized state within the federal framework, and to create a new legal order to allow the effective functioning of a social and participatory democracy, which would incorporate individuals and private institutions in the social, economic, and political process, and ensure political participation in the affairs of the state.

Nonetheless, the Constituent Assembly and the new Constitution it drafted did not respond to the demands of political transformation that were determined in the referendum of April 25, 1999: "transformation of the State" and "a new legal order," in order to strengthen democracy and the rule of law. It neither ensured nor established a basis for the transformation of the political system, and its content did not contribute to overcome the crisis of the system of centralized government of parties. That is, it did not structure a decentralized and participatory state that

---

[2]See Allan R. Brewer-Carías, *La Constitución de 1999*, Editorial Jurídica Venezolana, Caracas 2000; *La Constitución de 1999. Derecho Constitucional Venezolano*, 2 vols., Editorial Jurídica Venezolana, Caracas 2004.

could have preserved democracy. On the contrary, it consolidated both the prevailing state centralism, even moving backward the decentralization process initiated in 1989, and partisanship, which has been aggravated by the distortion of the electoral system and the substitution of the traditional multiparty system with a one-party system integrated into the state. A unique historical opportunity to introduce those reforms was lost, and despite of the convening of a national constituent assembly without a previous constitutional rupture, the lack of any agreements or consensus, produced a constitution that did not solve the existing central problems and did not establish the basis of effective democratic political change.

Instead of the Constitution helping to overcome the crisis of centralism, it aggravated it by establishing the constitutional basis for the development of a political authoritarianism based on regulations that reinforce the centralism, presidentialism, "statism," state paternalism, partisanship, and militarism, thus endangering democracy itself.[3]

In 2000, just a few months after the 1999 Constitution was approved and began to be enforced, the following were my initial thoughts regarding its provisions, as I considered it a constitution conceived of to promulgate authoritarianism:

> From the aforementioned results, regarding the 1999 political Constitution that, when analyzed globally, highlights an institutional framework

---

[3] For instance, the Inter-American Commission on Human Rights, in its Preliminary Observations N° 23/02 of Oct. 5, 2002, produced on the occasion of the on-site visit to Venezuela after the facts of Apr. 2002, pointed out the following aspects of the new Constitution: "22. Notwithstanding these significant constitutional advances, the Commission notes that the Constitution also includes various parts that may hinder effective observance of the rule of law. These provisions include the requirement for a preliminary proceeding on the merits (*antejuicio de mérito*) for high-ranking officers of the Armed Forces prior to starting any investigation into a crime (Article 266(3)); the stipulation of the Office of the Comptroller General of the National Armed Forces without clarifying its relationship with the Office of the Comptroller General of the Republic (Article 291); and the participation of the National Electoral Council in trade union elections. Article 58, which stipulates the right to timely, accurate, and impartial information, has been criticized, among others by this Commission. Furthermore, Article 203 includes the concept of enabling statutes, and allows for the possibility of a delegation of legislative powers to the President of the Republic, without establishing limits on the content of this delegation. In so doing, new crimes may be established by Executive decrees – as has already happened – and not through statutes adopted by the National Assembly, in violation of the requirements of the American Convention on Human Rights. In addition, the Constitution has suppressed some constitutional provisions that are important for the rule of law, such as legislative review of military promotions, the provision that established the non-involvement of the Armed Forces in political decision-making, and the prohibition on the military authority and the civilian authority being exercised simultaneously." See the text of the Preliminary Observations in Allan R. Brewer-Carías, *La crisis de la democracia venezolana. La Carta Democrática Interamericana y los sucesos de abril de 2002*, Los Libros de El Nacional, Colección Ares, Caracas 2002.

conceived for authoritarianism. It is derived from combining the State centralism, the exaggerated presidentialism, the democracy of parties, the concentration of power in the Assembly and the militarism that constitute the central elements designed for the organization of the Power of the State.

In my opinion, that is not the political Constitution required to improve democracy. On the contrary, it should be based on decentralization of power, a controlled presidentialism, politic participation to balance the powers of the state and the subjection of the military authority to the civil one.

Regarding the 1999 social constitution, when enumerating the human rights and guarantees and State obligations, the new Constitution, unfortunately, opens the door to their limitation by the Executive through delegated legislation. Moreover, analyzed globally, it shows a marginalization of society and private enterprises, falling on the State all the imaginable obligations, impossible to comply with. It is a Constitution conceived for paternalism, which leads to populism.

That is not the social Constitution needed to found a social and participating democracy. To that, it should re-value the participation of all private enterprises in educational, health and social security process, as activities in which a mutual responsibility between the state and Society must exist.

Finally, the new Constitution, in its component economic Constitution, completes the paternalist picture of social Constitution. It inclines the constitutional regime towards the state instead of the private enterprise, which originates an exaggerated statism. It creates the risk of increasing tax voracity that cannot be controlled, conceived to squash taxpayers, who aren't constitutionally protected.

That is not the economic Constitution needed to found the policy of economic development the country requires, which has to point to the creation of wealth and employment that the State is unable to accomplish without the decisive participation of private enterprises, which should be protected and stimulated.

Due to the aforementioned, in our opinion the Constitution of 1999 hasn't introduced the changes the country needed, on the occasion of the constituent moment that originated the crisis of the political model of Centralized State of Parties established from 1945 and restored in 1958. The country needed a radical change to improve the democracy, make it more representative and to structure a democratic decentralized and participating State. Nothing of this was accomplished, so only history will say if this Constitution is the last of the four politic historical periods of Venezuela or the first of the fifth.[4]

Unfortunately, the decade that has passed since the approval of the 1999 Constitution has proved the validity of these assertions: An authoritarian government has taken shape in Venezuela, using the Constitution and in many cases defrauding it, thereby undermining democracy from within.[5] This is the political frame of the new constitution, which I want to analyze referring to the three central elements that make up any constitution: first, the political constitution, which I comment on in this chapter; and second, the dogmatic constitution, referred to constitutional rights and guaranties, as well as the socioeconomic constitution, which I comment on in Chapter 4.

II. THE NEW "BOLIVARIAN" REPUBLIC AND ITS PARTISAN CHARACTER

The 1999 Constitution, in its first article, changed the name of Venezuela from the traditional *República de Venezuela* (Republic of Venezuela) to *República Bolivariana de Venezuela* (Bolivarian Republic of Venezuela). The motivation for the new name could be perceived as directed to refer to the ideas and actions of Simón Bolívar, who was not only the liberator of Venezuela but also of other "Bolivarian" republics in Latin America (Colombia, Ecuador, Bolivia an Peru). Although it has not been the first time in Venezuela's history that military and authoritarian rulers have evoked Simón Bolívar to attract followers and to give some

---

[4] Immediately after the approval of the Constitution, I expressed my critical comments in various lectures, which were published as "Reflexiones Críticas sobre la Constitución de 1999," in *Constitucionalismo Iberoamericano del Siglo XXI*, coords. Diego Valadés and Miguel Carbonell, Cámara de Diputados. LVII Legislatura, Universidad Nacional Autónoma de México, Mexico City 2000, 171-93; *Revista de Derecho Público* 81, Editorial Jurídica Venezolana, Caracas 2000, 7-21; *Revista Facultad de Derecho, Derechos y Valores* 3, Universidad Militar Nueva Granada, Santafé de Bogotá, D.C., Colombia, 2000, 9-26; and *La Constitución de 1999*, Biblioteca de la Academia de Ciencias Políticas y Sociales, Caracas 2000, 63-88. See also "The constitutional reform in Venezuela and the 1999 Constitution," Symposium on *Challenges to Fragile Democracies in the Americas: Legitimacy and accountability*, Faculty of Law, University of Texas, Austin, February 25, 2000, in *Texas International Law Journal* 36, 2001, 333-38.
[5] See Allan R. Brewer-Carías, "La demolición del Estado de derecho y la destrucción de la democracia en Venezuela (1999-2009)," in *La democracia en su contexto. Estudios en homenaje a Dieter Nohlen en su septuagésimo aniversario*, coords. José Reynoso Núñez y Herminio Sánchez de la Barquera y Arroyo, Instituto de Investigaciones Jurídicas, Universidad Nacional Autónoma de México, Mexico City 2009, 477-517.

doctrinal basis to their governments,[6] never before had adherence to a Bolivarian doctrine led to changing a republic's name and to the invention of a Bolivarian doctrine to justify the government's policies, including the socialist character that Chávez wanted to impose.[7]

The country had been named the Republic of Venezuela through most of its constitutional political history since 1811, when after independence from Spain, the Confederation of States of Venezuela was constituted. The sole exception to this situation was from 1819 to 1830, the constitutional period that followed the Congress of Angostura in 1819 up to the reconstitution of the Republic of Venezuela by the 1830 Convention of Valencia. In 1819, Simón Bolívar proposed the Congress of the Republic of Venezuela to sanction the Law of the Union of the Peoples of Colombia, through which the Republic of Venezuela would disappear as an autonomous state. A new law similar to the former one was approved in 1821, and in that same year, the Constitution of Cucuta established the Republic of Colombia, comprising both the former Captaincy General of

---

[6]It was the case of Antonio Guzmán Blanco in the nineteenth century and of Cipriano Castro, Juan Vicente Gómez, Eleazar López Contreras, and Marcos Pérez Jiménez in the twentieth century. John Lynch has pointed out: "The traditional cult of Bolivar has been used as a convenient ideology by military dictators, culminating with the regimes of Juan Vicente Gómez and Eleazar López Contreras; these had at least more or less respected the basic thought of the Liberator, even when they misrepresented its meaning." See John Lynch, *Simón Bolívar: A Life*, Yale University Press, New Haven, CT, 2007, 304. See also Germán Carrera Damas, *El culto a Bolívar, esbozo para un estudio de la historia de las ideas en Venezuela*, Universidad Central de Venezuela, Caracas 1969; Luis Castro Leiva, *De la patria boba a la teología bolivariana*, Monteávila, Caracas 1987; Elías Pino Iturrieta, *El divino Bolívar. Ensayo sobre una religión republicana*, Alfail, Caracas 2008; Ana Teresa Torres, *La herencia de la tribu. Del mito de la independencia a la Revolución bolivariana*, Editorial Alfa, Caracas 2009. See also the historiography study on these books in Tomás Straka, *La épica del desencanto*, Editorial Alfa, Caracas 2009.

[7]John Lynch has pointed out: "In 1998 Venezuelans were astonished to learn that their country had been renamed 'the Bolivarian Republic of Venezuela' by decree of President Hugo Chávez, who called himself a 'revolutionary Bolivarian.' Authoritarian populist, or neocaudillos, or Bolivarian militarists, whatever their designation, invoke Bolívar no less ardently that did previous rulers, though it is doubtful whether he would have responded to their calls…But the new heresy, far from maintaining continuity with the constitutional ideas of Bolívar, as was claimed, invented a new attribute, the populist Bolívar, and in the case of Cuba gave him a new identity, the socialist Bolívar. By exploiting the authoritarian tendency, which certainly existed in the thought and action of Bolívar, regimes in Cuba and Venezuela claim the Liberator as patron for their policies, distorting his ideas in the process." See John Lynch, *Simón Bolívar: A Life*, Yale University Press, New Haven, CT, 2007, 304. See also A.C. Clark, *The Revolutionary Has No Clothes: Hugo Chávez's Bolivarian Farce*, Encounter Books, New York 2009, 5-14. The last attempt to completely appropriate Simón Bolívar for the "Bolivarian Revolution," was the televised exhumation of his remains that took place at the National Pantheon in Caracas on July 26, 2010, conducted by President Chávez himself and other high officials, including the Prosecutor General, among other things, for the purpose of determining if Bolivar died of arsenic poisoning in Santa Marta in 1830, instead of from tuberculosis. See Simon Romero, "Building a New History By Exhuming Bolívar," *The New York Times*, August 4, 2010, p A7.

Venezuela (where the Republic of Venezuela had been established in 1811) and the former Viceroyalty of Nueva Granada. With the Constitution of 1821, part of Bolívar's dream for the union of the peoples of America came true.[8]

Thus, the idea of the "Bolivarian republic" from the point of view of Venezuela historically points to a political period and organization (1821-1830) in which Venezuela disappeared as an autonomous state, with its territory integrated in the Republic of Colombia. That is why the change of the republic's name in 1999 I considered was totally unacceptable being contrary to the idea of the country's sovereignty. But despite that approach, the renaming of the country in 1999 as a "Bolivarian republic" could also be explained as an intent to give the republic, in a certain way and ignoring two hundred years of history, a "definitive" national doctrine supposedly based on the thoughts of Bolívar. Nonetheless, what this approach can explain is that the real objective of the proposal was to give the new rulers the possibility to introduce their own socialist doctrine disguised as a Bolivarian one.

Conversely, another explanation of Venezuela's 1999 name change, other than evoking the ideas of Bolívar, who for instance rejected the federal form of government, can be found in exclusive political or partisan motivations. It must be remembered that the name of Chávez's initial political movement established in 1982 was the Bolivarian Revolutionary Movement 200 (MBR-200), which the president originally intended to transform into the Bolivarian Party. Nonetheless, because the Organic Law on Suffrage and Political Participation forbade using symbols of the motherland in parties' denominations, as a political movement its name needed to be changed in order to be converted into a political party. Thus, because it was impossible to use the Bolivarian denomination for the official party, the adherents of the president in the Constituent Assembly decided to use the name for the republic.[9] The party then became the Fifth Republic Movement (*Movimiento V República,* MVR) and later the United Socialist Party of Venezuela (PSUV), as a "Marxist" party.[10]

---

[8]See the texts of all these Laws in Allan R. Brewer-Carías, *Las Constituciones de Venezuela*, Academia de Ciencias Políticas y Sociales, Caracas 2008, 1:643-46.

[9]*Mutatis mutandi*, in a certain way it happened with the use of the name of Augusto C. Sandino in the name of the *Frente Sandinista de Liberación* and of the Sandinista Republic of Nicaragua.

[10]See "Declaration of Principles" of the United Socialist Party of Venezuela (Apr. 23, 2010), available at http://psuv.org.ve/files/tcdocumentos/Declaracion-de-principios-PSUV.pdf.

I was one of the few members of the Assembly who rejected the renaming proposal,[11] because I considered it not only as partisan motivated but also because a republic organized as "a federal decentralized State" was essentially anti-Bolivarian. Conversely, the last cry of Bolívar, on the eve of his death, was to abolish divisions and exclusions; and on the contrary, by adopting the new name of the republic in Article 1 of the Constitution, what the followers of the president were doing was to call for the bitter polarization of the country, between Bolivarian and those who are not and, consequently, between patriots and realists, good people and bad people, pure people and corrupt people, revolutionary and antirevolutionary or oligarchs; all that by manipulating history and popular feelings regarding the image of Bolivar.

The consequence of the constitutional reform on this matter has been that everything related to the new political regime has been called Bolivarian, beginning, for instance, with the "Bolivarian Circles" that were the first social or communal organizations promoted and supported by the government in order to react against any opposition to the government and to threaten anybody with views contrary to it.[12] In any event, after seven years of enforcing the Constitution, in the 2007 constitutional reform draft, it was proposed that the socialist "Bolivarian doctrine" be formally established as the fundamental doctrine of the state, defining the state's guiding doctrine as "Bolivarian socialism" and also guiding international relations. It was to be the "twenty-first century socialism," all of which was rejected through popular vote in the December 2007 referendum.[13] Despite such rejection, in 2008 the armed forces formally became the Bolivarian Armed Forces, and a new military component was also created, the Bolivarian Popular Militia, established by the 2008 Organic Law on the Bolivarian Armed Forces,[14] organized to be at the service of the president. Also in April 2010, the official United

---

[11]See Allan R. Brewer-Carías, *Debate constituyente (Aportes a la Asamblea Nacional Constituyente)* Fundación de Derecho Público–Editorial Jurídica Venezolana, Caracas 1999, 3 (Oct. 18–Nov. 30):237; 251-52.

[12]The general assembly of the Organization of American States, in its Report of Apr. 18, 2002, said about the Bolivarian Circles, that they "are groups of citizens or grassroots organizations who support the President's political platform. Many sectors consider them responsible for the human rights violations, acts of intimidation, and looting." See the reference in Allan R. Brewer-Carías, *La crisis de la democracia en Venezuela*, Libros El Nacional, Caracas 2002.

[13]See Allan R. Brewer-Carías, "Estudio sobre la propuesta de Reforma Constitucional para establecer un estado socialista, centralizado y militarista (Análisis del anteproyecto presidencial, Agosto de 2007)," *Cadernos da Escola de Direito e Relações Internacionais da UniBrasil* 7, Curitiba 2007, 265-308.

[14]Organic Law on the Bolivarian Armed Force, *Gaceta Oficial* N° 5.933, extra, Oct. 21, 2009.

Socialist Party of Venezuela, presided by the president of the "Bolivarian Republic," has adopted in its 'Declaration of Principles" as a "Marxist" party, the "Bolivarian socialism" doctrine, to be implemented through the "Bolivarian revolution."[15]

III. THE PROBLEM OF A POLITICAL CONSTITUTION DRAFTED FOR CENTRALISM AND AUTHORITARIANISM

The object of any political constitution is the organization of the state, and particularly of the constitutional branches of government and of the territorial distribution state power. That organization, in any constitution, can be determined differently. First, it can derive from the distribution of the state power, which creates either centralized (unitary) or decentralized states. Second, it can provoke distribution or division of powers, which results in either the concentration or the separation of powers. Last – the feature of democratic systems – organization is based on the separation, balance, and counterweight of powers of the state, which gives rise to the system of presidential or parliamentarian government. The political system, as laid out in the constitution, can also lead to autocracy or democracy, depending on whether sovereignty effectively lies in an autocrat or in the people through the electoral and party system.

With respect to Venezuela's Political Constitution of 1999, I want to highlight the most important substantive reforms that were introduced particularly in relation to the democratic system, bearing in mind that the Constitution, following the trends of the 1961 Constitution, contains all the provisions needed for the consolidation of the principles of the rule of law and justice (e.g., the excellent mechanisms of judicial review and of judicial reform established in the text).[16] Sadly, such mechanisms have been put out of action because of elements of authoritarianism set forth in the Constitution and the concentration of powers derived from other aspects of its text.

In effect, one of the great political changes that was to be made by the 1999 Constitution was to transform Venezuela's centralized federation of the past hundred years into an effectively decentralized federation, with distribution of power toward states and municipalities. The constitutional reform should have pointed in that direction in order to effectively

---

[15] See "Declaration of Principles" of the United Socialist Party of Venezuela (Apr. 23, 2010), available at http://psuv.org.ve/files/tcdocumentos/Declaracion-de-principios-PSUV.pdf.

[16] See, for instance, Allan R. Brewer-Carías, "Judicial Review in Venezuela," in *Duquesne Law Review*, Volume 45, Number 3, Spring 2007, 439-465.

conceive the state as a decentralized federal state (Art. 4). For such a purpose, it should have foreseen the political decentralization of the federation as a national policy of strategic character as it is formally defined in the Constitution (Article 158).

However, the approved constitutional scheme of territorial distribution of power has not resulted in any substantial advance regarding the previous process of decentralization initiated in 1989 through the Organic Law of Decentralization and Transfer of Competencies of Public Power.[17] That process was abandoned in 1994, not being able to achieve the needed relegitimization of the political system, which progressively collapsed.[18] Moreover, in many aspects, the new Constitution has meant an institutional step backward. It being a "decentralized federal state" is only nominal, and decentralization continues to be a desideratum, as it was in the Constitution of 1961. Although Article 4 of the 1999 Constitution defines the state as a federal decentralized state, and Article 158 defines decentralization as a national policy, the fact is that other sections of the Constitution allow for an entirely different reality.[19] Those sections allow the centralization of powers at the national level, thus progressively drowning any real possibility of political participation by the states and municipalities of the federation (local governments).[20]

Some historical analysis will help underscore the incongruity. As noted previously, before the convening of the 1999 Constituent Assembly, there had been great public demand for reforms in order to bring about the decentralization of the federal state. The reforms were initiated in 1989, by introducing the direct election of state governors and establishing the framework for the transfer of national powers to the states. These reforms, once initiated, were quickly abandoned, and in the text of the new Constitution, in contrast to the same general declaration of

---

[17] Sanctioned according to Article 137 of the 1961 Constitution. See the last reform of such statute in *Gaceta Oficial* N° 39 140 of Mar. 17, 2009.

[18] Ángel E. Álvarez, "State Reform before and after Chávez's Election," in *Venezuelan Politics in the Chávez Era: Class, Polarization & Conflicts*, eds. Steve Ellner and Daniel Hellinger, Lynne Rienner Publishers, London 2003, 147.

[19] In the 2007 constitutional reform draft proposals, Article 158 of the Constitution and all the constitutional provisions referring to political decentralization were proposed to be eliminated and changed to consolidate a centralized state. See *Proyecto de Reforma Constitucional. Elaborado por el ciudadano Presidente de la República Bolivariana de Venezuela, Hugo Chávez Frías*, Editorial Atenea, Caracas Aug. 2007.

[20] See Allan R. Brewer-Carías, *Federalismo y municipalismo en la Constitución de 1999 (Alcance de una reforma insuficiente y regresiva)*, Editorial Jurídica Venezolana, Caracas-San Cristóbal 2001.

decentralization policy contained in Article 158, other provisions have resulted in major setbacks to the prior reforms.

The Senate and the bicameral nature of the legislature, for instance, were eliminated in Article 159 of the Constitution, thus transforming Venezuela into the only federal state in the world with significant territory to function without a Senate. That has removed all possibility of equality among states that could be assured through equal number of votes in a senate or federal chamber and that are nonexistent in the new unicameral legislative chamber (National Assembly).[21] The unicameral organization of the National Assembly (Article 186) not only abandoned a tradition that goes back to 1811 but also contradicted the federal form of a state, which requires a legislative (federal) chamber with equal representation of states that serves as political counterweight to the chamber of people's representation (representation on which depends state populations). The elimination of the Senate was an attack on political decentralization, as it extinguished the instrument that made states equal in national affairs. It was also a step backward both in forming national laws and in exercising powers of parliamentary control over the executive branch.

With the new constitutional text, powers that previously had been designated as exclusive to the states were subjected to the regulations of national legislation (Article 164). Even the exercise of concurrent powers has become subject to the dictates of national law, thus contravening the autonomy of territorial entities. In particular, in the new Constitution, regulation of the functioning and organization of the state legislative councils is a competence of the National Assembly (Article 162), which contradicts the states' ability to dictate their own Constitution to organize their own branches of government. This regulation was an unacceptable interference of the national power into the regime of the states. The autonomy of the states was also seriously limited by constitutional provisions that allowed the National Assembly to regulate by means of a national statute the system of designation of the states' comptroller generals this being a competency of the states (Article 162).[22]

---

[21] See my dissenting vote in Allan R. Brewer-Carías, *Debate constituyente (Aportes a la Asamblea Nacional Constituyente)*, Fundación de Derecho Público, Caracas 1999, 3 (Oct. 18–Nov. 30):286ff.

[22] See Allan R. Brewer-Carías, "La 'federación descentralizada' en el marco de la centralización de la federación en Venezuela. Situación y perspectivas de una contradicción constitucional," in *Constitución, democracia y control el poder*, Centro Iberoamericano de Estudios Provinciales y Locales, Universidad de los Andes, Editorial Jurídica Venezolana, Mérida 2004, 111-43. See my proposals to the Constituent Assembly on political decentralization of the federation in Allan R. Brewer-Carías, *Debate constituyente (Aportes a la Asamblea Nacional Constituyente)*, Fundación de

Conversely, regarding the distribution of powers between territorial entities, the decentralization process required, above all, the effective allocation of taxation powers to states, specifically sales tax, as in almost all federations. The advances from discussions of the draft Constitution on this matter were abandoned; in the second discussion, all taxation powers assigned to states were removed, which was a step backward even regarding provisions that existed in the 1961 Constitution. Accordingly, the national government has been given authority, as a residual competence, in all tax matters not expressly delegated to the states and municipalities (Article 156, Section 12); the states have no taxing power, and even their power over sales tax has been eliminated (Article 156, Section 12). Article 167, Section 5, provides that states have tax powers only in the matters expressly assigned by national law. In that way, states continue to completely depend on the national financial contribution (*situado constitutional*), to be established in the national budget with an amount not more that 20% of the national public income. That limit did not exist in the Constitution of 1961, which established only a minimum. And even though the new Constitution established the Federal Council of Government (Article 185) as an "intergovernmental" organ, the one that was organized by an organic law in February 2010[23] has been established as an instrument for central planning and for the development of the "communal or popular power," which is not provided in the Constitution, setting aside the formal federal organization of the state.

Regarding municipalities, their autonomy, traditionally guaranteed in the Constitution, was also interfered by subjecting it to the limits established not only in the Constitution but also those established in national laws (Article 168). Therefore, the basic decentralizing principle, autonomy, was minimized, and municipalities in practice continued to be organized very far from the citizens' reach, thus impeding any kind of real political participation.[24] In fact, what the 1999 Constitution created was a centralized, antiparticipatory democratic system that deliberately confuses the instruments of direct democracy with effective political participation.

Derecho Público–Editorial Jurídica Venezolana, Caracas 1999, 1 (Aug. 8–Sept. 8): 155-70; 2 (Sept. 9–Oct. 17): 227-33.

[23]See *Official Gazette* N° 5.963 Extra. of Feb. 22, 2010.

[24]See Allan R. Brewer-Carías et al., *Ley Orgánica del Poder Público Municipal*, Editorial Jurídica Venezolana, Caracas 2005; and "El inicio de la desmunicipalización en Venezuela: La organización del Poder Popular para eliminar la descentralización, la democracia representativa y la participación a nivel local," in *AIDA, Opera Prima de Derecho Administrativo. Revista de la Asociación Internacional de Derecho Administrativo*, Asociación Internacional de Derecho Administrativo, Universidad Nacional Autónoma de México, Mexico City, 2007, 49-67.

That is why the citizen's assemblies and the communal councils, which began to be established in 2006, have gradually replaced local governments, being in contrast, directed from the center, and without any general electoral representative origin. Nonetheless, they create the idea that the people are participating. With the new Organic Law on the Federal Council of Government (2010), new base organizations of the popular power have been created, like the "communes," formally implementing through legislation the 2007 constitutional reform that was rejected by the people.[25]

In any case, the result is that the scheme of centralized federation of the Constitution of 1961 has been strengthened and aggravated in the 1999 Constitution and through its unconstitutional developments, despite it identifying the federation formally as a "decentralized federation" (Article 4).

The great reform of the political system that was needed to improve democracy was definitively to change the centralism of the state and to distribute political power throughout the territory. That was the only way to effect true political participation and a motive that could justify the Constituent Assembly. Decentralization, however, was postponed, and a great opportunity lost.

The Constituent Assembly, to overcome the political crisis, should have transformed the state, decentralizing power and establishing the basis for local government organizations to effectively approach the exercise of state power to the citizen. The Constituent Assembly did not do that – it neither transformed the state nor arranged the elements for effective participation. To participate is to be part of, to appertain, or to be associated with, and that is possible for citizens only with decentralized and accessible political local governments. Thus, participative democracy, besides elections or voting in referenda, is possible only with effective decentralization of power through expanding local governments in the

---

[25]In the 2007 constitutional reform draft proposals, a new branch of government was proposed to be created, the "popular power," and the "communes" seeking to consolidate the power of communal councils, with members who were not elected by popular vote and depended on the office of the head of state. See Allan R. Brewer-Carías, *Hacia la consolidación de un estado socialista, centralizado, policial y militarista. Comentarios sobre el alcance y sentido de la Reforma Constitucional 2007*, Editorial Jurídica Venezolana, Caracas 2007; and *La Reforma Constitucional de 2007 (Sancionada inconstitucionalmente por la Asamblea Nacional el 2 de Noviembre de 2007)*, Editorial Jurídica Venezolana, Caracas 2007.

territory. Thus, only democracies can be decentralized.[26] Democracy can be part of everyday life only when local governments are established throughout a country.[27]

IV. THE DEMOCRATIC REGIME AND POLITICAL PARTICIPATION

One of the fundamental values established in the 1999 Constitution is democracy (preamble), not only as a political regime and condition of government but also as a way of life, founded in the ideas of political pluralism and equal participation of everyone in political processes. In that sense, the concept of the democratic state (*estado democrático*) is a constitutional principle that gives roots to the political organization of the nation, as it derives from the preamble ("democratic society") and from Articles 2, 3, 5, and 6 of the Constitution.

Democracy is also established in Article 6 of the Constitution as an immutable regime of the government of the republic and its political entities (states and municipalities), in the sense that such government must always be "democratic, participative, elective, decentralized, alternative, responsible, pluralist, and of revocable mandates." The Constitution also establishes provisions regarding accountability (*rendición de cuentas*) (Article 197), particularly for elected officers, and the possibility of them being subject to recall referenda (Articles 6, 70, 72 and 198).

Regarding these provisions, the Constitutional Chamber of the Supreme Tribunal of Justice, in Decision No. 23 (January 22, 2003), pointed out that the 1999 Constitution intended to "establish a democratic, participative and protagonist society, which implies that it is not just the State who has to adopt and submit its institutions to the ways and principles of democracy, but it is also the society (formed by the Venezuelan citizens) who must play a decisive and responsible role in the conduction of the Nation."[28]

To establish a democratic government with all such elements, defined in *cláusulas pétreas* (rock–like clauses), which must always exist, Article 5

---

[26]See Allan R. Brewer-Carías, "Democracia municipal, descentralización y desarrollo local," in *Revista Iberoamericana de Administración Pública* 11, Ministerio de Administraciones Públicas, Madrid 2004, 11-34.

[27]See Allan R. Brewer-Carías, "Democratización, descentralización política y reforma del estado" and "El municipio, la descentralización política y la democracia," in *Reflexiones sobre el constitucionalismo en América,* Editorial Jurídica Venezolana, Caracas 2001, 105-41 and 243-53.

[28]See Case: *Interpretación del articulo 71 de la Constitución,* in *Revista de Derecho Público*, 93-96, Editorial Jurídica Venezolana, Caracas 2003, 530ff.

of the Constitution, after setting forth that "sovereignty resides in an nontransferable way in the people," declares that sovereignty can be exercised in two ways: First, in a direct way by means of referenda and other instruments for direct democracy established in the Constitution; second, and in an indirect way, "through suffrage, by the organs that exercise State Powers" (Article 5). The same enunciations are contained in Article 62 of the same Constitution, which sets forth citizens' political right to freely participate in all public affairs – that is, to participate in the formation, execution, and control of public activities to achieve their complete collective and individual development. It is the obligation of the state and society to facilitate and create the most favorable conditions for such participation. This political participation, an essential characteristic of any democracy, although not always accomplished, as already mentioned, is exercised in two ways according to the same provision of the Constitution: directly through instruments of direct democracy and indirectly through elected representatives, which is one of the essential elements of representative democracy (Article 62).

For the purpose of guaranteeing this right to political participation, Article 70 of the Constitution enumerates the following political means for citizens to exercise their sovereignty: by electing representatives to public office; by voting on referenda, including those to revoke mandates of elected officers; by participating in popular consultations; by assuming the initiative regarding legislative or constitutional reforms; and by participating in open town meetings and in citizens' assemblies (whose decisions are binding).

According to those constitutional provisions, the participatory democratic political system of Venezuela is characterized by the following elements: a representative democracy, assured by means of an electoral system that must guarantee free, universal, direct, and secret elections; a regime of plural political parties; an alternating system of government; and instruments of government accountability; and a direct democracy, assured by means of referenda, legislative initiatives, popular consultations, and the possibility of political participation in open town meetings and citizens' assemblies.

1. *Representative Democracy*

Representative democracy is a basic component of the participatory democratic system of Venezuela, through which citizens exercise sovereignty by electing representatives to state organs. This is an indirect means of exercising sovereignty, precisely "through suffrage, by the organs that exercise State Powers" (Article 5).

But suffrage and periodic fair and free elections, based on a universal, secret vote that expresses the will of the people, do not exhaust representative democracy. It has the following other essential elements: respect for human rights and fundamental liberties, access to power and its exercise with subjection to the rule of law, a regime of plural political parties and organizations, and separation and independence of public powers.

The exercise of sovereignty through representatives by means of elections not only is the most common element of representative democracy but also is irreplaceable. All head officials of the executive and legislative branches, in all levels of government, are elected by popular, direct, and secret vote. At the national level, the president is elected for a term of six years by popular, universal, direct, and secret vote by all citizens registered in the electoral registry by a simple majority of votes (Articles 228 and 230).

The representatives of the National Assembly are elected for a five-year term (Article 192) by citizens registered in the electoral registry by popular, universal, direct, and secret vote. In that case, the electoral system applied is mixed, combining a personal vote with proportional representation in a number fixed according to a population base of 1.1% of the country's total population (Article 186). In addition, three national representatives from each state must be elected. Also, the indigenous peoples have the right to elect three national representatives (Article 125). Each representative must have a substitute member, elected through the same process, who is called to act in cases of temporal or absolute absence of the principal (Article 186).

All other public officials of the branches of government (magistrates of the Supreme Tribunal of Justice, comptroller general, prosecutor general, peoples' defender, members of the National Electoral Council) are not elected in popular elections but appointed by the National Assembly (Articles 265, 279, and 296), in some cases, by a qualified majority of votes. That legislative election must be made with the participation of representatives of the various sectors of society that must integrate the nominating committees that must be established for such purposes.[29]

---

[29]See Allan R. Brewer-Carías, "La participación ciudadana en la designación de los titulares de los órganos no electos de los poderes públicos en Venezuela y sus vicisitudes políticas," *Revista Iberoamericana de Derecho Público y Administrativo* 5-2005, San José, Costa Rica 2005, 76-95.

Unfortunately, the latter provisions have been distorted by the National Assembly, reducing the participation scope of civil society by incorporating members of the National Assembly into such committees, controlling them.

At the state level, the governors of each state are elected, by a relative majority of votes, for a term of four years by popular, universal, direct, and secret vote of the citizens registered in the electoral registry from the constituency of the respective state (Article 160). The members of the legislative councils of each state are elected every four years, in a number of not more that fifteen or less than seven, also by the citizens registered in the electoral registry of each state. In this case, the same rules apply as for the election of the representatives to the National Assembly (Article 162). On the municipal level, mayors and members of municipal councils are elected every four years by popular, universal, direct, and secret vote of the majority of citizens registered in the electoral registry of the constituency of the respective municipality (Articles 174 and 175).

The 1999 Constitution initially established that the president, governors, and mayors could be reelected only once and in the immediately following constitutional term (Articles 160, 174, and 230) and that members of the National Assembly and the state legislative councils could be reelected for a maximum of two consecutive constitutional terms (Articles 162 and 192). Nonetheless, all the limits on the possible reelection of officials, which were a consequence of the principle of alternating government according to Article 6 of the Constitution, nonetheless were eliminated through a constitutional amendment approved by referendum on February 14, 2009.[30]

2. *The Mixed Electoral System and Its Distortion*

To guarantee representative democracy in the election of representatives and members of the National Assembly, legislative councils, and municipal councils, the Constitution has established an electoral system combining personalized and proportional representation ballots.[31] According to the 1961 Constitution, the election of representatives in general was governed by d'Hondt proportional representation system. In

---

[30] See *Official Gazette* N° 5.908 Extra. of Feb. 19, 2009.

[31] See Allan R. Brewer-Carías, "Reforma electoral en el sistema político de Venezuela," in *Reforma política y electoral en América Latina 1978-2007*, coords. Daniel Zovatto and J. Jesús Orozco Henríquez, Universidad Nacional Autónoma de México-IDEA internacional, Mexico City 2008, 953-1019.

1993, the Organic Law on Suffrage and Political Participation,[32] seeking to guarantee better representation in elections at the regional and local levels, introduced a combination of methods, mixing proportional representation with majority elections. That was finally constitutionalized in a general way in the 1999 Constitution as a "personalized proportional representation method" (Article 63). This mixed system required ensuring that in each state constituency a percentage of representatives is to be elected through majority ballot; and another percentage is to be elected in its subdividsions, through lists ballot (proportional representation), through blocked and closed lists. Until 2009, the elections of representatives were governed by the already mentioned Organic Law on Suffrage and Political Participation of 1993, reformed in 1998, providing that for the definitive allocation of representatives, regarding elected by both methods in one constituency from candidates of the same party, a deduction was to be made in the corresponding list in order to allow the effective application of the proportional–representation principle allowing the election of candidates from the other parties.[33] Nonetheless, this method of deducting elected candidates was restricted by means of a constitutional interpretation of the Constitution made by the Constitutional Chamber of the Supreme Tribunal of Justice on January 25, 2006, [34] before the election of the members of the National Assembly that same year. That decision legitimized the defrauding method applied by the parties supporting the government,[35] allowing those parties that have entered into agreements, for some of them to file nominations only for majority ballots and for others only to file nominations for proportional–representation ballots. Thus, being formally different parties (though part of the same coalition), no deduction of the elected candidates was to be applied, as it happens when it is the same party the one that elects candidates through both methods, distorting in this way the application of the proportional–representation method.[36] Accordingly, the system

---

[32] *Gaceta Oficial* Extra. N° 5.233, May 28, 1998.

[33] Articles 12 ff. See *Gaceta Oficial*. N° 5.233 Extra of May 28, 1998.

[34] Decision N° 74 (Case: *Acción Democrática vs. Consejo nacional Electoral y otras autoridades electorales*), in *Revista de Derecho Público* 105, Editorial Jurídica Venezolana, Caracas 2006, 122-44.

[35] The method was named "The Twins" (*Las Morochas*) allowing the same group of parties to use and benefit from both electoral systems in uninominal and plurinominal constituencies, without the deduction attached to the mixed system.

[36] See Allan R. Brewer-Carías, "El juez constitucional vs. el derecho al sufragio mediante la representación proporcional," in *Crónica sobre la "In"justicia constitucional. La Sala Constitucional y el autoritarismo en Venezuela*, Caracas 2007, 337ff.

became, in practice, a majority system that distorted proportional representation. In 2009, the new Organic Law on Electoral Processes was sanctioned, legalizing this distorted electoral method,[37] which is the one that was to be applied in the legislative election in September 2010.

3. *Principles of Participative Democracy and Their Distortion*

The 1999 Constitution, by establishing participation as a fundamental principle of democracy, also regulated it as a political constitutional right, "considering individuals as member of a determined political community, in order to take part in the formation of public decisions or of the will of the public institutions" – a right related to other political rights established in the Constitution, like the rights to vote (Article 63), to petition (Article 51), to have access to public offices (Article 62), to political association (Article 67), to demonstration (Article 68), and to be promptly informed by public administration offices on the course or result of petitions (Article 143). It also relates to social rights, like the right to health (Article 84); educational rights (Article 102); and environmental rights (Article 127).[38]

Participative democracy, besides representative (election) and direct democracy (referenda, citizens assembly whose decisions will be of binding force), also materializes in other constitutional instruments established for the direct intervention of citizens in public–affairs decision making such as the initiative for legislation, for constitutional reforms and for the constituent process, public consultations, and open town meetings (Article 70).

The Constitution also has directly regulated some mechanisms to guarantee direct participation of persons representing the different sectors of society in the adoption of some public decisions, particularly by integrating the nominating committees that are called to propose before the National Assembly the candidates to be appointed prosecutor general, comptroller general, people's defender, judges of the Supreme Court, and members of the Electoral National Council (Articles 270, 279, 295). With these provisions, the drafters of the Constitution were seeking to avoid the traditional agreements between political parties that characterized such

---

[37] *Gaceta Oficial* N° 5928, Extra., Aug. 12, 2009.

[38] See Case: *Interpretación del articulo 71 de la Constitución* in *Revista de Derecho Público*, N° 93-96, Editorial Jurídica Venezolana, Caracas 2003, 530ff.

"amplified" parliamentary commission of the National Assembly (Article 13) of which National Assembly members are integrated, even though National Assembly representatives are not considered representatives of civil society.

Also, in the case of the electoral power, to guarantee the autonomy of the National Electoral Council, the Constitution limited the discretional power that the previous Congress had to appoint its members, establishing the Electoral Nominating Committee also integrated by representatives of the different sectors of society. However, in the 2002 Organic Law of the Electoral Power,[46] regardless of the constitutional provisions, the integration of the Electoral Nominating Committee did not respect the Constitution. Instead, another "amplified" parliamentary commission was established as the nominating committee made up of "twenty-one (21) members, from which eleven (11) are representatives before the National Assembly, and ten (10) from sectors of society," all appointed by the same National Assembly. With that regulation, the right to political participation of different sectors of civil society, which had the exclusive right to conform the nominating committee, was confiscated.[47]

The same has occurred regarding the nomination and appointment of the high officials of the citizens' power (the branch of government comprising the prosecutor general, the comptroller general, and the peoples' defender), by means of the Organic Law of the Citizens Power of 2004.[48] That also resulted in a parliamentary commission.[49]

The National Assembly completely distorted the constitutional mechanism created to guarantee the possibility of citizens' direct participation, through representatives from various sectors of society, in selecting and nominating nonelected public officers of the state.

With the distortion of the nominating committees, the diverse branches of government have become more dependent on political power, which has given way in the constitutional order to a concentrated system of

---

[46] See *Gaceta Oficial* N° 37.573, Nov. 19, 2002.

[47] See comments in Allan R. Brewer-Carías, *La Sala Constitucional versus el estado democrático de derecho. El secuestro del poder electoral y de la Sala Electoral del Tribunal Supremo y la confiscación del derecho a la participación política*, Los Libros de El Nacional, Colección Ares, Caracas 2004.

[48] According to the 1999 Constitution, the citizen power is composed by three state organs: the prosecutor general, comptroller general, and peoples' defender. See *Gaceta Oficial* N° 37.310, Oct. 19, 2001.

[49] See Allan R. Brewer-Carías, "Sobre el nombramiento irregular por la Asamblea Nacional de los titulares de los órganos del poder ciudadano en 2007," *Revista de Derecho Público* 113, Editorial Jurídica Venezolana, Caracas 2008, 85-8.

powers that is contrary to the proclaimed principles of autonomy and independence of the different branches of government. Through legislative practice and the refusal of the Supreme Tribunal of Justice to exercise judicial review over such unconstitutional statutes, a very important constitutional innovation, unique in the world, has been neutralized. With this, unfortunately, the constitutionally guaranteed political participation of citizens has also been forgotten and has been manipulated by those who control power from the legislative branch.

Contrary to all the participative terminology it contains, the 1999 Constitution can be considered an interventionist and limiting text regarding the organizations of civil society. It establishes the jurisdiction of the National Electoral Council for "the organization of the elections of trade unions, professional associations and organizations with political objectives," in addition to its functions directed to guarantee "the equality, reliability, impartiality, transparency and efficiency of the electoral processes" (Article 293.6).

According to this provision, the internal elections that can take place within political parties, trade unions, and professional associations of any kind must be organized by the state, through one of the branches of government (electoral power). That openly contradicts the participatory feature attributed to the Constitution and its declared goal of promoting citizens' participation.

Consequently, all internal electoral processes in political parties in Venezuela, even those directed to select their candidates to general elections, from 2000 on must be organized by the National Electoral Council. That, in fact, has not always occurred because of the progressive configuration of the political arena in the country to one party.

With all those provisions, the state has actively intervened in civil–society organizations. For instance, even though trade unions are not considered "inside the structure of the Venezuelan public organization,"[50] the Electoral Chamber of the Supreme Court, in Decision No. 46 (March 11, 2002), has justified such anomalous state intervention and supervision of those social organizations.[51]

---

[50]See *Revista de Derecho Público* 84, Editorial Jurídica Venezolana, Caracas 2000, 132ff.

[51]See *Revista de Derecho Público* 89–92, Editorial Jurídica Venezolana, Caracas 2000, 148–49.

With respect to other civil associations of individuals or corporations —such as neighborhood associations;[52] social clubs or recreational associations;[53] and groups of a business, industrial, or commercial character[54]– on the basis of the same constitutional provision, the Electoral Chamber of the Supreme Tribunal of Justice has decided in many cases to participate in their internal functioning. In one emblematic case, the Electoral Chamber ruled on the obligatory intervention of the National Electoral Council in the electoral processes of civil associations, as occurred with the internal elections of the professors' association of Universidad Central de Venezuela.[55]

4. *Direct Democracy Institutions, Referenda, and the Distortion of the Recall Referendum*

Regarding direct democracy, the 1999 Constitution also established various mechanisms for its exercise to promote direct popular participation in conducting public affairs. In that context, Article 70 of the Constitution, referring to the need for prominent participation of the people, as aforementioned, enumerates as means for direct democracy: referenda; popular consultation; repeal of the public mandate; legislative, constitutional, and constituent initiatives; open town meetings (*cabildos abiertos*); and citizens' assemblies, "whose decisions shall have a binding character."

For referenda, the Constitution expressly established consultative referenda, recall referenda to revoke mandates, approbatory referenda of statutes and constitutional revisions, and referenda to abrogate statutes.[56]

---

[52] See Constitutional Chamber Decision N° 61 (May 29, 2001), Exp. 000064 (Case: *Asociación de Residentes de la Urbanización La Trinidad*). See also Allan R. Brewer-Carías, *Derecho administrativo*, Universidad Externado de Colombia, Bogotá 2005, 1:413ff.

[53] See Electoral Chamber Decision of Nov. 1, 2000, Exp. 0115 (Case: *Asociación Civil Club Campestre Paracotos*). See also Allan R. Brewer-Carías, *Derecho administrativo*, Universidad Externado de Colombia, Bogotá 2005, 1:413ff.

[54] See Electoral Chamber Decision N° 18 (Feb. 15, 2001), Exp. 000017 (Case: *Cámara de Comercios e Industrias del Estado Aragua*). This jurisprudence was ratified by the same chamber, according to verdict N° 162, Exp. 2002-000077 (Oct. 17, 2002) (Case: *Cámara de Comercio e Industrias del Estado Bolívar*). See Allan R. Brewer-Carías, *Derecho administrativo*, Universidad Externado de Colombia, Bogotá 2005, 1:413ff.

[55] See Electoral Chamber Decision N° 51 (May 19, 2000) (Case: *Asociación de Profesores de la Universidad Central de Venezuela*), in *Revista de Derecho Público* 82, Editorial Jurídica Venezolana, Caracas 2000, 92ff.

[56] See Cosimina G. Pellegrino Pacera, "Una introducción al estudio del referendo como mecanismo de participación ciudadana en la Constitución de 1999," in *El derecho público a*

Consultative referenda can be convened for questions of matters of preeminent national, state, or municipal importance. According to Article 71 of the Constitution, at the national level, they can be convened by the president in Council of Ministers; the National Assembly, by means of a resolution approved by a majority of members; and citizens, by means of a petition signed by at least 10% of registered voters. At the local level (e.g., parish[57] [*parroquias*], municipal, state), consultative referenda can be convened by municipal councils or state legislative councils on the initiative of two-thirds of members; by the mayor or governor; or by the people, with a petition signed by no less than 10% of registered voters in the specific jurisdiction.

The Constitution also establishes approval referenda regarding draft statutes, which are debated before the National Assembly. According to Article 73 of the Constitution, that occurs when at least two-thirds of members of the assembly so decide. If the referendum results in the approval of a statute, provided that at least 25% of registered voters have concurred, the corresponding bill will become law. Approval referenda also can be proposed by popular initiative (Article 204.7) when the National Assembly fails to take up debate on bills that also were proposed by popular initiative (Article 205).

According to Article 73 of the Constitution, treaties, conventions, and other international agreements that can compromise national sovereignty or transfer national powers or competencies to supranational entities, as with treaties for regional economic integration, may be subject to approbatory referenda. In that case, the initiative corresponds to the president in Council of Ministers; to the National Assembly, when approved by a vote of at least two-thirds of members; or to popular initiative, with a petition signed by at least 15% of registered voters.

The Constitution also regulates referenda for the abrogation of statutes regarding laws other than budgetary, tax, public debt, amnesty, and human rights laws, and those laws approving international treaties (Article 74). Abrogation referenda can be convened on the initiative of at least 10% of registered voters or on the initiative of the president in Council of Ministers. Decrees laws issued by the president (Article 236.8) also may be subjected to abrogation referenda, in which case the convention initiative only can be popular, through a petition signed by at least 5% of

---

comienzos del siglo XXI. Estudios homenaje al Profesor Allan R. Brewer-Carías, Instituto de Derecho Público, Universidad Central de Venezuela, Civitas Ediciones, Madrid 2003, 1:441-81.

[57]These are, of course, nonreligious territorial divisions of the municipalities.

registered voters. In all abrogation referenda, the concurrence of at least 40% of registered voters is necessary to abrogate a statute or decree law.

Revocation or recall referenda are the consequence of the principle established in the Constitution that all popular elected public officials are subject to revocation of their mandate (Article 6). Thus, Article 72 establishes recall referenda, which can take place only at the second half of the term in office. The popular revocation of mandates is one way that people have direct political participation in the exercise of their sovereignty (Article 70). Consequently, the corresponding petition for a recall referendum only can be of popular initiative and must be signed by at least 20% of registered voters in the corresponding jurisdiction.

For revocation of mandates, according to Article 72 of the Constitution, the following rules must be observed in the corresponding referendum. First, the recall referendum can be convened only once at the midpoint of the term of the elected officer. Second, the request to convene a recall referendum can be made only by popular initiative, signed by no less than 25% of registered voters in the corresponding constituency and filed before the National Electoral Council (Article 293.5). There cannot be more that one request for a recall referendum during the same constitutional term of the elected official. Third, in the convened recall referendum, a number greater than or equal to 25% of registered voters must concur as voting persons. Fourth, for approval of a mandate's recall, it is sufficient that a number of voters equal to or greater than that which elected the officer voted in the referendum to revoke the mandate. In that case, the official's mandate is considered revoked, and a new election must take place immediately to fill the absence (Articles 72 and 233).

Consequently, for a mandate to be recalled or revoked, the number of yes votes (to revoke) must be equal to or greater than the number of votes that originally elected the official, and voters must total at least 25% of registered voters in the corresponding jurisdiction. The Constitution says nothing about the fact that, in a recall referendum, voters who vote not to revoke the official's mandate could outnumber the votes to revoke. The provision is established for a recall referendum and not for a plebiscite; that is, it is established in order to decide the revocation of a mandate and not to decide on the confirmation or continuation of a mandate.

With respect to the president, because the revocation of his mandate has the effect of an absolute absence, in case a revocation occurs, replacement occurs as follows. If revocation takes place during the first four years of his mandate, there must be a new election of someone to complete the president's term. If the revocation takes place during the last two years of the presidential term, the executive vice president assumes the position of president until the end of the term (Article 233).

The Constitution also provides for revoking mandates of officials in the National Assembly. In that case, revoked representatives cannot seek a new election in the subsequent constitutional term (Article 198). This applies only to representatives in the National Assembly; the Constitution establishes nothing in this regard regarding the mandate revocation of other public elected officers.

On matters of recall referenda, Venezuela's only experience with them during the first decade of the 1999 Constitution is the recall referendum of the president (who was elected in 2000 by 3,757,774 votes), convened in 2004 by popular initiative signed by more than 3.5 million people.[58] That was distorted and illegitimately transformed, against the Constitution, into a sort of ratifying referendum of a plebiscite nature. In effect, in the 2004 referendum, 3,989,008 people voted to recall the president's mandate, a number of votes greater than the ones that elected him in 2000. Nonetheless, the votes not to revoke were 5,800,629 votes – and so, according to express provision of the Constitution, the president's mandate was revoked and there should have been a new election. However, the National Electoral Council, following a phrase in a Constitutional Chamber of the Supreme Tribunal decision,[59] converted the recall referendum into a "ratification referendum,"[60] which does not exist

---

[58]See Allan R. Brewer-Carías, "El secuestro del poder electoral y la confiscación del derecho a la participación política mediante el referendo revocatorio presidencial: Venezuela 2000-2004," *Revista Jurídica del Perú* 54, Lima 2004, 353-96; "El secuestro del poder electoral y de la Sala Electoral del Tribunal Supremo y la confiscación del derecho a la participación política mediante el referendo revocatorio presidencial: Venezuela: 2000-2004," *Revista Costarricense de Derecho Constitucional* 5, Instituto Costarricense de Derecho Constitucional, Editorial Investigaciones Jurídicas, San José 2004, 167-312; "El secuestro del poder electoral y la confiscación del derecho a la participación política mediante el referendo revocatorio presidencial: Venezuela 2000-2004," *Stvdi Vrbinati, Rivista tgrimestrale di Scienze Giuridiche, Politiche ed Economiche* 71, n.s., Università degli studi di Urbino, Urbino 2004, 379-436; "El secuestro del poder electoral y la confiscación del derecho a la participación política mediante el referendo revocatorio presidencial: Venezuela 2000-2004," *Boletín Mexicano de Derecho Comparado* 112, Instituto de Investigaciones Jurídicas, Universidad Nacional Autónoma de México, Mexico City 2005, 11-73.

[59]In Decision N° 2750 (Oct. 21, 2003) (Case: *Carlos E. Herrera Mendoza, Interpretación del artículo 72 de la Constitución*), the Chamber said: "It is a sort of relegitimizing [process] of the public official…so if in the referendum, more votes for the public official to remain in office are obtained, he must continue in it, even if enough number of persons votes for the revocation of his mandate." See in *Revista de Derecho Público*, N° 93-96, Editorial Juridica Venezolana, Caracas 2003.

[60]See Allan R. Brewer-Carías, "La Sala Constitucional vs. el derecho ciudadano a la revocatoria de mandatos populares: De cómo un referendo revocatorio fue inconstitucionalmente convertido en un 'referendo ratificatorio'," in *Crónica sobre la "in"justicia constitucional. La Sala Constitucional y el autoritarismo en Venezuela*, Colección Instituto de Derecho Público N° 2, Universidad Central de Venezuela, Caracas 2007, 349-78.

in the Constitution, because a greater number of voters cast no. A recall referendum asks the people if the mandate of an elected official should be revoked; it does not ask whether the elected official must remain in office. In the 2004 recall referendum, the National Electoral Council, when giving the voting results, converted it into a plebiscite ratifying the president.[61]

In any event, participation cannot be achieved only by inserting instruments of direct democracy in a representative democratic framework, as has occurred in modern constitutionalism. Referenda can be useful instruments to perfect democracy but, by themselves, they cannot satisfy the aim of participation. The result of the implementation of the 1999 Constitution is that the Venezuelan democracy has transformed into a centralized plebiscite democracy, in which effectively all power is in one hand, that of the president, who is supported by the military and a one-party system. The plebiscite democracy has created the illusion of popular participation, particularly by means of the uncontrolled distribution of state oil income among the poor through governmental social programs that are not precisely tailored to promote investment or generate employment.

The plebiscite democracy, without doubt, is less representative and less participatory than traditional representative democracy, which, notwithstanding all the warnings that were raised,[62] traditional parties have failed to preserve. All this is unfortunately contributing to the disappearance in Venezuela of democracy as a political system (which is much more than elections and referenda, as made clear by the 2001 Inter-American Democratic Charter), a development that the November 2, 2007, constitutional reforms sanctioned by the National Assembly intended to formalize, being rejected by popular vote in the December 2, 2007, referendum.

With respect to popular consultation, in addition to representatives of different sectors of society on nominating committees for appointment of high-ranking officials of the citizen, judicial, and electoral branches of

---

[61] That is why the 2004 recall referendum has been considered a "stunning victory" for Chávez that gave him an "overwhelming majority." See Richard Gott, *Hugo Chávez and the Bolivarian Revolution*, Verso, London 2005, 263. This is incorrect. The referendum was not a plebiscite, which does not exist in the Venezuelan Constitution. It was a referendum to revoke the mandate of the president. According to the Constitution, his mandate was revoked because more votes were cast to revoke than the president received in elections.

[62] See Allan R. Brewer-Carías, *El estado. Crisis y reforma*, Academia de Ciencias Políticas y Sociales, Caracas 1982; and *Problemas del estado de partidos*, Editorial Jurídica Venezolana, Caracas 1988.

government, Article 211 of the Constitution imposes on the National Assembly the obligation to always submit draft legislation to public consultation, asking the opinion of citizens and the organized society. Also, according to Article 206, the National Assembly before sanctioning statutes must consult states, through their legislative councils, when such statutes refer to matters concerning the states. Unfortunately, in practice, such consultations have not been made. Nonetheless, the wording of the general approach to participation has resulted in the fact that in all statutes that have been sanctioned under the 1999 Constitution, a chapter has always been included regarding popular participation in the matters regulated.

The Constitution also guarantees popular participation, not only for the introduction of draft legislation before the National Assembly by means of petitions signed by no less than 0.1% of registered voters (Article 204.7) but also for the purpose of convening consultative, approbatory, and abrogation referenda. In the case of the revocation or recall referendum, it is an exclusive right of the people, through popular initiative.

The Constitution conceives of municipalities as the primary political unit in the national organization (Article 168); thus, they were conceived to be the main institutional channel for political participation in matters belonging to local life, as ratified by Article 1 of the Organic Law on the Municipal Public Power.[63] That law sets forth that municipalities and other local entities, particularly the *parroquias* (parishes) to be established below municipalities, are the primary areas for citizens' participation in the planning, design, execution, control, and evaluation of public policies. For such purposes, municipal entities must create the needed mechanisms to guarantee participation of communities and social groups (Article 7), and they are obliged to promote them (Article 56). The law enumerates all the aspects of citizens' participatory rights (Articles 255 and 260), and for such purposes, it establishes that parishes (*parroquias*) must be the information, production, and promotion centers for participatory processes, for identifying budgetary priorities, and for promoting citizens' participation in public affairs (Article 37).

Article 70 of the Constitution specifically refers to town hall meetings, which are also regulated in the organic law, which can be convened by municipal councils, parish councils, and popular initiative according to what is established in municipal ordinances (Article 263). The decisions

---

[63] *Gaceta Oficial* N° 38.421, Apr. 21, 2006. See Allan R. Brewer-Carías et al., *Ley Orgánica del Poder Público Municipal*, Editorial Jurídica Venezolana, Caracas 2006.

adopted in such meetings are valid if approved by the majority of persons present, provided that the decisions refer to matters concerning municipal life (Article 264).

The other direct democracy means established in the Constitution are the citizens' assemblies (Article 70), conceived in the municipal organic law as local entities for participation, of deliberative character, established to enforce governance, drive planning, and decentralize services and resources, in which all citizens have the right to participate (Article 266). Their decisions have obligatory character (Article 70 of the Constitution), provided, as indicated in the municipal organic law, that they are not contrary to legislation or to the community and state interest. The law leaves regulation concerning citizens' assemblies to a special statute.

All these provisions regarding local governments (municipalities and parishes) have been set aside and have been progressively substituted by means of the organization of a so-called popular power not established in the Constitution and integrated by nonelected representative entities. Within these entities, the 2006 Communal Councils Law[64] has specifically regulated the citizens'assemblies an the communal councils that have been created at the communal level (subparish and submunicipal level) but without any relation whatsoever to the municipalities or parishes, except when the former transferred activities or services to them.

These communal councils are organized as nonrepresentative organs of the state, so their members are not elected by the people of the communities but rather appointed by the citizens' assemblies, which unfortunately are directly controlled by the official political party. In addition, these entities, from an institutional and financial point of view, depend directly on the president of the republic, initially through the Presidential Commission of the Popular Power and, since 2009, through a cabinet minister, minister of the popular power and for popular participation.[65]

---

[64]*Ley de los Consejos Comunales, Gaceta Oficial*, Extra N° 5.806, Apr. 10, 2006. This law was substituted in 2009 with the *Ley Orgánica de los Consejos Comunales, Gaceta Oficial* N° 39.335, Dec. 28, 2009. In June 2010, the National Assembly began the discussion of the Organic Law on the Communes (*Ley Orgánica de Comunas*).

[65]See Allan R. Brewer-Carías, "El inicio de la desmunicipalización en Venezuela: La organización del poder popular para eliminar la descentralización, la democracia representativa y la participación a nivel local," in *AIDA, Opera Prima de Derecho Administrativo. Revista de la Asociación Internacional de Derecho Administrativo*, Universidad Nacional Autónoma de México, Mexico City 2007, 49-67.

5. Plural Political Parties and the Move toward a Single-Party System

A democratic regime cannot exist without political parties and pluralism. As has been mentioned, that is why, after a short experiment with a dominant-party system from 1945 to 1948, the democratic parties that in 1958 signed the *Pacto de Punto Fijo* after the democratic revolution initiated that same year against the military dictatorship, committed to establishing a competitive, plural multiparty democratic system. That system functioned until 1999.

That democratic period during the second half of the twentieth century was characterized, from the beginning, by the fact of the predominance of the political parties that dominated all aspects of political life, particularly participation and representation (party state).[66] It was their crisis and the crisis of their leadership – because of the lack of reforms and updating the democratic system – that eventually provoked the collapse of the democratic system after 1998. After forty years of controlling political power and having democratized the country, the parties underestimated the country's need for more means of representation and political participation, failing to open the democratic system through, for instance, political decentralization that would allow effective participation. In any case, at the end of the twentieth century, all the political ills of Venezuela were attributed, particularly by the new authoritarian military and populist leadership that took control of the state, to the political parties, to the 1958 *Pacto de Punto Fijo*, and, to the Constitution of 1961.

The fact is that the presidential election of that year (1998) and the election of the Constituent Assembly in the following year (1999) were characterized by an antiparty trend, which was reflected in the drafting of the 1999 Constitution, which was conceived of as an antiparty instrument. Even the phrase "political party" was eliminated from its text and substituted with the more general expression "organizations with political purposes" (Article 67).[67] Of course, what the drafters of the new Constitution in 1999 tended to ignore, was the traditional political parties,

---

[66] See Allan R. Brewer-Carías, *Problemas del estado de partidos*, Editorial Jurídica Venezolana, Caracas 1989. See the critics on this characterization of the political system up to 1999 as a party state, in Juan Carlos Rey, "El sistema de partidos falló," in *Revista Sic,* N° 772, Centro Gumilla, Caracas 2010, 67-72.

[67] See Roberto V. Pastor and Rubén Martínez Dalmau, "La configuración de los partidos políticos en la Constitución venezolana," *Revista de Derecho Constitucional* 4, Editorial Sherwood, Caracas 2001, 375-89; Allan R. Brewer-Carías, "Regulación jurídica de los partidos políticos en Venezuela," in *Regulación jurídica de los partidos políticos en América Latina*, coord. Daniel Zovatto, Universidad Nacional Autónoma de México, International IDEA, Mexico City 2006, 893-937.

which until then, had been in power. For such purpose, the 1999 Constitution forbids public (state) financing of political organizations (a provision that the Supreme Tribunal of Justice has distorted through its interpretation),[68] as well as the existence of party parliamentarian groups. It requires voting by the members of the National Assembly according to their own conscience, forbidding any kind of voting instructions; a provision that is not in force, particularly due to the strict control exercised by the official party regarding its members in the National Assembly. Moreover, the Constitution, in principle, limits the possibility of parties reaching agreement on the appointment of nonelected public officials by requiring nominating committees to be formed only on the basis of representation of various sectors of civil society; a provision that as has been distorted aforementioned.

As aforementioned, not one of those prescriptions is really in force: The president is the acting head of his own official party, which completely controls the National Assembly. He is, in fact, director of his party parliamentary group, in which he has imposed rigid party discipline. Through such mechanisms, he has intervened in the designation of magistrates of the Supreme Tribunal and members of the National Electoral Council, as well as the other nonelected officials, thus disregarding the constitutional nominating committees. Those committees have effectively been converted into extended parliamentary commissions firmly controlled by the government party.[69]

The constitution-making process of 1999 and the sanctioning of the new Constitution unfolded in this context and gave way to new political parties that were established mainly for electoral purposes and by the government. Those parties crushed and then marginalized the old political parties, which abstained from participating in the 1999 constitution-making process. During subsequent years, the new political parties continued to support the new government and its president, and they

---

[68]See the Constitutional Chamber Decision N° 780 (May 8, 2008), in *Revista de Derecho Público* 114, Caracas 2008, 127ff. See Allan R. Brewer-Carías, "El juez constitucional como constituyente: El caso del financiamiento de las campañas electorales de los partidos políticos en Venezuela," *Revista de Derecho Público* 117, Caracas 2009, 195-203.

[69]See Allan R. Brewer-Carías, "La progresiva y sistemática demolición institucional de la autonomía e independencia del poder judicial en Venezuela 1999-2004," in *XXX Jornadas J.M Domínguez Escovar, Estado de derecho, Administración de justicia y derechos humanos*, Instituto de Estudios Jurídicos del Estado Lara, Barquisimeto 2005, 33-174; *La Sala Constitucional versus el estado democrático de derecho. El secuestro del poder electoral y de la Sala Electoral del Tribunal Supremo y la confiscación del derecho a la participación política*, Los Libros de El Nacional, Colección Ares, Caracas 2004; and *La crisis de la democracia en Venezuela (La Carta Democrática Interamericana y los sucesos de abril se 2002)*, Ediciones Libros El Nacional, Caracas 2002.

eventually became more centralized than the traditional parties, with internal governing structures linked to the president. The final result of this process was the presidential initiative, in 2006, to promote the single United Socialist Party, using state structures and services, over which President Hugo Chávez presides, which intends to unite all the various political parties that have supported his tenure. Nonetheless, complete unification has failed because, for instance, the Communist Party has refused to disappear, and other parties have left the official coalition.

The official United Socialist Party was in charge of supporting the presidential draft constitutional reforms submitted to referendum in 2007, which popular vote rejected, and was also the supporting instrument of government candidates in the regional and municipal elections of November 2008. The government's candidates lost elections in the most important and populated states and municipalities of the country, where opposition candidates to governors and mayors were elected. Nonetheless, their powers have been progressively eroded by the action of the national government privileging the communal councils organization.

The result of the first decade of political life under the 1999 Constitution, which seems to ignore political parties, has been an increase in partisanship and party autocracy, particularly regarding the official party that has been embodied in the state structures.

With respect to the constitutional provisions related to political organizations, the traditional lack of internal democracy in the parties, which traditionally elect leaders in perpetuity, led to a provision according to which not only members of governing boards must be elected by members of each party but also the choice of party candidates for elections to representative offices must be made through internal democratic elections (Article 67). To that end, the Constitution obligated the National Electoral Council to organize those internal elections (Article 293.6), which in practice, because of the lack of statutory development of the constitutional provisions, did not occur during the first decade of the Constitution's existence.

In addition, also as a reaction to the problems stemming from public funding of political parties, regulated under the 1998 Organic Law of Suffrage and Political Participation,[70] which led to a monopoly over those funds by the traditionally dominant parties, as aforementioned, the drafters of the 1999 Constitution simply prohibited public funding of organizations

---

[70] *Gaceta Oficial* Extra. N° 5.233, May 28, 1998.

with political purposes and established new controls for their private financing (Article 67). This was a regression in addressing what is a constant problem in the democratic world: the possibility of public funding of political parties to avoid irregular and illegitimate funding, particularly of governing parties.[71] Nonetheless, in a 2008 decision of the Constitutional Chamber of the Supreme Tribunal interpreting such Article 67 of the Constitution, the Chamber mutated the Constitution, ruling that the article intended to prohibit public financing of only "internal activities" of parties, not of their electoral activities.[72]

Article 67 of the Constitution refers to a statute with the task of regulating the scope of private contributions to and finances of "organizations with political purposes," including mechanisms to oversee the origins and management of funds. The statute must regulate political and election campaigns, oversee their duration and spending limits, and encourage democratization. Until 2009, these matters were regulated by the 1998 Organic Law of Suffrage and Political Participation, but they are now subject to the Organic Law on Electoral Processes of 2009.[73]

In the same trend against political parties, the Constitution established the principle that members of the National Assembly are representatives of the whole of the people and "are not to be subject to mandates or instructions other than their own conscience" (Article 200), seeking to eliminate parliamentary party groups. Nonetheless, in practice, the parliamentary factions have changed only their names; since 2000, they have been called "opinion groups." In any case, and particularly regarding the governing party, its board presided over by the president itself, has had more centralized control over representatives to the National Assembly than did parties before 1999.

The result of all these provisions, constitutional distortions, and absence of legislation has been that, in practice, under the new Constitution, parties have greater presence than they ever had, to the point that since 1999, the president of the republic is also president of the governing party, and

---

[71] See Allan R. Brewer-Carías, "Consideraciones sobre el financiamiento de los partidos políticos en Venezuela," in *Financiamiento y democratización interna de partidos políticos. Memora del IV Curso Anual Interamaricano de Elecciones,* San José, Costa Rica, 1991, 121-39.

[72] Decision N° 780, Constitutional Chamber of the Supreme Tribunal of Justice (May 8, 2008) (Interpretaton of Article 67 of the Constitution), in *Revista de Derecho Público* 114, Editorial Jurídica Venezolana, Caracas 2008, 126ff. See the comments in Allan R. Brewer-Carías, "El juez constitucional como constituyente: el caso del financiamiento de las campañas electorales de los partidos políticos en Venezuela," in *Revista de Derecho Público*, N° 117, Editorial Jurídica Venezolana, Caracas 2009, 195-203.

[73] *Gaceta Oficial* Extra. N° 5.928, Aug. 12, 2009.

almost all ministers are also members of the party's National Coordination Board. As never before, the symbiosis between the governing political party and the state and its public administration has been completely established in Venezuela, opening lines of communication and financial channels as could not have been envisioned during the golden age of party autocracy in the 1980s. The same party state has continued, with the same vices of clientelism, and the same control by officials who have not been chosen in free and democratic internal elections on governing boards at the helm of parties.

Finally, the Constitution conferred to one of the national braches of government, the public electoral power through the National Electoral Council, the duty not only to organize all electoral processes but also to "organize elections in the organizations with political purposes" (Article 293.6), thus establishing an intolerable principle of state intervention in the internal functioning of political parties.

6. *Institutions of Government Accountability and Liability*

The 1999 Constitution establishes the general principle of state liability, incorporated expressly in Article 140, which sets forth that "the State is liable for the damages suffered by individuals in their goods and rights, provided that the injury be imputable to the "normal or abnormal functioning of Public Administration." Although doubts can result from the wording of the article as to the liability of the state caused by legislative actions that nonetheless derive from general principles of public law, express provisions of Articles 49.8 and 255 of the Constitution clarify liability caused by judicial acts, such as judicial errors or delay.

Article 139 of the Constitution establishes the general principle of liability of public officials in the exercise of public functions, based on the "abuse or deviation of powers or on the violation of the Constitution or of the law." In addition, Article 25, following a long constitutional tradition, expressly establishes the specific civil, criminal, and administrative liability of any public officials when issuing or executing acts violating human rights guarantees in the Constitution and statutes. No excuse can be alleged based on executing orders received from superiors.

From a political point of view, the Constitution provides for the accountability (*rendición de cuentas*) of elected public officials, specifically establishing the possibility that they are subject to recall referenda (Article 6).

With respect to transparency, Article 143 of the Constitution guarantees citizens' rights to be informed and have access to administrative information. First, it provides for the right of citizens to be promptly and truly informed by public administration regarding the procedures in which they have direct interest and to know about the definitive resolutions therein adopted, to be notified of administrative acts, and to be informed of the course of administrative procedures.

Article 143 also establishes the individual right to access administrative archives and registries, without prejudice of the acceptable limits imposed in a democratic society related to the national or foreign security, to criminal investigation, or to the intimacy of private life, all according to statutes regulating secret or confidential documents. The same article prohibits the possibility to establish any previous censorship on public officials regarding the information they have and could divulge when referred to matters under their responsibility.

Finally, some duties that Constitution imposes on the president must be mentioned, like to formulate before the National Assembly in its ordinary sessions each year during the first ten days of its installment, the State of the Republic address, which gives an account of the political, economic, social, and administrative aspects of the president's actions during the previous year (Article 237). State governors must give an account of their actions not before legislative councils but only before the comptroller general of each state, and they only have to present a report (Article 161). Representatives to the National Assembly have the duty to give an annual account of their actions to their electors because they are subject to recall referenda (Article 197).

V. THE SYSTEM OF GOVERNMENT AND THE SEPARATION OF POWERS

1. *Presidential System and Its Reinforcement*

In the horizontal organization of the sovereign power, in the new Constitution, the presidential system continues, even though with some parliamentary elements, already introduced in the Constitution of 1961.

However, the new Constitution has reinforced presidentialism because it combines the following factors, which reverse the tradition of checks and balances. First, the president continues to be elected by a relative majority, even though an absolute majority had long been recommended (Article

228).[74] Second, the president's term was increased from five years to six years (Article 230).[75] Third, for the first time in a century, the president could be elected for a consecutive additional term (Article 230),[76] a provision that was amended in February 2009 to allow the continuous and unlimited election of all elected officials, thus affecting the principle of alternating government. Fourth, although recall referenda are established, the complexity of their implementation (Article 72) makes them almost inapplicable. Fifth, the National Assembly may delegate lawmaking power to the president, and there is no limit on the powers of such a delegation (Articles 203 and 236.8).[77] Sixth, the president has the power to dissolve the National Assembly after three votes of censure against the vice president (Article 236, Section 21), who nonetheless is conceived of as an executive–branch official (appointed by the president) with no parliamentary role. The parliamentary censure vote has a long tradition in Venezuela for cabinet ministers, but the provision concerning the vice president was an invention of the 1999 Constitution.

With this presidential model, presidentialism has been reinforced, with no balance in a bicameral system due to the elimination of the Senate. Moreover, it was reinforced in other reforms, as the provisions of enabling laws or the legislative delegation to the president by the National Assembly to enact decrees-laws, not limited only to economic and financial subjects (Article 203), as it was the case in the 1961 Constitution, but on any subject whatsoever.

---

[74]See my dissenting vote in Allan R. Brewer-Carías, *Debate constituyente (Aportes a la Asamblea Nacional Constituyente)*, Fundación de Derecho Público, Editorial Jurídica Venezolana, Caracas 1999, 3 (Oct. 18–Nov. 30):288ff.

[75]In the 2007 constitutional reform draft proposals, the term is extended to seven years. See *Proyecto de Reforma Constitucional. Elaborado por el ciudadano Presidente de la República Bolivariana de Venezuela, Hugo Chávez Frías,* Editorial Atenea, Caracas 2007.

[76]See my dissenting vote in Allan R. Brewer-Carías, *Debate constituyente (Aportes a la Asamblea Nacional Constituyente),* Fundación de Derecho Público–Editorial Jurídica Venezolana, Caracas 1999, 3 (Oct. 18–Nov. 30):289ff. The 2007 constitutional reform draft proposals establish the indefinite possible reelection of the president. See *Proyecto de Reforma Constitucional. Elaborado por el ciudadano Presidente de la República Bolivariana de Venezuela, Hugo Chávez Frías*, Editorial Atenea, Caracas 2007.

[77]See Allan R. Brewer-Carías, "Régimen constitucional de la delegación legislativa e inconstitucionalidad de los decretos leyes habilitados dictados en 2001," *Revista Primicia* (special issue), Caracas 2001.

2. Unbalanced Powers Due to Concentrated Power in the National Assembly

The Constitution adopts a separation-of-powers framework not only between the legislative and the executive but also between the judicial power, whose autonomy is repeatedly established, and two new powers of constitutional rank: the citizen power, which comprises the Public Ministry (prosecutor general of the republic), the people's defender, general controller of the republic, and the electoral power, exercised by the National Electoral Council.

The essence of the separation of powers in the Constitution is that each constitutionally established organ of the state exercises its respective function with independence and autonomy, in a system of checks and balances in which no branch of government is or can be subject to that of another, except on matters of judicial review, audit controls, and protection of human rights.[78] Nonetheless, the five-branched division of powers under the 1999 Constitution is deceiving because, in fact, it conceals that some of the principal branches of government are subject to the legislator, in a very dangerous system of democracy and rule of law that leaves an open door to the concentration of power in the state and to authoritarianism.

The Constitution, in fact, absurdly distorts separation of powers by giving to the National Assembly the authority not only to appoint but also to dismiss judges of the Supreme Tribunal of Justice, the prosecutor general, the comptroller general, the people's defender, and members of the National Electoral Council (Articles 265, 279, and 296); and, in some cases, they can do so even by simple majority.[79] The 2007 reform proposals suggested that the latter option be formally constitutionalized, and they sought to eliminate the guarantee of the qualified majority of

---

[78] See Allan R. Brewer-Carías, "La opción entre democracia y autoritarismo," in *Reflexiones sobre el constitucionalismo en América*, Editorial Jurídica Venezolana, Caracas 2001, 41-59; Allan R. Brewer-Carías, *Constitución, democracia y control del poder,* Centro Iberoamericano de Estudios Provinciales y Locales (CIEPROL), Universidad de Los Andes, Editorial Jurídica Venezolana, Mérida 2004.

[79] This was also the case for the magistrates of the Supreme Tribunal that, according to Article 23.4 of the Supreme Tribunal Organic Law, provided that the administrative act of their appointment by the National Assembly could be decided by "simple majority," in the sense of more than 50% of those representatives present and voting. In the 2010 reform of this Organic Law, such provision was eliminated.

members of the National Assembly for such dismissals and to establish a simple majority for that purpose.[80]

It is impossible to talk about separate powers or mutual control when the tenure of head officials of institutions depends on the political will of one branch of government.[81] The National Assembly's powers to dismiss alone make futile the formal consecration of the independence of powers – officials are aware that they can be removed at any time and precisely when they act effectively with independence.[82] In Venezuela, in practice, and together with the president, this has concentrated powers in the National Assembly and, because of the president's control over the assembly it has concentrated powers in the president. Consequently, the president has complete control regarding legislation, being the appropriation of the legislative framework a "key tool in the governmental practice to ensure its own perpetuity in power."[83] The other consequence has been the total absence of fiscal or audit control by the Comptroller General Office over the huge state income amount due to oil wealth; the total absence of protection from the people's defender, which is seen more as a defender of state power than of the people; the indiscriminate use by the public prosecutor of the judiciary and judicial procedures to persecute any political dissidence; and the absolute control exercised by the executive over the judiciary. In particular, the judiciary has lost its independence, which is confirmed by the fact that in 2009 at least 50% of judges were provisional or temporary judges and, thus, by definition, political dependents.[84] Unfortunately, the mastermind of this system of concentration of powers in the end has been the Supreme Tribunal itself, and particularly its Constitutional Chamber, which by means of successive constitutional interpretation has cleared all violations of the Constitution

---

[80]See Allan R. Brewer-Carías, *La reforma constitucional de 2007*, Editorial Jurídica Venezolana, Caracas 2007, 108, 110, 112.

[81]See Allan R. Brewer-Carías, "Democracia: sus elementos y componentes esenciales y el control del poder," in *Grandes temas para un observatorio electoral ciudadano, Tomo I, Democracia: retos y fundamentos*, comp. Nuria González Martín, Instituto Electoral del Distrito Federal, Mexico City 2007, 171-220.

[82]See Allan R. Brewer-Carías, *Constitución, democracia y control del poder*, CIEPROL, Universidad de Los Andes, Editorial Jurídica Venezolana, Mérida 2004.

[83] See the *Report of the Socialist International Mission to Venezuela, 20-23 January 2010*, 3. Available at www.socialistinternational.org

[84]The Inter-American Commission on Human Rights in its *2009 Annual Report* expressed that still in 2009, "more than 50% of judges in Venezuela do not enjoy tenure in their positions and can be easily removed when they make decisions that could affect government interests." IACHR Annual Report, 2009, para. 482. Available at http://www.cidh.org/annualrep/2009eng/Chap.IV.f.eng.htm.

committed by other branches of government.[85] The Constitutional Chamber has become a most effective tool for the existing consolidation of power in the person of the president.[86]

All these facts create the antithesis of the independence and balance between powers of the state; it is a model of concentrated power in the National Assembly, which is totally incompatible with a democratic society. The model has allowed for the development of a centralized and plebiscitary system of government that is crushing democracy. This inconsistency within the Constitution is a direct consequence of successful efforts by the president and his followers to use the constitution-making process to consolidate their power while maintaining the appearance of adherence to democratic norms.

3. *The State of Justice and Its Incongruence*

The preamble of the Constitution refers to justice as a global and "fundamental value" that must contribute to "the construction of a just and peace–loving society resulting from the democratic exercise of popular will" (Article 3). For such purpose, the Constitutional Chamber has considered that the power to administer justice that must be exercised in the name of the Republic comes from the citizens (Article 253) and "must be executed with independence and impartiality" by judges "free from subordinations and inadequate pressures" (Articles 254 and 256). This has been considered "a new paradigm about values and constitutional principles connected to the justice," which has led to the state of justice, which considers the judiciary not just one more branch of government but rather "the integrating and stabilizing State power with authority to control and even dissolve the rest of the branches of government" (judicial state).[87]

---

[85]See Allan R. Brewer-Carías, *Crónica sobre la "in"justicia constitucioal. La Sala Constitucional y el autoritarismo*, Editorial Jurídica Venezolana, Caracas 2007; in particular, "*Quis custodiet ipsos custodes: de la interpretación constitucional a la inconstitucionalidad de la interpretación*," paper submitted to the VIII Congreso Peruano de Derecho Constitucional. Colegio de Abogados de Arequipa, Sept. 22–24, 2005, 47ff.

[86]In 2001, when he approved more than forty-eight decree laws, via delegate legislation, the president said: "The law is me. The state is me" (*La ley soy yo. El estado soy yo.*). See Raquel Barreiro, "Chávez delega en la Asamblea Nacional cambios legales," in *El Universal*, Caracas Dec. 4, 2001, 1,1 and 2,1. Available at http://www.eluniversal.com/2001/12/04/eco_art_04201DD.shtml.

[87]See Decision N° 659 of the Political-Administrative Chamber (Mar. 24, 2000) (Case: *Rosario Nouel vs. Consejo de la Judicatura y Comisión de Emergencia Judicial*), in *Revista de Derecho Público* 81, Editorial Jurídica Venezolana, Caracas 2000, 103-4.

This concept of the state of justice (*estado de justicia*) results not only from the provisions of the preamble and Article 1 that declare justice a constitutional value but also from constitutional provisions establishing "the prevalence of the notion of material justice over formalities and technicalities"[88] and providing for the "effective judicial protection" of human rights by means of a system of justice that must be "free, available, impartial, transparent, autonomous, independent, responsible, fair and expeditious, without improper delays, formalisms or useless repositions" (Article 26).[89] To that effect, procedural laws must establish the "simplification, uniformity and efficiency of the proceedings and adopt a brief, oral and public procedure, without sacrificing justice because omission of nonessential formalities" (Article 257).

Article 253 provides that the system of justice comprise not only the organs of the judicial branch (the Supreme Tribunal of Justice and all other courts established by law) but also the Public Ministry (public prosecutor), the people's defender, criminal investigatory organs, judicial staff and assistants, the penitentiary system, alternative means of adjudication, citizens who participate in the administration of justice, and attorneys authorized to practice law. Article 258 imposes on the legislator the duty to promote arbitration, conciliation, mediation, and other means of conflict resolution.

Article 254 of the Constitution declares the independence of the judicial branch and establishes that the Supreme Tribunal has "functional, financial, and administrative autonomy." To guarantee the independence and autonomy of courts and judges, Article 255 provides for a specific mechanism to ensure the independent appointment of judges and to guarantee their stability. In that regard, the judicial office is considered a career, in which the admission and promotion of judges within it must be the result of a public competition or examinations, to ensure that candidates are adequately qualified. The candidates are to be chosen by panels from the judicial circuits, and judges are to be designated by the Supreme Tribunal of Justice. The Constitution also creates the Judicial Nominations Committee (Article 270) to assist the judicial branch in

---

[88] See Supreme Tribunal of Justice, in Decision N° 949 of the Political-Administrative Chamber (Apr. 26, 2000), in *Revista de Derecho Público* 82, Editorial Jurídica Venezolana, Caracas 2000, 163ff.

[89] The concept of the state of justice also has been analyzed by the Constitutional Chamber of the Supreme Tribunal of Justice, particularly in Decision N° 389 (Mar. 7, 2002), in which the principle of the informality of the process was repeated, also asserting *pro actione* as another principle of the state of justice. See *Revista de Derecho Público* 89–92, Editorial Jurídica Venezolana, Caracas 2002, 175ff.

selecting the magistrates for the Supreme Tribunal of Justice (Article 264) and to assist judicial colleges in selecting judges for the lower courts. The committee is to be composed of representatives from different sectors of society, as determined by law. The Constitution also guarantees the stability of all judges, prescribing that they can be removed or suspended from office only through judicial disciplinary procedures on trials led by judicial disciplinary judges (Article 255).

Unfortunately, those provisions have not been implemented and, in practice, the executive has completely controlled the judicial power. Contrary to the constitutional provisions regarding the appointment and stability of judges since 1999, the Venezuelan judiciary has been almost exclusively made up of temporary and provisional judges,[90] and no public competition processes for the appointment of judges with citizen participation has taken place. Consequently, in general, judges lack stability, and because the constitutional provisions creating the judicial disciplinary jurisdiction have not been implemented by legislation, matters of judicial discipline have been and are currently in the hands of the Functioning and Restructuring Commission of the judiciary[91] (not established in the Constitution but created by the National Constituent Assembly in 1999), which has the power to remove temporary judges without due–process guarantees.[92] The Judicial Commission of the Supreme Tribunal also has discretionary powers to remove all temporary judges.[93]

---

[90] See *Informe sobre la situación de los derechos humanos en Venezuela*; OAS/Ser.L/V/II.118. d.C. 4 rev. 2, Dec. 29, 2003, para. 11, 161.

[91] The Inter-American Commission on Human Rights, in its *2009 Annual Report,* has ratified that "Under that transitional regime, the Commission for the Functioning and Restructuring of the Judicial System was created, and this body has ever since had the disciplinary authority to remove members of the judiciary. This Commission, in addition to being a special, temporary entity, does not afford due guarantees for ensuring the independence of its decisions, since its members may also be appointed or removed at the sole discretion of the Constitutional Chamber of the Supreme Court of Justice, without previously establishing either the grounds or the procedure for such formalities." See IACHR, *Annual Report 2009*, Par. 481. Available at http://www.cidh.org/annualrep/2009eng/Chap.IV.f.eng.htm.

[92] The Politico-Administrative Chamber of the Supreme Tribunal has ruled that the dismissal of temporary judges is a discretional power of the Functioning and Restructuring Commission of the Judiciary. This commission, created after 1999, adopts its decisions without administrative procedure. See Decision N° 00463-2007. The same doctrine has been established by the Constitutional Chamber in Decision N° 2414 (Dec. 20, 2007), Decision N° 280 (Feb. 23, 2007), and Decision N° 00673-2008. See Allan R. Brewer-Carías, "La justicia sometida al poder y la interminable emergencia del poder judicial (1999-2006)," in *Derecho y democracia. Cuadernos Universitarios* 2, Órgano de Divulgación Académica, Vicerrectorado Académico, Universidad Metropolitana, Caracas 2007, 122-38.

[93] See Decision N° 1.939 of the Constitutional Chamber of the Supreme Tribunal of Dec. 18, 2008 (Case: *Gustavo Álvarez Arias y otros*).

With respect to dismissal of judges of the Supreme Tribunal, although Article 265 provides that dismissal is possible only by the vote of a qualified majority of two-thirds of the National Assembly, following a hearing, in cases of "grave faults" committed by the accused, based in a prior qualification by the citizens' power, the 2004 Organic Law of the Supreme Tribunal of Justice circumvented this requirement by authorizing the dismissal of magistrates by a simple majority vote, thus revoking the "administrative act of their appointment" (Article 23.4),[94] a power that the National Assembly has used to dismiss judges who have ruled on sensitive issues against the government's wishes. Nonetheless, this provision was abrogated in the 2010 reform of the Supreme Tribunal Organic Law.

The fact is that the constitutional principles that ensure the autonomy and independence of judges at all levels of the judiciary are yet to be applied, particularly the admission of candidates to a judicial career through public competition with citizens participation, and the prohibition on removing or suspending judges except through disciplinary trials before disciplinary courts and judges (Articles 254 and 267).

Since 1999, the Venezuelan judiciary has been dominated by politics, as commanded by the executive.[95] For example, in 2003, a contentious administrative court ruled[96] against the government in a politically charged case.[97] In response, the government intervened in (took over) the court and dismissed its judges.[98] After the Inter-American Court of Human Rights ruled in 2008 that the dismissal had violated the American

---

[94]See comments on this reform in Allan R. Brewer-Carías, *Ley Orgánica del Tribunal Supremo de Justicia*, 3rd ed., Editorial Jurídica Venezolana, Caracas 2006, 41ff.

[95]See Inter-American Commission on Human Rights, *Informe sobre la situación de los derechos humanos en Venezuela*, OEA/Ser.L/V/II.118, d.C. 4 rev. 2, Dec. 29, 2003, para. 11, 3.

[96]See First Contentious Administrative Court Decision of Aug. 21 2003, in *Revista de Derecho Público* 93–96, Editorial Jurídica Venezolana, Caracas 2003, 445ff.

[97]See Claudia Nikken, "El caso 'Barrio Adentro': La Corte Primera de lo Contencioso Administrativo ante la Sala Constitucional del Tribunal Supremo de Justicia o el avocamiento como medio de amparo de derechos e intereses colectivos y difusos," in *Revista de Derecho Público* 93–96, Editorial Jurídica Venezolana, Caracas 2003, 5ff.

[98]See Allan R. Brewer-Carías, "La progresiva y sistemática demolición institucional de la autonomía e independencia del Poder Judicial en Venezuela 1999–2004" in *XXX Jornadas J.M. Domínguez Escovar, Estado de derecho, Administración de justicia y derechos humanos,* Instituto de Estudios Jurídicos del Estado Lara, Barquisimeto 2005, 33-174; "La justicia sometida al poder (La ausencia de independencia y autonomía de los jueces en Venezuela por la interminable emergencia del poder judicial (1999-2006)," in *Cuestiones internacionales. Anuario Jurídico Villanueva 2007,* Centro Universitario Villanueva, Marcial Pons, Madrid 2007, 25-57.

Convention on Human Rights and Venezuela's international obligations,[99] the Constitutional Chamber upheld the government's argument that the decision of the Inter-American Court could not be enforced in Venezuela.[100] This is one of the leading cases that clearly show the subordination of the Venezuelan judiciary to the policies, wishes, and dictates of the president. In December 2009, another astonishing case was the detention of a criminal judge (María Lourdes Afiuni Mora) for having ordered the release from detention of a banker in order for him to face criminal trial while in freedom. The decision was based on a previous recommendation of the UN Working Group on Arbitrary Detention. The same day of the decision, the president publicly asked for the judge to be incarcerated, asking to apply to the judge a 30–year prison term, which is the maximum punishment for horrendous or grave crimes. The judge has remained in detention without trial.[101]

4. *The Constitutional Base for Militarism*

The 1999 Constitution substantially departed from the provisions of the 1961 Constitution regarding the national security and defense system and the military. The 1961 Constitution contained three provisions on the subject: Article 131, prohibiting the simultaneous exercise of civilian and military authority by any public official other than the president as commander–in–chief of the armed forces; Article 132, referring to the general regulation of the armed forces subjected to civil government; and Article 133, establishing restrictions regarding the possession of arms.

The 1999 Constitution, on the contrary, gave a marked militarist shape to the state, with board provisions regarding not only the military but also the security and defense system – without precedent in Venezuelan constitutionalism.

Article 322 of the 1999 Constitution states that the security of the nation falls within the essential competence and responsibility of the state, founded on the state's "integral development." The defense of the state is the responsibility of Venezuelans and of all natural and legal persons,

---

[99]See Decision of Aug. 5, 2008 (Case: *Apitz Barbera y otros ("Corte Primera de lo Contencioso Administrativo") vs. Venezuela*) at http://www.corteidh.or.cr. Excepción Preliminar, Fondo, Reparaciones y Costas, Serie C, N° 182.

[100]See the Constitutional Chamber Decision N° 1939 (Dec. 12, 2008).

[101]On Dec. 16, a panel of three independent UN human rights experts described the case as "a blow by President Hugo Chávez to the independence of judges and lawyers in the country," demanding the immediate freedom of the judge. Available at http://www.unog.ch/unog/website/news_media.nsf/%28httpNewsByYear_en%29/93687E8429BD53A1C125768E00529DB6?OpenDocument&cntxt=B35C3&cookielang=fr. In July 2010, the judge was still in detention without trial.

whether of public or private law, found within the geographic territory of the state.

In addition, Article 326 sets forth the general principles of national security, declaring that its preservation in "economic, social, political, cultural, geographic, environmental and military areas" mutually corresponds ("co-responsibility") to the state and to civil society, to fulfill the principles of "independence, democracy, equality, peace, liberty, justice, solidarity, promotion and conservation of the environment, the affirmation of human rights, and the progressive satisfaction of the individual and collective needs of Venezuelans on the basis of sustainable and productive development fully covering the national community." All those principles are also enumerated in Articles 1, 2, and 3 of the 1999 Constitution. To implement the principles of national security in the country's territorial border regions, Article 327 provides for the establishment of a special regime.

Also, the Constitution created a new council, the National Council of Defense (Article 323), the nation's highest authority for defense planning, advice, and consultation to the state (public powers) on all matters related to the defense and security of the nation's sovereignty, territorial integrity, and strategy. The president presides over the council, which also includes the executive vice president, the president of the National Assembly, the president of the Supreme Tribunal of Justice, the president of the Moral Republican Council (citizens' branch of government; Article 237), ministers of the defense sectors (interior security, foreign relations, and planning), and others whose participation is considered pertinent.

The Constitution integrated the traditional national armed forces (the army, the navy, the air force, and the national guard) into a single institution, the National Armed Force, called since the 2008 reform of the Organic Law on the Armed Force, the "Bolivarian Armed Force." Article 328 establishes that each unit works within its area of competence to fulfill its mission and with its own system of social security, as established by its respective organic legislation. The said 2008 reform of the Organic Law also created a new component of the Bolivarian Armed Force, the "Bolivarian Militia," which has been organized as a sort of personal guard of the president.

It must be mentioned that it was in the 2007 constitutional–reform project that the president proposed to change the name of the armed forces to the Bolivarian Armed Force, to create a Bolivarian military doctrine, to establish the Bolivarian Popular Militia as a new component of the armed forces, and to eliminate the character of the armed forces as an "essential professional institution, without political militancy," converting it into "an essentially patriotic, popular and anti-imperialist corp[s]." Despite the fact that those constitutional–reform proposals were rejected by popular referendum, the president approved all the proposed reforms, six months after the popular rejection, in the July 2008 Organic Law of the Bolivarian Armed Force issued through delegate legislation.[102]

According to Article 329 of the Constitution, the army, navy, air force, and national guard each has essential responsibilities for planning, executing, and controlling military operations necessary to ensure the defense of the nation. The national guard, however, has only a cooperative role in those functions and a basic responsibility to carry out operations necessary to maintain internal order in the country. The Constitution also establishes that the armed forces can carry out police administrative activities and criminal investigations as authorized by law.

As aforementioned, Article 328 of the Constitution defines the character of the armed forces as an essentially professional institution, without a militant political function, organized by the state to guarantee the independence and sovereignty of the nation and to ensure the integrity of the nation's geographic space by means of military defense and cooperation in the maintenance of internal order, as well as active participation in national development. According to the wording of Article 328, to fulfill those functions, the armed forces are at the exclusive service of the nation and in no case may be at the service of any particular person or political partiality. The foundations of the armed forces are discipline, obedience, and subordination.

The 1999 Constitution failed to provide for the "apolitical and non-deliberative" character of the armed forces established in Article 132 of the Constitution of 1961; it has no provision establishing the essential obligation of the armed forces to ensure "the stability of the democratic institutions" or "respect the Constitution and laws, the adherence which is above any other obligation," as was declared in Article 132 of the 1961 Constitution. Where the 1999 Constitution was innovative on these matters was in giving the military the right to vote (Article 325).

In addition, the Constitution established the general regime applicable to military promotions, providing that they are to be based on merit, seniority, and availability of vacancies and are the exclusive competence of the National Armed Force (Article 331). Consequently, the traditional intervention of the legislative branch in approving promotions of high-

---

[102] See Organic Law on the Bolivarian Armed Force, *Gaceta Oficial* N° 5.933, Extra. Oct. 21, 2009.

ranking military officials (Article 150.5, 1961 Constitution) was eliminated.

These constitutional provisions conform to a normative framework with clear marks of a militarist structure, thus "expanding the military's role in Venezuelan politics."[103] When combined with the tendency to centralize state power and concentrate power in the president, the result is a system that unfortunately has led to authoritarianism. In particular, in the 1999 Constitution's provisions on military matters, the idea of the subjection or subordination of military authority to civilian authority has disappeared; instead, what has been consecrated is a greater autonomy of the National Armed Force, whose four branches (and, since 2008, five branches) have been unified into one institution with the possibility of intervention in civilian functions. All these provisions paint a picture of militarism, unique in Venezuelan constitutional history, not even found in former military regimes, which has led to a global takeover of the civil administration of the state by the military, conducted by the president, himself as a retired officer. This has lead to the creation of the already mentioned Bolivarian militia (reserve force)[104] directly controlled by the president, tending toward the effective consolidation of a military party.

---

[103] See Deborah L. Norden, "Democracy in Uniform: Chávez and the Venezuelan Armed Forces," in *Venezuelan Politics in the Chávez Era: Class, Polarization & Conflicts*, eds. Steve Ellner and Daniel Hellinger, Lynne Rienner Publishers, London 2003, 99.

[104] The 2007 draft constitutional reforms proposed a new component of the armed forces: the Popular Bolivarian Militia. See *Proyecto de Reforma Constitucional. Elaborado por el ciudadano Presidente de la República Bolivariana de Venezuela, Hugo Chávez Frías,* Editorial Atenea, Caracas 2007, 58. Although rejected by the people, the proposal was implemented through the reform of the Organic Law on the Bolivarian Armed Force, *Gaceta Oficial* 5.933, Extra. Oct. 21, 2009.

Chapter 4

THE 1999 SOCIAL AND ECONOMIC CONSTITUTION AND ITS PROBLEMS

The second part of every constitution in modern constitutionalism, as supreme law, is composed by the regulations referred to as constitutional rights and guarantees, including social rights, and to regulate from the economic and social point of view the relation between state and society.

The 1999 Constitution had signs of advances not only in the extensive enumeration of individual, social, economic, cultural, and environmental rights but also in the incorporation of international treaties on human rights, with preferential application when providing for a more favorable regime regarding internal law (Article 23). On economic matters, the Constitution has established a general framework for the development of a system of mixed economy, allowing important participation of the state, which has been used during the past decade in order to construct a capitalism of state system, through confiscation and expropriation of public property and enterprises. I refer in this chapter to this socioeconomic framework of the 1999 Constitution, as well as to the general values and principles on the matter declared in its text.

I. CONSTITUTIONAL VALUES AND DECLARATIVE PRINCIPLES

The 1999 Constitution formally establishes the general trends of a democratic regime and the rule of law, defining the country as a social democratic state of law and justice (*estado democrático y social de derecho y de justicia*) (Article 2) and declaring that the rule of law (*estado de derecho*) is the state submitted to the "empire of the Law." The Constitution also includes the principle of "supremacy of the Constitution" (Article 7), which submits all state entities to the Constitution and the laws (Article 137). It also establishes a complete judicial review system to ensure constitutionality (Articles 334 and 336) and legality of all state acts and actions (Article 259) (constitutional jurisdiction and administrative contentious jurisdiction).

On matters of principles and values, the 1999 Venezuelan Constitution is one of the recent Constitutions in the contemporary world containing not only an extensive amount of articles devoted to enumerating human rights (120) but also a rich text full of values, principles, and global declarations. It has, perhaps, one of the most florid constitutional wordings that can be found in constitutional texts,[1] establishing its axiological foundations, which in principle are set forth for the National Assembly and all branches of government, and particularly by the courts, to follow. For such purposes, the Constitutional Chamber of the Supreme Tribunal of Justice has said that the Constitution is "an instrument with legal spirit that connects, according to the nature of the applicable precept, both the bodies of the State and the individuals" and that imposes constitutional juridical situations "with reference to indispensable values for the assurance of the human freedom, equality and dignity" guaranteed by the judiciary.[2]

The global values that are declared in the Constitution are those "values generally share[d] by the society" as "declarations of intent" that "have an indubitable value, both for the bodies of the State that must be guided by them, and for the judges."[3] For such purposes, as ruled by the same Constitutional Chamber, "Constitutions are, among other things, texts in which 'legally organized societies regulate their structures and functioning, and determine the scope of the citizen rights and the public authorities' powers"; they also are texts "in which the wishes of this same society are exposed – sometimes difficult to satisfy – and the means that have been created to satisfy them...The diverse duties that the State assumes are orders that must be executed. A text lacking of compulsory

---

[1] See Allan R. Brewer-Carías, *La Constitución de 1999. Derecho Constitucional Venezolano*, 2 vols., Editorial Jurídica Venezolana, Caracas 2004; Hildegard Rondón de Sansó, *Análisis de la Constitución Venezolana de 1999*, Editorial Ex Libris, Caracas 2001; Ricardo Combellas, *Derecho constitucional: Una introducción al estudio de la Constitución de la República Bolivariana de Venezuela*, McGraw Hill, Caracas 2001; Alfonso Rivas Quintero, *Derecho constitucional*, Paredes Editores, Valencia 2002.

[2] See Decision N° 963 (June 5, 2001). Case: *José A. Guía y otros vs. Ministerio de Infraestructura*, in *Revista de Derecho Público* 85–88, Editorial Jurídica Venezolana, Caracas 2001, 447.

[3] See Constitutional Chamber Decision N° 1278 (June 17, 2005). Case: *Aclaratoria de la sentencia de interpretación de los artículos 156, 180 y 302 de la Constitución*, in *Revista de Derecho Público* 102, Editorial Jurídica Venezolana, Caracas 2005, 56ff.

character for its addressees (public authorities and individuals) would be of little use."[4]

Constitutional values in the Venezuelan Constitution are expressed not only in the preamble but also in many of its articles – where they are enumerated in a formal way – as goals to guide the state, the society, and individuals' general conduct.[5] Consequently, in Venezuela, global values and principles derive not only from the courts' interpretation and application of the Constitution but also from what is set forth expressly in the Constitution itself.[6]

The values expressed in the 1999 Constitution apply to the state (the republic, the nation), its organization (distribution of state powers and branches of government) and its functioning (government and public administration), and to the legal system. In that sense, the preamble of the Constitution begins by declaring that the representatives of the Venezuelan people adopted it aiming to achieve a series of goals "guided by social, economical, political and judicial values"[7] and to inspire the action of the state, "which must respond to equalitarian, international, democratic, moral and historical principles."

The state is defined as a "State of justice, federal and decentralized," that must enforce the values of "freedom, independence, peace, solidarity, common good, territorial integrity, cohabitation and the empire of the law, for these and all future generations," in a society that is "democratic, participatory, multiethnic and multicultural." The latter is confirmed, for instance, by the express recognition in the Constitution of the indigenous populations' status (Articles 119–126).

The goals constitute, without a doubt, the fundamental principles and constitutional values that inspire the constitutional text as a whole. As such, they have the same binding and constitutional rigidity as constitutional provisions and, consequently, are enforceable. As affirmed by the Constitutional Chamber of the Supreme Tribunal, "The statutes must have

---

[4]See Case: *Aclaratoria de la sentencia de interpretación de los artículos 156, 180 y 302 de la Constitución*, Decision N° 1278 (June 17, 2005), in *Revista de Derecho Público* 102, Editorial Jurídica Venezolana, Caracas 2005, 56ff.

[5]See Allan R. Brewer-Carías, "La constitucionalización del derecho administrativo," in *Derecho administrativo*, Universidad Externado de Colombia, Bogotá 2005, 1:215ff.

[6]See Allan R. Brewer-Carías, *Principios fundamentales del derecho público*, Editorial Jurídica Venezolana, Caracas 2005.

[7]On the nature of the preamble and its constitutional value, see the decision of the former Supreme Court of Justice, Political-Administrative Chamber (Aug. 8, 1989), in *Revista de Derecho Público* 39, Editorial Jurídica Venezolana, Caracas 1989, 102.

those values as their purpose, so those that do not follow them or that are contrary to those objectives, become unconstitutional."[8]

Besides the values guiding the configuration of the state declared in the preamble, the Constitution also enumerates the following as superior values of the legal system and of all state activity: "life, freedom, justice, equality, solidarity, democracy, social responsibility and, in general, the preeminence of the human rights, the ethics and the political pluralism" (Article 2).

Additionally, the Constitution identifies "the defense and the development of the individual and the respect of his or her dignity, the democratic exercise of the popular will, the construction of a fair and peace–loving society, the promotion of the prosperity and well-being of the people and the guaranty of the fulfillment of all principles, rights and duties recognized and enshrined in the Constitution" as essential goals of the state. It considers "education and work" fundamental processes to reach those ends (Article 3).

However, the "refoundation of the Republic" intended by the constitutional text responded to a series of social ends specified in the preamble, ensuring "the right to a life, work, culture, education, social justice and equality without discrimination nor subordination of any kind." Reference is also made to the social goals of society and of the state to achieve "social justice." Social justice is also mentioned as a fundamental social goal, the assurance of "equality without discrimination or subordination of any kind."

Referring to the republic, the Constitution expressly emphasizes a few fundamental values. In addition to the already-mentioned values of freedom, equality, justice, and international peace, there is the principle that the nation's rights ("independence, freedom, sovereignty, immunity, territorial integrity and the national self-determination"; Article 1) cannot be renounced or abandoned.

Regarding public administration, the Constitution provides that it must be "at the service of the people," enumerating the following principles and values on which it must be based: "honesty, participation, celerity, efficiency, effectiveness, transparency, the accounting and responsibility in the execution of the public function, with complete subjection to the statutes and to the Law" (Article 141).

---

[8] See Case: *Deudores hipotecarios vs. Superintendencia de Bancos*, in *Revista de Derecho Público* 89–92, Editorial Jurídica Venezolana, Caracas 2002, 94ff.

As for the bodies of the electoral power, the Constitution enumerates the following principles that must be guaranteed in electoral processes: "equality, reliability, impartiality, transparency and efficiency," as well as "personalization of the vote and . . . proportional representation" (Article 293).

With respect to public services corresponding to the state, the Constitution enumerates a series of governing principles. For instance, the national public health system must be "inter-sectorial, decentralized and participative, and managed by the principles of gratuitousness, universality, integrality, impartiality, social integration and solidarity" (Article 84). Moreover, the social security system must be "universal, integral, of solidarity, unitary, [and] efficient and [have] participative financing, from direct or indirect contributions" (Article 86). The Constitution expresses that education must be "democratic, free and mandatory, based on the respect to all thought tendencies, in order to develop the creative potential of every human being and the complete exercise of his/her personality inside a democratic society based on the ethical valuation of the labor and the active, conscientious and solidarity participation in the processes of social transformation related with the values of the national identity and with a Latin American and universal vision" (Article 102).

With respect to socioeconomics, the Constitution enumerates the following principles on which the system must be based: "social justice, democracy, efficiency, free competition, environment protection, productivity and solidarity, in order to guarantee the integral human development, a dignified and prosperous existence for the collectivity, the generation of labor sources, high national added value, elevation of the standard of living of the people and to strengthen the economical supremacy of the country, guaranteeing juridical security, stability, dynamism, supportability, permanence and equity of the economy growth, in order to achieve a fair distribution of the wealth by means of a democratic, participative and of open consultation strategic planning" (Article 299). In particular, the Constitution states the principles that must rule fiscal management: "efficiency, solvency, transparency, responsibility and fiscal balance" (Article 311). Taxation must be ruled by the following principles: "progressiveness, protection of the national economy and the elevation of the standard of living of the population" (Article 316).

With respect to international relations, the preamble also mentions "peaceful cooperation between nations" as one of the goals of the state, which implies the commitment to look for peaceful solutions of controversies and the rejection of war. Peaceful cooperation must be executed in accordance with the principle of nonintervention in the affairs of other countries and with the principle of self-determination of the people. Also, it is said in the Preamble that international cooperation must be carried out "according to the universal and indivisible guarantee of human rights and the democratization of the international society."

The Preamble also refers to other values that must guide the international relations of the republic, like "nuclear disarmament, ecological balance and environment," which is considered as a "common and nonrenounceable patrimony of humanity." In particular, according to the Preamble, another fundamental goal that must guide the state's actions is "the impulse and consolidation of the Latin-American integration" also mentioned in Article 153.

But the fact has been that, despite all the constitutional values and principles, in political practice, they have been distorted. During the past decade, an authoritarian, militaristic, and centralized state has taken shape, based in populist policies of socialist trends. That state has demolished the principles of rule of law, separation of powers, and federation (decentralization). Thus, it has weakened the effectiveness of the protection of constitutional rights by subjecting the judicial review system and other checks and balances to the executive and by progressively destroying representative democracy itself in the name of participatory democracy.

In this sense, also, in Decision No. 23 (January 22, 2003) on the constitutional interpretation of Article 71 of the Constitution, the Constitutional Chamber of the Supreme Tribunal transformed the values incorporated in the Constitution into provisions subjected to the interpretation by the politically controlled constitutional judge. That is, the decision put aside the universal meaning of the values, considering that: "to interpret the legal system according to the Constitution, means to protect the Constitution itself from every diversion of principles and from every separation from the political project that it embodies by will of the people."[9] The Constitutional Chamber also said:

> [A] system of principles, assumed to be absolute and supra historical, cannot be placed above the Constitution, nor that its interpretation could eventually contradict the political theory that supports it. From this perspective, any theory that proposes absolute rights or goals must be rejected and,…the interpretation or integration [of the Constitution] must

---

[9] Case: *Interpretación del artículo 71 de la Constitución*, in *Revista de Derecho Público*, N° 93-96, Editorial Jurídica Venezolana, Caracas 2003, 107.

be done according to the living culture tradition whose sense and scope depend on the specific and historical analysis of the values shared by the Venezuelan people. Part of the protection and guarantee of the Constitution is established then, in an *in fieri* politic perspective, reluctant to the ideological connection with theories that can limit, under pretext of universal validities, the supremacy and the national self-determination, as demanded in article 1° *eiusdem*.[10]

This doctrine of subjecting global constitutional values to a political project – as in the previous case – was ratified in Decision No. 1,939 (December 18, 2009) (Case *Gustavo Álvarez Arias y otros*).[11] In that case, the Constitutional Chamber declared a decision of the Inter-American Court of Human Rights to be unenforceable in Venezuela of August 5, 2008 (*Apitz Barbera et al. [Corte Primera de lo Contencioso Administrativo] vs. Venezuela*) condemning the republic for violating the rights of dismissed judges,[12] thus rejecting the existence of values superior to those of the Venezuelan government. The chamber argued that the legal order "is a normative theory at the service of politic defined in the axiological project of the Constitution"; that the standard for resolving conflicts between principles and provisions must be "compatible with the political project of the Constitution," and such provisions "cannot be affected with interpretations that could give prevalence to individual rights or that could give prevalence to the international order regarding the national one affecting the State sovereignty"; that no system of principles "supposedly absolute and supra-historic can be placed above the Constitution"; and that "theories based on universal values that pretend to limit the sovereignty and national auto-determination are unacceptable."[13]

---

[10]Case: *Interpretación del artículo 71 de la Constitución*, in *Revista de Derecho Público*, N° 93-96, Editorial Jurídica Venezolana, Caracas 2003, 107-108 and 530-33.

[11]See http://www.tsj.gov.ve/decisiones/scon/Diciembre/1939-181208-2008-08-1572.html.

[12]Inter-American Court of Human Rights, *Apitz Barbera et al. (Corte Primera de lo Contencioso Administrativo) v. Venezuela* (Judgment of Aug. 5, 2008), *available at* www.corteidh.or.cr.

[13]See http://www.tsj.gov.ve/decisiones/scon/Diciembre/1939-181208-2008-08-1572.html.

II. THE GENERAL FRAMEWORK ON MATTERS OF HUMAN RIGHTS

1. *General Declarations*

One of the main values declared in the Constitution is "human dignity," considered by the courts "as inherent to the human condition" and existing "before the State"; all branches of government need to be "at the service of the human being."[14] This implies not only the existence of constitutional rights considered "inherent to human beings" but also the emergence of the "principle of progressiveness" in their interpretation and enforcement expressly adopted in the constitutional text (Article 19). According to the criteria of the Constitutional Chamber of the Supreme Tribunal, in this regard, the courts have an obligation "to interpret the entire legal system in the light of the Right of the Constitution . . . which also means that they have to interpret the system congruently with the fundamental rights or human rights, that must be respected above all, making a progressive and complete interpretation."[15]

The Constitution refers to this value in many articles, when guaranteeing to anybody deprived of liberty the right to be "treated with respect due to the inherent dignity of the human being" (Article 46); when guaranteeing that the judicial seizure of a person's home be made "always respecting human dignity" (Article 47); when obligating the state's security offices to always "respect the human dignity and rights of all persons" (Article 55); when establishing the duty of the State to protect senior citizens and disabled persons always respecting their "human dignity" (Articles 80 and 81); and when guaranteeing that the salary of every worker be "sufficient to enable him or her to live with dignity" (Article 91).

In that regard, the Constitutional Chamber of the Supreme Tribunal of Justice has considered human dignity "one of the values on which the Social rule of law and Justice State is based, and around which all the legal system and all the actions of the branches of government [public powers] must turn." On the basis of that approach, the Constitutional Chamber has defined human dignity in Decision 2442 (September 1, 2003) as "the supremacy that persons have as an inherent attribute of its rational being, which imposes public authorities the duty to watch for the protection and safe-conduct of the life, freedom and autonomy of men and

---

[14]See decision of the First Court of the Administrative Jurisdiction (June 1, 2000) (Case: *Julio Rocco A.*), in *Revista de Derecho Público* 82, Editorial Jurídica Venezolana, Caracas 2000, 287ff.
[15]Id.

women for the sole fact of their existence, independently of any other consideration." That is why, "the sole existence of man grants him the right to exist and to obtain all the guarantees needed to assure him a dignified life, that is, his own existence, proportional and rational to the recognition of his essence as a rational being." This concept of human dignity according to the Tribunal ruling imposes "upon the State of the duty to adopt the necessary protective measures to safeguard the legal assets that define man as a person, that is, life, integrity, freedom, autonomy."[16]

In this same sense, the Political-Administrative Chamber of the same Supreme Tribunal of Justice has specially emphasized dignity, considering it the "axiological" element representing "the ideological base that supports the dogmatic order of the current Constitution," limiting the exercise of public power, and establishing an effective judicial guarantee system." That is why this "prevalent position of human dignity," considered a "superior value of the legal system," obligates "the State and of all its bodies to protect and guarantee human rights as the main purpose and objective of its public action." Consequently, the defense and development of human dignity is considered by the Supreme Tribunal "one of the superior values of the legal system," and its "defense and development [is] one of the essential objectives of the State" (Articles 2 and 3)."[17]

Human dignity, however, implies the idea of the "preeminence of human rights" (Preamble), which according to the "principle of progressiveness" (Article 19), means that statutes must be interpreted in the most favorable way for their enjoyment. In this regard, Article 19 of the 1999 Constitution begins "Duties, Rights and Constitutional Guarantees," setting forth that the state must guarantee every person, "according to the progressiveness principle and without discrimination whatsoever, the enjoyment and nonrenounceable, indivisible and interdependent exercise

---

[16]See Decision N° 2442 (Sept. 1, 2003) (Case: *Alejandro Serrano López*) in *Revista de Derecho Público* 93–96, Editorial Jurídica Venezolana, Caracas 2003, 183ff. With this purpose, in the same Decision, the Tribunal said that Article 3 of the Constitution "establishes that the recognition of the human dignity constitutes a structural principle of the Social rule-of-law State and for that, it forbids, in its Title III, Chapter III, the forced disappearances, the degrading treatments, the tortures or cruel treatments that could harm the life as an inviolable right, the degrading punishments and all other inherent rights of the human person (Articles 43ff.)."

[17]See Decision N° 224 (Feb. 24, 2000) in *Revista de Derecho Público* 81, Editorial Jurídica Venezolana, Caracas 2000, 131ff. See also Decision 3215 of the Constitutional Chamber of the Supreme Tribunal (June 15, 2004) in *Revista de Derecho Público* 97–98, Editorial Jurídica Venezolana, Caracas 2004, 428.

of human rights." The provision adds that "the respect and the guarantee of the rights are mandatory to all State bodies in accordance with the Constitution, the treaties on human rights signed and ratified by the Republic and the statutes."[18] That is, as affirmed by the courts, "the interpretation of the corresponding constitutional provisions and any future constitutional revision, must be performed in the most favorable way for the exercise and enjoyment of the rights." Courts have added that "this principle is so important that its application obliges the State to update legislation in favor of the defense of the human rights and in view to dignify the human condition, adapting the interpretation of the norms 'to the sensibility, thought and needs of the new times' in order to adapt them to the new established order and to reject any anachronisms that opposes to their effective force." [19]

To give human dignity its complete shape, Article 23 of the 1999 Constitution granted constitutional rank to international treaties on human rights signed and ratified by Venezuela, adding that they "prevail in the internal order, when containing more favorable provisions regarding their enjoyment than those contained in the Constitution and the laws of the Republic." This means that they have supraconstitutional rank when containing more favorable provisions regarding the exercise of rights. The same article provides for the immediate and direct application of treaties by the state bodies, particularly courts.[20] The inclusion of such provisions

---

[18] About this principle, the Constitutional Chamber of the Supreme Tribunal of Justice, quoting Article 2 of the American Convention on Human Rights, in Decision N° 1154 (June 29, 2001), based on the same principle, has ruled that it is necessary "to adapt the legal system in order to ensure the efficiency of said rights, being unacceptable the excuse of the inexistence or unsuitability of the means provided in the internal order for their protection and application." See *Revista de Derecho Público* 85–88, Editorial Jurídica Venezolana, Caracas 2001, 111ff.

[19] In this sense, the First Court of the Administrative Jurisdiction has considered its obligation "to interpret the entire legal system in the light of the Right of the Constitution, even more, when acting in exercise of the constitutional power for protection, which also means, that we have to interpret the system congruently with the fundamental rights or human rights, that must be respected above all, making a progressive and complete interpretation." See Decision from June 1, 2000 (Case: *Julio Rocco A.*), in *Revista de Derecho Público* 82, Editorial Jurídica Venezolana, Caracas 2000, 287ff.

[20] The Constitutional Court of the Supreme Tribunal has, for instance, applied this provision regarding due process, applying preferentially Article 8 of the American Convention on Human Rights. See the Decision from Mar. 14, 2000 (Case: *C.A. Electricidad del Centro y C.A. Electricidad de los Andes*), in *Revista de Derecho Publico* 81, Editorial Jurídica Venezolana, Caracas 2000, 157-58; quoted in Decision N° 328 (Mar. 9, 2001), of the same chamber, in *Revista de Derecho Publico* 85–88, Editorial Jurídica Venezolana, Caracas 2001, 108. The Political-Administrative Chamber of the Supreme Tribunal interpreted and developed the criteria established by the Constitutional Chamber regarding the lack of applications of Article 185 of the Organic Law of the Supreme Court of Justice in Decision N° 802 (Apr. 13, 2000) (Case: *Elecentro vs. Superintendencia Procompetencia*), in *Revista de Derecho Publico* 82, Editorial Jurídica Venezolana, Caracas 2000, 270. On a similar matter, see also Decision N° 449 (Mar. 27, 2001) (Case: *Dayco de Construcciones*

in the Constitution was a significant advancement in protecting human rights.

However, to reinforce the constitutional value of human dignity, the human rights that are guaranteed and protected are not only the ones enumerated in the Constitution but also those that, although not enumerated, are considered "inherent to the human person" (Article 22).[21] That is why the last phrase of Article 22 establishes that "the lack of regulatory statutes regarding human rights do not diminish their exercise"; that is, their application "cannot be conditioned by the existence of a statute developing it; and on the contrary, the lack of legal instruments regulating them, do not diminish their exercise, being such rights of immediate and direct application by the courts and all other bodies of the State" (Articles 22 and 23).[22]

But in light of these progressive provisions, in practice, the supraconstitutional rank that the Constitution has given to international instruments of human rights and to their direct and immediate and direct application by all courts has been curtailed. In effect, contrary to the provision of Article 23 of the Constitution, in judicial practice and particularly regarding the provisions of the American Convention on Human Rights, the doctrine of the Supreme Tribunal also has been progressively restrictive, eventually rejecting the supraconstitutional rank of international instruments of human rights. This restrictive approach by the Constitutional Chamber that has affected the role to be played on matters of international protection of human rights by the Inter-American institutions, began with a decision dated May 5, 2000, in which the Constitutional Chamber objected to the "quasi-jurisdictional" powers of the Inter-American Commission in issuing provisional protective measures regarding a state, qualifying them as "unacceptable." The Constitutional Chamber stated that they "impl[y] a gross intrusion in the country Judiciary, like the suspension of the judicial proceeding against the

---

vs. INOS) in *Revista de Derecho Publico* 85–88, Editorial Jurídica Venezolana, Caracas 2001. Nonetheless, the Political-Administrative Chamber has denied giving prevalence to Article 8 of the American Convention regarding requests by corporate persons, understanding that the convention refers only to the "human" rights of individuals. See Decision N° 278 (Mar. 1, 2001), in *Revista de Derecho Publico* 85–88, Editorial Jurídica Venezolana, Caracas 2001, 104.

[21] This open clause is more extensive than the original wording of the U.S. Constitution (Amendment 9), in that it refers to rights and guarantees not enumerated in the Constitution and also in the international instruments on human rights, which creates a truly unlimited cast of unstated but protected rights inherent to the human person.

[22] See Decision N° 723 (May 15, 2001) in *Revista de Derecho Público* 85–88, Editorial Jurídica Venezolana, Caracas 2001, 111.

plaintiff, measures that can only be adopted by the judges exercising their judicial attributions and independence, according to what is stated in the Constitution and the statutes of the Republic."[23]

This unfortunate ruling questioned the superior role of the international institutions on matters of human rights and can be considered contrary to Article 31 of the Constitution, which establishes the right of everybody to bring before international institutions on human rights, precisely the Inter-American Commission on Human Rights, petitions or complaints to seek protection (*amparo*) of their violated constitutional rights.

The restrictive approach regarding the role and value of international institutions for the protection of human rights was also applied in Decision No. 1942 (July 15, 2003) (Case: *Impugnación de artículos del Código Penal, Leyes de desacato*),[24] in which the Constitutional Chamber, in referring to international courts, stated that "in Venezuela, in general, in relation to Article 7 of the Constitution, no jurisdictional organ could exist above the Supreme Tribunal of Justice, and even in such case, its decisions when contradicting constitutional provisions are unapplicable in the country." The restrictive approach on the matter has finished with Decision No. 1939 of December 18, 2008 (Case *Abogados Gustavo Álvarez Arias y otros*), in which the Constitutional Chamber declared unenforceable a decision of the Inter-American Court of Human Rights. The decision of the Inter-American Court of August 5, 2008 (Case *Apitz Barbera y otros ["Corte Primera de lo Contencioso Administrativo"] vs. Venezuela*)[25] condemned the Venezuelan state for violating the judicial guarantees of three former judges of the First Contentious Administrative Court, who were dismissed by a special commission of the Supreme Tribunal. The Constitutional Chamber rejected the supraconstitutional character of the provisions of the American Convention on Human Rights, considering that in the case of contradiction of a provision of the Constitution and a provision of an international treaty, the judiciary will determine applicable provisions. [26]

---

[23]See Case: *Faitha M. Nahmens L. y Ben Ami Fihman Z.* (*Revista Exceso*), Exp. N° 00-0216, Decision N° 386 (May 17, 2000). See Carlos Ayala Corao, "Recepción de la jurisprudencia internacional sobre derechos humanos por la jurisprudencia constitucional," *Revista del Tribunal Constitucional* 6, Sucre, Bolivia 2004, 275ff.

[24]See *Revista de Derecho Público* 93–96, Editorial Jurídica Venezolana, Caracas 2003, 136ff.

[25]See http://www.corteidh.or.cr. Excepción Preliminar, Fondo, Reparaciones y Costas, Serie C, N° 182.

[26]See http://www.tsj.gov.ve/decisiones/scon/Diciembre/1939-181208-2008-08-1572.html.

The result has been that on the basis of sovereignty principles, the decisions adopted by international courts cannot be considered enforceable in Venezuela, except if they accord with what is stated in the Constitution as interpreted by the Constitutional Chamber. Thus, the Constitutional Chamber has eliminated the supraconstitutional rank of treaties that establish more favorable human rights regulations. The Constitutional Chamber has assumed an absolute monopoly over constitutional interpretation to determine when a treaty provision prevails in the internal order–power that, according to the Constitution, the Constitutional Chamber does not have.

This political-positivistic conception of the Constitution unfortunately leaves interpretation of the very rich constitutional values and principles extensively enumerated in the Constitution, and of the Constitution itself, to the mercy of the Constitutional Chamber. Because it unfortunately is controlled by the executive,[27] this implies the rejection of the power of all courts established in Article 23 of the Constitution to apply in a direct and immediate way to international instruments on human rights to resolve judicial cases. The Constitutional Chamber has established, contrary to the intention of the Constituent Assembly,[28] its own monopoly to interpret when a constitutional provision is of immediate application and, particularly, when its content is justiciable.[29] In Decision No. 1942 of July 7, 2003,[30] the Constitutional Chamber ruled that once the provisions of the international instruments have been incorporated to the constitutional hierarchy, "the maximum and last interpreter of them [including international instruments] regarding internal law, is the Constitutional Chamber, which must determine the content and scope of the constitutional norms and principles" (Article 335). From that proposition,

---

[27]See Allan R. Brewer-Carías, "El juez constitucional al servicio del autoritarismo y la ilegítima mutación de la constitución: El caso de la Sala Constitucional del Tribunal Supremo de Justicia de Venezuela (1999-2009)," in *Revista de Administración Pública* 180, Centro de Estudios Políticos y Constitucionales, Madrid 2009, 383-418.

[28]Allan R. Brewer-Carías, "Quis Custodiet ipsos Custodes: De la interpretación constitucional a la inconstitucionalidad de la interpretación," in *VIII Congreso Nacional de derecho Constitucional, Perú,* Fondo Editorial 2005, Colegio de Abogados de Arequipa, Arequipa, Sept. 2005, 463-89.

[29]See Case: *Aclaratoria de la sentencia de interpretación de los artículos 156, 180 y 302 de la Constitución,* Decision N° 1278 (June 17, 2005), in *Revista de Derecho Público* 102, Editorial Jurídica Venezolana, Caracas 2005, 56ff. The Constitutional Chamber ruled in Decision N° 332 (Mar. 14, 2001) that "it is the constitutional jurisdiction represented by this Constitutional Chamber, who will resolve the controversies that might arise as the result of the legislatively undeveloped constitutional provisions, until the laws that regulate the constitutional jurisdiction decide otherwise." See Case: *INSACA vs. Ministerio de Sanidad y Asistencia Social,* in *Revista de Derecho Público* 85–88, Editorial Jurídica Venezolana, Caracas 2001, 492.

[30]See *Revista de Derecho Público* 93–96, Editorial Jurídica Venezolana, Caracas 2003, 136ff.

the Constitutional Chamber concluded that "the Constitutional Chamber [is] the only one that determines which norms on human rights contained in treaties, covenants and conventions prevail in the internal legal order; as well as which human rights nonincorporated in such international instruments have effects in Venezuela." It concluded:

> This power of the Constitutional Chamber on the matter, derived from the Constitution, and cannot be diminished by adjective norms contained in the treaties or in other international texts on human rights subscribed by the country, which allows the States parties to ask international institutions for the interpretation of rights referred to in the Convention or covenant, as it is established in Article 64 of the Approbatory statute of the American Convention of Human Rights, San José Covenant, because otherwise, the situation would be of a constitutional amendment, without following the constitutional procedures, diminishing the powers of the Constitutional Chamber, transferring it to international or transnational bodies, with the power to dictate obligatory interpretations.[31]

2. *Social Rights and the Social State*

Article 2 of the 1999 Constitution defines the Venezuelan state as one of social-democratic rule of law, in which the principle of social responsibility (Preamble) prevails in public policies, thus configuring the state as a social state, with specific social duties to society. In particular, the Constitution refers to the social goal of society and the state to ensure "social justice," guaranteeing the equitable participation of all in the enjoyment of wealth, preventing its concentration only in a few hands, avoiding unfair income differences, and seeking the guarantee of a dignified and prosperous existence for the collectivity (Articles 112 and 299).

This idea of a social state (*estado social*) refers to a state with social obligations that strive for social justice as a welfare state, which allows for its intervention in social and economic activities. Such a social character mainly derives from the fundamental constitutional value of equality and nondiscrimination, in the Preamble and Article 1, but also from Article 21, which declares these as fundamental rights; Article 2, which establishes them as the benchmark of state performance; and Article 299, which establishes social justice as the basis of the economic system.

---

[31] See *Revista de Derecho Público* 93–96, Editorial Jurídica Venezolana, Caracas 2003, 136ff.

The Constitutional Chamber of the Supreme Court – in Decision No. 85 (January, 24 2002) – defined the social state as follows: "it searches for the harmony between classes, avoiding that the dominant class, having the economic, political or cultural power, abuses and subjugates the other classes or social groups, preventing their development and submitting them to poverty and ignorance; as natural exploited without the possibility to redeem their situation." The Constitutional Chamber continued:

> The Social State must protect people or groups that regarding others are in a situation of legal weakness, regardless of the principle of equality before the law, which in practice does not resolve anything, because unequal situations cannot be treated with similar solutions. In order to achieve the balance, the Social State not only intervenes in the labor and social security factor, protecting the salaried workers nonrelated to the economical or political power, but it also protects their health, housing, education and economical relations. That is why the Economic Constitution must be seen from an essentially social perspective. . . .
>
> The State is obligated to protect the weak, defend their interests protected by the Constitution, particularly through the courts; and regarding the strong, its duty is to watch that their freedom is not a load for everybody. As a juridical value, there cannot be constitutional protection at the expense of the fundamental rights of others. . . .
>
> The Social State tries to harmonize the antagonistic interests of society, without allowing unlimited actions from social forces, based on the silence of the statutes or their ambiguities, because otherwise that would lead to the establishment of an hegemony over the weak by those economically and socially stronger, in which the private power positions become an excessive diminution of the real freedom of the weak, in a subjugation that constantly encourages the social crisis.[32]

Regarding solidarity as the social state's goal, it tends to reaffirm that people have social and community duties in addition to rights. Thus, the right of each individual necessarily finds its limits and boundaries in the right of others (Article 20). "Common good" ensures the satisfaction of all individual and collective needs, where the latter take priority over the former, which also implies that reasons of public and social order can always limit individual rights (Article 20).

---

[32] See Case: *Deudores hipotecarios vs. Superintendencia de Bancos*, in *Revista de Derecho Público* 89–92, Editorial Jurídica Venezolana, Caracas 2002, 94ff.

On the basis of this conception of the social state, the Constitution contains very extensive declarations of social rights,[33] including family and social protection, health and social security, labor, education and culture, environment, and indigenous peoples' rights. However in many cases, the declarations are more aims or public policy regarding social welfare than specific justiciable rights. In effect, an essential principle of constitutional rank in the establishment of human rights is the altering principle, which implies that every right carries an obligation, and that everyone who is entitled to a right must have a relation with somebody who has a correlative obligation. Therefore, there are no rights without obligations. So, the establishment of rights that do not create obligations are no more than declarations of principles or intent.

This has happened with several social rights and guarantees as established in the Constitution whose satisfaction is simply impossible. Rather, they are indubitably teleological declarations of principles and intent, and they hardly can be considered constitutional rights: Nobody is or can be obliged to satisfy them. The right to health, for example, is established as a fundamental social right; the state is obligated by it and guarantees it as "part of the right to life" (Article 83). But, in fact, it is impossible that someone could guarantee somebody's health and that the right to health could be constitutionally established. The wording used in the article is incorrect because the Constitution, of course, cannot establish the right to not get sick, which is impossible. The right that, for instance, can be established and is in fact established is the constitutional right to health care, which is the one that could obligate the state to establish and provide public services of preventive and curative medicine that can be judicially claimed, including by means of amparo actions.

The same can be said of the right established in the Constitution in favor of "every person" "to an adequate, secure, comfortable, hygienic house with essential basic services that include a habitat that makes more human the familiar, neighboring and community relations" (Article 82). In the way it is established, this "right" is more a definition of public policy beautifully structured than a "right" that does not lead to anyone being obligated to satisfy. The wording that was used in the Constitution was

---

[33]See Mercedes Pulido de Briceño, "La Constitución de 1999 y los derechos sociales," in *La cuestión social en la Constitución Bolivariana de Venezuela,* Editorial Torino, Caracas 2000, 15-28; Carlos Aponte Blank, "Los derechos sociales y la Constitución de 1999," in id., 113-34; Emilio Spósito Contreras, "Aproximación a los derechos sociales en la Constitución de la República Bolivariana de Venezuela," in *Revista de derecho del Tribunal Supremo de Justicia* 9, Caracas 2003, 381-98.

also incorrect, for instance, regarding the case of the right to social security (Article 86), conceived more as a political aim than a justiciable right, except if it exists in a particular link based on legislation on social security between a person and a social public service, in order to claim some benefits. In this matter, in many cases, good intentions and social declarations were mistaken with constitutional rights and obligations that create other types of legal relations.

On the other hand, in regulating social rights, the Constitution puts in the state's hands excessive burdens, obligations, and guarantees in many cases of impossible compliance and execution; in parallel minimizing, and even excluding, private initiatives. In this way, public services, essentially and traditionally concurrent between the state and individuals, such as education, health care, and social security, are regulated with a marked state–exclusive accent, which in practice has curtailed private initiatives.

For example, regarding health, "to guarantee it, State will create, exercise the ruling and arrange a national public health system, . . . integrated to the social security system, ruled by principles of free health, universality, comprehensiveness, equity, social integration and solidarity" (Article 84). Therefore, this is really about a public health system, ruled as a free public service that is part of the social security system. Nothing is said in the article about private health services, even though another article indicates that the state "will regulate public and private health institutions" (Article 85).

Moreover, social security is declared a free public service. The state is obligated "to ensure the effectiveness of this right, creating a universal, comprehensive, unitary, efficient and participatory social security system of joint financing and of direct or indirect contributions." The obligatory contributions "can be administrated with social purposes under the ruling of the state" (Article 86). Thus, all private enterprise regarding social security is excluded, and private participation in the administration of pension funds is minimized.

Regarding education, the tendency is similar. Education is regulated, in general, as a human right and a fundamental social duty. It is declared "democratic, free and obligatory" and is defined as "a public service," which the state should assume as "a function that cannot be declined" (Article 102). Nothing is said of private education except that there is the people's right to "found and maintain private educational institutions under the strict inspection and surveillance of the State, previous its acceptance" (Article 106). The possibility of turning education into a state exclusive service does not have limits in the Constitution; and an article regarding the subject in the Constitution of 1961, which established that "the State will stimulate and protect private education given according to the principles established in this Constitution and laws" (Article 79), was eliminated.

3. *Limits to the Exercise of Constitutional Rights That Can Only Be Established through Statutes*

The progression characterizing the enumeration of constitutional rights has a general guarantee by establishing that any limit or restriction to their exercise can only be established by the legislator, through statutes. This means that the matter has been reserved for the National Assembly (*reserva legal*) implying the need for the sanctioning of formal statutes (laws), to limit or restrict human rights; statutes being defined in the Constitution as the acts issued by the legislative organ (National Assembly) (Article 103), which is the one integrated by representatives elected in a democratic way.

Nonetheless, this guarantee was diminished in the same 1999 Constitution, which provides for a system of delegated legislation through laws that can be decided by the National Assembly (Article 203) in a way that has no comparison with any other Latin American constitution. The system confers the possibility of the National Assembly to delegate authority on the ruling of any subject to the president, which in practice can signify the curtailment of the exhaustive list of rights established in the Constitution.

This possibility for legislative delegation by means of enabling laws in the extended way of referring to any matters is an innovation of the 1999 Constitution, without precedent in other constitutions. The 1999 Constitution substituted the provisions of the 1961 Constitution, which limited the authorization by enabling laws to the president to adopting extraordinary measures exclusively on economic and financial matters (Article 190.8). In contrast, the 1999 Constitution extends the possibility of legislative delegation, without limits regarding the matters that the executive can regulate, which contradicts the general constitutional guarantee of certain matters that must be reserved to the legislator (as a body composed of elected representatives), like establishing limits to the exercise of human rights, the approval of taxes (no taxation without representation), and the creation of criminal offenses.[34]

---

[34]See Pedro Nikken, "Constitución venezolana de 1999: La habilitación para dictar decretos ejecutivos con fuerza de ley restrictivos de los derechos humanos y su contradicción con el derecho internacional," *Revista de Derecho Público* 83, Editorial Jurídica Venezolana, Caracas 2000, 5-19.

The fact is that according to this provision, the fundamental legislation of the country sanctioned from 1999 to 2009 has been contained in the decree laws issued by the president to execute those enabling laws, particularly in 2002 and 2008, which even were approved without ensuring the mandatory constitutional provision for public hearings, established in the Constitution (Article 211) to take place before the sanctioning of all statutes. That is contrary to the way the Constitution tends to ensure the exercise of the political participation right in the process of drafting legislation. This constitutional obligation, of course, also must be complied with by the president when a legislative delegation takes place. Nonetheless, in 2007 and 2008, the president, following the same steps he took in 2001,[35] extensively legislated without any public hearing or consultation. In this way, defrauding the Constitution by means of legislative delegation, President Chávez enacted decree laws without complying with the obligatory public hearings, thus violating citizens' right to political participation.

4. *Freedom of Expression and Its Limitations*

On matters of freedoms, the 1999 Constitution established a complete enunciation of all civil rights and freedoms, although in some cases it provided the basis for excessive state control. This has been the case particularly for the freedom of expression.

In this respect, Article 57 of the Constitution states that "everyone has the right to express freely his or her thoughts, ideas or opinions orally, in writing or by any other form of expression, and to use for such purpose any means of communication and diffusion, and no censorship shall be established." Anyone making use of this right assumes full responsibility for everything expressed. Anonymity, war propaganda, discriminatory messages, or those promoting religious intolerance are not permitted. Also, Article 57 provides that censorship restricting the ability of public officials (*funcionarios públicos*) to report on matters for which they are responsible is prohibited, a provision that is not applicable to judges.

For such purposes, Article 58 guarantees that communications are free and plural, and involve the duties and responsibilities indicated by law, thus providing citizens with the right to respond and to ask for

---

[35]See Allan R. Brewer-Carías, "Apreciación general sobre los vicios de inconstitucionalidad que afectan los Decretos Leyes Habilitados," in *Ley Habilitante del 13-11-2000 y sus Decretos Leyes*, Academia de Ciencias Políticas y Sociales, Serie Eventos N° 17, Caracas 2002, 63-103.

rectification.[36] Additionally, the Constitution establishes everyone's right to information – that is, to be informed – by incorporating the adjectives "impartial, opportune and reliable" (Article 58). The problem with this enunciation is that it could originate a political or public control that can eventually lead to the possible definition of an "official" truth and, therefore, the rejection or persecution of any other possible truth. Following this in 2003, the Law on Social Responsibility of the Media was sanctioned, considerably expanding official control over radio and television.[37]

On the other hand, through judicial interpretations of the Constitution, the Supreme Tribunal of Justice has progressively been limiting freedom of information. In Decision No. 1155 (May 18, 2000), the Political-Administrative Chamber of the Supreme Tribunal (Case: *Tulio A. Álvarez et al. vs. Gobernación del Estado Apure*), in a decision ordering the media not to transmit certain information, developed a collective versus an individual aspect of freedom regarding impartiality, opportuneness, and the reliable nature of information to admit limits to be imposed to the media regardless of the general prohibition of censorship.[38]

The following year, in Decision No. 1013 (June 12, 2001) (Case: *Elías Santana y Asociación Civil Queremos Elegir vs. Presidente de la República y Radio Nacional de Venezuela*), the Constitutional Chamber of the Supreme Tribunal dismissed an *amparo* action against the president filed by a citizen and the nongovernmental organization he represented asking for the exercise of his right to response. Through an interpretation of Articles 57 and 58 of the Constitution, the scope of freedom of information was extremely reduced, and the right to response and rectification was eliminated regarding opinions in the media when they were expressed by the president in his weekly televised program (*Aló*

---

[36]See, in general, Allan R. Brewer-Carías, "La libre expresión del pensamiento y el derecho a la información en la Constitución venezolana de 1999," in *Anuario de Derecho Constitucional Latinoamericano,* Konrad Adenauer Stiftung, Montevideo 2002, 267-76; Héctor Faúndez Ledesma, "Las condiciones de las restricciones a la libertad de expresión," in *El derecho público a comienzos del siglo XXI. Estudios homenaje al Profesor Allan R. Brewer-Carías,* Instituto de Derecho Público, UCV, Civitas Ediciones, Madrid 2003, 3:2598-664; Rafael Ortiz-Ortiz, "Las implicaciones jurídico positivas del derecho a la información y a la libertad de expresión en el nuevo orden constitucional," *Revista de la Facultad de Derecho de la Universidad de Carabobo* 1, Valencia 2002, 163-246.

[37]See Ley de Responsabilidad Social en Radio y Televisión in *Gaceta Oficial* N° 38.333, Dec. 12, 2005. See comments on this statute in Allan R. Brewer-Carías, Asdrúbal Aguiar, José Ignacio Hernández, Margarita Escudero, Ana Cristina Núñez Machado, Juan José Raffalli, Carlos Urdaneta Sandoval and Juan Cristóbal Carmona Borjas, *Ley de Responsabilidad Social de Radio y Televisión*, Colección Textos Legislativos 35, Editorial Jurídica Venezolana, Caracas 2006.

[38]See *Revista de Derecho Público* 82, Editorial Jurídica Venezolana, Caracas 2000, 291ff.

and the Venezuelan people, which is unique, sovereign, and indivisible. Consequently, the indigenous peoples have the duty to protect national integrity and sovereignty, and in no case will the term *people* be interpreted in the sense that it has in international law tending to the recognition of states.

In particular, Article 125 of the Constitution consecrates the right of indigenous peoples to political participation, which is established in Article 182, which guarantees "indigenous representation in the National Assembly and deliberating bodies of federal entities and of local entities where indigenous populations exist, in accordance with law."[44]

III. THE PROBLEM OF AN ECONOMIC CONSTITUTION CONCEIVED FOR STATE APPROPRIATION ("STATIZATION") OF THE ECONOMY

The third part of the Constitution, as in any contemporary constitution, is devoted to regulating the economics,[45] establishing the rules of the economic system of the country.

The 1999 Constitution established a mixed economy, recognizing private enterprise and the right of property and economic freedom; declaring the principles of social justice; and allowing the state to intervene in the economy, significantly in some cases.

1. *The Mixed Economic System*

Since the beginning of oil production in Venezuela, and particularly during the second half of the twentieth century, a mixed "social market economy"[46] has been developed that combines economic freedom, private initiative, and a free–market economic model (as opposed to a state-directed economy) with the possibility of state intervention in the

---

[44]See Ricardo Colmenares Olívar, "El derecho de participación y consulta de los pueblos indígenas en Venezuela," *Revista del Tribunal Supremo de Justicia* 8, Caracas 2003, 21-48.

[45]See Allan R. Brewer-Carías, "Reflexiones sobre la Constitución Económica," in *Estudios sobre la Constitución Española. Homenaje al Profesor Eduardo García de Enterría*, Madrid 1991, 3839-53.

[46]See Henrique Meier, "La Constitución económica," *Revista de Derecho Corporativo* 1, Caracas 2001, 9-74; Ana C. Núñez Machado, "Los principios económicos de la Constitución de 1999," *Revista de Derecho Constitucional* 6, Editorial Sherwood, Caracas 2002, 129-40; Claudia Briceño Aranguren and Ana C. Núñez Machado, "Aspectos económicos de la nueva Constitución," in *Comentarios a la Constitución de la República Bolivariana de Venezuela*, Vadell Hermanos Editores, Caracas 2000, 177ff.; Jesús Ollarves Irazábal, "La vigencia constitucional de los derechos económicos y sociales en Venezuela," in *Libro Homenaje a Enrique Tejera París, Temas sobre la Constitución de 1999*, Centro de Investigaciones Jurídicas (CEIN), Caracas 2001, 159-92.

economy to uphold principles of social justice. This has been possible particularly because of the special position of the state as owner of the subsoil and the oil industry, which has been nationalized since 1975.[47] This has made the state the most powerful economic entity in the nation, leading it to intervene in the country's economic activities in important ways.

It is precisely within this context that Article 299 of the 1999 Constitution sets forth that the social-economic regime of Venezuela shall be based on the principles of social justice, democratization, efficiency, free competition, environmental protection, productivity, and solidarity, with a view to ensuring overall human development and a dignified and useful existence for the community. Thus, Article 299 expressly establishes that the state must "jointly with private initiative" promote "the harmonious development of the national economy for the purpose of generating sources of employment, a high national level of added value, in order to elevate the standard of living of the population and strengthen the nation's economic sovereignty, guaranteeing legal certainty, solidity, dynamism, sustainability, permanence, and economic growth with equity, in order to guarantee a just distribution of wealth by means of strategic democratic, participative and open planning."

The economic system is therefore based on economic freedom, private initiative, and free competition in combination with the state as promoter of economic development, regulator of economic activity, and planner together with civil society. As the Constitutional Chamber of the Supreme Tribunal of Justice stated in Decision No. 117 (February 6, 2001),[48] this is "a socioeconomic system that is in between a free market (in which the state acts as a simple programmer [*programador*] for an economy that is dependent upon the supply and demand of goods and services) and an interventionist economy (in which the state actively intervenes as the 'primary entrepreneur')." The Constitution promotes "joint economic activity between the state and private initiative in the pursuit of, and in order to concretely realize the supreme values consecrated in the Constitution," and to pursue "the equilibrium of all the forces of the market, and joint activity between the State and private initiative." In

---

[47]See Organic Law That Reserves to the State the Industry and Commerce of Hydrocarbons, *Gaceta Oficial* Extra, N° 1.769, Aug. 29, 1975. See Allan R. Brewer-Carías, "Introducción al régimen jurídico de las nacionalizaciones en Venezuela," *Archivo de Derecho Público y Ciencias de la Administración* 3, Instituto de Derecho Público, Facultad de Ciencias Jurídicas y Políticas, Universidad Central de Venezuela, Caracas 1981, 23–44.

[48]See *Revista de Derecho Público* 85–88, Editorial Jurídica Venezolana, Caracas 2001, 212-18.

accord with that system, the Supreme Tribunal ruled that the Constitution "advocates a series of superior normative values with respect to the economic regime, consecrating free enterprise within the framework of a market economy and, fundamentally, within the framework of the Social State under the Rule of Law (the *Welfare State*, the State of Well-being or the Social Democratic State). This is a social State that is opposed to authoritarianism."[49] Nonetheless, in practice, particularly during the past decade (1999–2009), this framework has been changed as a result of the authoritarian government that developed, inclining the balance toward state participation in the economy through a process of progressive state appropriation ("statization") of the economy, reduction of economic freedoms, and an increase in the country's dependency on oil production.[50]

2. *Reduced Property Rights and Economic Freedoms*

Title 3 of the 1999 Constitution also contains a declaration of economic rights (Chapter 7, Articles 112–118), including economic freedom and the right to private property.

Regarding economic freedom, Article 112 of the Constitution declares the right of all persons to develop the economic activity of their choice, without other limits than those established by statute for reasons of human development, security, sanitation, environmental protection, and other social interests. In any case, the state must promote private initiative, guaranteeing the creation of wealth and its just distribution, as well as the production of goods and services to satisfy the needs of the population; freedom to work; and free enterprise, commerce, and industry – without prejudice to the power of the state to promulgate measures to plan, rationalize, and regulate the economy and promote the overall development of the country.

In 2007, by means of the draft constitutional reforms (rejected by referendum held in December of that same year), the president proposed to

---

[49] The values alluded to, according to the doctrine of the Constitutional Chamber, "are developed through the concept of free enterprise" (*libertad de empresa*), which encompasses both a subjective right "to dedicate oneself to the economic activity of one's choice" and a principle of economic regulation, "according to which the will of the business (*voluntad de la empresa*) to make its own decisions is manifest. The State fulfills its role of intervention in this context. Intervention can be direct (through businesses) or indirect (as an entity regulating the market)," id.

[50] As reported by Simón Romero, "Chávez Reopens Oil Bids to West as Prices Plunge," *New York Times*, Jan. 12, 2009, 1: in 2009, Venezuela was "reliant on oil for about 93 percent of its export revenue in 2008, up from 69 percent in 1998."

eliminate this constitutional provision, substituting it with one defining as a matter of state policy the obligation to promote "the development of a Productive Economic Model, that is intermediate, diversified and independent . . . founded upon the humanistic values of cooperation and the preponderance of common interests over individual ones, guaranteeing the meeting of the people's social and material needs, the greatest possible political and social stability, and the greatest possible sum of happiness." The proposal added that the state, in the same way, "shall promote and develop different forms of businesses and economic units from social property, both directly or communally, as well as indirectly or through the state." According to that norm, the state was to promote "economic units of social production and/or distribution, that may be mixed properties held between the State, the private sector, and the communal power, so as to create the best conditions for the collective and cooperative construction of a Socialist Economy."[51]

Article 115 of the Constitution, although following the orientation of the previous 1961 Constitution in the sense of guaranteeing the right to property, did not establish private property as having a social function to be accomplished, as did the 1961 Constitution.[52] Nonetheless, it provides that property shall be subject to such contributions, restrictions, and obligations as may be established by law in the service of the public or general interest. However, Article 115 defines the attributes of the right to property that traditionally were enumerated only in the Civil Code (Article 545); that is, the right to use, enjoy, and dispose of property are now in the Constitution.

The 2007 constitutional reforms proposed radical changes to this constitutional regime regarding property rights. The president sought to eliminate private property as a constitutionally protected right and to substitute a recognition of private property as "assets for use and consumption or as means of production," together with other forms of properties and, in particular, public property. The proposed reform regarding Article 115 of the Constitution recognized and guaranteed "different forms of property" instead of guaranteeing the right to private property, enumerating them as follows: public property, which belongs to

---

[51]See Allan R. Brewer-Carías, *La Reforma Constitucional de 2007 (Sancionada inconstitucionalmente por la Asamblea Nacional el 2 de Noviembre de 2007)*, Editorial Jurídica Venezolana, Caracas 2007,127ff.

[52]See Allan R. Brewer-Carías "El derecho de propiedad y libertad económica. Evolución y situación actual en Venezuela," in *Estudios sobre la Constitución. Libro Homenaje a Rafael Caldera*, Caracas 1979, 2:1139-246.

state entities; social property, which belongs to the people jointly and to future generations; collective property, which pertains to social groups or persons and is exploited for their common benefit, use, or enjoyment, and may be of social or private origin; mixed property, ownership of which is by the public, social, collective, and private sectors in different combinations, for the exploitation of resources or the execution of activities, subject always to the absolute economic and social sovereignty of the nation; and private property, which is owned by "natural or legal persons, only regarding assets for use or consumption, or as means of production legitimately acquired."[53]

With respect to expropriation, Article 115 of the Constitution establishes that expropriation can be decreed for any kind of property only for reasons of public benefit or social interest, and then by means of a judicial process and payment of just compensation.[54] Consequently, the Constitution prohibits confiscation (expropriation without compensation), except in cases permitted by the Constitution itself, regarding property of persons responsible for crimes committed against public property or who have illicitly enriched themselves in exercising public office. Confiscations may also take place regarding property deriving from business, financial, or any other activities connected with illicit trafficking of psychotropic or narcotic substances (Articles 116 and 271).

Article 307 of the Constitution declares the regime of large private real estate holdings (*latifundio*) to be contrary to social interests, charging the legislator with taxing idle lands and establishing necessary measures to transform them into productive economic units, as well as to recover arable land. The same constitutional provision entitles peasants to own land, thus constitutionalizing the obligation of the state to protect and promote associative and private forms of property to guarantee agricultural production and to oversee sustainable arrangements on arable lands to guarantee their food-producing potential. In exceptional cases, the same article requires that the legislature use federal tax revenue to fund financing, research, technical assistance, transfer of technology, and other activities aimed to raise productivity and competitiveness of the agricultural sector.

---

[53] See Allan R. Brewer-Carías, *La Reforma Constitucional de 2007 (Sancionada inconstitucionalmente por la Asamblea Nacional el 2 de Noviembre de 2007)*, Editorial Jurídica Venezolana, Caracas 2007, 122ff.

[54] See José L. Villegas Moreno, "El derecho de propiedad en la Constitución de 1999," in *Estudios de derecho administrativo: Libro homenaje a la Universidad Central de Venezuela*, Imprenta Nacional, Caracas 2001, 2:565-82.

3. The Almost-Unlimited Possibility of State Intervention in the Economy

In the economic arena, the Constitution is marked by statism, as it attributes to the state the fundamental responsibility in the arrangement and provision of basic public services in health, education, and social security areas and those pertaining to homes: distribution of water, gas, and electricity. It is also derived from the regulation of state power to control and plan economic activities.

Consequently, the articles of the Constitution regarding the economy are those destined for state intervention. Only succinct rules are devoted to regulating economic freedom (Article 112) and private property (Article 115); the necessary balance between public and private sectors is absent. In the latter, only activities not fundamental to generating wealth and employment are privileged, such as agricultural (Article 305), crafts (Article 309), small and medium enterprises (Article 308), and tourism (Article 310).

In effect, the Constitution also regulates various forms of state economic intervention that have developed in Venezuela in the past decades. The Constitution regulates the state as a promoter – that is, without substituting private initiatives – to foster and order the economy to ensure the development of private initiative. Article 112 sets forth that in any case, the state must promote private initiative, guaranteeing the creation of wealth and its just distribution, as well as the production of goods and services to satisfy needs of the population; freedom to work; and free enterprise, commerce, and industry – without prejudice to the power of the state to promulgate measures to plan, rationalize, and regulate the economy and promote the overall development of the country.

In this same regard, Article 299 sets forth that the state, jointly with private initiative, shall promote the harmonious development of the national economy to the end of generating sources of employment, a high rate of domestic added value, an increased standard of living for the population, and strengthened economic sovereignty of the country. It also guarantees the reliability of the law, as well as the solid, dynamic, sustainable, continuing, and equitable growth of the economy, to ensure just distribution of wealth through participatory democratic strategic planning with open consultation.

Specifically regarding agricultural activities, Article 305 of the Constitution establishes that the state shall promote sustainable agriculture as the strategic basis for overall rural development and, consequently, shall guarantee the population a secure food supply, defined as the sufficient and stable availability of food within the national sphere and timely and uninterrupted access to the same for consumers. A secure food supply must be achieved by developing and prioritizing internal agricultural and livestock production, understood as production deriving from the activities of agriculture, livestock, fishing, and aquaculture. Food production is in the national interest and is fundamental to the economic and social development of the nation. To that end, the state shall promulgate such financial, commercial, and technological transfer; land tenancy; infrastructure; training; and other measures as may be necessary to achieve strategic levels of self-sufficiency. In addition, it shall promote actions in the national and international economic context to compensate for the disadvantages inherent to agricultural activity. The state shall protect the settlement and communities of nonindustrialized fishermen, as well as their fishing banks in continental waters and those close to the coastline, as defined by law.

Regarding rural development, Article 306 imposes on the state the duty to promote conditions for overall rural development, for the purpose of generating employment and ensuring the rural population an adequate level of well-being, as well as their inclusion in national development. It shall likewise promote agricultural activity and optimum land use by providing infrastructure projects, supplies, loans, training services, and technical assistance.

Regarding industrial activities, Article 308 obligates the state to protect and promote small- and medium-sized manufacturers, cooperatives, savings funds, family-owned businesses, small businesses, and any other form of community association for purposes of work, savings, and consumption, under an arrangement of collective ownership, to strength the country's economic development based on the initiative of the people. Training, technical assistance, and appropriate financing are guaranteed. However, Article 309 provides that typical Venezuelan crafts and folk industries enjoy special protection of the state, to preserve their authenticity, and receive credit facilities to promote production and marketing.

On commercial matters, Article 301 reserves to the state the use of trade policy to protect the economic activities of public and private Venezuelan enterprises. In this regard, more advantageous status than that established for Venezuelan nationals will not be granted to foreign persons, enterprises, or entities. Foreign investment is subject to the same conditions as domestic investment.

Finally, Article 310 of the Constitution declares tourism an economic activity of national interest and of high priority in the country's strategy of diversification and sustainable development. As part of the foundation of the socioeconomic regime the Constitution contemplates, the state will promulgate measures to guarantee the development of tourism and will create and strengthen a national tourist industry.

Regarding economic planning, Article 112 empowers the state to promulgate measures to plan, rationalize, and regulate the economy and promote the overall development of the country. The president must formulate the National Plan of Development and, once approved by the National Assembly, direct its execution (Articles 187.8 and 236.18).

The Constitution establishes no provisions for the state to promote highly qualified or heavy industries, though it does establish that the state can reserve for its own exploitation, through an organic law and by reasons of national convenience, the petroleum industry (already nationalized since 1975) and other industries, operations, and goods and services that are in the public interest and of a strategic nature. The state shall promote the domestic manufacture of raw materials deriving from the exploitation of nonrenewable natural resources, with a view to assimilating, creating, and inventing technologies; generating employment and economic growth; and creating wealth and well-being for the people (Article 302).

As aforementioned, on the basis of a similar constitutional provision establishing the power of the state to reserve for its own exploitation services or resources (Article 97 of the 1961 Constitution), the oil industry was nationalized in 1975 and is managed by the state-owned enterprise Petróleos de Venezuela S.A. Article 303 of the 1999 Constitution set forth that for reasons of economic and political sovereignty and national strategy, the state shall retain all shares of that public enterprise, with the exception of its subsidiaries, strategic joint ventures, enterprises, and any other venture established or to be established as a consequence of carrying on the business of Petróleos de Venezuela. This last possibility has been considered a loosening of the strict nationalization process carried out through the 1975 organic law that reserves to the state the industry and commercialization of hydrocarbons.[55] The 2000 Organic Law on Hydrocarbons allowed for the establishment of mixed companies for the

---

[55]See Allan R. Brewer-Carías, "El régimen de participación del capital privado en las industrias petrolera y minera: Desnacionalización y regulación a partir de la Constitución de 1999," in *VII Jornadas Internacionales de Derecho Administrativo Allan R. Brewer-Carías, El Principio de Legalidad y el Ordenamiento Jurídico-Administrativo de la Libertad Económica,* Fundación de Estudios de Derecho Administrativo FUNEDA, Caracas 2004, 15-58.

exploitation of primary hydrocarbons activities, although with the state as majority shareholder[56] – that law was implemented in 2006–7.[57]

With respect to public enterprises in general, Article 300 of the Constitution refers to the statutes to determine the conditions for the creation of functionally decentralized entities to carry out social or entrepreneurial activities, with a view to ensuring the reasonable economic and social productivity of the public resources invested in such activities.

All the aforementioned provisions regarding the participation of the state in the economy were proposed to be radically changed in the 2007 draft constitutional reforms, which attempted to reduce the whole economic role of the state to promote and develop economic and social activities "under the principles of the socialist economy" (Article 300).

Thus, under the Constitution, the state is responsible for almost everything and is able to regulate everything. Private enterprise appears to be shunned. The 1999 Constitution did not assimilate the previous decades' experience of regulating, controlling, and planning an entrepreneurial state. The necessity of granting privileges to private enterprises and stimulating the generation of wealth and employment to society was not understood.

Globally, the result of the constitutional text regarding the economy is a Constitution created for state intervention in the economy, not for the development of the economy by private sectors under the principle of subsidiary state intervention.

---

[56]Ley Orgánica de Hidrocarburos, *Gaceta Oficial* N° 38.493, Aug. 4, 2006.

[57]See Allan R. Brewer-Carías, "The 'Statization' of the Pre-2001 Primary Hydrocarbons Joint Venture Exploitations: Their Unilateral Termination and the Assets Confiscation of Some of the Former Private Parties," in *Oil, Gas & Energy Law Intelligence* 6. Available at http://www.gasandoil.com/ogel/; and "La estatización de los convenios de asociación que permitían la participación del capital privado en las actividades primarias de hidrocarburos sucritos antes de 2002, mediante su terminación anticipada y unilateral y la confiscación de los bienes afectos a los mismos," in *Nacionalización, libertad de empresa y asociaciones mixtas*, coord. Víctor Hernández Mendible, Editorial Jurídica Venezolana, Caracas 2008, 123-88.

PART TWO

INSTITUTIONAL DEVELOPMENT TOWARD CONSOLIDATING AUTHORITARIANISM

The 1999 Constitution established express provisions to construct a democratic rule-of-law state, based on the main following trends: first, the vertical distribution of state powers between territorial entities with self-government, according to the "federal decentralized" form of the state; second, the autonomy and independence of five different branches of government according to the principles of separation of powers; third, the attribution to an independent and autonomous Supreme Tribunal of Justice of the power to control the supremacy of the Constitution; and fourth, a mixed economic system that combines private initiative and economic freedom with state participation.

Nonetheless, and despite those express provisions, in practice, the institutions that have developed during the past decade – in many cases, manipulating constitutional provisions (Chapter 5) – have been used, first, to consolidate the centralized federation that the 1999 constitution-making process aimed to surpass, thus abandoning all the decentralization policies defined in the 1990s (Chapter 6); second, to concentrate power, blurring the principle of separation between the branches of government; third, to subject the Supreme Tribunal of Justice to the will of the executive (Chapter 7), converting its judicial review powers into an illegitimate means of distorting the Constitution (Chapter 8); and fourth, to establish a completely "statized" economy, by nationalizing, expropriating, and confiscating private assets and extinguishing private initiatives (Chapter 9), which has affected activities, enterprises, and assets in the oil, iron, steel, agriculture, electricity, telephone, and cement industries.

In addition, similar to what happened during the 1999 constitution-making process, in which the judicial interpretation of the Constitution was used to justify violation of the Constitution (constitutional fraud), and with the endless constitutional transitory regime established over the past decade, the political regime that began with fraud in 1999 has used representative democracy to progressively dismantle it and substitute a so-called participatory democracy of the popular power. This is participatory and democratic only in name – it is fraud.

Because of this fraud committed against the popular will by means of electoral means, the democratic rule of law has been and is being progressively substituted for with a "state of the popular power." In such a state, all power is concentrated in the head of state; thus, it is not democratic, representative, or participatory. On the contrary, it is severely controlled and directed from the summit of the political power that the president exercises as head of the executive and of the single governing party. He has proclaimed himself, de facto, as "president of the popular power" and has formally named the ministers of the executive cabinet as "Ministers of the Popular Power for...."[1] The final purpose of this policy, as announced by the vice president of the republic in January 2007 during the sanctioning of the legislative delegation law (Enabling Act) in favor of the president, is the installment of a "dictatorship of democracy,"[2] in which no other political group or party different from the one controlled by the president can govern or control political power.

In democracy, no dictatorship is acceptable, not even a "dictatorship of democracy." More than ninety years after the failed dictatorship of the proletariat in the Soviet Union, in Venezuela, communal councils have been created, which depend directly on the executive through a minister to channel the popular power, with the supposed participation of the people, and to install a dictatorship of democracy. Such popular dictatorships have been and are fraudulent instruments of power that in the name of the popular power, end every trace of democracy and impose, by force, a socialist regime in a country whose citizens have not voted for it.[3]

---

[1] See Decree on the Organization of National Public Administration, N° 5246 of Mar. 20, 2007, *Gaceta Oficial* N° 38.654 of Mar. 28, 2007.

[2] Vice President Jorge Rodríguez, in Jan. 2007, said: "Of course we want to install a dictatorship, the dictatorship of the true democracy and the democracy is the dictatorship of everyone, you and us together, building a different country. Of course we want this dictatorship of democracy to be installed forever," in Cecilia Caione, "Queremos instaurar la dictadura de la verdadera democracia," in *El Nacional*, Caracas Feb. 19, 2007, A-2.

[3] On the contrary, in the Dec. 2007 referendum on constitutional reforms, the people voted rejecting the proposed reforms, including those that referred to the establishment of a socialist state.

Chapter 5

CONSTITUTIONAL FRAUD AND DEFRAUDING DEMOCRACY

At the beginning of the twenty-first century, Latin America has witnessed in Venezuela the birth of a new model of authoritarian state that did not immediately originate in a military coup, as had occurred on many other occasions during the long decades of the previous century. In Venezuela, the authoritarian government has had its origin in popular elections, which despite its militaristic nature and its final goal of destroying representative democracy, have provided it the convenient camouflage of "constitutional" and "elective" marks.

We are talking about militarist authoritarianism with alleged popular support, like all fascist and communist authoritarianism regimes of the past century, in many cases with some electoral origin. Authoritarian political systems, no matter how constitutionally and electively disguised, cannot be democratic or considered to allow a state to be subject to the rule of law, particularly because they lack the essential components of democracy, which are much more than the sole popular or circumstantial election of governments.

I. POPULAR AUTHORITARIANISM AND CONCENTRATED STATE POWERS

In particular, among all the essential elements and components of democracy, the one regarding the separation and independence of public powers is maybe the most fundamental pillar of the rule of law, because it can allow other factors of democracy to become political reality.[1] To be precise, democracy, as a political regime, can function only in a constitutional system of rule of law where control of power exists; that is, one that seriously considers the classic and clear advice, with all its political consequences, left as a legacy to the world by Charles Louis de Secondat, Baron of Montesquieu, decades before the French Revolution: "But constant experience shows us that every man invested with power is apt to abuse it, and to carry his authority as far as it will go.... To prevent this abuse, it is necessary from the very nature of things that power should be a check to power."[2]

Decades later, as a legacy of the North American and French revolutions,[3] this important political postulate about the separation of public powers began to be the inevitable premise of democracy as a political regime, such that democracy cannot exist without separation and power finds limits and can be stopped by power itself.

Consequently, for democracy to be a political system to ensure the government of the people, which is the legitimate holder of sovereignty, through the indirect means of representation and even through instruments for its direct exercise, it must be forged in a constitutionally political system that, above all, impedes the abuse of those who control any branches of government. This is the essence of the rule of law: For a democracy to effectively exist and function, a constitutional framework must exist that establishes and allows the control of power, both in its horizontal division regarding the branches of government and in its vertical or territorial distribution regarding regional and local government. Thus can the diverse powers of the state limit one another. This framework ensuring the separation of powers is the essential guarantee of all the values of democracy itself, among which are respect of popular will, enjoyment of freedoms and human rights, political pluralism, republican alternation, and submission to rule of law.

In Latin America, in one way or another, with all the ups and downs of the effectiveness of the rule of law, during the democratic periods of its

---

[1] On the Inter-American Democratic Charter and the crisis of Venezuelan democracy, see Allan R. Brewer-Carías, *La crisis de la democracia venezolana. La Carta Democrática Interamericana y los sucesos de abril de 2002*, Ediciones El Nacional, Caracas 2002, 137ff.

[2] Charles de Secondat, Baron of Montesquieu, *The Spirit of Laws*, Book XI, Chapter 4, translation by Thomas Nugent (1752), revised by J.V. Prichard. Based on a public-domain edition published in 1914 by G. Bell & Sons, Ltd., London. Available at http://www.constitution.org/cm/sol.txt.

[3] See Allan R. Brewer-Carías, *Reflexiones sobre la Revolución Americana (1776) y la Revolución Francesa (1789) y sus aportes al constitucionalismo moderno*, Editorial Jurídica Venezolana, Caracas 1992.

countries, there have always been institutions aiming to ensure respect for human rights, subjection of power to the law, elections almost regular and free, and a plural regime of political parties. But if, as in many cases, democracy has not settled completely and the rule of law has not absolutely taken over political institutions, it is because those countries have failed to effectively establish the last of the essential elements of democracy: the implementation of effective separation and independence of powers. That is to say, the constitutional order that must exist in every democracy and that gives sense to the rule of law, devoted to controlling and limiting political power, is the one that can allow for effective political representation – a true possibility of citizens' political participation, a transparent and responsible government, and the effective force of the rule of law.

Without control of power, there is no true democracy – and one cannot exist – or effective rule of law. Moreover, without such control of power, none of the essential elements of democracy can be guaranteed because only by controlling power can absolutely free and fair elections take place, thus achieving efficient representation; only by controlling power can political pluralism be developed; only by controlling power can effective democratic participation be ensured; only by controlling power can effective transparency in the exercise of government be ensured with real government accountability; only by controlling power can a government submitted to the Constitution and the rule of law be structured; only by controlling power can there be effective access to justice, which functions with valuable autonomy and independence; and only by controlling power can there be a true and effective guarantee of human rights.

On the contrary, the excessive concentration and centralization of power, as occurs in any authoritarian government, despite its electoral origins, inevitably leads to tyranny if there are no efficient controls over governments – and, even worse, if those have or believe to have popular support. This is part of the history of humankind during the first half of the twentieth century: tyrants who used the vote of the majority to rise to power and apply, from there, authoritarian practices to eliminate democracy and all its elements, beginning with respect for human rights and alternating government.

It is useful to remember that since the beginnings of modern constitutionalism, in the French Declaration of the Rights of Man and of the Citizen (1789), the principle of the separation of powers was proclaimed, denying the existence of a constitution in "any society in which the guaranty of rights is not assured, nor the separation of powers is determined" (Article 16). That is why, during the two centuries that have passed and because of the progress experienced in implementing democracy, particularly during the past five decades, because both the principle of division or organic separation of powers as manifestation of the horizontal distribution of power and the principle of territorial or vertical distribution of power as a sign of political decentralization have been the strongest tools of contemporary constitutionalism. However, they are not necessarily the most developed in practice to ensure freedom, democratic government, and the rule of law. That is precisely why they have been progressively and systematically demolished and dismantled in Venezuela.

The authoritarian government that has taken root in Venezuela during the first decade of the twenty-first century finds its main support not only in how separation of powers was conceived of in the 1999 Constitution but also in how it has been deformed, allowing power to concentrate in the hands of the executive power because of its control over the National Assembly and, consequently, over all other branches of government. In a certain way, the 1999 Constitution, despite that it formally separates powers, had the germ of the concentration of powers that would lead to authoritarianism.

Along the same line, regarding the federal system of territorial distribution of power, despite the proclaimed "federal decentralized state" (Article 4 of the Constitution), what the Constitution continued to establish was a centralized federation, reinforced by the elimination of the Senate, an institution that had existed since 1811 as an instrument to ensure equal participation of the representatives of the states in national policies. After the 1999 Constitution, Venezuela became a rare example of a federation without a federal chamber, as is the case of a few existing federations in very small states. The authoritarian roots of the 1999 Constitution derived not only from its potential to concentrate powers but also from the centralized framework of the state it designed.

If interpreters limit themselves to the words of the 1999 Constitution, they can deduce that what the Constitution has established is a democratic government based on the participatory and protagonist role of citizens, based on the principles of organic separation of different branches of government and on territorial distribution of public power by means of a decentralized federation. However, in reality, the formal and sometimes misleading words designed the foundations of a government based on the concentration of public powers and on political centralization of the state.

The result has been the development of a new form of constitutional authoritarianism in Latin America that is based on the concentration and centralization of state powers, which impede any possibility of effective democratic participation. This is contrary to what a democratic rule-of-law state should be, built on the principles of separation of powers and political decentralization that could allow for effective democratic participation and representation.

II. THE PROCESS OF CONCENTRATING POWER SINCE 1999

The process of concentrating power in Venezuela in the hands of the executive was possible because of the majority votes the executive controlled for the 2000 elections of the National Assembly and the absolute and total control it obtained in the 2005 National Assembly. In the latter case, because of the decision of opposition parties not to participate in the 2005 legislative elections, given manipulation of the electoral rules in applying the mixed electoral system established in the Constitution, by a National Electoral Council that was completely controlled by the Executive, after its members were appointed by the Constitutional Chamber of the Supreme Tribunal, without complying with the constitutional provisions on the matter, kidnapping the citizen's rights to political participation.[4]

Once complete control of the National Assembly was obtained, authoritarianism took hold in Venezuela, given the concentration and centralization of powers allowed for in the 1999 Constitution. That is why when the Constitution was approved in the referendum on December 15, 1999, I warned – in a document to justify the reasons I advocated to vote no for the referendum – that, in Venezuela, the following would be established on approval of the Constitution:

> An institutional scheme conceived for the authoritarianism derived from the combination of centralism of State, aggravated presidential system, democracy of political parties, militarism and concentration of power in the Assembly that constitutes the central element intended for the organization of the State powers. In my opinion, this is not what was required in order to perfect democracy; which, on the contrary, should be based on the decentralization of power, a controlled and moderated

---

[4] *See* decisions N° 2073 of Aug. 4, 2003 (Caso: *Hermánn Escarrá Malaver y oros*) and N° 2341 of Aug. 25, 2003 (Caso: *Hermánn Escarrá M. y otros*) in Allan R. Brewer-Carías, *La Sala Constitucional versus el Estado Democrático de Derecho. El secuestro del poder electoral y de la Sala Electoral del Tribunal Supremo y la confiscación del derecho a la participación política*, Los Libros de El Nacional, Colección Ares, Caracas 2004, p. 172; "El secuestro del Poder Electoral y la confiscación del derecho a la participación política mediante el referendo revocatorio presidencial: Venezuela 2000-2004," in *Boletín Mexicano de Derecho Comparado* 112, Instituto de Investigaciones Jurídicas, Universidad Nacional Autónoma de México, México City 2005, 11-73.

presidential system, a political participation system to balance the power of the State and the subjection of the military authority to the civil authority.[5]

Unfortunately, a decade later, my 1999 warnings had become a reality. The process began with the coup d'état given by the 1999 Constituent Assembly, which, without any authority whatsoever, assaulted and concentrated all power of the state under the in-effect 1961 Constitution. This had devastating results and produced unusual institutional sequels, like the endless and unfinished constitutional transitory regime of the country.[6] With this, the fundamental principles of democratic control over state power and the rule of law have been undermined.[7]

The Constitution framed by the 1999 Constituent Assembly contained an authoritarian institutional framework that has impeded the development of democracy and the consolidation of the rule of law. On the contrary, the Constitution that Venezuela needed in 1999 for its political development at the beginning of the twenty-first century was one that needed to ensure improved democracy by means of designing and effectively implementing organic separation of powers as an effective antidote to authoritarianism. Unfortunately, the formal progress from the establishment of the separation of powers beyond the three classical powers of the state (legislative, executive, and judicial), granting constitutional rank to the classic control institutions (e.g., comptroller general, prosecutor general, people's defender and electoral council) did not produce the desired results, particularly because of their factual dependence regarding the legislative power.

---

[5]Document dated Nov. 30, 1999. See Allan R. Brewer-Carías, *Debate constituyente (Aportes a la Asamblea Nacional Constituyente)*, Fundación de Derecho Público–Editorial Jurídica Venezolana, Caracas 1999, 3 (Oct. 18–Nov. 30):339.

[6]See Allan R. Brewer-Carías, *Golpe de estado y proceso constituyente en Venezuela*, Universidad Nacional Autónoma de Mexico, Mexico City 2003, 179ff.

[7]See, e.g., Allan R. Brewer-Carías, *La Sala Constitucional versus el estado democrático de derecho. El secuestro del poder electoral y de la Sala Electoral del Tribunal Supremo y la confiscación del derecho a la participación política*, Los Libros de El Nacional, Colección Ares, Caracas 2004; "La progresiva y sistemática demolición institucional de la autonomía e independencia del poder judicial en Venezuela 1999-2004," in *XXX Jornadas J.M. Dominguez Escovar, Estado de derecho, Administración de justicia y derechos humanos*, Instituto de Estudios Jurídicos del Estado Lara, Barquisimeto 2005, 33-174.

1. *The Germ of Concentrated Power: The National Assembly's Authority to Remove State Officials*

In effect, the 1999 Constitution (Article 136) established in Venezuela separation of powers defining five different branches of government: legislative, executive, judicial, citizen, and electoral. Nonetheless, for that separation to become effective, the independence and autonomy among those branches had to be consolidated to ensure the limitation and control of power by power. This, however, was not designed – the Constitution provided for an absurd distortion of separation by granting one branch of government, the National Assembly, the exercise of legislative power, as well as the power to appoint and remove judges of the Supreme Court of Justice, the prosecutor general, the comptroller general, the people's defender, and members of the National Electoral Council from their positions (Articles 265, 279, and 296). In some cases, they could do so by simple majority votes.

It is simply impossible to understand how the autonomy and independence of separate powers can function and exercise mutual control when the tenure of the officials of the branches of government (except the president) depends on the political will of one branch of government – that is, the National Assembly. The fact that the National Assembly can dismiss the heads of other branches makes futile the formal consecration of the autonomy and independence of powers, because the officials of the state are aware that they can be removed from office at any time, and especially if they act independently.[8]

Unfortunately, this has happened in Venezuela during the past decade. When there have been minimal signs of autonomy from some officials in state institutions who have dared to adopt their own decisions that distance them from the executive will, they have been dismissed. This occurred, for instance, in 2001 with the people's defender and the prosecutor general, originally appointed in 1999 by the Constituent Assembly, who were dismissed for failing to follow the dictates of the executive power.[9] This also happened with some judges of the Supreme Tribunal who dared to

---

[8] See "Democracia y control del poder," in Allan R. Brewer-Carías, *Constitución, democracia y control de poder*, Centro Iberoamericano de Estudios Provinciales y Locales, Universidad de Los Andes, Mérida 2004.

[9] The prosecutor general, appointed in Dec. 1999, thought he could initiate criminal impeachment proceedings against the then-minister of the interior; and the people's defender also thought she could challenge the special law of the 2001 National Assembly on appointment of judges to the Supreme Tribunal without complying with constitutional requirements. They were both dismissed in 2001.

issue decisions questioning the executive action; they were immediately subjected to investigation, and some were removed or "retired" from their positions.[10]

The consequence of this factual "dependency" of state organs on the National Assembly has been the total absence of fiscal or audit control in all state entities. The Comptroller General Office has ignored the results of the massive, undisciplined expenditure of oil–wealth public income, not always in accordance with budgetary discipline rules, which has provoked the classification of Venezuela among the lowest ranks on government transparency in the world.[11] Nonetheless, the most important decisions of the comptroller general have been those directed at disqualifying many opposition candidates from the November 2008 regional and municipal elections, on the basis of "administrative irregularities," although the Constitution establishes that the right to run for office can be suspended only when a judicial criminal decision has been adopted (Articles 39 and 42).[12] Unfortunately, the Constitutional Chamber of the Supreme Tribunal instead of declaring the unconstitutionality of such administrative decisions has upheld them, defrauding the Constitution.[13]

The people's defender has been perceived more as a defender of state powers than of the peoples' rights, even if the Venezuelan state never before has been denounced so many times as in the past years before the

---

[10]Franklin Arrieche, vice president of the Supreme Tribunal of Justice, delivered the decision of the Supreme Tribunal of Aug. 14, 2002, regarding the criminal process against the generals who acted on Apr. 12, 2002, declaring that there were no grounds on which to judge them given that, on that occasion, no military coup took place. The case of Alberto Martini Urdaneta, president of the Electoral Court, and Rafael Hernandez and Orlando Gravina, judges of the same court who undersigned Decision N° 24 (Mar. 15, 2004) (Case: *Julio Borges, César Pérez Vivas, Henry Ramos Allup, Jorge Sucre Castillo, Ramón Jose Medina y Gerardo Blyde vs. the National Electoral Council*), suspended the effects of Resolution N° 040302-131 (Mar. 2, 2004) of the National Electoral Council, which in that moment stopped the presidential-recall referendum.

[11]See http://www.transparencia.org.ve.

[12]In Oct. 2008, the European Parliament approved a resolution asking the Venezuelan government to end those practices (political incapacitation to make difficult the presence of opposition leaders in regional and local elections) and to promote a more global democracy with complete respect of the principles established in the 1999 Constitution. See http://venezuelanoticia.com/ archives/8298.

[13]Teodoro Petkoff has pointed out that with this decision, "the authoritarian and autocratic government of Hugo Chávez has clearly shown its true colors in this episode," explaining, "The political right to run for office is only lost when a candidate has receive a judicial sentence that has been upheld in a higher court. The recent sentence by the Venezuelan Supreme Court, upholding the disqualifications, as well as the constitutionality of Article 105 [of the Organic Law of the Comptroller General Office], constitute a Constitution defrauding, and the way in which the decision was handed down was an obvious accommodation to the president's desire to eliminate four significant opposition candidates from the electoral field." See Teodoro Petkoff, "Election and Political Power: Challenges for the Opposition," *ReVista: Harvard Review of Latin America*, David Rockefeller Center for Latin American Studies, Harvard University, Cambridge, MA 2008, 11.

Inter-American Commission on Human Rights. Finally, the public prosecutor has been characterized as using its powers to prosecute by using the controlled judiciary indiscriminately to persecute any political dissidence.

The effects of this dependency, of course, have been catastrophic regarding the judicial power, in which the Constituent Assembly intervened in 1999 by creating a special commission for such purpose that in 2010 continues to exist, with the unfortunate consent and complicity of the Supreme Tribunal of Justice itself. This has allowed for the judiciary reorganization commission, which has been legitimated, to cohabit with it, with disciplinary powers contrary to those established in the Constitution. In addition, the National Assembly has taken over political control of the magistrates of the Supreme Tribunal, who have the always-convenient warning that they can be investigated or removed, even by absolute majority vote, as has been unconstitutionally established in the 2004 Organic Law of the Supreme Court of Justice.[14]

2. *The Political Supremacy of the Executive and the Absence of Checks and Balances*

If the supremacy of the National Assembly over the judicial, citizen, and electoral powers is the most outstanding sign of the concentration of powers in the 1999 Constitution, the distortion of the separation of powers it declares also derives from the supremacy that from a political partisan point of view, the executive power has developed over the National Assembly.

In the 1999 Constitution, the presidential system was aggravated because of, among other factors, the extension to six years of the presidential term and provisions for the immediate reelection of the president (Article 203), contrary to the previous tradition of no reelection, which violates the principle of alternating government. This provision allowed for a possible administration term of up to twelve years, particularly because of the complexity of the government recall referendum (Article 72), which makes any referenda of that sort practically inapplicable. Nonetheless, in 2009, the provisions were radically changed through a constitutional amendment establishing continuous reelection for all public elected officials.

---

[14] In the reform to the Organic Law of the Supreme Tribunal of Justice approved in 2010, this possibility was eliminated.

Another constitutional provision reinforcing the presidential system is the establishment of the possibility of an unlimited legislative delegation to the president by means of enabling laws, which authorize the president to issue decree laws on any matters, not only on economic and financial matters as established in the 1961 Constitution (Article 203). This constitutes an assault on the constitutional guarantee of the "legal reserve" (legislation that is always reserved to an elected representative body), particularly regarding the regulation of constitutional rights. The truth is that the fundamental legislation that has been sanctioned during the past decade (2002–9) is contained in these decree laws has been sanctioned without respect for the constitutionally imposed public hearing (Article 211).

In effect, the legislative power that can be delegated to the president has as one of its fundamental limits imposed by the Constitution the ensuring of political participation in the drafting of said legislation, which is not only a fundamental value of the constitutional text but also one of the most relevant constitutional rights foreseen in it. The Constitution established the right "of the people to participate in the formation, execution and control of the public policies," having the state, as one of its obligations, to "enable the generation of the most favorable conditions for its practice" (Article 62). Also, the Constitution ensures the right to participate in political matters, among other means, through "popular consult" (Article 70).

To define that constitutional right, the Constitution specifically obligates the National Assembly to submit draft legislation to public hearings, as follows. First, with a general character, Article 211 requires the National Assembly and permanent commissions to submit to public consultation during the approval proceedings of draft laws and to listen to the opinion of the organs of the state, the citizens, and civil society. Second, Article 206 requires the National Assembly to consult the states' legislative councils when legislating on matters related to them. In this way, the Constitution ensures the exercise of political participation in the management of public matters and in the formation of laws.

Of course, the president also must comply with the constitutional obligation to submit draft laws to public consultation when legislative delegation takes place. Any delegation transfers powers as well as duties – among them is the constitutional obligation to submit draft decrees to public consultation, in execution of the enabling law. That is, independently of the organ sanctioning the legislation (National Assembly or president in virtue of legislative authorization), submission to public consultation is a compulsory part of the constitutional procedure for drafting statutes. Nonetheless, in 2001 and 2007, the president, after requesting and obtaining the sanction of enabling laws with broad content to enact legislation on many important matters, issued dozens of decree laws without any transparency, without informing the nation as to the draft laws, without debating them, and without required public consultation (Articles 206 and 211).

In this way, in evident constitutional fraud, the National Assembly transferred to the president the authority to legislate on matters of national interest, even if parties in support of the president completely controlled the assembly; as such, he would not find opposition of any kind on legislation that affected other branches of government, particularly the judicial, citizens, and electoral branches, as well as the territorial distribution of state powers.

With all these provisions undermining the separation of powers, Venezuela, whose Constitution is filled with contradictions (e.g., a centralized federation without a senate; legislative power and unlimited legislative delegation; and five-branched state powers with unusual concentration in the representative political organ), has constitutionalized the road to authoritarianism. Thus, democracy and even less the rule of law can hardly be effective in this constitutional framework.

3. *Continuous Interference and Subjection of the Judicial Power*

In Venezuela, after the National Assembly's unconstitutional intervention in the judicial power,[15] and despite the sanctioning of the 1999 Constitution, no effective independence and autonomy of the judicial branch has been ensured. On the contrary, there is a permanent and systematic process of demolishing independence and autonomy through submission to the political control of the president.[16]

In effect, according to the 1999 Constitution provision that eliminated the old Judicature Council, which since 1961 had administered the judiciary, the Supreme Tribunal has assumed the governance and

---

[15]See our reserved vote to the intervention of the judicial power by the Constituent Assembly in Allan R. Brewer-Carías, *Debate constituyente (Aportes a la Asamblea Nacional Constituyente)*, Fundación de Derecho Público–Editorial Jurídica Venezolana, Caracas 1999, 1 (Aug. 8–Sept. 8): 57-73. On the critiques of the process, see Allan R. Brewer-Carías, *Golpe de estado y proceso constituyente en Venezuela*, Universidad Nacional Autónoma de México, Mexico City 2002, 213ff.

[16]See Allan R. Brewer-Carías, "La progresiva y sistemática demolición de la autonomía e independencia del Poder Judicial en Venezuela (1999-2004)," in *XXX Jornadas J.M. Domínguez Escovar, Estado de derecho, Administración de justicia y derechos humanos*, Instituto de Estudios Jurídicos del Estado Lara, Barquisimeto 2005, 33-174.

management of the judiciary, controlling all the judicial system, particularly the appointment and removal of judges. The judges' instability, authorized and promoted by the same Supreme Tribunal, and their provisional appointment without the required public competition, is a main component of the Venezuelan courts' political subjection.

One of the basic principles concerning independence of the judiciary is stability of the judges,[17] considered by the Inter-American Court of Human Rights to be congruent with "the special nature and functions of the courts, because it guarantees the independence of the judges regarding all other branches of government and regarding the political-electoral changes."[18] Such stability is formally ensured in the 1999 Constitution by, first, the provision imposing the need for judges to be selected by public competition; and, second, the provision that to be removed, judges must be subjected to disciplinary trials carried out by disciplinary judges. Unfortunately, none of these provisions has been implemented, and with the complicity of the Supreme Tribunal, those provisions are dead letters.[19]

As a consequence, since 1999, the Venezuelan judiciary has been filled with provisional judges, a situation that since the 2003 Inter-American Commission on Human Rights has repeatedly noticed,[20] considering that provisional judges are susceptible to the political manipulation,[21] which alters the people's right to adequate administration of justice.[22] Since 2000, the Commission has also expressed worries that "the problem of the

---

[17]Basic Principles concerning the Independence of the Judicature adopted by the Seventh Congress of United Nations in Milan, Aug. 26–Sept. 6, 1985, confirmed by the General Assembly in its Resolutions 40/32 of Nov. 1985 and 40/146 of Dec. 1985.

[18]Inter-American Court on Human Rights, *Carranza vs. Argentina*; Case 10.087. Report N° 30/97, Dec. 30, 1997, para. 41.

[19]The Inter-American Commission on Human Rights, in its *2009 Annual Report*, reiterated "with concern the failure to organize public competitions for selecting judges and prosecutors, and so those judicial officials are still appointed in a discretionary fashion without being subject to competition. Since they are not appointed through public competitions, judges and prosecutors are freely appointed and removable, which seriously affects their independence in making decisions. The IACHR also observes that through the Special Program for the Regularization of Tenured Status, judges originally appointed on a provisional basis have been given tenured status, all without participating in a public competitive process," para. 479. Available at http://www.cidh.oas.org/annualrep/ 2009eng/Chap.IV.f.eng.htm.

[20]*Informe sobre la situación de los derechos humanos en Venezuela*; OAS/Ser.L/V/II.118. d.C. 4 rev. 2; Dec. 29, 2003, para. 11.3. It reads: "The Commission has been informed that only 250 judges have been appointed by opposition concurrence according to the constitutional text. From a total of 1,772 positions of judges in Venezuela, the Supreme Court of Justice reports that only 183 are holders, 1,331 are provisional and 258 are temporary."

[21]Id., paras. 11-12.

[22]Id.

provisional status of the judges had deepened and increased since the current Government began a judicial re-organization process,"[23] a statement that has been repeated in all its subsequent annual reports on the human rights situation in Venezuela. The result has been, as mentioned by the Commission in its 2006 report filed before the General Assembly of the Organization of American States, the failure to guarantee judicial independence in Venezuela, where there are cases of dismissals and substitutions in retaliation for decisions contrary to the government's position.[24] Finally, in its 2008 report, the Commission verified the provisional character of the judiciary as an "endemic problem" because the appointment of judges was made without applying constitutional provisions on the matter[25] – thus exposing judges to discretionary dismissal – which highlights the "permanent state of urgency" in which those appointments have been made.[26] In its 2009 Annual Report, the same Inter-American Commission noted "with concern that in some cases, judges were removed almost immediately after adopting judicial decisions in cases with a major political impact," concluding by saying that "The lack of judicial independence and autonomy vis-à-vis political power is, in the IACHR's opinion, one of the weakest points in Venezuelan democracy."[27]

What has happened in Venezuela with intervention in the judiciary, as stated by the Constitutional Chamber of the Supreme Tribunal after deciding that the rulings of the Inter-American Court of Human Rights were not enforceable in the country, has been a process of "cleansing [*depuración*] of the Judiciary."[28]

As described earlier, the constitutional principles tending to ensure autonomy and independence of judges at all levels of the judiciary are yet to be applied, particularly regarding the appointment of candidates through public competition, with citizen participation in their selection and appointment, and regarding the prohibition on removing or

---

[23]Id., para. 31.

[24]Id., paras. 295ff.

[25]*Annual Report 20*08 (OEA/Ser.L/V/II.134. Doc. 5 rev. 1. 25 febrero 2009), para. 39

[26]Id.

[27]See this conclusión of the Commission in ICHR, *Annual Report 2009*, para. 483. Available at http://www.cidh.oas.org/annualrep/2009eng/Chap.IV.f.eng.htm.

[28]Decision N° 1.939 (Dec. 18, 2008) (Case: *Abogados Gustavo Álvarez Arias y otros*), in which the Constitutonal Chamber decided the nonenforceability of the decision of the Inter American Court of Human Rights of Aug. 5, 2008 (Case: *Apitz Barbera y otros ["Corte Primera de lo Contencioso Administrativo"] vs. Venezuela [Corte IDH]*, Case: *Apitz Barbera y otros ["Corte Primera de lo Contencioso Administrativo"] vs. Venezuela*, Sentencia de 5 de agosto de 2008, Serie C, N° 182.

suspending judges except through disciplinary trials before a disciplinary court and judges (Articles 254 and 267). Unfortunately, none of these provisions has been implemented; therefore, since 1999, the Venezuelan judiciary has been composed by temporal and provisional judges that are subjected to the political manipulation, with the possibility for their discretionary dismissal without due process of law for political reasons.[29]

The worst of this irregular situation is that in 2006, there were attempts to solve the problem of the provisional status of judges by means of the Special Program for the Regularization of Tenures, addressed at accidental, temporary, or provisional judges, bypassing the entrance system constitutionally established by means of public competitive exams (Article 255) and consolidating the effects of the provisional appointments and their consequent power dependency.

Disciplinary jurisdiction of judges has not yet been established, and with the authorization of the Supreme Tribunal, the "transitional" Reorganization Commission of the Judicial Power created in 1999 has continued to function, removing judges without due process.[30]

This reality amounts to political control of the judiciary, as demonstrated by the dismissal of judges who have adopted decisions contrary to the policies of the governing political authorities. An example can illustrate this point. When a contentious administrative court ruled against the government in a politically charged case, the government responded by intervening in the court and dismissing its judges. After the Inter-American Court of Human Rights ruled that the dismissal violated the American Convention on Human Rights and Venezuela's international obligations, the Constitutional Chamber upheld the government's argument that the decision of the Inter-American Court cannot be enforced in Venezuela.

The case developed as follows: On July 17, 2003, the Venezuelan National Federation of Doctors brought an *amparo* action in the First Court on Contentious Administrative Matters in Caracas,[31] against the

---

[29]This was reported by the Inter-American Commission on Human Rights in 2003; see *Report on the Situation of Human Rights in Venezuela*, OEA/Ser.L/V/II.118, doc. 4, rev. 2, Dec. 29, 2003, para. 174. Acailable at http://www.cidh.oas.org/country-rep/Venezuela2003eng/toc.htm.: and also in its *2009 Annual Report*, para. 479; at http://www.cidh.oas.org/annualrep/2009eng/Chap.IV.f.eng.htm.

[30]See Allan R. Brewer-Carías, "La justicia sometida al poder y la interminable emergencia del poder judicial (1999-2006)," *in Derecho y democracia. Cuadernos universitarios* 2, Órgano de Divulgación Académica, Vicerrectorado Académico, Universidad Metropolitana, Caracas 2007, 122-38.

[31]Contentious administrative courts have competence to review administrative decisions.

mayor of Caracas, the Ministry of Health, and the Caracas Metropolitan Board of Doctors (Colegio de Médicos). The petitioners asked for a declaration of the nullity of certain measures of the defendant officials, who had hired Cuban doctors for a much-publicized government health program in the Caracas slums but without complying with the legal requirements for foreign doctors to practice medicine in Venezuela. The National Federation of Doctors argued that by allowing foreign doctors to practice medicine without complying with applicable regulations, the program was discriminatory and violated the constitutional rights of Venezuelan doctors.[32] One month later, on August 21, 2003, the court issued a preliminary protective *amparo* measure, on the grounds that there were sufficient elements to consider that the constitutional guarantee of equality before the law was being violated. The court preliminarily ordered the suspension of the Cuban doctors' hiring program and ordered the Metropolitan Board of Doctors to replace the Cuban doctors already hired with Venezuelan or foreign doctors who had fulfilled the legal requirements to practice medicine.[33]

In response to that preliminary *amparo* decision, the minister of health, the mayor of Caracas, and President Chávez made public statements to the effect that the decision would not be respected or enforced.[34] Following those statements, the government-controlled Constitutional Chamber of the Supreme Tribunal of Justice adopted a decision, without any appeal filed, assuming jurisdiction over the case and annulling the preliminary *amparo* ordered by the first court; a group of officials of the Ministry of the Interior Intelligence Services seized the first court's premises; and the president publicly called the president of the first court a "bandit," among other things.[35] A few weeks later, in response to the court's decision in an unrelated case challenging a local registrar's refusal to record a land sale, the unconstitutional Special Commission for the Intervention of the

---

[32]See Claudia Nikken, "El caso 'Barrio Adentro': La Corte Primera de lo Contencioso Administrativo ante la Sala Constitucional del Tribunal Supremo de Justicia o el avocamiento como medio de amparo de derechos e intereses colectivos y difusos," *Revista de Derecho Público* 93–96, Editorial Jurídica Venezolana, Caracas 2003, 5ff.

[33]See Decision of Aug. 21, 2003, in id., 445ff.

[34]The president said: "Váyanse con su decisión no sé para donde, la cumplirán ustedes en su casa si quieren" (You can all go with your decision to I don't know where; you will enforce it in your house if you want). See *El Universal*, Caracas Aug. 25, 2003; *El Universal*, Caracas Aug. 28, 2003.

[35]See Inter-American Court of Human Rights, *Apitz Barbera et al. (Corte Primera de lo Contencioso Administrativo) vs. Venezuela* (Decision of Aug. 5, 2008), available at http://www.corteidh.or.cr, para. 239. See also *El Universal,* Caracas Oct. 16, 2003; *El Universal*, Caracas Sept. 22, 2003.

Judiciary dismissed all five judges of the first court.[36] Despite nationwide protests from bar associations and the International Commission of Jurists,[37] the first court remained suspended and its premises closed for about nine months,[38] during which no judicial review of administrative action could be sought in the country.[39]

The dismissed judges of the first court brought a complaint to the Inter-American Commission on Human Rights for their unlawful removal by the government and for violations of their constitutional rights. The Commission, in turn, brought the case, *Apitz Barbera et al. (Corte Primera de lo Contencioso Administrativo vs. Venezuela)* before the Inter-American Court of Human Rights. On August 5, 2008, the Inter-American Court ruled that the Republic of Venezuela had violated the rights of the dismissed judges established in the American Convention on Human Rights and ordered the state to pay them due compensation, to reinstate them to a similar position in the judiciary, and to publish part of the decision in Venezuelan newspapers.[40] Nonetheless, on December 12, 2008, the Constitutional Chamber issued Decision No. 1.939, declaring that the August 5, 2008, decision of the Inter-American Court of Human Rights was unenforceable (*inejecutable*) in Venezuela. The Constitutional Chamber also accused the Inter-American Court of having usurped powers of the Supreme Tribunal of Justice, and it asked the executive branch to denounce the American Convention on Human Rights.[41]

---

[36] See *El Nacional*, Caracas Nov. 5, 2003, A2. The dismissed president of the first court said: "La justicia venezolana vive un momento tenebroso, pues el tribunal que constituye un último resquicio de esperanza ha sido clausurado." (The Venezuelan judiciary is living a dark moment, because the court that was a last glimmer of hope has been shut down."). id. The Commission for the Intervention of the Judiciary had also dismissed almost all judges in the country without due process and had replaced them with provisionally appointed judges beholden to the ruling power.

[37] See *El Nacional*, Caracas Oct. 10, 2003, A-6; *El Nacional*, Caracas Oct. 15, 2003, A-2; *El Nacional*, Caracas Sept. 24, 2003, A-4; *El Nacional*, Caracas Feb. 14, 2004, A-7.

[38] See *El Nacional*, Caracas Oct. 24, 2003, A-2; *El Nacional*, Caracas July 16, 2004, A-6.

[39] See, generally, Allan R. Brewer-Carías, "La progresiva y sistemática demolición institucional de la autonomía e independencia del poder judicial en Venezuela 1999–2004," in *XXX Jornadas J.M. Domínguez Escovar, Estado de derecho, Administración de justicia y derechos humanos,* Instituto de Estudios Jurídicos del Estado Lara, Barquisimeto 2005, 33-174; Allan R. Brewer-Carías, "La justicia sometida al poder (La ausencia de independencia y autonomía de los jueces en Venezuela por la interminable emergencia del poder judicial [1999-2006])," in *Cuestiones internacionales. Anuario Jurídico Villanueva 2007,* Centro Universitario Villanueva, Marcial Pons, Madrid 2007, 25-57, available at http://www.allanbrewercarias.com (N° 550, 2007).

[40] Inter-American Court of Human Rights, *Apitz Barbera et al. (Corte Primera de lo Contencioso Administrativo) vs. Venezuela* (Decision of Aug. 5, 2008), available at http://www.corteidh.or.cr.

[41] Supreme Tribunal of Justice, Constitutional Chamber, Decision N° 1.939 (Dec. 18, 2008) (Case: *Abogados Gustavo Álvarez Arias et al.*) (Exp. N° 08-1572).

The case just discussed, including in particular the ad hoc response of the Constitutional Chamber to the decision of the Inter-American Court of Human Rights, shows clearly the present subordination of the Venezuelan judiciary to the policies, wishes, and dictates of the president. The Constitutional Chamber has become a most effective tool for consolidating power in the person of President Chávez.

III. CENTRALIZING POWER AND THE ABSENCE OF EFFECTIVE POLITICAL PARTICIPATION

The authoritarian government that has taken root in Venezuela over the past decade has been possible thanks to the constitutionalization of elements contributing to the concentrated power of the state and to the reinforcement of the traditional centralized federation and the distortion of the exercise of democracy and popular participation – covered over by a false populist speech that pretends to replace representative democracy with participatory democracy and that has lead to the progressive dismantling of democracy.

1. *The Meaning of Democracy and the Illusion of Participatory Democracy*

Political participation – that is, the possibility for citizens to participate in political decision making – is possible only when power is available to the people in a decentralized power system based on the multiplication of self-governed local authorities.[42] On the contrary, in a centralized federation like the one reinforced in the 1999 Constitution, political participation turns into a rhetorical illusion, and the political system becomes an easy instrument of authoritarianism.[43]

For this reason, also on occasion of the referendum on the 1999 Constitution, I warned:

---

[42]See proposals for the reinforcement of the decentralization of the federation and the dismantling of its centralization in Allan R. Brewer-Carías, *Debate constituyente (Aportes a la Asamblea Nacional Constituyente),* Fundación de Derecho Público–Editorial Jurídica Venezolana, Caracas 1999, 1 (Aug. 8–Sept. 8):155ff.

[43]See the studies "La opción entre democracia y autoritarismo (Julio 2001)," 41-59; "Democracia, descentralización política y reforma del Estado (Julio-Octubre 2001), 105-25; "El municipio, la descentralización política y la democracia (Octubre 2001), 127-41, in Allan R. Brewer-Carías, *Reflexiones sobre el constitucionalismo en América,* Editorial Jurídica Venezolana, Caracas 2001.

The great reform of the political system necessary and essential to perfect democracy, was to dismantle the State centralism and to distribute the Public Power in the territory; the only way to make political participation a reality. The Constituent Assembly, in order to overcome the political crisis, had to design the transformation of the State, decentralizing power and setting the basis to make it more available to people. By not doing it, it neither transformed the State nor did it dispose of the necessary elements to make participation more effective.[44]

However, despite the centralized framework of state power clearly expressed in the Constitution, the word *participation* is used on multiple occasions. Moreover, it proclaims so-called participatory democracy as a global value but without allowing effective political participation of the people in public affairs through autonomous and decentralized political local entities. Thus, participation remains no more than the exercise of the right to vote in several mechanisms of direct democracy, like referenda, citizens' assemblies, and the communal councils. These, however, have no political autonomy; they are instruments established parallel to municipalities, conducted in a centralized way by a minister of the executive.

In fact, in authoritarian speech related to participatory democracy, expertly used as a response to the political failures of many representative democracies dominated by political parties, the term *participatory democracy* sometimes is confused with elements of direct democracy. It mainly is used as part of a misleading strategy to attack representative democracy as a political regime, aggravated by the popular distrust developed regarding the political parties and the state institutions, which are far too distant from citizens.

The confusion produced by the clamor of participation in many Latin American countries, which is by essence contrary to authoritarianism, forces a reestablishing of the true concept of democracy to situate political participation where it belongs, precisely in the local ambit of political decentralization. Without a doubt, the two fundamental principles of democracy in the contemporary world continue to be representation and participation. Representation can be confronted with direct democracy; thus, the dichotomy in this case is between representative (or indirect) democracy and direct democracy.

---

[44]Document dated Nov. 30, 1999. See Allan R. Brewer-Carías, *Debate constituyente (Aporte a la Asamblea Nacional Constituyente),* Fundación de Derecho Público—Editorial Jurídica Venezolana, Caracas 1999, 3 (Oct. 18–Nov. 30):323.

Participation cannot be confronted with representation but rather with political exclusion, so the dichotomy in this case is between participatory democracy (democracy of inclusion) and exclusionary democracy (democracy of exclusion). This is precisely what is not clear in speeches on participatory democracy: In certain cases, it is used to refer to mechanisms of direct democracy; in others, the concepts are deliberately confused to eliminate or minimize representation and establish an alleged direct relation between a leader, generally a messianic one, and the people. In the case of Venezuela, this means nonelected institutional entities disposed to make the people believe that they are participating when in fact they are only being mobilized and submitted to control by centralized power.

Representative democracy will continue to be the essence of democracy.[45] Its substitution is essentially impossible in democracy, without detriment that it could be perfected, for instance, with the introduction of mechanisms of direct democracy in the political systems, like those included in the 1993 Organic Law on Suffrage and Political participation and in the 1999 Constitution, that complement it but will never replace it.

In the contemporary world, there can never be only direct democracy, based on plebiscites, referenda, or permanent open municipal or town hall councils. But this does not impede the fact that all contemporary constitutional systems have incorporated popular consultation mechanisms and citizens' assemblies to complement representation. In that sense, as in the case of the 1999 Venezuelan Constitution, all imaginable types of referenda have been regulated: consulting, approving, deciding, abrogating, authorizing, and recalling – as well as popular initiatives. Without doubt, this has contributed to popular mobilization and to the relative direct manifestation of the will of the people. But it is clear that those mechanisms cannot replace democracy driven by elected representatives. The challenge here, to contribute to the consolidation of the democratic rule of law, is to ensure that representatives truly regard the communities they represent and that they be elected by direct, universal, and secret–ballot systems, where political pluralism prevails, and by means of transparent electoral processes ensuring access to power with submission to the rule of law.

---

[45]See the proposal on the regulation of the participatory and representative democratic principle in the 1999 Constitution in Allan R. Brewer-Carías, *Debate constituyente (Aportes a la Asamblea Nacional Constituyente),* Fundación de Derecho Público–Editorial Jurídica Venezolana, Caracas 1999, 1 (Aug. 8–Sept. 8):183ff.

Without doubt, though, the second basic principle of democracy has more contemporary interest. Political participation, it has been said, is not more than a democratic regime of political inclusion, where the citizen is part of its politically autonomous organized community and contributes to decision-making processes. To participate means to be included; for that reason, the opposite of political participation is political exclusion, which also can be of social and economic character. Unfortunately, however, in the democratic political doctrine, too often the concepts have been confused, and participatory democracy is often confused and reduced to mechanisms of direct democracy. But participatory democracy is much more than that.

To participate, in fact, in common language, is to be part of, to belong, to be incorporated, to contribute, to be associated or committed to; it is to have a role in, to have an active part in, to be involved in, or to lend a hand to; it is to be related, to share, or to have something to do with. Participation, then, in the political language, means nothing more than to be part of a political community, which, in essence, must have self-government with political autonomy in which individuals have a specific, active role according to which they contribute to decision making. This, consequently, cannot be exhausted by the sole exercise of the right to vote (which is undoubtedly a minimal form of participation); by being a member of intermediate societies, even those of political character, as political parties; by voting in referenda (another minimal form of participation); or by being part of citizens' assemblies controlled by the central power.[46]

Democratic political participation means, in reality, to be included in the political process and to be an active part of it, without interventions; it means, then, the ability to access the decision-making process in public matters to be decided by autonomous entities. This cannot be permanently accomplished in any democratic society solely with ballots in referenda or popular consultation. Nor is it accomplished with manifestations, even though they are multitudinous, and even less with those manifestations that are obedient and submissive to a leader. History, including the fascist authoritarianism of the previous century, has taken care to teach us this in all of its aspects; it should not be confused with political participation.

---

[46]See Allan R. Brewer-Carías, "Democracia municipal, descentralización y desarrollo local" (Conferencia Inaugural del XXVI Congreso Iberoamericano de Municipios, Organización Iberoamericana de Cooperación Intermunicipal, Ayuntamiento de Valladolid; Valladolid, Oct. 13–15, 2004), *Revista Iberoamericana de Administración Pública* 11, INAP, Madrid 2003, 11-34.

For democracy to be inclusive or of inclusion, it must allow citizens to be an effective part of political communities that, above all, are autonomous; it must allow them to develop their effective pertinence, that is, the sense of belonging in the political and social order, such as to a community, a place, a land, a field, a district, a town, a region, a city – in short, to a state – and to be elected for that purpose as a representative of the people.

Because of this, participatory democracy is not something new in political history. It has always been there, even since the revolutions of the nineteenth century, in the democratic political theories and practices. In all countries with a consolidated democracy, it exists imperceptibly, deeply rooted in the lowest level of the territories of the states, in the autonomous political entities, like municipalities or communes – in the base of the territorial distribution of power.

The great issue of political participation in democracies lacking participation is to determine where and how one can really participate. The answer points to the entities that result from the political decentralization of power and that are, above all, self-governed. Consequently, without replacing the vote and the instruments of direct democracy, political participation as democracy of inclusion, in which citizens can personally be part of a decision-making process regarding public activities of general interest, can exist only in the most politically reduced, decentralized, and autonomous territorial bodies – that is, at the local, community, or municipal level. Only in the lowest autonomous levels of self-government can a participatory organization be structured and allow incorporation of individual citizens, groups, or communities into the public life, particularly in the general public decision-making process or in administrative matters.

Thus, the central issue to be solved when talking properly about participatory democracy is that of determining the territorial level required for participation to be effective as a democratic routine. The classic answer is the municipality, as a self-governing political entity scattered throughout all parts of a state, in every village, town, and county, located very close to the citizen – not great urban or rural municipalities located far from the citizens.

Finally, in all of the democratically developed countries prevails many municipalities, and among them, small municipalities.[47] In contrast, in

---

[47]For instance, in approximate numbers: 2,350 municipalities in Austria, with an average population of 3,400; 589 municipalities in Belgium, with an average population of 17,000; 36,550

Latin America, municipalities are extremely distant from citizens.[48] In Europe and Latin America, municipalities were tributaries of the same basic principles derived from the French Revolution. The great difference is that since the beginning of the nineteenth century in Europe, municipalities were located in every borough, town, village, and city, very close to the citizen. In Latin America, municipalities that had their roots in colonialism have continued to have that same position after independence as metropolitan town councils, very far from citizens.

In Europe, and also in the United States, political participation is a daily life matter that many times passes by imperceptibly. In the second case, there is no participation of any kind because the territorial ambit is so distant from citizens that municipalities are useless in properly managing local interests or allowing for real political participation of the people in the management of their own communal affairs.

Therefore, participatory democracy is possible only when it is indissolubly linked not to direct democracy mechanisms, like referenda, popular consultation, popular initiatives, and citizens' assemblies, but rather to political decentralization, establishing local governments at the lowest level of the territory (municipalities). That is, participatory democracy cannot be mistaken for direct democracy, as often occurs when introducing means to perfect democracy.[49]

Political participation as a democratic routine or way of life can occur only at local levels of government. Consequently, political participation or participatory democracy is eventually related to localism and political decentralization, designed to limit the exercise of political power. That is why there cannot be and have never been decentralized authoritarianisms; the latter is always cemented in centralized government, not effectively allowing political participation. That is, centralized political power is essential to authoritarianism and opposite to democracy because it

---

municipalities in France, with an average population of 1,600; 16,120 municipalities in Germany, with an average population of 5,000; 7,100 municipalities in Italy with an average population of 7,100; 8,050 municipalities in Spain, with an average population of 4,800; or 75,500 municipalities in the Unites States, with an average population of 3,880. See references in Allan R. Brewer-Carías, *Reflexiones sobre el constitucionalismo en América*, Editorial Jurídica Venezolana, Caracas 2001, 139-41.

[48]For instance, in approximate numbers: 1,617 municipalities in Argentina, with an average population of 22,000; 5,580 municipalities in Brazil, with an average population of 30,000; 1,068 municipalities in Colombia, with an average population of 39,000; 2,418 municipalities in México with an average population of 40,116; 1,800 municipalities in Peru, with an average population of 13,800; or 338 municipalities in Venezuela, with an average population of 71,006, in id.

[49]See, e.g., in Venezuela, the set of studies published in *Participación ciudadana y democracia*, Comisión Presidencial para la Reforma del Estado, Caracas 1998.

prevents real participation. The latter can occur only in a system of government where power is politically decentralized and close to citizens. There is no other instance in the state's organization for citizens to participate. The rest is falsehood and deceit, or direct democracy mechanisms. This is why political decentralization is not a noticeable political issue in the developed and consolidated European democracies, where participation is part of daily life in local questions that can be dealt with in small urban and rural municipalities.

Consequently, because political decentralization is the basis for participatory democracy and a means for controlling power, no political participation can exist without political or territorial decentralization, without the existence of a multiplicity of local and regional governments. Centralism, however, is the basis of political exclusion: It concentrates power in those few who are elected and it discredits representative democracy.[50]

Only authoritarianism fears and rejects both political decentralization and political participation. Thus, in Venezuela since 1999, the government has progressively dismantled the work of the 1990s to promote decentralization and, in the name of participatory democracy, has been centralizing all state power, dismantling what was left of the federal form of government – and, with it, representative democracy – but without allowing real and effective political participation.

2. *The Reaction against the Federation as a Decentralized State*

In Venezuela, the great political transformation that should have taken place during the 1999 constitution-making process to improve democracy,[51] which should have been its key motivation, was the effective substitution of the centralized federal system that had developed during the twentieth century with an effectively decentralized federation of two territorial levels: states and multiple autonomous municipalities.

---

[50]See Allan R. Brewer-Carías, "El municipio, la descentralización política y la democracia," in *XXV Congreso Iberoamericano de Municipios, Guadalajara, Jalisco, Mexico, Octubre 23-26, 2001*, Fundación Española de Municipios y Provincias, Madrid 2003, 453ff.

[51]See the proposal during the discussion of the draft constitution in Allan R. Brewer-Carías, "Propuesta sobre la forma federal del estado en la nueva Constitución: Nuevo federalismo y nuevo municipalismo," in *Debate constituyente (Aportes a la Asamblea Nacional Constituyente)*, Fundación de Derecho Público–Editorial Jurídica Venezolana, Caracas 1999, 1 (Aug. 8-Sept. 8):150-70; "El reforzamiento de la forma federal del estado venezolano en la nueva Constitución: Nuevo federalismo y nuevo municipalismo," Report to the International Conference on Federalism in an Era of Globalization, Quebec Oct. 1999, available at http://www.allanbrewercarias.com (N° 734, 1999).

In practice, though, decentralization was not achieved, even if Article 4 declares that "the Bolivarian Republic of Venezuela is a decentralized federal State." The fact is that it is so, of course, "in the terms established in this Constitution; which as occurred in the 1961 Constitution, organized a centralized State with just a federal veil, because of the absence of any real vertical distribution of State power.[52] The "decentralized federation" mentioned in Article 4 of the Constitution is no more than void words, with the power of the state organized in an even more centralized way.[53]

In the 1999 Constitution, as it has been said before, there was not much progress regarding the content of the previous 1961 Constitution, except for the provisions incorporated in 1999 partially following the content of some articles of the 1989 Organic Law of Decentralization, Delimitation, and Transfer of Competencies of the Public Power. Nonetheless, there was no progress or transformations to make decentralization of the federation a reality. Rather, there was an institutional backwardness on the matter. The Senate was eliminated and, for the first time in the constitutional history of Venezuela, the unicameral National Assembly was established, with the consequent formalization of a permanent institutional equality between the states (Article 186). Also, the Constitution provides for the possibility of establishing limits to the autonomy of the states (Article 162) and even the municipalities (Article 168) by means of national statutes. This fact denies, first, the idea of political decentralization, and second, of the territorial autonomy of local governments. The Constitution also established a precarious ambit of the state powers, whose exercise, additionally, was subject to the provisions of national legislation; and it centralized taxation, which increased states' financial dependency.

---

[52]See Allan R. Brewer-Carías, "Los problemas de la federación centralizada en Venezuela," *Revista Ius et Praxis* 12, Facultad de Derecho y Ciencias Políticas, Universidad de Lima, Peru 1988, 49-96; "Problemas de la federación centralizada (A propósito de la elección directa de gobernadores)," in *IV Congreso Iberoamericano de Derecho Constitucional*, Universidad Nacional Autónoma de México, Mexico City 1992, 85-131.

[53]See Allan R. Brewer-Carías, *Federalismo y municipalismo en la Constitución de 1999 (Alcance de una reforma insuficiente y regresiva)*, Cuadernos de la Cátedra Allan R. Brewer-Carías de Derecho Público 7, Universidad Católica del Táchira–Editorial Jurídica Venezolana, Caracas–San Cristóbal 2001, 187. See also Allan R. Brewer-Carías, "El 'estado federal descentralizado' y la centralización de la federación en Venezuela. Situación y perspectiva de una contradicción constitucional," *Revista de Estudios de la Administración Local (REAL)* 292–293, Madrid 2003, 11-43.

3. *The Reaction against Local Governments and the Centralized Communal Councils*

For local government (municipalities), the great democratic reform that should have been introduced with the 1999 Constitution was, essentially, to place municipal institutions closer to citizens by extending local governments in the territory, by increasing instead of reducing the number of municipalities. None of this was done; no important reform on this matter was introduced. Instead, through the sanctioning of the Organic Law of the Municipal Public Power of 2005,[54] the expansion of local governments was prevented by establishing new limits for their creation. Instead of increasing municipalities or local governments, the Communal Councils Law of 2006, reformed in 2009, established communal councils as nonrepresentative institutions that function without elected members subject to the citizens' assemblies.[55] In June 2010, the National Assembly began the discussion of the new Law of the Communes, conceived as "the socialist local entity, from which the socialist society is to be edified" (Article 5), controlled by the central government.[56]

In effect, given the mechanisms of direct democracy established in the Constitution, like citizens' assemblies with binding decisions (Article 70), the Law on Communal Councils in 2006 established a centralized institutional system, parallel to the local government (municipalities), to replace it and to pretend to be ensuring popular participation. The result was to replace local governments in their constitutional task of being the basic instance for political participation. In the end, what has been established are the basic elements to construct a centralized state, without regional or local elected government, directed from the apex of the national executive through an organization called the "Popular Power," in which the citizens supposedly participate but according to the dictates of the central power diffused by the official party. The president announced this in January 2007, referring to "the revolutionary explosion of the communal power" by means of creating "some sort of regional, local and

---

[54]See *Gaceta Oficial* N° 38.204, June 8, 2005. The Organic Law was the subject of reform in Nov. 2005; *Gaceta Oficial* N° 38.327, Dec. 2, 2005, and then in Apr. 2006, *Gaceta Oficial* N° 5,806, Extra. Apr. 10, 2006, reprinted by material error in *Gaceta Oficial* N° 38.421, Apr. 21, 2006. See Allan R. Brewer-Carías et al., *Ley Orgánica del Poder Público Municipal*, Editorial Jurídica Venezolana, Caracas 2005.

[55]See *Gaceta Oficial* N° 5.806, Extra., Apr. 10, 2006; *Gaceta Oficial* N° 39.335, Dec. 28, 2009.

[56]See Eugenio G. Martínez, "Poca independencia tendrán comunas. Poder central debe aprobar todos los proyectos de las comunas," in *El Universal,* Caracas July, 5, 2010. Available at http://politica.eluniversal.com/2010/07/05/pol_art_poca-independencia-t_1961543.shtml

national Confederation of Communal Councils" to "march towards the conformation of a communal state," thus progressively dismantling the "old middle-class state that is still alive" and raising "the communal state, the socialist state, the Bolivarian state."[57] Two days later, on his second–term Inauguration Day, Chávez added that the objective was "to transit towards the road of a communal city, where no mayor's office or local government [municipal] boards are needed, only the communal power."[58] All these proposals, based on nondemocratic organizations, were incorporated in the constitutional reform draft he submitted to the National Assembly and that eventually was rejected by the people in the referendum of December 2, 2007.

The great difference between this communal entities is that and democratic local governments, is that in the latter, mayors and municipal councils are elected by popular universal and secret vote; on the contrary, in the framework of the so-called communal power, members of the communal councils are supposedly appointed directly in citizens' assemblies, which the executive controls through ministers of the central government and the official party.

In this centralized system, communal councils do not have any political autonomy, so they are not part of the representative democratic system established in the Constitution. They supposedly result from the functioning of the "community" conceived outside local governments (municipalities), which, according to the Constitution, are the primary political unit in the national organization. Ignoring these provisions, the communal councils have been created as "instances for participation, articulation and integration between the different community organizations, social groups and the people," but without any autonomy – they are not even decentralized entities. The result of this process has been, with the establishment of nonautonomous parallel institutions, a process of dismantling representative democracy.

With the 2006 Law of Communal Councils, councils were established without any type of relation with local governments (municipalities) or any kind of democratic representation. They were initially organized through a pyramidal frame of regional and national presidential commissions that provided funds. In such councils, organized in a centralized way, the "organized people" supposedly "exercise directly the management of public politics and projects directed to respond to the

[57]Speech of Hugo Chávez, 01-08-2007.
[58]Speech of Hugo Chávez, *El Nacional*, Caracas Nov. 1, A2.

needs and aspirations of the communities in the construction of a society of equality and social justice" (Article 2). In the 2009 reform of the Organic Law of Communal Councils, they also have been established without any sort of self-government or autonomy, and now they completely depend on the president.[59] In addition, in 2010 has been sanctioned the Organic Law on the Federal Council of Government,[60] in which the "organized society" is defined as constituted by "communal councils, communes and others base organizations of the Popular power" (Article 4). According to this new law, the "decentralization" process, bypassing states and municipalities, has been established for the purpose of transferring competencies to the "base organization of the popular power" (Article 2) and to newly created "Motor Districts for Development" (Article 7), in order "to achieve the integral development of the regions and the strengthening of the popular power for the purpose of facilitating the transition toward socialism" (Article 6). Finally, in June 2010, the National Assembly began the discussion of the Law of the Communes.

Within this centralist framework of the organization of popular power, what will ensure participation seems to be nothing less than the United Socialist Party that the head of state presides over himself, imbricate in the state bureaucracy as has never been seen in Venezuela, and that as a governmental political system was demolished in the world with the fall of the Berlin Wall.

IV. THE FORESEEABLE OUTCOME: THE DICTATORSHIP OF DEMOCRACY

For democratic rule of law to exist, the declarations contained in constitutional texts that speak of participatory and protagonist democracy or of the political decentralization of the state are not enough; neither is it enough to establish an elective system that allows the election of public officials through suffrage. The system must effectively ensure representation, political pluralism, and access to public offices according to rule of law and procedures.

Also, for a true democratic rule of law to exist, it is necessary and indispensable that the constitutional framework in which it is intended to

---

[59] *Gaceta Oficial* N° 39.335 of Dec. 28, 2009. See Allan R. Brewer-Carías, "Introducción general al régimen de los consejos comunales,"in *Ley de los Consejos Comunales*, Editorial Jurídica Venezolana, Caracas 2010.

[60] See in *Official Gazette* N° 5.963 Extra. of Feb. 22, 2010

function effectively allows for control of state power by power itself, in a checks-and-balances system, including the supreme power of the people. This is the only way to ensure rule of law, democratic principles, and full enjoyment of freedom and human rights.

Control of the state power under democratic rule of law can be achieved only by dividing, separating, and distributing public power, either horizontally among different branches of government or vertically among different territorial levels of government. Concentrations of power and its centralization are essentially antidemocratic state structures.

It is precisely within these principles where lie the problems of the formally declared rule of law in Venezuela – whose deformation rests in the proper constitutional text of 1999. Unfortunately, constitutional provisions encouraging authoritarianism were established, allowing neutralization of any form of power control and the centralization of power, thereby initiating the dismantling of federalism and municipalism. This has led to authoritarianism and, despite the direct democracy mechanisms established, has challenged the possibility of effective political participation. The result is constitutional authoritarianism that, although electoral in origin, negates the democratic rule of law.

On the basis of this framework of constitutional authoritarianism, in January 2007 at the beginning of his second term, President Chávez began to expose the steps to definitively dismantle democracy in Venezuela, by means of configuring a system of total concentration of state power – the popular power or communal power to construct a communal or socialist state) – totally concentrated and centralized, and politically conducted by the United Socialist Party directly connected with the head of state. Thus, both the popular power and the United Socialist Party instate a dictatorship of democracy, led by a single person.

As a result, the president began to refer to his ministries as "Ministries of the Popular Power for (Foreign Relations, Environment, etc.)," and he began to promote a general reform of the Constitution to transform a democratic, rule-of-law state into a centralized, socialist state.

Nonetheless, before drafting the constitutional-reform proposals and defrauding the Constitution, he began to implement some of the reforms by means of decree. He submitted to the National Assembly in January 2007 a draft of an enabling law to be authorized to enact statutes contrary to the Constitution "to update and transform the legal system that regulates State institutions" and to establish "the mechanisms of popular participation, by means of the social control, the social technical inspection and the practice of the voluntary enlistment of the organized community in the application of the judicial system and the economical scope of the State; also, to adapt the organization structure of the State institutions, to allow the direct exercise of the popular supremacy." All these "constitutional" statutes were to be sanctioned by means of decrees to advance the path toward constitutional reform and, after its approval, to further consolidate the socialist project.[61] That is, during another precise process of defrauding the Constitution, the president asked the National Assembly to enact an enabling law to prepare the way for implementation of a constitutional reform that was not yet approved or even drafted.

The general purpose of those reforms directed at the organization of the popular power was the elimination of democracy as a plural and representative political regime that allows for election of public officials at all levels by means of the universal, direct, and secret ballot: mayors and councilors in the municipalities, governors and legislators in the states, and representatives to the National Assembly.

Representative and indirect democracy was due to be substituted by alleged direct, participatory democracy in which there would be no popular election of any kind. It would be based on citizens' assemblies and communal councils whose members would not be elected but would be chosen in the community by citizens' assemblies, of course, with the ideological direction of the United Socialist Party, the only one with access to the state power organizations at all levels.

In the framework that could be foreseen from the presidential announcements, the communal councils would appoint representatives to regional communal councils or to those of the federal cities ("regional and local confederation of communal councils"); and the last step would be to appoint their representatives in the "National Assembly for the Popular Power" ("national confederation of communal councils"), which will eventually replace the National Assembly. In this way, every trace of direct, universal, secret election of representatives to state and national legislative organs would disappear. Finally, the National Assembly for the

---

[61] As it was written in the newspaper on Jan. 31, 2007: "The 18 month length period of force of the enabling Law, has the object of allowing Hugo Chávez, President of the Republic, to wait for the reform of the Constitution to be approved in order to write the norms that will base the socialist model of State he wants to instate." According to the opinions of members of parliament, during the first months the law decrees written by the Executive will be adapted to the 1999 Magna Charta, and in some of them, the omissions of the Legislative Power will be filled. . . . After the popular consult for the approval of the reforms of the Constitution, several representatives have expressed that it could happen in Sept., the president would have time enough to adapt the legislation to the political model he proposes. Thus, representatives assume that every legal instrument related to the State system will be announced by the end of 2007 or the beginning of 2008." *El Nacional,* Caracas Jan. 31, 2007, A2.

Popular Power, configured as such, would appoint the National Council (of government) for the Popular Power, which, of course, would be presided over by the same person who would be president of the Socialist Party.

All these political reforms eliminating representative democracy in the country began to be implemented a few months before the presidential decrees, during 2006, with the sanctioning of the Law of Communal Councils (Popular Power), substituted in 2009 by the Organic Law of the Communal Councils, in a new and evident defrauding coup against the Constitution, establishing a parallel structure for existing municipalities, to definitively replace the local self-government framework of municipalities.

It is obvious that once the base structure of the "Popular Power" announced in the 2009 Organic Law of Communal Councils, in the 2010 Organic Law of the Federal Council of Government and in the 2010 Law of the Communes draft, finished to be completed, and provided enormous resources directly managed by the national Executive that are not given to municipalities, the following step that could be taken would be the elimination of the municipalities. In 2007, the president announced his intention to proceed simultaneously with the elimination of the states and any trace of direct election and political decentralization and, therefore, of the real possibility of political participation. What he announced was the elimination of all municipal and regional, representative, and elected bodies.[62] On a state level, only certain federal cities or regional confederations of communal councils would remain, whose leaders, again, would be appointed by the communal councils.

Following this framework of proposed reforms, what was next was the proposal to eliminate the National Assembly as a national representative organ and establish the National Assembly of the Popular Power (national confederation of communal councils) in its place, which would be the summit of the popular power, formed by persons appointed by the federal cities and communal councils; all of these, of course, are duly controlled, from the summit, by the United Socialist Party.

In the 2007 constitutional reforms, the president also referred to a proposal he initially expressed in 2006 on the possibility of his indefinite reelection. In the interim, after popular rejection of such a constitutional reform in 2007, the president managed to have approved in 2009 a

---

[62]See the article on the president's statement in Laura Weffer Cifuentes, "Chávez: Empecemos a raspar a alcaldes y gobernadores," in *El Nacional*, Caracas Jan. 29, 2007, A2.

constitutional amendment on the matter. Nonetheless, it was obvious that the purpose was to establish reelection in a system based on appointment by the National Confederation of the Popular Power, which would be the National Assembly of the Popular Power. That is, the continuous reelection of the president would be based not on his popular election but rather on his appointment.

These were in general terms the proposals announced to ensure the dictatorship of democracy, not different from the dictatorship of the proletariat that was supposed to be established by the Soviets in the Soviet Union since 1918, or from the popular power in Cuba since 1958, where the Popular Assembly appoints the council of state and, for many decades, always elected the same person to preside.

In conclusion, the main purpose of the reform proposals, many of which have already been implemented, is the complete elimination of representative democracy and its replacement by a supposed direct participatory democracy.

Chapter 6

THE REINFORCED CENTRALIZATION OF THE FEDERATION

As it is provided in the 1999 Constitution, federalism in Venezuela is a contradictory form of government.[1] Typically, a federation is a politically decentralized state organization based on the existence and functioning of autonomous states. The power of that decentralized state is distributed among the national state and the member states. In contrast, the federation in Venezuela is a centralized federation, which is a contradiction in itself.

Unfortunately, Venezuela is not a good example of the importance of federalism in Latin America because it is a federation based on a very centralized national government, with twenty-three formal autonomous states and one capital district. Each of these twenty-three formal autonomous states is without its own effective public policies and its own substantive subnational constitutions; and if it is true that they have elected authorities, those have been weakened by the central government. Regarding the capital district, against the provisions of the 1999 Constitution, it has been regulated in 2009 by a national law with the same trends as the former federal district; that is, without self-government, dependent of the national executive.[2]

---

[1] See, in general, Allan R. Brewer Carías, *Federalismo y municipalismo en la Constitución de 1999 (Una reforma insuficiente y regresiva)*, Editorial Jurídica Venezolana, Caracas 2001; "El estado federal descentralizado y la centralización de la federación en Venezuela. Situación y perspectiva de una contradicción constitucional," in *Federalismo y regionalismo,* coord. Diego Valadés and José María Serna de la Garza, Tribunal Superior de Justicia del Estado de Puebla, Instituto de Investigaciones Jurídicas, Universidad Nacional Autónoma de México, Mexico City 2005, 717-50; and *Constitución, democracia y control del poder,* Universidad de Los Andes, Mérida 2004, 135-38.

[2] See the Special Law on the Organization and Regime of the Capital District, *Gaceta Oficial* Nº 39.156 of Apr. 13, 2009. See in general the comments in Allan R. Brewer-Carías et al, *Leyes sobre régimen de gobierno del Distrito Capital y del Área Metropolitana de Caracas*, Editorial Jurídica Venezolana, Caracas 2009.

But the federation in the country's history has not always been like it is now. The centralization of the federation occurred progressively during the twentieth century and has been particularly accentuated during the past decade.

Centralization began with the installment of the authoritarian government of the dictator Juan Vicente Gómez, who ruled for approximately three decades in the first half of the twentieth century. During those years, no democratic institutions were developed.

The transition from autocracy to democracy began in Venezuela between 1945 and 1958, when a democratic regime came into power and subsequently developed in accordance with the democratic Constitution of 1961. That Constitution was the longest Constitution in force in all of Venezuelan history (1961–99) and, as a product of the *Pacto de Punto Fijo* (1958), ensured the dominance of a centralized political–party system that due to its democratic centralized structure impeded the reinforcement of federal institutions.

Nonetheless, important efforts were made during the 1990s to politically decentralize the federation,[3] efforts that were later abandoned, mainly because of the crisis of the centralized party system and to the consequential political void in the country. That void was to be resolved with the constitution-making process of 1999, resulting in the approval of the 1999 Constitution of the Bolivarian Republic of Venezuela, which, under a democratic veil, has allowed the development of an authoritarian regime based on a centralized government that concentrates all powers of the state. The Constitution makes excellent declarations, including the definition of the state as a decentralized federal state, which other regulations in the same Constitution contradict and allow conduct to the contrary.

Nonetheless, as I already mentioned, the federation in Venezuela has not always been centralized. During the nineteenth century, notwithstanding the political turmoil of the institution-building process of the national state facing the regional caudillo powers, a federal system of government was established (1864). In it, as in many federations, development of the centrifugal and centripetal political forces took place, thus provoking the classical political pendulum between centralization and decentralization.

---

[3] I conducted that process as minister of state for decentralization (1993–94). See, in general, *Informe sobre la descentralización en Venezuela 1993, Memoria del Dr. Allan R. Brewer-Carías, Ministro de Estado para la Descentralización (junio 1993-febrero 1994)*, Presidencia de la República, Caracas 1994.

In general terms, during the nineteenth century, federalism prevailed, particularly because of its historical roots.

I. HISTORY AND DEVELOPMENT OF THE VENEZUELAN FEDERATION

It is important to bear in mind when studying federalism in Venezuela that the first constitution of an independent Latin American state was sanctioned in Venezuela two centuries ago, the Federal Constitution for the States of Venezuela, by an elected General Congress, on December 21, 1811, at the beginning of the independence wars. The Constitution declared the states or provinces as sovereign states, all of which in 1810–11 had declared independent from Spain and adopted their own provincial constitutions or form of government.

By means of the 1811 Constitution, the country adopted a federal form of government, following the influence of the U.S. Constitution. At that time, it must be remembered, a federation was the only new constitutional framework for the organization of states different from the centralized monarchical frame, which had been recently invented in the United States. The framers of the new Venezuelan state followed that invention to unite the seven former Spanish colonial provinces that formed the Venezuelan state and had never been previously united. In the territory of Venezuela, there were no viceroyalties or *audiencias* (until 1786), and a general captaincy for military purposes, to integrate the provinces was established only in 1777. Thus, Venezuela was the second country in constitutional history to adopt federalism, an important aspect of its constitutional history.[4]

It was after the endless civil conflict that marked the history of Venezuela during the nineteenth century that the federal form of government began to be limited. The conflict stemmed from the permanent struggles between the regional caudillos and the weak central power that had formed. This was the consequence of centralizing tendencies, which derived from the consolidation of the national state, a process that was particularly reinforced during the first half of the twentieth century.

During those decades, the authoritarian regimes of the country, aided by income from the new exploitation of oil by the national state (oil and the

---

[4]After U.S. independence (1776) and federation (1777), the first Latin American country to declare independence and adopt a constitution was Venezuela, in 1811; it adopted the federal form of state.

subsoil always has been the public property of the state), contributed to the consolidation of the national state in all aspects. Contributions included the creation of a national army, a national public administration, national taxation, and national legislation.[5] These centralizing tendencies almost provoked the disappearance of the federation, the territorial distribution of power, and the effective autonomy of the states and the federal district, which compose the formal federal organization of the state.

The 1961 democratic Constitution, which kept the federal form of the state but with a highly centralized national organization, allowed for the possibility of state decentralization, a process that began in 1989, when the party–system crisis exploded with the transfer of powers and services from the national level of government to the state level and the provision for the election of governors, which until that year were public officials appointed by the president. The democratic pressure exercised against the political parties, all of which were in the middle of a severe leadership crisis, forced the process.

According to those reforms, in December 1989, for the first time since the nineteenth century, state governors were elected by universal, direct, and secret suffrage, and regional political life began to play an important role in the country, thereby increasing the appearance of regional and local political leaders, many of whom were from outside traditional political parties. During the 1990s, the transfer of public competencies from the national level to the states marked the political life of the country, giving life to the decentralization process.[6]

All these decentralizing policies were abandoned after the approval of the 1999 Constitution, which did not have the necessary provisions to undertake the most needed democratic changes in Venezuela – namely political decentralization of the federation and the reinforcement of state and local political powers. The Constitution of 1999, in fact, continued with the same centralizing foundation embodied in the previous Constitution and, in some cases, centralized even more aspects. If it is true that it defined the decentralization process as a "national policy devoted to

---

[5]See Allan R. Brewer-Carías, "El desarrollo institucional del Estado centralizado en Venezuela (1899-1935) y sus proyecciones contemporáneas," *Revista Paramillo* 7, Universidad Católica del Táchira, San Cristóbal 1988, 439-80.

[6]See Organic Law on Decentralization, Delimitation and Transfer of Competencies of Public Power, *Gaceta Oficial.* Extra. N° 4.153, Dec. 28, 1989. See the comments in Allan R. Brewer-Carías et al., *Leyes y Reglamentos para la descentralización política de la Federación,* Editorial Jurídica Venezolana, Caracas 1990.

strengthened democracy" (Article 158), then in contrast, the national public policy executed during the past decade can be characterized as progressive centralization of government without any real development of local or regional authorities. Consequently, in Venezuela, federalism has been postponed and democracy has been progressively weakened.

II. FEDERALIST CONSTITUTIONAL PROVISIONS IN THE 1999 CONSTITUTION

A federation is, above all, a form of government in which public power is territorially distributed among various levels of government with autonomous political institutions. That is why, in principle, federalism and political decentralization are intimately related. Specifically, decentralization is the most effective instrument not only for guaranteeing civil and social rights but also for allowing effective participation of citizens in the political process. In this context, the relation between local government and the population is essential. That is why all consolidated democracies in the world today are embodied in clearly decentralized forms of governments, such as federations or the new "regional" states progressively established in countries like Spain, Italy, and France.[7] Thus, it can be said that the strong centralizing tendencies that have been developing in Venezuela in recent years are contrary to democratic governance and political participation.

According to Article 4 of the 1999 Constitution, the Republic of Venezuela is formally defined "as a decentralized Federal State under the terms set out in the Constitution," governed by the principles of "territorial integrity, solidarity, concurrence and co-responsibility." Nonetheless, "the terms set out in the Constitution" are without a doubt centralizing, and Venezuela continues to be a contradictory centralized federation.

Article 136 of the Constitution states that "public power is distributed among the municipal, state and national entities," thus establishing a federation with three levels of political governments and autonomy (similar to the Brazilian federation): a national level, exercised by the republic (federal level); the state level, exercised by the 23 states and a capital district; and the municipal level, exercised by the 338 existing municipalities or local governments. On each of the three levels, the Constitution requires that government always be "democratic, participatory, elected, decentralized, alternative, responsible, plural and

---

[7]Decentralized states based on political regions or autonomous communities.

with revocable mandates" (Article 6). The capital district substituted for the former federal district established in 1863, eliminating the traditional federal interventions that existed regarding the authorities of the capital city. Nonetheless, in 2009, by means of a statute contrary to the Constitution, the capital district was organized without any self-government and completely controlled by the national executive.[8]

According to the Constitution, the organization of the political institutions on each territorial level is formally guided by the principle of the organic separation of powers. On the national level, with a presidential system of government, the national public power is separated among five branches of government, including the "Legislative, Executive, Judicial, Citizen (which includes the Prosecutor General Office, the Comptroller General Office, and the People's Defender Office) and Electoral" (Article 136).

The new citizens and electoral branches, as well as the judiciary, only exist at the national or federal level of government. Therefore, Venezuela does not have a judiciary or an electoral power at the state level. Regarding the judicial branch, since 1945, it is reserved to the national level of government, basically because of the national character of all major legislation and codes (civil, commercial, criminal, labor, and procedural). Consequently, because all courts are national (federal), there is no room for state constitution regulations on those matters.

With respect to the legislative branch, it must be noted that the 1999 Constitution established the one-chamber National Assembly, thus ending the country's federalist tradition of bicameralism by eliminating the Senate. In the National Assembly, there are no state representatives, and members are global representatives of the citizens and of all states collectively. Theoretically, the global representatives are not subject to mandates or instructions, only to the "dictates of their conscience" (Article 201). This has effectively eliminated all vestiges of territorial representation.

Regarding the states, the 1999 Constitution established two branches of government: executive and legislative. Accordingly, each state has a governor who must be elected by a universal, direct, and secret vote (Article 160); and a legislative council, with elected representatives

---

[8] See the Special Law on the Organization and Regime of the Capital District, *Gaceta Oficial* N° 39.156 of Apr. 13, 2009. See the comments in Allan R. Brewer-Carías, "La problemática del régimen jurídico del 'Distrito Capital' en la estructura federal del estado en Venezuela, y su inconstitucional regulación legal," *AIDA Opera Prima de Derecho Administrativo* 5, Universidad Nacional Autónoma de México, Mexico City 2009, 81-119.

according to the principle of proportional representation (Article 162). According to the Constitution, it is the responsibility of each state's legislative council to enact its own Constitution "to organize their branches of government" along the guidelines of the national Constitution, which in principle guarantees the autonomy of the states (Article 159).

III. LIMITING THE CONTENTS OF SUBNATIONAL CONSTITUTIONS

Consequently, each state has constitutional power to enact its own subnational constitution to organize the state legislative and executive public branches of government and to regulate the states' own organ for audit control. Despite the regulations on the organization and functioning of the state branches of government, the 1999 Constitution has seriously limited the scope of state powers. Specifically, for the first time in federal history, the Constitution refers to a national legislation for the establishment of general regulation on this matter.

In effect, and in relation to the states' legislative branch of government, the 1999 Constitution states that the organization and functioning of the states' legislative councils must be regulated by a national statute (Article 162), which was a manifestation of centralism that had never before been envisioned. In any federation, it is inconceivable for the national (federal) congress to be able to enact legislation to determine the organization and functioning of all state legislatures.

In contrast, in Venezuela, according to the Constitution, the National Assembly sanctioned in 2002 the Organic Law for the State Legislative Councils, which established detailed regulations,[9] related not only to the organization and functioning of the state legislative councils (as the national Constitution allowed) but also the status and attributes of the council's members, as well as the general rules for the exercise of the legislative functions. With that national regulation, the effective contents of the state constitutions regarding their legislative branch have been voided and are limited to repeating what is established in the national organic law or statute.

Additionally, the possibility of organizing the executive branch of each state's government is also limited by the 1999 Constitution, which has established the basic rules concerning the governor as the head of the executive branch. The Constitution has additional regulations referring to the public administration (national, states, and municipal), public

---

[9] See *Gaceta Oficial* N° 37.282, Sept. 13, 2001.

employees (civil service), and the administrative procedures and public contracts in all of the three levels of government. All of the pertinent rules were also developed in two 2001 national Organic Laws on Public Administration and on Civil Service.[10] Therefore, state constitutions have been voided of real content, and their norms tend to repeat what has been established in the national organic laws or statutes.

Finally, regarding other aspects of states' organizations, in 2001, the National Assembly also sanctioned a law on the appointment of the states controllers,[11] which limits the powers of the states' legislative councils without constitutional authorization.

On the other hand, it must be pointed out that the Constitutional Chamber of the Supreme Tribunal of Justice has intervened in the process of limiting the scope of the states autonomy, in particular, in decisions adopted between 2000 and 2004 annulling articles of three state constitutions that have created the Office of the State Citizens' Rights Defender, on the grounds that citizens' rights are a matter reserved to the national (federal) level of government.[12]

As mentioned, the national Constitution establishes three levels of territorial autonomy and regulates the distribution of state powers, directly and extensively regulating local or municipal government. Therefore, the state constitutions and legislation can regulate municipal or local government only according to what is established in the national Constitution and the national Organic Law on Municipal Government,[13] which leaves very little room for state regulation.

Thus, without any possibility for the state legislatures to regulate anything related to civil, economic, social, cultural, environmental, or political rights, and with limited powers to regulate their own branches of government and other state organizations, including the comptroller general and peoples' defenders, there is very little scope left to subnational constitutions.

---

[10]See *Gaceta Oficial* N° 37.522, Sept. 6, 2002.

[11]See *Gaceta Oficial* N° 37.304, Oct. 16, 2001.

[12]See Decisions N° 1182 (Oct. 11, 2000), N° 1395 (Aug. 7, 2001), and N° 111 (Feb. 12, 2004), in *Revista de Derecho Público*, N° 84, Editorial Jurídica Venezolana, Caracas 2000, 177ff.; *Revista de Derecho Público*, N° 85-88, Editorial Jurídica Venezolana, Caracas 2001; 192ff. See the references in Allan R. Brewer-Carías, *La Constitución de 1999. Derecho constitucional venezolano*, Editorial Jurídica Venezolana, Caracas 2004, 1: 363ff.

[13]See *Gaceta Oficial* N° 38.421, Apr. 21, 2006. See the comments in Allan R. Brewer-Carías et al., *Ley Orgánica Del Poder Público Municipal*, Editorial Jurídica Venezolana, Caracas 2007.

IV. CONSTITUTIONAL DISTRIBUTION OF POWERS

Federalism is based on effective distribution of powers across the various levels of government, and in Venezuela's case, among the national, state, and municipal levels. Accordingly, the Constitution enumerates the competencies attributed exclusively to the national (Article 156), state (Article 154), and municipal (Article 178) levels of government. Those regulations, however, assigned most matters to the national level and an important portion of such matters to municipalities.[14] In contrast, few exclusive matters are attributed to the states.

According to Article 156, the national power has exclusive competencies in the following matters: international relations; security and defense; nationality and alien status; national police; economic regulations; mining and oil industries; national policies and regulations on education, health, the environment, land use, transportation, and industrial and agricultural production; the post; and telecommunications. The administration of justice, as mentioned, also falls under the exclusive jurisdiction of the national government (Article 156.31).

Article 178 assigned the municipalities competencies including urban land use, housing, urban roads and transport, advertising regulations, urban environment, urban utilities, electricity, water supply, garbage collection and disposal, basic health and education services, and municipal police. Some of the powers regarding these matters are exclusive, but most are concurrent with the national government. The autonomy of municipalities is set forth in the Constitution but without any constitutional guarantees, because national statute can limit municipal autonomy (Article 168).

The national Constitution fails to enumerate substantive matters of exclusive state jurisdiction and concentrates on formal and procedural ones. Furthermore, the competencies related to a limited number of matters are established in a concurrent way, common to all levels of government —only some aspects of the competencies are exclusive. This applies to municipal organizations, nonmetallic mineral exploitation, police, state roads, administration of national roads, and commercial airports and ports (Article 164). Nonetheless, regarding the latter matters, although defined as exclusive of the states, after the 2007 constitutional reform was rejected proposing to transform it into a national competency, the Constitutional Chamber of the Supreme Tribunal, at the request of the

---

[14]Exclusive matters are matters attributed to only one state level.

Attorney General of the Republic, interpreting Article 164.10 of the Constitution, mutated the Constitution and declared it as a concurrent competency subjected to the intervention of the national executive.[15]

On the other hand, the possibility of the state legislature regulating its own local government is also very limited, because it is subject to what is established in the national organic municipal law or statute.

According to the Constitution, state legislative councils can enact legislation on matters that are in the states' scope of powers (Article 162). However, those powers are referred to concurrent matters and, according to the Constitution, their exercise depends on the previous enactment of national statutes and regulations. As a result, the legislative powers of the States are very limited.

The concurrent matters formerly provided a broad scope for possible action by state bodies. However, now that their exercise is subject to what the National Assembly has previously established in "general statutes," the possibility for states to regulate is very small. The national Constitution also states that the legislation that refers to concurrent competencies must always adhere to the principles of "interdependence, coordination, cooperation, co-responsibility and subsidiarity," which theoretically allows for a broad possibility for judicial review (Article 165).

In terms of residual competencies, the principle of favoring the states as in all federations also is a constitutional tradition in Venezuela. Nonetheless, the 1999 Constitution limited that residual power of the states by expressly assigning the national government a parallel and prevalent residual taxation power in matters not expressly attributed to the states or municipalities (Article 156.12).

Also, the 1999 Constitution, following the provisions of the 1961 Constitution, established the possibility of decentralizing competencies by transfer from the national level to the states. This process was regulated in the 1989 Law on Decentralization and Transfer of Competencies.[16] Even though important efforts for decentralization were made between 1990 and 1994 to revert the centralizing tendencies, the process, unfortunately, was later abandoned. Since 2003, the transfers of competencies that occurred,

---

[15]See Decision N° 565 (Apr. 15, 2008) at http://www.tsj.gov.ve/decisiones/scon/Abril/565-150408-07-1108.htm. See the comments in Allan R. Brewer-Carías, "La Sala Constitucional como poder constituyente: la modificación de la forma federal del estado y del sistema constitucional de división territorial del poder público," in *Revista de Derecho Público*, N° 114, Editorial Jurídica Venezolana, Caracas 2008, 247-62

[16]See *Gaceta Oficial* N° 37.753, Aug. 14, 2003.

including health services, started the reversion process; and, since 2006, according to the Communal Councils Law, reformed in 2009,[17] and to the 2010 Organic Law on the Federal Council of Government,[18] the process of transfer of competencies from the national level toward states and municipalities has been stopped and has been diverted toward new nondecentralized entities related to "organized society," particularly, the communal councils, and even new non–decentralized territorial bodies, like the development district, created within the centralized planning system.

V. THE FINANCING RULES OF THE FEDERATION

The constitutional rules regarding the financing of the federation should also be mentioned. Virtually everything in the 1999 Constitution concerning taxation is more centralized than in the previous 1961 Constitution, and the powers of the states in tax matters have essentially been eliminated.

The national Constitution lists the national government competencies with respect to basic taxes, including income tax; inheritance and donation taxes; taxes on capital, production, and value added; taxes on hydrocarbon resources and mines; taxes on the import and export of goods and services; and taxes on the consumption of liquor, alcohol, cigarettes, and tobacco (Article 156.12). The Constitution also expressly allocates local taxation powers to the municipalities, including property, commercial, and industrial activities taxes (Article 179). The Constitution gives the national government residual competencies in tax matters (Article 156.12).

In contrast, the Constitution does not grant the states competencies in matters of taxation, except with respect to official stationery and revenue stamps (Article 164.7). Thus, the states can collect taxes only when the National Assembly expressly transfers the power to them, by a statute that contains specific taxation powers (Article 167.5). No such statute has yet been approved and likely none will be approved in the near future.

Lacking their own resources from taxation, state financing is accomplished by the transfer of national financial resources through three different channels, which the national government controls. The first channel is the *situado constitucional* established as a constitutional contribution established to be incorporated in the national budget

---

[17] See *Gaceta Oficial* N° 5.806 Extra. Apr.10, 2006.
[18] See *Gaceta Oficial* N° 5.963 Extra. Feb 22, 2010.

equivalent to a minimum of 15% and a maximum of 20% of the total estimated ordinary national income (Article 167.4), must be distributed among the states according to population. The second channel is a nationally established system of special economic allotments for the benefit of those states in which mining and hydrocarbon projects are being developed. The benefits that accompany this statute have also been extended to include other nonmining states (Article 156.16).[19] The third channel of financing for states and municipalities is national funds, such as the former Intergovernmental Fund for Decentralization (*Fondo Intergubrenamental para la Descentralización, [FIDES]*), created in 1993 as a consequence of the national regulation of value-added tax,[20] or the Interstate Compensation Fund, established in the Constitution (Article 167.6) and created in the 2010 Organic Law on the Federal Council of Government.[21]

Following a long tradition, the states and municipalities cannot borrow or have public debt because of the requirement of a special national statute to approve state borrowing.

VI. THE RECENTRALIZATION OF THE FEDERATION

As mentioned, the 1999 Constitution, in a very contradictory way, introduced elements to centralize power to the detriment of states, although it continued with the federal form of the government. All the centralizing elements have been used during the past decade to produce a very centralized government that has suffocated the regional and local autonomy of states and municipalities.

This process has been completed since 2008, when the government reverted to the centralization trend, abandoned the decentralization efforts of the 1990s, and recentralized competencies that had been transferred in areas like health and education.

Also in 2008, as mentioned, the Constitutional Chamber of the Supreme Tribunal interpreted the Constitution at the request of the attorney general and ruled in Decision No. 565 (April 15, 2008),[22] contrary to the

---

[19] See the Law on the special contributions for the states derived from mines and hydrocarbons, *Gaceta Oficial*, N° 5.824, Oct. 13, 2006.

[20] See *Gaceta Oficial*, Extra. N° 5.805, Mar. 22, 2006.

[21] See *Gaceta Oficial*. N° 5.963 Extra. Feb. 22, 2010.

[22] Decision N° 565 of the Constitutional Chamber (Apr. 15, 2008) (Case: *Procuradora General de la República, Recurso de interpretación del artículo 164 de la Constitución*), http://www.tsj.gov.ve/decisiones/scon/Abril/565-150408-07-1108.htm. See comments in Allan R.

provisions of the Constitution, that a very important exclusive attribution of the states to administer national highways, ports, and airports was not an exclusive attribution but only a concurrent one, subject to control of the national government, thus authorizing the central government to interfere in the exercise of that administration.

On the basis of that decision, which distorted the Constitution, and after opposition candidates won in the regional elections in December 2008, a few governorship and mayors in important states and cities (Maracaibo and Caracas), in a very quick way the National Assembly reformed the 1989 Decentralization Law[23] allowing a process of centralization that in fact was applied in such entities during 2009, completing the reversion of the decentralization process initiated in 1993.[24] In this regard, the Inter-American Commission on Human Rights in its 2009 Annual Report noted "how the State has taken action to limit some powers of popularly-elected authorities in order to reduce the scope of public functions in the hands of members of the opposition," noticing that "a series of legal reforms have left opposition authorities with limited powers, preventing them from legitimately exercising the mandates for which they were elected."[25]

Even the local government in Caracas has been almost extinguished by the unconstitutional re-creation of a nineteenth-century federal district as a capital district governed by an executive authority appointed by the president and with the National Assembly as its legislative authority.[26]

As can be deduced from the foregoing, the declaration of Article 4 of the 1999 Constitution regarding the "federal decentralized" form of the Venezuelan government is mere wording. It is a formula that is contradicted by all the other regulations regarding federalism contained in the Constitution, which, on the contrary, shows that the federation in Venezuela is a very centralized one, affecting the democratic regime and governance deeply.

Decentralization is the most effective instrument not only to guarantee civil and social rights but also to allow effective participation of citizens in

---

Brewer-Carías, "La Sala Constitucional como poder constituyente: La modificación de la forma federal del estado y del sistema constitucional de división territorial del poder público," *Revista de Derecho Público* 114, Editorial Jurídica Venezolana, Caracas 2008, 247-62.

[23] *Gaceta Oficial* N° 39 140, Mar. 17, 2009.

[24] For instance, it happened on matters of ports and airports. See General Port Law, *Gaceta Oficial* N° 39.140, Mar. 17, 2009; Civil Aviation Law, *Gaceta Oficial* N° 39.140, Mar. 2009.

[25] See IACHR 2009 Annual report, at http://www.cidh.oas.org/annualrep/2009eng/Chap.IV.f.eng.htm.

[26] Special Law on the Organization and Regime of the Capital District, *Gaceta Oficial* N° 39.156, Apr. 13, 2009.

the political process and to consolidate democracies. That is why decentralization in the contemporary world is a matter of democracies and is contrary to authoritarianism. That is, there have never been decentralized authoritarian governments; only democracies can be decentralized. And that is precisely why the authoritarian government developed in Venezuela has centralized all power at the national level of government, suffocating state and local governments and weakening democracy.

Although democracy is based on elections, it cannot be consolidated without real separation of powers and the real possibility of political participation. Because of an existing controlled judiciary and a judicial review organization controlled by the executive, instead of enforcing the democratic constitutional principles embodied in the Constitution, those bodies have acted as the main instrument of authoritarian government.

Over the past years, the most important democratic element of the Venezuelan political process was the weak federalist system, which in 2000 had allowed more than half of the municipal mayors and one-third of the elected state governors to be opposition leaders, thus ensuring some kind of political pluralism. Unfortunately, all of this was affected in the regional elections of 2004, in which almost all the candidates supported by the president were elected, except for two governors and with more than 75% of the electorate abstaining. In the 2008 regional elections, a few opposition governors and mayors were elected, provoking the already mentioned reaction from the central government to a point of politically suffocating the scope of action of states and municipalities.

Ultimately, this has resulted in a concentration of powers, which is almost complete. In addition to the horizontal concentration of powers caused by the predominance of the executive over the legislative, judicial, citizens', and electoral branches, the executive in Venezuela has also vertically concentrated powers through the centralized form of government. In that framework, it is very difficult to talk about federalism and democracy, in Venezuela.

Chapter 7

CONCENTRATION OF POWERS AND AUTHORITARIAN GOVERNMENT

I. THE SEPARATION OF POWERS IN MODERN CONSTITUTIONALISM AND THE VENEZUELAN CONSTITUTIONAL TRADITION

The principle of separation of powers in modern constitutionalism has its origin in the constitutions of the former colonies of North America. For example, the Constitution of Virginia of June 29, 1776, set forth the following:

> SEC. 3. The legislative, executive, and judiciary department, shall be separate and distinct, so that neither exercise the powers properly belonging to the other: nor shall any person exercise the powers of more than one of them, at the same time.[1]

This provision and similar ones incorporated after 1776 in other constitutions of the former colonies of North America[2] have their theoretical backgrounds in the writings of Locke,[3] Montesquieu,[4] and

---

[1] "The Constitution or Form of Government Agreed to and Resolved upon by the Delegates and Representatives of the Several Counties and Corporations of Virginia," June 29, 1776. This article has been considered "the most precise statement of the doctrine which had at that time appeared." M.J.C. Vile, *Constitutionalism and the Separation of Powers*, Oxford 1967, 118.

[2] The Constitution of Massachusetts (1780) also contained the following categorical expression: "Article XXX: In the government of this Commonwealth, the legislative department shall not exercise the executive and judicial powers, or either one of them: The executive shall never exercise the legislative and judicial powers, or either one of them: The judicial shall never exercise the legislative and executive powers, or either one of them: to the end it may be a government of laws not of men."

[3] See J. Locke, *Two Treatises of Government*, ed. Peter Laslett, Cambridge 1967, 371, 383-85, 350.

[4] It is always adequate to remember the famous proposition of Montesquieu: "But constant experience shows us that every man invested with power is apt to abuse it, and to carry his authority as far as it will go.... To prevent this abuse, it is necessary from the very nature of things that power should be a check to power.... In order to avoid the abuse of power, steps must be taken for power to

Rousseau,[5] which were the most important weapons used during the eighteenth-century American and French revolutions in the battle against the absolute state – in North America to fight against the sovereignty of British Parliament, and in France to fight against the sovereignty of the monarch. The consequence of both revolutions was the replacement of the absolute state by a constitutional state, subject to the rule of law, based precisely on separation of powers as a guarantee of liberty, although with different trends of government: the presidential system of government in the United States resulting from the American Revolution and, decades after the French Revolution, the consolidation of the parliamentary system of government in Europe.

Separation of powers thus became the most important and distinguishing principle of modern constitutionalism.[6] According to Madison:

> The accumulation of all powers, legislative, executive, and judiciary in the same hands, whether of one, a few, or many, and whether hereditary, self–appointed or elective, may justly be pronounced the very definition of Tyranny.[7]

---

limit power." That is why, in the well-known chapter 6, Book XI of his *De l'Ésprit of laws*, he formulated his theory of the separation of power into three categories: "the legislative; the executive in respect to things dependent on the law of nations; and the executive in regard to matters that depend on the civil law. By virtue of the first, the prince or magistrate enacts temporary or perpetual laws, and amends or abrogates those that have been already enacted. By the second, he makes peace or war, sends or receives embassies, establishes the public security, and provides against invasion. By the third, he punishes criminals, or determines the disputes that arise between individuals. The latter we shall call the judiciary power, and the other simply the executive power of the state." He added: "When legislative and executive powers are united in the same person, or in the same body of magistrates, there can be no liberty; because apprehensions arise, lest the same monarch or senate should enact tyrannical laws, to execute them in a tyrannical manner. Again, there is no liberty, if the judiciary be not separated from the legislative and the executive. Were it joined with the legislative, the life and liberty of the subject would be exposed to arbitrary control; for the judge would be then the legislator. Were it joined to the executive power, the judge might behave with violence and oppression. There would be an end of everything, were the same man or the same body, whether of the nobles or of the people, to exercise those three powers, that of enacting laws, that of executing the public resolutions, and of trying the causes of individuals." Charles de Secondat, Baron de Montesquieu, *The Spirit of Laws*, translation by Thomas Nugent (1752), revised by J.V. Prichard. Based on a public-domain edition published in 1914 by G. Bell & Sons, Ltd., London. Available at http://www.constitution.org/cm/sol.txt.

[5] See J.J. Rousseau, *Du contrat social*, ed. Ronald Grimsley, Oxford 1972, bk. 1, chap. 4, p. 153.

[6] See Allan R. Brewer-Carías, *Reflexiones sobre la Revolución norteamericana (1776), la Revolución francesa (1789) y la Revolución hispanoamericana (1810-1830) y sus aportes al constitucionalismo moderno*, 2nd rev. ed., Serie Derecho Administrativo N° 2, Universidad Externado de Colombia, Editorial Jurídica Venezolana, Bogotá 2008.

[7] See J. Madison, *The Federalist*, ed. B. F. Wright, Cambridge, MA, 1961, 336 (N° 47).

That explains the provision of Article 16 of the French Declaration of Rights of Man and of the Citizen (1789), according to which: "every society in which the guarantee of rights is not assured or the separation of powers not determined has no Constitution."

All these principles inspired the first modern constitution adopted in Latin America, the Federal Constitution of the States of Venezuela, sanctioned on December 21, 1811, by an elected general Congress, even before the Constitution of the Spanish monarchy of Cádiz of 1812 was sanctioned.[8] The 1811 Constitution adopted the principle of separation of powers, setting forth in the preamble: "The exercise of authority conferred upon the Confederation never could be reunited in its respective functions. The Supreme Power must be divided in the Legislative, the Executive and the Judicial, and conferred to different bodies, independent between them and regarding their respective powers."

To that proposition, Article 189 of the same 1811 Constitution added: "The three essential Departments of government, that is, the Legislative, the Executive and the Judicial, must be always kept separated and independent one from the other according to the nature of a free government, which is convenient in the connexion chain that unite all the fabric of the Constitution in an indissoluble way of Friendship and Union."[9]

Consequently, since the beginning of modern constitutionalism, separation of constitutional powers also was adopted in Venezuela, in particular according to the trends of the presidential system of government with checks and balances and granting the judiciary specific powers of judicial review. The latter, according to the objective guarantee of the Constitution, was established in Article 227 of the 1811 Constitution: "The laws sanctioned against the Constitution will have no value except when fulfilling the conditions for a just and legitimate revision and sanction [of the Constitution]" and, in Article 199, in the sense that any law sanctioned by the federal legislature or by the provinces contrary to the fundamental rights enumerated in the Constitution "will be absolutely null and void."

---

[8]See Allan R. Brewer-Carías, "El paralelismo entre el constitucionalismo venezolano y el constitucionalismo de Cádiz (o de cómo el de Cádiz no influyó en el venezolano)," in *Libro Homenaje a Tomás Polanco Alcántara, Estudios de derecho público*, Universidad Central de Venezuela, Caracas 2005, 101-89.

[9]See the text of the 1811 Constitution and all other Venezuelan constitutions in Allan R. Brewer-Carías, *Las constituciones de Venezuela*, 2 vols., Academia de Ciencias Políticas y Sociales, Biblioteca de la Academia de Ciencias Políticas y Sociales, Caracas 2008.

Since 1811, all the constitutions in Venezuelan history have established and guaranteed the separation of powers, particularly among the three classic legislative, executive, and judicial branches of government (powers), in a system of checks and balances, and always giving the judiciary the judicial review power. For such purpose, the independence and autonomy of the branches of government have been the most important aspects regulated in the constitutions, particularly during the democratic regimes, because the separation of powers in contemporary constitutionalism has become one of the basic conditions for democracy and for the possibility of guaranteeing the enjoyment and protection of fundamental rights. On the contrary, without separation of powers and autonomy and independence between the branches of government, no democratic regime can develop and no guarantee of fundamental rights can exist.

II. SEPARATION OF POWERS AND DEMOCRACY

In effect, the essential components of democracy are much more than the sole popular or circumstantial election of government officials, as was formally recognized in the Inter-American Democratic Charter adopted by the Organization of American States in 2001,[10] in which the separation and independence of powers – that is, the possibility of controlling the different branches of government – is enumerated as one of the "essential elements of the representative democracy" (Article 3). The separation and independence of the branches of government is conceived of in such an important way; it allows for all the other "fundamental components of democracy" to be politically possible. To be precise, democracy, as a political regime, can function only in a system of constitutional rule of law where the control of power exists; that is, a system of checks and balances based on the separation of powers with their independence and autonomy guaranteed, so that power itself can stop power.

Consequently, without separation of powers, no free and fair elections and political pluralism can exist; no effective democratic participation can be possible; no effective transparency in the exercise of government can be ensured; no subjection of the government to the Constitution and the laws can be guaranteed; no effective access to justice with autonomy and

---

[10]On the Inter-American Democratic Charter, see Allan R. Brewer-Carías, *La crisis de la democracia venezolana. La Carta Democrática Interamericana y los sucesos de abril de 2002*, Ediciones El Nacional, Caracas 2002, 137ff.

independence can de expected; and no true and effective respect for human rights can be ensured.[11]

The constitutional situation in Venezuela since the constitution-making process of 1999, which resulted in the complete takeover of all powers of the state and the sanctioning of the current 1999 Constitution, unfortunately has been of a very weak democracy, precisely because of the progressive demolishing of the separation of powers. In it, a process of concentrating powers has taken place, first with the 1999 constitution-making process, which intervened in all branches of government before sanctioning the new Constitution; second, because of the provisions of the 1999 Constitution, which do not guarantee the effective independence and autonomy of branches of government.

In effect, the 1999 Constitution, if read in a vacuum ignoring the political reality of the country, can be misleading. It is the only Constitution in the contemporary world that has established not only a tripartite separation of powers among the traditional legislative (*asamblea nacional*), executive (president and executive offices), and judicial (Supreme Tribunal of Justice and lower courts) branches of government but also a five-branched separation of powers adding to the traditional three two more branches of government: the electoral attributed to the National Electoral Council, in charge of the organization and conduction of the elections; and the citizens' power, attributed to three different state entities: the Prosecutor General Office (Public Ministry) (Fiscalía General de la República), the Comptroller General Office (Contraloría General de la República), and the Peoples' Defender (Defensor del Pueblo) (Article 136). The last two new branch of government was the culmination of a previous constitutional process and tendency initiated in 1961 with the consolidation in the Constitution of state organs with constitutional rank not subjected to the classical powers.[12]

But, as mentioned, despite the division of powers among five branches, the autonomy and independence of the branches of government is not completely and consistently ensured in the Constitution. Its application leads, on the contrary, to a concentration of state powers in the National Assembly and, through it, in the executive power.

---

[11]See Allan R. Brewer-Carías, "Democracia: Sus elementos y componentes esenciales y el control del poder," in *Grandes temas para un observatorio electoral ciudadano, Tomo I, Democracia: retos y fundamentos,* comp. Nuria González Martín, Instituto Electoral del Distrito Federal, Mexico City 2007, 171-220.

[12]See comments in Allan R. Brewer-Carías, *La Constitución de 1999*, Caracas 2000, 106ff.

In effect, in any system of separation of powers, even with five separate branches of government, for such separation to become effective, the independence and autonomy among them has to be ensured to allow for checks and balances – that is, the limitation and control of power by power itself. This was the aspect that was not designed as such in the 1999 Constitution, and an absurd distortion of the principle was introduced by giving the National Assembly the authority not only to appoint but also to dismiss judges of the Supreme Tribunal of Justice, the prosecutor general, the comptroller general, the people's defender, and members of the National Electoral Council (Articles 265, 279, and 296), and in some cases, even by a simple majority of votes. This latter solution was even proposed to be formally introduced in the rejected 2007 constitutional-reform proposals, which sought to eliminate the guarantee of the qualified majority of members of the National Assembly for such dismissals.[13]

III. DEFRAUDING POLITICAL PARTICIPATION IN APPOINTING OFFICIALS

The process of concentrating powers that Venezuela has experienced during the past decade also has been the result of a process of defrauding the Constitution, particularly by ignoring the limits the Constitution established to reduce the discretional power of the National Assembly in the process of appointing the heads of the different branches of government.

In effect, independently of the constitutional provisions regarding the possible dismissal by the National Assembly of the heads of nonelected branches of government, and the distortions of that, one of the mechanisms established to ensure their independence was the provision in the Constitution of a system to ensure that their appointment by the National Assembly was to be limited by the necessary participation of special collective bodies, called nominating committees, that must be integrated with representatives from different sectors of society (Articles 264, 279, and 295). The nominating committees are in charge of selecting and nominating candidates, thus guaranteeing the political participation of citizens in the process.

---

[13]See Allan R. Brewer-Carías, *Hacia la consolidación de un estado socialista, centralizado y militarista. Comentarios sobre el alcance y sentido de las propuestas de reforma Constitucional 2007*, Editorial Jurídica Venezolana, Caracas 2007, 133ff.; *La reforma constitucional de 2007 (Comentarios al proyecto inconstitucionalmente sancionado por la Asamblea Nacional el 2 de noviembre de 2007)*, Colección Textos Legislativos N° 43, Editorial Jurídica Venezolana, Caracas 2007, 108ff.

Consequently, the appointment of the judges of the Supreme Tribunal, the members of the National Electoral Council, the prosecutor general, the people's defender, and the comptroller general can be made only among candidates proposed by the corresponding nominating committees, which are in charge of selecting and nominating candidates before the assembly. These constitutional provisions seek to limit the discretional power that the political-legislative organ traditionally had to appoint those officials through political–party agreements by ensuring political citizenship participation.[14]

Unfortunately, these exceptional constitutional provisions have not been applied because the National Assembly during the past years, also to defraud the Constitution, has deliberately transformed those committees into simple parliamentary commissions, thus reducing civil society's right to political participation. The assembly in all the statutes sanctioned regarding such committees and the appointment process has established the composition of all the nominating committees with a majority of parliamentary representatives (who, by definition, cannot be representatives of civil society), although providing, in addition, for the incorporation of some other members chosen by the National Assembly itself from strategically selected nongovernmental organizations.[15]

The result has been complete control of the nominating committees and the persistence of the discretional political and partisan way of appointing the head officials of the nonelected branches of government, which the provisions of the 1999 Constitution intended to limit, by a National Assembly, which, since 2000, has been completely controlled by the executive.[16]

It was even attempted to constitutionalize this practice, with the proposal in the rejected constitutional reforms of 2007 to formally

---

[14]See Allan R. Brewer-Carías, "La participación ciudadana en la designación de los titulares de los órganos no electos de los Poderes Públicos en Venezuela y sus vicisitudes políticas," *Revista Iberoamericana de Derecho Público y Administrativo* 5, San José, Costa Rica, 2005, 76-95.

[15]See Ley Orgánica del Poder Ciudadano, *Gaceta Oficial* N° 37.310 of Oct. 25, 2001; Ley Orgánica del Poder Electoral, *Gaceta Oficial* N° 37.573 of Nov. 19, 2002; Ley Orgánica del Tribunal Supremo de Justicia, *Gaceta Oficial* N° 37.942 of May 20, 2004.

[16]Regarding the appointment of the prosecutor general in 2007, see Allan R. Brewer-Carías, "Sobre el nombramiento irregular por la Asamblea Nacional de los titulares de los órganos del poder ciudadano en 2007," in *Revista de Derecho Público*, N° 113, Editorial Jurídica Venezolana, Caracas 2008, pp. 85-88.

establish exclusive parliamentary nominating committees rather than have them comprise representatives from various sectors of civil society.[17]

IV. THE SUPREMACY OF THE EXECUTIVE AND THE ABSENCE OF CHECKS AND BALANCES

If the supremacy of the National Assembly over the judicial, citizen, and electoral powers is the most characteristic sign of the implementation of the Constitution of 1999 during the past decade, the distortion of separation of powers by a power concentration system also derives from the political – and, in this case, party – supremacy that the executive power has over the National Assembly.

The Constitution of 1999 reinforced the presidential system because, among other factors, it extended to six years the presidential term, it authorized the immediate reelection for an immediate period of the president (Article 203), and it maintained its election by simple majority (Article 228). In the rejected constitutional reforms of 2007, it was proposed that the term of the president be extended to seven years, and the indefinite reelection of the president was a main proposal.[18] The latter proposal eventually was the object of a constitutional amendment approved in the 2009 referendum establishing the possibility of the continuous and indefinite reelection of all elected positions.[19]

This presidential model that allows for the possibility of the president's dissolving of the National Assembly even in exceptional cases (Articles 236.22 and 240) has been reinforced by the weakening of checks and balances – for instance, with the elimination of the Senate in 1999.

Also, the presidential system has been reinforced with other reforms, like the provision for legislative delegation to authorize the president, through delegating statutes (enabling laws), to issue decree laws on any

---

[17]See Allan R. Brewer-Carías, *Hacia la consolidación de un estado socialista, centralizado y militarista. Comentarios sobre el alcance y sentido de las propuestas de reforma Constitucional 2007*, Editorial Jurídica Venezolana, Caracas 2007, 1337ff.; *La reforma constitucional de 2007 (Comentarios al proyecto inconstitucionalmente sancionado por la Asamblea Nacional el 2 de noviembre de 2007)*, Colección Textos Legislativos N° 43, Editorial Jurídica Venezolana, Caracas 2007, 108ff.

[18]See Allan R. Brewer-Carías, *Hacia la consolidación de un estado socialista, centralizado y militarista. Comentarios sobre el alcance y sentido de las propuestas de reforma Constitucional 2007*, Editorial Jurídica Venezolana, Caracas 2007, 136; *La reforma constitucional de 2007 (Comentarios al proyecto inconstitucionalmente sancionado por la Asamblea Nacional el 2 de noviembre de 2007)*, Colección Textos Legislativos N° 43, Editorial Jurídica Venezolana, Caracas 2007, 62.

[19]See in *Gaceta Oficial* N° 5.908 of Feb. 19, 2009.

topic, not only on economic and financial matters (Article 203). According to this provision, the fact is that the fundamental legislation of the country sanctioned during the past decade is contained in those decree laws, which have been approved without ensuring the mandatory constitutional provision for public hearings, which should take place before the sanctioning of all statutes (Articles 206 and 211).

To enforce this constitutional right of citizens' participation, the Constitution has specifically set forth that the National Assembly must submit draft legislation to public consultation, thus asking the opinion of citizens and the organized society (Article 211). This is the concrete way the Constitution tends to ensure the exercise of the right of political participation in the process of drafting legislation. The president also must carry out this obligation with legislative delegation. But, nonetheless, in 2007 and 2008, the president, following the same steps he took in 2001, extensively legislated without any public hearing or consultation. In that way, defrauding the Constitution by means of legislative delegation, the president enacted decree laws without complying with the obligatory public hearings, thus violating citizens' right to political participation.[20]

V. THE RUPTURE OF THE RULE OF LAW AND THE REJECTED 2007 CONSTITUTIONAL REFORM

As it can be deducted, for a state of democratic rule of law to exist, declarations contained in constitutional texts on separation of powers are not enough; they are indispensable to effective checks and balances among state powers. This is the only way to ensure the enforcement of the rule of law, democracy, and the effective enjoyment of human rights.

Moreover, under democratic rule of law, checks and balances can be achieved only by dividing, separating, and distributing public power, either horizontally by means of the guarantee of the autonomy and independence of the different branches of government, to avoid the concentration of power; or vertically, by means of distributing it or spreading it in the territory, thus creating autonomous political decentralized entities with representatives elected by votes, to avoid its centralization. Concentrations of power and its centralization, then, are essentially antidemocratic state structures.

---

[20] See comments in Allan R. Brewer-Carías, "Apreciación general sobre los vicios de inconstitucionalidad que afectan los decretos leyes habilitados" in *Ley Habilitante del 13-11-2000 y sus decretos leyes*, Academia de Ciencias Políticas y Sociales, Serie Eventos N° 17, Caracas 2002, 63-103.

It is precisely there where lie the problems of the formally declared rule of law and democracy in Venezuela – whose deformation rests in the same constitutional text of 1999. Unfortunately, the institutional framework established in the Constitution encourages authoritarianism, thus affecting the possibility of controlling power. This has permitted the centralization of power, thereby provoking the dismantling of federalism and municipalism and distorting the possibility of the effective political participation, despite the direct democracy mechanisms established.

This centralization of powers was to be constitutionalized in 2007 by means of the rejected constitutional reform proposed by President Hugo Chávez and sanctioned by the National Assembly. In doing so, he aimed to transform the democratic rule-of-law and decentralized social state established in the 1999 Constitution into a socialist, centralized, repressive, and militaristic state, grounded in a so-called Bolivarian doctrine, identified with twenty-first century socialism and an economic system of state capitalism, lead by a Marxist party.[21]

Despite its refusal by the people through referendum, it is important to stress that the president submitted it and the National Assembly sanctioned it, thus evading the procedure established in the 1999 Constitution for such fundamental changes. That is, the proposed reform also proposed defrauding the Constitution, to deceive the people.[22]

Article 347 of the 1999 Constitution required for those reforms to be approved at the convening and election of a national Constituent Assembly, which could not be undertaken by means of mere "constitutional reform" procedure, which is reserved exclusively for "a partial revision of the Constitution and a substitution of one or several of its norms without modifying the structure and fundamental principles of the Constitutional text." Consequently, following that procedure to achieve substantial constitutional changes, in 2007, the president and the National Assembly tried to repeat the political tactic that has become all

---

[21]See Allan R. Brewer-Carías, *Hacia la consolidación de un estado socialista, centralizado y militarista. Comentarios sobre el alcance y sentido de las propuestas de reforma Constitucional 2007*, Editorial Jurídica Venezolana, Caracas 2007, 11ff.; *La reforma constitucional de 2007 (Comentarios al proyecto inconstitucionalmente sancionado por la Asamblea Nacional el 2 de noviembre de 2007)*, Editorial Jurídica Venezolana, Caracas 2007, 19ff. See the "Declaration of Principles" of the United Socialist Party (Apr. 23, 2010), available at http://psuv.org.ve/files/tcdocumentos/Declaracion-de-principios-PSUV.pdf.

[22]See Allan R. Brewer-Carías, "Estudio sobre la propuesta de Reforma Constitucional para establecer un estado socialista, centralizado y militarista (Análisis del Anteproyecto Presidencial, Agosto de 2007)," *Cadernos da Escola de Direito e Relações Internacionais da UniBrasil* N° 07, Curitiba 2007; and "El sello socialista que se pretendía imponer al Estado," in *Revista de Derecho Público*, N° 112, Editorial Jurídica Venezolana, Caracas 2007, 71-76.

too common in the authoritarian regime installed since 1999: acting fraudulently with respect to the Constitution.

As the Constitutional Chamber of the Supreme Tribunal of Justice ruled in another matter, in Decision No. 74 (January 25, 2006), defrauding of the Constitution (*fraude a la Constitución*) occurs when democratic principles are destroyed "through the process of making changes within existing institutions while appearing to respect constitutional procedures and forms." The Constitutional Chamber also ruled that a "falsification of the Constitution" (*falseamiento de la Constitución*) occurs when "constitutional norms are given an interpretation and a sense different from those that they actually possess: this is in reality an informal modification of the Constitution itself." The Constitutional Chamber concluded by affirming, "A Constitutional reform not subject to any type of limitations would constitute a defrauding of the constitution."[23] This is to say, a defrauding of the Constitution occurs when the existing institutions are used in a manner that appears to adhere to constitutional forms and procedures to proceed, as the Supreme Tribunal warned, "towards the creation of a new political regime, a new constitutional order, without altering the established legal system."[24]

As has been mentioned, this was precisely what occurred in February 1999 in the convening of a consultative referendum on whether to convene a constituent assembly when that institution was not prefigured in the Constitution of 1961; it occurred with the December 1999 Decree on the Transitory Regime of the Public Powers with respect to the Constitution of 1999, issued by the Constituent Assembly, which was never the subject of an approbatory referendum; and it continued to occur in the subsequent years with the progressive destruction of democracy through the exercise of power and the kidnapping of successive constitutional rights and liberties, all supposedly carried out on the basis of legal and constitutional provisions.[25]

---

[23] See *Revista de Derecho Público* N° 105, Editorial Jurídica Venezolana, Caracas 2006, 76ff.
[24] Id.
[25] See Allan R. Brewer-Carías, "Constitution Making in Defraudation of the Constitution and Authoritarian Government in Defraudation of Democracy: The Recent Venezuelan Experience," *Lateinamerika Analysen* 19, German Institute of Global and Area Studies, Institute of Latin American Studies, Hamburg 2008, 119-42; "El autoritarismo establecido en fraude a la Constitución y a la democracia y su formalización en Venezuela mediante la reforma constitucional (De cómo en un país democrático se ha utilizado el sistema eleccionario para minar la democracia y establecer un régimen autoritario de supuesta 'dictadura de la democracia' que se pretende regularizar mediante la reforma constitucional)," in *Temas constitucionales. Planteamientos ante una reforma*, Fundación de Estudios de Derecho Administrativo, Caracas 2007, 13-74.

In the case of the 2007 constitutional reforms, constitutional provisions were fraudulently used for ends other than those for which they were established – that is, to try to introduce a radical transformation of the state, disrupting the civil order of the social-democratic state under the rule of law and justice through the procedure for constitutional reform that is established for other purposes. The aim of the 2007 reform was the conversion of the rule-of-law constitutional state into a socialist, centralized, repressive, militarist state in which representative democracy, republican alternating of office, and the concept of decentralized power were to disappear, with all power concentrated in the decisions of the chief of state.[26] But despite the deliberate use of an erroneous constitutional review procedure, the Supreme Tribunal deliberately refused to adopt any decision on judicial review regarding the unconstitutional procedure followed by the president, the National Assembly, and the National Electoral Council regarding the 2007 constitutional-reform process.[27]

In any case, although the popular rejection of the 2007 constitutional reform constituted a very important step back to the authoritarian government of President Chávez, and although according to the Constitution itself, the proposed reform could not be formulated again in the same constitutional term of government, the president announced his intention to seek to impose the rejected constitutional reform, again, thus defrauding the Constitution. In particular, for instance, he suggested that to ensure the possibility of his indefinite reelection, he could call himself for a recall referendum, seeking to convert the eventual rejection of such referendum into a plebiscite for his reelection.[28] Nonetheless, on this matter, it was the National Assembly that defrauding the Constitution proposed a "constitutional amendment" to achieve the same purpose, establishing the possibility of the continuous and indefinite reelection of

---

[26]See the comments on all the Constitutional Chamber decisions dissmising the cases in Allan R. Brewer-Carías, *Hacia la consolidación de un estado socialista, centralizado y militarista. Comentarios sobre el alcance y sentido de las propuestas de reforma Constitucional 2007*, Editorial Jurídica Venezolana, Caracas 2007; *La reforma constitucional de 2007 (Comentarios al proyecto inconstitucionalmente sancionado por la Asamblea Nacional el 2 de noviembre de 2007)*, Editorial Jurídica Venezolana, Caracas 2007.

[27]See Allan R. Brewer-Carías, "El juez constitucional vs. la supremacía constitucional. O de cómo la jurisdicción constitucional en Venezuela renunció a controlar la constitucionalidad del procedimiento seguido para la 'reforma constitucional' sancionada por la Asamblea Nacional el 2 de noviembre de 2007, antes de que fuera rechazada por el pueblo en el referendo del 2 de diciembre de 2007," *Revista de Derecho Público* 112 (*Estudios sobre la Reforma Constitucional*), Editorial Jurídica Venezolana, Caracas 2007, 661ff.

[28]See *El Universal*, Caracas Jan. 27, 2008.

all elected officials, which was eventually approved in the February 2009 referendum.[29]

In any case, during July and August of 2007, the president, defrauding the Constitution, proceeded to implement the rejected constitutional reforms using the powers to legislate by decree that were delegated to him by his completely controlled National Assembly in January 2007. He, in effect, sanctioned twenty-six very important new statutes[30] implementing – of course, fraudulently – many of the constitutional-reform proposals that the people rejected in the December 2007 referendum.[31]

Unfortunately, even though they all are unconstitutional, those decree laws were enacted and have been applied without any possibility of control or judicial review. The president was sure that no Constitutional Chamber judicial review decision would be adopted because the Constitutional Chamber is a wholly controlled entity that has proved his most effective tool to consolidate his authoritarian government.

This entire situation is the only explanation we can find to understand why a head of state of our times, as is the case of President Chávez in Venezuela, can say the following in challenging his opponents in a political rally held a few years ago, on August 28, 2008:

> I warn you, group of Stateless, putrid opposition.
>
> Whatever you do, the 26 Laws will go ahead! And the other 16 Laws . . . also. And if you go out in the streets, like on April 11 [2002]...we will sweep you in the streets, in the barracks, in the universities. I will close the

---

[29]See *Gaceta Oficial* N° 5,908 of Feb. 19, 2009.

[30]Regarding the 2008 decree laws, Teodoro Petkoff has pointed out: "In absolute contradiction to the results of the Dec. 2, 2007[,] referendum in which voters rejected constitutional reforms, in several of the laws promulgated the president presents several of the aspects of the rejected reforms almost in the same terms. The proposition of changing the name of the Venezuelan Armed Forces to create the Bolivarian National Militia was contained in the proposed reforms; the power given to the President to appoint national government officials over the governors and mayors to, obviously, weaken those offices and to eliminate the last vestiges of counterweight to the executive in general and the presidency in particular, was also contained in the reforms; the recentralization of the national executive branch of powers that today belong to the states and decentralized autonomous institutes was also part of the reforms: the enlargement of government powers to intervene in economic affairs was also contained in the reform. To ignore the popular decision about the 2007 proposal to reform the constitution in conformity with the will and designs of an autocrat, without heed to legal or constitutional norms, is, *stricto sensu*, a tyrannic act." See Teodoro Petkoff, "Election and Political Power: Challenges for the Opposition," *ReVista: Harvard Review of Latin America*, David Rockefeller Center for Latin American Studies, Harvard University, Cambridge, MA, 2008, 12.

[31]See the comments to all the 2007–2008 decree laws in *Revista de Derecho Público* 115, *(Estudios sobre los Decretos Leyes 2008)*, Editorial Jurídica Venezolana, Caracas 2008.

golpista media; I will have no compassion whatsoever.... This Revolution came to stay, forever!

You can continue talking stupid thinks.... I am going to intervene all communications and I will close all the enterprises I consider that are of public usefulness or of social interest! Out [of the country] contractors and Fourth Republic corrupt people!

I am the Law.... I am the State !!³²

Nonetheless, this was not the first time that the president had declared himself to be the law and the State. In 2001, when he approved more than forty-eight decree laws, also via delegate legislation, he said in a different way: "The law is me. The State is me."³³

This phrase – attributed to Louis XIV, although he never said it³⁴ – expressed now by a head of state in our times, is enough to understand the tragic institutional situation that Venezuela is currently facing: a complete absence of separation of powers and, consequently, of a democratic government.³⁵

---

³²"*Yo soy la Ley..., Yo soy el Estado*!!" See references at the blog of Gustavo Coronel, *Las Armas de Coronel*, Oct. 15, 2008, http://las armasdecoronel.blogspot.com/2008/10/yo-soy-la-leyyo-soy-el-estado.html.

³³"*La ley soy yo. El Estado soy yo.*". See Raquel Barreiro, "Chávez delega en la Asamblea Nacional cambios legales," in *El Universal*, Caracas Dec. 4, 2001, 1,1 and 2,1. Available at http://www.eluniversal.com/2001/12/04/eco_art_04201DD.shtml.

³⁴This famous phrase was attributed to Louis XIV when, in 1661, he decided to govern alone after the death of Cardinal Mazarin, but he never actually uttered it. See Yves Giuchet, *Histoire constitutionnelle française (1789–1958)*, Ed. Erasme, Paris 1990, 8.

³⁵Teodoro Petkoff, editor and founder of *Tal Cual*, an important newspaper in Caracas, recently summarized this situation as follows: "Chávez controls all the political powers. More than 90% of the Parliament obey his commands; the Venezuelan Supreme Court, whose number were raised from 20 to 32 by the parliament to ensure an overwhelming official's majority, has become an extension of the legal office of the Presidency.... The Prosecutor General's Office, the Comptroller's Office and the Public Defender are all offices held by 'yes persons,' absolutely obedient to the orders of the autocrat. In the National Electoral Council, four of five members are identified with the government. The Venezuelan Armed Forces are tightly controlled by Chávez. Therefore, from a conceptual point of view, the Venezuelan political system is autocratic. All political power is concentrated in the hands of the President. There is no real separation of Powers." See Teodoro Petkoff, "Election and Political Power: Challenges for the Opposition," *Revista: Harvard Review of Latin America*, David Rockefeller Center for Latin American Studies, Harvard University, Cambridge, MA, 2008, 12.

Chapter 8

THE CATASTROPHIC DEPENDENCE AND POLITICAL SUBJECTION OF THE SUPREME TRIBUNAL OF JUSTICE

The effects of the dependency of the branches of government subjected to the legislative power, and through it to the executive, have been particularly catastrophic for the judiciary. The Constituent Assembly initially intervened in the judiciary's powers in 1999,[1] and such intervention continued with the Supreme Tribunal of Justice's unfortunate consent and complicity. In the past decade, the country has witnessed permanent and systematic demolition of the autonomy and independence of the judicial power, aggravated by the fact that, according to the 1999 Constitution, the Supreme Tribunal, which is completely controlled by the executive, is in charge of administering the entire Venezuelan judicial system, particularly by appointing and dismissing judges.[2]

I. THE SUBJECTION OF THE SUPREME TRIBUNAL OF JUSTICE

The process began with the appointment, in 1999, of new Magistrates of the Supreme Tribunal of Justice without complying with the constitutional

---

[1] See Allan R. Brewer-Carías, *Debate constituyente (Aportes a la Asamblea Nacional Constituyente)*, Fundación de Derecho Público–Editorial Jurídica Venezolana, Caracas 1999, 1 (Aug. 8–Sept. 8):57ff.

[2] See Allan R. Brewer-Carías, "La progresiva y sistemática demolición de la autonomía e independencia del Poder Judicial en Venezuela (1999-2004)," in *XXX Jornadas J.M. Dominguez Escovar, Estado de derecho, Administración de justicia y derechos humanos*, Instituto de Estudios Jurídicos del Estado Lara, Barquisimeto 2005, 33-174; "La justicia sometida al poder (La ausencia de independencia y autonomía de los jueces en Venezuela por la interminable emergencia del Poder Judicial (1999-2006)," in *Cuestiones internacionales. Anuario Jurídico Villanueva 2007*, Centro Universitario Villanueva, Marcial Pons, Madrid 2007, 25-57.

conditions, made by the Constituent Assembly itself, by means of a constitutional transitory regime sanctioned after the Constitution was approved by referendum.[3] From that point, intervention in the judiciary has continued, including the fact that the president has politically controlled the Supreme Tribunal of Justice and, through it, the complete Venezuelan judicial system.

1. *The Confiscation of Civil Society's Right to Participate in the Appointment of the Magistrates of the Supreme Tribunal in 2000*

As mentioned, one of the principal purposes of the constitution-making process of 1999 was to reform the procedure for the appointment of the nonelected officials of the state, in a way out of the reach of the political parties' control and with citizens' participation in such appointments, thus removing the absolute discretion that the former Congress had on the matter. Consequently, the 1999 Constitution regulated a precise system of active participation of society in those appointments by creating various nominating committees, composed of representatives from different sectors of society, with the exclusive authority to nominate candidates before the National Assembly. In a Constitution with more that fifty articles referring to citizens' participation, the only means for such participation that the Constitution provides for directly is to ensure the participation of "different sectors of society" in the nominating committees. In this case, the provision is not established as a means for consultation, much less for dialogue, but rather as a mechanism for active participation. The consequence of this system is that under the Constitution, the National Assembly cannot directly nominate nonelected officials; the committees must bring those nominations beforehand. The National Assembly has no constitutional authority to appoint persons not presented by the committees.

Following those principles, regarding the judicial branch Article 270 of the Constitution of 1999 provides that only the Judicial Nominating Committee may nominate candidates for Magistrates to the Supreme Tribunal of Justice. Candidates may file their proposals before the committee on their own initiative or through organizations with activities in legal and judicial matters. To propose candidates before the National Assembly, the committee must follow a very complex procedure of

---

[3]On this transition regime, see Allan R. Brewer-Carías, *Golpe de estado y proceso constituyente en Venezuela*, Universidad Nacional Autónoma de México, Mexico City 2002, 345ff.

selection, with citizens' participation, and the participation of the citizen power branch of government.

Nonetheless, the Constituent Assembly, when issuing the Decree on the Transition Regime of December 22, 1999, provisionally appointed Magistrates to the Supreme Tribunal who were to remain in office until the new National Assembly could make permanent appointments "according to the requirements of the Constitution" (Article 20), without following the strict constitutional procedure or guaranteeing the citizens' right to participation. Thus, the new National Assembly elected on August 2000 had a constitutional obligation to make permanent the Magistrates' appointments in accord with constitutional procedure. The same was to be done regarding appointments by the National Assembly of the prosecutor general, the comptroller general, the people's defender, and members of the National Electoral Council (Articles 279 and 295). However, this was never done.

In effect, to create the nominating committees according to the provisions of the Constitution, the National Assembly elected in August 2000 was obligated to enact the respective organic laws of the different entities, and particularly the organic law of the Supreme Tribunal of Justice. The assembly could not "legislate in order to not legislate," which it did when sanctioning on November 14, 2000, the Special Law for the Ratification or Appointment of Officials of the Citizens' Power and Magistrates to the Supreme Tribunal of Justice,[4] thus providing for the appointments of nonelected state officials without following the constitutional provisions, and thus violating Articles 264, 270, and 279 of the Constitution, as well as Articles 20 and 33 of the National Constituent Assembly's Decree on the Transitory Regime. The special law, in effect, organized the nominating committees as a parliamentary commission of fifteen representatives and six other persons elected by the assembly (Articles 3 and 4), not as provided in the Constitution. The special law thus extended rather than ended the transitional regime, thereby confiscating the right to political participation guaranteed in express form in the Constitution.[5]

---

[4] *Gaceta Oficial* N° 37.077, Nov. 14, 2000.

[5] *Gaceta Oficial*, N° 37.105, Dec. 22, 2000. That is why the Inter-American Commission on Human Rights, in its *2003 Report on the Situation of Human Rights in Venezuela*, noted that "the constitutional amendments introduced for the election of these authorities as guarantees of their independence and impartiality were not put into practice in this instance," para. 186. Available at http://www.cidh.oas.org/countryrep/Venezuela2003eng/chapter1.htm#B.

This motivated the people's defender to file an action presenting the unconstitutionality of the special law and to seek its judicial review and annulment by the Supreme Tribunal.[6] Even though the Supreme Tribunal never decided the case, in preliminary Decision No. 1.562 (December 12, 2000) (asking the people's defender to clarify the *amparo* petition filed together with the nullity action), the Tribunal recognized that "the full normalization of new institutions such as the Citizens' Power and the Supreme Tribunal of Justice requires Organic Laws developed in the constitutional context" and affirmed that, "as long as these are not enacted, these institutions are governed by two co-existent formative bodies of law, the Decree for the Transition of the Public Powers and the Constitution of the Bolivarian Republic of Venezuela," which form a single "constitutional block" – the Constitutional Chamber decided similarly in its decisions of March 14 and 28, 2000.[7] The consequence was that the transitory provisions of the Constitution and the transitional regime enacted by the Constituent Assembly were to remain in effect until the National Assembly enacted those organic laws. But instead of exhorting the National Assembly to enact the needed organic laws, by annulling the special law that failed to apply the Constitution, the Constitutional Chamber legitimized the contents of the previously mentioned special law.[8]

Is important to point out that the Justification Report of the Special Law Draft referred to the "absence of express provisions regulating the appointment of the members of the Citizens' Power and of the Magistrates to the Supreme Tribunal" (which only the National Assembly could

---

[6]See Clodovaldo Hernández, "Designaciones de la Asamblea bajo juicio de nulidad," in *El Universal,* Caracas Dec. 13, 2000, 1–2.

[7]See *Revista de Derecho Público* 84, Editorial Jurídica Venezolana, Caracas 2000, 108ff.

[8]The director general of the Office of the People's Defender, Juan Navarrete, characterized the decision of the Supreme Tribunal of Justice as an abuse of power. See *El Universal,* Caracas Dec. 14, 2000, 1–2. In its *2003 Report on the Situation of Human Rights in Venezuela,* the Inter-American Commission on Human Rights, noted "with concern that the Supreme Court of Justice itself justified the mechanism imposed by this law, by upholding the legality of the transition process," para. 187; and reiterated its concern regarding what has been called the "Transitional Regime," which, in its opinion, undermines the full currency of the Constitution. The aforesaid Transitional Government Regime was enacted by the National Assembly as a mechanism intended to ensure the survival of provisions that would have been tacitly repealed under the new constitution until such time as the corresponding legislation could be enacted. The implementation of this regime, as explained previously, led to the failure to implement the mechanisms enshrined in the constitution for the appointment of Supreme Court magistrates, the People's Defender, the Prosecutor General, and Comptroller General of the Republic. This is all because the Supreme Court of Justice has maintained that the full currency of the Constitution requires the adoption of a set of specific laws that, to date, have not yet been enacted. See para. 188. OEA/ser.L/V/II.118 doc.4 rev 2. Acailable at http://www.cidh.oas.org/countryrep/ Venezuela2003eng/chapter1.htm#B.

enact), and to the fact that the nominating committees for the appointments "[did] not yet exist" (only the National Assembly could regulate their existence); instead of enacting the required organic law, the special law was a draft for the "the National Assembly to fill the legal vacuum," without ending the provisional regime or forfeiting its obligation to legislate.

2. *The Appointment of the Magistrates of the Supreme Tribunal of Justice*

The systematic violation of the 1999 Constitution on this matter of appointment of Magistrates of the Supreme Tribunal in 2000 reached its zenith when the Constitutional Chamber of the Supreme Tribunal of Justice held that eligibility requirements for Magistrates of the tribunal, set forth very precisely in Article 263 of the Constitution, were inapplicable to the Magistrates sitting on the Supreme Tribunal in 2000 who were issuing the provisional ruling in the aforementioned case filed by the people's defender.

The Magistrates decided that they could be "ratified" in their positions by the National Assembly, without complying with the conditions set forth in the Constitution for appointment. The Constitution, as supreme norm, was deemed to be mandatory for all people and institutions (Article 7), except for the Magistrates of the Supreme Tribunal of Justice, whose signatures appeared at the foot of the decision. For such purpose, the Constitutional Chamber created the argument that ratification was a concept not foreseen in the Constitution; therefore, Article 263 applied only to *ex novo* appointments of Magistrates, not to the tenure of those provisionally appointed. This concept of ratification, instead, was incorporated in the Decree for the Transition Regime enacted by the Constituent Assembly, only applicable to the Magistrates of the Supreme Tribunal. Because the decree only provided the need to appoint new Magistrates "according to the Constitution," the Tribunal concluded that ratification of the Magistrates did not need to respect the Constitution.

Accordingly, with a single stroke, the Constitutional Chamber – the institution established to guarantee the supremacy of the Constitution – decided that it was inapplicable precisely to its own Magistrates, who were the deciding judges in this case. Those who stood to benefit from the decision handed down "justice."[9]

The result was that the Magistrates of the Constitutional Chamber created and defined a special regime concerning the conditions of eligibility for their own offices, applicable only to them. They found that to require conditions other than the effective accomplishment of their functions would be to discriminate against those whose positions were to be ratified and favor those who have not been Magistrates but aspire to sit on the Supreme Tribunal of Justice.

The consequence of this decision was the decision of the National Assembly in December 2000 ratifying or appointing the Magistrates of the Supreme Tribunal of Justice, many of whom did not fill the conditions set forth in the Constitution to be Magistrates,[10] and almost all were close allies of the government. With this, the political control of the Supreme Tribunal was consolidated and, consequently, began the endless intervention of the judiciary by the Commission on the Functioning and Restructuring of the Judicial System, established during the 1999 constitution-making process.

3. *The Consolidation of the Commission on the Functioning and Restructuring of the Judicial System and the Complete Political Control of the Judiciary*

Since 2001–2, the Commission on the Functioning and Restructuring of the Judicial System has continued to exist parallel to the Supreme Tribunal of Justice and with its recognition. This has consolidated the political intervention of the judiciary, making inapplicable the 1999 constitutional provisions that guarantee the independence and autonomy of judges.

In effect, according to the 1999 Constitution, judges can enter the judicial career only by means of public competition with citizens'

---

[9] Because of this situation, the People's Defender (Dilia Parra) asked the Judges to recuse themselves, because being in the case "judges and party" (*Ellos son juez y parte*). See in Taynem Hernández, "Solicitan inhibición del TSJ," in *El Nacional*, Caracas Dec. 16, 2000, 1–4.

[10] The Inter-American Commission on Human Rights, in its *2003 Report on the Situation of Human Rights in Venezuela*, mentioned as another issue of concern with respect to the guarantees of judicial independence and impartiality in Venezuela "the failure to follow the mechanisms set forth in the new Constitution for the election of its top authorities. The Commission believes that this failure to apply the procedures established by the Constitution as the guarantees of domestic law for ensuring the independence of the members of the judiciary means that the institutional legitimacy of that branch of government is undermined and the rule of law is weakened," para. 178. Available at http://www.cidh.oas.org/countryrep/Venezuela2003eng/chapter1.htm#B.

participation (Article 255) in order to choose the most competent persons. Unfortunately, this provision a decade later had not been enforced. That is why the Inter-American Commission on Human Rights in 2010 noted:

> with concern the failure to organize public competitions for selecting judges and prosecutors, and so those judicial officials are still appointed in a discretionary fashion without being subject to competition. Since they are not appointed through public competitions, judges and prosecutors are freely appointed and removable, which seriously affects their independence in making decisions.[11]

On the other hand, also in order to guarantee the independence of the Judiciary, according to the Constitution, judges can be dismissed from the their tenure only through disciplinary processes, conducted by disciplinary courts and judges conforming to a disciplinary judicial jurisdiction (Article 253). Consequently, according to the constitutional provisions it is completely illegitimate and contrary to the due-process guarantee (Article 49) to assign disciplinary judicial functions regarding judges to an ad hoc commission, as the aforementioned one. If the original purpose was to provisionally assign the disciplinary jurisdiction to specific entities before the formal creation of the disciplinary jurisdiction, then that function must have been attributed to preexisting courts or judges, not to an ad hoc commission not integrated by judges. Doing so violated the due process guaranteed and the right of everybody to be judged by their "natural judge" (Article 49).

The fact is that the ad hoc commission has continued to exist, to the extent that the Inter-American Commission, in its *2009 Annual Report*, pointed out that:

> even though the 1999 Constitution states that legislation governing the judicial system is to be enacted within the first year following the installation of the National Assembly, a decade later the Transitional Government Regime, created to allow the Constitution to come into immediate effect, remains in force. Under that transitional regime, the Commission for the Functioning and Restructuring of the Judicial System was created, and this body has ever since had the disciplinary authority to remove members of the judiciary. This Commission, in addition to being a special, temporary entity, does not afford due guarantees for ensuring the independence of its decisions, since its members may also be

---

[11]See IACHR, *2009 Annual Report*, para. 479. Available at http://www.cidh.oas.org/annualrep/2009eng/Chap.IV.f.eng.htm.

appointed or removed at the sole discretion of the Constitutional Chamber of the Supreme Court of Justice, without previously establishing either the grounds or the procedure for such formalities.[12]

In effect, after its creation in the December 22, 1999, Transitory Regime Decree of the Constituent Assembly, it enacted two more decrees on the matter on January 18, 2000, also in exercise of a supposedly "original constituent power." It appointed a tribunal inspector and members of the Commission on the Functioning and Restructuring of the Judicial System.[13]

The situation of the lack of complete inapplicability of the Constitution due to the transitory regime has been indefinitely prolonged because the omission of the legislature and the Supreme Tribunal as head of the judiciary, despite the regulations the same Supreme Tribunal enacted on August 2, 2000 – the Rules on the Direction, Government and Administration of the Judiciary, by which supposedly the provision of Article 267 would by satisfied to "end the effects of the transitory regime issued by the Constituent Assembly," a fact that did not occur.

In effect, Article 1 of the rules issued by the Supreme Tribunal had the purpose of creating the Executive Office of the judiciary to exercise by delegation the functions of direction, government, and administration of the judiciary assigned to the Supreme Tribunal. Nonetheless, in matters of disciplinary jurisdiction, through Article 30 of the rules, the Supreme Tribunal without any authority, and defrauding the Constitution, extended the existence of the Commission on the Functioning and Restructuring of the Judicial System, which was to continue in its transitional functions according to the rules to be established by the Supreme Tribunal, assigning it "disciplinary functions while the corresponding legislation is enacted and the Disciplinary Judicial Courts are created."

With those rules, the Supreme Tribunal declined to exercise its own normative attributions on judicial-organization matters, and it was the Commission on the Functioning and Restructuring of the Judicial System that enacted, without any constitutional or legal basis, the new rules to punish and dismiss judges.[14]

---

[12]See IACHR, *2009 Annual Report,* para. 481. Available at http://www.cidh.oas.org/annualrep/2009eng/Chap.IV.f.eng.htm.

[13]See *Gaceta Oficial* N° 36.878, Jan. 26, 2000.

[14]See *Gaceta Oficial* N° 37.080, Nov. 17, 2000.

It has been according to those new rules that the Commission has "cleansed"[15] the judiciary of judges not in line with the new political authoritarian regime. The extraordinary thing about the rules is that they were not even issued by the Supreme Tribunal, which, according to the Constitution, is the branch of government precisely in charge of the government and of administering the judiciary. It also is extraordinary that the Supreme Tribunal accepted them, thus endorsing the functioning of an unconstitutional entity and allowing that it could enact not only its own functioning rules but also the disciplinary regime for judges; that is, it established the rules and reasons for judges' dismissal.

Accordingly, the ad hoc commission continued to exist with the endorsement of the Supreme Tribunal; and its existence was again extended, this time by the legislature in the Organic Law of the Supreme Tribunal of May 2004,[16] which included a transitory disposition (Paragraph 2.e) setting forth that the following:

> (e) The Commission on the Functioning and Restructuring of the Judicial System will only have disciplinary functions while legislation is enacted, and the disciplinary jurisdiction and the corresponding disciplinary courts are created.

Consequently, during all the years of enforcing the 1999 Constitution, the constitutional provision requiring that "the disciplinary jurisdiction will be in charge of disciplinary courts determined by law" (Article 267) has never been applied; and, until 2010, judges have not had any guarantee of their stability – their permanence in the judiciary has been at the mercy of a nonjudicial, ad hoc commission that has cleansed the judiciary, particularly removing judges in a discretionary way, particularly when they have issued decisions not within the complacency of the government. As it was observed by the Inter-American Commission on Human Rights in its *2009 Annual Report*:

> in Venezuela, judges and prosecutors do not enjoy the guaranteed tenure necessary to ensure their independence following changes in policies or

---

[15]The word used by the Constitutional Chamber to describe the commission's functions is *depurar*, which means "to cleanse." See Decision N° 1.939 (Dec. 18, 2008) (Case: *Abogados Gustavo Álvarez Arias et al.*) on the unenforceability in Venezuela of the Aug. 8, 2008, decision of the Inter-American Court of Human Rights in the case of former Judges of the First Court of Contentious Administrative Matters (Case: *Apitz Barbera y otros ["Corte Primera de lo Contencioso Administrativo"] vs. Venezuela*). See *Revista de Derecho Público* 116, Editorial Jurídica Venezolana, Caracas 2008.

[16]See *Gaceta Oficial* N° 37942, May 20, 2004.

government. Also, in addition to being freely appointed and removable, a series of provisions have been enacted that allow a high level of subjectivity in judging judicial officials' actions during disciplinary proceedings. Even the Code of Ethics of Venezuelan Judges, adopted in August 2009, contains provisions that, by reason of their breadth or vagueness, allow disciplinary agencies broad discretion in judging the actions of judges.[17]

Unfortunately, on those judicial matters, the judicial activism of the Constitutional Chamber was deployed in other fields. For instance, it has decided ex officio cases of unconstitutional legislative omissions like the one referred to in the Organic Municipal Power Law.[18] On the contrary, the Political-Administrative Chamber of the Supreme Tribunal affirmed in Decision No. 673 (2008) that "the exercise of disciplinary functions in all its extension, that is, regarding titular judges that have attained stability by means of public competition, and regarding provisional judges, is today attributed in an exclusive way to the Commission on the Functioning and Restructuring of the Judicial System, as an organ created with transitory character while the disciplinary jurisdiction is created."[19]

The same Constitutional Chamber of the Supreme Tribunal of Justice summarized this situation in Decision No. 1.939 (December 18, 2008), issued to declare and justify that an August 2008 decision of the Inter-American Court of Human Rights, condemning Venezuela for violating the due-process rights of the judges of the First Court on Administrative Contentious Matters, was not enforceable in Venezuela. The tribunal, in addition to recognizing the powers on disciplinary matters of the Commission on the Functioning and Restructuring of the Judicial System, confirmed that the Supreme Tribunal itself through its Judicial Commission has the power to dismiss, in any case, in a discretionary way, without due process, any provisionally appointed judge. Therefore, the Constitutional Chamber rejected the Inter-American Court's decision, considering it contrary to the sovereignty of the Republic of Venezuela

---

[17]See IACHR, *2009 Annual Report*, para. 480. Available at http://www.cidh.oas.org/annualrep/2009eng/Chap.IV.f.eng.htm.

[18]See Decision N° 3118 (Oct. 6, 2003), in *Revista de Derecho Público* 93-96, Editorial Jurídica Venezolana, Caracas 2003. See Allan R. Brewer-Carías, *La Constitución de 1999. Derecho constitucional venezolano*, Editorial Jurídica Venezolana, Caracas 2004, 2:970ff.

[19]Quoted in Decision N° 1.939 (Dec. 18, 2008) (Case: *Abogados Gustavo Álvarez Arias et al.*), in *Revista de Derecho Público* 116, Editorial Jurídica Venezolana, Caracas 2008, 89ff.

and not enforceable, because such a court cannot impose its decisions on the Venezuelan judicial power.[20]

The fact is that the absence of stability of judges has led, in practice, to the dismissal of judges when adopting decisions contrary to the will or intterest of the executive branch. This was also pointed out by the Inter-American Commission on Human Rights, in its *2009 Annual Report*, noting:

> with concern that in some cases, judges were removed almost immediately after adopting judicial decisions in cases with a major political impact. The lack of judicial independence and autonomy vis-à-vis political power is, in the IACHR's opinion, one of the weakest points in Venezuelan democracy.[21]

4. *The 2004 Reform of the Supreme Tribunal Organic Law and the Reinforcement of Executive Control over the Judiciary*

After the National Assembly sanctioned the special law to provisionally appoint the Magistrates of the Supreme Tribunal without complying with the Constitution, the transitory situation continued in 2004, led again by the National Assembly with its sanctioning of the Organic Law of the Supreme Tribunal of Justice, which increased the number of magistrates from twenty to thirty-two and distorted the constitutional conditions for their appointment and dismissal.[22] The sanctioning of such a law allowed the government to assume absolute control of the Supreme Tribunal, particularly of its Constitutional Chamber.[23] The reform, as the Inter-American Commission emphasized in 2004, "takes no account of the concerns expressed by the IACHR in its report over possible threats to the

---

[20] Id.

[21] See IACHR, *2009 Annual Report*, para. 483. Available a http://www.cidh.oas.org/annualrep/2009eng/Chap.IV.f.eng.htm.

[22] The Inter-American Commission on Human Rights, in its *2003 Report on the Situation of Human Rights in Venezuela*, raised "its concern regarding certain provisions set forth in the draft Organic Law of the Supreme Court of Justice; these, were they to become positive law, could have a negative impact on the independence of the Venezuelan judiciary. These provisions entail several innovations: the increase in the number of Supreme Court magistrates; the granting of powers to the National Assembly whereby it can increase or decrease, by an absolute majority vote, the number of judges in the different chambers of the Supreme Court; and the empowerment of the Assembly to decree, by a simple majority vote, the revocation of Supreme Court magistrates' appointments," para. 158. OEA/ser.L/V/II.118 doc.4 rev 2. Available at http://www.cidh.oas.org/ countryrep/Venezuela2003eng/ chapter1.htm#B.

[23] See comments on this statute in Allan R. Brewer-Carías, *Ley del Tribunal Supremo de Justicia*, Editorial Jurídica Venezolana, Caracas 2004.

independence of the judiciary."[24] In its *2009 Annual Report*, the same Inter-American Commission "reiterates what it has said on previous occasions: that the rules for the appointment, removal, and suspension of magistrates set out in the Organic Law of the Supreme Court of Justice lack the safeguards necessary to prevent other branches of government from undermining the Supreme Court's independence and to keep narrow or temporary majorities from determining its composition."[25]

After the reform of 2004, the final process for selecting new judges, although being an exclusive competency of the National Assembly to be exercised without intervention of the executive, was submitted to the president, and on the eve of appointments, the president of the parliamentary commission declared:

> Although we, the representatives, have the authority for this selection, the President of the Republic was consulted and his opinion was very much taken into consideration.... Let's be clear, we are not going to score auto-goals. In the list, there were people from the opposition who comply with all the requirements. The opposition could have used them in order to reach an agreement during the last sessions, but they did not want to. We are not going to do it for them. There is now one in the group of postulates that could act against us.[26]

With good reason, the Inter-American Commission on Human Rights suggested in its *2004 Annual Report* that "These provisions of the Organic Law of the Supreme Court of Justice also appear to have helped the executive manipulate the election of judges during 2004."[27]

---

[24]See IACHR, *2004 Annual Report* (Follow-Up Report on Compliance by the State of Venezuela with the Recommendations made by the IACHR in its Report on the Situation of Human Rights in Venezuela [2003]), para. 174. Available at http://www.cidh.oas.org/annualrep/2004eng/chap.5b.htm

[25]See IACHR *2009 Annual Report*, para. 478. Available at http://www.cidh.oas.org/annualrep/2009eng/Chap.IV.f.eng.htm.

[26]See declaration of Pedro Carreño in *El Nacional*, Caracas Dec. 13, 2004. That is why the Inter-American Commission suggested in its report to the General Assembly of the Organization of American States in 2004 that "these regulations of the Organic Law of the Supreme Court of Justice would have made possible the manipulation, by the Executive Power, of the election process of judges that took place during 2004." See Inter-American Commission on Human Rights, *2004 Report on Venezuela*, para. 180.

[27]The IACHR added: "The IACHR learned of complaints filed from various quarters, including law faculties, international observers and opposition forces, to the effect that a simple majority of the National Assembly, composed of government supporters, had arranged for the election of judges to *pack* the Supreme Court with a clear government majority. As a result, the 49 judges (17 full judges and 32 alternates) elected were politically sympathetic to the government, and they included among their number two judges who are sitting parliamentary members for the government majority," para. 180. See IACHR, *2004 Annual Report* (Follow-Up Report on Compliance by the State of Venezuela

This configuration of the Supreme Tribunal, as highly politicized and subjected to the will of the president, has eliminated all autonomy of the judicial power and even the basic principle of the separation of powers.

The president admitted his own influence on the Supreme Tribunal when he publicly complained that the Supreme Tribunal had issued an important ruling in which it "modified" the Income Tax Law without previously consulting the "leader of the Revolution"; he also warned courts against decisions that would be "treason to the People" and "the Revolution." That was a very controversial case, decided by the Constitutional Chamber in Decision No. 301 (February 27, 2007).[28] The president said:

> Many times they come, the National Revolutionary Government comes and wants to make a decision against something that, for instance, deals with or has to pass through judicial decisions, and then they begin to move against it in the shadows, and many times they succeed in neutralizing decisions of the Revolution through a judge, or a court, and even through the very same Supreme Tribunal of Justice, behind the backs of the Leader of the Revolution, acting from within against the Revolution. This is, I insist, treason to the people, treason to the Revolution.[29]

To ensure the control of the Supreme Tribunal, another important provision of the new Organic Law of the Supreme Tribunal of Justice concerned dismissal of Judges. According to Article 265 of the 1999 Constitution, a judge can be dismissed in cases of "grave faults" (*faltas graves*) committed by the accused, only by the vote of a qualified majority of two-thirds of the National Assembly, following a hearing and prior qualification by the citizens' power. The Organic Law of the Supreme Tribunal of Justice defines "grave faults" broadly, leaving open the

---

with the Recommendations made by the IACHR in its Report on the Situation of Human Rights in Venezuela [2003]). Available at http://www.cidh.oas.org/annualrep/2004eng/chap.5b.htm.

[28] Supreme Tribunal of Justice, Constitutional Chamber, Decision N° 301 (Feb. 27, 2007) (Case: *Adriana Vigilanza y Carlos A. Vecchio*) (Exp. N° 01-2862), in *Gaceta Oficial* N° 38.635, Mar. 1, 2007. See Allan R. Brewer-Carías, "El juez constitucional en Venezuela como legislador positivo de oficio en materia tributaria," in *Revista de Derecho Público* 109, Editorial Jurídica Venezolana, Caracas 2007, 193-212; and "De cómo la jurisdicción constitucional en Venezuela, no sólo legisla de oficio, sino subrepticiamente modifica las reformas legales que 'sanciona,' a espaldas de las partes en el proceso: El caso de la aclaratoria de la sentencia de Reforma de la Ley de Impuesto sobre la Renta de 2007," *Revista de Derecho Público* 114, Editorial Jurídica Venezolana, Caracas 2008, 267-76.

[29] *Discurso en el Primer Encuentro con Propulsores del Partido Socialista Unido de Venezuela desde el teatro Teresa Carreño* (Speech in the First Event with Supporters of the Venezuela United Socialist Party at the Teresa Carreño Theater), Mar. 24, 2007, available at http://www.minci.gob.ve/alocuciones/4/13788/primerencuentrocon.html, 45.

possibility of dismissal based exclusively on political motives.[30] Furthermore, the Constitution required the qualified two-thirds majority to avoid leaving the tenure of Judges in the hands of a simple majority of legislators. Unfortunately, this provision was distorted by the 2004 Organic Law of the Supreme Tribunal of Justice, which established that Judges could be dismissed by simple majority when the "administrative act of their appointment" is revoked (Article 23.4).[31] This distortion, contrary to the independence of the judiciary, was attempted to be constitutionalized in the rejected 2007 constitutional reforms, which proposed that Magistrates of the Supreme Tribunal could be dismissed in case of grave faults but only by the vote of the majority of members of the National Assembly.[32] The National Assembly used this power to dismiss Judges who have ruled against the government's wishes on sensitive issues.

All of this has allowed the government to assume absolute control of the Supreme Tribunal of Justice in general, and of every one of its chambers, especially the Constitutional Chamber.

II. THE SUPREME TRIBUNAL AS A TOOL TO DISTORT THE CONSTITUTION AND RECOURSE FOR CONSTITUTIONAL INTERPRETATION

If Constitutions are superior laws that support the validity of a legal order, then the institutional solution to ensure their enforcement is the existence of a supreme court that can act as guardian of the Constitution, with powers to annul unconstitutional state acts or declare their unconstitutionality. In democracies, such courts have always been the main institutional guarantee of freedom and the rule of law. Nonetheless, the same courts in authoritarian governments, far from ensuring the rule of law, have been used to demolish the foundations of the democracy. Unfortunately, the latter has been the case in Venezuela over the past decade (1999–2010), notwithstanding the formal provisions on judicial review in the Constitution.

---

[30]See Allan R. Brewer-Carías, *Ley Orgánica del Tribunal Supremo de Justicia*, Editorial Jurídica Venezolana, Caracas 2004, 41.

[31]Id., 39-41. The provision was abrogated in the 2010 reform of the Organic Law of the Supreme Tribunal of Justice.

[32]See Allan R. Brewer-Carías, *La reforma constitucional de 2007 (Comentarios al proyecto inconstitucionalmente sancionado por la Asamblea Nacional el 2 de noviembre de 2007)*, Editorial Jurídica Venezolana, Caracas 2007, 108.

The 1999 Constitution, in effect, expressly established constitutional supremacy (Article 7), according to which the Constitution must prevail above the will of all the constituted bodies of the state, including, of course, the Supreme Tribunal of Justice itself. This supremacy is ensured by means of two provisions: those regarding the absolute, rigid character of the Constitution implying that its modification can take place only with the necessary and indispensable popular intervention, and those concerning the constitutional judicial review system to guarantee said supremacy.

As for the institutional system of constitutional reform, three different procedures have been established in the Constitution: constitutional reform, constitutional amendment, and constituent assembly – the last is needed in cases of transforming the state to establish a new legal order and to fully reform the Constitution (Article 347). In the other two cases, constitutional review procedures are designed to introduce reforms without changing or modifying the structure or fundamental principles of the Constitution (Articles 340 and 342). The common trend in all cases is the intervention of the people through referendum by convening the Constituent Assembly or to approve the constitutional reforms or the amendments. Any modification of the Constitution carried out differently from those three procedures is considered unconstitutional and illegitimate.

The constitutional judicial review system,[33] as a result of the principles of constitutional supremacy and rigidity, has been established with a mixed or integral character that combines diffused and concentrated methods of judicial review.[34] That is, the guarantee for constitutional supremacy is ensured, first, by assigning all judges of the republic the obligation to "guarantee the integrity of the Constitution" (Article 334); and second, by assigning the Supreme Court of Justice, as "the higher and

---

[33] See Mauro Cappelletti, *Judicial Review in the Contemporary World*, Bobbs-Merrill, Indianapolis 1971; Allan R. Brewer-Carías, *Judicial Review in Comparative Law,* Cambridge University Press, Cambridge 1989; *Instituciones políticas y constitucionales,* Universidad Católica del Táchira–Editorial Jurídica Venezolana, San Cristóbal–Caracas 1996, 6 (La justicia constitucional):131ff.; *El control concentrado de la constitucionalidad de las leyes (Estudio de derecho comparado),* Editorial Jurídica Venezolana, Caracas 1994.

[34] See Manuel Arona Cruz, "El control de la constitucionalidad de los actos jurídicos en Colombia ante el derecho comparado," in *Archivo de Derecho Público y Ciencias de la Administración, Derecho público en Venezuela y Colombia,* Instituto de Derecho Público, UCV, Caracas 1986, 7:39-114; Allan R. Brewer-Carías, *El sistema mixto o integral de control de la constitucionalidad en Colombia y Venezuela,* Universidad Externado de Colombia, Pontificia Universidad Javeriana, Bogotá 1995; *El sistema de justicia constitucional en la Constitución de 1999,* Editorial Jurídica Venezolana, Caracas 2000; *La justicia constituticonal. Procesos y procedimientos constitucionales,* Universidad Nacional Autónoma de México, Mexico City 2007; "La justicia constitucional en la nueva Constitución," *Revista de Derecho Constitucional* 1, Editorial Sherwood, Caracas 1999, 35-44.

last interpreter of the Constitution," the task of ensuring "the supremacy and effectiveness of constitutional provisions and principles" and their "uniform interpretation and application" (Article 335). The Constitution also assigns constitutional jurisdiction to the Constitutional Chamber of the Supreme Tribunal (Articles 266.1 and 336), through which it has the power to annul unconstitutional statutes and other state acts of statutory character exercising the concentrated method of judicial review.

In accordance with these provisions, the Constitutional Chamber is, without a doubt, the most powerful instrument for ensuring the supremacy of the Constitution and the rule of law. As a guardian of the Constitution, it is of course subject to it, a matter that is in any rule-of-law system, is absolutely understood and is not subject to discussion. It would be inconceivable that a constitutional court can violate the Constitution it is called on to apply and interpret. As a matter of principle, other state bodies might violate it, but not its guardian. For such purpose and to ensure that this does not occur, the constitutional court must have absolute independence and autonomy. On the contrary, a constitutional court submitted to the will of the political power, instead of being the guardian of the Constitution, becomes the most atrocious instrument of authoritarianism. Thus, the best constitutional justice system, in the hands of judges subjected to political power, is a dead letter for individuals and is an instrument to defraud the Constitution.

Unfortunately, the latter has been occurring in Venezuela since 2000. The Constitutional Chamber of the Supreme Tribunal, as constitutional judge, far from acting within the expressed constitutional attributions, has been adopting decisions that, in some cases, contain unconstitutional constitutional interpretations,[35] not only of its own powers of judicial review but also of substantive matters. It changed or modified constitutional provisions, in many cases to legitimize and support the progressive building of the authoritarian state. That is, it has distorted the Constitution through illegitimate and fraudulent "constitutional mutations" (*mutaciones constitutionales*)."[36] These illegitimate modifications, of course, have been

---

[35]See Allan R. Brewer-Carías, "*Quis Custodiet Ipsos Custodes*: De la interpretación constitucional a la inconstitucionalidad de la interpretación," in *VIII Congreso Nacional de derecho Constitucional, Perú*, Fondo Editorial 2005, Colegio de Abogados de Arequipa, Arequipa 2005, 463-89; and *Revista de Derecho Público* 105, Editorial Jurídica Venezolana, Caracas 2006, 7-27. See also Allan R. Brewer-Carías, *Crónica sobre la "in"justicia constitucional. La Sala Constitucional y el autoritarismo en Venezuela*, Editorial Jurídica Venezolana, Caracas 2007.

[36]A "constitutional mutation" (distortion) occurs when the content of a constitutional provision is modified in such a way that even when the provision maintains its content, it receives a different meaning. See Néstor Pedro Sagüés, *La interpretación judicial de la Constitución*, Abeledo-Perrot,

made by the Constitution's supreme guardian, exercising a sort of derived constituent power that does not belong to it and is not regulated in the Constitution. The eternal question arising from the uncontrolled power – *Quis custodiet ipsos custodes* – is particularly relevant.

One of the most important instruments for distorting the Constitution that has been used in Venezuela is the abstract recourses of interpretation of the Constitution, created by the Constitutional Chamber of the Supreme Tribunal from the interpretation of Article 335 of the Constitution, which grants the Supreme Tribunal the character of "maximum and final interpreter of the Constitution." In other words, this autonomous recourse for the abstract interpretation of the Constitution, which is not established in the Constitution or in any statute, has served as the main tool for adopting some of the most distinguishable and illegitimate distortions (*mutaciones*) of the Constitution. Many of the latter have their origin in the decision on autonomous requests for the abstract interpretation of the Constitution, in many cases filed by the national executive through the attorney general.

The 1999 Constitution grants the Supreme Tribunal of Justice only the power to "decide the recourses of interpretation on the content and scope of the legal texts" (statutes) (Article 266.6), a faculty that is to be exercised "by all the Chambers [of the Tribunal] pursuant to the provisions of this Constitution and the law" (Article 266). No reference is made in the Constitution to a recourse for the abstract interpretation of the Constitution itself.

Nonetheless, before the Supreme Tribunal of Justice's organic law was sanctioned in 2004, and without any constitutional or legal support, in 2000 the Constitutional Chamber created an autonomous "recourse of interpretation of the Constitution."[37] The court's ruling was founded on Article 26 of the Constitution, which established the right to access justice, considering that, although the action was not set forth in any statute, it was not forbidden, either. Therefore, the Constitutional Chamber

---

Buenos Aires 2006, 56-59, 80-81, 165ff.; Salvador O. Nava Gomar, "Interpretación, mutación y reforma de la Constitución. Tres extractos," in *Interpretación constitucional*, coord. Eduardo Ferrer Mac-Gregor, Ed. Porrúa, Universidad Nacional Autónoma de México, Mexico City 2005, 2:804ff.; Konrad Hesse, "Límites a la mutación constitucional," in *Escritos de derecho constitucional*, Centro de Estudios Constitucionales, Madrid 1992.

[37] Decision N° 1077 of the Constitutional Chamber (Sept. 22, 2000), Case: *Servio Tulio León Briceño;* see in *Revista de Derecho Público*, N° 83, Editorial Jurídica Venezolana, Caracas 2000, 247ff.

decided that "citizens do not require statutes establishing the recourse for constitutional interpretation, in particular, to raise it."[38]

To raise this recourse for constitutional interpretation, the Constitutional Chamber has considered that a particular interest shall exist in the plaintiff. The court ruled:

> a public or private person shall have a current legitimate legal interest, grounded in a concrete and specific legal situation, which necessarily requires the interpretation of constitutional rules applicable to the case, in order to cease the uncertainty impeding the development and effects of said legal situation.[39]

Regarding the purpose of the recourse for constitutional interpretation, in Decision No. 1077 (August 22, 2001), the Constitutional Chamber considered that it is "a declaration of certainty on the scope and content of a constitutional provision," seeking for a constitutional interpretation in order to "clear doubts and ambiguities about the supposed collision." The Constitutional Chamber added that the petition for interpretation might be inadmissible "if it does not specify which is the obscurity, ambiguity or contradiction between the provisions of the constitutional text."[40] The petition, if applicable, also must specify "the nature and scope of the applicable principles" or "the contradictory or ambiguous situations aroused between the Constitution and the rules of its transitory regime."[41] The interpretation of the Constitution by the Constitutional Chamber in these cases is binding.[42]

This extraordinary interpretive power, although theoretically an excellent judicial means for interpreting the Constitution, unfortunately has been extensively abused by the Constitutional Chamber to distort important constitutional provisions, to interpret them contrary to the text, and to justify constitutional solutions according to the will of the executive.[43] That is, this instrument for abstract interpretation of the

---

[38]This criterion was ratified later in Decision N° 1347 (Sept. 11, 2000), in *Revista de Derecho Público* 84, Editorial Jurídica Venezolana, Caracas 2000, 264ff.

[39]Id.

[40]Case: *Servio Tulio León Briceño*, in *Revista de Derecho Público* 83, Editorial Jurídica Venezolana, Caracas 2000, 247ff.

[41]Id.

[42]Decision N° 1347 of the Constitutional Chamber (Nov. 9, 2000), in *Revista de Derecho Público* 84, Editorial Jurídica Venezolana, Caracas 2000, 264ff.

[43]See Decision N° 1139 (June 5, 2002) (Case: *Sergio Omar Calderón Duque y William Dávila Barrios*); N° 137 (Feb. 13, 2003) (Case: *Freddy Lepage y otros*); N° 2750 (Oct. 21, 2003) (Case:

Constitution, without a doubt, has distorted the Constitution and has amplified the constitutional powers of the Constitutional Chamber. This autonomous recourse for abstract interpretation of the Constitution has no precedent in comparative law.[44]

As I have mentioned, an autonomous recourse for abstract interpretation of the Constitution, in the hands of an autonomous and independent constitutional judge, can be an efficient instrument for adapting the norms of the Constitution to the changes in the constitutional order of a country at a point in time. However, a recourse of that nature in the hands of a constitutional judge who is absolutely dependant on the executive power, in an authoritarian regime like the one in Venezuela during the past decade, is an instrument for the illegitimate distortion (*mutación*) of the Constitution. That is, through a series of judicial-review decisions interpreting the Constitution, many of which issued at the request of executive through the attorney general filing recourses for the abstract interpretation of the Constitution, the Constitutional Chamber eventually has "reformed" the Constitution. It is what has been called a process of *mutación ilegítima* of the Constitution – in many cases, even enforcing proposals for constitutional reforms that were formulated in 2007 and were rejected by the people in the December 2007 referendum.[45]

Carlos E. Herrera Mendoza); N° 2432 (Aug. 29, 2003) (Case: *Luis Franceschi y otros*); and N° 2404 (Aug. 28, 2003) (Case: *Exsel Alí Betancourt Orozco, Interpretación del articulo 72 de la Constitución*), in Allan R. Brewer-Carías, *La Sala Constitucional versus el estado democrático de derecho. El secuestro del poder electoral y de la Sala Electoral del Tribunal Supremo y la confiscación del derecho a la participación política*, Los Libros de El Nacional, Colección Ares, Caracas 2004, 172; "El secuestro del Poder Electoral y la confiscación del derecho a la participación política mediante el referendo revocatorio presidencial: Venezuela 2000-2004," *Boletín Mexicano de Derecho Comparado* 112, Instituto de Investigaciones Jurídicas, Universidad Nacional Autónoma de México, Mexico City 2005, 11-73.

[44] See Allan R. Brewer-Carías, "Le recours d'interprétation abstrait de la Constitution au Vénézuéla," in *Le renouveau du droit constitutionnel, Mélanges en l'honneur de Louis Favoreu*, Dalloz, Paris 2007, 61-70; "La ilegítima mutación de la Constitución por el juez constitucional: la inconstitucional ampliación y modificación de su propia competencia en materia de control de constitucionalidad," in *Libro Homenaje a Josefina Calcaño de Temeltas,* Fundación de Estudios de Derecho Administrativo (FUNEDA), Caracas 2009, 319-62.

[45] See Allan R. Brewer-Carías, *Reforma constitucional y fraude a la Constitución (1999-2009),* Academia de Ciencias Políticas y Sociales, Caracas 2009, 217ff;

Chapter 9

STATE APPROPRIATION, NATIONALIZATION, EXPROPRIATION, AND CONFISCATION OF PRIVATE ASSETS

A general trend of the economic policy of the authoritarian government that has taken shape in Venezuela, following the framework established in the 1999 Constitution, has been the progressive appropriation by the state of private industries and services; a public policy that has been fueled during the past decade because of the state's uncontrolled expenditure of outstanding fiscal revenues derived from increased oil prices in the nationalized oil industry.

This process of state appropriation of the economy has occurred through the consensual acquisition of industries and services by means of private law contracts and agreements, as was the case with the main electricity (Electricidad de Caracas C.A.) and telephone (C.A. Teléfonos de Venezuela) companies. It also has occurred through public law instruments allowed for in the Constitution, like the nationalization of economic sectors, which always implies expropriation of private assets. But, in many cases, the forced appropriation of private assets occurred through unconstitutional confiscations.[1]

I. THE COMPULSORY ACQUISITION OF PRIVATE ASSETS

In the Venezuelan legal system, the term *nationalization* refers to the public law institution through which the state, by means of a statute,

---

[1] See, in general, Antonio Canova González, Luis Alfonso Herrera Orellana, and Karina Anzola Spadaro, *¿Expropiaciones o vías de hecho? (La degradación continuada del derecho fundamental de propiedad en la Venezuela actual*," Funeda, Universidad Católica Andrés Bello, Caracas 2009.

reserves for itself an economic sector or activity, followed by the acquisition, normally through expropriation, of the private assets used in that sector or activity. The institution of nationalization was established in the 1961 Constitution (Article 97) and was first applied in the 1970s, through processes in which always was combined a legislative decision to reserve to the state the economic sector or activity and the administrative process of expropriation of the needed private assets, in order to make the reservation effective."[2]

In effect, Article 97 of the 1961 Constitution established the possibility of the state, through organic law and based on motives of national convenience or interest, reserving for itself some industries and services. That article was initially used to nationalize the natural gas industry in 1971 and the iron mineral exploitation industry in 1974.[3]

The oil industry and commerce were nationalized in 1975 by means of the 1975 Organic Law Reserving to the State the Industry and Commerce of Hydrocarbons,[4] which reserved that activity to the state; terminated foreign enterprises' existing concessions for the exploration and exploitation of oil; and established a procedure to expropriate private assets used for that activity, including payment to private industry participants.

The state's reservation institution was maintained in Article 302 of the 1999 Constitution, which establishes that "the State reserves for itself, by means of the corresponding organic law and for reasons of national convenience, the oil activity and other industries, exploitations, services and assets of public interest and strategic character." Regarding the reservation of the oil industry to the state, which, as mentioned, was

---

[2] See Allan R. Brewer-Carías, "Introducción al Régimen Jurídico de las Nacionalizaciones en Venezuela", in *Archivo de Derecho Público y Ciencias de la Administración*, III (1972-1979), Instituto de Derecho Público, Universidad Central de Venezuela, Caracas 1981, 2:23-44.

[3] *Ley que Reserva al Estado la Industria del Gas Natural*, in Gaceta Oficial N° 29.594, Aug. 26, 1971; Decree Law N° 580, Nov. 26, 1974 (*Decreto Ley que Reserva al Estado la Industria de la Explotación del Mineral de Hierro*), in Gaceta Oficial N° 30.577, Dec. 16, 1974.

[4] *Gaceta Oficial*, Extra. N° 1.769, Aug. 29, 1975. The 1975 Organic Nationalization Law reserved to the state all matters "related to the exploration of the national territory in search for petroleum, asphalt and any other hydrocarbons; to the exploitation of reservoirs thereof, the manufacturing or upgrading, transportation by special means and storage; internal and external trade of the exploited and upgraded substances, and the works required for their handling" (Article 1). Article 5 ordered that the activities be exercised directly by the national executive or entities owned by it, and it authorized private participation through operating agreements or association agreements in certain circumstances. See Allan R. Brewer-Carías, "Comentarios en torno a la nacionalización petrolera," in *Revista Resumen* 5, Caracas 1974, 22; Román J. Duque Corredor, *El derecho de la nacionalización petrolera*, Editorial Jurídica Venezolana, Caracas 1975, 22.

decided in 1975, was ratified in the 2001 Organic Hydrocarbons Law, providing in Article 9 that:

> activities relating to the exploration in search of hydrocarbon reservoirs encompassed in this Decree-Law, to their extraction in natural state, to their initial production, transport and storage, are denominated as primary activities for purposes of this Decree-Law. In accordance with what is provided in Article 302 of the Constitution of the Bolivarian Republic of Venezuela, the primary activities indicated, as well as those relating to works required by their management, remain reserved to the State in the terms established in this Decree-Law.[5]

Other constitutional mean for compulsory acquisition of private rights and property is expropriation, defined in Article 115 of the Constitution as the compulsory acquisition by the state of any privately owned assets, rights, or property through a specific procedure (due process) and with payment of just compensation; which applies regardless of whether the economic sector or activity affected has been or not reserved to the state, and of whether the decision is taken regarding a specific private asset or assets affected to an economic activity. According to the constitutional provision, the 2002 Expropriation Law defines expropriation in Article 2 as:

> an institution of Public Law, by which the State acts for the benefit of a cause of public utility or social interest, with the purpose of obtaining the compulsory transfer of the right to property or any other right of private individuals to its [the state's] patrimony, through a final judicial decision and timely payment of just compensation.[6]

Expropriation can be made through an act of general effects, like a special statute. This was the case, for instance, with the 1970 expropriations in connection with the iron and oil industries. In those cases, the statutes implementing nationalization declared the reservation and ordered expropriation of the interests of the former concessionaries following specific rules of procedure.

The 2002 Expropriation Law establishes the general procedure for expropriation and contemplates the possibility of an expropriation decree

---

[5] 2001 Organic Law of Hydrocarbons in *Gaceta Oficial* N° 37.323, Nov. 13, 2001.

[6] *Gaceta Oficial* N° 37.475, July 1, 2002. See the comments to this Law in Allan R. Brewer-Carías et al., *Ley de Expropiación por causa de utilidad pública o social*, Editorial Jurídica Venezolana, Caracas 2002, 7-100.

applying to more than one asset of more than one individual or entity (Articles 5 and 6). The Expropriation Law also contemplates that through special laws it is possible to provide for other procedures and rules to be applied to specific expropriation cases, including expropriation of multiple assets of multiple subjects (Article 4).

The former Supreme Court of Justice held that "the institution of expropriation applies not only when the State resorts to it, through the organisms authorized to do so, in compliance with the Law that governs it, but also within its conceptual amplitude, its principles are applied by extension to all the cases of deprivation of private property, or of patrimonial diminution, for reasons of public utility or public interest."[7]

Consequently, in Venezuela, all property, rights, and assets are subject to lawful expropriation and protected from unlawful expropriation, being an important change introduced in the 1999 Constitution and the 2002 Expropriation Law the clarification that expropriation, as the compulsory acquisition of assets by the state, can refer to the right to property (*derecho de propiedad*) and to any other right of private parties (*algún otro derecho de los particulares*) (Article 2) or assets of any nature (*bienes de cualquier naturaleza*) (Article 7). Accordingly, expropriation is conceived in Article 115 of the Constitution as a constitutional guarantee of the right to property, any other rights or assets of any nature, which cannot be taken by the state except through a judicial procedure (juridical guarantee) and with just compensation (patrimonial or economic guarantee). The consequence of these provisions is that any appropriation of private rights by the state without compensation is a confiscation, and it is unconstitutional except as a criminal sanction imposed by judges in cases of corruption or drug trafficking (Article 116). That is, any taking of private property, rights, or assets by the state, or any termination of private individual rights by the state without following expropriation procedures or other means for acquiring property (e.g., requisition, seizure, reversion, criminal sanction) is considered confiscation, which is prohibited in the Constitution.

Consequently, any limitations, contributions, restrictions, or obligations imposed on property, rights, or assets implying deprivation of the essence of the right or asset or when such regulations annihilate the property, right, or asset in question, must be considered as an expropriation. As it was ruled by the Constitutional Chamber of the Supreme Tribunal with respect

---

[7] See Supreme Court of Justice, Politico-Administrative Chamber, Decision of Oct. 3, 1990 (Case: *Inmobiliaria Cumboto, C.A.*), in *Jurisprudencia Ramírez & Garay* 114, Caracas 1990, 551-52.

to Articles 115 and 116 of the Constitution, the limits that can be established regarding private rights and property "must be established on the basis of a legal text, as long as said restrictions do not constitute an absolute or irrational impairment of such property right. That is, impeding the patrimonial capacity of the individuals in such a way that it eventually extinguishes it."[8] In the same sense, the former Supreme Court explained:

> Article 99 of the Constitution establishes the guarantee of the right to property.... [T]he limitation imposed on that right cannot represent an impairment that implies absorption of its attributions to the extent that it eliminates it.... This is, the right to property may be limited, restricted with respect to most of its content, attributions and scope, but this cannot exceed the limit – it is emphasized – by virtue of which such right is left completely empty, there is a central core of that right that is not susceptible of being impaired by the legislator, since if this were so, we would find ourselves before another legal institution (for example, expropriation).[9]

With regard to the prohibition on confiscation, the Court also explained:

> The prohibition of confiscation is related to the principle of reasonability that must guide the adjustment between the actions of the State and the impact on the legal sphere of those subject to the law, for which care must be taken that the activity does not formally or substantially reach the confiscation of the assets of the person, which occurs with the total dispossession of the assets or their equivalent.[10]

The aforementioned, in general terms, the constitutional and legal framework established in Venezuela in order for the state to acquire private assets and rights, whether or not the state has reserved for itself an economic sector or activity, except in cases of confiscation imposed as a criminal judicial sanction, always implies the right of the affected individual or enterprise to be compensated. Nonetheless, during the past decade and as a state unconstitutional policy, in numerous cases the state has appropriated private rights and assets without compensation.

---

[8]Supreme Tribunal of Justice, Constitutional Chamber, Decision N° 3003 of Oct. 14, 2005 (Exp. 04-2538).

[9]See Supreme Court of Justice, Decision of Apr. 29, 1997, in *Revista de Derecho Público* 69–70, Editorial Jurídica Venezolana, Caracas 1997, 391-92.

[10]Supreme Tribunal of Justice, Constitutional Chamber, Decision N° 2152 of Nov. 14, 2007, in *Revista de Derecho Público* 112 (*Estudios sobre la refroma constitucional*), Editorial Jurídica Venezolana, Caracas 2007, 519ff.

II. THE 2006–2007 STATE APPROPRIATION OF PRIVATE ENTERPRISES IN THE NATIONALIZED OIL INDUSTRY

The 1975 Nationalization Organic Law, notwithstanding the decision it contained to reserve the oil industry to the state, provided for private enterprises to participate in primary hydrocarbons activities (Article 5) in two ways: operating agreements and association agreements, including exploration-at-risk and profit-sharing agreements.[11] Consequently, according to the state policy named "oil opening" (*Apertura petrolera*) defined during the 1990s through Congress resolutions (Acuerdos), [12] the state-owned oil nationalized enterprises entered into agreements with private foreign and national enterprises. Consequently, pursuant to such public policy, private oil companies did in fact participate in primary hydrocarbon activities in Venezuela through Operating Agreements, Association Agreements for the Exploration at Shared-Risk-and-Profit, and Association Agreements for the development of the Orinoco Oil Belt (*Faja Petrolífera del Orinoco*).

Although the 2001 Organic Hydrocarbons Law changed the legal framework for the participation of private enterprises in the oil industry, reshaping such participation to only mixed companies – thus repealing the 1975 Nationalization Organic Law – in light of the nonretroactive nature of laws (Article 24 of the 1999 Constitution), the association agreements signed in the 1990s and also those signed in 2001,[13] remained as valid compromise executed by the state that continued to be in force.

---

[11] Regarding the interpretation of Article 5 of the 1975 Organic Nationalization Law and the participation of private companies in the oil industry activities, see Isabel Boscán de Ruesta et al., *La Apertura Petrolera, I Jornadas de Derecho de Oriente*, Fundación Estudios de Derecho administrativo, Caracas 1997.

[12] On these legislative decisions, see Allan R. Brewer-Carías, "El régimen nacional de los hidrocarburos aplicable al proceso de la apertura petrolera en el marco de la reserva al Estado de la Industria Petrolera," in *La apertura petrolera, I Jornadas de Derecho de Oriente*, Fundación de Estudios de Derecho Administrativo FUNEDA, Caracas 1997, 2-3.

[13] Still in 2001, after the sanctioning of the new Hydrocarbons Law (*Gaceta Oficial* N° 37.323 Nov. 13, 2001), the "Oil Opening" policy was applied by the government according to Article 5 of the 1975 Organic Nationalization Law. For such purpose, legislative authorization was sough for the signing of an association agreement with the China National Oil and Gas Exploration and Development Corporation, a subsidiary of China National Petroleum Corporation, for the production of bitumen and the design, construction, and operation of a unit for production and emulsification of natural bitumen for the elaboration of *orimulsión* (BITOR Agreement). The agreement was authorized by the National Assembly on Dec. 17, 2001 (*Gaceta Oficial* N° 37.347 of Dec. 17, 2001), just days before the entry into force of the new 2001 Hydrocarbons Organic Law (Jan. 1, 2002). The approval of the BITOR Agreement was possible because when enacting the 2001 Organic Hydrocarbons Law thorugh a Decree Law, the National Executive included a provision postponing its entry into force until Jan. 1, 2002, that is, after the BITOR agreement was already authorized and signed. See the

Starting in 2006, Venezuela initiated a state appropriation policy of the oil industry through the gradual elimination or reduction, by law, of private capital in oil industry activities. This was not a process of nationalization, which, as aforementioned, in Venezuela combines the decision to reserve to the state certain activities followed by expropriation (with compensation) of the affected assets. The oil industry and commerce, as aforementioned, was nationalized in 1975, so in the process developed in 2006–7, based on the 2001 Hydrocarbon Law, no reserve of activities to the state was decided because the reserve of the oil industry to the state already existed. The new policy produced what was the termination of the agreements entered with private companies but without compensation.[14]

This elimination or sharp reduction of private capital in the industry was achieved through three legislative instruments.

First, the Law Regulating Private Participation in Primary Activities, of April 18, 2006, declared the early and unilateral termination of existing operating agreements,[15] considering that they have denaturalized the oil industry "as a result of the so-called Oil Opening, to a point where it violated the higher interests of the State and the basic elements of sovereignty" (Article 1). Hence, Article 2 of that law declared that the content of the operating agreements that arose as a result of the oil "opening" was "incompatible with the rules set forth in the oil nationalization regime." Moreover, "they will be extinguished and the execution of their precepts will no longer be possible as of the publication of this Law in the *Official Gazette*" (Article 2). The termination constitutes an expropriation of rights, even if done through legislative act.[16] Article 3 of the Decree Law ratified the principle set forth in the 2001 Hydrocarbons Organic Law, whereby private capital could

---

comments in Allan R. Brewer-Carías, "La estatización de los convenios de asociación que permitían la participación del capital privado en las actividades primarias de hidrocarburos suscritos antes de 2002, mediante su terminación anticipada y unilateral y la confiscación de los bienes afectos a los mismos," in *Nacionalización, Libertad de Empresa y Asociaciones Mixtas*, coord.. Víctor Hernández Mendible, Editorial Jurídica Venezolana, Caracas 2008, pp. 123-88.

[14]On the concept of nationalization in Venezuela, see Allan R. Brewer-Carías, "Introducción al régimen jurídico de las nacionalizaciones en Venezuela," in *Archivo de derecho público y ciencias de la administración*, Instituto de Derecho Público, Facultad de Ciencias Jurídicas y Políticas, Universidad Central de Venezuela, Caracas 1981, 1:23-44.

[15]*Gaceta Oficial* N° 38.419, Apr. 18, 2006.

[16]See Allan R. Brewer-Carías, "Algunas reflexiones sobre el equilibrio financiero en los contratos administrativos y la aplicabilidad en Venezuela de la concepción amplia de la Teoría del Hecho del Príncipe," in *Revista Control Fiscal y Tecnificación Administrativa* 13, Contraloría General de la República, Caracas 1972, 86-93.

participate in primary hydrocarbons activities only by incorporating as mixed companies, which was exactly what had been proposed in the draft constitutional reforms that were rejected in a 2007 referendum.[17] To such end, the National Assembly adopted in March 2006 the Accord Approving the Terms and Conditions for the Creation and Operation of Mixed Companies.[18]

Second, Decree-Law No. 5200 Concerning the Migration of the Association Agreements of the Orinoco Belt and of the Exploration-at-Risk and Profit-Sharing Agreements into Mixed Companies, of February 2007, started the early and unilateral termination of the existing association agreements entered into between 1993 and 2001, establishing the possibility for their transformation (migration) into new mixed companies with a minimum of 50% state equity participation (2001 Organic Hydrocarbon Law, Articles 22 and 27–32). The law required that if the private investors in associations did opt for a mixed company arrangement, they could only be shareholders of those companies with maximum equity participation of 40%. The state shareholder Corporación Venezolana de Petróleo, S.A., or an affiliate of PDVSA would have a 60% maximum equity share (Article 2). For those companies that could not reach an agreement with the state to transform the joint ventures into mixed enterprises, the Decree Law 5200 implied the expropriation of the contractual rights, and the right to be fairly compensated for the damages caused by the execution of such law.

On the other hand, the legislative decision to begin the unilaterally and prematurely end of the association contracts implied the need to ensure the state's immediate assumption of actual industrial operations of each association agreement. Nonetheless, Article 4 of the law gave the private-sector companies that had been party to terminated agreements four months from the date the law was published (February 26, 2007) – that is, until June 26, 2007 – to "agree on the terms and conditions of their possible participation in the new mixed companies" with the ministry of Energy and Mines. It also provided that in such a case they would be conceded two extra months "to submit the aforementioned terms and conditions to the National Assembly for the corresponding authorization, pursuant to the Organic Hydrocarbons Law." Once the four months had

---

[17]See Allan R. Brewer-Carías, *La Reforma Constitucional de 2007 (Comentarios al proyecto inconstitucionalmente sancionado por la Asamblea Nacional el 2 de Noviembre de 2007)*, Editorial Jurídica Venezolana, Caracas 2007, 129ff.

[18]*Gaceta Oficial*, N° 38.410, Mar. 31, 2006.

elapsed, "without having reached an agreement on the incorporation and operation of the mixed companies," then the republic, through Petróleos de Venezuela, S.A., or its affiliates, was to directly take over the activities exercised by the associations to ensure their continuity, by reason of their character of public use and social interest (Article 5), as it occurred in many cases. Nonetheless, the law mentioned nothing about indemnifying the private companies that did not agree to continue as mixed companies.

Regarding these two laws, by beginning the process of termination of existing public contracts, it can be said that according to the Constitution, they initiated an expropriation process of the contractual rights of private companies, and they did so directly by statute without following the general procedure set forth in the 2001 Expropriations Law. Pursuant to Article 115 of the Constitution, those two laws generated inalienable rights for the contracting companies to be fairly compensated for damages (expropriation of contractual rights) arising from the take over of assets derived from public contracts they validly entered into with the state.

Third, the Law on the Effects of the Migration Process to Mixed Companies of the Orinoco Belt Association Agreements and the Exploration-at-Risk and Profit-Sharing Exploration Agreements, of October 2007,[19] "confiscated" the interests, shares, participation, and rights of companies that had participated in such agreements and associations but had not complied with the requirement to migrate to mixed companies. That is, according to this law, what might have been expropriation initially became, by unilateral and early termination of contracts, a confiscation of rights – in this case, the rights of those companies that did not reach an agreement with the state to continue operating as mixed companies.

In effect, according to this Law on the Effects of the Migration Process, the associations referred to in the Law of the Migration "were extinguished" as of the publication date of such Law or of the "decree that ordered the transfer of the right to exercise primary activities to the mixed companies incorporated pursuant to such Law" in the *Gaceta Oficial* (Article 1).

Decree Law No. 5200 made no mention of the rights to compensation of the private companies that had not agreed to continue as partners of the new mixed companies. However, instead of proceeding to do this in the Law on the Effects of the Migration Process, the state definitively

---

[19]*Gaceta Oficial* N° 38.785, Oct. 8, 2007.

confiscated such rights by declaring the agreements "extinguished" in the dates established in the said Law on the Effects, of October 5, 2007.

For purposes of executing such confiscation, Article 2 of the Law on the Effects of the Migration Process expressly provided that "the interests, shares and participations" in the associations referred to in Article 1 of the migration law, in the companies incorporated to develop the corresponding projects, and in "the assets used to conduct the activities of such associations, including property rights, contractual and other rights," which, until June 26, 2007 (pursuant to the term established in Article 4 of the migration law), "belonged to the private sector companies with whom agreement was not reached for migrating to a mixed company, are hereby transferred, based on the principle of reversion, without the need for any additional action or instrument, to the new mixed companies incorporated as a result of the migration of the respective associations, except for the provisions of Article 2 herein." This provision, according to the Venezuelan constitutional regime constitutes a confiscation of such assets, which Article 116 of the Constitution prohibits.

In other words, the state, by law, ordered the forced transfer of privately owned assets to newly incorporated mixed companies without compensation or due process; constituting an unconstitutional confiscation. In these cases, in no way could the takeover be justified by the principle of reversion, which is essentially associated with the figure of administrative concessions, which do not exist in hydrocarbons matters, and is applicable only when the corresponding contract arrives to its term, once assets are duly amortized.[20]

III. THE 2008–2009 NATIONALIZATION AND STATE APPROPRIATION

1. *The Nationalization of the Iron and Steel Industry*

On April 30, 2008, in Decree Law No. 6,058[21] issued by the national executive according to the legislative delegation contained in the 2007 enabling law,[22] the iron and steel exploitation and transformation industry

---

[20] As has been said by Eduardo García de Enterría and Tomás R. Fernández, the reversion has lost "its old character of being an essential element of every concession and comes to be regarded as an accidental element of the business, that is, it is admissible only in the case of an express accord, like one more piece, when conceived in this way, of the economic formula that all concessions consist in," in their *Curso de derecho administrativo*, 13th ed., Thomson-Civitas, Madrid 2006, 1:763.

[21] *Gaceta Oficial* N° 38.928, May 12, 2008.

[22] *Gaceta Oficial* N° 38.617, Feb. 1, 2007.

located in the Guayana region was nationalized. The motives for nationalization were strategic, as Guayana has the highest iron mineral reserves of the country, and those reserves have been nationalized since 1975[23] (Article 1). As a direct consequence of the reservation to the state of this industry, and to complete the nationalization process by means of expropriation, all business activities of the company SIDOR, C.A., and those of any of its subsidiaries and affiliates were declared of "public utility and social interest" (Article 3).

Therefore, the iron and steel industry was reserved to the state as a consequence of the order to transform SIDOR, C.A., its subsidiaries, and it affiliates to state-owned companies, with state shareholder participation of at least 60%, according to Article 100 of the Organic Law of Public Administration (Article 3).

With regard to the managerial transformation, Article 4 of the decree law establishes that the republic, through the Popular Power Ministry for Basic and Mining Industries or any of its decentralized organizations, would be the legal stockowner of the percentage belonging to the public sector in the newly created state-owned companies. To ensure the proper transfer of all activities resulting from this transformation, and in accordance with Article 5 of the law, the Popular Power Ministry for Basic and Mining Industries or any of its decentralized organizations, within seven days of publication of the law, was to establish a transitional commission for each company that would be incorporated in SIDOR's executive board. For nationalized private companies, Article 5 mandated that they fully cooperate with the nationalization process to guarantee a successful and safe transition, which ended on June 30, 2008. Article 10 of the law exempted from any direct or indirect tax contribution all business agreements, title transfers, and negotiations, as well as any operation that could result in economic gains, needed to transfer the private companies to state-owned companies.

To ensure the transfer of property and compensation to private companies being nationalized, Article 6 provided for sixty continuous days, beginning on the publication date of the organic decree law – that is, until August 12, 2008 – to agree on the terms and conditions of their possible participation in the state-owned companies. A technical committee with state and private representation was formed in order to determine a fair value to base the appropriate compensation owned to the

---

[23]Decree Law N° 580, Nov. 26, 1974 (*Decreto Ley que Reserva al Estado la Industria de la Explotación del Mineral de Hierro*), in *Gaceta Oficial* N° 30.577, Dec. 16, 1974.

nationalized companies (Article 7). On March 25, 2009, it was announced that the state and the Argentine enterprise Techint, which previously held majority ownership of SIDOR shares, reached an agreement to fix compensation and establish a schedule for payment.

The decree law established that if no agreement for the transformation of the private companies into state-owned companies had been reached by August 12, 2008, as in fact occurred, then the republic, through the Popular Power Ministry for Basic and Mining Industries or any of its decentralized organizations, would assume total control and management of the private companies to ensure the continuous operation of the nationalized industry. Articles 9 and 11 provided that all layoffs were to be frozen from the time of the publication of the organic law until the transformation process was over, and that all employees of the iron and steel industry would be covered under their respective collective contracts.

Additionally, in case no agreement was reached for transformation, Article 8 provided an expropriation clause for the shares of such companies based on the Expropriation Law. However, Article 8 also provided that to estimate the "compensation or fair value" of the assets being expropriated, no lost profit or indirect damages would be taken into account.

2. *The Nationalization of the Cement Industry*

Following the same trend used to nationalize the iron and steel industry, on May 27, 2008, in Decree Law No. 6091, as part of the 2007 enabling law, the cement industry was nationalized. The motive for nationalization was strategic (Article 1), and as a direct consequence of the reservation to the state of this industry, and to complete the nationalization process by means of expropriation, the activities developed by the main existing cement companies[24] – as well as any of their subsidiaries and affiliates – were declared of public utility and social interest (Article 3).

Therefore, the cement industry was reserved to the state and transformed, in accordance with Article 100 of the Organic Law of Public Administration, into state-owned companies, with state shareholder participation of at least 60% (Article 3).

With regard to the managerial transformation, Article 4 of the decree law established that the republic, through the Popular Power Ministry for

---

[24]Cemex Venezuela, S.A.C.A.; Holcim Venezuela, C.A.; and C.A. Fábrica Nacional de Cementos, S.A.C.A. (Grupo Lafarge de Venezuela).

Basic and Mining Industries or any of its decentralized organizations, would be the legal stockowner of the percentage belonging to the public sector in the newly created state-owned companies. To ensure the proper transfer of all activities resulting from the transformation, and in accordance with Article 5 of the law, the Popular Power Ministry for Basic and Mining Industries or any of its decentralized organizations, within seven days of publishing the law would establish a transitional commission for each company to be incorporated into the executive board of the nationalized companies. In fact, no such committee was established, and public officials occupied the enterprises. In any case, Article 5 mandated that private shareholders fully cooperate with nationalization to guarantee a successful and safe transition, to be completed by December 31, 2008 (Article 6). Article 10 of the law exempted from any direct or indirect tax contribution, all business agreements, title transfers, and negotiations needed to conclude the transformation and any operation that could result in economic gains.

Because the takeover of the cement industry was formally a nationalization, to ensure the transfer of property and the compensation due to the private companies being nationalized, Article 6 of the decree law gave them sixty continuous days, beginning on the publication date of the organic decree law – that is, until September 18, 2008 – to agree on terms and conditions of possible participation in the new state-owned companies. A technical committee with the participation of state and private representation was formed to determine the fair value to base the appropriate compensation owned to the nationalized companies (Article 7).

The government signed a memorandum of understanding with two of the shareholders of the nationalized enterprises (Holcim and Lafarge), in which they agreed on the compensation price and payment conditions. The agreements were not effective, and at least one of the enterprises initiated international arbitration. The third enterprise (Cemex) did not reach an agreement with the state and submitted to international arbitration. In that latter case, however, the state signed an agreement for technical assistance with the company, with limited duration, that allowed the nationalized industry to continue operations but with the systems of the private company.

In this case of the cement industry, in similar terms to the provisions regarding the nationalization of the iron and steel industry, the decree law established that if no agreement for the transformation was reached by December 31, 2008, as in fact occurred, then the republic, through the Popular Power Ministry for Basic and Mining Industries or any of its decentralized organizations, would assume total control and management of the private companies to ensure continuous operations of the nationalized industry.

3. *The State Appropriation of Assets and Services Related to Primary Hydrocarbon Activities*

In May 2009, the National Assembly, also on the basis of strategy, sanctioned the organic law reserving for the state the assets and services related to the primary activities of the oil industry[25] established in the Hydrocarbon Law (Article 1), which were formerly conducted by Petróleos de Venezuela, S.A. (PDVSA) and its subsidiaries, and later assumed by private companies, being activities essential to the industry (Article 2). The consequence of the nationalization was according to Article 1 of the law, that activities were to be "directly executed by the Republic, by Petróleos de Venezuela, S.A. (PDVSA), or any of its designed subsidiaries, or by mixed companies under Petróleos de Venezuela, S.A. (PDVSA) control."

Article 7 of the law assigned "public order" character to its provisions, meaning that provisions "shall have preference over any other legal dispositions related to the matter." However, Article 5 established that all the aforementioned assets and services provided or required were to be considered "public services and of public and social interest." Such assets and services are enumerated in Article 2 of the law as follows: water, steam, or gas injections aimed to increase the oilfield's energy and improve the recovery factor; gas compression; and all goods and services connected to activities in the Lago de Maracaibo (boats for personnel transport, divers, and maintenance); cargo ships (including diesel, industrial waters, and any other supplies), crane ships, tug boats, buoys, padding and filling cranes, pipe and wire lines, ship maintenance, workshops, docks, floating docks, and ports of any nature.

To carry out the state appropriation, Article 3 of the Law empowered the Popular Power Ministry for Energy and Oil to define by unilateral administrative acts (resolutions) the assets and services listed in the provisions of Articles 1 and 2. In the case that such resolutions are issued, according to Article 3 of the organic law, all previous contracts and agreements regarding the reserved activities and signed between private companies and state-owned companies will be considered *ipso jure*

---

[25]See *Gaceta Oficial* N° 39.173, May 7, 2009.

extinguished by virtue of the law. The law recognized the contracts, for the purpose of their early termination, as "administrative contracts" (Article 3).

The reservation to the state of the assets and services related to primary hydrocarbon activities –different from previous nationalization processes– provided that as of the date of the law's publication (May 7, 2009), "Petróleos de Venezuela, S.A., (PDVSA) or any of its subsidiaries will take possession of any assets and control of all operations related to the reserved activities," which effectively occurred. That is, according to the law, an "expedite mechanism" was provided according to the needs of the oil industry, "allowing Petróleos de Venezuela, S.A. (PDVSA) or any of its subsidiaries, to take over assets and control the operations of related the reserved activities, as a previous step to complete the expropriation process."

To that effect, the law authorized the Popular Power Ministry for Energy and Oil to take all available measures to ensure the continuous operation of the reserved activities, with authorization to ask for support from any state organ or entity. In this case, the National Guard was chosen to achieve this goal. Additionally, the law compelled all actors in the process to fully and peacefully collaborate in the transfer of operations, facilities, documents, and property affected by the law provisions; otherwise, they could be subject to administrative or criminal sanctions (Article 4).

To ensure the transfer to the state of all assets and services, Article 8 provided that any permits, certifications, authorizations, and valid registries belonging to the private operating companies, or pertaining to any of the reserved activities, would *ipso jure* be transferred to Petróleos de Venezuela or a designated subsidiary.

Additionally, to facilitate the transfer, Article 9 establishes that any act, business, or agreement related to the transfer of assets and operations enshrined under the organic law would be exempt from any national taxes.

Also, Article 10 of the organic law, as part of the transfer process, gives power to the Popular Power Ministry for Energy and Oil to make any decisions regarding the transfer of all working personnel from the statized companies to Petróleos de Venezuela or any of its subsidiaries. The state appropriation and immediate takeover of all goods, services, and assets obligated the state to fairly compensate shareholders of the private companies that the state took over. Nonetheless, for such purpose, the law only referred to the expropriation process as a mere possibility, providing that the state could (*podrá*) decree total or partial expropriation of all shares and assets belonging to any company doing business or conducting any of the reserved, in accordance with the Expropriation Law. In such cases, Petróleos de Venezuela, S.A., or any of its subsidiaries would be the expropriating entity (Article 6).

In the case of the state appropriation of the oil industry assets and services, the law established restricted criteria regarding the just and fair compensation provided for in Article 115 of the Constitution. To estimate the fair value of the assets being expropriated, Article 6 provided that in no case could lost profits or indirect damages be taken into account and that valuation would be based on "book value less all wages, payroll and environmental passives determined by the proper authorities." Article 6 adds that the time to effectively take possession would be taken into account to establish fair value. Additionally, payments could be through cash, bonds, or obligations issued by public entities (Article 6).

In any event, the day after the publication of the organic law, on May 8, 2009, the Popular Power Ministry for Energy and Oil passed Resolution No. 051,[26] listing all services, sectors, goods, and companies "affected by the takeover measures" (Article 1), and instructing Petróleos de Venezuela, S.A., or any of its subsidiaries, "to take control over operations and immediate possession of the mentioned facilities, documents, capital assets and equipment" (Article 2).

To ensure immediate takeover, the law provided that to register all information related to all affected goods, services, and assets, within the following fifteen days an inventory must be made to be signed by Petróleos de Venezuela, S.A., or any of its subsidiaries and the private companies, or be made through a judicial inspection or notarized act (Article 2). In that same resolution, the Popular Power Ministry for Energy and Oil reserved to itself the right to apply any necessary measures to guarantee the continuous operation of the affected business, as well as the right to identify other assets, services, companies, or sectors that follow under the provisions of the organic law (Article 3).

A few days later, on May 13, 2009,[27] the Popular Power Ministry for Energy and Oil passed Resolution No. 54, naming an additional list of companies conducting business and in possession of essential capital assets (gas compression) connected with primary hydrocarbon activities in accordance with the Hydrocarbon Organic Law, the list being considered as a declarative not compelling one (Article 1).

---

[26] See *Gaceta Oficial* N° 39.174, May 8, 2009.
[27] See *Gaceta Oficial* N° 39.177, May 13, 2009.

The fact of all the provisions and actions was the immediate takeover of all the assets and services unilaterally enumerated by the state, without any compensation paid or expropriation process initiated. It simply was another confiscation of private property, prohibited in the Constitution.

4. *The Reservation to the State of Petrochemical Activities*

On June 2009, the Law for the Development of the Petrochemical Activities was sanctioned,[28] reserving to the state the basic and intermediate petrochemical industry, as well as the works, assets, and installations required for its accomplishment (Article 5). "Basic petrochemical" includes the industrial processes related to physical transformation of the basic components of hydrocarbons, understood as products obtained from hydrocarbons with a very specific chemical formula (Article 4.2). "Intermediate petrochemical" includes industrial processes related to the chemical or physical transformation obtained from the basic petrochemical (Article 4.3).

The reservation to the state of petrochemical activities means that only the state, enterprises it exclusively owns, or mixed enterprises it controls can undertake such activities. Mixed enterprises are subject to prior authorization from the National Assembly, once informed by the Ministry of Energy and Oil about the specific circumstances and conditions in each case (Article 5).

The same law declared that because of economic and political sovereignty and for reasons of national strategy, the state shall remain as the owner of all shares of Petroquímica de Venezuela, S.A., or of any other entity that in its substitution could be established to manage the petrochemical industry (Article 6).

IV. THE STATE APPROPRIATIONS OF RURAL LAND AND ALIMENTARY INDUSTRIES

Since the enactment of the Land and Farming Law,[29] not only the possibility for the state to occupy and expropriate private land was extended, leading to the massive appropriation of private land by the state, without compensation, but also the possibility for the state to take over rural land simply ignoring its condition of private own property supported in the due registered titles, imposing in many cases to the owner, without legal support,

---

[28]See *Gaceta Oficial* N° 39.203, June 18, 2009.
[29]See Ley de Tierras y Desarrollo Agrario in *Gaceta Oficial* N° 5.771 Extra. of May 18, 2005.

the impossible burden to proof a property tradition for almost two hundred years.[30]

On the other hand, sine 2007, a massive process of expropriation, in many cases without due compensation, and of forced occupation of assets and industries by public authorities, with the support of the national guard, have taken place, based on "strategic" or "alimentary sovereignty" motives. In the latter case, the process has been based on the provisions of the Organic Law on Farming and Alimentary Security and Sovereignty,[31] which assigns expropriation powers to the executive without the need of a previous declaration of a specific public interest or public utility, and allowing the State to occupy private industries without compensation.[32] Also, the Law for the defense of persons in their access to goods and services [33] has allowed indiscriminate occupations of private property and industries, supporting its take over by public authorities, in many cases *sine die* and without compensation. [34]

---

[30]See Antonio Canova González, Luis Alfonso Herrera Orellana and "Karina Anzola Spadaro, *¿Expropiaciones o Vías de hecho? (La degradación continuada del derecho fundamental de propiedad en la Venezuala actual)*, FUNEDA, Caracas 2009, 115ff. See also Allan R. Brewer-Carías, "El régimen de las tierras baldías y la adquisición del derecho de propiedad privada sobre tierras rurales en Venezuela," in *Estudios de derecho administrativo* 2005-2007, Editorial Jurídica Venezolana, Caracas 2007, 327-74.

[31] See Ley Orgánica de soberanía y seguridad alimentaria, *Gaceta Oficial* N° 5.889, Extra., July 31, 2008. See the comments in José Ignacio Hernández G., "Planificación y soberanía alimentaria," in *Revista de Derecho Público (Estudios sobre los Decretos Leyes)* 115, Editorial Jurídica Venezolana, Caracas 2008, 389-394.

[32]See Carlos García Soto, "Notas sobre la expansión del ámbito de la declaratoria de utilidad pública o interés social en la expropiación," in *Revista de Derecho Público*, N° 115 (Estudios sobre los Decretos Leyes), Editorial Jurídica Venezolana, Caracas 2008, 149-151; Antonio Canova González, Luis Alfonso Herrera Orellana and Karina Anzola Spadaro, *¿Expropiaciones o Vías de hecho? (La degradación continuada del derecho fundamental de propiedad en la Venezuala actual)*, FUNEDA, Caracas 2009, 143ff.

[33]See Decreto Ley N° 6,092 para la defensa de las personas en el acceso a los bienes y servicios, *Gaceta Oficial* N° 5,889 Extra. of July 31, 2008,

[34]See Juan Domingo Alfonzo Paradisi, "Comentarios en cuanto a los procedimientos administrativos establecidos en el decreto N° 6.092 con rango valor y fuerza de Ley para la defensa de las personas en el acceso a los bienes y servicios," in *Revista de Derecho Público* 115, *(Estudios sobre los Decretos Leyes)*, Editorial Jurídica Venezolana, Caracas 2008, 246ff.; Karina Anzola Spadaro, "El carácter autónomo de las 'medidas preventivas' contempladas en el artículo 111 del Decreto Ley para la defensa de las personas en el acceso a los bienes y servicios," in id., 271-79; Antonio Canova González, Luis Alfonso Herrera Orellana and Karina Anzola Spadaro, *¿Expropiaciones o Vías de hecho? (La degradación continuada del derecho fundamental de propiedad en la Venezuala actual)*, FUNEDA, Caracas 2009, 163ff.

PART THREE

CONSTITUTIONAL REFORMS DESIGNED TO CONSOLIDATE AUTHORITARIANISM

The 1999 Constitution, after being applied for one decade by an authoritarian government, during the years 2007 and 2009 was the object of two reform projects, one that has failed and the other that has succeeded – both marked by authoritarian trends. The president announced the first one in January 2007 and, at his initiative, submitted the proposed reforms to the National Assembly in August 2007. Once approved by the National Assembly as draft constitutional reforms, they were submitted to approval referendum in December 2007, where they were rejected by popular vote. The intent of this constitutional reform was to consolidate the authoritarian government that had taken shape in the country, by formalizing a constitutional framework for a socialist, centralist, military, and police state (Chapters 10, 11, and 12). Nonetheless, despite its popular rejection and contrary to the Constitution, many of the proposals have been unconstitutionally implemented through statutes and decree laws (Chapter 13) and through decisions adopted by the Constitutional Chamber of the Supreme Tribunal (Chapter 14). The president announced the second constitutional reform in 2008, after the first one had been rejected. That reform referred precisely to one of the rejected constitutional reform proposals, the one to substitute the constitutional limits on reelection of public officials –in particular, the president– with the possibility of continuous, unlimited reelection of public officials. This reform was conceived of as a constitutional amendment and elaborated as an initiative of the National Assembly. It was submitted to approval referendum in February 2009 and was approved by popular vote (Chapter 15).

Chapter 10

THE FAILED ATTEMPT TO CONSOLIDATE AN AUTHORITARIAN AND ANTIDEMOCRATIC POLITICAL SYSTEM IN THE CONSTITUTION

I. A NEW FRAUD ON THE CONSTITUTION

On November 2, 2007, the National Assembly of Venezuela, following President Chávez's proposals, sanctioned a major constitutional reform to transform the democratic rule-of-law and decentralized social state established in the 1999 Constitution into a socialist, centralized, repressive, and militaristic state.[1] In the referendum for the approval of the constitutional reform on December 2, 2007, the people rejected the proposed reform.[2]

The constitutional reform was intended to transform the most essential and fundamental aspects of the state, making it one of the most important reforms in all of Venezuelan constitutional history. With it, the decentralized, democratic, pluralistic, and social state built and consolidated since the Second World War would have been radically changed to create a socialist, centralized, repressive, and militaristic state grounded in a so-called Bolivarian doctrine, which has been identified with twenty-first-century socialism and an economic system of state

---

[1] See Allan R. Brewer-Carías, *La reforma constitucional de 2007 (Comentarios al proyecto inconstitucionalmente sancionado por la Asamblea Nacional el 2 de noviembre de 2007)*, Editorial Jurídica Venezolana, Caracas 2007.

[2] According to information from the National Electoral Council on Dec. 2, 2007, of 16,109,664 registered voters, only 9,002,439 voted (44.11% abstention); of voters, 4,504,354 rejected the proposal (50.70%). This means that there were only 4,379,392 votes to approve the proposal (49.29%), so only 28% of registered voters voted for the approval.

capitalism.³ This reform was sanctioned following the president's proposal, which evaded the procedure established in the Constitution for such fundamental change. Thus, the reform defrauded the Constitution, being sanctioned through a procedure established for other purposes, to deceive the people.⁴ That is why it has been qualified as one more step of the "permanent coup d'état" that has occurred in Venezuela.⁵

The most important consequence of this draft reform from citizens' perspective was that, with it, an official state ideology and doctrine was to be formally established in Venezuela. That ideology was socialist and supposedly Bolivarian, which as a state doctrine (despite its imprecision – therein lies the danger) would allow for no dissidence. It must not be forgotten that the citizens have a constitutional duty to ensure the enforcement of the Constitution (Article 131); thus, if this reform had been approved, all citizens would have had the duty to actively contribute to the implementation of the state's official doctrine. Even a neutral position would not have been admissible. Thus, any thought, expression of thought, action, or omission that could have been considered contrary to the official socialist and Bolivarian doctrine, or that the authorities might have considered as not contributing to the development of socialism, could have been determined a violation of constitutional duty, subject to possible criminalization and criminal sanctions. It was a unique and official way of thinking.

The rejected reforms were the conclusion of a process that the president began in January 2007, when he announced that he would propose a series of reforms to the Constitution of 1999.⁶ For such purpose, he designated

---

³See *Proyecto de exposición de motivos para la reforma constitucional, Presidencia de la República, Proyecto Reforma Constitucional. Propuesta del Presidente Hugo Chávez*, Caracas Agosto 2007, 19.

⁴See Rogelio Pérez Perdomo, "La Constitución de papel y su reforma," in *Revista de Derecho Público* 112 *(Estudios sobre la reforma constitucional)*, Editorial Jurídica Venezolana, Caracas 2007, 14; Gerardo Fernández, "Aspectos esenciales de la modificación constitucional propuesta por el Presidente de la república. La modificación constitucional en fraude a la democracia," in id., 21-25; Fortunato González, "Constitución histórica y poder constituyente," in id., pp. 33-36; Lolymar Herández Camargo, "Los límites del cambio constitucional como garantía de pervivencia del Estado de derecho," in id., 37-45; Claudia Nikken, "La soberanía popular y el trámite de la reforma constitucional promovida por iniciativa presidencial el 15 de agosto de 2007," in id., 51-58.

⁵See José Amando Mejía Betancourt, "La ruptura del hilo constitucional," in id., 47. The term was first used by Francois Mitterand, *Le coup d'État permanent*, Éditions 10/18, Paris 1993.

⁶See the 1999 Constitution in *Gaceta Oficial* N° 36.860, Dec. 30, 1999, republished in *Gaceta Oficial* N° 5452, Extra. Mar. 24, 2000. For commentary on the Constitution, see Allan R. Brewer-Carías, *La Constitución de 1999. Derecho constitucional venezolano*, 2 vols., Editorial Juridical Venezolano, Caracas 2004.

the Presidential Council for the Reform of the Constitution.[7] The council was presided over by the president of the National Assembly and composed of officials from each branch of government, including the second vice president of the National Assembly and four additional deputies, the president of the Supreme Tribunal of Justice, the people's defender, the minister of labor, the attorney general, and the prosecutor general. The president instructed the council by decree to "work according to the Chief of State's guidelines in strict confidentiality" (Article 2),[8] contrary to the principles of any form of constitutional reform in a democratic country.

Guidelines for the proposed reforms emerged from various discussions and speeches of the president. These pointed to, on the one hand, the formation of a state of popular power or of communal power, or a communal state (*estado del poder popular o del poder communal, o estado comunal*), built on the communal councils (*consejos comunales*) as primary political units or social organizations. The communal councils, whose members are not elected by means of universal, direct, and secret suffrage, had already been created by statute in 2006,[9] parallel to the municipal entities, supposedly to channel citizen participation in public affairs. However, they operate within a system of centralized management by the national executive power and without any territorial autonomy.[10] On the other hand, the guidelines for reform also referred to the structuring of a socialist state and the substitution of the existing system of economic freedom and mixed economy with a state and collectivist economic system subject to centralized planning, which minimizes the role of individuals and eliminates any vestige of economic liberties or private property as constitutional rights.

In accordance with these orientations, the 2007 rejected reform intended to radically transform the state by creating a completely new juridical order. A change of that nature, according to Article 347 of the 1999

---

[7]Decree N° 5138 (Jan. 17, 2007), in *Gaceta Oficial* N° 38.607, Jan. 18, 2007, establishing the Consejo Presidencial para la Reforma de la Constitución.

[8]Id., Art. 2. This was also declared publicly by the president of the National Assembly when she took her seat as part of the council. *El Universal*, Caracas Feb. 20, 2007.

[9]Ley de Consejos Comunales, *Gaceta Oficial, Extra.* 5.806, Apr. 10, 2006. This statute was replaced by Ley Orgánica de los Consejos Comunales. See *Gaceta Oficial* N° 39.335, Dec. 28, 2009.

[10]See Allan R. Brewer-Carías, "El inicio de la desmunicipalización en Venezuela: La organización del poder popular para eliminar la descentralización, la democracia representativa y la participación a nivel local," in *AIDA, Revista de la Asociación Internacional de Derecho Administrativo*, Universidad Nacional Autónoma de México, Asociación Internacional de Derecho Administrativo, Mexico City 2007, 49-67.

Constitution, required the convening and election of a Constituent Assembly and could not be undertaken by means of mere constitutional reform. The procedure for constitutional reform is applicable only to "a partial revision of the Constitution and a substitution of one or several of its norms without modifying the structure and fundamental principles of the Constitutional text." This limited constitutional change is obtained through debate and sanctioning in the National Assembly, followed by approval in popular referendum.[11]

Nonetheless, despite these constitutional provisions, with the rejected reforms, a political tactic that has been a common denominator in the actions of the authoritarian regime was repeated: acting fraudulently with respect to the Constitution. That is, existing institutions were used in a manner that appeared to adhere to constitutional form and procedure to proceed, as the Supreme Tribunal has warned, "towards the creation of a new political regime, a new constitutional order, without altering the established legal system."[12] This occurred in February 1999, in the convening of a consultative referendum on whether to convene a constituent assembly when that institution was not prefigured in the then-existing Constitution of 1961.[13] It occurred with the December 1999 Decree on the Transitory Regime of the Public Powers, with respect to the 1999 Constitution, which was never the subject of an approbatory referendum.[14] It has continued to occur in subsequent years with the progressive destruction of democracy through the exercise of power and the sequestering of successive public rights and liberties, all supposedly based on legal and constitutional provisions.[15]

---

[11] See Allan R. Brewer-Carías, *Hacia la consolidación de un estado socialista, centralizado y militarista. Comentarios sobre el alcance y sentido de las propuestas de reforma Constitucional 2007*, Editorial Jurídica Venezolana, Caracas 2007.

[12] See the decision of the Constitutional Chamber of the Supreme Tribunal of Justice N° 74 (Jan. 25, 2006), in *Revista de Derecho Público 105,* Editorial Jurídica Venezolana, Caracas 2006, 76ff.

[13] See Allan R. Brewer-Carías, *Asamblea constituyente y ordenamiento constitucional*, Academia de Ciencias Políticas y Sociales, Caracas 1999.

[14] See Allan R. Brewer-Carías, *Golpe de estado y proceso constituyente en Venezuela*, Universidad Nacional Autónoma de México, Mexico City 2002.

[15] See Allan R. Brewer-Carías, "Constitution-Making Process in Defraudation of the Constitution and Authoritarian Government in Defraudation of Democracy: The Recent Venezuelan Experience," paper presented at the VII International Congress of Constitutional Law, Athens, June 2007. See also Allan R. Brewer-Carías, "El autoritarismo establecido en fraude a la Constitución y a la democracia y su formalización en Venezuela mediante la reforma constitucional. (De cómo en un país democrático se ha utilizado el sistema eleccionario para minar la democracia y establecer un régimen autoritario de supuesta 'dictadura de la democracia' que se pretende regularizar mediante la reforma constitucional)," in *Temas constitucionales. Planteamientos ante una reforma*, Fundación de Estudios de Derecho Administrativo, Caracas 2007, 13-74.

In this instance, once again, constitutional provisions were fraudulently used for ends other than those for which they were established; they were used to radically transform the state, thus disrupting the civil order of the social-democratic state to convert the state into a socialist, centralized, repressive, and militarist state in which representative democracy, republican alternation in office, and the concept of decentralized power would have disappeared, with all power instead concentrated in the decisions of the head of state. As is constitutionally proscribed, and as the Constitutional Chamber of the Supreme Tribunal of Justice summarized in Decision No. 74 (January 25, 2006), a symbolic case, it occurred "with the fraudulent use of powers conferred by martial law in Germany under the *Weimar* Constitution, forcing the Parliament to concede to the fascist leaders, on the basis of terms of doubtful legitimacy, plenary constituent powers by conferring an unlimited legislative power."[16] In the case of the 2007 reforms, the various acts adopted (the presidential initiative, the sanction by the National Assembly, the convening of referendum by the National Electoral Council) were all challenged through judicial review through actions of unconstitutionality and *amparo* and, in all cases, the Supreme Tribunal diligently declared all as inadmissible.[17]

Nonetheless, the fraud on the Constitution was initially evidenced in the proposals elaborated by the president's Council for Constitutional Reform that began to circulate in June 2007, despite the president's ordered "pact of confidentiality,"[18] thus demonstrating the intent of the highest government and state officials who sat on the council. The proposals were later given concrete form in the first draft constitutional reforms, which the president presented to the National Assembly on August 15, 2007,[19] proposing a radical transformation of the state to create a new juridical

---

[16] See the Constitutional Chamber of the Supreme Tribunal of Justice, Decision N° 74 (Jan. 25, 2006) in *Revista de Derecho Público* 105, Editorial Jurídica Venezolana, Caracas 2006, 76ff.

[17] On these decisions, see Allan R. Brewer-Carías, "El juez constitucional vs. la supremacía constitucional. O de cómo la jurisdicción constitucional en Venezuela renunció a controlar la constitucionalidad del procedimiento seguido para la 'reforma constitucional' sancionada por la Asamblea Nacional el 2 de noviembre de 2007, antes de que fuera rechazada por el pueblo en el referendo del 2 de diciembre de 2007," in *Revista de Derecho Público* 112 *(Estudios sobre la reforma constitucional)*, Editorial Jurídica Venezolana, Caracas 2007, 661-94.

[18] The document circulated in June 2007 under the title *Consejo Presidencial para la Reforma de la Constitución de la República Bolivariana de Venezuela, "Modificaciones propuestas."* The complete text was published as *Proyecto de reforma constitucional. Versión atribuida al Consejo Presidencial para la reforma de la Constitución de la República Bolivariana de Venezuela*, Editorial Atenea, Caracas 2007, 146.

[19] The full text was published as *Proyecto de Reforma Constitucional. Elaborado por el ciudadano Presidente de la República Bolivariana de Venezuela, Hugo Chávez Frías*, Editorial Atenea, Caracas 2007.

order.[20] Finally, the defrauding of the Constitution was consummated in November 2007 with the National Assembly's sanctioning of the reform.

First, the state was to be converted into a centralized state of concentrated power under the illusory guise of a popular power, implying definitive elimination of the federal form of the state, rendering political participation impossible, and degrading representative democracy. All of this was to be done by means of the organization of the population to participate in the Councils of the Popular Power (Consejos del Poder Popular), such as the communal councils. These institutions wholly lacked autonomy, and their members are not directly elected; they are controlled by the head of the national government; in their functioning, they were to be controlled by the United Socialist Party, an instrument the government created in 2007.

Second, in addition, the state was to be converted into a socialist state, with a political official doctrine of socialist character – Bolivarian doctrine – by means of which any thoughts different from the official one were rejected, as the official political doctrine was incorporated into the Constitution itself, which established a constitutional duty for all citizens to ensure its compliance. As a consequence, the basis for criminalizing all dissidence has been formally established.

Third, the economic system was to be converted into a state-owned, socialist, centralized economy by means of eliminating economic liberty and private initiative as constitutional rights, as well as the constitutional right to private property; conferring the means of production to the state, to be centrally managed; and configuring the state as an institution on which all economic activity depended and to whose bureaucracy the totality of the population is subject. All the reforms collided with the ideas of liberty and solidarity proclaimed in the 1999 Constitution and

---

[20]In this sense, the director of the National Electoral Council, Vicente Díaz, stated on July 16, 2007, "The presidential proposal to reform the constitutional text modifies fundamental provisions and for that reason it would be necessary to convene a National Assembly to approve them." This council member was consulted on this matter on Unión Radio, Aug. 16, 2007, at http://www.unionradio.com.ve/Noticias/No-ticia.aspx?noticiaid=212503. The initiation of the reform process in the National Assembly could have been challenged before the Constitutional Chamber of the Supreme Tribunal on the basis of unconstitutionality. Nonetheless, the president of the Constitutional Chamber – who was also a member of the Presidential Council for the Reform of the Constitution – made clear that "no legal action related to modifications of the constitutional text would be heard until such modifications had been approved by citizens in referendum," adding that "any action must be presented after a referendum, when the constitutional reform has become a norm, since we cannot interpret an attempted norm. Once a draft reform has become a norm we can enter into interpretations of it and hear nullification actions." See Juan Francisco Alonso, *El Universal*, Caracas Aug. 18, 2007.

established a state that substitutes for society itself and private economic initiative.

Fourth, the state was to be converted into a repressive (police) state, given the regressive character of the regulations established in the reform regarding human rights, particularly civil rights, and the expansion of the president's emergency powers, under which he was authorized to indefinitely suspend constitutional rights.

Fifth, and finally, the state was to be converted into a militarist state, on the basis of the role assigned to the Bolivarian Armed Force (*Fuerza Armada Bolivariana*), which was configured to function wholly under the president, and the creation of the new Bolivarian National Militia (*Milicia Nacional Bolivariana*).

All the reforms implied the radical transformation of the Venezuelan political system; sought to establish a centralized socialist, repressive, and militaristic state of popular power; and departed fundamentally from the concept of a civil social-democratic state under the rule of law and justice based on a mixed economy.

Moreover, under the sanctioned reforms, representative democracy at the local level and territorial political autonomy would have materially disappeared, substituted with a supposed participatory and protagonist democracy that would, in fact, be controlled by the president and that proscribed any form of political decentralization and territorial autonomy.

In this way, eight years after the sanctioning of the 1999 Constitution by a Constituent Assembly that was totally controlled by the president, in 2007, further constitutional reforms were proposed, this time through the National Assembly.

As aforementioned, according to Article 344 of the Constitution, the reform sanctioned by the National Assembly on November 2, 2007,[21] was submitted to referendum on December 2, 2007, and the popular vote, expressing the will of the original constituent power, rejected it.

According to the Constitution, the consequence of the will expressed by the people was that no new constitutional reforms on the same matters

---

[21] On the reform proposals, see Allan R. Brewer-Carías, *Hacia la consolidación de un estado socialista, centralizado, policial y militarista. Comentarios sobre el sentido y alcance de las propuestas de reforma constitucional 2007,* Colección Textos Legislativos N° 42, Editorial Jurídica Venezolana, Caracas 2007; *La reforma constitucional de 2007 (Comentarios al proyecto inconstitucionalmente sancionado por la Asamblea Nacional el 2 de noviembre de 2007),* Colección Textos Legislativos N° 43, Editorial Jurídica Venezolana, Caracas 2007. See also all the articles published in *Revista de Derecho Público* 112 *(Estudios sobre la reforma constitucional),* Editorial Jurídica Venezolana, Caracas 2007.

could be again proposed during the constitutional term (2006–2012). Even though the people rejected the 2007 reform, it is important to analyze its contents, which clearly show the shape of the authoritarian government in Venezuela over the past decade (1999–2010). For such purpose, I analyze the meaning and scope of the reform, as sanctioned by the National Assembly, comparing in each case the proposed changes with the corresponding provision of the 1999 Constitution.

II. Proposed Changes to the Fundamental Principles of the Political System

Throughout 2007, particularly in a speech at the presentation of the draft reforms before the National Assembly, the president said that the reforms' main objective was "the construction of a Bolivarian and socialist Venezuela" – that is, to sow "socialism in the political and economic realms." [22] This is something that the 1999 Constitution did not do, and in 1998 and 1999, when the President proposed and convened the National Constitutent Assembly, he did not propose it for the purpose of "projecting the road of socialism." He just offered the convening of a Constituent Assembly. In contrast, in 2006, as candidate for reelection, he said: "Let us go to Socialism" and, consequently, he deducted that "everyone who voted for candidate Chávez then, voted to go to socialism."[23]

Thus, the draft constitutional reforms presented, according to the president's speech aimed to construct "Bolivarian Socialism, Venezuelan Socialism, our Socialism, and our socialist model," having "the community" (*la comunidad*), a "basic and indivisible nucleus," and considering that "real democracy is only possible in socialism." However, the democracy referred to was not a democracy because it was a nonrepresentative one, that was "not born of suffrage or from any election,

---

[22]See *Discurso de orden pronunciado por el ciudadano Comandante Hugo Chávez Frías, Presidente Constitucional de la República Bolivariana de Venezuela en la conmemoración del ducentécimo segundo aniversario del juramento del Libertador Simón Bolívar en el Monte Sacro y el tercer aniversario del referendo aprobatorio de su mandato constitucional*, special session, Aug. 15, 2007, Asamblea Nacional, División de Servicio y Atención legislativa, Sección de Edición, Caracas 2007, 4, 33.

[23]Id., 4. That is, it sought to impose the wishes of only 46% of registered voters who voted to reelect the president on the remaining 56% of registered voters who did not vote for presidential reelection. According to official statistics from the National Electoral Council, of 15,784,777 registered voters, only 7,309,080 voted to reelect the president.

but rather is born from the condition of organized human groups as the base of the population."[24]

The president in that speech summarized the aims of his reform proposals explaining that on the political ground, the purpose was to "deepen popular Bolivarian democracy"; on the economic ground, to "create better conditions to sow and construct a socialist productive economic model," which he considered "our model." That is, "in the political field: socialist democracy; on the economic, the productive socialist model; in the field of public administration, incorporate new forms in order to lighten the load, to leave behind bureaucracy, corruption, and administrative inefficiency, which are heavy burdens of the past still upon us like weights, in the political, economic and social areas."[25]

All his proposals to construct socialism were linked by the president to Simón Bolívar's 1819 Constitution of Angostura, which he considered "perfectly applicable to a socialist project" in the sense of considering that it was possible to "take the original Bolivarian ideology as a basic element of a socialist project."[26] Of course, this assertion has no serious foundations: it is enough to read Bolívar's 1819 Angostura discourse on presenting the draft constitution to realize that it has nothing to do with a "socialist project" of any kind.[27]

The rejected constitutional reform, without doubt, would have altered the basic foundations of the state.[28] This is true particularly with respect to the proposals on the constitutional amplification of the Bolivarian doctrine; the substitution of the democratic, social state with the socialist state; the elimination of decentralization as a policy of the state designed

---

[24]See *Discurso de orden pronunciado por el ciudadano Comandante Hugo Chávez Frías,* op cit., 32, 34, 35.

[25]Id., 74.

[26]Id., 42. Only one month before the president's speech on the proposed constitutional reforms, the former minister of defense, General in Chief Raúl Baduel, who was in office until July 18, 2007, stated on leaving the Ministry of Popular Power for the Defense that the president's call to "construct socialism for the twenty-first century, implied a necessary, pressing and urgent need to formalize a model of Socialism that is theoretically its own, autochthonous, in accord with our historical, social, political and cultural context." He added, "Until this moment, this theoretical model does not exist and has not been formulated." It is hard to imagine that it could have been formulated just one month later.

[27]See Simón Bolívar, *Escritos fundamentales*, Caracas 1982. See also Pedro Grases ed., *El Libertador y la Constitución de Angostura de 1819,* Caracas 1969; José Rodríguez Iturbe, ed., *Actas del Congreso de Angostura,* Caracas 1969.

[28]See Eugenio Hernández Bretón, "Cuando no hay miedo (ante la Reforma Constitucional)," in *Revista de Derecho Público* 112 *(Estudios sobre la reforma constitucional),* Editorial Jurídica Venezolana, Caracas 2007, 17-20; Manuel Rachadell, "El personalismo político en el Siglo XXI," in id., 65-70.

to develop public political participation; the dismantling of the public administration; and the elimination of budgetary discipline and the unity of the treasury.

1. *Bolivarian Doctrine*

An innovation of the 1999 Constitution was the change in the name of the Republic of Venezuela to Bolivarian Republic of Venezuela (Article 1). This substituted the name the republic had had since 1811, with the sole exception of the period between 1821 and 1830, when that denomination disappeared because Venezuela itself had disappeared as an autonomous state, integrated into the Republic of Colombia, precisely on the proposal of Simón Bolívar. This latter political organization can then be considered the Bolivarian conception of the state: one in which Venezuela, as such, simply does not exist as a sovereign state.

That is why the name change, in principle, had nothing to do with Bolívar and his thought or with the construction of socialism – just as the president stated in his August 15 speech, in 1999, socialism had not been proposed. The name change had a partisan political motivation, as the name derived from the political group established by the president, which could not legally use the word *Bolívar* in its name. In this manner, it was the Bolivarian party that gave the republic its name[29] and the teaching of the "*ideario bolivariano*" (Bolivarian ideology) became obligatory in schools (Article 170).

But, in 2007, the president, with his proposed reforms, and the National Assembly, through its sanctioning of the 2007 reform, identified the Bolivarian doctrine with the socialist political and economic model of the state and, thus, with the republic itself. It is in this sense, then, that the word *bolivariano* must be understood. The proposed reform to Article 100 of the 1999 Constitution declared the Bolivarian Republic "the historical product of a confluence of various cultures." It was in the same sense of the complete identification between socialism and Bolivarianism that the 2007 constitutional reform identified the Armed Force as the Bolivarian Armed Forces (Articles 156.8, 236.6, 328, and 329) and the components of the armed forces as the Bolivarian National Army, the Bolivarian

---

[29]According to the Political Parties Law, *Gaceta Oficial* N° 27.725, Apr. 30, 1965, political parties cannot use the name of the founders of the country or homeland symbols. The political organization the president formed before campaigning for the 1998 election was Movimiento Bolivariano 200. That name could not be used to identify the political party he founded, which became Movimiento V República.

National Navy, the Bolivarian National Air Force, the Bolivarian National Guard, and the Bolivarian National Militia (Article 329).

Moreover, the proposed reform to Article 328 of the Constitution stated that the functioning of the Bolivarian Armed Forces was to be realized "by means of the study, planning and execution of Bolivarian military doctrine" – that is, according to socialist doctrine, that they be enabled to guarantee the independence and sovereignty of the nation, to preserve it from external or internal attack, and ensure the integrity of the national geography.

In addition, the proposed reform of Article 103 of the Constitution attempted to seal the relationship between Bolivarianism and socialism by stating that the priority investment of the state in education must be done "according to the humanistic principles of the Bolivarian socialism."

2. *The Substitution of the Social-Democratic State for a Socialist State*

Article 2 of the 1999 Constitution, following the tradition of contemporary constitutionalism, defines Venezuela as a "social democratic state under the rule of law and justice." This phrase (*estado democrático y social de derecho y de justicia*) was constructed precisely to design a nonsocialist state, just as it was adopted in postwar contemporary constitutions like the Constitution of the Federal Republic of Germany of 1949 (Article 20.1), the Spanish Constitution of 1978 (Article 1), and the Constitution of Colombia of 1991 (Article 1).

This corresponds to a conception of a liberal, nonsocialist state in a mixed economy, which follows the contemporary trends of the social state, one with obligations to resolve problems of social justice. This leads the state to intervene in economic and social activity, as a provider of benefits, assistance, and services (*estado prestacional*). This social character of the state derives principally from the fundamental values of equality and nondiscrimination (Articles 2 and 21) and from the declaration of social justice as a foundation of the economic system (Article 299). The democratic state is the concept on which the whole of the political organization of the nation rests, which derives from the Preamble of the 1999 Constitution (with the phrase "democratic society"), and is present in Articles 2, 3, 5, and 6, which identify the fundamental value of constitutionalism as democracy exercised through representatives (elective democracy) and through instruments of direct democracy. The rule-of-law state (*estado de derecho*) is the concept of a state under the rule of law, or legality, as provided in the Preamble to the 1999 Constitution. This implies that all acts of the state and the public administration must adhere to the principle of legality (Article 141) and are subject to independent judicial control (Articles 7, 137, 258, 334, and 336). The state is also defined, for this reason, as a state of justice, in which justice, beyond the mere affording of formal procedure, is guaranteed (Article 26).

Even though the 2007 reform makes no mention of Article 2 of the 1999 Constitution, it is evident that its sense is radically altered by the creation of a socialist state[30] in place of the traditional social-democratic state under the rule of law and justice. This is so because the model of a socialist state is absolutely incompatible with that of the social-democratic state, with the rule of law and justice. This confirms, again, the deception of reforming the Constitution to establish a socialist state without changing its Article 2 and justifying the claims that reforms have left untouched fundamental aspects of the state and, thus, the convening of the Constituent Assembly was unnecessary to approve them.[31] The 2007 reform was the result of one more fraud on the Constitution.

Many articles of the reform contain references to the socialist state. Article 16 of the Constitution creates "the communes and communities" (*comunas y comunidades*) as "the basic and indivisible spatial nuclei of the Venezuelan Socialist State." Article 70 added to the definition of the "means of political participation and protagonist of the people in the direct exercise of their sovereignty" the only objective to be directed "for the construction of socialism"; the same article added a stipulation to various forms of citizens' political associations, requiring that they be "constituted to develop the values of mutual cooperation and socialist solidarity." Article 112 established that the economic model created, achieve "the best conditions for the collective and cooperative construction of a Socialist Economy" and Article 113 stated the need to constitute "mixed corporations and/or socialist units of production."

In the rejected reform, Article 158 read: "the State must promote people's participation as a national policy, devolving its power and

---

[30]See Rogelio Pérez Perdomo, "La Constitución de papel y su reforma," in *Revista de Derecho Público* 112 *(Estudios sobre la reforma constitucional)*, Editorial Jurídica Venezolana, Caracas 2007, 14; G. Fernández, "Aspectos esenciales de la modificación constitucional propuesta por el Presidente de la República. La modificación constitucional como un fraude a la democracia," *Id*, 22; Alfredo Arismendi, "Utopía Constitucional," in id., 31; Manuel Rachadell, "El personalismo político en el Siglo XXI," in id., 66; Allan R. Brewer-Carías, "El sello socialista que se pretendía imponer al Estado," in id., 71-75; Alfredo Morles Hernández, "El nuevo modelo económico para el Socialismo del Siglo XXI," in id., 233-36.

[31]The president of the National Assembly stated this on Aug. 23, 2007, on approval of the draft reforms, as a whole, in the first debate. See *El Universal*, Caracas Aug. 24, 2007.

creating the best conditions for the construction of a Socialist democracy." Article 168 referred to socialist means of production; Articles 184 and 300 mentioned the socialist economy; Article 299 mentioned the socialist principles of the socioeconomic system; and Articles 318 and 320 referred to the socialist state and the socialist development of the nation.

3. *The Elimination of Decentralization as a State Policy*

Article 4 of the 1999 Constitution states, "The Bolivarian Republic of Venezuela is a federal decentralized state in the terms consecrated by this Constitution." The Constitution incorporated some elements of the Organic Law of Decentralization, Delimitation, and Transfer of Competencies of the Public Powers of 1989,[32] which promoted the transfer of certain competencies of the national public power to the state powers. As a policy of the state, decentralization was also reflected in various other norms in the 1999 Constitution. Article 6 defines the government as "decentralized," and Article 16 refers to "municipal autonomy and political administrative decentralization"; Article 84, to a decentralized national public health system; Articles 269 and 272, to decentralized administration of justice and the penitentiary system; Article 285, to decentralized electoral administration; and Article 300, to the functional decentralization of the economic administrative organization of the state.

In addition, Article 158 defined decentralization as a general national policy to be implemented to "deepen democracy, to bring power closer to the population, creating the best conditions for the exercise of democracy and for the effective and efficient meeting of state commitments" with respect to all public activities.

Following the political practice of recent years, the 2007 reform, contrary to the 1999 Constitution, definitively centralized the state and eliminated any vestige of decentralization in public policy and organization in territorial autonomy and representative democracy at the local level, or the primary political units of the land. Without a doubt, this changed a fundamental characteristic of the state, which could not be achieved through constitutional reform.

---

[32]Ley Orgánica de Descentralización, Delimitación y Transferencia de Competencias del Poder Público de 1989, *Gaceta Oficial* N° 4.153, Dec. 28, 1989. This law was reformed in 2003, *Gaceta Oficial* N° 37.753, Aug. 14, 2003; and again in 2009, *Gaceta Oficial,* N° 39.140, Mar. 17, 2009.

The 2007 reform eliminated all vestiges of political decentralization beginning with the fundamental principle of territorial decentralization and autonomy established in Article 16 of the Constitution.[33] Autonomy and decentralization are basic elements of participatory democracy, and Article 16 of the 1999 Constitution requires the territorial political division of the republic to guarantee "municipal autonomy and public administrative decentralization." The reform, however, sought to create a new territorial division that guaranteed only "participation of the popular power," with no reference to political autonomy or decentralization.

The 2007 reform also tended to derogate Article 158 of the Constitution, which defined the national policy of decentralization to "deepen democracy"; establishing in its place only that "the State shall promote, as a national policy, the protagonist participation of the people, transferring power to them, and creating the best conditions for the construction of a Social Democracy." This fundamental change, as the president stated on August 15, constituted "the development of what we understand by decentralization, because the Fourth Republic concept of decentralization is very different from the concept we must work with. For this reason, we have here stated 'the protagonist participation of the people, transferring power to them, and creating the best conditions for the construction of social democracy.'"[34]

In addition, *decentralization* was to be eliminated, with the proposed reform of Articles 272 (decentralization of prisons), 295 (decentralized electoral administration), and 300 (decentralized public enterprises).

4. *Fragmentation of Public Administration*

One of the most important innovations in the 1999 Constitution is that it incorporated a normative framework of fundamental principles specifically designed to regulate and rationalize the public administration of the state. First, Article 141 provided that the public administration was to operate at the service of citizens; second, it was to be based on principles of honesty, public participation, speediness, effectiveness, efficiency, transparency, accountability, and responsibility in the exercise

---

[33] See Manuel Rachadell, "El personalismo político en el Siglo XXI," in *Revista de Derecho Público* 112 *(Estudios sobre la reforma constitucional)*, Editorial Jurídica Venezolana, Caracas 2007, 67; Ana Elvira Araujo, "Proyecto de reforma constitucional (agosto a noviembre 2007). Principios fundamentales y descentralización política," in id., 77-81; José Luis Villegas, "Impacto de la reforma constitucional sobre las entidades locales," in id., 119-23.

[34] See *Discurso de orden pronunciado por el ciudadano Comandante Hugo Chávez Frías*, op. cit., 50.

of public functions; and third, it was to fully operate under the law, thus implicating the constitutional formulation of the principle of legality.

The 2007 reform eliminated the requirement that the public administrative apparatus, as a single universe, exist at the service of citizens and replaced it with another – the public administration exists solely at the service of the state – which terminated the right of citizens to have the administration operate in their service. In this sense, it was further proposed to establish in Article 141 that "the public administrations are organizational structures destined to serve as instruments of the public powers, for the exercise of their functions and for the provision of services."

The new language proposed for Article 141 would have signified the fragmentation of public administration and departure from a universal regulation of one apparatus to a regulation of various public administrations.[35] These, contrary to any proper legislative technique, were classified in a way that was more suited to an academic "paper" than to a constitution. In the text of the proposed reform, public administrations were classified into two categories: "the bureaucratic or traditional public administrations," which were those that attend to structures established and regulated under the 1999 Constitution and the laws, and the "missions" (*misiones*), which were "organizations of a variety of natures, created to meet the most deeply felt and urgent needs of the population." Their provision of services would require the use of exceptional systems, including experimental systems, which were to be "established by the Executive Power by means of organizational and functional regulations."

Thus, the 2007 reform – instead of seeking to correct the almost decade-old administrative disaster produced by a lack of budgetary and administrative discipline from the creation of funds assigned to missions that existed outside of the general organization of the state – would constitutionalize administrative disorder by characterizing the administrative structures of the state as "bureaucratic or traditional." It would not convert the institutions into the proper instruments for meeting the most deeply felt, urgent needs of the population. Moreover, all this left

---

[35]See José Antonio Muco Borjas, "El trastocamiento de la Administración Pública en la reforma Constitucional de 2007," in *Revista de Derecho Público* 112 *(Estudios sobre la reforma constitucional)*, Editorial Jurídica Venezolana, Caracas 2007, 163-67; José Araujo Juárez, "Consideraciones sobre el cambio institucional de la Administración Pública en la reforma constitucional," in id., 169-73; José Ignacio Hernández, "La administración paralela como instrumento del Poder Público," in id., 175-78; Ninoska Rodríguez Laverde, "Las Administraciones Públicas: potestad sancionadora y ámbitos competenciales en el proyecto de reforma constitucional," in id., 183-89.

the public administration subject to the sole volition of the president, to be exercised by means of regulations.

5. *The Abandonment of Budgetary Discipline and the Unity of the Treasury*

Even though the 2007 reform did not contain express changes to Articles 313 and 314 of the Constitution – the principal articles establishing the general principle of budgetary discipline – it sought to eliminate the fundamental principle of state economic and financial administration through changes to Article 321.[36]

In effect, under Articles 313 and 314, the economic and financial administration of the entire national public administration must be governed by a budget approved annually through legislation of the National Assembly, which provides an estimate of public revenues and authorized public spending. Thus, Article 314 declares that "there shall be no form of spending that has not been provided for in the annual Budget law," the only exceptions being those provided by additional budget credits for unforeseen expenses and underfunded items, which also require approval of the National Assembly. That system is designed to guarantee that ordinary revenues are sufficient to cover ordinary expenses and that "the income generated from the exploitation of the wealth derived from the subsoil and minerals, in general, will tend to be used to finance real productive investments, education and health" (Article 311).

The rejected 2007 reform of Article 321 was intended to bring the whole system of budgetary discipline into complete chaos, through constitutional provisions. In that sense, it eliminated the constitutional provision requiring the creation of "a fund for macroeconomic stabilization destined to guarantee the expenses of the State at the municipal, regional and national levels, in the event of fluctuations in ordinary revenues" and declared that such funds must function under "basic principles of efficiency, equity, and nondiscrimination between the public entities that bring resources to it." Instead, it established that "at the end of each year, the Chief of State shall establish, in coordination with the Central Bank of Venezuela, the level of reserves needed for the national economy, as well as the amount of surplus reserves. The surplus reserves shall be destined to funds established by the National Executive for productive investments,

---

[36]See Enrique Sánchez Falcón, "La propuesta de modificación constitucional y el régimen de la Administración Financiera Pública," in *Revista de Derecho Público* 112 *(Estudios sobre la reforma constitucional)*, Editorial Jurídica Venezolana, Caracas 2007, 191-93.

development and infrastructure, financing of the Missions, and, definitively, to the integral, endogenous, humanist and socialist development of the nation." By means of the reform, the president was charged with administering international reserves (Article 318).

In this way, the definitive rupture of the unity of the treasury was to be constitutionalized, establishing a financial mechanism parallel to the budget of funds created solely by the national executive destined for the missions. As has been said, the missions are also under the charge of the national executive and exist as public administrative organizations parallel to the "bureaucratic and traditional Public Administration."

III. PROPOSED CHANGES IN THE POLITICAL SYSTEM: FROM REPRESENTATIVE DEMOCRACY TO PARTICIPATORY DEMOCRACY

1. *The Elimination of Representative Democracy at the Local Level*

Article 5 of the 1999 Constitution establishes that "sovereignty resides untransferrable in the people, who exercise it directly in the manner provided in this Constitution and the Law, and indirectly, by means of suffrage through the organs that exercise the Public Power." This norm followed Venezuela's republican tradition that began with the Constitution of 1811[37] by providing for the exercise of popular sovereignty through political representation (indirect democracy) and the direct exercise of democracy as complementary. The 1999 Constitution also establishes mechanisms for popular participation in Article 62, which consecrates the right of all citizens to "freely participate in public affairs, directly or through their representatives," as well as through the "means of participation" set forth in Article 70.

For democracy to exist as such, it must be representative, although it may contain mechanisms of direct democracy. For this reason, the 1999 Constitution requires that representative democracy always have its source in elections that are popular, universal, direct, and secret (Article 70) and that such elections are to select the titular heads of almost all organs of the different branches of government, established in the Constitution according to the principles of the separation and distribution of powers

---

[37] On the presence of this principle in all of Venezuela's constitutions, see Allan R. Brewer-Carías, *Las constituciones de Venezuela,* Academia de Ciencias Políticas y Sociales, Caracas 2008, 1:109-322.

(Article 136). In the 2007 reform, the right to vote was extended to all citizens over the age of sixteen years (Article 64).

This form of representative democracy is, of course, not contradictory to participative democracy, and both are different from mechanisms of direct democracy such as referenda (consultative, approbatory, abrogating, and recall) (Articles 71–74) that serve to perfect democracy and from the various forms of political participation regulated in the Constitution. The latter include popular consultations, legislative, constitutional and constituent initiatives, *cabildos abiertos* (open town hall meetings), and citizens' assemblies (Article 70).

In any case, participatory democracy cannot substitute for representative democracy, especially if participation is conducted from above. For democracy to be participatory, in addition to being essentially representative, it must allow citizens the possibility of participating in public affairs, which is possible only when they have access to power. This is possible only when power is near to citizens, which necessarily implies the presence of a well-established, well-developed autonomous local government in every locality and urban or rural settlement. This means that political participation can be founded only on political decentralization, through the creation of autonomous political entities that permit local self-government. It is possible to participate politically only when, through decentralized government, local authorities are established by means of elections through suffrage at the smallest territorial level. As a whole, this implies the spreading of public power throughout the territory of the state.

This is, of course, contrary to the concentration of power and centralization that the rejected reform of 2007 attempted to consolidate. The reform, as stated, attempted to eliminate from the Constitution all references to political decentralization and to definitively substitute representative democracy at the local level with a supposed participatory democracy. This would have finished off democracy itself as a political regime, substituting it with an authoritarian one that centralizes and concentrates power and impedes political participation because of the nonexistence of autonomous local entities.

This was to be achieved through proposals to eliminate all vestiges of local territorial autonomy and political decentralization, thereby precluding the possibility of participatory democracy. As mentioned, democratic participation requires the existence of autonomous territorial political entities; without them, the central power can develop simple and controlled mobilization of the population. But popular mobilization cannot be confounded with the democratic participation, as in that of the communal councils.[38] Members of the communal councils are not elected by means of direct suffrage (Article 136) but are appointed by citizens' assemblies under the control of the national executive power. The proposal to reform Article 16 of the Constitution sought to constitutionally consolidate this system through its reference to new territorial divisions that would guarantee "the participation of the popular power."

According to the rejected 2007 reform of Article 16 of the 1999 Constitution, a new "popular power" (*poder popular*) – a proposed new level of state power (in addition to the national, state, and municipal levels) – was to be created from the bottom up. This was to begin with communities (*comunidades*), each of which "shall constitute a basic and indivisible spatial nucleus of the Venezuelan Socialist State, where ordinary citizens will have the power to construct their own geography and their own history." The communities were to be grouped into communes (*comunas*) that were "geographic areas or extensions" and "geo-human cells of the territory."[39] The communes, in turn, were to be grouped into cities (*ciudades*), "the primary political unit in the organization of the national territory." The latter were to be understood as "all of the popular settlements within the municipality" (*municipio*). In this manner, from the community and the commune, "the Popular Power shall develop forms of political-territorial communal aggregation that are to be regulated by Law and shall constitute forms of Self-government and any other expression of direct democracy."

The rejected reform of Article 136 of the Constitution was precise in its reference to the popular power. It provided that the popular power "is expressed through the constitution of communities, communes, and the self-government of the cities, by means of the communal councils, workers' councils, peasant councils, student councils, and other entities

---

[38] *Ley de los Consejos Comunales, Gaceta Oficial* N° 5806, Extra., Apr. 4, 2006. See Giancarlo Henríquez Maionica, "Los Consejos Comunales (una breve aproximación a su realidad y a su proyección ante la propuesta presidencial de reforma constitucional)," in *Revista de Derecho Público* 112 *(Estudios sobre la reforma constitucional)*, Editorial Jurídica Venezolana, Caracas 2007, 89-99; Allan R. Brewer-Carías, "El inicio de la desmunicipalización en Venezuela: La organización del poder popular para eliminar la descentralización, la democracia representativa y la participación a nivel local," in *AIDA, Opera Prima de Derecho Administrativo. Revista de la Asociación Internacional de Derecho Administrativo*, Universidad Nacional Autónoma de México, Asociación Internacional de Derecho Administrativo, Mexico City 2007, 49-67. The 2006 law was replaced by *Ley Orgánica de los Consejos Comunales, Gaceta Oficial* N° 39.335, Dec. 28, 2009. See the comments on this Law in Allan R. Brewer-Carías, *Ley de los Consejos Comunales*, Editorial Jurídica Venezolana, Caracas 2010.

[39] The communes have been created in the statute on the Federal Council of Government. See *Ley Orgánica del Consejo Federal de Gobierno, Gaceta Oficial* N° 5.963 Extra. of Feb. 22, 2010). In June 2010, the National Assembly began the discusión of the Law on the Communes.

established by law." However, although "the people" (*el pueblo*) were designated as the "depositary of sovereignty," to be "exercised directly through the popular power," it was stated that the popular power "does not arise from suffrage or from any election, but arises from the condition of the organized human groups that form the base of the population."

What was sought, then, in that reform was to put an end to representative democracy at the local level, and with that, to put an end to any vestige of political territorial autonomy, which is necessary to public political participation. For such purpose, the reforms were proposed as creating participatory democracy, substituting representation with the supposed direct democracy of participation in citizens' assemblies, communities, communes, and cities that were not autonomous political territorial entities but rather controlled from the central power.

2. *Elimination of Republican Alternation in Office by Establishing the Possibility of Indefinite Reelection of the President*

According to Article 4 of the 1999 Constitution, the republic's government and all the political entities that constitute it are required to be democratic and alternating (*democrático* and *alternativo*). On the basis of this principle, the Constitution established term limits governing reelection of all officers.

With respect to the president, Article 230 of the Constitution, in a radical departure from the previous constitutional tradition forbidding immediate presidential election, allowed the immediate reelection of the president, but for only one more term. Regarding members (*diputados*) of the National Assembly, Article 192 provides that they may be reelected for no more than "two consecutive terms." Article 160 provides that state governors "may be immediately reelected for a new term, but only once," and Article 162 provides that members of the states' legislative councils may be reelected for only "two consecutive terms." Finally, Article 174 provides that mayors "may be immediately reelected for a new term, but only once."

Regarding these matters, the 2007 constitutional reform of Article 230 not only would have increased the length of the presidential term from six to seven years but also was designed to establish the possibility of the president being reelected. This would have signified the inclusion in the Constitution of the principle of indefinite reelection of the president, thus contradicting the democratic principle of alternation in office and perpetuating the president's power.[40]

Nonetheless, and despite that the reforms were rejected, in the following year, the National Assembly approved a constitutional amendment with the same purpose and extended the reelection principle to all elected officials, thereby defrauding the Constitution.[41]

3. *The Contradictory Restrictions on Citizens' Right to Political Participation*

Regarding the principle of political participation, the 1999 Constitution directly establishes regulations ensuring the participation of civil society in public affairs. This was the case with the mechanism created to ensure civil-society participation in the appointment of nonelected state officials (judiciary, citizens' power, and electoral power), with political participation by means of referenda, and with citizens' political participation in matters of constitutional review.

A. The Elimination of the Civil Society's Participation in Nominating State Officials

The rejected 2007 reform proposed to eliminate civil society's direct participation in public affairs (established in the 1999 Constitution as an institutional novelty) in nominating the magistrates of the Supreme Tribunal, members of the National Electoral Council, the people's defender, the comptroller general, and the prosecutor general. The nomination is to be made before the National Assembly by various nomination committees, required to comprise only "representatives of the various sectors of society" (Articles 264, 279, and 295).

The provisions of the 1999 Constitution were distorted through political praxis and subsequent legislation by the Constituent Assembly (1999), followed by the National Assembly (2000). This transformed the nominating committees into amplified parliamentary commissions (2002–

---

[40]See Carlos Ayala Corao, "Reforma constitucional 2007. El presidencialismo y la reelección," in *Revista de Derecho Público* 112 *(Estudios sobre la reforma constitucional)*, Editorial Jurídica Venezolana, Caracas 2007, 137-43; Carlos Luis Carrillo, "La desnaturalización del sistema presidencial en Venezuela. Del presidencialismo exacerbado consagrado en la Constitución de 1999 al ultrapresidencialismo pretendido en la reforma constitucional de 2007," in id., 145-49.

[41]See *Gaceta Oficial* N° 5.908 Extra. of Feb. 19, 2009.

4), thus limiting civil society's right to political participation.[42] This trend was intended to be constitutionalized in the 2007 reform, which sought to establish that the nominating committees, instead of comprising representatives from various sectors of civil society, comprise almost entirely state officials.

With respect to Article 270 on the Judicial Nominating Committee, the proposed reform established a parliamentary commission that was similar to that regulated in the 2004 Organic Law of the Supreme Tribunal of Justice.[43] The reform provided that the National Assembly would convene the Judicial Nominating Committee, to comprise "members of the Assembly, representatives of the Popular Power and representatives related to juridical activities," adding that the "Popular Power Councils, social sectors and organizations related to juridical activities can nominate candidates."

With respect to the Electoral Nominating Committee for the National Electoral Council, the rejected 2007 reform to Article 295 also established a parliamentary commission similar to that regulated in the 2002 Organic Law of the Electoral Power. The reform provided that the National Assembly would convene the committee, to comprise "members of the Assembly, and of representatives of the Popular Power, of social organizations and of sectors." Thus, it would be composed basically of representatives of state organs, thereby abandoning the principle of exclusive participation of civil society. The provision in the 1999 Constitution that provides that law faculties around the country are to propose candidates was to be eliminated by reform, whereby popular power representatives and representatives from the educational and social sectors would nominate candidates.

Finally, regarding the citizens' power nominating committee to appoint the people's defender, the comptroller general, and the prosecutor general, the rejected proposed reform to Article 279 also established that the National Assembly would convene a committee "of members of the Assembly, and of representatives of the different sectors of the Popular Power," and it eliminated any reference to civil society.

---

[42] See Allan R. Brewer-Carías, "La participación ciudadana en la designación de los titulares de los órganos no electos de los poderes públicos en Venezuela y sus vicisitudes políticas," in *Revista Iberoamericana de Derecho Público y Administrativo* 5, San José, Costa Rica, 2005, 76-95.

[43] See Allan R. Brewer-Carías, *Ley Orgánica del Tribunal Supremo de Justicia*, Editorial Jurídica Venezolana, Caracas 2006, 32ff.

B. Limits to Political Participation by Means of Referenda and Restrictions on Direct Democracy

Articles 5 and 62 of the 1999 Constitution establish that the right to political participation can be exercised indirectly by the election of representatives and directly through the means regulated in the Constitution. Political participation is exercised directly through those means provided for in Article 70 and by means of referenda, enumerated in Articles 71–74 as consultative, recall, approbatory, and abrogating referenda.

The important aspect of these provisions is the establishment of the popular initiative to convene the referendum, attributing to 10% of registered voters the right to call for convening consultative referenda (Article 71); to 20%, the right to call for convening recall referenda (Article 72); to 15%, the right to call for convening approbatory referenda of certain international treaties (Article 73); to 10%, the right to call for convening referenda to abrogate statutes (Article 74); and to 5%, the right to call for convening referenda to abrogate executive decree laws (Article 74).

The rejected reform sought to limit the political right to participate by increasing the percentage of registered voters required to file such popular initiatives as follows: 20% for consultative referenda (Article 71), 30% for recall referenda (Article 72), 30% for approbatory referenda (Article 73), 30% for convening approbatory referenda on certain international treaties (Article 73), 30% for referenda to abrogate statutes (Article 74), and 30% for referenda to abrogate executive decree laws (Article 74).[44]

The 2007 reform regarding Article 72 sought to change the system to make it less participatory and more difficult to initiate recall elections. The reform established, first, that instead of not less than 20% of registered voters directly convening a recall referendum, a petition was to be filed before the National Electoral Council to activate a proceeding through which no fewer than 30% of registered voters could petition for a recall referendum. Second, instead of fixing electoral participation in recall votes to at least 25% of registered voters, the reform would require participation of 40% of registered voters. Third, to achieve a recall, in addition to requiring that the number of votes for the recall be equal to or greater than

---

[44]See Alberto Blanco Uribe Quintero, "Menoscabo al derecho humano a la participación, por la reforma constitucional," in *Revista de Derecho Público* 112 *(Estudios sobre la reforma constitucional)*, Editorial Jurídica Venezolana, Caracas 2007, 191-202.

the number of votes through which the official in question was originally elected (as is provided in the 1999 Constitution), the reform would add the new requirement that the final vote in favor of a recall must be greater than the total number of votes against it, even though the number of votes for the recall would be greater than the number of votes that elected the official to begin with. Thus, the recall referendum was to be converted into a ratification referendum, which had already occurred de facto in 2004.[45]

C. Limits on the Right to Political Participation in Constitutional Review Procedures

The 1999 Constitution provides for three means or procedures for constitutional review according to the importance of the reforms to be implemented: amendment, constitutional reform, and constituent assembly.

Amendments can apply only in matters of adding or modifying one or various articles, without altering the fundamental structure of the Constitution (Article 340). The amendment process initiates with a popular initiative of at least 15% of registered voters. The 2007 reform sought to augment the requirement to 20% of registered voters (Article 341.1), making the process more difficult to initiate. In addition, the reform proposed that the National Assembly, distorting the character of the popular initiative, was to approve amendments.

Amendments must be approved by referendum in which at least 25% of registered voters participate. The rejected 2007 reform sought to raise that percentage to 30% of registered voters.[46]

The constitutional reform procedure, according to Article 342 of the 1999 Constitution, is intended to partially review the Constitution and to substitute one or various articles but without modifying the structure and fundamental principles of the constitutional text. The initiative for the constitutional reform procedure is popular initiative of at least 15% of

---

[45]See Allan R. Brewer-Carías, "La Sala Constitucional vs. el derecho ciudadano a la revocatoria de mandatos populares: De cómo un referendo revocatorio fue inconstitucionalmente convertido en un 'referendo ratificatorio,'" in *Crónica sobre la "in"justicia constitucional. La Sala Constitucional y el autoritarismo en Venezuela*, Colección Instituto de Derecho Público, Universidad Central de Venezuela–Editorial Jurídica Venezolana, Caracas 2007, 349-78.

[46]See Alberto Blanco Uribe Quintero, "Menoscabo al derecho humano a la participación, por la reforma constitucional," in *Revista de Derecho Público* 112, *(Estudios sobre la reforma constitucional*, Editorial Jurídica Venezolana, Caracas 2007, 191-202.

registered voters. The rejected reform sought to augment the requirement to 25% of registered voters (Article 342).

Finally, constituent assembly, under Article 347 of the 1999 Constitution, can occur to "transform the state, create a new legal order and write a new Constitution." The initiative for the convening of a constituent assembly is popular initiative of at least 15% of registered voters. The rejected 2007 reform sought to augment the requirement to 30% of registered voters (Article 342), making it much more difficult to initiate.

4. *Reducing the Right to Political Participation to Implementing Socialist Ideology*

Article 62 of the 1999 Constitution declares it to be a political right of citizens "to freely participate in public affairs, directly or through their elected representatives," and it refers to "the people's participation in the conception, execution and control of public management [as a] necessary means to be protagonist in order to guarantee complete individual and collective development." For this purpose, the article establishes the "obligation of the state and duty of society to provide for the generation of more favorable conditions for its practice."

Article 62 is complemented by Article 70 of the 1999 Constitution, which provides for the following means for people's participation and the exercise of popular sovereignty: From the political point of view, the election of public officials, referenda, popular hearings, mandate recalls, legislative and constitutional review initiatives, open town hall meetings, and citizens' assemblies whose decisions are of an obligatory nature. From the social and economic point of view, citizens' attention, self-management, cooperatives in all their forms, including those of a financial character, savings institutions, community enterprises, and other associative means guided by mutual cooperation and solidarity.

The end result of the rejected 2007 reform was that it restricted political participation. On the one hand, the enumeration of means of participation in Article 70 was expanded to include "the councils of popular power, the communal councils, the workers' councils, the students' councils, the peasants councils, the artisans' councils, the fishermen's councils, the sporting councils, the youth councils, the senior citizens' councils, the women's councils, and the disabled people's councils." On the other hand, all of them restricted citizens' right to freely participate in public affairs because the means of political participation were reduced to one purpose: "the construction of socialism." Consequently, those who do not want to construct socialism would be excluded from the right to political participation, which was reserved for developing "socialist solidarity" and was not free, as is provided in Article 62 of the Constitution.

5. *Political Parties, Political Association, and Public Financing of Electoral Activities*

In a marked reaction against political parties, the 1999 Constitution omitted express reference to "political parties," and instead it established a set of provisions regulating "associations for political purpose," guaranteeing citizens "the right to associate for political ends by means of democratic methods, organization, functioning and leadership" (Article 67).

A traditional problem associated with political parties is the financing of their activities through public funds, established in the former Organic Law of Suffrage and Political Participation of 1998,[47] which led to inequitable concentrations of funds in hands of official (governmental) parties. The drafters of the 1999 Constitution reacted to this problem in Article 67 by inconveniently prohibiting public financing of all "associations for political purposes." This was considered a regression in the context of contemporary democratic trends regarding public (state) financing of political activity because it could open the door to irregular and illegitimate public financing of political parties supporting the government.

The 2007 rejected reform sought to modify the prohibition on state funding of political parties, instead proposing that "the state may finance electoral activities" without indicating whether that referred to political parties in general or also to self-nominated candidates. The proposal provided for the enactment of a law to establish "means for the financing, for the use of public space, and for access to social communications media in elections campaigns." In any event, if an official state ideology were to be established, the financing of electoral activities other than those tending to consolidate socialism would have been considered contrary to the Constitution. Nonetheless, this reform was carried out in an illegitimate way through constitutional interpretation by the Constitutional Chamber of the Supreme Tribunal in 2008.[48]

---

[47]Ley Orgánica del Sufragio y Participación Política, *Gaceta Oficial* N° 5.233, Extra., May 28, 1998.

[48]See the comments in Allan R. Brewer-Carías, "El juez constitucional como constituyente: El caso del financiamiento de las campañas electorales de los partidos políticos en

The 2007 rejected reform attempted to eliminate from Article 67 the general prohibition directed to "the directors of associations with political ends" to "contract with public sector entities." In a system in which the proposal was to consolidate the United Socialist Party, such elimination could have completely intertwined the party and the state. The reform proposal also established in Article 67 a general prohibition against "the financing of associations with political ends or of persons participating in electoral processes by any foreign public or private entity."

Venezuela," in *Revista de Derecho Público* 117, Editorial Jurídica Venezolana, Caracas 2009, 195ff.

Chapter 11

THE FAILED ATTEMPT TO CONSOLIDATE A CENTRALIZED STATE IN THE CONSTITUTION

In addition to consolidating an authoritarian and nondemocratic state in the Constitution, the rejected 2007 constitutional reform sanctioned by the National Assembly, also sought to consolidate a centralized state in the Constitution in complete substitution of the federation.

I. PROPOSED CHANGES IN THE STATE FORM: FROM CENTRALIZED FEDERATION TO CENTRALIZED STATE

From the time the Republic of Venezuela was established in 1811, and from when it was subsequently reconstituted in 1830, the Venezuelan state, in formal terms, has always been that of a federation – a state whose public powers are distributed between autonomous political-territorial entities on three levels: national (republic), state (individual states), and municipal (municipalities). The respective autonomies of each level have been constitutionally guaranteed.

Despite its vicissitudes and a tendency toward centralization, the Venezuelan federation has implied a vertical distribution of the public powers. Although it is not expressly eliminated in formal terms, the 2007 reform was to result in the disappearance of the federation. This was to perpetuate fraud on the Constitution.

1. *The Destruction of the Federation*

A. Taking Away Territoriality from the Federation

Although the 2007 reform did not expressly propose eliminating the federal form, its content was designed to eliminate the federation.[1] With respect to the states and municipalities (Article 16 of the Constitution of 1999), on which the concept of federalism is built, the 2007 reform sought to eliminate the constitutional guarantee of municipal autonomy and political-administrative decentralization, thus laying the groundwork to remove any jurisdictional competencies and power from those territorial entities. The reforms also proposed stripping municipalities of their traditional constitutional characterization as primary political units of the republic (Article 168). They proposed instead that "the primary political unit of the national territory shall be the city, by which is understood all of the populated settlements within the municipality, which are composed of geographic areas or extensions called communes."

According to the proposed reform to Article 15 of the Constitution, the communes forming the popular power (a new vertical level of government) were conceived to be the basic human cells of the territory "composed of communities, each of which shall constitute an indivisible spatial nucleus of the Venezuelan Socialist State, in which the citizens shall have the power to construct their own geography and their own history." It concluded: "from the community and the commune, the popular power shall develop forms of political-territorial communal aggregation that are to be regulated by law, and which shall constitute forms of self-government and any other expression of direct democracy."

The reform of Article 16 added that "the communal city [*ciudad comunal*] shall be constituted when, within the totality of its perimeter, the organized communities, the communes, and communal self-government have been established," and once approved by popular referendum to be convened by the president.

Furthermore, the proposed reform to Article 136, which addressed the popular power, sets forth that

---

[1] See Manuel Rachadell, "El personalismo político en el Siglo XXI," in *Revista de Derecho Público* 112 *(Estudios sobre la reforma constitucional)*, Editorial Jurídica Venezolana, Caracas 2007, 67; Ana Elvira Araujo, "Proyecto de reforma constitucional (agosto a noviembre 2007). Principios fundamentales y descentralización política," in id., 77-81; José Luis Villegas, "Impacto de la reforma constitucional sobre las entidades locales," in id., 119-23.

the popular power is expressed through the constitution of communities, communes, and the self-government of the cities, by means of the communal councils, workers' councils, peasant councils, student councils, and other entities established by law....[The popular power] does not arise from suffrage or from any election, but arises from the condition of the organized human groups that form the base of the population.

This definitively sought to eliminate representative democracy and local political autonomy and to eliminate political decentralization as a condition of political participation. What the reform sought to achieve was to cease democratic election of local public powers, contrary to the constitutional principle of representative democracy.

B. A Territorial Division of the Republic Tied to the Central Power

The territorial scheme proposed in the 2007 reform had the purpose of dismembering the federation – that is, to eliminate any sort of organization of the territory into political entities enjoying political territorial autonomy with elective governments as it is provided in Article 6 of the Constitution.

Instead of the political organization of the republic based on division of the national territory into states, the capital district, and municipalities with democratically elected governments, as laid out in the Constitution of 1999, the 2007 rejected reform of Article 16 provided for the establishment of a new division of the national territory, according to a "new geometry of power,"[2] composed "by a federal district in which the capital of the republic shall have its seat, by the states, by the maritime regions, by the federal territories, by the federal municipalities and by the island districts."

Rather than organizing the national territory in municipalities, as set forth in the 1999 Constitution, the 2007 reform stated that "the states are organized in municipalities" (Article 16), which would have disappeared when the new entities engulfed their territories. Thus, in the reform, the municipality was to disappear as the primary political unit.

The proposed reforms to Article 16 sought to authorize the president to decide with the intervention of the National Assembly, the creation of "maritime regions [*regiones marítimas*], federal territories [*territorios*

---

[2]See Gustavo Tarre Briceño, "La nueva geometría del poder," in *Revista de Derecho Público* 112 *(Estudios sobre la reforma constitucional)*, Editorial Jurídica Venezolana, Caracas 2007, 115-18.

federales], federal municipalities [*municipios federales*], insular districts [*distritos insulares*], federal provinces [*provincias federales*], federal cities [*ciudades federales*], and functional districts [*distritos funcionales*], and any other entity established by law." Under the reform, therefore, the territorial political division of the republic would have ceased to have constitutional rank, as it always has been, or even to be regulated by legislation; it would become solely the subject of executive regulation. It would be difficult to centralize power more than that.

All the territorial entities, according to the proposed reforms, were not conceived of as political entities with autonomy. They were to be subject to the central national power, which would designate their respective authorities.

C. The Capital City: No Political Autonomy or Democratic Government

An important reform introduced in the 1999 Constitution was to definitively ensure decentralized, democratic local government in Caracas, the capital and federal city, guaranteeing municipal autonomy and political participation of the diverse entities in the urban area. To that end, a two-tiered metropolitan government structure was created to ensure a general (metropolitan) government for the city as well as the existence of a democratically elected local government with political autonomy. The 1999 Constitution thus eliminated the federal district, which was a vestige of the traditional nineteenth-century federation, in which the capital city had no self-government.

On the contrary, the rejected 2007 constitutional reform sought to return to the nineteenth-century model in which local government in the capital city was absent, a model that all federations of the world have abandoned. For such purpose, the proposed reform of Article 18 of the Constitution sought to eliminate the capital district and its municipal organization, substituting for it a revived federal district with no constitutional guarantee of municipal or territorial autonomy and no guarantee of a "democratic and participative character of government," as is established in the 1999 Constitution. The intent was to pass the city to control by the national power, so that in the capital of the republic (and the seat of the national power), only national government organs, not local ones, could act.

This reform, nonetheless, and despite its popular rejection, was carried out unconstitutionally in 2009, by means of the Law on the Government Regime of the capital District and the metropolitan Area of Caracas.[3] In it, violating Article 18 of the Constitution, Caracas as the capital of the republic and the seat of the organs of the national branches of government was regulated as a "political territorial unit," wholly dependent on the central power, without any local political autonomy whatsoever. The proposed norm added that "the National Power, through the Executive Power, and with the collaboration and participation of all of the entities of the national, state and municipal public powers, in addition to those of the popular power, its communities, communes, and communal councils and other social organizations, shall provide for all that is necessary for urban reorganization, the restructuring of roadways, environmental recuperation, optimal results in public and personal security, the comprehensive strengthening of neighborhoods, urban development, the provision of systems for health, education, sports, culture and entertainment, the total restoration of the historic city center and historical sites, the construction of a system of small and midsized satellite cities along the territorial axes." That is, the reform sought to nationalize and centralize the entire government in Caracas.

In addition, Article 18 included a provision regarding the establishment of a national system of cities and declared the right to a city (*derecho a la ciudad*) to be understood as "the equitable benefit that each of the inhabitants receives, in conformity with the strategic role that the city formulates regrading both the urban regional context and the national system of cities."

2. *Abandoning Vertical Distribution of the Public Powers*

In the history of Venezuela's constitutions, the federation has always materialized through a vertical system of distribution of the public powers among the municipal, state, an national levels of government, as it is stated in Article 136 of the 1999 Constitution.

The rejected 2007 reform of Article 136 proposed a radical change to this traditional distribution of powers adding to it a new territorial level, that of the popular power, which was to express itself through the already

---

[3]See *Gaceta Oficial* N° 39.156 of Apr. 13, 2009. See the comments on this Law in Allan R. Brewer-Carías et al., *Leyes sobre el Distrito Capital y el Área metropolitana de Caracas*, Editorial Jurídica Venezolana, Caracas 2009.

mentioned councils of popular power.[4] It was supposed that through the councils, people, as the depository of sovereignty, would exercise that sovereignty directly, with the particularity that the communal councils were not representatives. On the contrary, it was expressly provided in the reform proposal that the popular power arises not "from suffrage or from any election, but arises from the condition of the organized human groups that form the base of the population."

In addition, popular power was incorporated in the rejected constitutional reform as to the composition of the nominating committees to appoint various offices of the government.

3. *Nationalizing Federated States' Competencies*

Article 136 of the 1999 Constitution, in organizing the federal state, distributes and assigns various competencies among three levels of government – national, state, and municipal – which are to be exercised autonomously and according to vertical distribution of power. Nonetheless, in political practice, the tendency has been to centralize almost all competencies in the national power, which has left very few competencies to the states and municipalities.

In this same tendency, the 2007 rejected reform sought to materially centralize all competencies of the public powers at the national level by assigning new competencies to the national powers, centralizing the states' competencies under the 1999 Constitution, and obligating states and municipalities to transfer their competencies to communal councils. The reforms would have left the states as voided entelechies.

The reject reform sought to attribute to the national level of government various competencies to organize the state. The first sought to confer competency to the central national government in order to regulate and administer the territory, and in particular to establish the regime "of the territorial regime of the federal district, of the states, of the municipalities, of the federal dependencies and of other regional entities" (Article 156.10). The second sought to confer competency to the national power with respect to "the creation, regulation and administration of federal provinces, federal and communal territories, and federal and communal cities" (Article 156.11). Under the reforms, states and municipalities

---

[4]See Gustavo Linares Benzo, "Sólo un Poder Público más. El Poder Popular en la reforma del 2007," in *Revista de Derecho Público* 112 *(Estudios sobre la reforma constitucional)*, Editorial Jurídica Venezolana, Caracas 2007, 102-105; Arturo Peraza, "Reforma, Democracia participativa y Poder Popular," in id., 107-13.

would have become totally dependent on the national-level government, as organs without autonomy of any kind, peripheral administrations of the central power, subject to the regulation and administration of the national power.

The reform also proposed attributing to the national power competency for administrative legislation (Article 156.32), which was to imply the total centralization of all legislation governing public administration, whether national, state, or municipal.

The reform also sought to reassign several competencies that the 1999 Constitution attributed to states and municipalities to the national power. In particular, proposed changes to Article 156.27 sought to nationalize, or attribute to the national power, the competency that Article 164.10 assigned to states regarding the "conservation, administration, and use of national roads and highways." Approval would also have implied modifications to Sections 9 and 10 of Article 164 of the Constitution, which assigns states the competency for the "conservation, administration, and use of national roads and highways, and of ports and airports of commercial use, in coordination with the national executive." Nonetheless, and despite the popular rejection of these reforms proposal, they were illegitimately carried out in 2008 through a judicial constitutional interpretation of the provision of the Constitution issued by the Constitutional Chamber of the Supreme Tribunal of Justice.[5]

Finally, in the area of shared national and municipal competencies, Article 156.14 of the 1999 Constitution assigns to the national power the creation and organization of land taxes on rural lands and real property transactions, whereas their "collection and control corresponds to the municipalities, in accord with this Constitution." The 2007 reform proposed to eliminate all references to the municipal role and added "collection of land taxes on rural lands" to the competencies of the national power.

Following this centralizing orientation, the 2007 reform proposed to eliminate the competency of the states in the exploitation of nonmetallic minerals, salt deposits, and oyster beds (Article 164.5), which was to be transferred to the national level and could only be delegated to states (Article 157.17).

---

[5]See the comments in Allan R. Brewer-Carías, "La Sala Constitucional como poder constituyente: La modificación de la forma federal del estado y del sistema constitucional de división territorial del poder público," in *Revista de Derecho Público* 114, Editorial Jurídica Venezolana, Caracas 2008, 247-62.

In a definitive coup de grace, the rejected 2007 reform proposed to eliminate the residual competency of the states, something inherent in every federation and established in Article 164.11 of the Constitution of 1999, regarding "all those that do not correspond to the national or municipal competency, according to this Constitution." The rejected reform sought to substitute the provision with one that established the rule inversely and attributed residual competency to the national power. This change was proposed in the reform to Article 156 that states that the competency of the national public power embraces all other subject matters "that by their kind or nature correspond to it, or that are not expressly attributed to state or municipal competencies."

4. *Obligating States and Municipalities to Transfer Their Competencies to the Organs of the Popular Power*

In Article 184, the 1999 Constitution establishes that the law must create open and flexible mechanisms through which states and municipalities can decentralize and transfer the rendering of their respective public services to communities and organized neighborhood organizations, once those have demonstrated the ability to provide those services. The article intends to promote the provision of services in the areas of health, education, housing, sports, culture, social programs, the environment, the maintenance of industrial areas, the maintenance and conservation of urban areas, neighborhood prevention and protection, works in construction, and other public services. The policy intends to promote the participation of communities and citizens through neighborhood associations and nongovernmental organizations; to have state and municipal authorities formulate investment proposals; and to participate in the implementation, evaluation, and monitoring of public works, social programs, and public services provided in their jurisdictions. In addition, the policy is intended to promote the creation of new subjects of decentralization at the submunicipal level of the *parroquias* ("parishes"), communities, neighborhoods, and localities. This needs to be done to guarantee the principle of coresponsibility (*corresponsabilidad*) in public business in local and state government and to develop self-management and comanagement in the administration and control of state and municipal services.

The rejected 2007 constitutional reform, seeking to redefine the federal decentralized democratic state and to convert it into a communal, centralized, nondemocratic state, proposed to establish that the "decentralization and transferring" required by the Constitution was to be done in "the organized communities, the communal councils, the communes, and other entities of the popular power" (Article 184). This implied "the assumption of the activity of municipal and/or state public enterprises by the communal organizations" (Article 184.2) and "the transference of the administration and control of state and municipal public services to the Communal organizations, on the basis of the principle of coresponsibility in public business" (Article 184.7).

The rejected 2007 reform defined the structure of "the organized community" (*la comunidad organizada*), which "shall have as its maximum authority the assembly of citizens [*asamblea de ciudadanos*] of the popular power, which, in that capacity, was to designate and revoke the organs of the communal power [*poder comunal*] in the communities, communes, and other political-territorial entities constituting the city, as the primary political unit of the territory." It also stated that "the communal council constitutes the executive organ for the decisions of the citizen's assemblies, formulating and composing the diverse communal organizations and social groups." The proposed reform to Article 184 also added that the communal council "shall assume the role of the justice of the peace and the provision of neighborhood prevention and protection services," which traditionally were competencies of municipalities. Finally, it was proposed that "a fund for the financing of the projects of the communal councils shall be created through legislation." This institutional framework must, of course, be adequately linked to what the rejected reform proposed with respect to Article 136 of the Constitution relative to the popular power and elimination of any vestige of representative democracy.[6]

5. Eliminating the Constitutional Guarantee of Municipal Autonomy

Under Article 168 of the 1999 Constitution, municipalities constitute the primary political unit (*unidad política primaria*) of national organization. They have juridical personality and enjoy autonomy. This status includes the election of their authorities; the management and administration of matters within their competencies; the creation, collection, and investment of revenues; and the constitutional protection that provides that municipal acts "may not be challenged except before the competent courts, according with the Constitution and the laws." Thus, municipal acts are not subject

---

[6]See Arturo Peraza, "Reforma, Democracia participativa y Poder Popular," in *Revista de Derecho Público* 112 *(Estudios sobre la reforma constitucional)*, Editorial Jurídica Venezolana, Caracas 2007, 113.

to any form of review – other than judicial – by the organs of the national level of government or of the states.

The rejected 2007 reform attempted to eliminate this final element of the legal and institutional autonomy of municipalities. The reform would have left open the possibility of establishing by law that the acts of municipalities be challenged and reviewed by organs of the executive powers of the states or of the national power, and would eliminate the guarantee that municipal acts can be reviewed only by judicial authorities.[7]

II. PROPOSED CHANGES IN THE ORGANIZATION OF THE NATIONAL LEVEL OF GOVERNMENT

1. *Proposed Reforms Regarding the International Activities of the Republic*

The rejected 2007 constitutional reform sought to substantially modify Articles 152 and 153 of the Constitution, which define the basis for the international activities of the republic, as well as the participation of Venezuela in regional Latin American economic-integration processes.

The proposed reform to Article 152 redefined the guidelines for international activity of the state adding to all those established in the 1999 Constitution, that the external policy must be oriented "in an active way toward the configuration of a multipolar world, free from the hegemony of any center of imperial, colonial, and neocolonial power."

The reform proposed completely eliminating the republic's participation in Latin American economic integration processes.[8] Instead, it established few principles of foreign affairs: "The republic must promote the integration, the confederation and the union of Latin America and the Caribbean in order to configure a political, economic and social great regional block." The provision added that "to attain that objective, the state will privilege the structure of new models of integration and union on our continent, allowing the creation of geopolitical spaces, within which

---

[7]See José Luis Villegas Moreno, "Impacto de la Reforma Constitucional sobre las entidades locales," in *Revista de Derecho Público* 112, *(Estudios sobre la reforma constitucional)*, Editorial Jurídica Venezolana, Caracas 2007, 119-23.

[8]See Jorge Luis Suárez, "La reforma del artículo 153 de la Constitución de 1999: un severo retroceso luego de un gran avance," in id., 125-30; Maria Auxiliadora Andrade, "la integración económica latinoamericana en la Constitución de 1999 y en la reforma Constitucional de 2007," in id., 131-35.

peoples and governments of our America could construct a single great national [*gran nacional*] project, which Simón Bolívar called 'A Nation of Republics.'" Thus, the reform would have allowed Venezuela "to subscribe to international treaties and covenants based on the most ample political, social, economic, cultural, great national, productive, complementarily, solidarity and just trade cooperation."[9]

2. *Proposed Reforms to the Executive Power and Reinforcing the Presidential System*

With the rejected 2007 reform, the presidential system was sought to be reinforced, particularly through the extension of the president's term of office, the possibility of indefinite reelection of the president, the establishment in addition to the existent position of executive vice president, of new position of vice presidents, and the expansion of presidential powers and attributions.

A. The Extension of the President's Term and Unlimited Reelection

The 2007 reform, in addition to ensuring the possibility of the president's indefinite reelection, sought to extend the presidential term from six to seven years (Article 230).[10] Never has there been such a lengthy presidential term in the whole of the country's constitutional history. Never in the whole of Venezuela's political history has a president exercised the executive power continuously for as many years as the current president has governed the country. Nonetheless, after the popular rejection of the 2007 constitutional reform, the president managed to

---

[9]See for instance, regarding the tight international relations that have been established with Cuba, Fernando Olivares Méndez (Interview), "Agustín Blanco Muñoz/ Fidel es el presidente de Venecuba" (July 5, 2010), available at http://www.enfoques365.net/N6902-agustn-blanco-muoz---fidel-es-el-presidente-de-venecuba.html. See also the discussion organized the same Agustín Blanco Muñoz, in the Cátedra Pío Tamayo, Central University of Venezuela, on the subject "¡Aqui manda Fidel! Venezueba, ¿un proyecto montado por y para la traición a la patria?," May 2010. Available at http://www.vlinea.com/index.php?option=com_content&view=article&id=9182:iaqui-manda-fidel-venecuba-iun-proyecto-montado-por-y-para-la-traicion-a-la-patria&catid=1:nacionales&Itemid=64; and http://www.gentiuno.com/articulo.asp?articulo=8934. In contrast, on July 22, 2010, the president broke off all diplomatic relations with Colombia, after the Colombian ambassador before the Organization of American States presented at a meeting of the organization evidence of Colombian rebel camps and bases inside Venezuela, asking for independent observers to visit the country. See "Chávez Cuts Ties with Colombia," *The New York Times*, July 23, 2010, A7.

[10]See Carlos Ayala Corao, "Reforma constitucional 2007: El presidencialismo y la reelección," in id., 137-43; Carlos Luis Carrillo Artles, "La desnaturalización del sistema presidencial en Venezuela. Del presidencialismo exacerbado consagrado en la Constitución de 1999 al ultrapresidencialismo pretendido en la reforma constitucional de 2007," in *id.*, 145-49.

succeed in his objective of establishing the possibility for his continuous and indefinite reelection, by means of the constitutional amendment approved in February 2009.[11]

B. The New Executive Organs: Vice Presidents

An innovation of the 1999 Constitution was the creation of the office of the executive vice president (*vicepresidente ejecutivo*), as a nonelected officer freely named and removed by the president, thus rendering the office completely subject to the political will of the president (Article 225).

The rejected 2007 reform of Article 225 sought to increase the number of vice presidents by changing the title from executive vice president to first vice president (*primer vicepresidente*) and by enabling the president to designate the number of vice presidents he "deems necessary." The new vice presidents also would have exercised the executive power and, as was publicly announced, would have been assigned to determined territories, sectors, or subject matters, in particular to conduct what the president and the reform proposal called the "new geometry of power."[12] Consequently, these public officials would have reinforced the direct action of the president in the territory or determined subject areas, independently of the vertical distribution of the public powers that could exist.

C. Extending the Powers of the President

Article 236 of the Constitution of 1999 enumerates the competencies of the president, which the 2007 constitutional reform sought to expand and amplify[13] as follows.

First, in addition to the power to direct the government, as is provided in Article 236.2, the reform sought to give him the power to direct the state and to coordinate relations between the other national public powers while acting in his capacity as head of state. This reform sought to assign to the

---

[11] See *Gaceta Oficial* N° 5,908 of Feb. 19, 2009. See the comments in Allan R. Brewer-Carías, "El juez constitucional vs. la alternabilidad republicana," in *Revista de Derecho Público* 117, Caracas 2009, 205ff.

[12] See Gustavo Tarre Briceño, "La nueva geometría del poder," in *Revista de Derecho Público* 112 *(Estudios sobre la reforma constitucional)*, Editorial Jurídica Venezolana, Caracas 2007, 115-18.

[13] See Margarita Escudero León, "La concentración de poderes en el Presidente de la república de acuerdo con la propuesta de reforma constitucional sancionada por la Asamblea Nacional el 2 de noviembre de 2007," in id., 151-55; Aurilivi Linares Martínez, "La ampliación de los poderes presidenciales en la práctica y en el proyecto de reforma constitucional de 2007," in *id.*, 157-61.

president the power to direct the actions of the state, which implied that the president was to direct not only the actions of the national executive power but also those of all organs of the national power (including the other branches of government) and of all the state and municipal powers. This implies complete centralization of the state.

Second, a new power was proposed to be conferred to the president in Article 236.3 regarding not only matters of territorial organization and land use planning but also the "regime of the federal district, the states, the municipalities, the federal dependencies and other regional entities." With these powers, all vestiges of autonomy and territorial division would have disappeared, granted exclusively to the executive.

Third, the reform of Article 236.4 sought to assign the president the power to create "the federal provinces, federal territories, federal cities, functional districts, federal municipalities, maritime regions and insular districts, as provided in the Constitution, and to designate their authorities as established by law." This implied the creation of territorial entities that would have been totally dependent on the national executive and would be superimposed upon states and municipalities.

Fourth, Article 236.19 sought to attribute to the president the competence to "formulate a national plan for development and direct its execution," eliminating the requirement of the assembly's approval of the plan (Article 236.18).[14] This change would have eliminated all participation in the planning process of the popular representation (in the National Assembly).

Fifth, the reforms of Articles 236.5 and 236.6 sought to reinforce the role of the president in "command[ing] the Bolivarian Armed Forces as commander in chief, exercising supreme hierarchical authority in all of its corps, components and units, determining its contingent," Article 236.7 added the power to "promote officials in all [of the armed force's] ranks and hierarchies and designate their corresponding positions." Under the reforms, the whole of the Bolivarian Armed Forces would have become directly subject to the will of the president and, of course, his political project.

Sixth, the proposed reform to Article 236.9 sought to empower the president to "decree the suspension and restriction of constitutional guaranties" when declaring state of exception, in contrast to the 1999 Constitution, which authorizes the president only to "restrict" guarantees,

---

[14]See Juan M. Raffalli A., "El Consejo de Estado y el Plan nacional de Desarrollo," in id., 182.

not to suspend them. This attribution was also ratified in the proposed reform to Article 337, which expanded the president's powers in cases of states of exception (Articles 338 and 339).[15]

Finally, in addition to the classical attribution to the president to "administer the national treasury," the constitutional reform also proposed assigning the president the power to administer "the international reserves, as well as to establish and regulate the monetary policy, in coordination with the central bank."

The proposed reforms also attributed entirely new and broad competencies to the president. First, the reform to Article 11 of the Constitution established a new competency for the president to create by "decree special military regions in order to guarantee the sovereignty, the security and the defense in any part of the territory and geographic spaces of the republic," as well as to create by "decree special authorities in the event of contingencies, disasters, or any other requiring immediate and strategic intervention of the state."

Second, the reform to Article 16 sought to assign the president the power to create, by decree, communal cities within organized communities, communes, and communal self-governments. The reforms also sought to confer to the president the competency to "create by decree maritime regions, federal territories, federal municipalities, insular districts, federal provinces, federal cities and functional districts, as well as any other entity established in the Constitution or in statute."

Third, the reforms to Article 16 also assigned to the national government (directed by the president) the power to develop and activate a district mission with the corresponding functional-strategic plan to create a functional district.

Fourth, the reform to Article 16 also assigned the national executive power competency to designate and dismiss authorities of the maritime regions, federal territories, federal district, federal municipalities, insular districts, federal provinces, federal cities, and functional districts, as well as any other entity established in the Constitution or by statute.

Fifth, the reform to Article 13 sought to attribute competency to the executive power – with the collaboration and participation of all entities of the national, state, and municipal public powers, as well as of the popular power, its communities, communes, councils, and other social organizations – to provide for "all that is necessary for urban

---

[15] See Jesús María Casal, "Los estados de excepción en la reforma constitucional," in id., 325-29.

reorganization; the restructuring of roadways; environmental recuperation; the achievement of optimal results in public and personal security; the comprehensive strengthening of neighborhoods; urban development; the provision of systems for health, education, sports, culture and entertainment; the total restoration of the historic city center; and, the construction of a system of small and midsized satellite cities along its territorial axes of expansion." Under the provisions, the legislative power would have been left materially void of competency in all of these areas.

Sixth, the reform of Article 141 sought to confer competencies to the executive power to establish missions as "public administrations" by means of organizational and functional regulations. Missions were understood to be "organizations of varied of natures, created to meet the most deeply felt and urgent needs of the population, requiring the use of exceptional systems, including experimental systems." The consequence of this reform was that organization and regulation concerning all the public administration would have been the exclusive competency of the national executive, beyond the reach of the legislature. These rejected constitutional reforms, nonetheless, were illegitimately carried out through a decree law on the Organic Law on Public Administration in 2008.[16]

Seventh, the reform to Article 318 proposed conferring competency to the president or executive power to establish "monetary policies and exercise the monetary competencies of the national power" in coordination with the Central Bank of Venezuela. This power was conferred so that the president or the executive power could jointly, with the Central Bank of Venezuela, "achieve stability in prices and preserve the internal and external value of the currency," and share with the Central Bank of Venezuela the functions "of participating in the formulation and execution of monetary policy, the design and execution of exchange policy, the regulation of money and credit, and the fixing of interest rates." As administrator of the National Public Treasury (Hacienda Pública Nacional), competency was proposed to be passed to the president to administer and direct the republic's international reserves, which are to be managed by the Central Bank of Venezuela. Nonetheless, and despite the popular rejection of the 2007 constitutional reform, many of these reforms

---

[16]See *Gaceta Oficial* N° 5,890 of July 31, 2008. See the comments in Allan R. Brewer-Carías, "El sentido de la reforma de la Ley Orgánica de la Administración Pública," in *Revista de Derecho Público* 115, *(Estudios sobre los Decretos Leyes),* Caracas 2008, 155-62.

have been implemented by means of successive reforms of the Law on the Central Bank of Venezuela.[17]

Last, the reform to Article 321 assigned competency to the chief of state, within the framework of his administration of international reserves, to establish, in coordination with the Central Bank of Venezuela, at the end of each year, the level of reserves necessary for the national economy, as well as the amount of surplus reserves, which were to be directed to funds "established by the national executive for productive investments, development and infrastructure, financing of the missions, and, definitively, to the integral, endogenous, humanist and socialist development of the nation." That is, under the proposed reforms, all competencies in the area of monetary and fiscal policy would have been in the hands of the president.

3. *Proposed Reforms Regarding the Legislative Power and Political Permeability*

The 1999 Constitution, following the principle of separation of powers, to ensure separation between the executive and the legislative powers, established that members of the National Assembly could not be appointed to executive positions without losing their legislative tenure (Article 191). This means that once appointed to an executive post, a former member of the legislative body cannot return to the assembly.

The proposed reform diluted this separation by seeking to establish that members of the National Assembly could accept executive positions without losing legislative tenure. It was proposed that, when named to a position by the president, they could return to the assembly once finished with the executive appointment, to finish the period of the legislative tenure for which they were elected (Article 191). This provision, of course, is inconceivable in presidential systems of government. It is normal in parliamentary systems, where parliament is in charge of forming the government with its members.

4. *Proposed Reforms Regarding the Appointing and Dismissing of the Head Officers of the Nonelected Branches of Government*

As aforementioned, one of the important reforms introduced in the 1999 Constitution in order to ensure the independence and autonomy of the

---

[17]See *Gaceta Oficial* 39.300, Nov. 5, 2009. In Mar. 2010, a new reform of the Central Bank of Venezuela Law was sanctioned by the Nacional Assembly.

different branches of government was to establish limits on the National Assembly powers to appoint the head officers of the nonelected branches of government – that is, the magistrates of the Supreme Tribunal of Justice, the prosecutor general, the comptroller general, the peoples' defender and the members of the National Electoral Council. For such purpose, the Constitution created different nominating committees integrated by representatives of the different sectors of society, in charge of selecting and proposing the candidates before the National Assembly.

The 2007 constitutional reform sought to change the composition of the committees, transforming it into a parliamentary commission of members of the National Assembly, other public officials (e.g., the representative of the popular power), and representatives of social organizations (Article 279).

In addition, regarding the appointment of the officials, the reform sought to eliminate the guarantee of the qualified majority of members of the National Assembly for such appointments (Article 279), seeking to establish a simple majority for that purpose as well.

In the same sense as the proposed changes to nominations of members of the National Electoral Council, the proposed reforms aimed to change the requirement that the Electoral Nominating Committee comprise representatives from various sectors of society (Article 292). The reform provided that the National Assembly, to make appointments, must itself convene a nominating committee composed of members of the assembly, representatives of the popular power, and representatives of other social organizations (Article 295). That is, the nominating committee was to be composed of a majority of public officials. The reform also sought to eliminate the requirement that candidates be nominated by civil society and law faculties of the country; instead, it is established that such nominations are to be made by the councils of popular power and other educational and social sectors (Article 296). The proposed reforms follow the trend established in the 2002 Organic Law of the Electoral Power, which unconstitutionally converted the nominating committee into a parliamentary commission.

The reform was also to eliminate the provision of the 1999 Constitution imposing the need for a majority of two-thirds of assembly members to appoint members of the National Electoral Council (Article 296); instead, it established that a simple majority vote was sufficient (Article 295). The reform also established that a majority of votes of members of the National Assembly was sufficient to dismiss members of the electoral power (Article 296).

III. Proposed Changes in the Armed Forces: From a Civil Managed State to a Militarist State

Another area of innovation in the 1999 Constitution was the regime of the National Armed Forces, established under the regime of security and defense. The changes in 1999 reinforced militarism.

The 2007 reforms proposed radical changes in the military institution. The proposed reforms for Articles 328 and 329 sought to transform the military from a professional, apolitical institution that does not deliberate and that operates at the service of the republic into a militia that operates at the service of the chief of state and at the service of his political party.

In effect, the rejected 2007 reform regarding Article 328 sought, first, to eliminate the constitutional clause that states that the armed forces "is an institution that is essentially professional, without political affiliation." In its place, it was proposed that the Constitution state that the armed forces is "a corps that is essentially patriotic, popular, and anti-imperialist." Under the reform, the military as a professional institution would have disappeared, as would the prohibition on the military's political partisanship. The definition of the institution as "patriotic, popular, and anti-imperialist" would have opened an avenue to integrate the armed forces into the political party of the commander in chief, who would, under the proposed reforms for Article 236.6, exercise supreme hierarchical authority in each of its corps, components, and units. Unfortunately, this was implemented in an unconstitutional way by means of the Organic Law of the Bolivarian Armed Forces.[18]

Second, although Article 328 sets forth the objectives of the armed forces "to guarantee the independence and sovereignty of the nation, and assure the integrity of its geographic space," the reform proposed to add "to reserve [the nation] from any internal or external attack."

Third, instead of stating that the objectives of the armed forces are to be achieved "through military defense, through cooperation in the maintenance of internal order, and through active participation in national development," the reform established that the objectives be obtained "by means of study, planning and execution of Bolivarian military doctrine, by means of the application of principles of comprehensive military defense and the popular war of resistance [*guerra popular de resistencia*], by means of permanent participation in the tasks of maintaining citizen security and the conservation of internal order, and in the same sense, by

---

[18]See *Gaceta Oficial* N° 5.891 of July 31, 2008.

means of actively participating in the plans for the economic, social, scientific and technical development of the nation." In this way, the Bolivarian military doctrine would be incorporated into the Constitution as an essential element of the armed forces, even though the exact content of the doctrine remains unknown. Guerrilla elements were proposed to be incorporated as "popular war of resistance," and the armed forces was to be converted into a national police organization, charged with citizen security and conservation of internal order. In addition, providing that the armed force is to, among other functions, "actively participate in the plans for the economic, social, scientific and technical development of the nation," the reform sought to constitutionalize the militarization of the state and the public administration.

Fourth, instead of providing, as the Constitution of 1999 does, that in fulfilling its function the armed forces operates "exclusively at the service of the nation, and not of any person or political partiality," the 2007 reform proposed that the armed forces, "in the fulfillment of its function, shall always be at the service of the Venezuelan people in defense of their sacred interests, and in no case shall be at the service of any oligarchy or foreign imperial power." The consequence of this change would have been to eliminate the constitutional prohibition on the armed forces from operating in the service of any person or political preference. This proposal, again, sought to open a path to the integration of the armed forces into the political party of the commander in chief, who could place the armed forces at his service or at the service of the government's party.

It should be remembered, also, that the reform for Article 236.7 sought to attribute to the president, acting in his or her capacity as commander in chief, the power to "promote officials in all [of the armed forces'] ranks and hierarchies and to assign them to their corresponding positions." This power would have constituted an instrument for securing a political hold on such officials.

Fifth, where Article 328 asserts that the fundamental pillars of the armed forces are the Constitution and the laws, discipline, obedience, and subordination, the reform proposed adding: "its historic pillars stand in the mandate of Bolívar: 'Liberate the homeland, take up the sword in defense of the social guarantees and be deserving of the people's blessings.'"

Article 329 of the Constitution of 1999 states that "the army, the navy and the air force have, as an essential responsibility, the duty to plan, execute and oversee those military operations that are required to assure the defense of the nation." The national guard is to "cooperate in the development of those operations and shall have as a basic responsibility, the duty to carry out operations necessary for maintaining the internal order of the country." The provision adds that "the armed forces may exercise those administrative police and criminal investigative activities that are assigned by law."

The reform proposed to change Article 329. It proposed increasing the number of military components of the Bolivarian Armed Forces to five, including land, air, and sea corps, and to administratively organize these into the Bolivarian National Army, the Bolivarian National Navy, the Bolivarian National Air Force, the Bolivarian National Guard, and the Bolivarian National Militia. The reform also established that the Bolivarian Armed Forces "could accomplish police activities attributed by law."

All the reforms sought to reinforce the political character of the armed forces and the militarism of the state that began with the Constitution of 1999. The provision asserting the "apolitical and nondeliberating character" of the armed forces established in Article 132 of the 1961 Constitution had already disappeared from the 1999 constitutional text, as had the essential obligation of the armed forces to ensure "the stability of the democratic institutions and respect of the Constitution and the laws, whose obedience is always above any other obligation," in the same article. The traditional prohibition against the simultaneous exercise of military and civil authority contained in Article 131 of the Constitution of 1961, and the control held by the former Senate over military promotions in the upper levels under Article 331 of the Constitution of 1961, had already disappeared in the Constitution of 1999.

Notwithstanding the popular rejection of all these reforms in 2007, they were all implemented fraudulently and illegitimately by means of a decree law enacted by the president in 2008 to reform the Organic Law of the Bolivarian Armed Forces,[19] in which the National Bolivarian Militia was created without any constitutional support.[20] This National Bolivarian Militia, directly dependent on the president, is composed of a Military Reserve and a Territorial Militia, the latter integrated not only by Venezuelan citizens but also by non-Venezuelans, resulting in a new military component structured in parallel to the army.

---

[19] See Jesús María Alvarado Andrade, "La nueva Fuerza Armada Bolivariana (comentarios a raíz del Decreto N° 6.239, con rango, valor y fuerza de Ley Orgánica de la Fuerza Armada Nacional Bolivariana)," in *Revista de Derecho Público* 115, *(Estudios sobre los Decretos Leyes 2008)*, Editorial Jurídica Venezolana, Caracas 2008, 205ff.

[20] See *Gaceta Oficial* N° 5.891 Extra. of July 31, 2008.

Chapter 12

THE FAILED ATTEMPT TO CONSOLIDATE A SOCIALIST CENTRALIZED ECONOMIC SYSTEM IN THE CONSTITUTION

In addition to the aforementioned reform proposals sanctioned by the National Assembly in 2007 regarding the organization of the State, the rejected 2007 constitutional reform also sought to transform the socio-political foundations of the state's order of mixed economy, establishing instead a Socialist system.

According to the trends in constitutionalism developed since the middle of the past century, the economic constitution of Venezuela has been established on the model of the mixed economy, which is based on the principle of liberty as opposed to the directed economy – this is similar to the economic models of all Western nations.[1] This economic system, then, is founded on economic liberty, private initiative, and free competition, without excluding the participation of the state as a promoter of economic development, regulator of economic activity, and planner together with the civil society.

Following this orientation, the 1999 Constitution establishes a mixed economic system, a social market economy. This is an economic system that is based on economic liberty but must be developed according to principles of social justice – therefore, it requires the intervention of the state.[2] This socioeconomic regime, in accord with Article 299 of the

---

[1] See Allan R. Brewer-Carías, "Reflexiones sobre la Constitución económica," in *Estudios sobre la Constitución Española. Homenaje al Profesor Eduardo García de Enterría*, Editorial Civitas, Madrid 1991, 5:3.839-3.853.

[2] On the economic constitution in the 1999 Constitution see Allan R. Brewer-Carías, *La Constitución de 1999. Derecho Constitucional Venezolano*, Editorial Jurídica Venezolana, Caracas 2004, 1:818-82.

Constitution, rests on the following principles: social justice, democratization, efficiency, free competition, environmental protection, productivity, and solidarity. These aim to ensure comprehensive human development, existence with dignity, and the maximum benefit for the collective. For these purposes, Article 299 expressly sets forth that the state must, "jointly with private initiative," promote "the harmonious development of the national economy for the purpose of generating sources of employment and a high national level of added value to elevate the standard of living of the population and strengthen the nation's economic sovereignty, thus guaranteeing legal certainty, solidity, dynamism, sustainability, permanence, and economic growth with equity, to guarantee a just distribution of wealth by means of strategic democratic, participative, and open planning."

As the Constitutional Chamber of the Supreme Tribunal of Justice stated in Decision No. 117 (February 6, 2001),[3] this is "a socioeconomic system that is intermediate between a free market (in which the State acts as a simple programmer [*programador*] for an economy that is dependent upon the supply and demand of goods and services) and an interventionist economy (in which the State actively intervenes as the 'primary entrepreneur')." The Constitution promotes "joint economic activity between the State and private initiative in the pursuit of, and in order to concretely realize the supreme values consecrated in the Constitution," and to pursue "the equilibrium of all the forces of the market, and, joint activity between the State and private initiative." In accord with that system, the Tribunal ruled, the Constitution "advocates a series of superior normative values with respect to the economic regime, consecrating free enterprise within the framework of a market economy and, fundamentally, within the framework of the Social State under the Rule of Law (the Welfare State, the State of Well-being or the Social Democratic State). This is a social State that is opposed to authoritarianism."[4]

The practical application of this constitutional model brought about the development of an economy based on economic freedom and private initiative but subject to important and necessary intervention by the state

---

[3]See *Revista de Derecho Público* 85–88, Editorial Jurídica Venezolana, Caracas 2001, 212-18.

[4]The values alluded to, according to the doctrine of the Constitutional Chamber, "are developed through the concept of free enterprise" (*libertad de empresa*), which encompasses both the notion of a subjective right "to dedicate oneself to the economic activity of one's choice" and a principle of economic regulation according to which the will of the business (*voluntad de la empresa*) to make its own decisions is manifest. The state fulfills its role of intervention in this context. Intervention can be direct (through businesses) or indirect (as an entity regulating the market)." Id.

to ensure the constitutionally required orientation of social justice. State intervention has increased because the state owns title, within the public domain, to the petroleum-rich subsoil, as it always has in Venezuela's legal history.

In 2007, the rejected constitutional reform proposed to radically alter this model in order to accentuate the existing disequilibrium between the public and private sectors and to transform the system into a state economy based on central planning within a socialist state and socialist economy.[5]

I. PROPOSED CHANGES ON MATTERS OF ECONOMIC FREEDOM AND PRIVATE PROPERTY

1. *Eliminating Economic Freedom as a Constitutionally Protected Right*

As a fundamental principle of the constitutional system, Article 112 of the 1999 Constitution establishes the right of every person to freely dedicate him- or herself to the economic activity of choice, without limitations beyond those established in the Constitution and the laws based on reasons related to human development, security, public health, the protection of the environment, or other social interests. Thus, under the 1999 Constitution, the state is obligated to promote "private initiative, in order to guarantee the creation and just distribution of wealth, the production of goods and services meeting the needs of the population, the freedom to work, free enterprise, and commercial and industrial liberty, while not diminishing [the state's] power to take measures in order to plan, rationalize, and regulate the economy to promote comprehensive development within the nation."

The reform proposed to eliminate both the constitutional right to develop economic activities and economic freedom by seeking to substitute such provision by one reduced to define, as only a matter of state policy, the obligation to promote "the development of a productive economic model, that is intermediate, diversified and independent."

---

[5] See Rogelio Pérez Perdomo, "La Constitución de papel y su reforma," in *Revista de Derecho Público* 112 *(Estudios sobre la reforma constitucional)*, Editorial Jurídica Venezolana, Caracas 2007, 14; Alfredo Arismendi, "Utopía Constitucional," in id., 31; Gerardo Fernández, "Aspectos esenciales de la modificación constitucional propuesta por el Presidente de la República. La modificación constitucional como un fraude a la democracia," in id., p. 22; Manuel Rachadell, "Personalismo político en el Siglo XXI," p. 65; Allan R. Brewer-Carías, "El sello socialista que se pretendía imponer al Estado," in id., 71-75; Alfredo Morles Hernández, "El nuevo mdelo económico para erl Socialismo del Siglo XXI," in id., 233-36.

Moreover, the proposed model was to be "founded upon the humanistic values of cooperation and the preponderance of common interests over individual ones, guaranteeing the meeting of the people's social and material needs, the greatest possible political and social stability, and the greatest possible sum of happiness." The proposal added that the state, in the same way, "shall promote and develop different forms of businesses and economic units from social property, both directly or communally, as well as indirectly or through the state." According to that norm, the state was to promote "economic units of social production and/or distribution, that may be mixed properties held between the State, the private sector, and the communal power, so as to create the best conditions for the collective and cooperative construction of a socialist economy."

The reforms sought simply to derogate and eliminate the right to the free exercise of economic activities as a constitutional right and economic freedom itself.[6] This would, of course, have been contrary to the principle of progressivism in human and constitutional rights that Article 19 of the 1999 Constitution guarantees. It also would have fundamentally transformed the state, which cannot be accomplished through the constitutional-reform procedures.

The 1999 Constitution confers a set of attributes to the state for it to regulate the exercise of economic rights. In particular, the Constitution prohibits monopolies, declaring activities that tend to establish them or that can lead to their existence as contrary to the fundamental principles of the Constitution (Article 113). The abuse of a position of market dominance, independent of the cause of such dominance, is also declared as contrary to the fundamental principles of the Constitution. In each case, the norm affords the state the power to take measures necessary to avoid the harmful and restrictive effects of monopoly, the abuse of market dominance, and the concentration of demand for the purpose of protecting consumers and producers and to protect effective conditions for competition in the economy.

---

[6]See Gerardo Fernández, "Aspectos esenciales de la modificación constitucional propuesta por el Presidente de la República. La modificación constitucional como un fraude a la democracia," in *Revista de Derecho Público* 112 *(Estudios sobre la reforma constitucional)*, Editorial Jurídica Venezolana, Caracas 2007, 24; Alfredo Arismendi, "Utopía Constitucional," in id., 31; José Antonio Muci Borjas, "La suerte de la libertad económica en el proyecto de Reforma de la Constitución de 2007," in id., 203-208; Tamara Adrián, "Actividad económica y sistemas alternativos de producción," in id., 209-14; Víctor Hernández Mendible, "Réquiem por la libertad de empresa y derecho de propiedad," in id., 215-18; Alfredo Morles Hernández, "El nuevo modelo económico para el Socialismo del Siglo XXI," in id., 233-236.

The rejected constitutional reform on these matters also proposed to radically alter the regime of economic activity. The reform for Article 113 provided for a series of limitations that far exceeded restrictions on monopoly and abuse of market dominance; it moved to establish a privileged public or state economy and privileged socialist means of production.

In this context, the reform included a norm that prohibited activities, agreements, practices, conduct, and omissions by individuals that could damage the methods and systems of social and collective production and affect social and collective property. This norm was also to prohibit acts by individuals that prevent or make difficult the just and equitable confluence of goods and services. This norm would therefore have rendered all the private economic activity the subject of the absolute discretion of public authorities.

The reform also added that in cases involving the exploitation of natural resources or other assets within national domain that are of a strategic character or that involve the provision of essential services, the state may reserve the exploitation of resources or the provision of services to itself, either directly or through state-owned corporations. This was to be made, however, "without prejudice to the establishment of corporations were to be direct social property, of mixed corporations, and/or socialist units of production that ensure social and economic sovereignty, that respect the oversight of the state, and meet their imputed social responsibilities in accordance with the terms of legislation corresponding to their respective sector of the economy."

2. *Eliminating Property as a Constitutionally Protected Right*

In addition to economic liberty, another fundamental pillar of the Constitution of 1999 is the guarantee of the right to private property – that is, the right of every person "to the use, enjoyment, benefit, and disposition of his or her assets" (Article 115). The right to an asset is subject to "those contributions, restrictions, and obligations established by law for the purposes of public utility or general interest," and it is "only for the cause of public utility or social interest, and on the basis of a final judicial decision and timely payment of just indemnification," that any asset may be expropriated.

The constitutional reforms sought to alter radically the regime of the right to private property by eliminating private property as a constitutionally protected right[7] and by "recognizing" private property (*propiedad privada*) as one sort of property among many. The supposed "right" to property was reduced only regarding "assets for use and consumption or as means of production," which minimized the protections of private property in comparison with other properties recognized, particularly public property.

With respect to Article 115 of the Constitution, the proposed reform, in effect, recognized and guaranteed "different forms of property" as follows:

1. "Public property [*propiedad pública*] is that which belongs to the entities of the state; social property [*propiedad social*] is that which belongs to the people jointly and to future generations, and can be of two kinds: (a) indirect social property [*propiedad social indirecta*] when exercised by the state in the name of the community, and (b) direct social property [*propiedad social directa*], when the state assigns property, in its different forms, and within the ambit of demarcated territories, to one or several communities, or to one or several communes, so that it constitutes communal property [*propiedad comunal*]; or the property is assigned to one or several cities, so that it constitutes citizens' property [*propiedad ciudadana*]."

2. "Collective property [*propiedad colectiva*] is property pertaining to social groups or persons, exploited for their common benefit, use, or enjoyment, that may be of social or private origin."

3. "Mixed property [*propiedad mixta*] is property that is constituted between the public sector, the social sector, the collective sector and the private sector, in different combinations, for the exploitation of resources or the execution of activities, subject always to the absolute economic and social sovereignty of the nation."

4. "Private property [*propiedad privada*] is that which is owned by natural or legal persons, is recognized as assets for use or consumption, or as means of production legitimately acquired."

The reforms aimed to reduce private property to assets for use or consumption or means of production. What is to be understood by assets for consumption remained to be defined but, in common parlance, they are those assets not used to produce others goods; they are used to meet the

---

[7]See Román José Duque Corredor, "La reforma constitucional y la desnaturalización del derecho de propiedad y su transformación en una simple relación de hecho permitida por el Estado," in *Revista de Derecho Público* 112 *(Estudios sobre la reforma constitucional)*, Editorial Jurídica Venezolana, Caracas 2007, 241-48; Gustavo A. Grau Fortoul, "Aproximación preliminar al tratamiento de la propiedad privada en la primera propuesta de modificación de la Constitución de 1999," in id., 249-55; Uxúa Ojer, "La propiedad en la propuesta de cambio constitucional," in id., 257-60.

specific needs of the consumers who acquire them. "Means of production" refers to a set of work objects used in production to create material assets.

With respect to the guarantee of private property being taken only by expropriation, the proposed reform to Article 115 sought to add express "authority to organs of the State to previously occupy assets that are the object of expropriation during judicial proceedings," and thus constitutionalized a mechanism for prior occupation. Nonetheless, and despite the popular rejection to the 2007 constitutional reform, many of the Decree Laws subsequently enacted have implemented these means of affecting private property, allowing takeover and occupations, in many cases *sine die*, of industries and private assets, as it was provided in Law for the defense of persons in their access to goods and services.[8]

3. *The Elimination of the* Latifundio

Article 307 of the 1999 Constitution declares the latifundio as contrary to social interests. In common usage, *latifundio* refers to large tracts of privately owned rural land subject to agricultural exploitation on a large scale but that make inefficient use of the available resources. To correct the situation, the Constitution indicates that the legislature must pass legislation "in the area of taxation, in order to levy taxes on idle lands and to establish the measures necessary to transform these into productive economic units, and, equally, recover lands with agricultural potential."

The norm contained in Article 307 also establishes property rights for rural workers (*campesinos*) and other agricultural and livestock producers working the land according to the forms established in respective legislation. However, the article places an obligation on the state to protect and promote associational and private forms of property to guarantee agricultural production and to safeguard the sustainable organization of arable lands with the objective of ensuring their agricultural and alimentary potential. The same article states that the legislature shall on an exceptional basis create non-tax-based contributions for the purpose of facilitating the funding of financing, research, technical assistance,

---

[8] See Decreto Ley N° 6,092 para la defensa de las personas en el acceso a los bienes y servicios, *Gaceta Oficial* N° 5,889 Extra. of July 31, 2008. See Juan Domingo Alfonzo Paradisi, "Comentarios en cuanto a los procedimientos administrativos establecidos en el decreto N° 6.092 con rango valor y fuerza de Ley para la defensa de las personas en el acceso a los bienes y servicios," in *Revista de Derecho Público* 115, *(Estudios sobre los Decretos Leyes 2008)*, Editorial Jurídica Venezolana, Caracas 2008, 246ff.; Karina Anzola Spadaro, "El carácter autónomo de las 'medidas preventivas' contempladas en el artículo 111 del Decreto Ley para la defensa de las personas en el acceso a los bienes y servicios," in id., 271-79.

technical transfers, and other activities aimed to promote the competitiveness and productivity of the agricultural sector.

The rejected reforms regarding Article 307 sought to eliminate any concept of the public policy of promoting the disappearance of the *latifundio* through tax measures by taxing idle lands, and to eliminate the policy of transforming the *latifundios* into productive economic units while recovering lands with agricultural potential. Instead, the reform established that "the republic shall determine by law the form in which the latifundios will be transferred into the property of the state, or into that of public entities or public corporations, cooperatives, communities, or social organizations that are capable of administering them and of making the lands productive." Consequently, the reform was not a matter of making any privately own *latifundio* productive but rather of transferring the property to the state.[9]

The reform also added to this norm that for purposes of guaranteeing agricultural production, the state shall protect and promote social property, and legislation shall be enacted to tax productive lands that are not devoted to agriculture or livestock.

Finally, it was proposed that a clause be added stating that "farms whose owners execute irreparable actions of environmental destruction, or dedicate farms to the production of psychotropic substances or narcotics, or trade in persons, or use the farms, or permit the farms to be used as areas for the commission of crimes against the security and defense of the nation, shall be confiscated."

II. Proposed Changes on Matters of Public Economy Management

1. *The Regime Governing State Intervention in the Economy*

One of the classic forms of active state intervention in the economy is through the constitution of public corporations or public enterprises. Regarding the regulation of such corporations, Article 300 of the 1999 Constitution refers only to national legislation for the establishment of conditions for the creation of public corporations as "entities that are functionally decentralized." The purpose of the public enterprises, under

---

[9]In the Land and Farming Law, the possibility for the state to occupy and take over private land was extended. See Ley de Tierras y Desarrollo Agrario in *Gaceta Oficial* N° 5.771 Extra. of May 18, 2005.

Article 300, is to realize social or entrepreneurial activities aimed to ensure the reasonable economic and social productivity of the public resources invested.

The rejected 2007 reform sought to alter this regulation by eliminating any reference to decentralization and by reducing the scope of possible purposes serving as the basis for creating public enterprises or entities to the single purpose of promoting and realizing the ends of the socialist economy. In particular, the reform proposed that Article 300 referred only to the creation of "regional corporations or entities for the promotion and realization of economic and social activities under the principles of the socialist economy," and that these established "mechanisms for oversight and accounting that ensure transparency in the management of the public resources invested in them and their reasonable economic and social productivity."

Article 301 of the 1999 Constitution requires the state to defend the economic activity of national public and private enterprises and establishes that foreign investments are subject to the same regulatory conditions as national investments. The rejected reform, however, not only placed the defense of the economic activities of public and private enterprises within the scope of the state's trade policy but also added the defense of the communal, mixed, collective, and social enterprises. The proposed reform also eliminated all reference to foreign investment.

With respect to economic activities to be reserved to the state, Article 302 of the 1999 Constitution sets forth that "by means of the respective organic legislation and for reasons of national interest, the state shall reserve to itself the oil industry and activity," adding that activities in other "industries, forms of exploitation, and areas of goods and services that are in the public interest and are of a strategic character" also may be reserved to the state. In this way, the state's reservation of the oil industry that had already been effectuated through the organic law of the nationalization of the oil industry in 1975 acquired constitutional rank. However, the constitutional text tied the terms of the reservation to what was established in the organic law, which could be changed legislatively, as in fact occurred in 2000.[10] The reservation of the petroleum industry to the state was thus neither rigid nor absolute but rather flexible, in accord with what was established in the corresponding organic law.

---

[10]See Organic Law on Hydrocarbons, in *Gaceta Oficial* N° 37.323 of Nov. 13, 2001. Reformed in 2006. See in *Gaceta Oficial* N° 38.493 of Aug. 4, 2006.

The rejected reform sought to radically change the conception of this regulation by establishing the reservation in the Constitution itself, for reasons of national interest, with respect to "the exploitation of liquid, solid and gaseous hydrocarbons, as well as to the initial recollection, transport and manufacturing and the works required for it." The reform added that "the state shall promote national manufacture to process the raw material, assimilating, creating or innovating national technology, in particular referred to the Orinoco Oil Belt [Faja Petrolífera del Orinoco], gas belts in land and offshore and the petrochemical corridors, in order to develop productive forces, to drive economic growth and achieve social justice." In addition, "the state by means of organic legislation can reserve for itself any other activity related to hydrocarbons."

Reforms of the same article sought to add that the activities reserved to the state were to be accomplished "directly by the national executive, or through entities or enterprises of its exclusive property, or by means of mixed enterprises in which the state have the control and majority of shares," therefore constitutionalizing the mixed-enterprise regime established in 2006 and 2007.[11]

In addition, the proposed reform to Article 113 provided that the state could also reserve for itself, directly or by means of enterprises of its property, the exploitation or execution of natural resources or any other public of the domain of the nation (*dominio de la nación*) considered by the Constitution or by the law of a strategic character, as well as the rendering of vital public services (public utilities) considered as such in the Constitution or in the law.

Finally, regarding reserved activities, the proposed reform of Article 303 sought to establish the absolute prohibition on privatization of any of those resources and activities.

Another important innovation of the 1999 Constitution was the regulation of principles and policies in the area of sustainable agricultural production and nutritional security in Article 305. The reform proposed to add to this article that "if necessary to guarantee nutritional security, the republic may assume indispensable sectors of agricultural, livestock, fishing and aquatic production, and transfer their operation to autonomous entities, public corporations and social, cooperative, or communal

---

[11]See the comments in Allan R. Brewer-Carías, "The 'Statization' of the Pre 2001 Primary Hydrocarbons Joint Venture Exploitations: Their Unilateral Termination and the Assets' Confiscation of Some of the Former Private Parties" in *Oil, Gas & Energy Law Intelligence*, available at www.gasandoil.com/ogel/ ISSN: 1875-418X, Vol. 6, Issue 2 (OGEL/TDM Special Issue on Venezuela: The Battle of Contract Sanctity vs. Resource Sovereignty, Elizabeth Eljuri ed.), Apr. 2008.

organizations." Further, the proposal added that the republic might "fully utilize its powers of expropriation, encumbrance, and occupation according to the terms established by this Constitution and the law."

2. *Proposed Changes in the State's Fiscal and Economic Regime*

In the area of the fiscal regime, for the first time in Venezuelan constitutionalism, the 1999 Constitution incorporated a set of norms relating to the Central Bank of Venezuela and the macroeconomic policy of the state (Articles 318–21). In particular, the Constitution attributes the national power's competencies relating monetary policy to the Central Bank of Venezuela, requiring exercise exclusively and obligatorily for the fundamental objectives of achieving stability in prices and preserving the internal and external values of the currency. The Constitution guarantees the bank's autonomy in formulating policies within its competency. In addition, so that the Bank could adequately meet its objectives, the Constitution assigns to it competencies to formulate and execute monetary policy, to participate in the design and execution of exchange policy, to regulate money and credit, to set interests rates, to administer international reserves, and to assume all of those attributes established by law.

A. Eliminating the Autonomy of the Central Bank of Venezuela

Contrary to the provisions of the 1999 Constitution, the constitutional reforms sought to change the regime governing monetary policy and the Central Bank of Venezuela by seeking to eliminate the Bank's competencies and autonomy, thus rendering the bank totally and directly dependent on the national executive.[12]

To this end, the following reforms were proposed regarding Article 318 of the Constitution. First is the requirement that "the national monetary system be directed toward the achievement of the essential ends of the socialist state and the well-being of the people, above any other consideration." Second, the competencies to fix monetary policies would be attributed to the national executive and the Central Bank "in strict and obligatory coordination." Third, the autonomy of the bank was formally eliminated through language stating that the bank "is a person in public

---

[12]See Manuel Rachadell, "Personalismo político en el Siglo XXI," in *Revista de Derecho Público* 112 *(Estudios sobre la reforma constitucional)*, Editorial Jurídica Venezolana, Caracas 2007, 67; Enrique J. Sánchez Falcón, "La propuesta de modificación constitucional y el régimen de la Administración Financiera Pública," in id., 192.

law without autonomy in the formulation and execution of the corresponding policies." The Bank's functions were to be subordinated to general economic policy and the national development plan to achieve the superior objectives of the socialist state and the greatest possible sum of happiness for the whole of the people. Fourth, it was established that the functions of the Central Bank were to be "shared with the executive power," and that for the adequate fulfillment of its specific objectives, the bank "shall have, among its functions, shared with the national executive power," only the power to "participate in the formulation and execution of monetary policy, in the design and execution of exchange policy, in the regulation of money and credit, and the fixing of interest rates."

Last, competency to "administer international reserves" was entirely removed from the bank, so the norm stated instead that "the international reserves of the republic shall be managed by the Central Bank of Venezuela, under the administration and direction of the president of the republic, as administrator of the National Public Treasury."

Nonetheless, through successive reforms of the Central Bank Law, many of the rejected proposed reforms affecting the autonomy of the institution have been implemented.[13]

B. Macroeconomic Policy at the Mercy of the National Executive

Article 320 of the 1999 Constitution establishes detailed regulation in relation to the coordination of macroeconomic policy, first relating to economic stability and second to the Macroeconomic Stabilization Fund (Fondo de Estabilización Macroeconómica). The rejected reform sought radically to change both regulations.[14]

Article 320 sets forth that "the state must promote and defend economic stability, avoid economic vulnerability and safeguard the price stability in order to ensure social well-being." The provision establishes the obligation "of the ministry responsible for the finances and of the Central Bank of Venezuela" to contribute "to the harmonization of fiscal policy with monetary policy, facilitating the achievement of the macroeconomic objectives." The Constitution further states that, "in the exercise of its functions, the Central Bank of Venezuela shall not be subordinated to the

---

[13] See *Gaceta Oficial* 39.300, Nov. 5, 2009. In Mar. 2010, a new reform of the Central Bank of Venezuela Law was sanctioned by the National Assembly.

[14] See Enrique J. Sánchez Falcón, "La propuesta de modificación constitucional y el régimen de la Administración Financiera Pública," in *Revista de Derecho Público* 112 (*Estudios sobre la reforma constitucional*), Editorial Jurídica Venezolana, Caracas 2007, 193.

directives of the executive power and shall not validate or finance deficit fiscal policies."

In addition, the constitutional norm requires that the coordinated action of the executive power and the bank be realized "through an annual policy agreement," which must include the "final growth objectives and their social repercussions, the foreign exchange balance, inflation, fiscal, exchange and monetary policy, as well as the levels of intermediate and instrumental variables necessary for the achievement of the indicated final objectives." Article 320 sets forth the formal procedures required for the approval of the agreement, which included the signature of the president of the bank, the signature of the head of the Ministry of Finances, and the presentation of the agreement to the National Assembly at the time of the assembly's approval of the budget. The Constitution provides that the institutions signatory to the agreement are responsible for ensuring that its "policy actions are consistent with its objectives" and that it specifies "the anticipated results, and the policies and actions directed towards reaching those results."

The rejected 2007 reform sought to eliminate the entire detailed regulatory framework designed to guarantee economic stability and coordination between the national executive and the bank, proposing instead that Article 320 contain the following language: "the state must promote and defend economic stability, avoid economic vulnerability and safeguard the monetary and price stability, in order to assure social well being. Equally, the state shall safeguard the harmonization of fiscal and monetary policies to achieve the macro-economic objectives." The changes would have eliminated any principle of coordination between the national executive and the Central Bank. Under the reforms, the Central Bank would have remained without autonomy as an executing arm of the executive's disposal.

With respect to the regime governing the Fund for Macroeconomic Stabilization, Article 321 of the 1999 Constitution refers to it as "destined to guarantee the expenditures of the state at the municipal, regional and national levels in the event of fluctuations in ordinary revenues." The article requires that the functioning of the fund be tied to "basic principles of efficiency, equity, and nondiscrimination among the public entities that bring resources to it." The rejected reform totally eliminated the Fund for Macroeconomic Stabilization and instead proposed that Article 321 attribute the "administration of international reserves . . . to the Head of State" and authorize the head of state "in coordination with the Central Bank of Venezuela, to establish the level of reserves needed for the national economy, at the end of each year, as well as the amount of surplus reserves." The express indication was added that the surplus reserves shall be destined to funds established by the national executive for productive investments, development, and infrastructure; financing of the missions; and, definitively, to the integral, endogenous, humanist, and socialist development of the nation.

III. PROPOSED CHANGES IN MATTERS OF HUMAN RIGHTS

With respect to human rights, the 1999 Constitution introduced very important and notable reforms, marked by progressiveness, which was expressly included in Article 19. Unfortunately, a few important and radical changes were incorporated into the reforms, like restrictive changes in matters of political rights and political participation, in matters of economic freedom and property rights, and in matters of right to education, in particular the right to university autonomy. In addition, in matters of emergency or states of exception, the reforms were notably regressive, and the state was configured as a repressive (police) state.[15] Other reforms in matters of human rights referred to the right of nondiscrimination and labor rights. Reforms in the latter category do not require a constitutional reform because they can be achieved through legislation.

1. *The Extension of the Principle of Equality*

Article 21 of the 1999 Constitution extensively regulated equality and nondiscrimination, with very rich content. The proposed reform extended those principles by enumerating forms of forbidden discrimination. Where the 1999 Constitution referred to discriminatory motives based on "race, sex, religion and social condition," the reform proposed adding discrimination based on "ethnic, gender, age, sex, health, creed, political orientation, sexual orientation, social, and religious conditions."[16]

---

[15] See Manuel Rachadell, "Personalismo político en el Siglo XXI," in *Revista de Derecho Público* 112 *(Estudios sobre la reforma constitucional)*, Editorial Jurídica Venezolana, Caracas 2007, 67; in id., 68; Verónica Espina Molina, "El principio de progresividad de los derechos humanos," in id., 261-66; Víctor Herández Mendible, "La regresión constitucional en materia de derechos humanos," in id., 267-86; Alberto Blanco Uribe Quintero, "Menoscabo al derecho humano a la participación, por la reforma constitucional," in id., 199; Ana Cristina Núñez Machado, "La eliminación del derecho a la información del artículo 337 de la Constitución: Violación del 'principio de progresividad' de los derechos humanos," in id., 331-35.

[16] See Carlos Urdaneta Sandoval, "El principio de igualdad en el proyecto de reforma constitucional de 2007," in id., 275-93; Tamara Adrián, "Protección constitucional de la mujer y de la diversidad sexual" in id., 295-300.

2. *Proposed Changes in the States of Exception*

Chapter 2 of Title 8 of the 1999 Constitution ("Protection of the Constitution") aims to establish the regime governing exceptional circumstances that could originate states of exception or emergency that could gravely affect the security of the nation, its institutions, and persons, and impose the need to adopt exceptional measures (Article 337).

The proposed reform would radically change the protective regulations established in the 1999 Constitution regarding human rights, including revocation of the Organic Law on the States of Exception of 2001 in the only derogatory disposition of the reform.[17]

A. The Expansion of States of Exception

According to Article 338 of the 1999 Constitution, a "state of alarm" can be decreed "when catastrophes, public calamities and other similar situations could constitute a serious peril for the security of the nation or its citizens."

The proposed reform extended states of alarm, establishing two sorts: first, one that established hypothetical situations that could originate the new form of a state of alarm, in cases where "a certain and imminent possibility exists for the occurrence of situations capable of originating catastrophes, public calamities and other similar situations, in order to adopt the necessary measures to protect the nation and its citizens"; and second, the previous "state of alarm" became "state of emergency."

B. The Elimination of the Duration of a State of Emergency

The 1999 Constitution establishes that the states of exception (alarm, emergency, or commotion) must necessarily be limited to a duration that varies from thirty to ninety days, with the possibility of an extension. The reforms sought to eliminate from Article 338 the terms of duration from the various states of exception (thirty days for state of alarm; sixty days for state of economic emergency; and ninety days for states of interior or exterior commotion). It proposed converting them to situations without temporal limits whose enforcement was subject to the sole will and discretion of the president.

---

[17]See Jesús María Casal, "Los estados de excepción en la reforma constitucional," in id., Editorial Jurídica Venezolana, Caracas 2007, 325-29.

The consequence of this reform was that the National Assembly would lose its power according to the 1999 Constitution to approve or deny extensions of states of emergency.

C. The Possibility of Suspending Constitutional Guarantees

The 1999 Constitution expressly eliminated the possibility of the president to "suspend" the constitutional guarantees of human rights, as had been authorized in the 1961 Constitution and had in the past led to unacceptable institutional abuses.[18] In states of exception, the president's power was reduced to only temporarily "restrict" (Article 236.7) those constitutional guarantees.

The reform proposed, regressively, reestablishing that the President could suspend constitutional guarantees, which is inadmissible in a democratic society.

D. Changes Regarding the Constitutional Guarantees of Human Rights That Can Be Suspended or Restricted in Situations of Exception

Within the constitutional guarantees that, according to the 1999 Constitution, could not be affected in states of exception are the right to life, the prohibition on incommunicado detentions, the prohibition on torture, the right to due process of law, the right to be informed, and all the other intangible human rights. The latter includes the guarantees that, according to the International Covenant of Civil and Political Rights and to the American Convention on Human Rights, cannot be suspended, such as the guarantee of equality and nondiscrimination, the guarantee to not be condemned to prison on the basis of contractual obligations, the guarantee against ex post facto laws, the right to personality, the right to religious liberty, the principle of legality, the protection of the family, the rights of the child, the guarantee against being arbitrarily deprived of nationality, the exercise of political rights, and the right to access public functions.

The proposed reforms aimed to eliminate from Article 337 the prohibition on suspending or restricting due process of law, the right to be

---

[18]See, e.g., Allan R. Brewer-Carías, "Consideración sobre la suspensión o restricción de las garantías constitucionales," in *Revista de Derecho Público* 37, Editorial Jurídica Venezolana, Caracas 1989, 5-25.

informed,[19] and all the other intangible human rights. Nonetheless, in a contradictory way, the reform added to the reduced list of unsuspended rights, a few specific rights conforming the due process, as are the prohibition on the disappearance of persons, the right to self-defense, the right to personal integrity, the right to be judged by a competent natural court, and the right not be condemned to punishment in excess of thirty years.

E. The Elimination of the Control Mechanisms of States of Exception

The 1999 Constitution, in its provisions on states of exception, establishes three mechanisms for controlling the executive powers: the National Assembly, the Constitutional Chamber of the Supreme Tribunal, and international organizations. The constitutional reforms proposed eliminating all of these mechanisms.

First, the reform eliminated the possibility of the National Assembly to control and revoke the executive decree declaring states of exception (including the possibility to extend their term) and established that only the president could end the decree "when their motivating cause ceases" (Article 339). The decree declaring the state of exception was to be presented to the assembly, but the assembly would retain no power to revoke it, as established in the 1999 Constitution.

Second, the reform also eliminated from Article 339 the obligatory constitutional control attributed to the Constitutional Chamber of the Supreme Tribunal regarding decrees on states of exception. Nonetheless, the competency of the Supreme Tribunal remained in Article 336.6, which attributed to the Constitutional Chamber the power to review the constitutionality of the decrees, even ex officio, on the basis of its own initiative.

Third, the reforms also proposed eliminating the constitutional provision established in Article 339 that requires that executive decrees of states of exception comply with "the conditions, principles and guarantees established in the International Covenant on Civil and Political Rights and in the American Convention on Human Rights."

---

[19]See Ana Cristina Núñez Machado, "La eliminación del derecho a la información del artículo 337 de la Constitución: Violación del 'principio de progresividad' de los derechos humanos," in *Revista de Derecho Público* 112 *(Estudios sobre la reforma constitucional)*, Editorial Jurídica Venezolana, Caracas 2007, 331-35.

3. *Proposed Changes in Education Rights: The Limits to University Autonomy*

On matters of social rights, the 2007 constitutional reforms also proposed changed in Article 109 of the 1999 Constitution in which the autonomy of universities is guaranteed. The proposed reform sought to incorporate workers within the university academic community with full rights, including those in order to elect the authorities of the universities. Also, the reform pretended to give equal electing votes to students and professors and extended the right to vote to all teachers even without permanent tenure.[20] The purpose was to eliminate the autonomy of the Universities, for which purpose, in 2010, proposals were made to initiate a "university constituent" process.[21]

4. *Proposed Changes in Labor Rights: A Useless Constitutional "Reform"*

The constitutional reforms also proposed changes to two articles from the chapter of the 1999 Constitution on labor rights. First, Article 87 referred to social security for nondependent workers; second, Article 90 concerned the maximum length of the workday. The content of the proposed reforms, however, was not a matter for constitutional review and required no constitutional modification for their implementation, which could be achieved through legislation.[22]

---

[20] See Juan Domingo Alfonzo Paradisi, "La autonomía universitaria y el proyecto de reforma constitucional de 2007," in *Revista de Derecho Público* 112 *(Estudios sobre la reforma constitucional)*, Editorial Jurídica Venezolana, Caracas 2007, 301-11. See also Eugenio Herández Bretón, ""Cuando no hay miedo (ante la reforma Constitucional)," in id., 18; Manuel Rachadell, "Personalismo político en el Siglo XXI," in id., 67.

[21] See regarding the threats against the national autonomous Universities, Gustavo Méndez, "Universidades bajo amenaza de constituyente e intervención. Ejecutivo y Asamblea Nacional enfilan sus baterías contra las instituciones," in *El Universal*, Caracas July 4, 2010. Available at http://politica.eluniversal.com:80/2010/07/04/pol_art_universidades-bajo-a_1961598.shtml..

[22] See, on this matter of labor rights in the reform proposal, Juan Carlos Pro Rísquez, "Las reformas laborales," in *Revista de Derecho Público* 112 *(Estudios sobre la reforma constitucional)*, Editorial Jurídica Venezolana, Caracas 2007, 313-18.

Chapter 13

THE IRREGULAR FRAUDULENT IMPLEMENTATION OF THE REJECTED CONSTITUTIONAL REFORM THROUGH LEGISLATION

Once the 2007 constitutional reforms were rejected by popular vote, the president and main officials of the National Assembly publicly announced that, despite such rejection, they would implement the reforms by means of statutes and decree laws, contrary to the Constitution.

Consequently, many of the rejected constitutional reforms were illegitimately and fraudulently implemented by means of decree laws issued by the president in execution of the February 1999 enabling law.[1] This legislative delegation was sanctioned by the National Assembly parallel to the announcement by the president at the beginning of the 2007 constitutional reform process. Nonetheless, and assuming that the presidential constitutional-reform proposal was to be approved by the people, the president began implementing it before even being sanctioned by the National Assembly and, of course, without popular approval, by means of the execution of the enabling law (delegate legislation) sanctioned in 2007 that was then used fraudulently to implement the rejected reforms,[2] particularly in economic and social matters, to structure

---

[1] *Gaceta Oficial,* 38.617, Feb. 1, 2007.

[2] See Lolymar Hernández Camargo, "Límites del poder ejecutivo en el ejercicio de la habilitación legislativa: Imposibilidad de establecer el contenido de la reforma constitucional rechazada vía habilitación legislativa," in *Revista de Derecho Público* 115 *(Estudios sobre los Decretos Leyes),* Editorial Jurídica Venezolana, Caracas 2008, 51ff.; Jorge Kiriakidis, "Breves reflexiones en torno a los 26 Decretos-Ley de julio-agosto de 2008, y la consulta popular refrendaría de diciembre de 2007," in id., 57ff.; José Vicente Haro García, "Los recientes intentos de reforma constitucional o de cómo se está tratando de establecer una dictadura socialista con apariencia

a socialist centralized state.³ This process, on the other hand, was developed in absolute secrecy with any public consultation and participation, in violation of Article 210 of the Constitution.⁴

The process began even before the draft reforms were even submitted to the National Assembly, when Decree Law No. 5,841 was enacted on June 12, 2007,⁵ containing the organic law creating the Central Planning Commission. This was the first formal state act devoted to building the socialist state.⁶ Once this reform was rejected in referendum, on December 13, 2007, the National Assembly approved the 2007–13 Economic and Social Development National Plan, established in Article 32 of the Decree Law enacting the Planning Organic Law,⁷ in which the basis of the "planning, production and distribution system oriented towards socialism" is established, providing that "the relevant matter is the progressive development of social property of the production means." For such purpose, the proposed 2007 rejected constitutional reforms to assign the state all powers over farming, livestock, fishing, and aquaculture, and in particular the production of food, materialized in the decree law Organic Law on Farming and Food Security and Sovereignty.⁸ That law assigned

---

de legalidad (A propósito del proyecto de reforma constitucional de 2007 y los 26 decretos leyes del 31 de julio de 2008 que tratan de imponerla)," in id., 63ff.

³See Ana Cristina Nuñez Machado, "Los 26 nuevos Decretos-Leyes y los principios que regulan la intervención del Estado en la actividad económica de los particulares," in id., 215-20.

⁴See Aurilivi Linares Martínez, "Notas sobre el uso del poder de legislar por decreto por parte del Presidente venezolano," in id., 79-89; Carlos Luis Carrillo Artiles, "La paradójica situación de los Decretos Leyes Orgánicos frente a la Ingeniería Constitucional de 1999," in id., 93-100; Freddy J. Orlando S., "El "paquetazo," un conjunto de leyes que conculcan derechos y amparan injusticias," in id., 101-104.

⁵*Gaceta Oficial* N° 5.841, Extra., June 22, 2007.

⁶See Allan R. Brewer-Carías, "Comentarios sobre la inconstitucional creación de la Comisión Central de Planificación, centralizada y obligatoria," in *Revista de Derecho Público* 110, Editorial Jurídica Venezolana, Caracas 2007, 79-89; Luis A. Herrera Orellana, "Los Decretos-Leyes de 30 de julio de 2008 y la Comisión Central de Planificación: Instrumentos para la progresiva abolición del sistema político y del sistema económico previstos en la Constitución de 1999," in *Revista de Derecho Público* 115, *(Estudios sobre los Decretos Leyes)*, Editorial Jurídica Venezolana, Caracas 2008, 221-32.

⁷*Gaceta Oficial* N° 5.554 of Nov. 13, 2001.

⁸*Gaceta Oficial* N° 5.889, Extra., July 31, 2008. See José Ignacio Hernández G., "Planificación y soberanía alimentaria," in *Revista de Derecho Público* 115, *(Estudios sobre los Decretos Leyes)*, Editorial Jurídica Venezolana, Caracas 2008, 389-94; Juan Domingo Alfonso Paradisi, "La constitución económica establecida en la Constitución de 1999, el sistema de economía social de mercado y el decreto 6.071 con rango, valor y fuerza de Ley Orgánica de seguridad y soberanía agroalimentaria," in id., 395-415; Gustavo A. Grau Fortoul, "La participación del sector privado en la producción de alimentos, como elemento esencial para poder alcanzar la seguridad alimentaria (Aproximación al tratamiento de la cuestión, tanto en la Constitución de 1999 como en la novísima Ley Orgánica de soberanía y seguridad alimentaria)," in id., 417-24.

to the state power not only to authorize food imports but also to prioritize production and directly assume distribution and commercialization. The law also expanded expropriation powers of the executive violating the constitutional guarantee of the previous declaration of a specific public interest or public utility involved, and allowing the State occupation of indutries without compensation.[9]

Decree Law No. 6,130 of June 3, 2008, enacted the Popular Economy Promotion and Development Law, establishing a "socio-productive communal model," with different socio-productive organizations following the "socialist model."[10] In the same openly socialist orientation, Decree Law No. 6,092 was issued enacting the Access to Goods and Services Persons Defense Law,[11] which derogated the previous Consumer and Users Protection Law,[12] with the purpose of regulating all commercialization and different economic aspects of goods and services, extending the state powers of control to the point of establishing the possibility of confiscating goods and services, by means of their takeover and occupation through administrative decisions.[13]

Regarding the 2007 reforms related to eliminating local-level representative democracy, the same began to be implemented in 2006 with the sanctioning of the Communal Councils Law,[14] which created them as

---

[9]See Carlos García Soto, "Notas sobre la expansión del ámbito de la declaratoria de utilidad pública o interés social en la expropiación," in id., 149-51.

[10]*Gaceta Oficial* N° 5.890, Extra., July 31, 2008. See Jesús María Alvarado Andrade, "La desaparición del bolívar como moneda de curso legal (Notas críticas al inconstitucional Decreto N° 6.130, con rango, valor y fuerza de la ley para el fomento y desarrollo de la economía comunal, de fecha 3 de junio de 2008," in *Revista de Derecho Público* 115, *(Estudios sobre los Decretos Leyes)*, Editorial Jurídica Venezolana, Caracas 2008, 313-20.

[11]*Gaceta Oficial* N° 5,889 Extra of July 31, 2008; José Gregorio Silva, "Disposiciones sobre el Decreto-Ley para la defensa de las personas en el acceso a bienes y servicios," in id., 277-79; Carlos Simón Bello Rengifo, "Decreto N° 6.092 con rango, valor y fuerza de la ley para la defensa de las personas en el acceso a los bienes y servicios (Referencias a problemas de imputación)," in id., 281-305; Alfredo Morles Hernández, "El nuevo modelo económico del socialismo del siglo XXI y su reflejo en el contrato de adhesión," in id., 229-32.

[12]*Gaceta Oficial* N° 37.930, May 4, 2004.

[13]See See Juan Domingo Alfonso Paradisi, "Comentarios en cuanto a los procedimientos administrativos establecidos en el Decreto N° 6.092 con rango, valor y fuerza de Ley para la defensa de las personas en el acceso a los bienes y servicios," in *Revista de Derecho Público* 115, *(Estudios sobre los Decretos Leyes)*, Editorial Jurídica Venezolana, Caracas 2008, 245-60; Karina Anzola Spadaro, "El carácter autónomo de las 'medidas preventivas' contempladas en el artículo 111 del Decreto-Ley para la defensa de las personas en el acceso a los bienes y servicios," in id., 271-76.

[14]Ley de Consejos Comunales, *Gazeta Oficial* N° 5806, Extra., Apr. 10, 2006. See Allan R. Brewer-Carías, "El inicio de la desmunicipalización en Venezuela: La organización del poder popular para eliminar la descentralización, la democracia representativa y la participación a nivel local," in

social units and organizations not directed by popularly elected officials, without any sort of territorial autonomy, supposedly devoted to channeling citizens' participation but in a centralized conducted system from the apex of the national executive.[15]

A primary purpose of the 2007 constitutional reforms was to complete the dismantling of the federal form of the state by centralizing power attributions of the states, creating administrative entities to be established and directed by the national executive, attributing powers to the president to interfere in regional and local affairs, and voiding state and municipal competency by means of compulsory transfer of that competency to communal councils.[16] The implementation of the rejected constitutional reforms regarding the organization of the "Public Power" based on the strengthening of the communes and communal councils has been completed with the approval in 2010 of the Law on the Federal Council of Government.[17]

To implement these reforms, not only the last mentioned aspect has been achieved forcing the states and municipalities to transfer its attributions to local institutions controlled by the central power (communal councils) but also by means of Decree Law No. 6217 of July 15, 2008, on the Organic Law of Public Administration[18] that is now directly applicable to the States' and Municipalities' Public Administrations, the national executive has implemented the principle of centralized planning, subjection regional and local authorities to the Central Planning Commission. This Organic Law also assigns to the president, as proposed in the 2007 reforms, the power to appoint regional authorities with powers to plan, execute, follow

---

AIDA, Opera Prima de Derecho Administrativo. Revista de la Asociación Internacional de Derecho Administrativo, Universidad Nacional Autónoma de México, Mexico City, 2007, 49-67.

[15]Ley Orgánica de los Consejos Comunales, *Gazeta Oficial* N° 39.335, Dec. 28, 2009. See Juan M. Raffali A., "Límites constitucionales de la Contraloría Social Popular," in Revista de Derecho Público, 115, *(Estudios sobre los Decretos Leyes)*, Editorial Jurídica Venezolana, Caracas 2008, in *id.*, 133-47.

[16]See See Manuel Rachadell, *"La centralización del poder en el Estado federal descentralizado,"* in id., 111-131.

[17]See *Ley Orgánica del Consejo Federal de Gobierno, Gaceta Oficial* N° 5.963 Extra. of Feb. 22, 2010.

[18]*Gaceta Oficial* N° 5.890, Extra., July 31, 2008. See Allan R. Brewer-Carías, "El sentido de la reforma de la Ley Orgánica de la Administración Pública," in *Revista de Derecho Público* 115, *(Estudios sobre los Decretos Leyes)*, Editorial Jurídica Venezolana, Caracas 2008, 155161; Cosimina G. Pellegrino Pacera, "La reedición de la propuesta constitucional de 2007 en el Decreto N° 6.217, con Rango, Valor y Fuerza de Ley Orgánica de la Administración Pública," in id., 163-68; Jesús Caballero Ortíz, "Algunos comentarios sobre la descentralización funcional en la nueva Ley Orgánica de la Administración Pública," in id. 169-74; Alberto Blanco-Uribe Quintero. "Afrenta a la Debida Dignidad frente a la Administración Pública. Los Decretos 6.217 y 6.265," in id., 175-79.

up on, and control land use and territorial development policies, thus subjecting all programs and projects to central planning approval.

Regarding the vertical distribution of state attributions between the national level and the states, the proposed and rejected constitutional reforms sought to eliminate the exclusive attribution assigned to the states in Article 164.10 of the Constitution to "maintain, administrate and profited use of national roads and highways, as well as ports and airports of commercial use, in coordination with the national power." In this case, the fraudulent implementation of the rejected constitutional reform was made by the Constitutional Chamber of the Supreme Tribunal of Justice, when deciding recourse for constitutional interpretation filed by the attorney general representing the national executive. In Decision No. 565 of April 15, 2008,[19] the Supreme Tribunal through an obligatory interpretation simply "modified" the content of the mentioned constitutional provision, urging the National Assembly to approve legislation in accordance with the judicial made constitutional reform. This was effectively accomplished in May 2009 by reforming the Organic Law on Decentralization, Delimitation, and Transfer of Public Attributions,[20] eliminating the exclusive attributions of the states established in its Articles 11.3 and 11.5, and adding two new provisions authorizing the national executive to revert the transfer of competencies already made to the states (Article 8) and to decree the intervention of transferred assets and public services (Article 9). With the reforms, the fraud on the Constitution was completed, and the federation disrupted.[21]

The rejected 2007 constitutional reforms also sought to eliminate the capital district, created in the federal framework of the Constitution as one political entity in the territory. Notwithstanding popular rejection of the 2007 reform proposals, in April 2009, the reform was unconstitutionally implemented by the National Assembly, defrauding once more the Constitution by sanctioning the Special Law on the Organization and

---

[19]See Constitutional Chamber Decision N° 565 (Apr. 15, 2008) (Case: *Procuradora General de la República*), interpretation recourse of Article 164.10 of the 1999 Constitution, at http://www.tsj.gov.ve/de-cisiones/scon/Abril/565-150408-07-1108.htm.

[20]*Gaceta Oficial* N° 39.140, Mar. 17, 2009.

[21]See Allan R. Brewer-Carías, "La Sala Constitucional como poder constituyente: La modificación de la forma federal del estado y del sistema constitucional de división territorial del poder público," in *Revista de Derecho Público* 114, Editorial Jurídica Venezolana, Caracas 2008, 247-62; Manuel Rachadell, "*La centralización del poder en el Estado federal descentralizado,*" in *Revista de Derecho Público*, N° 115 (Estudios sobre los Decretos Leyes), Editorial Jurídica Venezolana, Caracas 2008, 120.

Regime of the Capital District.[22] In it, instead of creating a democratic entity to govern the capital district, the law established an organization completely dependent on the national level of government in the same territorial jurisdiction that "used to be one of the extinct federal district" equivalent to one of the current Libertador municipality in Caracas. According to this law, the capital district, contrary to what is provided for in the Constitution, has no elected authorities of government and is governed by the national level by means of a "special regime" consisting of the exercise of the legislative function by the National Assembly itself and a chief of government in charge of the executive branch (Article 3) and appointed by the president. This means that through a national statute, in the same territory of Libertador, a new national structure has been unconstitutionally imposed.

Finally, although the 2007 constitutional reforms proposed regarding the military and the Armed Force, seeking to transform them into the Bolivarian Armed Force organized for the purpose of reinforcing socialism, were rejected in the December 2007 referendum, the radical changes it contained have been implemented by the president, usurping the constituent power, by means of a decree law reforming the Organic Law on the Armed Force,[23] creating the Bolivarian National Armed Force subjected to a "military Bolivarian Doctrine," and creating in it the "National Bolivarian Militia" – all of this according to what was proposed and rejected by the people in the 2007 Constitutional Reform.[24]

---

[22]*Gaceta Oficial* N° 39.156, Apr. 13, 2009. See the comments on this Law in Allan R. Brewer-Carías et al., *Leyes sobre el Distrito Capital y el Área Metropolitana de Caracas*, Editorial Jurídica Venezolana, Caracas 2009.

[23]Decree Law N° 6.239, on the Organic Law of the National Bolivarian Armed Force, in *Gaceta Oficial* N° 5.933, Extra., Oct. 21, 2009.

[24] See Alfredo Arismendi A., "*Fuerza Armada Nacional: Antecedentes, evolución y régimen actual,*" in *Revista de Derecho Público*, N° 115 (Estudios sobre los Decretos Leyes), Editorial Jurídica Venezolana, Caracas 2008, 187-206; Jesús María Alvarado Andrade, "La nueva Fuerza Armada Bolivariana (Comentarios a raíz del Decreto N° 6.239, con rango, valor y fuerza de Ley Orgánica de la Fuerza Armada Nacional Bolivariana),*"* in id., 207-14.

Chapter 14

THE ILLEGITIMATE MUTATION OF THE CONSTITUTION THROUGH JUDICIAL CONSTITUTIONAL INTERPRETATION

According to the 1999 Constitution, its provisions can be reviewed and modified only through the specific means established for such purpose, that is, the convening of a National Constituent National Assembly; the proposing, sanctioning, and popular approving of a "constitutional reform"; or the proposing and popular approving of a "constitutional amendment" (Articles 340-349). The common trend of all these constitutional review procedures is that the intervention of the people through referenda is always required for the Constitution to be modified,[1] so no constitutional review is possible without the vote of the people. Any other modification, reform, or amendment to the Constitution adopted through any other means is to be considered illegitimate.

That is why, in 2007, in order to modify the Constitution for the purpose of reinforcing the authoritarian, socialist, centralized, and militaristic state that has been built during the past decade, the president proposed an extensive "constitutional reform" that after being sanctioned by the National Assembly was rejected by the people in the December 2007 referendum. After this defeat, the following year, the National Assembly sanctioned a "constitutional amendment" draft in order to implement one aspect of the 2007 reforms proposals rejected by the people, referred to the continuous and indefinite possibility for reelection of the president and

---

[1] See Allan R. Brewer-Carías, "La intervención del pueblo en la revisión constitucional en América latina," en *El derecho público a los 100 números de la Revista de Derecho Público 1980-2005*, Editorial Jurídica Venezolana, Caracas 2006, 41-52.

other elected officials, which eventually was approved in the referendum that took place in February 2009.

Notwithstanding the limits imposed in the rigid constitution for their review, it is accepted that without any formal review of the Constitution, the sense of one of its provisions can be changed, particularly in the case of old constitutions, when its meaning is judicially interpreted particularly by constitutional judges, in order to adapt its content to the current social development of a society, applying democratic principles and values that derive from the same Constitution. In these cases of constitutional interpretation, the result can be what has been called a "constitutional mutation" (*mutación constitutional*) that may occur when the content of the constitutional-provision is modified in such a way that even if the provision maintains its textual content, it receives a different meaning, which is generally accepted according to the democratic values of society.[2]

The problem with these "constitutional mutations" is that they can be illegitimate when the judicial constitutional interpretation is the result of a deliberate process directed to distort the Constitution, in order to force the modification of the meaning of its provisions without altering its text, for the purpose of reinforcing authoritarianism and defrauding democracy, as it has occurred, for instance, in Venezuela when via judicial constitutional interpretation issued by the Constitutional Chamber of the Supreme Tribunal of Justice, the government succeeded in implementing many of the constitutional-reform proposals that were rejected by the people through the 2007 referendum.

This process of illegitimate distortion of the Constitution began in Venezuela in 2000, when the Constitutional Chamber, deciding on the unconstitutionality of the challenged Decree of Transitory Regime issued in December 1999 by the National Constituent Assembly after the popular approval of the Constitution, admitted the existence of constitutional provisions that were not included in the text of the 1999 Constitution as it was approved by the people. The process has continued during the past decade through multiple decisions of the Constitutional Chamber through which the Constitution has been illegitimately distorted or "mutated."

---

[2]See Néstor Pedro Sagüés, *La interpretación judicial de la Constitución*, Abeledo-Perrot, Buenos Aires 2006, 56-59, 80-81, 165ff.; Salvador O. Nava Gomar, "Interpretación, mutación y reforma de la Constitución. Tres extractos," in *Interpretación constitucional*, coord. Eduardo Ferrer Mac-Gregor, Ed. Porrúa, Universidad Nacional Autónoma de México, Mexico City 2005, 2:804ff.; Konrad Hesse, "Límites a la mutación constitucional," in *Escritos de derecho constitucional*, Centro de Estudios Constitucionales, Madrid 1992.

Following are a few examples of this process that could only be explained due to the tragic subjection of the Supreme Tribunal of Justice to the executive.[3]

I. THE ACCEPTANCE OF A TRANSITORY CONSTITUTIONAL REGIME NOT APPROVED BY THE PEOPLE

The first constitutional mutation (distortion) regarding the 1999 Constitution was decided by the Constitutional Chamber of the Supreme Tribunal of Justice a few weeks after approval of the Constitution. It admitted the existence of constitutional transitory provisions different from those approved by popular vote and embodied in the text of the Constitution. The 1999 Constitution was approved by referendum on December 15, 1999, with a text that included transitory provisions. The popular approval of the Constitution, in principle, concluded the mission of the Constituent Assembly.

However, one week after the approval of the Constitution, on December 22, 1999, the Constituent Assembly sanctioned the Decree of the Regime of Transition of the Public Power,[4] "to give effect to the transition process towards the regime established in the Constitution of 1999." In that decree, it decided, without any attribution foreseen in the new Constitution, to eliminate the prior Congress, along with its senators and deputies, and to assign legislative power to the National Legislative Commission, not established in the Constitution; to dissolve the states' legislative assemblies; to assign legal attributions in their place to state legislative commissions, which were not provided for in the Constitution; to take control of the mayor's offices and municipal councils; to eliminate the former Supreme Court of Justice, create new chambers of the Supreme Tribunal and assign them a fixed number of judges –not established in the Constitution– and to appoint them without complying with what the

---

[3]On this process of illegitimate mutations of the constitution see, in general, the comments in Allan R. Brewer-Carías, *Reforma constitucional y fraude a la Constitución (1999-2009)*, Academia de Ciencias Políticas y Sociales, Caracas 2009, 217ff.; "El juez constitucional al servicio del autoritarismo y la ilegítima mutación de la Constitución: el caso de la Sala Constitucional del Tribunal Supremo de Justicia de Venezuela (1999-2009)," in *Revista de Administración Pública*, N° 180, Madrid 2009, 383-418; "La fraudulenta mutación de la Constitución en Venezuela, o de cómo el juez constitucional usurpa el poder constituyente originario," in *Anuario de Derecho Público*, Centro de Estudios de Derecho Público de la Universidad Monteávila, Año 2, Caracas 2009, 23-65; "La ilegítima mutación de la Constitución por el juez constitucional y la demolición del Estado de derecho en Venezuela," in *Revista de Derecho Político*, N° 75-76, Homenaje a Manuel García Pelayo, Universidad Nacional de Educación a Distancia, Madrid 2009, 289-325.

[4]*Gaceta Oficial* N° 36.859, Dec. 29, 1999.

Constitution demanded; to create the Commission for the Reorganization and Functioning of the Judiciary to take it over, removing judges from office without due process; to appoint the officials of the different branches of government; and to dictate an electoral statute without any constitutional provision supporting it.

None of these reforms was constitutional – they were not approved by the people. Consequently, the transition regime decree was challenged before the Constitutional Chamber on the basis of the violation of the Constitution that the people had recently approved. The result was that the same Constitutional Chamber decided in its own cause, holding that the Constituent Assembly had supraconstitutional power to create constitutional provisions without popular approval and that, as a consequence, in Venezuela there were two transitional constitutional regimes: that contained in the transitory provisions approved by the people and that approved by the Constituent Assembly without popular approval.

In Decision No. 6 (January 27, 2000), the Constitutional Chamber decided that because the transition regime of December 22, 1999, was adopted by the Constituent Assembly prior to publication of the Constitution on December 31, 1999, it was not subject to that Constitution or to the previous Constitution of 1961 still in force.[5] Later, in Decision No. 186 (March 28, 2000) (Case: *Allan R. Brewer-Carías et al.*), when deciding the constitutionality of the electoral statute of the public power adopted by the Constituent Assembly on January 30, 2000,[6] the Constitutional Chamber ratified that to create a new legal order and adopt a new Constitution, the Constituent Assembly had several alternatives for regulating the transitory constitutional regime. First was to incorporate transitory dispositions that would be part of the Constitution to be approved by the people via referendum. Second was to dictate separate acts, of constitutional scope and value, which would create a parallel constitutional transitory regime not approved by the people.[7]

With those decisions, the constitutional judge proceeded to illegitimately interpret and distort the Constitution, violating popular sovereignty, by holding that the Constituent Assembly could dictate constitutional provisions not approved by the people through referendum.

---

[5] See *Revista de Derecho Público* 81, Editorial Jurídica Venezolana, Caracas 2000, 81ff.

[6] See *Gaceta Oficial* N° 36,884, Feb. 3, 2000.

[7] On the illegitimate transitory regime created outside the Constitution, see in Allan R. Brewer-Carías, *Golpe de Estado y Proceso Constituyente en Venezuela*, Universidad Nacional Autónoma de México, México 2002, 345ff.

This began a long period of constitutional instability that, ten years later, has not ended; it is evidenced, for instance, in the survival of judiciary interference. Thus, Venezuela has been under a constitutional transitory regime not approved by the people, by the grace of a constitutional judge who legitimized the usurpation of the popular will.

II. FROM REVOCATION REFERENDA TO RATIFYING REFERENDA

In Venezuela, Article 72 of the Constitution established, as a political right of the people, the revocation of mandates of all popularly elected offices. The recall is required after the midterm for which the official was elected, by popular initiative of no less than 20% of voters registered in the corresponding constituency. The Constitution determined that when equal to or greater than 25% of registered voters vote in the referendum and "a number of electors equal or higher than that of those who elected the official, vote in favor of the revocation," the official's mandate is considered revoked and that void must be covered immediately through a new election.

That is, the necessary votes to revoke a mandate must be equal to or greater than the votes that elected the officer, independent of the number of votes cast against the revocation – the Constitutional Chamber ratified this in several decisions.[8] The Constitution provides for a revocation referendum of popular election mandates, not a ratifying referendum (plebiscite) of mandates. Precisely for that reason, there is nothing in the Constitution regarding the case when a number of electors, greater than the number of votes obtained by the official at the time of election, could vote for no revocation. This could occur but, according to the constitutional text, it would have no effect at all, because the regulation establishes the revocation referendum. To be revoked, it is enough for the votes to revoke to be equal to or greater than those obtained by the official at the time of election.

Nevertheless, clearly in an unconstitutional way, in 2003, when a recall referendum was first called by popular initiative to revoke the president's mandate, the National Electoral Council issued a regulation on the matter.[9]

---

[8] See Decision N° 2750 (Oct. 21, 2003) (Case: *Carlos Enrique Herrera Mendoza, Interpretación del artículo 72 de la Constitución*), Exp. 03-1989; Decision N° 1139 (June 5, 2002) (Case: *Sergio Omar Calderón Duque and William Dávila Barrios*). See *Revista de Derecho Público* 89–92, Editorial Jurídica Venezolana, Caracas 2002, 171. The same criterion was followed in Decision N° 137 (Feb. 13, 2003) (Case: *Freddy Lepage Scribani et al.*) (Exp. 03-0287).

[9] See *Normas para regular los procesos de referendos revocatorios de mandatos de elección popular*, Res. N° 030925-465, Sept. 25, 2003.

That regulation held that even though a mandate is considered revoked, "if the number of votes in favor of the revocation is equal or higher to the number of the electors that vote for the officer," but added a phrase providing that: "the number must not be lower than the number of electors that voted against the revocation" (Article 60), changing the constitutional provisions on the matter. With that addition – in a regulation of sublegal scope – the right of the people to politically participate by revoking popular mandates was restricted, thus disrupting the nature of the referendum regulated by Article 72 of the Constitution and, in evident fraud to the Constitution, turning it into a ratifying referendum of mandates of popular election.

What was without precedent in this constitutional fraud was that the illegitimate constitutional "reform" was endorsed by the Constitutional Chamber of the Supreme Court when it decided a recourse on the abstract interpretation of the Constitution in Decision No. 2750 (October 21, 2003) (Case: *Carlos E. Herrera Mendoza, Interpretación del artículo 72 de la Constitución*) stating:

> It has to do with some kind of re-legitimating the officer and, even, in this democratic process of majorities, *if the option of his permanence obtains more votes in the referendum, he should remain in office*, even if a sufficient number of people vote against him to revoke his mandate.[10]

In this way, the constitutional judge illegitimately distorted the Constitution.[11] Actually, in a revocation referendum, there cannot be votes in favor of the permanence of the official. There can be votes to revoke the mandate and votes not to revoke. The vote not to revoke cannot be turned into a vote to ratify the official. With this distortion, the Constitutional Chamber changed the nature of the revocation referendum, turning it into a vote to relegitimate or ratify mandates of popular election, when that was not the intention of the Constitution. The only issue regulated in Article 72 of the Constitution is the revocation of mandates, and for that, the only thing it demands in regard to the voting process is that "a number of electors equal or higher than that of those who elected the official, vote in favor of the revocation."

---

[10] Exp. 03-1989.

[11] See Allan R. Brewer-Carías, "La Sala Constitucional vs. el derecho ciudadano a la revocatoria de mandatos populares: de cómo un referendo revocatorio fue inconstitucionalmente convertido en un "referendo ratificatorio," in *Crónica sobre la "In" Justicia Constitucional. La Sala Constitucional y el autoritarismo en Venezuela*, Editorial Jurídica Venezolana, Caracas 2007, 349-78.

This illegitimate distortion of the Constitution, nonetheless, had a precise objective: to avoid the revocation of President Hugo Chávez's mandate in 2004. He was elected in August 2000 with 3,757,744 votes – the number of votes to revoke had to surpass that number to revoke his mandate. As the National Electoral Council announced on August 27, 2004, the number of votes to revoke the president's mandate, casted in the referendum of August 15, 2004, was 3,989,008, and so his mandate was constitutionally revoked.

However, the Constitution had already been illegitimately distorted, and regardless of fraud accusations, the National Electoral Council (on August 27, 2004), because more people (5,800,629) voted not to revoke his mandate, decided to ratify the president in his position until the culmination of the constitutional term in January 2007.[12]

III. THE ELIMINATION OF THE CONSTITUTIONAL PRINCIPLE OF ALTERNATE GOVERNMENT AND THE LIMITS TO CONTINUOUS REELECTION

Article 6 of the Constitution establishes the fundamental principles of republican government:

> The government of the Bolivarian Republic of Venezuela and its political entities is and will always be democratic, participative, elective, decentralized, alternate, responsible, pluralist and of revocable mandates.

Consequently, among the fundamental principles of the constitutional system that cannot be modified either by means of constitutional reform or amendment are those principles of government, and with them the

---

[12] In fact, on the Web page of the National Electoral Council, the following appeared on Aug. 27, 2004: "Francisco Carrasquero Lopez, President of the National Electoral Council, addressed the country in national broadcast, to announce the definite and official results of the electoral act that took place on Aug. 15th, which ratified Hugo Rafael Chávez Frías, as President of the Republic with a total of 5 million 800 thousand 629 votes in favor of the option 'NO.' 9 million 815 thousand 631 electors participated in the election, of which 3,989,008 voted in favor of the option 'YES' to revoke the mandate of President Chávez. The total showed that the option 'NO' represented 59.25% of the ballot, while the option 'YES' achieved 40.74% of the grand total, with a 30.02% of non-participation. It must be said that for these elections, the Electoral Registry increased significantly, reaching a universe of 14,027,607 electors with the right to vote in the Revocation Referendum. On this Friday, Aug. 27, based on the expression of the popular will, the National Electoral Council will ratify Hugo Chávez Frías in the Presidency of the Bolivarian Republic of Venezuela, whose constitutional term will culminate in the year 2006." In fact, during a solemn act that took place the same day, the National Electoral Council agreed to ratify the president in his position, despite the fact that a number of electors greater than that which had elected him had voted in favor of revoking his mandate. See *El Nacional*, Caracas Aug. 28, 2004, A-1 and A-2.

principle that the government must be not only democratic but also elective and alternate.

This latter principle was incorporated for the first time in Venezuela's constitutional history as a reaction to the continuation in the exercise of political power, and was based on the very "doctrine of Simón Bolívar," on which the republic is based according to Article 1 of the Constitution:

> There is nothing as dangerous as to allow the long term permanence in office of a single citizen. The people gets used to obeying him and he gets used to rule over them.... [O]ur citizens must fear, with abundant justice, that the same Judge who has ruled them for a long time, rules them forever.[13]

According to this doctrine, which as Bolivarian must be considered part of the values of the constitution itself (Article 1), in Venezuelan constitutionalism, the alternating of government has always meant that people take turns in certain positions or that positions are carried out in terms. As stated by the Electoral Chamber of the Supreme Tribunal of Justice in Decision No. 51 (March 18, 2002), the alternate principle means "the successive exercise of a position by different persons, belonging or not to the same party."[14]

This principle of alternating government was historically conceived to face the desires to remain in power – that is, continuation – and also to avoid the advantages in electoral processes that those occupying positions when being candidates to occupy the same positions could have. The principle of alternating government, thus, is not equivalent to that of elective government. Election is one thing, but the need for people to take turns in office is another. Thus, the principle has always been reflected in the establishment of limits on the reelection of officials, which is common in presidential systems. This is what happened in the Constitutions of 1830, 1858, 1864, 1874, 1881, 1891, 1893, 1901, 1904, 1909, 1936, 1845, and 1947 – they prohibited the reelection of the president of the republic for the immediate constitutional term.[15]

---

[13]See Simón Bolívar, "Discurso de Angostura" (1819), in *Escritos fundamentales*, Monteávila Ediciones, Caracas 1982.

[14]Case *Francisco Caracciolo vs. Consejo Nacional Electoral*. Available at http://www.tsj.gov.ve/decisiones/selec/ Marzo/51-180302-000207.htm.

[15]Actually, in the constitutional history of the country, the prohibition on immediate presidential reelection was eliminated in the constitutions of authoritarian governments: the Constitution of 1857; the Constitutions of Juan Vicente Gómez of 1914, 1922, 1925, 1928, 1929, and 1931; and the Constitution of Marcos Pérez Jiménez of 1953.

This prohibition regarding the president, during the democratic period that began in 1958, was extended in the Constitution of 1961 for the two subsequent terms (ten years). The 1999 Constitution softened that principle to allow for the possibility of immediate presidential reelection, only once, for a new term. That is why President Chávez, after being elected in 1998, and again in 2000 under the new constitutional regime, and being "ratified" in 2004, was reelected in 2006.

The alternation of government, thus, is a principle of constitutionalism that contests continuation or permanence in power by the same person; for that reason, any provision that would allow for permanence or continuation is contrary to it. Thus, the principle cannot be confused with the elective principle of government or the most general democratic principle established by Article 6 of the Constitution. It is one thing to elect government officials, different to the principle of alternation tending to impede the successive election of the same government official.

Thus, it is contrary to the Constitution to interpret – as the Constitutional Chamber did in Decision No. 53 of February 3, 2009[16] – that the principle of alternation "demands that the people, as the holder of sovereignty, have the periodical possibility to choose their government officials or representatives," thus confusing alternate government with elective government. What the Constitutional Chamber stated was wrong in deciding that the principle of alternating "would only be violated" if the possibility of election is impeded. With its decision, once more, the Constitutional Chamber illegitimately distorted the constitutional text. Contrary to what has been said, the elimination of the ineligibility clause derived from the fact of a citizen being currently in the exercise of a public position misrepresents the alternation principle in the exercise of power.[17]

What the Constitutional Chamber decided allowing the possibility of continuous reelection alters the fundamental principle of alternate government, a democratic value that informs Venezuelan juridical order. Because the formula used in Article 6 of the Constitution ("is and always will be"), alternating government cannot be the object of any constitutional reform, and in the event that it could be modified, it could not be modified through constitutional amendment or reform but only through the convening of a Constituent Assembly.

---

[16] See *Revista de Derecho Público* 117, Editorial Jurídica venezolana, Caracas 2009, 205-11.

[17] See Allan R. Brewer-Carías, "El Juez Constitucional vs. La alternabilidad republicana (La reelección continua e indefinida)," in id., 2009, 205-11.

With its decision, the Constitutional Chamber smoothed the road for the referendum that took place a few days later, on February 15, 2009, in which people approved a constitutional amendment project proposed by the National Assembly regarding Articles 160, 162, 174, 192, and 230 of the Constitution. Even though the same proposal was rejected in the 2007 "constitutional reform" referendum, this time, using the procedure for a "constitutional amendment," a modification of the Constitution was approved (2009) in order to establish in Venezuela the possibility of continuous reelection of elective positions, which antagonizes the constitutional republican alternating principle (Article 6), which consequently in this regard resulted as void and ineffective.

IV. LIFTING THE PROHIBITION ON REPEATING REFERENDA FOR CONSTITUTIONAL REVIEW

In the aforementioned Decision No. 53 of February 3, 2009,[18] of the Constitutional Chamber regarding the illegitimate change of alternate government, the chamber also adopted another illegitimate distortion of the Constitution. It loosened the constitutional prohibition on calling for a popular referendum on constitutional reforms that the people had already rejected in the same constitutional term (Article 345).

Article 345 of the Constitution, regarding constitutional reforms, expressly prohibits the submission to the National Assembly during the same constitutional term any initiative for constitutional reform that has already been rejected in referendum. Notwithstanding, the Constitution establishes nothing regarding the effects of the rejection of a "constitutional reform" proposal on the possibility to proceed to submit the same matter again to referendum but through the "constitutional amendment" procedure.

In December 2007, a constitutional-reform proposal sanctioned by the National Assembly – including a provision to allow for the continuous reelection of the president – was rejected by popular vote. Thus, as the populace had already expressed its will on the matter, according to the teleological interpretation of Article 345 of the Constitution, it was not possible to submit the same matter to popular vote again during the same constitutional term. Nonetheless, and notwithstanding popular rejection, in January 2009, the National Assembly took the initiative and approved a

---

[18]See *Revista de Derecho Público* 117, Editorial Jurídica Venezolana, Caracas 2009, 205-211. Also available at http://www.tsj.gov.ve/decisiones/scon/Febrero/53-3209-2009-08-1610.html.

constitutional amendment to modify Article 230 of the Constitution regarding limits to presidential reelection and to modify Articles 160, 162, 174, and 192 regarding reelection of other elective officials. It eliminated all established limits.

Instead of looking at the intent of the constitutional provision establishing the rules for not repeating referenda on the same constitutional issues (Article 345), the Constitutional Chamber, in the aforementioned Decision No. 53 of February 3, 2009,[19] confusing the sense of the prohibition, sustained that the provision established was not directed to fix limits to successive popular votes on the same matter, only to provide limits for the National Assembly to consider reforms initiatives. In that way, they reasoned, the National Assembly could not be asked to twice discuss the same constitutional modifications it had already rejected. Nonetheless, the Constitutional Chamber "forgot" that the constitutional principle aimed to regulate popular expression of will in matters modifying the Constitution and their effects, and not to regulate the debates in the National Assembly, being its purpose to avoid for the people asked, again and again in the same constitutional term about the same constitutional modification once it has already been rejected.

Any way, by admitting the possibility to modify the Constitution in the same constitutional period through an amendment procedure when the matter has been rejected through a reform procedure, as was resolved in Decision No. 53 can be considered another defrauding of the Constitution. The fact is that, in 2007, the National Assembly sanctioned a "constitutional reform" to establish the continuous and indefinite reelection of the president, which the people rejected. In the same constitutional term, in 2009, the same National Assembly sanctioned a proposal for reforming the Constitution for the same purpose, this time through the "constitutional amendment" procedure; it only added to the original proposal – perhaps to try to differentiate both – all the other elected representatives.

The result, then, was that, although the people had rejected the proposal for the continuous and indefinite reelection of the president, the same proposal was submitted to referendum in 2009, again, and was approved. For such purpose, the Constitutional Chamber issued a constitutional interpretation of Article 345 that ignored that citizens cannot be

---

[19]See *Revista de Derecho Público* 117, Editorial Jurídica Venezolana, Caracas 2009, 205-11.

summoned during the same constitutional term, consecutively and without limits, to express their will on the same matter.[20]

V. ILLEGITIMATE TRANSFORMATION OF THE FEDERAL SYSTEM

Article 4 of the 1999 Constitution establishes that the republic "is a decentralized federal State in the terms expressed in this Constitution," wording that as it has been analyzed contradicts the real sense of the constitutional provisions that qualify the state as a "centralized federation."[21] But, despite those limits, and notwithstanding any contradiction, the Constitution expressly distributed some state powers to various public and territorial levels of government – that is, the municipalities, the states, and the national government. Those powers cannot be changed except by means of constitutional reform (Articles 136, 156, 164, 178, and 179).[22]

Specifically, the Constitution provides that the conservation, administration, and use of roads and national highways, as well as of national ports and airports of commercial use, correspond exclusively to the states, which they must exercise in "coordination with the National Power" (Article 164.10).

A general purpose of the rejected 2007 constitutional reform was to change the federal form of the state and the territorial distribution of the competencies established in Articles 156 and 164 of the Constitution, thus centralizing the state even more by concentrating almost all competencies of the public power at the national level. Particularly, one purpose of the reform was to "nationalize" the competency set forth in Article 164.10 of the Constitution, which attributes to the states jurisdiction on the

---

[20] See the comments on the Constitutional Chamber decision in Allan R. Brewer-Carías, "El Juez Constitucional vs. La alternabilidad republicana (La reelección continua e indefinida), en *Revista de Derecho Público* 117, Editorial Jurídica Venezolana, Caracas 2009, 205-11.

[21] See Allan R. Brewer-Carías, *Federalismo y municipalismo en la Constitución de 1999 (Alcance de una reforma insuficiente y regresiva)*, Unversidad católica del Táchira–ditorial Jurídica Venezolana, Caracas–San Cristóbal 2001; "El estado federal descentralizado y la centralización de la federación en Venezuela. Situación y perspectiva de una contradicción constitucional," in *Federalismo y regionalismo*, coord. Diego Valadés and José María Serna de la Garza, Universidad Nacional Autónoma de México, Supreme Court of Justice of the State of Puebla, Instituto de Investigaciones Jurídicas, Mexico City 2005, 717-50.

[22] See Allan R. Brewer-Carías, "Consideraciones sobre el régimen de distribución de competencias del poder público en la Constitución de 1999," in *Estudios de derecho administrativo. Libro homenaje a la Universidad Central de Venezuela, Facultad de Ciencias Jurídicas y Políticas, con ocasión del vigésimo aniversario del Curso de Especialización en Derecho Administrativo*, eds. Fernando Parra Aranguren and Armando Rodríguez García, Tribunal Supremo de Justicia, Caracas 2001, 1:107-36.

conservation, administration, and use of national highways, roads, ports, and airports.[23]

Because the people rejected the constitutional reforms in a December 2007 referendum, Article 164.10 did not change. However, the Constitutional Chamber, in Decision No. 565 (April 15, 2008),[24] deciding an autonomous recourse for abstract constitutional interpretation filed by the attorney general of the republic, ruled to modify the content of that constitutional provision. It held that the exclusive attribution was not exclusive but concurrent – meaning that the national government could also exercise that competency interfering with the states' powers. The attorney general said the provision "was not clear enough to establish, in an efficient and precise way, the scope and performance of the National Executive, regarding the coordination with the States about the administration, conservation and use of national roads and highways, as well as ports and airports of commercial use." The Constitutional Chamber decided, accordingly, that the National Public Administration, "in exercise of its coordination authority, can directly assume the conservation, administration and use of the national roads and highways, as well as all ports and airports of commercial use" and that it corresponds to the national executive (the president and cabinet ministers) to decree such intervention and assume the rendering of services and assets when considered deficient or inexistent.

With that interpretation, the chamber illegitimately modified the Constitution usurping popular sovereignty and changed the federal form of the state by misrepresenting the territorial distribution system of powers between the national power and the states. Particularly, it nationalized what the Constitution expressly established as attributions that are exclusive to the states. As a result, the Constitutional Chamber "reformed" the Constitution and eliminated the exclusive competency of the states in that matter. By turning the competency into a concurrent one, being subjected to possible decentralization, it also can be reverted to the

---

[23]See Allan R. Brewer-Carías, *Hacia la consolidación de un estado socialista, centralizado, policial y militarista. Comentarios sobre el sentido y alcance de las propuestas de reforma constitucional 2007*, Editorial Jurídica Venezolana, Caracas 2007, 41ff.; and *La Reforma Constitucional de 2007 (Comentarios al proyecto inconstitucionalmente sancionado por la Asamblea Nacional el 2 de noviembre de 2007)*, Editorial Jurídica Venezolana, Caracas 2007, 72ff.

[24]See Decision N° 565 of the Constitutional Chamber (Apr. 15, 2008) (Case: *Procurador General de la república, Interpretación del artículo 164.10 de la Constitución*), available at http://www.tsj.gov.ve/decisio-nes/scon/Abril/565-150408-07-1108.htm.

national government.²⁵ The chamber held: "it corresponds to the National Executive, to decree the intervention in order to assume the rendering of services and assets of national roads and highways, as well as ports and airports of commercial use, in those cases where, even though said competencies had been transferred, the rendering of the service, either by the States, is deficient or inexistent." ²⁶

This judicial made illegitimate constitutional modification, as warned by the same Constitutional Chamber, generated the need for a "revision and modification of great scope and magnitude of the current legal system," leading the Chamber to warn the National Assembly to "proceed to the revision and corresponding modification of the legal provisions related to the obligatory interpretation established in this decision, and to sanction statutes congruent with the constitutional principles derived from the interpretation established by this Chamber in exercise of its competencies."²⁷ That is, the chamber forced the legislator to issue legislation against the provisions of the 1999 Constitution and in line with the illegitimate constitutional modification imposed. So, after the electoral triumph of opposition governors and mayors in key states and municipalities in the elections of December 2008, the National Assembly, in March 2009, diligently reformed the Organic Law for Decentralization,²⁸ to eliminate the exclusive attribution to the states of those powers established in Articles 11.3 and 11.5 of said Law. It added, according to the illegitimate Constitutional Chamber Decision, two new provisions allowing the national executive to "revert, for strategic reasons, of merit, opportunity or convenience, the transfer of attributions to the States, for the conservation, administration and use of assets and services considered to be of general public interest" (Article 8); and to decree the intervention of the said assets and rendering of public services transferred to ensure users and consumers quality service (Article 9). With this, the National Assembly completed the defrauding of the Constitution that the

---

[25] See the comments on the Constitutional Chamber decision in Allan R. Brewer-Carías, "La ilegitima mutación de la Constitución y la legitimidad de la jurisdicción constitucional: la "reforma" de la forma federal del Estado en Venezuela mediante interpretación constitucional," in *Memoria del X Congreso Iberoamericano de Derecho Constitucional,* Instituto Iberoamericano de Derecho Constitucional, Asociación Peruana de Derecho Constitucional, Instituto de Investigaciones Jurídicas-UNAM y Maestría en Derecho Constitucional-PUCP, IDEMSA, Lima 2009, 1:29-51

[26] See Decision N° 565 of the Constitutional Chamber (Apr. 15, 2008) (Case: *Procurador General de la República, Interpretación del artículo 164.10 de la Constitución),* available at http://www.tsj.gov.ve/decisio-nes/scon/Abril/565-150408-07-1108.htm.

[27] Id.

[28] *Gaceta Oficial* N° 39 140, Mar. 17, 2009.

Constitutional Chamber had started – a constitutionally assigned exclusive attribution became a concurrent one.

VI. THE LIFTING OF THE PROHIBITION ON GOVERNMENT FINANCING OF ELECTORAL ACTIVITIES

Article 67 of the Constitution of 1999 expressly established that "the financing of political associations with Government funds will not be allowed," a provision that was an emphatic, radical change from the previous regime of public financing of political parties, established in Article 230 of the Organic Law of Suffrage and Political Participation of 1998. That law sought to establish greater balance and impartiality for parties' participation in democratic life and, especially, in electoral campaigns, in an attempt to mitigate any imbalances or perversions resulting from only private financing (e.g., possible drug financing) and the possible indirect, irregular, corrupt public financing.[29] The constitutional prohibition, by derogating such article of the organic law, eliminated any public funding of political parties, abandoning the technique that predominates in comparative law.[30]

This express constitutional prohibition regarding public financing of political parties was also one of the matters referred to in the 2007 constitutional reform,[31] which proposed modification of Article 67 by providing that "the State…. be able to finance electoral activities." As already mentioned, the constitutional reform was rejected by popular vote in referendum on December 2, 2007, with which the governmental financing of political parties regarding their electoral activities continued to be prohibited in the Constitution.

However, despite those constitutional prohibitions and the popular rejection of its modification, the Constitutional Chamber of the Supreme Court of Justice, in Decision No. 780 (May 8, 2008)[32] by means of

---

[29]See Allan R. Brewer-Carías, "Consideraciones sobre el financiamiento de los partidos políticos en Venezuela," in *Financiamiento y democratización interna de partidos políticos. Memoria del IV Curso Anual Interamericano de Elecciones,* San José, Costa Rica, 1991, 121-39.

[30]See Allan R. Brewer-Carías, "Regulación jurídica de los partidos políticos en Venezuela," in *Estudios sobre el estado constitucional (2005-2006)*, Cuadernos de la Cátedra Fundacional Allan R. Brewer Carías de Derecho Público N° 9, Universidad Católica del Táchira, Editorial Jurídica Venezolana, Caracas 2007, 655-86.

[31]See *Proyecto de Exposición de Motivos para la Reforma Constitucional, Presidencia de la República, Proyecto Reforma Constitucional. Propuesta del presidente Hugo Chávez Agosto 2007,* Editorial Atenea, Caracas 2007, 19.

[32]File N° 06-0785. See *Revista de Derecho Público* 114, Editorial Jurídica Venezolana, Caracas 2008, 127ff.

constitutional interpretation, has illegitimately distorted the Constitution. It has substituted itself for the popular will and the original constitutional power in holding that, "regarding the scope of the prohibition of public financing of political associations," the norm only "limits the possibility to provide resources for the internal expenses of the different forms of political associations, but…said limitation, is not extensive to the electoral campaign, as a fundamental stage of the electoral process."

That is, the Constitutional Chamber, facing a clear though censurable constitutional provision in Article 67 of the Constitution, usurped the constituent power, substituting itself for the people. It ruled to reform the provision in the same way that of the constitutional-reform draft that was rejected by the people in the December 2007 referendum, expressly allowing governmental financing of the electoral activities of the political parties and associations – the opposite of what is provided for in the Constitution.[33]

Therefore, the constitutional judge decided simply that the Constitution does not say what it actually says but the opposite. That when the Constitution says that "the financing of political associations with Government funds will not be allowed," the Constitution actually means to prohibit only "financing of current and internal expenses of the political associations with resources coming from the State"; thus, expenses of electoral campaigns can be financed with funds from the state.

The absurd conclusion, against any democratic logic, derives from the false premise that, supposedly, in democratic systems, the state can finance current and internal expenses of the parties. This is not conceived of in democracies, and so it does not require any prohibition. In democracies, the operations of parties are financed but always with a view to electoral campaigns. That financing is withdrawn if parties do not obtain a certain percentage of votes in the elections.

The result of this Supreme Tribunal Decision is that through it, the constitutional judge has reformed the Constitution, usurped the original constituent power of the people, and went against the people's express wish in the December 2007 referendum rejecting state electoral financing.

---

[33] See the comments on the Constitutional Chamber decision in Allan R. Brewer-Carías, "El juez constitucional como constituyente: el caso del financiamiento de las campañas electorales de los partidos políticos en Venezuela," in *Revista de Derecho Público* 117, Editorial Jurídica Venezolana, Caracas 2009, 195-203.

VII. THE ILLEGITIMATE ELIMINATION OF THE SUPRACONSTITUTIONAL RANK OF INTERNATIONAL HUMAN RIGHTS TREATIES

A contemporary universal trend has allowed constitutional courts to directly apply international treaties for the protection of human rights, thus progressively widening the scope for their protection. For such purpose, contemporary constitutions have progressively recognized the normative scope of those treaties, assigning them, regarding internal law, supraconstitutional, constitutional, supralegal, and legal rank.[34]

Article 23 of Venezuela's 1999 Constitution expressly sets forth the following:

> Treaties, pacts and conventions regarding human rights, subscribed and ratified by Venezuela, have constitutional rank and prevail in the internal order, as long as they contain norms about their enjoyment and exercise, more favorable than those established in this Constitution and in the laws of the Republic, and are to be direct and immediately applicable, by the courts and other bodies of the State.

Without a doubt, this article and the norms it expresses are among the most important in matters of human rights in the country. The formulation is unique in Latin America because it grants international human rights treaties, not only constitutional rank but also supraconstitutional rank; that is, they rank superior to the Constitution itself in the case that they contain more favorable regulations. The article also establishes the direct and immediate application of treaties by the courts and other authorities of the country. This provision of the Constitution was, without a doubt, a significant advance in constructing the human rights protection framework, which the courts have applied, for instance, in declaring that the American Convention on Human Rights prevails over certain legal and constitutional provisions.

---

[34]On this general classification, see Rodolfo E. Piza R., *Derecho internacional de los derechos humanos: La Convención Americana*, San José, Costa Rica, 1989; Carlos Ayala Corao, "La jerarquía de los instrumentos internacionales sobre derechos humanos," in *El nuevo derecho constitucional latinoamericano*, vol. 2, IV Congreso Venezolano de Derecho Constitucional, Caracas 1996; *La jerarquía constitucional de los tratados sobre derechos humanos y sus consecuencias*, Ed. Porrúa, Mexico City, 2003; Humberto Henderson, "Los tratados internacionales de derechos humanos en el orden interno: La importancia del principio pro homine," in *Revista IIDH* 39, Instituto Interamericano de Derechos Humanos, San José, Costa Rica, 2004, 71ff. See also Allan R. Brewer-Carías, *Mecanismos nacionales de protección de los derechos humanos*, Instituto Internacional de Derechos Humanos, San José, Costa Rica, 2004, 62ff.

For example, the right to appeal before a second judicial instance invoked before the contentious administrative jurisdiction was been excluded in the former 1976 Organic Law of the Supreme Court of Justice. The Constitution of 1999 establishes a constitutional right to appeal only in matters of criminal procedures in favor of the person declared guilty (Article 40.1). So, in contentious administrative suit, there was no express constitutional guarantee of appeal and, therefore, the decisions of the First Court of Contentious Administrative matters were not appealable. Nonetheless, the content of Article 23 of the Constitution finally led the Constitutional Chamber of the Supreme Tribunal to rule in 2000 on the prevailing application of the American Convention on Human Rights, considering:

> That article 8.1 and 8.2.h of the American Convention on Human Rights, are part of the Venezuelan constitutional order; that its dispositions, containing the right to appeal judicial decision, are more favorable, concerning the benefit and exercise of said right, than that foreseen in article 49,1 of said Constitution; and that are of immediate and direct application by the courts and other State bodies.[35]

However, in Decision No. 1,939 (December 18, 2008) (Case: *Gustavo Álvarez Arias et al.*),[36] by declaring unenforceable a decision of the Inter-American Court of Human Rights of August 5, 2008 – the case of former judges of the First Court on Contentious Administrative matters (*Apitz Barbera et al. vs. Venezuela, First Court on Contentious Administrative*),[37] the Constitutional Chamber definitely resolved that Article 23:

> does not grant supraconstitutional rank to international treaties on human rights, thus, in case of antinomy or contradiction between one disposition of the Constitution and a provision of an international pact, it would correspond to the Judicial Power to determine which would be applicable, considering both what is established in the referred provision, and in the jurisprudence of this Constitutional Chamber of the Supreme Court of Justice, paying attention to the content of articles 7, 266.6, 334, 335, 336.11 *ejusdem* and to Decision No. 1.077/2000 of this Chamber.[38]

---

[35] Decision N° 87 (Mar. 13, 2000) (Case: *C.A. Electricidad del Centro (Elecentro) y otra vs. Superintendencia para la Promoción y Protección de la Libre Competencia (Procompetencia)*, in Revista de Derecho Público 81, Editorial Jurídica Venezolana, Caracas 2000, 157ff.

[36] See http://www.tsj.gov.ve/decisiones/scon/Diciembre/1939-181208-2008-08-1572.html.

[37] See www.corteidh.or.cr. Excepción Preliminar, Fondo, Reparaciones y Costas, Serie C, N° 182.

[38] See at http://www.tsj.gov.ve/decisiones/scon/Diciembre/1939-181208-2008-08-1572.html.

To base this Decision rejecting superior values that could not be modifiable by any political project, the chamber clarified, "that law is a normative theory at the service of politics that underlines behind the axiological project of the Constitution," adding that "the standards to resolve the conflict between the principles and the provisions have to be compatible with the political project of the Constitution (Democratic and Social State of Law and Justice) and cannot affect the force of said project with ideological interpretative elections that privilege individual rights decisively, or that welcome the supremacy of the international judicial order over national law at the sacrifice of the sovereignty of the State."[39]

The Constitutional Chamber concluded in its Decision No. 1,939 (December 18, 2008) by declaring that "a system of principles, supposedly absolute and supra-historic, cannot be above the Constitution" and that the theories that pretend to limit "under the pretext of universal legalities, the sovereignty and the national auto-determination" are unacceptable;[40] quoting in support another of its decisions (Decision N° 1265/2008) in which the Chamber considered "that when a contradiction is evidenced between the Constitution and an international convention or treaty, "the constitutional provision that privilege the general interest and the common well-being must prevail, applying the dispositions that privilege the collective interests ... over particular interests."[41]

With this decision, the Constitutional Chamber illegitimately distorted the Constitution, reforming Article 23 of the Constitution by eliminating the supraconstitutional rank of the American Convention on Human Rights in cases where that document contains more favorable provisions for the benefit and exercise of human rights than the Constitution.[42]

Moreover, the matter decided by the Constitutional Chamber also was one of the express reform proposals made in 2007 by the Presidential Council for the Constitutional Reform.[43] Regarding Article 23, the intention of the proposal was to completely eliminate the constitutional

---

[39] Id.

[40] See http://www.tsj.gov.ve/decisiones/scon/Diciembre/1939-181208-2008-08-1572.html.

[41] Quoted in http://www.tsj.gov.ve/decisiones/scon/Diciembre/1939-181208-2008-08-1572.html.

[42] See the comments on the Constitutional Chamber Decision N° 1,939/2008 in Allan R. Brewer-Carías, "La interrelación entre los Tribunales Constitucionales de America Latina y la Corte Interamericana de Derechos Humanos, y la cuestión de la inejecutabilidad de sus decisiones en Venezuela," in *Gaceta Constitucional. Análisis multidisciplinario de la jurisprudencia del Tribunal Constitucional*, Gaceta Jurídica, Tomo 16 Año 2009, Lima 2009, 17-48.

[43] See the comments on the draft in Allan R. Brewer-Carías, *Hacia la consolidación de un estado socialista, centralizado, policial y militarista. Comentarios sobre el sentido y alcance de las propuestas de reforma constitucional 2007*, Editorial Jurídica Venezolana, Caracas 2007, 122ff.

hierarchy of the provisions of international human rights treaties, and their prevalence over the internal order, by reformulating Article 23 as follows: "treaties, pacts and conventions related to human rights, subscribed and ratified by Venezuela, as long as they remain current, are part of the internal order, and are of immediate and direct application by the bodies of the public power."

This proposal for constitutional reform formulated by the presidential commission in 2007 was a hard blow to the progressiveness in protecting the rights established in Article 19 of the Constitution, which does not allow for regressions in their protection. However, what the authoritarian regime was not able to accomplish through constitutional reform, the Constitutional Chamber of the Supreme Court carried out through constitutional interpretation.

VIII. THE ELIMINATION OF JUDGES' POWER TO IMMEDIATELY AND DIRECTLY APPLY INTERNATIONAL HUMAN RIGHTS TREATIES

In matters of human rights, Article 23 of the Constitution, after granting supraconstitutional rank to the provisions of international treaties, pacts, and conventions on human rights, "as long as they contain provisions more favorable to their enjoyment and exercise," it also expressly declares that those instruments are "of direct and immediate application by the courts and other bodies of the State."

Regarding that provision, the Constitutional Chamber, reaffirming its role as maximum and ultimate interpreter of the Constitution and treaties on human rights, established in Decision No. 1492 (July 15, 2003) (Case: *Impugnación de diversos artículos del Código Penal*) that, because those treaties have constitutional rank, the Constitutional Chamber itself is the only body capable of interpreting them, determining which of their provisions prevail in the internal legal order, and deciding which human rights not contemplated in those international instruments have force in Venezuela.[44] With this unconstitutional decision, the Constitutional Chamber again illegitimately distorted the Constitution. According to Article 23, not only the Constitutional Chamber but also all courts of the republic, have those powers when acting as constitutional judges, for instance, when declaring the unconstitutionality of a statute (diffused judicial review) or when deciding *amparo* cases proceeding. The intent of the Constitutional Chamber to concentrate all constitutional justice

---

[44]See *Revista de Derecho Público* 93–96, Editorial Jurídica Venezolana, Caracas 2003, 135ff.

Chapter 15

THE ALTERNATE PRINCIPLE OF GOVERNMENT AND THE 2009 CONSTITUTIONAL AMENDMENT ON CONTINUOUS REELECTION

One of the main reform proposals contained in the 2007 rejected constitutional reform was the one seeking to establish the continuous and indefinite reelection of the president of the republic, eliminating the restrictions established in the 1999 Constitution.

Nonetheless, and despite the popular rejection of the reform, the matter continued to be proposed and eventually was the object of a constitutional amendment approved by the National Assembly, submitted to a referendum held on February 15, 2009. The result was the popular approval of the constitutional amendment, which changed the traditional principle of the alternate character of the democratic government of Venezuelan constitutionalism, allowing the continuous and indefinite reelection not only of the president but also of all elected public officials. This constitutional amendment defrauded the prohibition established in the Constitution to submit to popular vote the same constitutional reform proposal during the same constitutional term and, in addition, violated the Constitution by eliminating one of the unchangeable constitutional principles as it was the alternation in government.[1]

---

[1] The president considered this constitutional amendment "vital for the Revolution" (in his weekly program *Aló President*, Jan. 11, 2009), but in reality, it modified a vital principle for the future of democracy.

I. THE REPUBLICAN PRINCIPLE OF ALTERNATE GOVERNMENT AND THE VENEZUELAN TRADITION OF NO REELECTION

In effect, the general restriction on elected officials' continuous reelection has been a tradition of Venezuela's constitutional history – since Venezuela adopted the presidential system of government in 1811, as occurred in all Latin America countries.[2]

The restriction on presidential reelection was first established in the 1830 Constitution as a reaction to continuity in office (*continuísmo*), precisely to confront individuals' desire to perpetuate themselves in power and to avoid the advantages that public officials might have in electoral processes.

Simón Bolívar clearly expressed his thoughts against continuity in power in his famous Angostura speech (1819):

> The continuation of the authority in the same individual has frequently been the end of democratic governments. Repeated elections are essentials in popular systems, because nothing is more dangerous than to leave for a long term the same citizen in power. The people get used to obey him, and he gets used to command them; from where usurpation and tyranny is originated…. Our citizens must fear with more than enough justice that the same Official, who has governed them for a long time, could perpetually command them.[3]

In Venezuela, this principle of limiting the term of elected officials imposing the need for changing the head of elected public offices is called the principle of *alternabilidad*, from the Latin word *alternatium*, which means "interchangeably" or "by turns." This principle of alternate government refers to the idea that elected public offices must be occupied by turns, not continuously by the same elected person. It is in that sense that the Electoral Chamber of the Supreme Tribunal of Justice of

---

[2] Restrictions to presidential reelection are traditional in the presidential system of government, not in the parliamentary system of government mainly followed in Europe. See Allan R. Brewer-Carías, *Reflexiones sobre la Revolución norteamericana (1776), la Revolución francesa (1789) y la Revolución hispanoamericana (1810-1830) y sus aportes al constitucionalismo moderno*, Universidad Externado de Colombia, Bogotá 2008, 106ff.

[3] "La continuación de la autoridad en un mismo individuo frecuentemente ha sido el término de los gobiernos democráticos. Las repetidas elecciones son esenciales en los sistemas populares, porque nada es tan peligroso como dejar permanecer largo tiempo en un mismo ciudadano el poder. El pueblo se acostumbra a obedecerle y él se acostumbra a mandarlo; de donde se origina la usurpación y la tiranía…nuestros ciudadanos deben temer con sobrada justicia que el mismo Magistrado, que los ha mandado mucho tiempo, los mande perpetuamente." See Simón Bolívar, *Escritos fundamentales*, Monteávila Ed., Caracas 1982.

Venezuela, in Decision No. 51 (March 18, 2002) ruled that *alternabilidad* means "the successive exercise of public offices by different persons."[4] The principle is not the same as the "elective" principle or election to public office. To be elected is one thing; it is another to occupy public offices by turns.

The principle has always been established as an immutable constitutional clause (*cláusula pétrea*) that must never be changed. Article 6 of the Constitution establishes that the government of the Republic and of its political entities *"is and will always be"* alternate, as well as "democratic, participatory, elective, decentralized, responsible, plural and of recall mandates" (Article 5), which means that the principle cannot be changed.

Regarding the president of the republic, the principle has been included in almost all the Venezuelan constitutions since 1830 (1830, 1858, 1864, 1874, 1881, 1891, 1893, 1901, 1904, 1909, 1936, 1845, and 1947),[5] by establishing a general prohibition for the immediate reelection of the president for the subsequent term. In the 1961 Constitution, the prohibition on reelection was extended up to two terms (ten years), and in the 1999 Constitution, that provision was made more flexible by establishing for the first time in more than a century the possibility for the immediate reelection of the president, but only once and in the subsequent term (Article 230).

In Venezuelan history, the only constitutions not prohibiting presidential reelection were the short-lived 1857 Constitution, the authoritarian constitutions of the period of Juan Vicente Gómez (1914–33), and the 1953 Constitution of Marcos Pérez Jiménez – both military dictators of the previous century. Now, in the twenty-first century, Hugo Chávez Frías proposed the same, having been the object of the amendment to the 1999 Constitution approved by referendum in February 2009.

On the other hand, Venezuelan history shows that each time the principle of no reelection has been changed through disputed constitutional reforms, the outcome has been a political crisis ending in overthrow of the government. It occurred in 1858 with the continuation attempt of President José Tadeo Monagas, who after reforming the

---

[4]Quoted in the dissenting vote to the Constitutional Chamber of the Supreme Tribunal of Justice, Decision N° 53 (Feb. 2, 2009) (Case: *Interpretation of Articles 340.6 and 345 of the Constitution*), http://www.tsj.gov.ve/decisions/scon/Febrero/53-3209-2009-08-1610.html.

[5]For text of all the Constitutions, see Allan R. Brewer-Carías, *Las Constituciones de Venezuela*, Academia de Ciencias Políticas y Sociales, Caracas 2008, 709-1341.

Constitution in 1857, was ousted a few months later by the Julián Castro March Revolution. It happened in 1891, when President Raimundo Andueza Palacios reformed the Constitution to allow for his reelection – he was overthrown the following year by the Joaquin Crespo Legalist Revolution. It also occurred, although in another context, in 1945, with the constitutional reform promoted by President Isaías Medina Angarita that failed to establish direct presidential election, thus allowing for the continuation of indirect presidential election of government candidates by Congress, a fact that contributed to the 1945 October Revolution. Finally, it occurred in 1957, when Marcos Pérez Jiménez convened a referendum (plebiscite) to approve his own reelection, which led in the next year to the Democratic Revolution of 1958.[6] This shows that countries do not always follow the lessons of history, and frequently the result is the unwanted repetition of similar facts.

In any case, the restriction established in the 1999 Constitution for the reelection of the president (Article 230) and similar provisions establishing reelection restrictions for governors, mayors, and representatives to the National Assembly and state legislative councils (Articles 160, 162, 174, 192) were proposed by the National Assembly to be changed through constitutional amendment, which the Venezuelan people approved in the February 2009 referendum.

II. THE LIMITS IMPOSED BY THE CONSTITUTION ON CONSTITUTIONAL REVIEW

The 1999 Constitution establishes three institutional mechanisms for constitutional review, distinguishable according to the importance and magnitude of the changes proposed: constitutional amendment, constitutional reform, and constituent assembly. The constitutional amendment procedure is established to add or modify one or more provisions to the Constitution without altering its fundamental structure (Article 340); constitutional reforms are designed for partial revisions of the Constitution and for the substitution of one or several provisions, but without modifying its structure and fundamental principles (Article 342). Both procedures need to be approved by referendum and cannot be used to change fundamental constitutional principles or the structure of the Constitution. Only through a national constituent assembly can the

---

[6]See Allan R. Brewer-Carías, *Historia constitucional de Venezuela*, Editorial Alfa, Caracas 2008, 2:9-31.

Constitution be reviewed to "transform the State, to create a new legal order, and to write a new Constitution" (Articles 347).

The Constitution establishes the effects of popular rejection of a constitutional reform, in the sense that a similar proposal cannot be filed again as another "constitutional reform" before the National Assembly in the remainder of the constitutional term (Article 345). Nothing is expressly established in the Constitution on the effects of the rejection of constitutional amendments, and nothing is established on the possibility to file the same rejected constitutional reform proposal through constitutional amendment, as occurred in 2009.

This provision needed to be interpreted in order to determine the intent of the constituent assembly for the inclusion of the constitutional limit to the possibility of repeatedly asking for the direct expression of the will of the people by referenda. That is, once the people have expressed their popular will in referendum, it is not possible to ask the people, again and again, without limits, on the same matters in the same constitutional term.

The matter of the continuous presidential reelection, as aforementioned, had been already proposed through the draft constitutional reform formulated by the president in 2007 and rejected by the people in the referendum on December 2007.[7] Nonetheless, at the suggestion of the president one year later, the National Assembly voted on January 15, 2009, to modify the Constitution, this time through constitutional amendment, initially intended to establish the possibility of indefinite and continuous reelection of the president, which was later extended to all elected public offices.[8]

---

[7] See Allan R. Brewer-Carías, *La reforma constitucional de 2007 (Comentarios al proyecto inconstitucionalmente sancionado por la Asamblea Nacional el 2 de noviembre de 2007)*, Editorial Jurídica Venezolana, Caracas 2007, 62ff.

[8] One constitutional implication of the Feb. 15 referendum remained unsolved. The question approved in referendum, in fact, was "Do you approve of the amendment of Articles 160, 162, 174, 192, and 230 of the Constitution of the Republic prepared by initiative of the National Assembly, which extends the political rights of the people to allow any citizen in exercise of a public office by popular election to become a candidate to the same office for the constitutionally established term, his or her election depending exclusively from the popular vote?" As the amendment aimed to eliminate restrictions on reelection of all elected public officials and representatives, it is is not clear why the question submitted to referendum did not clearly state this or use the words *reelection, indefinite*, or *continuous reelection*. However, according to the Constitution, any approved constitutional amendment must be published as a continuation of the Constitution without altering the original text – amended articles carry a footnote referring to the number and date of their amendment. With the question as formulated, the result was to eliminate the limits imposed in Articles 162 and 192 of the Constitution on representatives to the state legislative councils and the National Assembly (reelection only for up to two terms) and in Articles 160, 174, and 230 on the president, the governors, and municipal mayors (reelection only once for an immediate new term). In the publication of the

III. THE BINDING CONSTITUTIONAL INTERPRETATION

Two questions with constitutional implication result from the amendment proposal and were the object of endless constitutional discussions and legal contention in the country. First is the possibility of using a constitutional amendment procedure through which no fundamental constitutional principle can be changed, to alter and change the principle of *alternabilidad* of the government, a fundamental republican principle formulated in Article 6 of the Constitution. Second is the possibility of using the constitutional amendment to effect the continuous election of the president, thus changing the limits imposed in the Constitution (reelection only once and in the subsequent period), a proposal already submitted to referendum in December 2007 and rejected by the people.

It was on these matters that the Constitutional Chamber of the Supreme Tribunal of Justice issued on February 3, 2009, two decisions (Decisions Nos. 46 and 53),[9] which established a binding interpretation of the Constitution.

First, on the possibility of submitting to popular vote a modification of the Constitution via constitutional amendment on the same matter already rejected by referendum, the Constitutional Chamber argued that the limit imposed in the Constitution was directed only to the National Assembly to discuss again a constitutional reform on the same subject once rejected by the people, without considering the substantive aspect of the prohibition regarding the limits to ask the people to express again, and endlessly, their will through referenda.

Second, on the possibility of using the constitutional amendment to change the fundamental principle of *alternabilidad* in government, the Constitutional Chamber said that the principle of *alternabilidad* imposes "for the people as sovereign to have the possibility to periodically elect their representatives," confusing alternate government (*gobierno alternativo*) with elective government (*gobierno electivo*). According to the Chamber decision, confusing the terms, the principle of alternate

---

Constitution, after the constitutional amendment was approved, the text of the articles was changed, including in all of them the expression that the officer "can be reelected." See *Gaceta Oficial* N° 5,908 Extra. of Feb. 19, 2009.

[9] See the Constitutional Chamber of the Supreme Tribunal of Justice, Decision N° 53 (Feb. 3, 2009) (Case: *Interpretación de los artículos 340,6 y 345 de la Constitución* Case), http://www.tsj.gov.ve/decisions/scon/Febrero/53-3209-2009-08-1610.html. On that decision, see Allan R. Brewer-Carías, "El Juez Constitucional vs. La alternabilidad republicana (La reelección continua e indefinida), in *Revista de Derecho Público* 117, Editorial Jurídica Venezolana, Caracas 2009, 205-11

government (*gobierno alternative*) can be infringed only if the possibility of having elections (*gobierno electivo*) is impeded.

With those decisions, the Supreme Tribunal resolved the constitutional challenges to the February referendum and, through constitutional interpretation, modified the text of the Constitution.

FINAL REFLECTIONS

THE RIGHT TO DEMOCRACY AND ITS VIOLATION BY VENEZUELA'S AUTHORITARIAN GOVERNMENT: SOME RELEVANT FACTS FROM THE PAST DECADE

I. REPRESENTATIVE DEMOCRACY AND THE VENEZUELAN AUTHORITARIAN GOVERNMENT

The Inter-American Democratic Charter of September 11, 2001,[1] recognized democracy as a right of the peoples of the Americas, with the consequent obligations of Latin American governments to promote and defend it as essential to their social, political, and economic development. Democracy, in this context, is indispensable to the effective exercise of fundamental freedoms and human rights in their universality, indivisibility, and interdependence, embodied in the national constitutions and in international human rights instruments (Article 7).

The charter considered the effective exercise of representative democracy as the basis for the rule of law, enumerating its essential elements as follows: respect for human rights and fundamental freedoms; access to and the exercise of power in accordance with the rule of law; the holding of periodic, free, and fair elections based on secret balloting and universal suffrage as an expression of the sovereignty of the people; a pluralistic system of political parties and organizations; and separation of powers and independence of the branches of government (Article 3). In addition, Article 4 of the charter enumerated the following essential components of the exercise of democracy: transparency in government activities, probity and

---

[1] See http://www.oas.org/charter/docs/resolution1_en_p4.htm.

responsible public administration, respect for social rights, and freedom of expression and of the press (Article 4). Furthermore, the charter considered equally essential to democracy the constitutional subordination of all state institutions to the legally constituted civilian authority and respect for the rule of law on the part of all institutions and sectors of society.

Regarding political parties and other political organizations, their strengthening is considered a priority for democracy (Article 5), which highlights the special attention that must be paid to the problems associated with the high cost of electoral campaigns and the establishment of a balanced and transparent system for their financing.

Finally, regarding participation, Article 6 of the charter declared it a right and responsibility of all citizens to participate in decisions relating to their own development in order to promote and foster diverse forms of participation, a necessary condition for the full and effective exercise of democracy.

The general importance of these provisions of the Inter-American Democratic Charter is that they impose a standard of conduct on all Latin American states to preserve democracy, understanding democracy as a system not only in which elections are held but also in which all the aforementioned essential elements and components of democracy are enforced. Consequently, the violation of the charter occurs when a coup d'état is carried out against the constituted organs of a state and when the constituted organs of the state violate the essential elements and components of representative democracy, as when they use them fraudulently. This is what has been happening with the progressive configuration of a new model of an authoritarian state in Venezuela of a supposed "popular power." Despite the elective origin of its government and its camouflage of "constitutional" forms, the model has been designed precisely to destroy representative democracy itself.[2]

All the aforementioned essential elements and components of democracy have been ignored or fractured in Venezuela, thereby dismantling representative democracy in the name of a participatory democracy. The

---

[2] See Allan R. Brewer-Carías, "Constitution Making in Defraudation of the Constitution and Authoritarian Government in Defraudation of Democracy: The Recent Venezuelan Experience," in *Lateinamerika Analysen* 19, German Institute of Global and Area Studies, Institute of Latin American Studies, Hamburg 2008, 119-42; "El autoritarismo establecido en fraude a la Constitución y a la democracia y su formalización en Venezuela mediante la reforma constitucional (De cómo en un país democrático se ha utilizado el sistema eleccionario para minar la democracia y establecer un régimen autoritario de supuesta 'dictadura de la democracia' que se pretende regularizar mediante la reforma constitucional)," in *Temas constitucionales. Planteamientos ante una reforma*, Fundación de Estudios de Derecho Administrativo, Caracas 2007, 13-74.

result is that in the past decade, there have been more violations of human rights than ever before, as confirmed by the numerous petitions that have been filed before the Inter-American Commission on Human Rights and the numerous decisions of the Inter-American Court of Human Rights condemning the Republic of Venezuela.[3] The access to power in many instances has been achieved contrary to the provisions established in the Constitution, as that for appointing heads of the judicial, citizens', and electoral branches of government.[4]

The basic rule of representative democracy by means of elections has also been violated through the creation of communal councils, which substitute electoral representation with citizens' assemblies and councils whose members are not elected but rather appointed by citizens' assemblies that are controlled by the national executive.[5] The plural regime of parties has been destroyed, and the government has created the official "Marxist" *Partido Socialista Unido de Venezuela* (PSUV) (United Socialist Party of Venezuela),[6] using public funds, directly controlled by the president, which functions in a completely imbricate way with the state apparatus. In such a party, public employees are forced to be registered as members. Consequently, because everything depends on the oil income of the

---

[3] See http://www.corteidh.or.cr/buscar.cfm?clave=casos%20venezuela.

[4] See Allan R. Brewer-Carías, "El secuestro del poder electoral y la confiscación del derecho a la participación política mediante el referendo revocatorio presidencial: Venezuela 2000-2004," *Revista Jurídica del Perú* 54, Lima 2004, 353-96; "El secuestro del poder electoral y de la Sala Electoral del Tribunal Supremo y la confiscación del derecho a la participación política mediante el referendo revocatorio presidencial: Venezuela: 2000-2004," *Revista Costarricense de Derecho Constitucional* 5, Instituto Costarricense de Derecho Constitucional, Editorial Investigaciones Jurídicas S.A., San José 2004, 167-312; "El secuestro de la Sala Electoral por la Sala Constitucional del Tribunal Supremo de Justicia, in *La Guerra de las Salas del TSJ frente al Referendum Revocatorio*," Editorial Aequitas, Caracas 2004, 13-58; "El secuestro del poder electoral y la confiscación del derecho a la participación política mediante el referendo revocatorio presidencial: Venezuela 2000-2004," *Stvdi Vrbinati, Rivista Trimestrale di Scienze Giuridiche, Politiche ed Economiche* 71, n.s., Università degli Studi di Urbino, Urbino 2004, 379-436; "El secuestro del poder electoral y la confiscación del derecho a la participación política mediante el referendo revocatorio presidencial: Venezuela 2000-2004," *Boletín Mexicano de Derecho Comparado* 112, Instituto de Investigaciones Jurídicas, Universidad Nacional Autónoma de México, Mexico City 2005, 11-73.

[5] See Allan R. Brewer-Carías, "El inicio de la desmunicipalización en Venezuela: La organización del poder popular para eliminar la descentralización, la democracia representativa y la participación a nivel local," *AIDA, Opera Prima de Derecho Administrativo. Revista de la Asociación Internacional de Derecho Administrativo*, Universidad Nacional Autónoma de México, Facultad de Estudios Superiores de Acatlán, Coordinación de Postgrado, Instituto Internacional de Derecho Administrativo "Agustín Gordillo," Asociación Internacional de Derecho Administrativo, Mexico City 2007, 49-67.

[6] See the "Declaration of Principles" of the United Socialist Party (Apr. 23, 2010). Available at http://psuv.org.ve/files/tcdocumentos/Declaracion-de-principios-PSUV.pdf.

resource-rich state, only those who are part of the United Socialist Party and its entities can have effective access to political and administrative life.

This entire institutional democratic distortion has been established without real separation or independence of the different branches of government, not only in their horizontal division but also in their vertical distribution. What was left of the federation has been progressively dismantled. Consequently, the powers of the federated states and municipalities have been minimized by means of eliminating every trace of political decentralization of the autonomous entities in the territory, thereby preventing any real possibility of democratic participation.

Moreover, the governmental activity of the rich and wealthy oil state has ceased to be transparent – there are no checks and balances, and so it is not possible to demand any kind of accountability or responsibility from the government. The consequence is rampant governmental corruption developed in a way never seen before and promoted by the different agencies of the state, as the 2009-10 financial and banking crisis has shown. In addition, freedom of speech and the press has been systematically threatened as has been evidenced in the case of *Globovisión*,[7] and the state has closed or appropriated media outlets as has happened with *Radio Caracas Televisión*.[8] In other cases, self-censorship has been imposed by journalists and dissidents who fear systematic persecution.

So it is that, during the past years, all essential elements and fundamental components of representative democracy have been progressively dismantled in Venezuela, particularly the principle of separation of powers, to the point that the Inter-American Commission on Human Rights has said in its *2009 Annual Report* that the conditions analyzed in it "indicates the absence of due separation and independence between the branches of government in Venezuela."[9] In December 2009, the president of the

---

[7] In June 2010, the main shareholders of Globovisión were persecuted by the government, using for such purpose criminal judicial accusations "motivated" on supposed commerce or financial offences. See Juan Francisco Alonso, "Ministerio Público solicitó extradición de Zuloaga, El Universal, June 30, 2010. Available al http://www.eluniversal.com/2010/06/30/pol_art_ministerio-publico-s_1956783.shtml; and "Mezerhane: No regresará hasta que haya seguridad jusrídica," (En entrevista con CNN en Español), in El Universal, June 14, 2010. Available at http://www.eluniversal.com/2010/06/14/pol_ava_mezerhane:-no-regres_14A4022131.shtml.

[8] See, e.g., the case of the shutdown of Radio Caracas Televisión, in Allan R. Brewer-Carías, "El juez constitucional en Venezuela como instrumento para aniquilar la libertad de expresión y para confiscar la propiedad privada: El *caso RCTV*" (I de III), *Gaceta Judicial*, Santo Domingo, República Dominicana, 2007, 24-27.

[9] See IACHR, *2009 Annual Report*, para. 472. See http://www.cidh.oas.org/annualrep/2009eng/Chap.IV.f.eng.htm. The President of the Commission, Felipe González, said in Apr. 2010: "Venezuela is a democracy that have grave limitations, because democracy implies the functioning of

Supreme Tribunal of Justice considered such separation an element designed to "debilitate the State."[10]

Consequently, the country has faced an excess of concentrated and centralized power, as occurs in any authoritarian government, despite their electoral origin. In such cases, as history has shown, and in the current case of Venezuela, an inevitable tendency toward tyranny develops, particularly when there are no efficient means of control over those who govern – it is even worse when those who govern have or believe to have popular support. In Venezuela, the authoritarian government that has taken root during the past decade has concentrated all power in the hands of the executive, President Chávez, who at once controls the National Assembly and all other branches of government.

This situation is in contrast to the democratic system that, with all its defects, had consolidated in Venezuela during the second half of the twentieth century, and democracy still was among the most important historical, political, and cultural heritages of Venezuela's population at the beginning of the twenty-first century. At the end of the twentieth century, after forty years of democratic rule, Venezuela had Latin America's oldest, most tested stable contemporary democracy. Since 1999, that legacy has been systematically destroyed against the people's will.[11]

II. REPRESENTATIVE DEMOCRACY AND ITS DEFORMATIONS

The Inter-American Democratic Charter began by stating that the effective exercise of representative democracy is the basis for the rule of law and for constitutional regimes (Article 2), revaluating representative democracy as a political system that is the antithesis of a regime based on the popularity of a populist leader supported by the armed forces.[12] Representative democracy

---

the principle of separation of powers, and a Judiciary free of political factors." See Juan Francisco Alonso, "Últimas medidas judiciales certifican informe de la CIDH," in *El Universal*, Apr. 4, 2010. Available at http://universo.eluniversal.com/2010/04/04/pol_art_ultimas-medidas-jud_1815569.shtml.

[10] See Juan Francisco Alonso, "La división de poderes debilita al estado. La presidenta del TSJ [Luisa Estela Morales] afirma que la Constitución hay que reformarla," *El Universal*, Caracas Dec. 15, 2009, http://www.eluniversal.com/2009/12/05/pol_art_morales:-la-divisio_1683109.shtml.

[11] Still in Dec. 2009, according to a Latinobarómetro poll of eighteen Latin American countries, Venezuela and Uruguay were the countries with the highest number of people expressing that "democracy is preferable to any other type of government," and with the lowest percentage of people expressing that "in certain circumstances an authoritarian government can be preferable to a democratic one." See *Economist* 393, Dec. 12, 2009, 42.

[12] The express inclusion of the reference to representative democracy in the charter was despite suggestions to replace it with "participatory democracy," as in the meeting of heads of state and governments of the Americas (3rd Summit of the Americas), Quebec City, 2001, and in the General Assembly of the Organization of American States, in San José, Costa Rica, in 2001.

is contrary to the well-known nonelective relationship of leader, people, and military that created the fascist and national-socialist praxis of the first half of the twentieth century and was used to confiscate democracy in the second half.

In the Venezuela of 1999, representative democracy as basis of the rule of law and the constitutional regime, without doubt needed to be improved to make it more representative of the people, regarding their organizations, regions, communities, and neighborhoods, and not only of the political parties that monopolized it. That was the great political change that Venezuelans called for, and that call provoked the electoral process of 1998. In those elections, a vast majority did not vote for traditional parties and many voted against them. But instead of perfecting representative democracy, during the past decade, representative democracy has been distorted, particularly through the systematic manipulation of the electoral system and the progressive destruction of pluralism. The result has been the adoption of a political system with reduced representation. Instead of allowing representation of various political parties, representation has been reduced to only one governmental party, with no other representation. That is why, even in 2000, the organization secretary of the government party, facing the possibility of losing the majority in the National Assembly, expressed that if the majority were lost, "it would be the end of the democratic way of the process due to the fact that through parliament it is possible to abrogate statutes, to censure ministries, to indict the president."[13] Eight years later, President Chavez, facing a possible setback for the government in the regional elections of 2008 said that if the opposition groups would eventually win important positions of governorships and mayors in Caracas and states like Miranda, Carabobo, Táchira or Anzoategui, "the next step will be war."[14] The following year, in 2009, it was also President Chávez, who in referring to the September 2010 elections of new members of the National Assembly, said:

> The vital objective in order to maintain the stability of the country, to maintain peace in the country, is for the Revolution to obtain next year a resonant triumph in the Assembly, obtaining a majority of representatives. Just imagine for a minute, on the possibility for the counterrevolution, due to any factor, to obtain a majority in the National Assembly. They will

---

[13] See *El Universal,* Caracas Dec. 28, 2001, 1–2.

[14] See report of Chavez's speech, "Al ganar la oposición vendrá la Guerra," *El Universal,* Caracas Jan. 21, 2008, iavailable at http://noticias.eluniversal.com/2008/01/21/pol_art_al-ganar-la-oposici_680614.shtml.

begin to reverse the statutes, this law would be quickly abrogated, and as the people will not keep quiet, and then the country would take the violent way. The same happens with the government: just suppose for an instant that a recall referendum could take place next year. Suppose that my mandate would be revoked. The country would enter into an earthquake, violence, destabilization, which is their objective. The government is their objective, and again to control the State as they did so for a long time.[15]

That is, for Chávez and his followers, a "democratic" system in Venezuela is conceivable only if it exclusively represents his supporters. It is simply inconceivable if it represents any in the opposition. In fact, the political system in Venezuela has progressively moved toward a supposed "democracy" representing only one party, which has declare itself as a "Marxist" party, monopolizing most of the representative bodies, manipulating election rules, and taken control of the electoral branch of government. The fact is, in Venezuela, during the last four decades of the past century, there was never a party autocracy as the one now seen that admits no dissidence.

That is why since the beginning of his government, Chávez and his followers have not admitted that the composition of the National Assembly could be democratically changed. This was true even in January 2001, when threatened by the possible defection of some representatives supporting the government, the majority in the National Assembly could be changed. As aforementioned, in 2009, Chávez himself considered such change the beginning of violence.

For the government to arrive at this political monopoly on representation, it has changed the electoral system. Members of the National Assembly were traditionally elected by the method of d'Hondt proportional representation introduced in 1946 and reformed by the 1993 Organic Law on Suffrage and Political Participation.[16] Following the reforms introduced in the law, the 1999 Constitution provided for a combination of methods, adding to the proportional representation a parallel majority method to be applied in the constituency: the "personalized proportional representation method" (Article 63).[17] This mixed system requires ensuring the election in each constituency of a percentage of representatives elected in uninominal ballot and another percentage in plurinominal ballot through blocked and

---

[15]See Joaquin Chaffardet, "Amenaza presidencial y pasividad opositora," Nov. 1, 2009, at http://webarticulista.net.

[16]*Gaceta Oficial* Extra. No. 5.233, May 28, 1998.

[17]See Decision No. 74 (Jan. 25, 2006) of the Constitutional Chamber of the Supreme Tribunal of Justice, in *Revista de Derecho Público* 105, Editorial Jurídica Venezolana, Caracas 2006, 122-44.

closed lists. This was the method applied in the elections of representatives to the National Assembly in 2000, but it was distorted in 2005 regarding the election of the same members of the National Assembly when the parties supporting the government applied the fraudulent "*Las Morochas*" method. This distortion was later legitimized through a constitutional interpretation of the Constitutional Chamber of the Supreme Tribunal of Justice on January 25, 2006.[18] The method allowed the various parties supporting official candidates to enter into agreements for some of them to file nominations only for the uninominal election and others only for the plurinominal one in the respective constituencies. As they formally were different parties (although part of the same government coalition) no deduction of the elected candidates would be applied.[19] In that way, the system in practice became one of a preponderant majority, thus distorting proportional representation. In 2009, the Organic Law on the Electoral Processes was sanctioned, "regularizing" the method.[20] In addition to the distortion of the mixed system, the complete lack of independence and autonomy of the National Electoral Council must be mentioned because it has prevented any possible guarantee of impartiality. All these facts forced opposition parties not to participate in the legislative elections of 2005, with catastrophic consequences for democracy.

Another important distortion of the electoral system has been the deliberate use of the comptroller general's office, illegitimately controlled by the executive, to disqualify many opposition candidates' participation in electoral process through supposed administrative "irregularities" that they committed while in public positions. This is notwithstanding the provision of the Constitution guaranteeing that the political right to run for office can be suspended only by a criminal judicial decision (Articles 39 and 42).[21] On this matter, the Inter-American Commission on Human Rights, in its *2009 Annual Report*, has highlighted this mechanism restricting "the possibilities of candidates opposed to the government for securing access to power," emphasizing that "through administrative resolutions of the Office of the

---

[18]Decision No. 74 (Case: *Acción Democrática vs. National Electoral Council and other electoral authorities*), in *Revista de Derecho Público* 105, Editorial Jurídica Venezolana, Caracas 2006, 122-44.

[19]See Allan R. Brewer-Carías, "El juez constitucional vs. el derecho al sufragio mediante la representación proporcional," in *Crónica sobre la "in"justicia constitucional. La Sala Constitucional y el autoritarismo en Venezuela,* Caracas 2007, 337ff.

[20]*Gaceta Oficial* No. 5.928 Extra. of Aug. 12, 2009.

[21]In Oct. 2008, the European Parliament approved a resolution asking the Venezuelan government to end these practices (political disqualification to prevent election of opposition leaders in regional and local elections) and to promote a more global democracy with complete respect for the principles established in the 1999 Constitution. See http://venezuelanoticia.com/ archives/8298.

Comptroller General of the Republic, whereby 260 individuals, mostly opposed to the government, were disqualified from standing for election," and pointing out that "these disqualifications from holding public office were not the result of criminal convictions and were ordered in the absence of prior proceedings, in contravention of the American Convention's standards."[22]

Unfortunately, the Constitutional Chamber of the Supreme Tribunal legitimized these unconstitutional administrative measures limiting this right, defrauding the Constitution.[23] The result was the elimination of many possible opposition candidates from the November 2008 regional and municipal elections. The same sort of decision was publicly announced in November 2009, when many possible opposition candidates for the National Assembly in 2010 were disqualified from participating in such elections.[24]

But one of the biggest distortions of the electoral system occurred in 2004, before the recall presidential referendum that year. First, the date of the referendum was delayed without justification to allow the sudden and indiscriminate incorporation to the electoral list of almost 2 million new voters, many of whom were formerly illegal immigrants whose status had been regularized.[25] Second, more that 1 million voters were illegally moved to voting centers in other cities. Third, more that eighteen thousand members of the electoral centers were dismissed for having signed the petition to convene the 2004 recall referendum. Fourth, in general, the names of all 3.5 million persons who signed that petition were incorporated in a public list ("*Lista Tascón*") that was published for political purposes by one member of the National Assembly, who and thus were massively discriminated against in their relations with the public administration. Fifth, public servants who signed the same petition were openly dismissed from their positions.

Of all these distortions that have affected the implementation of free and fair elections, the most serious one has been the complete absence of

---

[22]See IACHR, *2009 Annual Report*, para. 473. See http://www.cidh.oas.org/annualrep/2009eng/Chap.IV.f.eng.htm.

[23]See Teodoro Petkoff, "Election and Political Power: Challenges for the Opposition," in *ReVista: Harvard Review of Latin America*, David Rockefeller Center for Latin American Studies, Cambridge, MA, Harvard University, 2008, 11.

[24]On May 25, 2010, the disqualification of two former governors (from the states of Zulia and Sucre) opposing Chávez as candidates for the Sept. 2010 legislative elections was announced. See http://www.globovision.com/news.php?nid=150031.

[25]See Decree No. 2,823 of Feb. 3, 2004, *Gaceta Oficial* No. 37,871 of Feb. 2, 2004, reformed by Decree No. 3,041 of Aug. 3, 2004, *Gaceta Oficial* No. 38,002 of Aug. 17, 2004. See the comments on this process in Allan R. Brewer-Carías, *Régimen de la nacionalidad, Ciudadanía y Extranjería*, Editorial Jurídica Venezolana, Caracas 2005, pp. 57ff.

independence and autonomy of the National Electoral Council, which according to the Constitution was to comprise five members with no ties to political organizations and appointed by the National Assembly, following the nominations of an electoral nominating committee exclusively composed of representatives from different sectors of society. That nominating committee was to receive nominations from the law and political science faculties of national universities, the citizens' branch of government, and civil society organizations.

In any event, since 2000, the configuration of the Committee for Electoral Nominations and those of all other nominating committees has been distorted. The committees were never structured as provided for in the Constitution with representatives from various sectors of civil society. They have mainly included elected members of the National Assembly and members of the official party. This began in 2002, after the Organic Law of the Electoral Power[26] was sanctioned and the National Assembly was due to appoint new members of the National Electoral Council. Because representatives supporting the government did not have the qualified majority to approve such appointments and did not want to agree on the matter with the opposition, the National Assembly failed to appoint members of the National Electoral Council. The consequence of this omission was that the Constitutional Chamber of the Supreme Tribunal of Justice, controlled by the executive, decided an action filed against such unconstitutional legislative omission and directly appointed members of the Electoral Council, without complying with the conditions established in the Constitution. That move ensured the government's complete control of the state electoral organ.[27]

The provisions of the Organic Law of the Electoral Power tending to guarantee political participation of civil society converted the nominating committee into a parliamentary commission, with some additional members appointed by the same assembly. The result is that members of the Electoral

---

[26]See *Gaceta Oficial* No. 37.573, Nov. 19, 2002.

[27]See Decisions No. 2073 (Aug. 4, 2003) (Case: *Hermánn Escarrá Malaver y otros*) and No. 2341 (Aug. 25, 2003) (Case: *Hermánn Escarrá M. y otros*) in Allan R. Brewer-Carías, *La Sala Constitucional versus el estado democrático de derecho. El secuestro del poder electoral y de la Sala Electoral del Tribunal Supremo y la confiscación del derecho a la participación política*, Los Libros de El Nacional, Colección Ares, Caracas 2004, 172; "El secuestro del poder electoral y la confiscación del derecho a la participación política mediante el referendo revocatorio presidencial: Venezuela 2000-2004," *Boletín Mexicano de Derecho Comparado* 112, Instituto de Investigaciones Jurídicas, Universidad Nacional Autónoma de México, Mexico City 2005, 11-73; Rafael Chavero G. et al., *La guerra de las salas del TSJ frente al referéndum revocatorio*, Editorial Aequitas, Caracas 2004, 13-58.

Council have been, in their great majority, supporters of the government or members of the United Socialist Party, which has been confirmed in the appointment of new members of the council in November 2009, a decision that opposition parties formally challenged before the Supreme Tribunal.

Consequently, the elections held in Venezuela during the past decade have been organized by a politically dependent branch of government without any guarantee of independence or impartiality. This is the only explanation, for instance, of the complete lack of official information on the final voting results of the December 2007 referendum, in which the people rejected the president's draft constitutional reforms. The country, in June 2010, still ignored the number of votes that effectively rejected the proposed reform for the establishment in Venezuela of a socialist, centralized, militaristic, and police state, as proposed by President Chávez.

The constitutional regime of political parties was designed in the 1999 Constitution, following the antiparty trends resulting from the political crisis of the 1990s, which was reflected in the drafting of the new Constitution. That text eliminated the phrase "political party" from its text and substituted the more general "organizations with political purposes" (Article 67).[28] Of course, what in 1998 and 1999 were ignored were the traditional political parties that, until then, had been in control of power. Those parties were completely crushed and marginalized, with weak possibilities of participating in the political process. In the subsequent years, new political parties controlled by the government developed, with more centralized organizations than the traditional ones, directly controlled by the president. The final result was the presidential initiative, in 2006, to promote the founding of the United Socialist Party of Venezuela, using for such purposes the state structures and services, which in its first Congress in April 2010 declared to be a "Marxist" party. This official party is, of course, led by the president himself, with the intention of uniting all the various political parties that have supported his government. Only the tiny Communist Party initially refused to disappear, and others have abandoned their support to the government.[29]

---

[28] See Roberto V. Pastor and Rubén Martínez Dalmau, "La configuración de los partidos políticos en la Constitución venezolana," *Revista de Derecho Constitucional* 4, Editorial Sherwood, Caracas 2001, 375-89; Allan R. Brewer-Carías, "Regulación jurídica de los partidos políticos en Venezuela," in *Regulación jurídica de los partidos políticos en América Latina*, coord. Daniel Zovatto, Universidad Nacional Autónoma de México, International IDEA, Mexico City 2006, 893-937.

[29] The case of the party *Patria para Todos* PPT, which after supporting the government until 2010, Chávez sentenced: "The PPT is finished, that party does not exist." See http://elobservador.rctv.net/Noticias/VerNoticia.aspx?NoticiaId=283197&Tipo=14.

The United Socialist Party was in charge of supporting the presidential draft constitutional reforms submitted to referendum in 2007, which was rejected by popular vote. The party was also the supporting instrument of government candidates in regional and municipal elections of November 2008 – the government's candidates lost elections in the most important and populated states and municipalities of the country, where some opposition candidates were elected as governors and mayors. This latter fact provoked the reaction of the government affecting the constitutional right to hold elected positions. This has been highlighted by the Inter-American Commission on Human Rights in its *2009 Annual Report*, in which it noticed "how the State has taken action to limit some powers of popularly-elected authorities in order to reduce the scope of public functions in the hands of members of the opposition," particularly through "a series of legal reforms [that] have left opposition authorities with limited powers, preventing them from legitimately exercising the mandates for which they were elected."[30]

In any case, the result of the first decade of political life under the 1999 Constitution, which seems to ignore political parties in its regulations, has been to increase partisanship and party autocracy, particularly regarding the official party, in a way never before seen. The traditional multiparty government of the second half of the twentieth century has been substituted with a single-party government that is completely imbricate with the state.

The traditional lack of internal democratic rules of parties, with their traditional pattern of leaders in perpetuity, led to a provision in the 1999 Constitution according to which not only the members of governing boards must elect the members of each party, but also the party candidates for elections to representative offices must be selected through democratic internal elections (Article 67). To that end, the Constitution required that the National Electoral Council organize such internal elections (Article 293.6). In practice, because of the lack of statutory development of the constitutional provisions, that has not occurred.

Also as a reaction against problems stemming from the public funding of political parties that was established in the 1998 Organic Law of Suffrage and Political Participation,[31] the application of which led the traditionally dominant parties to monopolize those funds, the drafters of the 1999 Constitution simply prohibited public funding of organizations with political

---

[30]See IACHR, *2009 Annual Report*, para. 474. See http://www.cidh.oas.org/annualrep/2009eng/Chap.IV.f.eng.htm.

[31]*Gaceta Oficial* Extra. No. 5.233, May 28, 1998.

purposes and established new controls for their private financing (Article 67). This was a regression in addressing what is a constant problem in the democratic world: the possibility for public funding of political parties to avoid irregular and illegitimate funding, particularly of governing parties.[32] Nonetheless, in a 2008 decision of the Constitutional Chamber of the Supreme Tribunal interpreting such Article 67 of the Constitution, the chamber distorted the Constitution, concluding contrary to the constitutional provision that the article intended to prohibit only public financing regarding internal activities of parties, not their electoral activities.[33] Of course, because of the monopoly of the United Socialist Party over the electoral branch of government, it is easy to understand that public funding will eventually end up in the official party's budget.

Also as a reaction against political parties, the Constitution established that members of the National Assembly are representatives of the people as a whole and "are not to be subject to mandates or instructions other than their own conscience" (Article 200), thus seeking to eliminate parliamentary party groups and blind voting. Nonetheless, in practice, parliamentary factions have only changed their names – since 2000, they have been called "opinion groups." On the vote of members of the National Assembly, particularly those elected by the official party, the president of the National Assembly was emphatic in 2002 that they "are not independent at all, but are subject to discipline. The one who pretend[s] to act as an independent must resign, and just be an independent candidate."[34]

In any case, the governing party has had more centralized control over members of the National Assembly than had parties before 1999. As a result, the constitutional provision aimed to guarantee the internal renovation of the political directors of the parties is a dead letter – the president of the republic presides over the official party, and the board of directors is made up of state officers appointed by the president.

---

[32]See Allan R. Brewer-Carías, "Consideraciones sobre el financiamiento de los partidos políticos en Venezuela," in *Financiamiento y democratización interna de partidos políticos. Memora del IV Curso Anual Interamaricano de Elecciones,* Instituto Interamericano de Derechos Humanos, San José, Costa Rica, 1991, 121-39.

[33]Decision No. 780 (May 8, 2008),of the Constitutional Chamber of the Supreme Tribunal of Justice (Case: *Interpretación del artículo 67 de la Constitución*), in *Revista de Derecho Público* 114, Editorial Jurídica Venezolana, Caracas 2008, 126ff. See the comments in "El juez constitucional como constituyente: el caso del financiamiento de las campañas electorales de los partidos políticos en Venezuela," in *Revista de Derecho Público* 117, Editorial Jurídica Venezolana, Caracas 2009, 195-203.

[34]See *El Nacional,* Caracas Dec. 27, 2001, D-2.

The result of all these provisions, constitutional distortions, and the absence of legislation is that after the enactment of the 1999 Constitution, the political parties have greater presence than they ever had. In addition, the symbiosis between the governing political party and the state and its public administration that has been established in the past years confirms that a party state has continued to exist, with the same vices of clientelism and the same control by officials sitting permanently on the governing boards. The consequence has been that the constitutional provision establishing the prohibition on public officers serving any party (Article 145) has been forgotten. As never before, the country has a president who has continued acting more like the chief of a political party than a head of government and state. This has been the situation in the country since 2000.[35]

In Venezuela, representative democracy has not been based on pluralism, tolerance, dissidence, discussion, dialogue, and consensus. It is a system in which only the government parties and the supporters of the president are "represented"; the opposition parties and organizations are completely excluded or marginalized from political life.

III. PARTICIPATORY DEMOCRACY AND THE VIOLATION OF THE CITIZENS' RIGHT TO PARTICIPATION

The Inter-American Democratic Charter not only reaffirms the need for an effective exercise of representative democracy as basis for the rule of law and of the constitutional regime but also states that such representative democracy shall be strengthened and deepened by permanent, ethical, and responsible participation of the citizenry within a legal and constitutional order (Article 2). Furthermore, the charter adds that citizens' participation in decisions relating to their own development is a right, a responsibility, and a necessary condition for the full and effective exercise of democracy. Therefore, it affirms that promoting and fostering diverse forms of participation strengthens democracy (Article 6).

It can be said that the 1999 Constitution is marked by the concept of participation, not only by declaring the government of the republic and all political entities as participatory (Article 6) but also by formally establishing the right to political participation (Article 62), for which purpose the Constitution lists, beyond the election of public representatives, the diverse

---

[35]On May 25, 2010, for instance, it was Chávez who officially announced the Party candidates for the Sept. 2010 legislative elections. See Alejandra M. Hernández F., "Chávez anuncia candidatos que encabezan lista para la AN," in *El Universal*, May 25, 2010. See http://politica.eluniversal.com/2010/05/25/pol_art_chavez-anuncia-candi_25A3904931.shtml.

ways to participate in political matters: election, referenda, popular consultation; revocation of mandates; legislative, constitutional, and constituent initiatives; open town hall meetings; and citizens' assemblies of binding character (Article 70).

In addition to all these participatory political means that must be developed through legislation for their complete exercise, the Constitution has established through self-executing provisions two specific ways to participate in public management. First is the exercise of the legislative function by obligating the National Assembly to consult state organs, citizens, and the organized society to hear their opinions on draft statutes (Article 211) and obligating it to consult the states' legislative councils on draft laws on matters regarding the states (Article 206). This obligation of the National Assembly, without doubt, applies to the president when, through enabling laws, the assembly authorizes the president to issue decree laws (Article 203). The converse would be to defraud the Constitution.

Second is the process of appointing the head officers of the organs of the citizens' power (attorney general, comptroller general, and human rights ombudsman), the electoral power (National Electoral Council), and the judicial power (magistrates of the Supreme Tribunal of Justice) by imposing limits to the former discretional power of the former Congress to make those appointments. According to provisions of the Constitution, in all those cases, the National Assembly can make those appointments only from candidates proposed by the corresponding nominating committees integrated by "representatives of the diverse sectors of society" (Articles 270, 279, and 295).

Nonetheless, these two direct means for political participation have been completely ignored and distorted over the past decade. On the need for public consultation on matters of legislation, the violation of the constitutional provisions was made in all cases of decree laws approved by the president in execution of the 2001 and 2007 Enabling Laws authorizing the President of the Republic to enact them, through which the main legislation of the country has been enacted. It occurred in November 2001, when the president issued forty-eight decree laws regulating matters of primary importance in the country without submitting drafts to public consultation, as required by the Constitution and as established in the Organic Law of Public Administration of October 2001, which punishes with absolute nullity (Article 137) any statute approved without following the procedure of public consultation set forth.[36] It also happened in 2007–8, also through the approval of more that fifty decree laws, many of which were to implement the rejected 2007 constitutional reforms of the president that were not submitted to popular consultation.[37]

Constitutional provisions regarding citizens' rights to participate in the appointment of officials of the judicial, citizens', and electoral powers has also been systematically violated during the past decade. The text of the Constitution was ignored by the National Assembly when it issued the transitional Special Law for the Ratification or Designation of Officers of the Citizen Power and Magistrates of the Supreme Court of Justice for the first constitutional period of November 2000,[38] and when it approved laws regulating the electoral power, the citizens' power and the Supreme Tribunal of Justice.[39]

Because of the unconstitutionality of the 2000 special law, even the people's defender challenged it before the Supreme Tribunal.[40] The tribunal never ruled on the claim, but in a preliminary decision of December 12, 2000, it decided that the Constitution was not to be applied to the magistrates deciding the case who were expecting to be "ratified,"[41] in violation of the most elemental principle of the rule of law: no one shall be judge and a party in the same process. The Tribunal justified its ruling on the basis of the 1999 Transitory Constitutional Regime.[42]

---

[36]See Allan R. Brewer-Carías, "Apreciación general sobre los vicios de inconstitucionalidad que afectan los decretos leyes habilitados," in *Ley Habilitante del 13-11-2000 y Sus Decretos Leyes*, No. 17, Academia de Ciencias Políticas y Sociales, Caracas 2002, 63-103. See also *El Universal*, Caracas Nov. 25, 2001, 1-1 and 1-2; *Revista Primicia* 206, Caracas Dec. 11, 2001, special report; *La Nación*, San Cristóbal, Nov. 23, 2001, 1-C.

[37]For essays on the 2008 decree laws, see *Revista de Derecho Público* 115 *(Estudios sobre los Decretos Leyes 2008)*, Editorial Jurídica Venezolana, Caracas 2008.

[38]See Allan R. Brewer-Carías, *Golpe de estado y proceso constituyente en Venezuela*, Universidad Autónoma de México, Mexico City 2002, 389ff.

[39]See Ley Orgánica del Poder Ciudadano, *Gaceta Oficial* No. 37.310, Oct. 25, 2001; Ley Orgánica del Poder Electoral, *Gaceta Oficial* No. 37.573, Nov. 19, 2002; Ley Orgánica del Tribunal Supremo de Justicia, *Gaceta Oficial* No. 37.942, May 20, 2004. On the 2007 appointment of the prosecutor general, see Allan R. Brewer-Carías, "Sobre el nombramiento irregular por la Asamblea Nacional de los titulares de los órganos del poder ciudadano en 2007," in *Revista de Derecho Público* 113, Editorial Jurídica Venezolana, Caracas 2008, 85-88.

[40]The people's defender considered that the statute "was a fault against the democratic system, and the kidnapping of the right to citizen right, excluding the possibility to be plural." See *El Universal*, Caracas Nov. 21, 2000, 1-4.

[41]The general director of the People's Defender Office stated that this was because "many of the magistrates do not fulfill the necessary conditions to be ratified." See *El Universal*, Caracas Dec. 14, 2000, 1-2.

[42]On this, see the statements by one of the magistrates of the Supreme Tribunal (Delgado Ocando) in *El Universal*, Caracas Jan. 12, 2001, 1-4.

The Inter-American Commission on Human Rights highlighted these violations in its Preliminary Observations of May 10, 2002, issued after its last visit to Venezuela, noting that at that time members of the Supreme Court of Justice, as well as the Peoples' Defender, the Prosecutor General, and the Comptroller General, "were not nominated by such committees as required by the Constitution," whose provisions "were aimed precisely at limiting undue interference, ensuring greater independence and impartiality, and allowing various voices of society to be heard in the selection of such high-level authorities." The commission concluded by urging the state "to adopt the organic laws so as to establish the mechanisms provided for in the Constitution for the selection of the members of the Supreme Court of Justice, as well as the Peoples' Defender, the Prosecutor General, and the Comptroller General."[43]

After 2002, the corresponding statutes regarding all those public offices were sanctioned, but in all of them, instead of being integrated by representatives of diverse sectors of civil society, as mandated in the Constitution, they are appointed by simple parliamentary commission of a majority of National Assembly representatives.[44] Civil society was discriminated against, and the heads of the citizens', electoral, and judicial powers were appointed by the National Assembly and directly controlled by the executive – sometimes without observing the strict conditions established in the Constitution. This was also the case regarding the appointment of members of the National Electoral Council in 2009. Although the Constitution expressly prohibits them to be members of any political party, some were formally registered members of the United Socialist Party.[45]

Participatory democracy, in all cases provided for directly in the Constitution by means of self-executing provisions, has been postponed by state organs. The same has occurred with the statutory development and application of other constitutional provisions regarding participatory democracy. As aforementioned, on matters of referenda, one of the most important ones established in the Constitution is the recall referendum that

---

[43]Paras. 26-29. See the reference in Allan R. Brewer-Carías, *La crisis de la democracia venezolana. La Carta Democrática Interamericana y los sucesos de abril de 2002,* Los Libros de El Nacional, Colección Ares, Caracas 2002, 154.

[44]See Ley Orgánica del Poder Ciudadano, *Gaceta Oficial* N° 37.310 of Oct. 25, 2001; Ley Orgánica del Poder Electoral, *Gaceta Oficial* N° 37.573 of Nov. 19, 2002; Ley Orgánica del Tribunal Supremo de Justicia, *Gaceta Oficial* N° 37.942 of May 20, 2004.

[45]Juan M. Raffalli A. "Rectores del partido. Se ha consumado otro fraude a la Constitución y quedó al descubierto," in *El Universal*, Caracas May 7, 2010. See http://guarenasguatire.eluniversal.com/2010/05/07/opi_art_rectores-del-partido_1884615.shtml.

must be convened by popular initiative to revoke the mandate of elected officials. The only referendum of this type convened during the past decade – after a petition signed by more than 3.5 million people – was the recall or recall referendum regarding the mandate of President Chávez. In violation of the constitutional right to political participation, the National Electoral Council, following a ruling of the Constitutional Chamber of the Supreme Tribunal of Justice,[46] illegitimately converted the recall referendum of the president into a ratifying referendum[47] which does not exist in the Constitution.

Prior to the 2004 recall referendum, attempts to convene a consultative referendum, also by popular initiative, to ask the people about the permanence or resignation of the president in his position, were systematically frustrated. First, in 2003, more than 3 million signatures supporting the petition were openly ignored and rejected by the National Electoral Council, a process that ended with a decision by the Electoral Chamber of the Supreme Tribunal to annul the convening of the referendum. In the interim, police seized copies of the signatures. Second, regarding the 2004 recall referendum, prior to carrying it out, the National Electoral Council annulled more that half of the 3 million signatures in support of the petition. Third, in the same process, the National Electoral Council converted the process of signing for a petition of this kind from an open process to an administrative procedure subject to strict public control. Fourth, the decision of the National Electoral Council annulling the signatures was challenged before the Electoral Chamber of the Supreme Tribunal, which issued a preliminary ruling suspending the National Electoral Council decision, thus allowing the referendum to be held. The Constitutional Chamber, without any power to do so, annulled the electoral chamber decision, ratifying the annulment of signatures decided by the National Electoral Council. In the end, after it had been tactically *ex profeso* postponed, the referendum took place in 2004, but after all the legal battles

---

[46]See Decision No. 2750 (Oct. 21, 2003) (Case: *Carlos E. Herrera Mendoza, Interpretación del artículo 72 de la Constitución*), in *Revista de Derecho Público* 93-96, Editorial Jurídica Venezolana, Caracas 2003, 229ff.

[47]See Allan R. Brewer-Carías, "La Sala Constitucional vs. el derecho ciudadano a la revocatoria de mandatos populares: De cómo un referendo revocatorio fue inconstitucionalmente convertido en un "referendo ratificatorio," in *Crónica sobre la "in"justicia constitucional. La Sala Constitucional y el autoritarismo en Venezuela*, Universidad Central de Venezuela–Editorial Jurídica Venezolana, Caracas 2007, 349-78.

developed before entities completely controlled by the executive, it was eventually converted into a ratifying referendum.[48]

Another distortion that has occurred during the past decade regarding political participation is the progressive interference of the state in civil society organizations. First, in 2000, the Constitutional Chamber of the Supreme Tribunal denied citizens' right to participate through organizations of civil society that had any sort of financing from transnational or foreign institutions or foundations, improperly limiting the freedom of the people.[49] Second, in 2003, the Supreme Electoral Council suspended internal elections of all professional boards in the country, improperly limiting the rights of professionals to choose their boards of directors. Third, in particular, regarding the elections of the capital district's Colegio de Abogados (Lawyers' Board), in 2008, the Constitutional Chamber ignored the lawyers' election and appointed new members to that board.[50]

Finally, mention must be made of the communal councils, established since 2006 as the supposed means for citizens participation, substituting for municipalities, which were, according to Article 168 of the Constitution, the "primary political unit of the national organization" and the basis for political participation. In lieu of developing these local government structures with elected members (mayors and councilors), the authoritarian regime preferred to create a parallel structure of centrally controlled

---

[48]See Allan R. Brewer-Carías, "El secuestro del poder electoral y la confiscación del derecho a la participación política mediante el referendo revocatorio presidencial: Venezuela 2000-2004," *Revista Jurídica del Perú* 54, Lima 2004, 353-96; "El secuestro del poder electoral y de la Sala Electoral del Tribunal Supremo y la confiscación del derecho a la participación política mediante el referendo revocatorio presidencial: Venezuela: 2000-2004," *Revista Costarricense de Derecho Constitucional* 5, Instituto Costarricense de Derecho Constitucional, Editorial Investigaciones Jurídicas, San José 2004, 167-312; "El secuestro del poder electoral y la confiscación del derecho a la participación política mediante el referendo revocatorio presidencial: Venezuela 2000-2004," *Stvdi Vrbinati* 71, n.s., Università degli Studi di Urbino, Urbino 2004, 379-436; "El secuestro del poder electoral y la confiscación del derecho a la participación política mediante el referendo revocatorio presidencial: Venezuela 2000-2004," *Boletín Mexicano de Derecho Comparado* 112, Instituto de Investigaciones Jurídicas, Universidad Nacional Autónoma de México, Mexico City, 11-73.

[49]In its *2009 Annual Report*, the Inter-American Commission on Human Rights has express its concern about the provisions included in an "International Cooperation Bill." And the vague language used in it giving a broad margin of discretion to the authorities responsible for regulating it, which could result in the violation of rights including freedom of association, freedom of expression, political participation, and equality, affecting the functioning of nongovernmental organizations. Regarding the limits on NGO funding, the Commission noted that it "could hamper freedom of association in a way that is incompatible with the American Convention's standards," para. 498. See http://www.cidh.oas.org/annualrep/2009eng/Chap.IV.f.eng.htm.

[50]See Decision No. 11 of Feb. 14, 2008 (Case, *Juan Carlos Velásquez Abreu y otro*), N° Expediente: 04-1263.

communal councils,[51] whose members are not elected by the people but designated by local "assemblies of the citizens" (Article 70), controlled by the central government through the president and channels of the United Socialist Party. The citizens' assemblies according to the 2009 reform of the Law are the "highest deliberation and decision instance for the exercise of the communal power" (Article 20), but being directly controlled by a Ministry for the Popular Power on Political Participation, in fact they are the instrument of the official party and the central government in politically interfering in all social and economic activities, through control of the Ministry (Article 56).[52]

IV. DISRESPECTING HUMAN RIGHTS

Among the essential elements of representative democracy listed in the Inter-American Charter is respect for human rights and fundamental freedoms (Article 3). The relation between democracy and constitutional rights and freedoms is so important that the charter specifies that democracy is indispensable to the effective exercise of fundamental freedoms and human rights, in their universality, indivisibility, and interdependence, which are embodied in the Constitution and in inter-American and international human rights instruments.

However, in the past decade, in Venezuela, human rights have suffered in a way never seen before in the country.[53] This critical situation has been systematically denounced during the past decade by organizations dealing with their protection, including the Inter-American Commission on Human Rights. It is enough to analyze the annual reports from the commission on the situation of human rights in Venezuela, and the many decisions adopted by the Inter-American Court of Human Rights condemning Venezuela, for a complete panorama of the situation. Never before has the Inter-American Commission on Human Rights received so many petitions to protect human rights from the state, including violations of the freedom to form and join trade unions; attacks on freedom of association; violations of judicial

---

[51]*Gaceta Oficial* No. 5.806, Extra., Apr. 10, 2006. See Allan R. Brewer-Carías, "El inicio de la desmunicipalización en Venezuela: La organización del poder popular para eliminar la descentralización, la democracia representativa y la participación a nivel local," in *Revista de la Asociación Internacional de Derecho Administrativo,* Mexico City 2007, 49-67.

[52]The 2006 law was substituted with the 2009 Organic Law on Communal Councils. See *Gaceta Oficial* No. 39.335, Dec. 28, 2009.

[53]See, in general, Human Right Watch, *A Decade under Chávez: Political Intolerance and Lost Opportunities for Advancing Human Rights in Venezuela,* Sept. 2008, http://www.hrw.org/reports/2008/venezuela0908/.

guarantees and due process; interference of the executive branch in other branches of government, including submission of the judicial branch to the executive; disrespect of the right to life – as denounced in 2002, over extrajudicial executions and death squads of local police units[54]; and attacks on the freedom of expression and violations of the right to privacy of communications. On the matter of death squads, the Inter-American Commission on Human Rights, since 2002, expressed its concerns regarding various extrajudicial executions perpetrated by those groups, pointing out that, in many cases, they operate within the state's police force.[55]

Violent actions by social groups have also transferred to the political arena and, during the past decade, the country has witnessed open harassment, intimidation, and significant acts of vandalism and looting, exercised by groups connected with the government or with the official government party, against institutions, demonstrators, media, and even the freedoms of opposition members of the National Assembly and legislative councils. All this recalls fascist practices of harassment, threats, and destruction.[56]

The situation of human rights after the decade of authoritarian government can be summarized as follows. First, the constitutional rank of human rights declared and contained in international treaties of human rights recognized in Article 23 of the Constitution has been distorted by the Constitutional Chamber of the Supreme Tribunal of Justice in various decisions (No. 1.013 of 2001, No. 1.492 of 2003, and No. 1.939 of 2008) that have denied the direct applicability of such international provisions.[57] Also, the state has denied enforcement in the country of provisional protective measures adopted by the Inter-American Commission on Human Rights and the Inter-American Court of Human Rights, as in the case of the television station Globovisión, where the president publicly declared in 2003 that the

---

[54]See, e.g., the statement of Human Rights Watch representative on death squads; impunity surrounding their activities; and indifference of the government, judges, and state police. See *El Universal*, Caracas Jan. 18, 2002, 1-5.

[55]See the Preliminary Observation of May 10, 2002.

[56]In its *2009 Annual Report,* the Inter-American Commission on Human Rights noted "extreme concern that in Venezuela, violent groups such as the *Movimiento Tupamaro, Colectivo La Piedrita, Colectivo Alexis Vive, Unidad Popular Venezolana, and Grupo Carapaica* are perpetrating acts of violence with the involvement or acquiescence of state agents. These groups have similar training to that of the police or the military, and they have taken control of underprivileged urban areas. The IACHR has received alarming information indicating that these violent groups maintain close relations with police forces and, on occasion, make use of police resources." Para. 509. See http://www.cidh.oas.org/annualrep/2009eng/Chap.IV.f.eng.htm.

[57]See the comments on these decisions in Allan R. Brewer-Carías, "El juez constitucional vs. La justicia internacional en materia de derechos humanos," in *Revista de Derecho Público* 116, Editorial Jurídica Venezolana, Caracas 2008, 249-60

government would not respect those bodies. The state has also formally declared the decision of the Inter-American Court of Human Rights of August 5, 2008 (*Apitz Barbera et al. (Corte Primera de lo Contencioso Administrativo) vs. Venezuela*)[58] condemning the republic for violating the rights of dismissed judges, as unenforceable in Venezuela (2008).[59]

Neither has the right to life and personal security been guaranteed. To understand this tragic situation, during the past decade, the annual toll of homicides in the country rose from 5,968 to 14,800, an average of more than 10,000 homicides per year.[60] In 2008, according to the information made available to the Inter-American Commission, "there were a total of 13,780 homicides in Venezuela, which averages out to 1,148 murders a month and 38 every day."[61] Caracas was considered the murder capital of the world.[62]

The right to equality and nondiscrimination has also been massively violated, particularly on political matters. As a consequence of the exercise in 2003 and 2004 of the right to petition for a presidential recall referendum, all those who signed the petition (more than 3.5 million people) were included in a list used to openly discriminate them. In this respect, in general, in its *2009 Annual Report*, the Inter-American Commission on Human Rights found that "in Venezuela, not all persons are ensured full enjoyment of their rights irrespective of the positions they hold vis-à-vis the government's policies," highlighting "that the State's punitive power is being used to intimidate or punish people on account of their political opinions."[63]

---

[58] Inter-American Court of Human Rights, *Apitz Barbera et al. (Corte Primera de lo Contencioso Administrativo) v. Venezuela* (Judgment of Aug. 5, 2008), available at www.corteidh.or.cr.

[59] See Decision No. 1,939 (Dec. 18, 2009) (Case *Gustavo Álvarez Arias y otros*), available at http://www.tsj.gov.ve/decisiones/scon/Diciembre/1939-181208-2008-08-1572.html.

[60] In contrast, in New York City, only 461 homicides occurred in 2009, and about 500 per year over the past decade. In the past fifty years, the highest rate of homicides in New York was 2,245 in 1990. See Al Baker, "Homicides Near Record Low in New York City," *New York Times*, Dec. 29, 2009, A1 and A3.

[61] Inter-American Commission on Human Rights, *2009 Annual Report*, para. 505, available at http://www.cidh.oas.org/annualrep/ 2009eng/Chap.IV.f.eng.htm.

[62] See "The List: Murder Capitals of the World," *Foreign Policy*, Sept. 2008, http://www.foreignpolicy.com/story/cms.php?story_id=4480; David Paulin, "Caracas: Murder Capital of the World," Oct. 1, 2008, *American Thinker*, http://www.americanthinker.com/ 2008/10/ caracas_murder_capital_of_the.html.

[63] Inter-American Commission on Human Rights, *2009 Annual Report*, para. 472. In para. 475 of this *Report*, the Commission also noted "a troubling trend of punishments, intimidation, and attacks on individuals in reprisal for expressing their dissent with official policy. This trend affects both opposition authorities and citizens exercising their right to express their disagreement with the policies pursued by the government. These reprisals are carried out through both state actions, including harassment, and acts of violence perpetrated by civilians acting outside the law as violent groups. The Commission notes with concern that in some extreme cases, criminal

Moreover, the right to privacy in correspondence has been openly violated. In 2000–1, the National Assembly tapped telephone conversations of individuals without any judicial order, and transcripts were later published in state-owned media. The same sort of privacy rights were violated in 2002, when the Bank Supervision Agency ordered banks to inform the state's secret police of the accounts of opposition leaders, also without any judicial order.

Against expressions of tolerance in the Constitution, during the past decade, the country has witnessed the most bitter attacks by the president himself against the Catholic Church, the Cardinal and clerics[64]; in 2003, the foreign minister, at a meeting of the Organization of American States in Chile, promoted religious discrimination, denigrated the Catholic faith, and disqualified opposition; and then there were raids on Jewish schools and synagogues in 2008–9. The president himself promoted divisions in the Catholic Church in Venezuela,[65] and in July 2010, again he publicly insulted the Venezuelan Cardinal.[66]

With respect to labor rights, particularly the freedom to organize and manage trade unions has been violated since 2000. Trade unions have been subjected to administrative control. This is why, the Inter-American Commission on Human Rights, in its *2009 Annual Report*, noted "that Venezuela is still characterized by constant intervention in the functioning of its trade unions, through actions of the State that hinder the activities of union leaders and that point to political control over the organized labor movement, as well as through rules that allow government agencies to interfere in the election of union leaders," observing "with concern that in

---

proceedings have been brought against dissidents, accusing them of common crimes in order to deny them their freedom on account of their political positions." Available at http://www.cidh.oas.org/annualrep/2009eng/Chap.IV.f.eng.htm.

[64] The open attacks against the Catholic Church began in 2002, when the president qualified it as "one of the tumors the country has," rejecting the right of Cardinal Velasco to censure the use of churches for political purposes "without consulting anybody." See *El Nacional,* Caracas Jan. 25, 2002, D-4; *El Nacional,* Caracas Jan. 27, 2002, D-2; *El Universal,* Caracas Jan. 28, 2002, 1-4.

[65] That is why the rector of the Catholic University Andrés Bello (Luis Ugalde, S.J.) expressed his contrary opinion, affirming that "Chávez could not divide the Church." See *El Universal,* Caracas Jan. 31, 2002, 1-1. Another Jesuit (Jesús Gazo, S.J.) dissented. See *El Universal,* Caracas Oct. 16, 2000, 1-12.

[66] The Cardinal responded from Rome to the insults, insisting that "the president and his government wants to take the country through the road of Marxist socialism that fill all spaces, is totalitarian and lead to dictatorship." See "Cardenal Urosa Savino rechazó acusaciones del presidente Chávez," Rome, July 7, 2010, available at http://www.globovision.com/news.php?nid=154155.

Venezuela, trade-union membership is subject to pressure related to the political position or ideology of the particular union."[67]

A massive violation of the right to work occurred in 2003, with the dismissal of more than nineteen thousand workers of the state-owned Petróleos de Venezuela, S.A., after a general strike that took place in 2003, paralyzing the oil industry. The dismissals were compulsory, without any recognition of accumulated labor rights. The workers also saw their right to dwelling openly violated when they were violently evicted by the government from their homes in oilfield settlements by the national guard, with riot equipment.

Since 2002, exercise of the right to demonstrate has been severely reduced given continuous, systematic armored attacks of public police and military forces against any opposition demonstrations. In this regard, in its *2009 Annual Report*, the Inter-American Commission on Human Rights noted "that exercising the right of peaceful demonstration in Venezuela frequently leads to violations of the rights to life and humane treatment, which in many cases are the consequence of excessive use of state force or the actions of violent groups." In addition, the Commission noted the tendency "toward the use of criminal charges to punish people exercising their right to demonstrate or protest against government policies" (e.g., "blocking public highways, resisting the authorities, damage to public property, active obstruction of legally-established institutions, offenses to public officials, criminal instigation and criminal association, public incitement to lawbreaking, conspiracy, restricting freedom of employment, and breaches of the special secure zones regime, among others"), stressing that "this practice constitutes a restriction of the rights of assembly and freedom of expression guaranteed in the American Convention, the free exercise of which is necessary for the correct functioning of a democratic system that includes all sectors of society."[68] In addition, since 2002, the president has declared extensive urban areas to be military and security zones, completely excluding demonstrations in key areas of Caracas and other important cities.

In the realm of economic rights, property rights in particular have been systematically violated by means of the continuous seizure of rural land through the application of a land law and through confiscation (expropriation without compensation) of industrial assets, rights, and

---

[67]Inter-American Commission on Human Rights, *2009 Annual Report*, para. 477, available at http://www.cidh.oas.org/annualrep/ 2009eng/Chap.IV.f.eng.htm.

[68]Inter-American Commission on Human Rights, *2009 Annual Report*, para. 476, available at http://www.cidh.oas.org/annualrep/ 2009eng/Chap.IV.f.eng.htm.

enterprises in the oil, iron, steel, and cement industries (2006–9). There was the case of the confiscation of the rights and assets of Radio Caracas Televisión, considered to be opposition, after the government arbitrarily decided not to renew its concession. In that case, the Supreme Tribunal of Justice supported the confiscation of private property and assigned private rights to a state-owned entity without trial or compensation.[69]

For judicial guarantees of human rights, the general trend of the past decade has been systematic violation of due process. In some cases, by allowing impunity, like the massacre of peaceful demonstrators on April 11, 2002, that led to the resignation of the president,[70] and by transforming its authors into "heroes of the revolution" (Case: *Pistoleros de Puente Llaguno*). In that case, the police who were protecting demonstrators became criminals, condemned to a maximum prison term without due-process guarantees.[71]

Due process has been systematically violated in all cases regarding the dismissal of judges.[72] In other cases, the government has ignored judicial decisions, as was the case in 2003 with a decision of the First Court on Contentious Administrative, matters provisionally suspending the process of hiring foreign physicians not licensed to practice medicine. The president ignored the decision and ordered the dismissal of those judges without due process. After a decision of the Inter-American Court of Human Rights was issued in 2008 condemning the state for violating the dismissed judges' judicial guarantees, in 2008, the state considered the decisions of that court unenforceable in Venezuela.[73]

---

[69] See, in general, Antonio Canova González, Luis Alfonso Herrera Orellana, and Karina Anzola Spadaro, *Expropiaciones o vías de hecho? (La degradación continuada del derecho fundamental de propiedad en la Venezuela actual)*, Funeda, Universidad Católica Andrés Bello, Caracas 2009.

[70] On the facts surrounding the resignation of the president Chávez on Apr. 11, 2002, see Allan R. Brewer-Carías, *La crisis de la democracia venezolana. La Carta Democrática Interamericana y los sucesos de abril de 2002,* Los Libros de El Nacional, Colección Ares, Caracas 2002, 63ff.

[71] See "Ex comisarios Simonovis, Forero y Vivas sentenciados a 30 años de prisión," Apr. 3, 2009. See http://www.globovision.com/news.php?nid=113766 and http://www.vtv.gov.ve/noticias-nacionales/16500.

[72] The Inter-American Commission on Human Rights, in its *2009 Annual Report*, observed "that in Venezuela judges and prosecutors do not enjoy the guaranteed tenure necessary to ensure their independence following changes in policies or government. Also, in addition to being freely appointed and removable, a series of provisions have been enacted that allow a high level of subjectivity in judging judicial officials' actions during disciplinary proceedings," para 480. See http://www.cidh.oas.org/annualrep/2009eng/Chap.IV.f.eng.htm.

[73] See Decision No. 1,939 (Dec. 18, 2009) (Case *Gustavo Álvarez Arias y otros*), in http://www.tsj.gov.ve/decisiones/scon/Diciembre/1939-181208-2008-08-1572.html.

But the violation of due process also has occurred in past years through a systematic process of criminalizing dissidence, in which the government uses criminal prosecution and processes to persecute persons in opposition to the government.[74] In this regard, the Inter-American Court has already condemned the state for such violations, as in the 2009 case of a former minister of finance of Chávez's government who defected from government ranks once the president resigned in April 2002.[75] Afterward, he was condemned for insulting the armed forces when he explained on television how a flamethrower functions; a fact for which the Venezuelan state was condemned in 2009 by the Inter-American Court of Human Rights, for violation of his rights.[76]

In all cases in which judicial processes have been used to criminalize dissidence, the government has used the tools of the Public Prosecutor's Office to persecute elected opposition leaders, governors and mayors, opposition presidential candidates, and even former ministers and supporters of the government – in many cases, they have been detained and condemned (Case: *Baduel* – Former Minister of Defense-) or forced to leave the country (Case: *Peña* – Former Mayor of Caracas; Case: *Rosales* – Former Governor of Zulia state; Case: *Lapi* – Former Governor of Yaracuy state). In other cases, the docile and manageable public prosecutor has been used by the government to persecute entrepreneurial leaders not aligned with official policies (Case: *Anderson*). The most outrageous and scandalous case was that of a criminal judge (Case: *María Lourdes Afiuni Mora*) who, in 2009, and after recommendations by an independent panel of the United Nations on arbitrary detention, ordered the release from preventive prison (after more than two years without trial) of a businessman accused of financial crimes, to be prosecuted in freedom. The president ordered the judge to be imprisoned, violating all of his constitutional guarantees.[77]

---

[74]See Inter-American Commission on Human Rights, *2009 Annual Report*, para. 475. See http://www.cidh.oas.org/annualrep/ 2009eng/Chap.IV.f.eng.htm.

[75]On the resignation of president Chávez on Apr. 11, 2002, see Allan R. Brewer-Carías, *La crisis de la democracia venezolana. La Carta Democrática Interamericana y los sucesos de abril de 2002*, Los Libros de El Nacional, Colección Aries, Caracas 2002, 63ff; Humberto de la Calle, *El día que Chávez renunció. El golpe en la intimidad de la OEA*, Ediciones B, Bogotá 2008.

[76]Decision of Nov. 20, 2009, Case *Usón Ramírez vs. Venezuela*, available at http://www.corteidh.or.cr/ docs/casos/articulos/seriec_207_esp.pdf.

[77]See http://www.unog.ch/ unog/website/news_media.nsf/%28httpNewsByYear_en%29/ 93687E8429BD53A1C125768E00529DB6?OpenDocument&cntxt=B35C3&cookielang=fr. Also http://www.unionradio.net/ Actualidad/#&&NewsId=35473.

V. ACCESS TO POWER AND ITS EXERCISE CONTRARY TO THE RULE OF LAW

The second essential element of democracy according to the Inter-American Democratic Charter is access to and exercises of power in accordance with the rule of law. This implies that for democracy to exist, access to power must be in line with prescribed constitutional rules; furthermore, power must be exercised in accordance with the rule of law. There is no democracy without respect for the Constitution.

The first violation to the rule of law in the past decade was in 1999, by means of convening the Constituent Assembly in violation of the provisions of the 1961 Constitution. That process was completely controlled by Chávez's supporters, which excludd all other political actors from participating, leading to a constituent coup d'état. The Constituent Assembly assumed all state powers without any authority from the people and even issued transitional constitutional provisions without power to do so. Ex post facto, the same Supreme Tribunal of Justice appointed in the transitory constitutional regime, and challenged on the grounds of its unconstitutionality, ruled in 2000 that the Constituent Assembly had supraconstitutional powers and accepted two constitutional provisions: one approved by the people and the other not. It thus prolonged *sine die* the existence of the transitory and malleable constitutional regime. The fact is that, as mentioned by the Inter-American Commission on Human Rights in its *2009 Annual Report*, for instance, "even though the 1999 Constitution states that legislation governing the judicial system is to be enacted within the first year following the installation of the National Assembly, a decade later the Transitional Government Regime, created to allow the Constitution to come into immediate effect, remains in force."[78]

This regime was also the main tool that allowed the access to power in violation of the Constitution and the rule of law. In effect, in December 1999, the Constituent Assembly dismissed elected and unelected officials of the state and appointed, transitionally, new public servants, without complying with the Constitution. The Supreme Tribunal of Justice in 2001 extended the constitutional term of the president to allow "reelection" according to the provisions of the new Constitution[79]; and the transitory

---

[78] See Inter-American Commission on Human Rights, *2009 Annual Report*, para. 481. See http://www.cidh.oas.org/annualrep/ 2009eng/Chap.IV.f.eng.htm.

[79] The decision was adopted according to the public request formulated by the president. On Decision No. 457 (Apr. 5, 2001), see Allan R. Brewer-Carías, "Formas constitucionales de terminación del mandato del Presidente de la República," *Revista Primicia* 199, Caracas 2001, 2.

National Legislative Commission, exercising legislative powers without any constitutional authorization, appointed members of the National Electoral Council without following constitutional procedure. In 2000, the newly elected National Assembly, to nominate and appoint head officials, sanctioned a "special law" to regulate appointment for the first constitutional term, without complying with the constitutional provisions. The people's defender challenged the special law before the Supreme Tribunal. The judicial action was never decided; the people's defender and transitional magistrates were ratified in their positions. Later in 2002, members of the National Electoral Council were appointed by the Constitutional Chamber of the Supreme Tribunal, thus bypassing some constitutional provisions and violating others. In the same year, the Constitutional Chamber appointed the deputy prosecutor general, an appointment that corresponded to the National Assembly.

The result of all this is that, yes, many electoral processes have taken place to elect the president; governors; mayors; and members of the National Assembly, regional councils, and municipal councils. Nonetheless, access to power in accordance with the rule of law has been openly violated in other cases, particularly those of the organs of the citizens' power, electoral power, and judicial power. There, the provisions of the Constitution were set aside, and so it is that the executive completely controls all branches of government.

This situation, together with others facts observed by the Inter-American Commission on Human Rights in 2002, led it to point out the necessity of strengthening the rule of law in the country in its Preliminary Observations:

> 17. The IACHR considers that the lack of independence of the Judiciary, the limitations on freedom of expression, the proclivity of the Armed Forces to engage in politics, the extreme polarization of society, the action of the death squads, the scant credibility of the oversight institutions due to the uncertainty surrounding the constitutionality of their designation and the partiality of their actions, and the lack of coordination among the security forces, represent a clear weakness of the basic elements of the rule of law in a democracy, in the terms of the American Convention and the Inter-American Democratic Charter. Accordingly, the Commission calls for the rule of law to be strengthened in Venezuela as soon as possible.[80]

---

[80] See Allan R. Brewer-Carías, *La crisis de la democracia venezolana. La Carta Democrática Interamericana y los sucesos de abril de 2002*, Los Libros de El Nacional, Colección Ares, Caracas 2002.

But the second essential element of democracy defined in the Inter-American Democratic Charter not only imposes the need for a political system to ensure the access to power in accordance with the rule of law but also expressly prescribes the need for its exercise to be in accordance with the rule of law. When government violates the Constitution and legal order, or defrauds the Constitution, it violates the rule of law and it violates democracy. During the past decade, this has been the pattern of conduct of the authoritarian government of Venezuela.

In the legislative branch, during the past decade, particularly when representatives backing the government did not control a majority of votes, the interior regulations of the assembly were openly manipulated and reformed in 2003 and 2004 to allow the incorporation of deputies without formal requirements and to allow the assembly to annul its own previous decisions by simple majority. Sessions of the assembly were held outside the parliament official headquarters, in public spaces, to prevent the participation of opposition representatives because of violent threats from so-called Bolivarian circles. The provision of the Constitution guaranteeing representatives their right to vote according to their conscience has never been enforced, and never during the past decade have representatives been accountable to their constituency, as provided for in the Constitution.

Many Organic Laws were sanctioned by the National Assembly without complying with the need for a qualified majority to begin discussions, a procedure that the Constitutional Chamber of the Supreme Tribunal supported in 2004. That same year, it sanctioned the Organic Law of the Supreme Tribunal, which allowed the National Assembly to dismiss the tribunal's magistrates by simple majority vote. That is why in its *2009 Annual Report*, the Inter-American Commission on Human Rights has reiterated that "the rules for the appointment, removal, and suspension of magistrates set out in the Organic Law of the Supreme Court of Justice lack the safeguards necessary to prevent other branches of government from undermining the Supreme Court's independence and to keep narrow or temporary majorities from determining its composition."[81]

The National Assembly has renounced its basic function of legislating. In 2001, by sanctioning an enabling law, it delegated the legislative function to the president, who has since enacted all basic statutes through decree laws. The same occurred in 2007. Through such legislative delegations, the executive has violated the principle of the legislative reserve – that the

---

[81] See Inter-American Commission on Human Rights, *2009 Annual Report*, para. 478. See http://www.cidh.oas.org/annualrep/ 2009eng/Chap.IV.f.eng.htm.

Constitution place in the National Assembly certain legislative power that cannot be delegated, such as human rights, taxation, and criminal provisions. The 2007 delegation was the worst – it authorized the executive to legislate on matters that needed the approval of constitutional reform. The people rejected the 2007 draft constitutional reforms; nonetheless, the president issued decree laws implementing the reforms, thereby defrauding the will of the people.[82]

Also, special reference must be made to the role of the Constitutional Chamber as "positive legislator" by means of constitutional interpretation. In many cases, the Constitutional Chamber has openly issued legislation, as when reforming the procedural rules regarding *amparo*[83]; when it decided an action of unconstitutionality of various articles of the Income Law, it reformed ex officio one article that was not even challenged.[84] By means of a recourse for the abstract interpretation of the Constitution, the Constitutional Chamber has illegitimately reformed the Constitution, changing the meaning of its provisions and, in some cases, even implementing through judicial means the rejected constitutional reforms.[85]

---

[82] On these decree laws, see the articles published in *Revista de Derecho Público* 115 *(Estudios sobre los decretos leyes 2008)*, Editorial Jurídica Venezolana, Caracas 2008.

[83] See Allan R. Brewer-Carías, "El juez constitucional como legislador positivo y la inconstitucional reforma de la Ley Orgánica de Amparo mediante sentencias interpretativas," in *La ciencia del derecho procesal constitucional. Estudios en homenaje a Héctor Fix-Zamudio en sus cincuenta años como investigador del derecho*, coords. Eduardo Ferrer Mac-Gregor and Arturo Zaldívar Lelo de Larrea, Instituto de Investigaciones Jurídicas, Universidad Nacional Autónoma de México, Mexico City 2008, 5:63-80.

[84] See Allan R. Brewer-Carías, "El juez constitucional en Venezuela como legislador positivo de oficio en materia tributaria," in *Revista de Derecho Público* 109, Editorial Jurídica Venezolana, Caracas 2007, 193-212.

[85] See Allan R. Brewer-Carías, "La fraudulenta mutación de la Constitución en Venezuela, o de cómo el juez constitucional usurpa el poder constituyente originario," *Anuario de Derecho Público* 2, Centro de Estudios de Derecho Público de la Universidad e Monteávila, Caracas 2009, 23-65; "El juez constitucional al servicio del autoritarismo y la ilegítima mutación de la Constitución: El caso de la Sala Constitucional del Tribunal Supremo de Justicia de Venezuela (1999-2009)," *IUSTEL, Revista General de Derecho Administrativo* 21, Madrid 2009; "La ilegitima mutación de la Constitución y la legitimidad de la jurisdicción constitucional: La 'reforma' de la forma federal del estado en Venezuela mediante interpretación constitucional," in *Memoria del X Congreso Iberoamericano de Derecho Constitucional,* Instituto Iberoamericano de Derecho Constitucional, Asociación Peruana de Derecho Constitucional, Instituto de Investigaciones Jurídicas-UNAM y Maestría en Derecho Constitucional-PUCP, IDEMSA, Lima 2009, 1:29-51; "El juez constitucional como constituyente: el caso del financiamiento de las campañas electorales de los partidos políticos en Venezuela," *Revista de Derecho Público* 117, Caracas 2009, 195-203.

VI. BROKEN REPRESENTATIVE DEMOCRACY

Another essential element of democracy according to the Inter-American Democratic Charter is periodic, free, and fair elections based on secret balloting and universal suffrage as an expression of the sovereignty of the people. Therefore, elections are essential in representative democracy, and the impartiality and independence of the organ of electoral control are essential to its effectiveness and the fair character of the elections.

The 1999 Constitution makes the electoral power one of the branches of government with due autonomy and independence, in which no political party can have any sort of participation – also, citizens' participation must be guaranteed. This electoral body must function according to the principles of decentralized electoral administration, transparency, speed of balloting, and scrutiny (Article 294).

Nonetheless, in 1999–2000, members of the National Electoral Council were appointed transitionally, first by the National Constituent Assembly and later by the National Legislative Commission, in violation of Article 295 of the Constitution. This regime violated the Constitution by infringing on the autonomy of the electoral branch.

In 2002, after the sanctioning of the Organic Law of the Electoral Power, the National Assembly was due to appoint members of the National Electoral Council, but the Assembly failed to do so because representatives supporting the government could not achieve the two-thirds majority required for appointments and did not want to agree on the matter with the opposition. The consequence of this legislative omission was that the Constitutional Chamber of the Supreme Tribunal of Justice, when deciding an action filed against it, directly appointed members of the Electoral Council, without complying with conditions in the Constitution. Again in 2009, appointments did not respect the constitutional prohibition on electing members with party affiliation.[86]

---

[86] See Decisions No. 2073 (Aug. 4, 2003) (Caso: *Hermánn Escarrá Malaver y oros*) and No. 2341 (Aug. 25, 2003) (Caso: *Hermánn Escarrá M. y otros*), in Allan R. Brewer-Carías, *La Sala Constitucional versus el estado democrático de derecho. El secuestro del poder electoral y de la Sala Electoral del Tribunal Supremo y la confiscación del derecho a la participación política*, Los Libros de El Nacional, Colección Ares, Caracas 2004, 172; "El secuestro del poder electoral y la confiscación del derecho a la participación política mediante el referendo revocatorio presidencial: Venezuela 2000-2004," *Boletín Mexicano de Derecho Comparado* 112, Instituto de Investigaciones Jurídicas, Universidad Nacional Autónoma de México, Mexico City 2005, 11-73; Rafael Chavero G. et al., *La guerra de las salas del TSJ frente al referéndum revocatorio*, Editorial Aequitas, Caracas 2004, 13-58.

The foregoing has served to weaken progressively representative democracy in Venezuela – the elections are directed by an organ in which civil society and most political parties have no confidence. In 2002, again, the Inter-American Commission on Human Rights, on its last visit to the country, pointed out the following regarding the composition of the National Electoral Council:

> 51. The organs of public power with jurisdiction to settle claims regarding the transparency and legality of elections should be endowed with the utmost impartiality, and should resolve such matters fairly and promptly, as the best way to ensure the effective exercise of the right to elect and be elected established in Article 23 of the American Convention. Accordingly, the Commission recommends that the full and definitive composition of the National Electoral Council proceed as regulated in the Constitution.[87]

VII. WEAKENED DEMOCRACY DUE TO THE ABSENCE OF PLURALISM

The fourth essential element of representative democracy is a pluralistic system of political parties and organizations, for which the strengthening of political parties and other political organizations is a priority (Article 5). Political pluralism is opposed to all ideas of concentrated power and political organization of society promoted by the state or from the state.

Thus, a plural democratic regime is always opposed to state power. In it, parties and political organizations try to be outside the sphere of the state and its influence so individuals and social groups can freely develop. Pluralism, furthermore, ought to ensure free elections, government alternation, political participation, and power decentralization. A plural regime of parties and political organizations is the antidote to authoritarianism.

Political pluralism, therefore, implies the need for the democratic existence of a multiplicity of political groups, parties, and organizations, outside the reach of the state. The Constitution in several provisions refers to associations or organizations with political purposes (Article 67), to organizations of civil society (Articles 293.6 and 296), and to organized society (Article 211). In contrast, the Constitution grants the electoral power interference in the organizations of civil society through the power to organize the internal elections not only of trade unions and professional

---

[87]See Allan R. Brewer-Carías, *La crisis de la democracia venezolana. La Carta Democrática Interamericana y los sucesos de abril de 2002,* Los Libros de El Nacional, Colección Ares, Caracas 2002, 164.

groups but also of organizations with political purposes (Article 293.6). This, in itself, is a step back for political pluralism and an inconvenient transformation of social organizations into part of the state.

Social groups outside the ambit of state power guarantee political pluralism as an essential element of democracy. Thus, the Constitution bestows on public officers the obligation to be "at the service of the state and not at the service of any party" (Article 145), to clearly separate the political organization of the society (the state) from the organized groups of society (parties and organizations of civil society), preventing in the Constitution, even though inconvenient and contrary to the provisions of the Democratic Charter (Article 5), the financing of the associations with political purposes with funds from the state (Article 67). This constitutional prohibition was "reformed" in 2008 by the Constitutional Chamber, which allowed public financing of electoral activities.[88]

In Venezuela, political pluralism has been severely harmed by the integration of the government party into the state in a way never known before in Venezuelan political history. The United Socialist Party has been created from within the state, and with public funds, and its authorities are the officials of the state. The president has been president of the government party and the ministers have been directors of the same.[89] The state, therefore, is at the service of the official government party, and the latter is at the service of the state. Other political organizations and parties different from that of the government have been discriminated against – and now the official party could receive all the public financing.

The integration of the government party into the state has provoked the complete inapplicability of all constitutional rules regarding civil service, for instance, appointment of officers only by means of public competition and their stability. In the imbricate grid between state and party, the appointments of public servants are discretionary, as is their dismissal. Public Administration, having been cleansed, is the exclusive "booty" of the

---

[88] See the Constitutional Chamber Decision No. 780 (May 8, 2008), in *Revista de Derecho Público* 114, Caracas 2008, 127ff. See Allan R. Brewer-Carías, "El juez constitucional como constituyente: El caso del financiamiento de las campañas electorales de los partidos políticos en Venezuela," in *Revista de Derecho Público* 117, Caracas 2009, 195-203.

[89] Since the beginning of the Chávez government, the "political command of the revolution" was established by the president with officials of the state. See *El Nacional,* Caracas Nov. 11, 2001, D-4, and Jan. 20, 2002, D-6. See Angela Zago, Felipe Mújica, and Pablo Medina, *El Nacional,* Caracas Jan. 20, 2002, H-1.

government party.⁹⁰ Consequently, the new public service comprises exclusively members of the government party or those who support its policies.

During the past decade, the state has tried to politically organize society. At the beginning, this was carried out through so-called Bolivarian circles, groups that were the antithesis of pluralism because of their full dependence of the organs of power. They were used for political purposes, threatening and violently attacking institutions, organizations, or persons not supporting the government. They have acted as shock troops to verbally and physically assault those identified as enemies of the political process, particularly leaders of the opposition, including members of the National Assembly and municipal authorities, journalists and communicators, and social leaders, especially in the trade union and university movements. In his report to the general assembly of the Organization of American States, the secretary-general of that organization said: "The Bolivarian Circles are groups of citizens or grassroots organizations who support the President's political platform. Many sectors consider them responsible for the human rights violations, acts of intimidation, and looting." The secretary-general added: "The state, and let there be no doubt about this, must retain a monopoly on the legitimate use of force. The accusations that certain sectors are jeopardizing the legitimate use of force must be investigated. In all cases, any use of force must occur under authorization and within the normative framework to which the military adheres."⁹¹

The Inter-American Commission on Human Rights asserted also in 2002: "The international responsibility of the State is triggered if groups of civilians act freely violating rights, with the support or acquiescence of the Government. Accordingly, the Commission called on the Government to investigate seriously the acts of violence attributed to some 'Bolivarian Circles,' and to take, as urgently as possible, all measures necessary to prevent these acts from recurring. In particular, it is essential that the monopoly of force be maintained exclusively by the public security forces;

---

⁹⁰In 2002, the head of the "political command of the revolution," Guillermo García Ponce, announced the definitive cleansing of public administration to sack all civil servants "not identified politically with the process." See *El Nacional*, Caracas Jan. 22, 2002, D-1.

⁹¹See Allan R. Brewer-Carías, *La crisis de la democracia en Venezuela*, Libros El Nacional, Caracas 2002, 168.

complete disarmament of any group of civilians should immediately be guaranteed."[92]

These Bolivarian circles, informally created by the government to attack any opposition institution, have lost their protagonist role – many have remained "institutionalized" in certain urban sectors as instruments for political control of the population; many of them are armed by the government and remain at its disposal.

The interference of the state in trade unions must be highlighted, as well, and even the interference of the president himself in their elections, such as by ignoring their results or promoting a government candidate to the Venezuelan Confederation of Workers.[93]

The Inter-American Commission on Human Rights in 2002 gave a particular treatment to the subject of the right to form and join trade unions in the country as well. In a May 2002 press release, stressing that it was informed "that once the elections were held, in keeping with the rules of the National Electoral Council, the elected directors of the union federation (*Confederación de Trabajadores de Venezuela CTV*) were not recognized by the national authorities," urging "Venezuelan State to resolve as soon as possible, and in keeping with Venezuela's international obligations, the conflict that came about due to the failure of the authorities to recognize the freely elected authorities of the CTV.[94]

Sadly, since 2000, the Supreme Tribunal of Justice has been in charge of regimenting and distorting the organizations of civil society, as when it denied that members of the Catholic Church be "representatives" of society[95]; when it excluded from the concept of civil society the associations, groups, and institutions that receive foreign financial help (as from international solidarity); and has said that whoever acts on behalf of a social organization shall do so "elected by someone to fulfill such

---

[92]Paras. 57-58. See Allan R. Brewer-Carías, *La crisis de la democracia venezolana. La Carta Democrática Interamericana y los sucesos de abril de 2002,* Los Libros de El Nacional, Colección Ares, Caracas 2002, 170.

[93]See *El Nacional,* Caracas Jan. 8, 2002, D-1; *El Nacional,* Caracas Sept. 3, 2001, D-1.

[94]See Allan R. Brewer-Carías, *La crisis de la democracia venezolana. La Carta Democrática Interamericana y los sucesos de abril de 2002,* Los Libros de El Nacional, Colección Ares, Caracas 2002, 171-72.

[95]See *El Nacional,* Caracas Nov. 24, 2000, D-1; *El Universal,* Caracas Sept. 18, 2000, 1-4. See Liliana Ortega, *El Nacional,* Caracas Nov. 27, 2000, D-4; and references to the tribunal decisions in Pedro Nikken, "El Tribunal Supremo de Justicia ¿Juez o parte?," in Allan R. Brewer-Carías et al., *La libertad de expresión amenazada. Sentencia 1.013,* Instituto Interamericano de Derechos Humanos, Editorial Jurídica Venezolana, Caracas 2001, 130ff.

representation."[96] Political pluralism, as an essential element of democracy, has been seriously threatened in Venezuela by the State power.

VIII. VANISHING DEMOCRACY AND ABSENT SEPARATION OF POWERS

The fifth essential element of representative democracy according to the Inter-American Democratic Charter is separation and independence of branches of government: checks and balances.

With no institutional control of power, democracy could not exist: only by controlling state power can respect for human rights and fundamental freedoms exist; only by controlling state power can the rule of law be achieved; only by controlling state power can periodic, free, and fair elections be held; and only by controlling state power can a plural regime of parties and political organizations exist. Without separation and independence of all branches of government, vertically and horizontal, there is no effective democracy.

The 1999 Constitution provides a double distribution (separation and independence) of branches of government and state powers. The vertical distribution establishes that the public power is distributed among municipalities, states, and the national government, each with political autonomy. The horizontal distribution is made across five branches – legislative, executive, judicial, citizen, and electoral – each with independence and autonomy (Article 136).

From the horizontal point of view, as has been highlighted throughout this book, separation of powers has progressively vanished as a fundamental principle of the constitutional state, to the point that in December 2009, the president of the Supreme Tribunal of Justice proposed a final reform of the 1999 Constitution to definitively eliminate the principle of separation of powers that she considered "debilitates the State" and one of the aspects of the Constitution that contradicts the implementation of "the regime."[97] Unfortunately, it has been precisely because of this, that control on the exercise of state power has disappeared[98] and, in particular, that the Judiciary

---

[96] See the comments on the Supreme Trubunal decisions in Allan R. Brewer-Carías, *Derecho Administrativo,* Universidad Externado de Colombia, Bogotá 2005, 1:413ff.

[97] See Juan Francisco Alonso on the statement of Luisa Estela Morales, "Morales: 'La división de poderes debilita al estado.' La presidenta del TSJ afirma que la Constitución hay que reformarla," *El Universal*, Caracas Dec. 5, 2009. See the entire text of the statement of the president of the Supreme Tribunal at http://www.tsj.gov.ve/informacion/notasde prensa/notasdeprensa.asp?codigo=7342.

[98] See Allan R. Brewer-Carías, *Constitución, democracia y control del poder*, Centro Iberoamericano de Estudios Provinciales y Locales, Universidad de Los Andes/Editorial Jurídica Venezolana. Mérida, octubre 2004.

has been progressively subjected to the executive for the purpose of assuring the support of the "regime." That is why, for instance, in 2010 the constitutional provision establishing disciplinary jurisdiction for judges (Article 267) is not in force. The provisional status of judges has been the common trend of the judiciary and with it, unfortunately, the break in their autonomy and independence. In this regard, the Inter-American Commission on Human Rights in its *2009 Annual Report* noted "with concern the failure to organize public competitions for selecting judges and prosecutors, and so those judicial officials are still appointed in a discretionary fashion without being subject to competition. Since they are not appointed through public competitions, judges and prosecutors are freely appointed and removable, which seriously affects their independence in making decisions"; observing, in addition, that "in Venezuela judges and prosecutors do not enjoy the guaranteed tenure necessary to ensure their independence following changes in policies or government."[99]

This situation has led during the past decade to the long-standing problem of a Judiciary mainly composed by provisional judges, a situation that has a negative impact on the stability, independence, and autonomy that should govern the Judiciary. This situation has been raised with concern since 2002 by the Inter-American Commission on Human Rights in all its *Annual Reports* on the situation of human rights in Venezuela,[100] having expressed in its Preliminary Observations issued in its last visit to the country that "the problem of provisional judges has become more severe and more widespread since the current administration began the process of restructuring the Judiciary."[101]

Unfortunately, none of those recommendations have been implemented, and the commission continued to make those observations through 2009. The procedure established in the Constitution to appoint judges through public competition has not yet been implemented, and the disciplinary jurisdiction to guarantee judges' stability did not yet exist in 2010. The Supreme Tribunal has continued to accept their discretionary dismissal.

The final expression of the absolute lack of judges' autonomy and stability occurred in December 2009, when a criminal judge (María Lourdes Afiuni Mora) ordered the conditional release pending trial of a detainee whose

---

[99]See IACHR, *2009 Annual Report*, para. 479-480. See http://www.cidh.oas.org/annualrep/2009eng/Chap.IV.f.eng.htm.

[100]See Allan R. Brewer-Carías, *La crisis de la democracia venezolana. La Carta Democrática Interamericana y los sucesos de abril de 2002,* Los Libros de El Nacional, Colección Ares, Caracas 2002, 180.

[101]Id.

which in Venezuela has suffered severe attacks from government and in particular from the president.[114] Even the Supreme Tribunal has limited those freedoms, contrary to the Constitution.[115]

There also have been governmental threats and harassment of the media and media directors, particularly after sanctioning of the Telecommunications Law and of the Law on the Social Responsibility of Media.[116] Regarding the provisions of this law dealing with accusations of incitement, the Inter-American Commission on Human Rights in its 2009 Annual Report has stated "that because of their extreme vagueness, the severity of the associated punishments, and the fact that their enforcement is the responsibility of a body that depends directly on the executive branch…may lead to arbitrary decisions that censor or impose a subsequent disproportionate penalty on citizens or the media for simply expressing criticisms or dissent that may be disturbing to public officials temporarily holding office in the enforcement agency."[117] In this regard, the case of the former state governor and opposition leader Oswaldo Álvarez Paz, who was detained in February 2010 for expressing criticisms against government policies, is pathetic. After arbitrarily being detained for a few weeks, he was submitted to prosecution for crimes such as "diffusion of false information" and "hate public instigation."[118]

Regarding freedom of information violations, the Inter-American Court of Human Rights since 2002 has condemned the actions of the state and of groups related to it and has issued protective preliminary measures for

---

[114]Since 2002, the president has openly attacked editors and media directors: Andrés Mata, *El Universal*; Alberto Federico Ravell, *Globovisión;* and Miguel Enrique Otero, *El Nacional*. See *El Universal*, Feb. 10, 2002, 1-4. The threats against Globovisión began in Oct. 2001. See the statement by the president of the station, Guillermo Zuloaga, in *El Universal*, Caracas Oct. 29, 2001, 1-6. See my comment in *El Nacional*, Caracas Oct. 6, 2001, A-1 and D-2; *El Impulso*, Barquisimeto, Oct. 6, 2001, A-1 and D-6.

[115]See *El Nacional*, Caracas June 29, 2001, D-2, and Jan. 2, 2002, D-1; *El Universal*, Caracas July 23, 2001, 1-4. On Decision No. 1.013 (June 12, 2001), see *El Universal*, Caracas June 15, 2001, 1-4; *El Nacional*, Caracas June 15, 2001, D-1; June 16, 2001, D-4; June 24, 2001, H-1; June 23, 2001, P. D-1. On this decision, see Allan R. Brewer-Carías, Héctor Faúndez Ledesma, Pedro Nikken, Carlos M. Ayala Corao, Rafael Chavero Gazdik, Gustavo Linares Benzo, and Jorge Olavarría, *La libertad de expresión amenazada. Sentencia 1.013*, Instituto Interamericano de Derechos Humanos, Editorial Jurídica Venezolana, Caracas 2001.

[116]See Allan R. Brewer-Carías et al., *Ley de Responsabilidad Social de Radio y Televisión*, Editorial Jurídica Venezolana, Caracas 2006.

[117]See Inter-American Commission on Human Rights, *2009 Annual Report*, para. 489. See http://www.cidh.oas.org/annualrep/ 2009eng/Chap.IV.f.eng.htm.

[118]See Rafael Rodríguez, "Tribunal ordena juicio contra Oswaldo Alvarez Paz, (Interview)," in El Universal June 27, 2010. See http://politica.eluniversal.com/2010/05/28/pol_ava_tribunal-ordena-juic_28A3924891.shtml.

THE RIGHT TO DEMOCRACY AND ITS VIOLATION

television stations and journalists, which the government has refused to enforce.[119] In general terms, as expressed by the executive secretary of the Inter-American Commission, "the harassment acts against journalist[s] and media have a very grave multiplied effect on the violations against human rights regarding all the people of Venezuela."[120] In its *2009 Annual Report*, the Inter-American Commission noted "that recent months have seen an increase in administrative proceedings sanctioning media that criticize the government," expressing concern that "in several of these cases, the investigations and administrative procedures began after the highest authorities of the State called on public agencies to take action against *Globovisión* and other media outlets that are independent and critical of the government."[121]

One tool for limiting freedom of information that the government, particularly that the president has used, is the systematic, compulsory, and abrupt interruption of programming on private radio and television signals, with long blanket broadcast of statements and political messages from the president.[122] The Inter-American Commission, in its *2009 Annual Report*, has referred to the use by the president of this powers "to broadcast his speeches simultaneously across the media, with no time constraints," expressing that "the duration and frequency of these presidential blanket broadcasts could be considered abusive on account of the information they contain, which might not always be serving the public interest."[123]

---

[119]See Carlos Ayala Corao, *El Nacional*, Caracas Jan. 11, 2002, D-2; Pedro Nikken, *El Universal*, Caracas Jan. 15, 2002, 1-5; Lileana Ortega, *El Nacional*, Caracas Jan. 18, 2002, D-1. See also *El Nacional*, Jan. 22, 2002; *El Nacional*, Caracas Jan. 22, 2002, D-4. The secretary-general of the Inter-American Commission, Santiago Cantón, compelled the government to execute preliminary measures. See *El Universal*, Feb. 8, 2002, 1-4. In Jan. 2002, the Inter-American Commission issued protective measures for the director of *El Universal*, Andrés Mata. See *El Universal*, Caracas Jan. 25, 2002, 1-8; *El Nacional*, Caracas Jan. 25, 2002, D-6. The premises of *El Universal* were also "visited" by groups supporting the government. See *El Universal*, Caracas Jan. 14, 2002, 1-9.

[120]See *El Universal*, Caracas Feb. 9, 2002, 1-6.

[121]See Inter-American Commission on Human Rights, *2009 Annual Report*, para. 486. See http://www.cidh.oas.org/annualrep/ 2009eng/Chap.IV.f.eng.htm.

[122]Opposition members of the National Assembly challenged before the Supreme Tribunal Article 209 of the Telecommunications Law that authorizes such blanket broadcasts "considering unconstitutional because "contrary to the right to information." See *El Nacional*, Caracas Feb. 8, 2002, D-6. The executive secretary of the Inter-American Commission on Human Rights considered the use of such blanket broadcast as acceptable only in cases of "extreme necessity to inform public interest matters" and that the president "has used it in an unreasonable way." See *El Nacional*, Caracas Feb. 9, 2002, D-4; *El Universal*, Caracas Feb. 10, 2002, 1-4.

[123]See Inter-American Commission on Human Rights, *2009 Annual Report*, para. 492. See http://www.cidh.oas.org/annualrep/ 2009eng/Chap.IV.f.eng.htm. As reported by Luís Carías, "From 1999 up to Jan. 2010, the president has transmitted 1995 *cadenas* [blanket broadcasts] through radio and TV, which is equal to 1,310 hours, 36 minutes and three seconds, which means almost two

XI. DEMOCRACY AND SUBMISSION OF THE MILITARY TO CIVIL POWER

The Inter-American Democratic Charter states furthermore that the constitutional subordination of all state institutions to civil authority legally constituted is a fundamental component of democracy (Article 4). That points to the subordination of the military to the civilian authority. However, in contrast, in Venezuela, the progressive militarization of the state as a governmental policy has broken that subordination, and the danger of a military party at the service of the president has arisen. This situation, denounced since 2001,[124] has worsened during the past decade, with the military and retired military occupying all high positions in the public administration; and with the military participating in administrative and police functions, or in upholding law and order, considered by the Inter-American Commission on Human Rights as "incompatible with a democratic approach to the defense and security of the State"; considering that "a democratic society demands a clear and precise separation between domestic security, as a function of the police, and national defense, as a function of the armed forces, since the two agencies have substantial differences in the purposes for which they were created and in their training and skills."[125]

The militaristic process of the state peaked in 2008 with the transformation of the armed forces, against the will expressed by the people in the 2007 constitutional reform referendum, into the Bolivarian Armed Force and the Bolivarian Militia at the service of the president.[126] That was the beginning of the consolidation of the "military party"[127] – since 2009, the president has been "president commander" (*comandante presidente*) of the republic.

---

months of broadcasts." See Luis Carías, "Mil 995 cadenas ha transmitido Chávez desde que asumió el poder," in *Diario El Carabobeno*, Jan. 28, 2010. Available at http://www.el-carabobeno.com/p_pag_hnot.aspx?art=a280110 e04&id=t280110-e04.

[124]See the criticisms by Pablo Medina, as secretary-general of the party Patria para Todos, which used to be part of the coalition of parties supporting the government, saying that what the president wanted was to impose an "authoritarian militarism," in *El Universal*, Caracas Mar. 23, 2000, 1-7; *El Nacional*, Caracas Jan. 12, 2002, D-3; *El Nacional*, Caracas Jan. 15, 2002, D-6. See the report *Consultores 21* for *Veneconomia* on the "Militarization of Government," *El Universal*, Caracas Dec. 23, 2001, 1-10.

[125]See IACHR, *2009 Annual Report*, para. 501. See http://www.cidh.oas.org/annualrep/2009eng/Chap.IV.f.eng.htm.

[126]See Organic Law on the Bolivarian Armed Force, *Gaceta Oficial* No. 5,891 of July 31, 2008; reformed in 2009, *Gaceta Oficial* No. 5.933, Extra., of Oct. 21, 2009.

[127]The first signs of the idea of a military party were expressed in 2001, when high officers of the Armed Forces made public a communiqué of adherence to the head of state and his revolution. See *El Nacional* (Caracas), Nov. 8, 2001, D-1, Nov. 9, 2001, D-1; Norberto Ceresole, foreign adviser to the

Also since 2001, the president has encouraged politics within the armed forces, as when justifying the elimination from the Constitution of the prohibition on them being deliberative. That has justified public expressions of generals supporting the president as party chief, not as commander in chief of the armed forces. In addition, a formal compulsory military salute was imposed for use on any occasion by the military: *patria, socialismo o muerte* ("patriotism, socialism, or death").[128]

The Inter-American Commission on Human Rights since 2002 expressed its concerns on the "undue influence of the Armed Forces in the political life of the country, and the existence of excessive involvement by the Armed Forces in political decisions" that could be "traced back to the fact that the 1999 Venezuelan Constitution removed a rule traditionally included in the constitutions that preceded it, according to which the Armed Forces are an '*apolitical and non-deliberating*' body." The Commission in its Preliminary Observations issued after its last visit to Venezuela in 2002 remained that "the reality in the region shows that the involvement of the armed forces in politics generally precedes departures from the constitution, which in almost all cases leads to serious human rights violations."[129]

All the aforementioned problems affecting democracy in Venezuela have been provoked by a government that does not believe in representative democracy and that conceives of participatory democracy as a tool to concentrate and centralize power – thus confusing mobilization with participation. This situation has provoked an extreme polarization and has caused bitter, apparently irreconcilable intolerance between the government and the opposition. Much hate has been spread by the president for what is now a long decade in his attempts to impose his so-called Bolivarian revolution and a socialist system, which in 2010 has been officially identified as a Marxist revolution and system, for which nobody has voted – and was indeed rejected by the people in the 2007 constitutional reform

---

president, considered the communiqué a "legitimate" expression of the "military party." *El Nacional* (Caracas), Nov. 11, 2001, D-4.

[128]See Alberto Muller Rojas (Military Presidential Chief of Staff), in Reuters, "Venezuelan military adopts Chavez socialism slogan," *El Universal*, Caracas May 13, 2007, in http://www.reuters.com/article/idUSN1142580120070511. On the official slogan of the United Socialist Party of Venezuela: "*Patria socilaista o muerte*," see its "Declaration of Principles" (Apr. 23, 2010), Available at http://psuv.org.ve/files/tcdocumentos/Declaracion-de-principios-PSUV.pdf

[129]See para. 65 in Allan R. Brewer-Carías, *La crisis de la democracia venezolana: La Carta Democrática Interamericana y los sucesos de abril de 2002,* Los Libros de El Nacional, Colección Ares, Caracas 2002, 195.

referendum – and the majority rejects.[130] That is, most Venezuelans want democracy as a political system with all its fundamental elements and essential components, as defined in the Inter-American Democratic Charter – precisely those that the government has systematically violated and demolished.

Unfortunately, the hate that has been spread by the president has led to the consolidation of irreconcilable extremes and, regrettably, there is only a short pace from hate to violence, particularly with devastating destruction of institutions, worsening economic and social conditions, and increasing poverty.[131]

The government has made every imaginable effort to provoke a political and social definitive confrontation and to complete its total destruction of the country, its institutions, and what remains of democracy after being progressively dismantled.[132]

---

[130] According to the results of a poll made by Alfredo Keller y Asociados, Consultoría en Asuntos Públicos, 74 % is against elimination of private property; 74% is against expropriation of all private enterprises; 66% is against substitute private property by a social property; 58% is against transforming Venezuela into a socialist country, and 83% is against converting Venezuela into a communist country like Cuba. See *Estudio de Opinión Pública*, 2d, Semester 2010, May 2010, 14.

[131] See Francisco Rodríguez, "An Empty Revolution: The Unfulfilled Promises of Hugo Chávez," *Foreign Affairs* 87, http://www.foreignaffairs.com/articles/63220/francisco-rodr%C3%83%C2%ADguez/an-empty-revolution.

[132] In the 2008 report of Human Rights Watch, the following was the conclusion of its executive summary: "A country's citizens cannot participate fully and equally in its politics when their rights to freedom of expression and association are at risk. Ensuring these essential rights requires more than constitutional guarantees and political rhetoric. It requires institutions that are capable of countering and curbing abusive state practices. Above all, it requires a judiciary that is independent, competent, and credible. It is also critical that non-state institutions – such as the media, organized labor, and civil society – are free from government reprisals and political discrimination. President Chávez has actively sought to project himself as a champion of democracy, not only in Venezuela, but throughout Latin America. Yet his professed commitment to this cause is belied by his government's willful disregard for the institutional guarantees and fundamental rights that make democratic participation possible. Venezuela will not achieve real and sustained progress toward strengthening its democracy – nor will it serve as a useful model for other countries in the region – so long as its government continues to flout the human rights principles enshrined in its own constitution." See Human Rights Watch, *A Decade under Chávez: Political Intolerance and Lost Opportunities for Advancing Human Rights in Venezuela,* Sept. 2008, http://www.hrw.org/reports/2008/venezuela0908/.

INDEX

-A-

abrogation referenda, 111-112, 115, 185, 281, 286
alternate government, 30, 67, 81, 99, 102-103, 122, 127, 168, 169, 175, 202, 223, 268, 283-284, 338, 341-344, 359-365, 398
approval referendum, 102-112, 185, 240, 287
arbitration, 127, 258
armed forces, 95, 131-133, 270, 273-274, 303, 307-310, 334, 371, 391, 394, 406, 409-410
authoritarian government, 1-3, 12-14, 22, 29-30, 40, 65, 91, 158, 167, 169-170, 183, 199, 211-212, 223-224, 239, 245, 262, 291, 367, 370-371, 387, 394
authoritarianism, 13, 27-28, 33, 89, 95-98, 123, 132, 152, 165, 167, 170-172, 177, 183-184, 186, 188-189, 193-195, 211, 220, 241, 262, 312, 336, 398

-B-

Bolivarian Armed Force, 97, 133-135, 272, 275-276, 305, 310-312, 336, 412
Bolivarian Circles, 93, 395, 401-403
Bolivarian doctrine, 92, 95, 221, 264-265, 269, 272-273, 334
Bolivarian republic, partisan character, 91-95, 273
Bolivarian revolution, 5, 6, 42, 93, 95, 113, 407, 411
budgetary discipline, 174, 273, 279

-C-

capital district, 196, 200-201, 208, 293-295, 336, 385, 405
Catholic Church, 389, 401
cement industry, nationalization, 165, 256-257, 390
Central Bank of Venezuela, autonomy, 281, 306-307, 323-325
centralized federation, 20, 28, 45, 87, 96, 99, 165, 170, 177, 183, 189-191, 198, 202, 291, 346
centralized socialist state, 22, 191, 194, 266, 272, 274-276, 282, 292, 313, 321-322, 331
centralized state, 20, 38, 42, 45, 89, 139, 190-191, 269, 291, 330
centralized state economy, 159, 164, 269, 275-276, 313-314, 319
checks and balances, 1, 21, 46-47, 122-123, 139, 175, 214-216, 219-220, 370, 401

citizen's power, 106, 109, 123, 228, 382
civil society, participation, 21, 35, 42, 47, 51, 62, 64, 103, 106-110, 117, 131, 157, 176, 218, 227, 284-285, 307, 311, 376, 383, 385, 397-398, 401, 406
Colombia, Constituent Assembly, 1-2, 11-12, 18, 38-39, 52, 53
communal councils, 14, 22, 25, 67, 99, 116, 118, 166, 184, 191-193, 195-196, 208, 266, 269, 282, 288, 293, 295-296, 298-299, 332, 369, 385
concentration of powers, 21, 28, 35, 65, 90, 95-96, 123-124, 147, 169-171, 175, 177, 193-194, 211-212, 216, 219-220, 281, 289, 314, 405
confiscation, 29, 134, 160, 227, 245, 248-249, 253-254, 260, 390, 406
Congress, extinction, 13, 16, 23, 59, 65, 73, 106, 337
constituent assemblies, exclusion, 9, 22, 27, 35, 53, 57, 60, 185
constituent assemblies, history, 7, 11, 18, 22, 37-38
constituent assemblies, nonconsensual, 7, 9
Constituent Assembly 1999, 12-13, 21, 35-67
Constituent Assembly 1999, election, 1-2, 9, 12, 15-16, 18-19, 24, 40, 50, 52, 55-57
Constituent Assembly 1999, judicial review, 53, 79
constituted powers, seizure, 57-60, 69-80
Constitution 1999, drafting, 60
Constitution 1999, illegitimate interpretation, 335-358
Constitution 1999, transitory regime, 64-66, 69-84
constitution-making process 1999, 49-63
constitutional declarations, 134, 141
constitutional fraud, 1, 7, 9, 13-15, 18, 22, 24-26, 28, 30, 33, 36, 49, 91, 132, 152, 165-167, 174, 177, 194-195, 217-218, 221-224, 233, 244, 264-265, 267-269, 275, 284, 291, 310, 329, 333-334, 336, 340-341, 345, 349, 359, 368, 373, 375, 381, 394-395
constitutional guarantees, suspension, 303, 326
constitutional interpretation, recourse, 51, 239, 242-244, 333, 340, 347, 396
constitutional rights, 134-164, 303-328
constitutional values, 134
constitutional reform, 209, 264-328
constitutional review, means, 2, 9, 15, 50, 223, 240, 284, 287-288, 328, 335, 344, 362
corruption, 31, 248, 349, 370, 404, 406

-D-

decentralization, 20, 45, 63, 87, 96, 98, 100, 170, 172, 187, 189, 201-202, 207, 281, 404
decentralization, crisis, 44, 65, 89, 97, 116, 139, 190, 193, 196, 209-210, 270, 272, 276, 293, 298, 319, 333, 347-348, 370, 405
defrauding democracy, 1, 7, 9, 13-15, 18, 22, 24-26, 28, 30, 33, 36, 49, 91, 132, 152, 165-167, 174, 177, 194-195, 217-218, 220-224, 233, 241, 264-265, 267-269, 275, 284, 291, 310, 329, 333-334, 336, 340-341, 345, 349, 359, 368, 373, 375, 381, 394-395

INDEX

delegate legislation, 123, 151-152, 176-177, 194-195, 219, 254, 256, 329, 381, 395
democracy, essential elements, 3, 7, 47, 101, 102, 167, 169, 215, 367-368, 370, 386
democracy, separation of powers, 7, 9, 43, 46, 87, 95, 122-123, 139, 168-177, 203, 210-216, 219-220, 225, 238, 306, 367, 370, 401-402
dictatorship of democracy, 25-26, 116, 166, 193-194, 196
direct democracy, institutions, 99, 101, 102, 105, 110-111, 114, 116, 184-189, 191, 194-195, 221, 274, 280-283, 285, 292

-E-

economic constitution, 15, 27, 31, 66, 90-91, 134, 136, 138, 147-148, 151, 155-163, 194, 221, 246, 264, 266, 269-277, 279, 288, 311-318, 328, 330, 390, 406
economic freedom, 156-158, 160, 266, 312-314, 324
economy intervention, 22, 156, 160, 163, 313, 318, 406
economy state appropriation, 29, 156, 158, 245, 248-249, 251, 254, 258-259
Ecuador, constituent assembly, 2, 11, 14-16, 18, 26, 37-39, 53
electoral power, dependency, 79, 108-109, 121, 124, 138, 175, 203, 219, 284-285, 307, 376, 381, 382, 394, 396-398
electoral system, distortions, 43, 52, 55, 89, 102, 104, 171, 372-375
executive, supremacy, 175, 219
expropriation, 29, 134, 160, 245-249, 251-253, 255-256, 259-260, 317, 321, 331, 390

-F-

federal system, history, 44, 199-201, 222
federal system, illegitimate transformation, 346
federation, 20, 22, 26, 28, 37, 44-45, 87, 92, 96-99, 139, 165, 169-170, 177, 180-181, 183, 189-191, 195-196, 198-204, 207-211, 213, 291-295, 298, 300, 333, 346, 370, 400, 404
federation, recentralization, 209
federation, financing rules, 208-209
freedom of press, 7, 21, 152, 154, 265, 368, 370, 390, 394, 405, 407
freedom of expression, 7, 21, 152, 154, 265, 368, 370, 390, 394, 405, 407

-G-

government transparency, 7, 47, 122, 137-138, 169, 174, 177, 215, 319, 367, 405-406
governmental accountability, institutions, 101/102, 121-122, 169, 277, 370, 406

-H-

Honduras, constituent assembly, 2, 9-10, 15, 26, 52

415

human rights, disrespect, 30, 182, 367, 379, 369, 380, 382, 386, 389-393, 396, 404, 408, 410
human rights, international protection, 73, 134, 143-144, 351-352, 354-355, 387
hydrocarbon industry, nationalization, 162, 246-247, 250-251, 319
hydrocarbon primary activities, state appropriation, 251, 253, 258-260

-I-

indigenous peoples, collective rights, 55, 63, 103, 149, 155-156
Inter-American Court of Human Rights, decision, unenforceability, 140, 145, 179, 182, 352, 355, 357-358, 387, 391
Inter-American Democratic Charter, 2, 3, 7-8, 30, 47, 115, 215, 367, 368, 371, 380, 392, 394, 396, 398, 401, 405, 407, 409, 411
international treaties, constitutional rank, 143-144, 146, 149, 344, 351, 352-354, 387
iron industry, nationalization, 254-256

-J-

judicial review, means, 46, 94, 109, 134, 182, 207, 214
judiciary, cleansing, 179
judiciary, subjection, 29, 85, 177-178, 226, 337, 339
judiciary, transitory commission, 59-60, 128, 145, 180, 403
justice state, substitution, 141

-L-

labor rights, 324, 328, 389
latifundio, elimination, 159, 317-318
legislation, public consultation, 115, 152, 176-177, 219-220, 381, 398
legislative assemblies, dissolution, 13, 56, 59, 75, 337
local governments, 13, 16, 21, 43, 57, 59, 75, 100, 103-104, 110, 115-116, 118, 174, 184-196, 201-202, 204-209, 211, 221, 235, 266, 276-277, 279, 282, 291-300, 302-305, 323, 332-334, 337, 346, 348, 370, 375, 377, 385, 394, 399, 401, 404-405

-M-

macroeconomic policy, 279, 321-323
Marxist party, 6, 93, 95, 221, 369, 373, 377
Marxist revolution, 5, 411
militarism, 4, 7, 19, 29, 35-36, 65, 87, 90-91, 130, 133, 139, 167, 171, 221, 223, 264, 268, 270, 307, 310, 335, 377, 410
mixed economy system, 134, 156, 266, 270, 274, 311
monetary policy, 304-306, 321-323
municipalities, 13, 16, 21, 43, 57, 59, 75, 100, 103-104, 111, 115-116, 119, 174, 184-196, 201-202, 204-209, 211, 221, 235, 266, 276-277, 279, 282, 291-300, 302, 305, 323, 332-334, 337, 346, 348, 370, 375, 377, 385, 394, 399, 401, 404-405

INDEX

-N-

National Assembly, supremacy, 175, 219
National Electoral Council, 23, 53-54, 64, 80, 103, 106, 108-110, 112, 114, 118, 121, 124, 171, 173, 216-217, 223, 228, 268, 284, 285, 286, 306-307, 339, 341, 374-376, 378, 381, 383-384, 393, 396-397, 400
National Legislative Commission, 23, 73-75, 79, 337, 393, 396
nationalization, 162, 245-247, 250, 251, 254-258, 261, 319
nondiscrimination, 147, 274, 279, 323-324, 326, 388

-O-

official party, 21, 25, 93, 95, 118, 193-196, 221, 269, 289, 369, 373, 376-377, 379, 383, 385, 399
oil industry, association agreements, 250, 252-253
oil industry, confiscation, 251, 253, 258-260
oil industry, nationalization, 162, 246-247, 250-251, 319

-P-

participation, nominating committees, 103, 106-109, 115, 117, 217-218, 227-228, 230, 284-285, 296, 306-307, 375-376, 381
participation, public consultation of statutes, 115, 152, 176-177, 219-220, 381, 398
participatory democracy, 8, 14, 19-20, 25, 33, 39, 41-43, 58, 61, 63-64, 87-88, 99-100, 102, 105, 109, 114, 115-116, 136, 139, 150, 161, 166, 170, 183-189, 193, 195, 197, 202, 270, 277, 280-281, 283, 286, 361, 368, 380, 383, 404, 410
petrochemical activities, reservation, 292
pluralism, absence, 33, 41, 57, 100, 116, 137, 169, 185, 193, 210, 215, 372, 378, 380, 398-399, 401
political parties, financing, 117, 119, 289-290, 349-350, 368, 378-379, 398-399
political system, crisis (1990s), 16, 18-21, 39, 41, 46, 47-49, 64, 88-90, 100, 116, 184, 199, 201, 377
president, reelection, 10, 22, 30, 55, 67, 103, 175, 196, 219, 223, 262-263, 283-284, 301, 335, 341-345, 359-364, 393
presidential system, 21-22, 35, 42, 47, 89-90, 95, 122-123, 170-172, 175-176, 203, 213-214, 219, 301, 306, 342, 360
proportional representation, 42-43, 102, 104-105, 138, 203, 373-374
public administration, fragmentation, 277-278

-R-

recall referendum, 17, 110-112, 113-114, 122-123, 175, 185, 223, 281, 286-287, 339, 361, 372, 375, 383-384, 388
recall referendum, distortion, 114, 287

INDEX

reelection, 10, 22, 30, 56, 67, 103, 175, 196, 219, 223, 263, 271, 283-284, 301, 335, 341-345, 359-364, 393
referenda, 191, 106, 111, 203, 270, 276, 351
representative democracy, 7-8, 13-14, 17, 19-20, 24-25, 33, 42-44, 52, 57, 74, 87, 90, 101-102, 104-106, 114, 116, 139, 166-167, 183-185, 189, 192, 195, 197, 215, 223, 268-270, 274, 276, 280-281, 283, 293, 299, 332, 367-372, 380, 386, 396-398, 401, 410
right to democracy, 8, 30, 367
rule of law, 3, 7-9, 25-26, 30, 47, 50-51, 64, 81, 87-88, 96, 102, 123, 134, 139, 141, 147, 158, 165-172, 185, 193-194, 213, 215, 220, 222, 239, 241, 270, 274-275, 312, 367-368, 371, 380, 382, 392-394, 401

-S-

separation of powers, 7, 9, 43, 46, 87, 95, 122-123, 139, 168-177, 203, 211-216, 219-220, 225, 238, 306, 367, 370, 401-402
social democratic state, 134, 158, 274, 312
social rights, 7, 105, 134, 147, 149-150, 202, 210, 328, 368, 405
socialist economy, 159, 163, 269, 275-276, 313-314, 319
socialist ideology, 22, 159, 163, 190, 194, 266, 269, 272, 274-276, 282, 292, 313-314, 319, 321-322, 330
socialist state, 22, 191, 194, 266, 272, 274-276, 282, 292, 313, 321-322, 330
state centralism, 20, 22, 28, 45, 87, 96, 99, 165, 170, 177, 183, 189-191, 194, 198, 202, 266, 272, 274-276, 282, 291, 292, 313, 321-322, 330, 346
state of justice, incongruence, 126-127, 136, 275
states of exception, 301, 324-327
steel industry, nationalization, 255-257
Supreme Tribunal of Justice, appointment of magistrates, 21, 27, 60, 74, 76, 79-81, 86, 117, 128, 226-230, 236, 284, 382, 393
Supreme Tribunal of Justice, Constitutional Chamber, decisions, 3, 13, 23, 29-30, 36, 65, 67, 74, 80, 85, 100, 104, 114, 119, 124-126, 130, 135-136, 139-141, 144-148, 153-154, 157, 171, 174, 179-183, 205-206, 209, 221-222, 224, 229-232, 235-236, 238-239, 241-244, 248, 268, 289, 297, 312, 327, 333, 336-340, 343-345, 347-350, 352-355, 357-358, 364, 373, 375-376, 379, 383-385, 387, 393, 395-398, 405
Supreme Tribunal of Justice, constitutional mutation, 30, 241, 335-358
Supreme Tribunal of Justice, political subjection, 29, 85, 177-178, 226, 337, 339

-T-

trade unions, interference, 42, 109-110, 386, 389, 398-400
transitory constitutional regime, 27, 33, 64, 69, 83, 85, 337-338, 382, 393

-U-

United Socialist Party of Venezuela, 6, 21, 25, 93, 95, 119, 193-196, 221, 269, 290, 369, 369, 373, 376-377, 379, 383, 385, 399